The ONE YEAR® Seasonal BIBLE

Fall Devotions

D1449762

Tyndale House Publishers, Inc.
Carol Stream, Illinois

Tyndale House Publishers and Wycliffe Bible Translators share the vision for an understandable, accurate translation of the Bible for every person in the world. Each sale of the *Holy Bible,* New Living Translation, benefits Wycliffe Bible Translators. Wycliffe is working with partners around the world to accomplish Vision 2025—an initiative to start a Bible translation program in every language group that needs it by the year 2025.

CONTENTS

OCTOBER
1

ISAIAH 62:6–65:25

◐ Jerusalem, I have posted
watchmen on your walls;
they will pray day and night,
continually.
Take no rest, all you who pray
to the LORD.
⁷ Give the LORD no rest until he
completes his work,
until he makes Jerusalem the
pride of the earth.
⁸ The LORD has sworn to Jerusalem
by his own strength:
"I will never again hand you over
to your enemies.
Never again will foreign warriors
come
and take away your grain and
new wine.
⁹ You raised the grain, and you will
eat it,
praising the LORD.
Within the courtyards of the Temple,
you yourselves will drink the
wine you have pressed."

¹⁰ Go out through the gates!
Prepare the highway for my
people to return!
Smooth out the road; pull out
the boulders;
raise a flag for all the nations
to see.
¹¹ The LORD has sent this message
to every land:
"Tell the people of Israel,*
'Look, your Savior is coming.
See, he brings his reward with
him as he comes.'"
¹² They will be called "The Holy People"
and "The People Redeemed
by the LORD."

And Jerusalem will be known as
"The Desirable Place"
and "The City No Longer Forsaken."

⁶³:¹WHO is this who comes from Edom,
from the city of Bozrah,
with his clothing stained red?
Who is this in royal robes,
marching in his great strength?

"It is I, the LORD, announcing
your salvation!
It is I, the LORD, who has the
power to save!"

² Why are your clothes so red,
as if you have been treading
out grapes?

³ "I have been treading the winepress
alone;
no one was there to help me.
In my anger I have trampled
my enemies
as if they were grapes.
In my fury I have trampled my foes.
Their blood has stained
my clothes.
⁴ For the time has come for me
to avenge my people,
to ransom them from their
oppressors.
⁵ I was amazed to see that no
one intervened
to help the oppressed.
So I myself stepped in to save them
with my strong arm,
and my wrath sustained me.
⁶ I crushed the nations in my anger
and made them stagger and
fall to the ground,
spilling their blood upon
the earth."

⁷ I will tell of the LORD's unfailing love.
I will praise the LORD for all he
has done.
I will rejoice in his great goodness
to Israel,

which he has granted according
to his mercy and love.

⁸ He said, "They are my very
own people.
Surely they will not betray
me again."
And he became their Savior.

⁹ In all their suffering he also suffered,
and he personally* rescued them.
In his love and mercy he redeemed
them.
He lifted them up and carried
them
through all the years.

¹⁰ But they rebelled against him
and grieved his Holy Spirit.
So he became their enemy
and fought against them.

¹¹ Then they remembered those
days of old
when Moses led his people
out of Egypt.
They cried out, "Where is the one
who brought Israel through
the sea,
with Moses as their shepherd?
Where is the one who sent his
Holy Spirit
to be among his people?

¹² Where is the one whose power
was displayed
when Moses lifted up his hand—
the one who divided the sea
before them,
making himself famous forever?

¹³ Where is the one who led them
through the bottom of the sea?
They were like fine stallions
racing through the desert, never
stumbling.

¹⁴ As with cattle going down into a
peaceful valley,
the Spirit of the LORD gave
them rest.
You led your people, LORD,
and gained a magnificent
reputation."

¹⁵ LORD, look down from heaven;
look from your holy, glorious
home, and see us.

Where is the passion and the might
you used to show on our behalf?
Where are your mercy and
compassion now?

¹⁶ Surely you are still our Father!
Even if Abraham and Jacob*
would disown us,
LORD, you would still be our Father.
You are our Redeemer from ages
past.

¹⁷ LORD, why have you allowed us to
turn from your path?
Why have you given us stubborn
hearts so we no longer fear you?
Return and help us, for we are
your servants,
the tribes that are your special
possession.

¹⁸ How briefly your holy people
possessed your holy place,
and now our enemies have
destroyed it.

¹⁹ Sometimes it seems as though we
never belonged to you,
as though we had never been
known as your people.

⁶⁴:¹*OH, that you would burst from
the heavens and come down!
How the mountains would quake
in your presence!

²*As fire causes wood to burn
and water to boil,
your coming would make the
nations tremble.
Then your enemies would learn
the reason for your fame!

³ When you came down long ago,
you did awesome deeds beyond
our highest expectations.
And oh, how the mountains
quaked!

⁴ For since the world began,
no ear has heard,
and no eye has seen a God like you,
who works for those who wait
for him!

⁵ You welcome those who gladly
do good,
who follow godly ways.
But you have been very angry with us,
for we are not godly.

We are constant sinners;
how can people like us be saved?
6 We are all infected and impure
with sin.
When we display our righteous
deeds,
they are nothing but filthy rags.
Like autumn leaves, we wither
and fall,
and our sins sweep us away like
the wind.
7 Yet no one calls on your name
or pleads with you for mercy.
Therefore, you have turned away
from us
and turned us over* to our sins.

8 And yet, O LORD, you are our Father.
We are the clay, and you are
the potter.
We all are formed by your hand.
9 Don't be so angry with us, LORD.
Please don't remember our
sins forever.
Look at us, we pray,
and see that we are all your people.
10 Your holy cities are destroyed.
Zion is a wilderness;
yes, Jerusalem is a desolate ruin.
11 The holy and beautiful Temple
where our ancestors praised you
has been burned down,
and all the things of beauty are
destroyed.
12 After all this, LORD, must you still
refuse to help us?
Will you continue to be silent
and punish us?

65:1 THE LORD says,

"I was ready to respond, but no one
asked for help.
I was ready to be found, but no
one was looking for me.
I said, 'Here I am, here I am!'
to a nation that did not call on
my name.*
2 All day long I opened my arms to a
rebellious people.*
But they follow their own
evil paths
and their own crooked schemes.

3 All day long they insult me to my face
by worshiping idols in their
sacred gardens.
They burn incense on pagan altars.
4 At night they go out among the graves,
worshiping the dead.
They eat the flesh of pigs
and make stews with other
forbidden foods.
5 Yet they say to each other,
'Don't come too close or you will
defile me!
I am holier than you!'
These people are a stench in
my nostrils,
an acrid smell that never goes away.

6 "Look, my decree is written out*
in front of me:
I will not stand silent;
I will repay them in full!
Yes, I will repay them—
7 both for their own sins
and for those of their ancestors,"
says the LORD.
"For they also burned incense
on the mountains
and insulted me on the hills.
I will pay them back in full!

8 "But I will not destroy them all,"
says the LORD.
"For just as good grapes are found
among a cluster of bad ones
(and someone will say, 'Don't
throw them all away—
some of those grapes are good!'),
so I will not destroy all Israel.
For I still have true servants there.
9 I will preserve a remnant of the
people of Israel*
and of Judah to possess my land.
Those I choose will inherit it,
and my servants will live there.
10 The plain of Sharon will again be
filled with flocks
for my people who have searched
for me,
and the valley of Achor will be
a place to pasture herds.

11 "But because the rest of you have
forsaken the LORD

and have forgotten his Temple,
and because you have prepared
    feasts to honor the god of Fate
and have offered mixed wine to
    the god of Destiny,
[12] now I will 'destine' you for the sword.
All of you will bow down before
    the executioner.
For when I called, you did not answer.
When I spoke, you did not listen.
You deliberately sinned—before my
    very eyes—
and chose to do what you know
    I despise."

[13] Therefore, this is what the Sovereign
    LORD says:
"My servants will eat,
    but you will starve.
My servants will drink,
    but you will be thirsty.
My servants will rejoice,
    but you will be sad and ashamed.
[14] My servants will sing for joy,
    but you will cry in sorrow and
    despair.
[15] Your name will be a curse word
    among my people,
    for the Sovereign LORD will
    destroy you
    and will call his true servants by
    another name.
[16] All who invoke a blessing or take
    an oath
    will do so by the God of truth.
For I will put aside my anger
    and forget the evil of earlier days.

[17] "Look! I am creating new heavens
    and a new earth,
    and no one will even think about
    the old ones anymore.
[18] Be glad; rejoice forever in my creation!
    And look! I will create Jerusalem
    as a place of happiness.
Her people will be a source
    of joy.
[19] I will rejoice over Jerusalem
    and delight in my people.
And the sound of weeping
    and crying
    will be heard in it no more.

[20] "No longer will babies die when only
    a few days old.
No longer will adults die before
    they have lived a full life.
No longer will people be considered
    old at one hundred!
Only the cursed will die that
    young!
[21] In those days people will live in the
    houses they build
    and eat the fruit of their own
    vineyards.
[22] Unlike the past, invaders will not
    take their houses
    and confiscate their vineyards.
For my people will live as long
    as trees,
    and my chosen ones will have
    time to enjoy their hard-won
    gains.
[23] They will not work in vain,
    and their children will not be
    doomed to misfortune.
For they are people blessed by
    the LORD,
    and their children, too, will
    be blessed.
[24] I will answer them before they even
    call to me.
While they are still talking about
    their needs,
    I will go ahead and answer their
    prayers!
[25] The wolf and the lamb will feed
    together.
The lion will eat hay like
    a cow.
But the snakes will eat dust.
In those days no one will be hurt
    or destroyed on my holy
    mountain.
I, the LORD, have spoken!"

62:11 Hebrew *Tell the daughter of Zion.*   **63:9** Hebrew *and the angel of his presence.*   **63:16** Hebrew *Israel.* See note on 14:1.   **64:1** Verse 64:1 is numbered 63:20 in Hebrew text.   **64:2** Verses 64:2-12 are numbered 64:1-11 in Hebrew text.   **64:7** As in Greek, Syriac, and Aramaic versions; Hebrew reads *melted us.*   **65:1** Or *to a nation that did not bear my name.*   **65:1-2** Greek version reads *I was found by people who were not looking for me. / I showed myself to those who were not asking for me. / All day long I opened my arms to them, / but they were disobedient and rebellious.* Compare Rom 10:20.   **65:6** Or *their sins are written out;* Hebrew reads *it stands written.*   **65:9** Hebrew *remnant of Jacob.* See note on 14:1.

PHILIPPIANS 2:19–3:4

If the Lord Jesus is willing, I [Paul] hope to send Timothy to you [Philippians] soon for a visit. Then he can cheer me up by telling me how you are getting along. 20I have no one else like Timothy, who genuinely cares about your welfare. 21All the others care only for themselves and not for what matters to Jesus Christ. 22But you know how Timothy has proved himself. Like a son with his father, he has served with me in preaching the Good News. 23I hope to send him to you just as soon as I find out what is going to happen to me here. 24And I have confidence from the Lord that I myself will come to see you soon.

25Meanwhile, I thought I should send Epaphroditus back to you. He is a true brother, co-worker, and fellow soldier. And he was your messenger to help me in my need. 26I am sending him because he has been longing to see you, and he was very distressed that you heard he was ill. 27And he certainly was ill; in fact, he almost died. But God had mercy on him—and also on me, so that I would not have one sorrow after another.

28So I am all the more anxious to send him back to you, for I know you will be glad to see him, and then I will not be so worried about you. 29Welcome him with Christian love* and with great joy, and give him the honor that people like him deserve. 30For he risked his life for the work of Christ, and he was at the point of death while doing for me what you couldn't do from far away.

3:1WHATEVER happens, my dear brothers and sisters,* rejoice in the Lord. I never get tired of telling you these things, and I do it to safeguard your faith.

2Watch out for those dogs, those people who do evil, those mutilators who say you must be circumcised to be saved. 3For we who worship by the Spirit of God* are the ones who are truly circumcised. We rely on what Christ Jesus has done for us. We put no confidence in human effort, 4though I could have confidence in my own effort if anyone

could. Indeed, if others have reason for confidence in their own efforts, I have even more!

2:29 Greek *in the Lord.*   3:1 Greek *brothers;* also in 3:13, 17.   3:3 Some manuscripts read *worship God in spirit;* one early manuscript reads *worship in spirit.*

PSALM 73:1-28

A psalm of Asaph.

1 Truly God is good to Israel,
   to those whose hearts are pure.
2 But as for me, I almost lost my footing.
   My feet were slipping, and I was
      almost gone.
3 For I envied the proud
   when I saw them prosper despite
      their wickedness.
4 They seem to live such painless lives;
   their bodies are so healthy
      and strong.
5 They don't have troubles like other
      people;
   they're not plagued with
      problems like everyone else.
6 They wear pride like a jeweled
      necklace
   and clothe themselves with cruelty.
7 These fat cats have everything
   their hearts could ever wish for!
8 They scoff and speak only evil;
   in their pride they seek to crush
      others.
9 They boast against the very heavens,
   and their words strut throughout
      the earth.
10 And so the people are dismayed and
      confused,
   drinking in all their words.
11 "What does God know?" they ask.
   "Does the Most High even know
      what's happening?"
12 Look at these wicked people—
   enjoying a life of ease while their
      riches multiply.

13 Did I keep my heart pure for nothing?
   Did I keep myself innocent for
      no reason?
14 I get nothing but trouble all day long;
   every morning brings me pain.
15 If I had really spoken this way
   to others,

I would have been a traitor to
your people.
16 So I tried to understand why the
wicked prosper.
But what a difficult task it is!
17 Then I went into your sanctuary,
O God,
and I finally understood the
destiny of the wicked.
18 Truly, you put them on a slippery
path
and send them sliding over the
cliff to destruction.
19 In an instant they are destroyed,
completely swept away by terrors.
20 When you arise, O Lord,
you will laugh at their silly ideas
as a person laughs at dreams in
the morning.

21 Then I realized that my heart
was bitter,
and I was all torn up inside.
22 I was so foolish and ignorant—
I must have seemed like a
senseless animal to you.
23 Yet I still belong to you;
you hold my right hand.
24 You guide me with your counsel,
leading me to a glorious destiny.
25 **Whom have I in heaven but you?**
I desire you more than anything
on earth.
26 **My health may fail, and my spirit**
may grow weak,
but God remains the strength
of my heart;
he is mine forever.

27 Those who desert him will perish,
for you destroy those who
abandon you.
28 But as for me, how good it is to be
near God!
I have made the Sovereign LORD
my shelter,
and I will tell everyone about the
wonderful things you do.

PROVERBS 24:13-14
My child,* eat honey, for it is good, and
the honeycomb is sweet to the taste. In

the same way, wisdom is sweet to your
soul. If you find it, you will have a bright
future, and your hopes will not be cut
short.

24:13 Hebrew *My son;* also in 24:21.

OCTOBER 2

ISAIAH 66:1-24
This is what the LORD says:

"Heaven is my throne,
and the earth is my footstool.
Could you build me a temple as
good as that?
Could you build me such a
resting place?
2 My hands have made both heaven
and earth;
they and everything in them
are mine.*
I, the LORD, have spoken!

"I will bless those who have humble
and contrite hearts,
who tremble at my word.
3 But those who choose their own ways—
delighting in their detestable
sins—
will not have their offerings
accepted.
When such people sacrifice a bull,
it is no more acceptable than a
human sacrifice.
When they sacrifice a lamb,
it's as though they had sacrificed
a dog!
When they bring an offering of grain,
they might as well offer the blood
of a pig.
When they burn frankincense,
it's as if they had blessed an idol.
4 I will send them great trouble—
all the things they feared.
For when I called, they did not answer.
When I spoke, they did not listen.

They deliberately sinned before my
very eyes
and chose to do what they know
I despise."

5 Hear this message from the LORD,
all you who tremble at his words:
"Your own people hate you
and throw you out for being loyal
to my name.
'Let the LORD be honored!' they scoff.
'Be joyful in him!'
But they will be put to shame.
6 What is all the commotion in the city?
What is that terrible noise from
the Temple?
It is the voice of the LORD
taking vengeance against his
enemies.

7 "Before the birth pains even begin,
Jerusalem gives birth to a son.
8 Who has ever seen anything as
strange as this?
Who ever heard of such a thing?
Has a nation ever been born in a
single day?
Has a country ever come forth in
a mere moment?
But by the time Jerusalem's* birth
pains begin,
her children will be born.
9 Would I ever bring this nation to the
point of birth
and then not deliver it?" asks
the LORD.
"No! I would never keep this nation
from being born,"
says your God.

10 "Rejoice with Jerusalem!
Be glad with her, all you who love
her
and all you who mourn for her.
11 Drink deeply of her glory
even as an infant drinks at its
mother's comforting breasts."

12 This is what the LORD says:
"I will give Jerusalem a river of peace
and prosperity.
The wealth of the nations will
flow to her.

Her children will be nursed at her
breasts,
carried in her arms, and held on
her lap.
13 I will comfort you there in Jerusalem
as a mother comforts her child."

14 When you see these things, your
heart will rejoice.
You will flourish like the grass!
Everyone will see the LORD's hand
of blessing on his servants—
and his anger against his enemies.
15 See, the LORD is coming with fire,
and his swift chariots roar like
a whirlwind.
He will bring punishment with the
fury of his anger
and the flaming fire of his
hot rebuke.
16 The LORD will punish the world
by fire
and by his sword.
He will judge the earth,
and many will be killed by him.

17"Those who 'consecrate' and 'purify'
themselves in a sacred garden with its
idol in the center—feasting on pork and
rats and other detestable meats—will
come to a terrible end," says the LORD.
18"I can see what they are doing, and I
know what they are thinking. So I will
gather all nations and peoples together,
and they will see my glory. 19I will perform a sign among them. And I will
send those who survive to be messengers to the nations—to Tarshish, to the
Libyans* and Lydians* (who are famous
as archers), to Tubal and Greece,* and to
all the lands beyond the sea that have
not heard of my fame or seen my glory.
There they will declare my glory to the
nations. 20They will bring the remnant
of your people back from every nation.
They will bring them to my holy mountain in Jerusalem as an offering to the
LORD. They will ride on horses, in chariots and wagons, and on mules and camels," says the LORD. 21"And I will appoint
some of them to be my priests and Levites. I, the LORD, have spoken!

[22] "As surely as my new heavens and
earth will remain,
so will you always be my people,
with a name that will never
disappear,"
says the LORD.
[23] "All humanity will come to
worship me
from week to week
and from month to month.
[24] And as they go out, they will see
the dead bodies of those who
have rebelled against me.
For the worms that devour them will
never die,
and the fire that burns them will
never go out.
All who pass by
will view them with utter horror."

66:2 As in Greek, Latin, and Syriac versions; Hebrew reads
these things are.   66:8 Hebrew Zion's.   66:19a As in
some Greek manuscripts, which read Put (that is, Libya);
Hebrew reads Pul.   66:19b Hebrew Lud.   66:19c Hebrew
Javan.

PHILIPPIANS 3:5-21

[I] [Paul] was circumcised when I was
eight days old. I am a pure-blooded citi-
zen of Israel and a member of the tribe
of Benjamin—a real Hebrew if there ever
was one! I was a member of the Phari-
sees, who demand the strictest obedience to the Jewish law. [6]I was so zealous
that I harshly persecuted the church.
And as for righteousness, I obeyed the
law without fault.

[7]I once thought these things were
valuable, but now I consider them worthless because of what Christ has done.
[8]Yes, everything else is worthless when
compared with the infinite value of
knowing Christ Jesus my Lord. For his
sake I have discarded everything else,
counting it all as garbage, so that I could
gain Christ [9]and become one with him. I
no longer count on my own righteousness through obeying the law; rather, I
become righteous through faith in
Christ.* For God's way of making us right
with himself depends on faith. [10]I want
to know Christ and experience the
mighty power that raised him from the
dead. I want to suffer with him, sharing

in his death, [11]so that one way or another
I will experience the resurrection from
the dead!

[12]I don't mean to say that I have already achieved these things or that I have
already reached perfection. But I press
on to possess that perfection for which
Christ Jesus first possessed me. **[13]No,
dear brothers and sisters, I have not
achieved it,* but I focus on this one
thing: Forgetting the past and looking
forward to what lies ahead, [14]I press
on to reach the end of the race and receive the heavenly prize for which
God, through Christ Jesus, is calling us.**

[15]Let all who are spiritually mature
agree on these things. If you disagree on
some point, I believe God will make it
plain to you. [16]But we must hold on to
the progress we have already made.

[17]Dear brothers and sisters, pattern
your lives after mine, and learn from
those who follow our example. [18]For I
have told you often before, and I say it
again with tears in my eyes, that there are
many whose conduct shows they are
really enemies of the cross of Christ.
[19]They are headed for destruction. Their
god is their appetite, they brag about
shameful things, and they think only
about this life here on earth. [20]But we are
citizens of heaven, where the Lord Jesus
Christ lives. And we are eagerly waiting
for him to return as our Savior. [21]He will
take our weak mortal bodies and change
them into glorious bodies like his own,
using the same power with which he will
bring everything under his control.

3:9 Or through the faithfulness of Christ.   3:13 Some
manuscripts read not yet achieved it.

PSALM 74:1-23
A psalm of Asaph.*

[1] **O** God, why have you rejected
us so long?
Why is your anger so intense
against the sheep of your
own pasture?
[2] Remember that we are the people
you chose long ago,

the tribe you redeemed as your
   own special possession!
And remember Jerusalem,* your
   home here on earth.
3 Walk through the awful ruins
   of the city;
   see how the enemy has destroyed
     your sanctuary.

4 There your enemies shouted their
   victorious battle cries;
   there they set up their battle
     standards.
5 They swung their axes
   like woodcutters in a forest.
6 With axes and picks,
   they smashed the carved paneling.
7 They burned your sanctuary
   to the ground.
   They defiled the place that bears
     your name.
8 Then they thought, "Let's destroy
   everything!"
   So they burned down all the
     places where God was
     worshiped.

9 We no longer see your miraculous
   signs.
   All the prophets are gone,
   and no one can tell us when
     it will end.
10 How long, O God, will you allow our
   enemies to insult you?
   Will you let them dishonor your
     name forever?
11 Why do you hold back your strong
   right hand?
   Unleash your powerful fist and
     destroy them.

12 You, O God, are my king from
   ages past,
   bringing salvation to the earth.
13 You split the sea by your strength
   and smashed the heads of the
     sea monsters.
14 You crushed the heads of Leviathan*
   and let the desert animals eat him.
15 You caused the springs and streams
   to gush forth,
   and you dried up rivers that never
     run dry.

16 Both day and night belong to you;
   you made the starlight* and the
     sun.
17 You set the boundaries of the earth,
   and you made both summer
     and winter.

18 See how these enemies insult
   you, LORD.
   A foolish nation has dishonored
     your name.
19 Don't let these wild beasts destroy
   your turtledoves.
   Don't forget your suffering
     people forever.

20 Remember your covenant
   promises,
   for the land is full of darkness
     and violence!
21 Don't let the downtrodden be
   humiliated again.
   Instead, let the poor and needy
     praise your name.

22 Arise, O God, and defend your cause.
   Remember how these fools insult
     you all day long.
23 Don't overlook what your enemies
   have said
   or their growing uproar.

74:TITLE Hebrew *maskil*. This may be a literary or musical
term.   74:2 Hebrew *Mount Zion*.   74:14 The
identification of Leviathan is disputed, ranging from an
earthly creature to a mythical sea monster in ancient
literature.   74:16 Or *moon;* Hebrew reads *light*.

PROVERBS 24:15-16
Don't wait in ambush at the home of
the godly, and don't raid the house
where the godly live. The godly may trip
seven times, but they will get up again.
But one disaster is enough to overthrow
the wicked.

OCTOBER 3

JEREMIAH 1:1–2:30

These are the words of Jeremiah son of Hilkiah, one of the priests from the town of Anathoth in the land of Benjamin. ²The LORD first gave messages to Jeremiah during the thirteenth year of the reign of Josiah son of Amon, king of Judah.* ³The LORD's messages continued throughout the reign of King Jehoiakim, Josiah's son, until the eleventh year of the reign of King Zedekiah, another of Josiah's sons. In August* of that eleventh year the people of Jerusalem were taken away as captives.

⁴The LORD gave me this message:

⁵ "I knew you before I formed you in
        your mother's womb.
    Before you were born I set
        you apart
    and appointed you as my prophet
        to the nations."

⁶"O Sovereign LORD," I said, "I can't speak for you! I'm too young!"

⁷The LORD replied, "Don't say, 'I'm too young,' for you must go wherever I send you and say whatever I tell you. ⁸And don't be afraid of the people, for I will be with you and will protect you. I, the LORD, have spoken!" ⁹Then the LORD reached out and touched my mouth and said,

    "Look, I have put my words
        in your mouth!
¹⁰ Today I appoint you to stand up
        against nations and kingdoms.
    Some you must uproot and tear
        down,
        destroy and overthrow.
    Others you must build up
        and plant."

¹¹Then the LORD said to me, "Look, Jeremiah! What do you see?"

And I replied, "I see a branch from an almond tree."

¹²And the LORD said, "That's right, and it means that I am watching,* and I will certainly carry out all my plans."

¹³Then the LORD spoke to me again and asked, "What do you see now?"

And I replied, "I see a pot of boiling water, spilling from the north."

¹⁴"Yes," the LORD said, "for terror from the north will boil out on the people of this land. ¹⁵Listen! I am calling the armies of the kingdoms of the north to come to Jerusalem. I, the LORD, have spoken!

    "They will set their thrones
        at the gates of the city.
    They will attack its walls
        and all the other towns of Judah.
¹⁶ I will pronounce judgment
        on my people for all their evil—
    for deserting me and burning
        incense to other gods.
    Yes, they worship idols made
        with their own hands!

¹⁷ "Get up and prepare for action.
        Go out and tell them everything
        I tell you to say.
    Do not be afraid of them,
        or I will make you look foolish in
        front of them.
¹⁸ For see, today I have made you strong
        like a fortified city that cannot
        be captured,
    like an iron pillar or a bronze wall.
    You will stand against the whole
        land—
        the kings, officials, priests, and
        people of Judah.
¹⁹ They will fight you, but they will fail.
    For I am with you, and I will take
        care of you.
    I, the LORD, have spoken!"

²:¹THE LORD gave me another message. He said, ²"Go and shout this message to Jerusalem. This is what the LORD says:

    "I remember how eager you were
        to please me
    as a young bride long ago,
    how you loved me and followed me
        even through the barren
        wilderness.

³ In those days Israel was holy
    to the LORD,
    the first of his children.*
All who harmed his people were
    declared guilty,
    and disaster fell on them.
    I, the LORD, have spoken!"

⁴Listen to the word of the LORD, people of Jacob—all you families of Israel!
⁵This is what the LORD says:

"What did your ancestors find
    wrong with me
    that led them to stray so far
    from me?
They worshiped worthless idols,
    only to become worthless
    themselves.
⁶ They did not ask, 'Where is the LORD
    who brought us safely out
    of Egypt
and led us through the barren
    wilderness—
    a land of deserts and pits,
a land of drought and death,
    where no one lives or even
    travels?'

⁷ "And when I brought you into a
    fruitful land
    to enjoy its bounty and goodness,
you defiled my land and
    corrupted the possession I had
    promised you.
⁸ The priests did not ask,
    'Where is the LORD?'
Those who taught my word
    ignored me,
    the rulers turned against me,
and the prophets spoke in the
    name of Baal,
    wasting their time on worthless
    idols.
⁹ Therefore, I will bring my case
    against you,"
    says the LORD.
"I will even bring charges against
    your children's children
    in the years to come.

¹⁰ "Go west and look in the land
    of Cyprus*;

go east and search through the
    land of Kedar.
Has anyone ever heard of anything
    as strange as this?
¹¹ Has any nation ever traded its gods
    for new ones,
    even though they are not gods
    at all?
Yet my people have exchanged their
    glorious God*
    for worthless idols!
¹² The heavens are shocked at such
    a thing
    and shrink back in horror and
    dismay,"
    says the LORD.
¹³ "For my people have done two evil
    things:
They have abandoned me—
    the fountain of living water.
And they have dug for themselves
    cracked cisterns
    that can hold no water at all!

¹⁴ "Why has Israel become a slave?
    Why has he been carried away
    as plunder?
¹⁵ Strong lions have roared against
    him,
    and the land has been destroyed.
The towns are now in ruins,
    and no one lives in them
    anymore.
¹⁶ Egyptians, marching from their
    cities of Memphis* and
    Tahpanhes,
    have destroyed Israel's glory
    and power.
¹⁷ And you have brought this upon
    yourselves
    by rebelling against the LORD
    your God,
    even though he was leading you
    on the way!

¹⁸ "What have you gained by your
    alliances with Egypt
    and your covenants with Assyria?
What good to you are the streams
    of the Nile*
    or the waters of the Euphrates
    River?*

¹⁹ Your wickedness will bring its own
        punishment.
    Your turning from me will
        shame you.
    You will see what an evil, bitter
        thing it is
        to abandon the LORD your God
            and not to fear him.
        I, the Lord, the LORD of Heaven's
            Armies, have spoken!

²⁰ "Long ago I broke the yoke that
        oppressed you
    and tore away the chains of
        your slavery,
    but still you said,
        'I will not serve you.'
    On every hill and under every
        green tree,
        you have prostituted
            yourselves by bowing down
            to idols.
²¹ But I was the one who planted you,
        choosing a vine of the purest
        stock—the very best.
    How did you grow into this
        corrupt wild vine?
²² No amount of soap or lye can make
        you clean.
    I still see the stain of your guilt.
    I, the Sovereign LORD, have spoken!

²³ "You say, 'That's not true!
        I haven't worshiped the images
        of Baal!'
    But how can you say that?
        Go and look in any valley in
            the land!
    Face the awful sins you have done.
        You are like a restless female camel
            desperately searching for a mate.
²⁴ You are like a wild donkey,
        sniffing the wind at mating time.
    Who can restrain her lust?
        Those who desire her don't need
            to search,
        for she goes running to them!
²⁵ When will you stop running?
        When will you stop panting after
            other gods?
    But you say, 'Save your breath.
        I'm in love with these foreign gods,
        and I can't stop loving them now!'

²⁶ "Israel is like a thief
        who feels shame only when he
            gets caught.
    They, their kings, officials, priests,
        and prophets—
        all are alike in this.
²⁷ To an image carved from a piece
        of wood they say,
        'You are my father.'
    To an idol chiseled from a block
        of stone they say,
        'You are my mother.'
    They turn their backs on me,
        but in times of trouble they cry
            out to me,
        'Come and save us!'
²⁸ But why not call on these gods you
        have made?
    When trouble comes, let them
        save you if they can!
    For you have as many gods
        as there are towns in Judah.
²⁹ Why do you accuse me of doing
        wrong?
    You are the ones who have
        rebelled,"
    says the LORD.
³⁰ "I have punished your children,
        but they did not respond to my
            discipline.
    You yourselves have killed your
        prophets
        as a lion kills its prey."

1:2 The thirteenth year of Josiah's reign was 627 B.C.
1:3 Hebrew *In the fifth month,* of the ancient Hebrew lunar
calendar. A number of events in Jeremiah can be cross-
checked with dates in surviving Babylonian records and
related accurately to our modern calendar. The fifth month
in the eleventh year of Zedekiah's reign occurred within the
months of August and September 586 B.C. Also see 52:12
and the note there.   1:12 The Hebrew word for "watching"
(*shoqed*) sounds like the word for "almond tree" (*shaqed*).
2:3 Hebrew *the firstfruits of his harvest.*   2:10 Hebrew
Kittim.   2:11 Hebrew *their glory.*   2:16 Hebrew *Noph.*
2:18a Hebrew *of Shihor,* a branch of the Nile River.
2:18b Hebrew *the river?*

PHILIPPIANS 4:1-23

Therefore, my [Paul] dear brothers and
sisters,* stay true to the Lord. I love you
and long to see you, dear friends, for
you are my joy and the crown I receive
for my work.

²Now I appeal to Euodia and Synty-
che. Please, because you belong to the
Lord, settle your disagreement. ³And I

ask you, my true partner,* to help these two women, for they worked hard with me in telling others the Good News. They worked along with Clement and the rest of my co-workers, whose names are written in the Book of Life.

⁴Always be full of joy in the Lord. I say it again—rejoice! ⁵Let everyone see that you are considerate in all you do. Remember, the Lord is coming soon.

⁶Don't worry about anything; instead, pray about everything. Tell God what you need, and thank him for all he has done. ⁷Then you will experience God's peace, which exceeds anything we can understand. His peace will guard your hearts and minds as you live in Christ Jesus.

⁸**And now, dear brothers and sisters, one final thing. Fix your thoughts on what is true, and honorable, and right, and pure, and lovely, and admirable. Think about things that are excellent and worthy of praise.** ⁹Keep putting into practice all you learned and received from me—everything you heard from me and saw me doing. Then the God of peace will be with you.

¹⁰How I praise the Lord that you are concerned about me again. I know you have always been concerned for me, but you didn't have the chance to help me. ¹¹Not that I was ever in need, for I have learned how to be content with whatever I have. ¹²I know how to live on almost nothing or with everything. I have learned the secret of living in every situation, whether it is with a full stomach or empty, with plenty or little. ¹³For I can do everything through Christ,* who gives me strength. ¹⁴Even so, you have done well to share with me in my present difficulty.

¹⁵As you know, you Philippians were the only ones who gave me financial help when I first brought you the Good News and then traveled on from Macedonia. No other church did this. ¹⁶Even when I was in Thessalonica you sent help more than once. ¹⁷I don't say this because I want a gift from you. Rather, I want you to receive a reward for your kindness.

¹⁸At the moment I have all I need—

and more! I am generously supplied with the gifts you sent me with Epaphroditus. They are a sweet-smelling sacrifice that is acceptable and pleasing to God. ¹⁹And this same God who takes care of me will supply all your needs from his glorious riches, which have been given to us in Christ Jesus.

²⁰Now all glory to God our Father forever and ever! Amen.

²¹Give my greetings to each of God's holy people—all who belong to Christ Jesus. The brothers who are with me send you their greetings. ²²And all the rest of God's people send you greetings, too, especially those in Caesar's household.

²³May the grace of the Lord Jesus Christ be with your spirit.

4:1 Greek *brothers;* also in 4:8.   4:3 Or *loyal Syzygus.*
4:13 Greek *through the one.*

PSALM 75:1-10

For the choir director: A psalm of Asaph. A song to be sung to the tune "Do Not Destroy!"

¹ **W**e thank you, O God!
    We give thanks because you
        are near.
    People everywhere tell of your
        wonderful deeds.

² God says, "At the time I have
        planned,
    I will bring justice against
        the wicked.
³ When the earth quakes and its
        people live in turmoil,
    I am the one who keeps its
        foundations firm.   *Interlude*

⁴ "I warned the proud, 'Stop your
        boasting!'
    I told the wicked, 'Don't raise
        your fists!
⁵ Don't raise your fists in defiance
        at the heavens
    or speak with such arrogance.'"

⁶ For no one on earth—from east
        or west,
    or even from the wilderness—
        should raise a defiant fist.*
⁷ It is God alone who judges;

he decides who will rise and
who will fall.
⁸ For the LORD holds a cup in his hand
that is full of foaming wine mixed
with spices.
He pours out the wine in judgment,
and all the wicked must drink it,
draining it to the dregs.

⁹ But as for me, I will always proclaim
what God has done;
I will sing praises to the God
of Jacob.
¹⁰ For God says, "I will break the
strength of the wicked,
but I will increase the power
of the godly."

75:6 Hebrew *should lift.*

PROVERBS 24:17-20

Don't rejoice when your enemies fall;
don't be happy when they stumble. For
the LORD will be displeased with you
and will turn his anger away from them.
□ Don't fret because of evildoers; don't
envy the wicked. For evil people have no
future; the light of the wicked will be
snuffed out.

JEREMIAH 2:31–4:18
"**O** my people, listen to the words
of the LORD!
Have I been like a desert to Israel?
Have I been to them a land of
darkness?
Why then do my people say, 'At last
we are free from God!
We don't need him anymore!'
³² Does a young woman forget her
jewelry?
Does a bride hide her wedding
dress?
Yet for years on end
my people have forgotten me.

³³ "How you plot and scheme to win
your lovers.
Even an experienced prostitute
could learn from you!
³⁴ Your clothing is stained with the
blood of the innocent and
the poor,
though you didn't catch them
breaking into your houses!
³⁵ And yet you say,
'I have done nothing wrong.
Surely God isn't angry with me!'
But now I will punish you severely
because you claim you have not
sinned.
³⁶ First here, then there—
you flit from one ally to another
asking for help.
But your new friends in Egypt will let
you down,
just as Assyria did before.
³⁷ In despair, you will be led into exile
with your hands on your heads,
for the LORD has rejected the
nations you trust.
They will not help you at all.

3:1 "IF a man divorces a woman
and she goes and marries
someone else,
he will not take her back again,
for that would surely corrupt
the land.
But you have prostituted yourself
with many lovers,
so why are you trying to come
back to me?"
says the LORD.
² "Look at the shrines on every hilltop.
Is there any place you have not
been defiled
by your adultery with other gods?
You sit like a prostitute beside the
road waiting for a customer.
You sit alone like a nomad in the
desert.
You have polluted the land with
your prostitution
and your wickedness.
³ That's why even the spring rains
have failed.

For you are a brazen prostitute
and completely shameless.
⁴ Yet you say to me,
'Father, you have been my guide
since my youth.
⁵ Surely you won't be angry forever!
Surely you can forget about it!'
So you talk,
but you keep on doing all the evil
you can."

⁶During the reign of King Josiah, the
LORD said to me, "Have you seen what
fickle Israel has done? Like a wife who
commits adultery, Israel has worshiped
other gods on every hill and under every
green tree. ⁷I thought, 'After she has
done all this, she will return to me.' But
she did not return, and her faithless
sister Judah saw this. ⁸She saw that I divorced faithless Israel because of her
adultery. But that treacherous sister Judah had no fear, and now she, too, has
left me and given herself to prostitution.
⁹Israel treated it all so lightly—she
thought nothing of committing adultery
by worshiping idols made of wood and
stone. So now the land has been polluted. ¹⁰But despite all this, her faithless
sister Judah has never sincerely returned
to me. She has only pretended to be
sorry. I, the LORD, have spoken!"

¹¹Then the LORD said to me, "Even
faithless Israel is less guilty than treacherous Judah! ¹²Therefore, go and give
this message to Israel.* This is what the
LORD says:

"O Israel, my faithless people,
come home to me again,
for I am merciful.
I will not be angry with you forever.
¹³ Only acknowledge your guilt.
Admit that you rebelled against
the LORD your God
and committed adultery against
him
by worshiping idols under every
green tree.
Confess that you refused to listen
to my voice.
I, the LORD, have spoken!

¹⁴ "Return home, you wayward
children,"
says the LORD,
"for I am your master.
I will bring you back to the land
of Israel*—
one from this town and two from
that family—
from wherever you are scattered.
¹⁵ And I will give you shepherds after
my own heart,
who will guide you with
knowledge and understanding.

¹⁶"And when your land is once more
filled with people," says the LORD, "you
will no longer wish for 'the good old
days' when you possessed the Ark of
the LORD's Covenant. You will not miss
those days or even remember them, and
there will be no need to rebuild the Ark.
¹⁷In that day Jerusalem will be known
as 'The Throne of the LORD.' All nations
will come there to honor the LORD. They
will no longer stubbornly follow their
own evil desires. ¹⁸In those days the
people of Judah and Israel will return
together from exile in the north. They
will return to the land I gave their ancestors as an inheritance forever.

¹⁹ "I thought to myself,
'I would love to treat you as my
own children!'
I wanted nothing more than to give
you this beautiful land—
the finest possession in
the world.
I looked forward to your calling
me 'Father,'
and I wanted you never to turn
from me.
²⁰ But you have been unfaithful to me,
you people of Israel!
You have been like a faithless wife
who leaves her husband.
I, the LORD, have spoken."

²¹ Voices are heard high on the
windswept mountains,
the weeping and pleading of
Israel's people.

He, Keeps Knocking 16

For they have chosen crooked paths
and have forgotten the LORD
their God.

22 "My wayward children," says the
LORD,
"come back to me, and I will heal
your wayward hearts."

"Yes, we're coming," the people reply,
"for you are the LORD our God.
23 Our worship of idols on the hills
and our religious orgies on the
mountains
are a delusion.
Only in the LORD our God
will Israel ever find salvation.
24 From childhood we have watched
as everything our ancestors
worked for—
their flocks and herds, their sons
and daughters—
was squandered on a delusion.
25 Let us now lie down in shame
and cover ourselves with
dishonor,
for we and our ancestors have
sinned
against the LORD our God.
From our childhood to this day
we have never obeyed him."

4:1 "O Israel," says the LORD,
"if you wanted to return to me,
you could.
You could throw away your
detestable idols
and stray away no more. *yes Lord*

2 Then when you swear by my name,
saying,
'As surely as the LORD lives,'
you could do so
with truth, justice, and
righteousness.
Then you would be a blessing to the
nations of the world,
and all people would come and
praise my name."

3 This is what the LORD says to the
people of Judah and Jerusalem:

"Plow up the hard ground
of your hearts!

Do not waste your good seed
among thorns.
4 O people of Judah and Jerusalem,
surrender your pride and power.
Change your hearts before the LORD,*
or my anger will burn like an
unquenchable fire
because of all your sins.

5 "Shout to Judah, and broadcast
to Jerusalem!
Tell them to sound the alarm
throughout the land:
'Run for your lives!
Flee to the fortified cities!'
6 Raise a signal flag as a warning for
Jerusalem*:
'Flee now! Do not delay!'
For I am bringing terrible
destruction upon you
from the north."

7 A lion stalks from its den,
a destroyer of nations.
It has left its lair and is headed
your way.
It's going to devastate your land!
Your towns will lie in ruins,
with no one living in them
anymore.
8 So put on clothes of mourning
and weep with broken hearts,
for the fierce anger of the LORD
is still upon us.

9 "In that day," says the LORD,
"the king and the officials will
tremble in fear.
The priests will be struck with horror,
and the prophets will be
appalled."

10 Then I said, "O Sovereign LORD,
the people have been deceived by
what you said,
for you promised peace for
Jerusalem.
But the sword is held at their
throats!"

11 The time is coming when the LORD
will say
to the people of Jerusalem,

This relates to last Sundays message.

"My dear people, a burning wind is
   blowing in from the desert,
   and it's not a gentle breeze useful
   for winnowing grain.
12 It is a roaring blast sent by me!
   Now I will pronounce your
   destruction!"

13 Our enemy rushes down on us like
   storm clouds!
   His chariots are like whirlwinds.
His horses are swifter than eagles.
   How terrible it will be, for we are
   doomed!
14 O Jerusalem, cleanse your heart
   that you may be saved.
   How long will you harbor
   your evil thoughts?
15 Your destruction has been announced
   from Dan and the hill country
   of Ephraim.

16 "Warn the surrounding nations
   and announce this to Jerusalem:
   The enemy is coming from a distant
   land,
   raising a battle cry against the
   towns of Judah.
17 They surround Jerusalem like
   watchmen around a field,
   for my people have rebelled
   against me,"
   says the LORD.
18 "Your own actions have brought
   this upon you.
   This punishment is bitter,
   piercing you to the heart!"

3:12 Hebrew *toward the north.*   **3:14** Hebrew *to Zion.*
4:4 Hebrew *Circumcise yourselves to the LORD, and take
away the foreskins of your heart.*   **4:6** Hebrew *Zion.*

COLOSSIANS 1:1-17

This letter is from Paul, chosen by the
will of God to be an apostle of Christ
Jesus, and from our brother Timothy.
   2 We are writing to God's holy people
in the city of Colosse, who are faithful
brothers and sisters* in Christ.
   May God our Father give you grace
and peace.
   3 We always pray for you, and we give
thanks to God, the Father of our Lord
Jesus Christ. 4 For we have heard of your
faith in Christ Jesus and your love for

all of God's people, 5 which come from
your confident hope of what God has
reserved for you in heaven. You have
had this expectation ever since you first
heard the truth of the Good News.
   6 This same Good News that came to
you is going out all over the world. It is
bearing fruit everywhere by changing
lives, just as it changed your lives from
the day you first heard and understood
the truth about God's wonderful grace.
   7 You learned about the Good News
from Epaphras, our beloved co-worker.
He is Christ's faithful servant, and he is
helping us on your behalf.* 8 He has told
us about the love for others that the
Holy Spirit has given you.
   9 So we have not stopped praying for
you since we first heard about you. We
ask God to give you complete knowledge
of his will and to give you spiritual wisdom and understanding. 10 Then the way
you live will always honor and please the
Lord, and your lives will produce every
kind of good fruit. All the while, you will
grow as you learn to know God better
and better.
   11 We also pray that you will be
strengthened with all his glorious power
so you will have all the endurance and patience you need. May you be filled with
joy,* 12 always thanking the Father. He
has enabled you to share in the inheritance that belongs to his people, who live
in the light. 13 **For he has rescued us
from the kingdom of darkness and
transferred us into the Kingdom of
his dear Son, 14 who purchased our
freedom* and forgave our sins.**

15 Christ is the visible image of the
   invisible God.
   He existed before anything
   was created and is supreme
   over all creation,*
16 for through him God created
   everything
   in the heavenly realms and
   on earth.
   He made the things we can see
   and the things we can't see—
   such as thrones, kingdoms, rulers,

and authorities in the
unseen world.
Everything was created through
him and for him.
¹⁷ He existed before anything else,
and he holds all creation together.

1:2 Greek *faithful brothers.* 1:7 Or *he is ministering on
your behalf;* some manuscripts read *he is ministering on
our behalf.* 1:11 Or *all the patience and endurance you
need with joy.* 1:14 Some manuscripts add *with his blood.*
1:15 Or *He is the firstborn of all creation.*

PSALM 76:1-12

*For the choir director: A psalm of Asaph.
A song to be accompanied by stringed
instruments.*

¹ God is honored in Judah;
his name is great in Israel.
² Jerusalem* is where he lives;
Mount Zion is his home.
³ There he has broken the fiery
arrows of the enemy,
the shields and swords and
weapons of war.   *Interlude*

⁴ You are glorious and more majestic
than the everlasting mountains.*
⁵ Our boldest enemies have been
plundered.
They lie before us in the sleep
of death.
No warrior could lift a hand
against us.
⁶ At the blast of your breath, O God
of Jacob,
their horses and chariots lay still.

⁷ No wonder you are greatly feared!
Who can stand before you when
your anger explodes?
⁸ From heaven you sentenced your
enemies;
the earth trembled and stood
silent before you.
⁹ You stand up to judge those who do
evil, O God,
and to rescue the oppressed
of the earth.   *Interlude*
¹⁰ Human defiance only enhances
your glory,
for you use it as a weapon.*

¹¹ Make vows to the LORD your God,
and keep them.

Let everyone bring tribute to the
Awesome One.
¹² For he breaks the pride of princes,
and the kings of the earth fear him.

76:2 Hebrew *Salem,* another name for Jerusalem. 76:4 As
in Greek version; Hebrew reads *than mountains filled with
beasts of prey.* 76:10 The meaning of the Hebrew is
uncertain.

PROVERBS 24:21-22

My child, fear the LORD and the king.
Don't associate with rebels, for disaster
will hit them suddenly. Who knows
what punishment will come from the
LORD and the king?

OCTOBER 5

JEREMIAH 4:19–6:15
My heart, my heart—I writhe
in pain!
My heart pounds within me!
I cannot be still.
For I have heard the blast of enemy
trumpets
and the roar of their battle cries.
²⁰ Waves of destruction roll over
the land,
until it lies in complete desolation.
Suddenly my tents are destroyed;
in a moment my shelters are
crushed.
²¹ How long must I see the battle flags
and hear the trumpets of war?

²² "My people are foolish
and do not know me," says
the LORD.
"They are stupid children
who have no understanding.
They are clever enough at doing
wrong,
but they have no idea how
to do right!"

²³ I looked at the earth, and it was
empty and formless.

I looked at the heavens, and
there was no light.
24 I looked at the mountains and hills,
and they trembled and shook.
25 I looked, and all the people were gone.
All the birds of the sky had
flown away.
26 I looked, and the fertile fields had
become a wilderness.
The towns lay in ruins,
crushed by the LORD's fierce anger.

27 This is what the LORD says:
"The whole land will be ruined,
but I will not destroy it
completely.
28 The earth will mourn
and the heavens will be draped
in black
because of my decree against
my people.
I have made up my mind and will
not change it."

29 At the noise of charioteers and
archers,
the people flee in terror.
They hide in the bushes
and run for the mountains.
All the towns have been
abandoned—
not a person remains!
30 What are you doing,
you who have been plundered?
Why do you dress up in beautiful
clothing
and put on gold jewelry?
Why do you brighten your eyes with
mascara?
Your primping will do you no good!
The allies who were your lovers
despise you and seek to kill you.

31 I hear a cry, like that of a woman in
labor,
the groans of a woman giving
birth to her first child.
It is beautiful Jerusalem*
gasping for breath and crying out,
"Help! I'm being murdered!"

5:1 "RUN up and down every street in
Jerusalem," says the LORD.

"Look high and low; search
throughout the city!
If you can find even one just and
honest person,
I will not destroy the city.
2 But even when they are under oath,
saying, 'As surely as the LORD lives,'
they are still telling lies!"

3 LORD, you are searching for honesty.
You struck your people,
but they paid no attention.
You crushed them,
but they refused to be corrected.
They are determined, with faces set
like stone;
they have refused to repent.

4 Then I said, "But what can we expect
from the poor?
They are ignorant.
They don't know the ways of
the LORD.
They don't understand God's laws.
5 So I will go and speak to their
leaders.
Surely they know the ways
of the LORD
and understand God's laws."
But the leaders, too, as one man,
had thrown off God's yoke
and broken his chains.
6 So now a lion from the forest will
attack them;
a wolf from the desert will
pounce on them.
A leopard will lurk near their towns,
tearing apart any who dare to
venture out.
For their rebellion is great,
and their sins are many.

7 "How can I pardon you?
For even your children have
turned from me.
They have sworn by gods that are
not gods at all!
I fed my people until they
were full.
But they thanked me by committing
adultery
and lining up at the brothels.
8 They are well-fed, lusty stallions,

each neighing for his neighbor's
    wife.
⁹ Should I not punish them for this?"
    says the LORD.
    "Should I not avenge myself
        against such a nation?

¹⁰ "Go down the rows of the vineyards
        and destroy the grapevines,
    leaving a scattered few alive.
    Strip the branches from the vines,
        for these people do not belong
            to the LORD.
¹¹ The people of Israel and Judah
        are full of treachery against me,"
    says the LORD.
¹² "They have lied about the LORD
        and said, 'He won't bother us!
    No disasters will come upon us.
    There will be no war or famine.
¹³ God's prophets are all windbags
        who don't really speak for him.
    Let their predictions of disaster
        fall on themselves!'"

¹⁴Therefore, this is what the LORD God
of Heaven's Armies says:

    "Because the people are talking
        like this,
    my messages will flame out of
        your mouth
    and burn the people like kindling
        wood.
¹⁵ O Israel, I will bring a distant nation
        against you,"
    says the LORD.
    "It is a mighty nation,
        an ancient nation,
    a people whose language you do
        not know,
    whose speech you cannot
        understand.
¹⁶ Their weapons are deadly;
    their warriors are mighty.
¹⁷ They will devour the food of your
        harvest;
    they will devour your sons
        and daughters.
    They will devour your flocks
        and herds;
    they will devour your grapes
        and figs.

And they will destroy your fortified
    towns,
    which you think are so safe.

¹⁸"Yet even in those days I will not
blot you out completely," says the LORD.
¹⁹"And when your people ask, 'Why did
the LORD our God do all this to us?' you
must reply, 'You rejected him and gave
yourselves to foreign gods in your own
land. Now you will serve foreigners in a
land that is not your own.'

²⁰ "Make this announcement to Israel,*
        and say this to Judah:
²¹ Listen, you foolish and senseless
        people,
    with eyes that do not see
    and ears that do not hear.
²² Have you no respect for me?
    Why don't you tremble in my
        presence?
    I, the LORD, define the ocean's sandy
        shoreline
    as an everlasting boundary that
        the waters cannot cross.
    The waves may toss and roar,
        but they can never pass the
            boundaries I set.
²³ But my people have stubborn and
        rebellious hearts.
    They have turned away and
        abandoned me.
²⁴ They do not say from the heart,
    'Let us live in awe of the LORD
        our God,
    for he gives us rain each spring
        and fall,
    assuring us of a harvest when the
        time is right.'
²⁵ Your wickedness has deprived you
        of these wonderful blessings.
    Your sin has robbed you of all
        these good things.

²⁶ "Among my people are wicked men
    who lie in wait for victims like a
        hunter hiding in a blind.
    They continually set traps
        to catch people.
²⁷ Like a cage filled with birds,
    their homes are filled with evil plots.

And now they are great
and rich.
28 They are fat and sleek,
and there is no limit to their
wicked deeds.
They refuse to provide justice
to orphans
and deny the rights of the poor.
29 Should I not punish them for this?"
says the LORD.
"Should I not avenge myself
against such a nation?
30 A horrible and shocking thing
has happened in this land—
31 the prophets give false prophecies,
and the priests rule with an iron
hand.
Worse yet, my people like it
that way!
But what will you do when the
end comes?

6:1 "RUN for your lives, you people of
Benjamin!
Get out of Jerusalem!
Sound the alarm in Tekoa!
Send up a signal at Beth-hakkerem!
A powerful army is coming from
the north,
coming with disaster and
destruction.
2 O Jerusalem,* you are my
beautiful and delicate
daughter—
but I will destroy you!
3 Enemies will surround you, like
shepherds camped around
the city.
Each chooses a place for his
troops to devour.
4 They shout, 'Prepare for battle!
Attack at noon!'
'No, it's too late; the day is fading,
and the evening shadows are
falling.'
5 'Well then, let's attack at night
and destroy her palaces!'"

6 This is what the LORD of Heaven's
Armies says:
"Cut down the trees for battering
rams.

Build siege ramps against the
walls of Jerusalem.
This is the city to be punished,
for she is wicked through and
through.
7 She spouts evil like a fountain.
Her streets echo with the sounds
of violence and destruction.
I always see her sickness and sores.
8 Listen to this warning, Jerusalem,
or I will turn from you in disgust.
Listen, or I will turn you into a heap
of ruins,
a land where no one lives."

9 This is what the LORD of Heaven's
Armies says:
"Even the few who remain in Israel
will be picked over again,
as when a harvester checks each
vine a second time
to pick the grapes that were
missed."

10 To whom can I give warning?
Who will listen when I speak?
Their ears are closed,
and they cannot hear.
They scorn the word of the LORD.
They don't want to listen at all.
11 So now I am filled with the
LORD's fury.
Yes, I am tired of holding it in!

"I will pour out my fury on children
playing in the streets
and on gatherings of young men,
on husbands and wives
and on those who are old and gray.
12 Their homes will be turned over to
their enemies,
as will their fields and their wives.
For I will raise my powerful fist
against the people of this land,"
says the LORD.
13 "From the least to the greatest,
their lives are ruled by greed.
From prophets to priests,
they are all frauds.
14 They offer superficial treatments
for my people's mortal wound.
They give assurances of peace
when there is no peace.

15 Are they ashamed of their
disgusting actions?
Not at all—they don't even know
how to blush!
Therefore, they will lie among the
slaughtered.
They will be brought down when
I punish them,"
says the LORD.

4:31 Hebrew *the daughter of Zion.* 5:20 Hebrew *to the house of Jacob.* The names "Jacob" and "Israel" are often interchanged throughout the Old Testament, referring sometimes to the individual patriarch and sometimes to the nation. 6:2 Hebrew *Daughter of Zion.*

COLOSSIANS 1:18–2:7
Christ is also the head of the church,
which is his body.
He is the beginning,
supreme over all who rise from
the dead.*
So he is first in everything.
19 For God in all his fullness
was pleased to live in Christ,
20 and through him God reconciled
everything to himself.
He made peace with everything in
heaven and on earth
by means of Christ's blood
on the cross.

21This includes you who were once far away from God. You were his enemies, separated from him by your evil thoughts and actions. 22Yet now he has reconciled you to himself through the death of Christ in his physical body. As a result, he has brought you into his own presence, and you are holy and blameless as you stand before him without a single fault.

23But you must continue to believe this truth and stand firmly in it. Don't drift away from the assurance you received when you heard the Good News. The Good News has been preached all over the world, and I, Paul, have been appointed as God's servant to proclaim it.

24I am glad when I suffer for you in my body, for I am participating in the sufferings of Christ that continue for his body, the church. 25God has given me the responsibility of serving his church by proclaiming his entire message to you. 26This message was kept secret for centuries and generations past, but now it has been revealed to God's people. 27For God wanted them to know that the riches and glory of Christ are for you Gentiles, too. And this is the secret: Christ lives in you. This gives you the assurance of sharing his glory.

28So we tell others about Christ, warning everyone and teaching everyone with all the wisdom God has given us. We want to present them to God, perfect* in their relationship to Christ. 29That's why I work and struggle so hard, depending on Christ's mighty power that works within me.

2:1I WANT you to know how much I have agonized for you and for the church at Laodicea, and for many other believers who have never met me personally. 2I want them to be encouraged and knit together by strong ties of love. I want them to have complete confidence that they understand God's mysterious plan, which is Christ himself. 3In him lie hidden all the treasures of wisdom and knowledge.

4I am telling you this so no one will deceive you with well-crafted arguments. 5For though I am far away from you, my heart is with you. And I rejoice that you are living as you should and that your faith in Christ is strong.

6**And now, just as you accepted Christ Jesus as your Lord, you must continue to follow him. 7Let your roots grow down into him, and let your lives be built on him. Then your faith will grow strong in the truth you were taught, and you will overflow with thankfulness.**

1:18 Or *the firstborn from the dead.* 1:28 Or *mature.*

PSALM 77:1-20
For Jeduthun, the choir director: A psalm of Asaph.

1 I cry out to God; yes, I shout.
Oh, that God would listen to me!
2 When I was in deep trouble,
I searched for the Lord.

All night long I prayed, with hands
        lifted toward heaven,
    but my soul was not comforted.
³ I think of God, and I moan,
    overwhelmed with longing
        for his help.   *Interlude*

⁴ You don't let me sleep.
    I am too distressed even to pray!
⁵ I think of the good old days,
    long since ended,
⁶ when my nights were filled with
        joyful songs.
    I search my soul and ponder the
        difference now.
⁷ Has the Lord rejected me forever?
    Will he never again be kind to me?
⁸ Is his unfailing love gone forever?
    Have his promises permanently
        failed?
⁹ Has God forgotten to be gracious?
    Has he slammed the door on his
        compassion?   *Interlude*

¹⁰ And I said, "This is my fate;
    the Most High has turned his
        hand against me."
¹¹ But then I recall all you have done,
        O Lord;
    I remember your wonderful
        deeds of long ago.
¹² They are constantly in my thoughts.
    I cannot stop thinking about your
        mighty works.

¹³ O God, your ways are holy.
    Is there any god as mighty as you?
¹⁴ You are the God of great wonders!
    You demonstrate your awesome
        power among the nations.
¹⁵ By your strong arm, you redeemed
        your people,
    the descendants of Jacob
        and Joseph.   *Interlude*

¹⁶ When the Red Sea* saw you, O God,
    its waters looked and trembled!
    The sea quaked to its very depths.
¹⁷ The clouds poured down rain;
    the thunder rumbled in the sky.
    Your arrows of lightning flashed.
¹⁸ Your thunder roared from
        the whirlwind;

the lightning lit up the world!
    The earth trembled and shook.
¹⁹ Your road led through the sea,
    your pathway through the
        mighty waters—
    a pathway no one knew was there!
²⁰ You led your people along that road
        like a flock of sheep,
    with Moses and Aaron as their
        shepherds.

77:16 Hebrew *the waters.*

PROVERBS 24:23-25
Here are some further sayings of the
wise: □It is wrong to show favoritism
when passing judgment. A judge who
says to the wicked, "You are innocent,"
will be cursed by many people and de-
nounced by the nations. But it will go
well for those who convict the guilty;
rich blessings will be showered on them.

OCTOBER 6

JEREMIAH 6:16–8:7
This is what the Lord says:
"Stop at the crossroads and
    look around.
    Ask for the old, godly way, and
        walk in it.
    Travel its path, and you will find
        rest for your souls.
    But you reply, 'No, that's not the
        road we want!'
¹⁷ I posted watchmen over you who said,
    'Listen for the sound of the alarm.'
    But you replied,
    'No! We won't pay attention!'

¹⁸ "Therefore, listen to this, all
        you nations.
    Take note of my people's situation.
¹⁹ Listen, all the earth!
    I will bring disaster on my people.
    It is the fruit of their own schemes,
    because they refuse to listen to me.

They have rejected my word.
²⁰ There's no use offering me sweet
frankincense from Sheba.
Keep your fragrant calamus
imported from distant lands!
I will not accept your burnt offerings.
Your sacrifices have no pleasing
aroma for me."

²¹ Therefore, this is what the LORD says:
"I will put obstacles in my
people's path.
Fathers and sons will both fall over
them.
Neighbors and friends will
die together."

²² This is what the LORD says:
"Look! A great army coming from
the north!
A great nation is rising against
you from far-off lands.
²³ They are armed with bows and spears.
They are cruel and show no mercy.
They sound like a roaring sea
as they ride forward on horses.
They are coming in battle formation,
planning to destroy you, beautiful
Jerusalem.*"

²⁴ We have heard reports about
the enemy,
and we wring our hands in fright.
Pangs of anguish have gripped us,
like those of a woman in labor.
²⁵ Don't go out to the fields!
Don't travel on the roads!
The enemy's sword is everywhere
and terrorizes us at every turn!
²⁶ Oh, my people, dress yourselves
in burlap
and sit among the ashes.
Mourn and weep bitterly, as for the
loss of an only son.
For suddenly the destroying
armies will be upon you!

²⁷ "Jeremiah, I have made you a tester
of metals,*
that you may determine the
quality of my people.
²⁸ They are the worst kind of rebel,
full of slander.

They are as hard as bronze and iron,
and they lead others into
corruption.
²⁹ The bellows fiercely fan the flames
to burn out the corruption.
But it does not purify them,
for the wickedness remains.
³⁰ I will label them 'Rejected Silver,'
for I, the LORD, am discarding
them."

^{7:1}THE LORD gave another message to
Jeremiah. He said, ²"Go to the entrance
of the LORD's Temple, and give this message to the people: 'O Judah, listen to this
message from the LORD! Listen to it, all of
you who worship here! ³This is what the
LORD of Heaven's Armies, the God of Israel, says:

"'Even now, if you quit your evil ways, I
will let you stay in your own land. ⁴But
don't be fooled by those who promise
you safety simply because the LORD's
Temple is here. They chant, "The LORD's
Temple is here! The LORD's Temple is
here!" ⁵But I will be merciful only if you
stop your evil thoughts and deeds and
start treating each other with justice;
⁶only if you stop exploiting foreigners,
orphans, and widows; only if you stop
your murdering; and only if you stop
harming yourselves by worshiping idols.
⁷Then I will let you stay in this land that I
gave to your ancestors to keep forever.

⁸"'Don't be fooled into thinking that
you will never suffer because the Temple
is here. It's a lie! ⁹Do you really think you
can steal, murder, commit adultery, lie,
and burn incense to Baal and all those
other new gods of yours, ¹⁰and then come
here and stand before me in my Temple
and chant, "We are safe!"—only to go
right back to all those evils again? ¹¹Don't
you yourselves admit that this Temple,
which bears my name, has become a den
of thieves? Surely I see all the evil going
on there. I, the LORD, have spoken!

¹²"'Go now to the place at Shiloh
where I once put the Tabernacle that
bore my name. See what I did there because of all the wickedness of my people, the Israelites. ¹³While you were

doing these wicked things, says the LORD, I spoke to you about it repeatedly, but you would not listen. I called out to you, but you refused to answer. [14]So just as I destroyed Shiloh, I will now destroy this Temple that bears my name, this Temple that you trust in for help, this place that I gave to you and your ancestors. [15]And I will send you out of my sight into exile, just as I did your relatives, the people of Israel.*'

[16]"Pray no more for these people, Jeremiah. Do not weep or pray for them, and don't beg me to help them, for I will not listen to you. [17]Don't you see what they are doing throughout the towns of Judah and in the streets of Jerusalem? [18]No wonder I am so angry! Watch how the children gather wood and the fathers build sacrificial fires. See how the women knead dough and make cakes to offer to the Queen of Heaven. And they pour out liquid offerings to their other idol gods! [19]Am I the one they are hurting?" asks the LORD. "Most of all, they hurt themselves, to their own shame."

[20]So this is what the Sovereign LORD says: "I will pour out my terrible fury on this place. Its people, animals, trees, and crops will be consumed by the unquenchable fire of my anger."

[21]This is what the LORD of Heaven's Armies, the God of Israel, says: "Take your burnt offerings and your other sacrifices and eat them yourselves! [22]When I led your ancestors out of Egypt, it was not burnt offerings and sacrifices I wanted from them. [23]This is what I told them: 'Obey me, and I will be your God, and you will be my people. Do everything as I say, and all will be well!'

[24]"But my people would not listen to me. They kept doing whatever they wanted, following the stubborn desires of their evil hearts. They went backward instead of forward. [25]From the day your ancestors left Egypt until now, I have continued to send my servants, the prophets—day in and day out. [26]But my people have not listened to me or even tried to hear. They have been stub-

born and sinful—even worse than their ancestors.

[27]"Tell them all this, but do not expect them to listen. Shout out your warnings, but do not expect them to respond. [28]Say to them, 'This is the nation whose people will not obey the LORD their God and who refuse to be taught. Truth has vanished from among them; it is no longer heard on their lips. [29]Shave your head in mourning, and weep alone on the mountains. For the LORD has rejected and forsaken this generation that has provoked his fury.'

[30]"The people of Judah have sinned before my very eyes," says the LORD. "They have set up their abominable idols right in the Temple that bears my name, defiling it. [31]They have built pagan shrines at Topheth, the garbage dump in the valley of Ben-Hinnom, and there they burn their sons and daughters in the fire. I have never commanded such a horrible deed; it never even crossed my mind to command such a thing! [32]So beware, for the time is coming," says the LORD, "when that garbage dump will no longer be called Topheth or the valley of Ben-Hinnom, but the Valley of Slaughter. They will bury the bodies in Topheth until there is no more room for them. [33]The bodies of my people will be food for the vultures and wild animals, and no one will be left to scare them away. [34]I will put an end to the happy singing and laughter in the streets of Jerusalem. The joyful voices of bridegrooms and brides will no longer be heard in the towns of Judah. The land will lie in complete desolation.

[8:1]"IN that day," says the LORD, "the enemy will break open the graves of the kings and officials of Judah, and the graves of the priests, prophets, and common people of Jerusalem. [2]They will spread out their bones on the ground before the sun, moon, and stars—the gods my people have loved, served, and worshiped. Their bones will not be gathered up again or buried but will be scattered on the ground like manure. [3]And the people of this evil nation who survive will wish to die rather than live where I will send them. I, the LORD of Heaven's Armies, have spoken!

4"Jeremiah, say to the people, 'This is what the LORD says:

"'When people fall down, don't they
    get up again?
When they discover they're on the
    wrong road, don't they turn back?
5 Then why do these people stay on
    their self-destructive path?
Why do the people of Jerusalem
    refuse to turn back?
They cling tightly to their lies
    and will not turn around.
6 I listen to their conversations
    and don't hear a word of truth.
Is anyone sorry for doing wrong?
    Does anyone say, "What a terrible
    thing I have done"?
No! All are running down the path
    of sin
    as swiftly as a horse galloping
    into battle!
7 Even the stork that flies across the sky
    knows the time of her migration,
as do the turtledove, the swallow,
    and the crane.*
    They all return at the proper time
    each year.
But not my people!
    They do not know the LORD's
    laws.'"

6:23 Hebrew *daughter of Zion.* 6:27 As in Greek version; Hebrew reads *of metals in my people a fortress.* 7:15 Hebrew *of Ephraim,* referring to the northern kingdom of Israel. 8:7 The identification of some of these birds is uncertain.

COLOSSIANS 2:8-23

Don't let anyone capture you [Colossians] with empty philosophies and high-sounding nonsense that come from human thinking and from the spiritual powers* of this world, rather than from Christ. 9**For in Christ lives all the fullness of God in a human body.*** 10**So you also are complete through your union with Christ, who is the head over every ruler and authority.**

11When you came to Christ, you were "circumcised," but not by a physical procedure. Christ performed a spiritual circumcision—the cutting away of your sinful nature.* 12For you were buried with Christ when you were baptized. And with him you were raised to new life because you trusted the mighty power of God, who raised Christ from the dead.

13 You were dead because of your sins and because your sinful nature was not yet cut away. Then God made you alive with Christ, for he forgave all our sins. 14He canceled the record of the charges against us and took it away by nailing it to the cross. 15In this way, he disarmed* the spiritual rulers and authorities. He shamed them publicly by his victory over them on the cross.

16So don't let anyone condemn you for what you eat or drink, or for not celebrating certain holy days or new moon ceremonies or Sabbaths. 17For these rules are only shadows of the reality yet to come. And Christ himself is that reality. 18Don't let anyone condemn you by insisting on pious self-denial or the worship of angels,* saying they have had visions about these things. Their sinful minds have made them proud, 19and they are not connected to Christ, the head of the body. For he holds the whole body together with its joints and ligaments, and it grows as God nourishes it.

20You have died with Christ, and he has set you free from the spiritual powers of this world. So why do you keep on following the rules of the world, such as, 21"Don't handle! Don't taste! Don't touch!"? 22Such rules are mere human teachings about things that deteriorate as we use them. 23These rules may seem wise because they require strong devotion, pious self-denial, and severe bodily discipline. But they provide no help in conquering a person's evil desires.

2:8 Or *the spiritual principles;* also in 2:20. 2:9 Or *in him dwells all the completeness of the Godhead bodily.* 2:11 Greek *the cutting away of the body of the flesh.* 2:15 Or *he stripped off.* 2:18 Or *or worshiping with angels.*

PSALM 78:1-31
A psalm* of Asaph.

1 **O** my people, listen to my instructions.
  Open your ears to what I am
      saying,
2   for I will speak to you in a parable.
  I will teach you hidden lessons
      from our past—
3   stories we have heard and known,
      stories our ancestors handed
      down to us.
4 We will not hide these truths from
      our children;
  we will tell the next generation
  about the glorious deeds of the LORD,
      about his power and his mighty
      wonders.
5 For he issued his laws to Jacob;
  he gave his instructions to Israel.
  He commanded our ancestors
      to teach them to their children,
6 so the next generation might
      know them—
  even the children not yet born—
  and they in turn will teach their
      own children.
7 So each generation should set its
      hope anew on God,
  not forgetting his glorious miracles
  and obeying his commands.
8 Then they will not be like their
      ancestors—
  stubborn, rebellious, and
      unfaithful,
  refusing to give their hearts to God.

9 The warriors of Ephraim, though
      armed with bows,
  turned their backs and fled on the
      day of battle.
10 They did not keep God's covenant
      and refused to live by his
      instructions.
11 They forgot what he had done—
  the great wonders he had
      shown them,
12 the miracles he did for their ancestors
      on the plain of Zoan in the land
      of Egypt.
13 For he divided the sea and led them
      through,

  making the water stand up
      like walls!
14 In the daytime he led them by
      a cloud,
  and all night by a pillar of fire.
15 He split open the rocks in the
      wilderness
  to give them water, as from a
      gushing spring.
16 He made streams pour from the rock,
  making the waters flow down
      like a river!

17 Yet they kept on sinning against him,
  rebelling against the Most High
      in the desert.
18 They stubbornly tested God in their
      hearts,
  demanding the foods they craved.
19 They even spoke against God
      himself, saying,
  "God can't give us food in the
      wilderness.
20 Yes, he can strike a rock so water
      gushes out,
  but he can't give his people bread
      and meat."
21 When the LORD heard them, he
      was furious.
  The fire of his wrath burned
      against Jacob.
  Yes, his anger rose against Israel,
22 for they did not believe God
  or trust him to care for them.
23 But he commanded the skies
      to open;
  he opened the doors of heaven.
24 He rained down manna for them
      to eat;
  he gave them bread from heaven.
25 They ate the food of angels!
  God gave them all they could hold.
26 He released the east wind in the
      heavens
  and guided the south wind by his
      mighty power.
27 He rained down meat as thick
      as dust—
  birds as plentiful as the sand on
      the seashore!
28 He caused the birds to fall within
      their camp

and all around their tents.
²⁹ The people ate their fill.
He gave them what they craved.
³⁰ But before they satisfied their
craving,
while the meat was yet in their
mouths,
³¹ the anger of God rose against them,
and he killed their strongest men.
He struck down the finest of
Israel's young men.

78:TITLE Hebrew *maskil*. This may be a literary or musical term.

PROVERBS 24:26
An honest answer is like a kiss of friendship.

OCTOBER
7

JEREMIAH 8:8–9:26
"'**H**ow can you say, "We are wise
because we have the word of
the LORD,"
when your teachers have twisted
it by writing lies?
⁹ These wise teachers will fall
into the trap of their own
foolishness,
for they have rejected the word
of the LORD.
Are they so wise after all?
¹⁰ I will give their wives to others
and their farms to strangers.
From the least to the greatest,
their lives are ruled by greed.
Yes, even my prophets and priests
are like that.
They are all frauds.
¹¹ They offer superficial treatments
for my people's mortal wound.
They give assurances of peace
when there is no peace.
¹² Are they ashamed of these
disgusting actions?
Not at all—they don't even know
how to blush!

Therefore, they will lie among the
slaughtered.
They will be brought down
when I punish them,
says the LORD.
¹³ I will surely consume them.
There will be no more
harvests of figs and grapes.
Their fruit trees will all die.
Whatever I gave them will soon
be gone.
I, the LORD, have spoken!'

¹⁴ "Then the people will say,
'Why should we wait here to die?
Come, let's go to the fortified towns
and die there.
For the LORD our God has decreed
our destruction
and has given us a cup of poison
to drink
because we sinned against
the LORD.
¹⁵ We hoped for peace, but no peace
came.
We hoped for a time of healing,
but found only terror.'

¹⁶ "The snorting of the enemies'
warhorses can be heard
all the way from the land of Dan
in the north!
The neighing of their stallions
makes the whole land
tremble.
They are coming to devour the
land and everything in it—
cities and people alike.
¹⁷ I will send these enemy troops
among you
like poisonous snakes you
cannot charm.
They will bite you, and you will die.
I, the Lord, have spoken!"

¹⁸ My grief is beyond healing;
my heart is broken.
¹⁹ Listen to the weeping of my people;
it can be heard all across
the land.
"Has the LORD abandoned
Jerusalem?*" the people ask.
"Is her King no longer there?"

"Oh, why have they provoked my
    anger with their carved idols
    and their worthless foreign
        gods?" says the LORD.

²⁰ "The harvest is finished,
    and the summer is gone," the
        people cry,
    "yet we are not saved!"

²¹ I hurt with the hurt of my people.
    I mourn and am overcome
        with grief.
²² Is there no medicine in Gilead?
    Is there no physician there?
    Why is there no healing
        for the wounds of my people?

^{9:1}*IF only my head were a pool of water
    and my eyes a fountain of tears,
    I would weep day and night
        for all my people who have been
            slaughtered.
²*Oh, that I could go away and forget
        my people
    and live in a travelers' shack
        in the desert.
    For they are all adulterers—
        a pack of treacherous liars.

³ "My people bend their tongues
        like bows
    to shoot out lies.
    They refuse to stand up for the truth.
        They only go from bad to worse.
    They do not know me,"
        says the LORD.

⁴ "Beware of your neighbor!
    Don't even trust your brother!
    For brother takes advantage of
        brother,
    and friend slanders friend.
⁵ They all fool and defraud each other;
        no one tells the truth.
    With practiced tongues they tell lies;
        they wear themselves out with
            all their sinning.
⁶ They pile lie upon lie
    and utterly refuse to acknowledge
        me,"
    says the LORD.

⁷ Therefore, this is what the LORD
    of Heaven's Armies says:

"See, I will melt them down
    in a crucible
    and test them like metal.
What else can I do with my people?*
⁸   For their tongues shoot lies like
        poisoned arrows.
    They speak friendly words to their
        neighbors
    while scheming in their heart
        to kill them.
⁹ Should I not punish them for this?"
    says the LORD.
    "Should I not avenge myself
        against such a nation?"

¹⁰ I will weep for the mountains
    and wail for the wilderness
        pastures.
    For they are desolate and empty
        of life;
    the lowing of cattle is heard no
        more;
    the birds and wild animals have
        all fled.

¹¹ "I will make Jerusalem into a heap
    of ruins," says the LORD.
    "It will be a place haunted by
        jackals.
    The towns of Judah will be
        ghost towns,
    with no one living in them."

¹² Who is wise enough to understand
all this? Who has been instructed by the
LORD and can explain it to others? Why
has the land been so ruined that no one
dares to travel through it?

¹³ The LORD replies, "This has hap-
pened because my people have abandoned my instructions; they have refused
to obey what I said. ¹⁴Instead, they have
stubbornly followed their own desires
and worshiped the images of Baal, as
their ancestors taught them. ¹⁵So now,
this is what the LORD of Heaven's Armies,
the God of Israel, says: Look! I will feed
them with bitterness and give them poi-
son to drink. ¹⁶I will scatter them around
the world, in places they and their ancestors never heard of, and even there I will
chase them with the sword until I have
destroyed them completely."

¹⁷ This is what the LORD of Heaven's
        Armies says:
  "Consider all this, and call for the
        mourners.
     Send for the women who mourn
        at funerals.
¹⁸ Quick! Begin your weeping!
     Let the tears flow from your eyes.
¹⁹ Hear the people of Jerusalem*
        crying in despair,
     'We are ruined! We are
        completely humiliated!
  We must leave our land,
     because our homes have been
        torn down.'"

²⁰ Listen, you women, to the words
        of the LORD;
     open your ears to what he has
        to say.
  Teach your daughters to wail;
     teach one another how to lament.
²¹ For death has crept in through our
        windows
     and has entered our mansions.
  It has killed off the flower of
        our youth:
     Children no longer play in the
        streets,
     and young men no longer gather
        in the squares.

²² This is what the LORD says:
  "Bodies will be scattered across
        the fields like clumps of
        manure,
     like bundles of grain after the
        harvest.
  No one will be left to bury them."

²³ This is what the LORD says:
  "Don't let the wise boast in
        their wisdom,
     or the powerful boast in
        their power,
     or the rich boast in their riches.
²⁴ But those who wish to boast
     should boast in this alone:
  that they truly know me and
        understand that I am the LORD
     who demonstrates unfailing love
     and who brings justice and
        righteousness to the earth,

  and that I delight in these things.
     I, the LORD, have spoken!

²⁵"A time is coming," says the LORD,
"when I will punish all those who are
circumcised in body but not in spirit—
²⁶ the Egyptians, Edomites, Ammonites,
Moabites, the people who live in the
desert in remote places,* and yes, even
the people of Judah. And like all these
pagan nations, the people of Israel also
have uncircumcised hearts."

8:19 Hebrew *Zion?*   **9:1** Verse 9:1 is numbered 8:23 in
Hebrew text.   **9:2** Verses 9:2-26 are numbered 9:1-25 in
Hebrew text.   **9:7** Hebrew *with the daughter of my people?*
Greek version reads *with the evil daughter of my people?*
9:19 Hebrew *Zion.*   **9:26** Or *in the desert and clip the
corners of their hair.*

COLOSSIANS 3:1-17

Since you have been raised to new life
with Christ, set your sights on the reali-
ties of heaven, where Christ sits in the
place of honor at God's right hand.
² Think about the things of heaven, not
the things of earth. ³For you died to this
life, and your real life is hidden with
Christ in God. ⁴And when Christ, who
is your* life, is revealed to the whole
world, you will share in all his glory.

⁵ So put to death the sinful, earthly
things lurking within you. Have nothing
to do with sexual immorality, impurity,
lust, and evil desires. Don't be greedy, for
a greedy person is an idolater, worshiping the things of this world. ⁶Because of
these sins, the anger of God is coming.*
⁷You used to do these things when your
life was still part of this world. ⁸But now
is the time to get rid of anger, rage, mali-
cious behavior, slander, and dirty language. ⁹Don't lie to each other, for you
have stripped off your old sinful nature
and all its wicked deeds. ¹⁰Put on your
new nature, and be renewed as you learn
to know your Creator and become like
him. ¹¹In this new life, it doesn't matter
if you are a Jew or a Gentile,* circumcised or uncircumcised, barbaric, un-
civilized,* slave, or free. Christ is all that
matters, and he lives in all of us.

¹²Since God chose you to be the holy
people he loves, you must clothe yourselves with tenderhearted mercy, kind-

ness, humility, gentleness, and patience. [13]Make allowance for each other's faults, and forgive anyone who offends you. Remember, the Lord forgave you, so you must forgive others. [14]Above all, clothe yourselves with love, which binds us all together in perfect harmony. [15]And let the peace that comes from Christ rule in your hearts. For as members of one body you are called to live in peace. And always be thankful.

[16]Let the message about Christ, in all its richness, fill your lives. Teach and counsel each other with all the wisdom he gives. Sing psalms and hymns and spiritual songs to God with thankful hearts. [17]**And whatever you do or say, do it as a representative of the Lord Jesus, giving thanks through him to God the Father.**

3:4 Some manuscripts read *our.*   3:6 Some manuscripts read *is coming on all who disobey him.*   3:11a Greek *a Greek.*   3:11b Greek *Barbarian, Scythian.*

PSALM 78:32-55

But in spite of this, the people
    kept sinning.
Despite his [God's] wonders, they
    refused to trust him.
[33] So he ended their lives in failure,
    their years in terror.
[34] When God began killing them,
    they finally sought him.
They repented and took God
    seriously.
[35] Then they remembered that God
    was their rock,
    that God Most High* was their
    redeemer.
[36] But all they gave him was lip service;
    they lied to him with their
    tongues.
[37] Their hearts were not loyal to him.
    They did not keep his covenant.
[38] Yet he was merciful and forgave
    their sins
    and did not destroy them all.
Many times he held back his
    anger
    and did not unleash his fury!
[39] For he remembered that they were
    merely mortal,

gone like a breath of wind that
    never returns.

[40] Oh, how often they rebelled against
    him in the wilderness
    and grieved his heart in that dry
    wasteland.
[41] Again and again they tested God's
    patience
    and provoked the Holy One
    of Israel.
[42] They did not remember his power
    and how he rescued them from
    their enemies.
[43] They did not remember his
    miraculous signs in Egypt,
    his wonders on the plain of Zoan.
[44] For he turned their rivers into blood,
    so no one could drink from the
    streams.
[45] He sent vast swarms of flies to
    consume them
    and hordes of frogs to ruin
    them.
[46] He gave their crops to caterpillars;
    their harvest was consumed
    by locusts.
[47] He destroyed their grapevines
    with hail
    and shattered their sycamore-figs
    with sleet.
[48] He abandoned their cattle
    to the hail,
    their livestock to bolts of lightning.
[49] He loosed on them his fierce anger—
    all his fury, rage, and hostility.
He dispatched against them
    a band of destroying angels.
[50] He turned his anger against them;
    he did not spare the Egyptians'
    lives
    but ravaged them with the plague.
[51] He killed the oldest son in each
    Egyptian family,
    the flower of youth throughout
    the land of Egypt.*
[52] But he led his own people like a
    flock of sheep,
    guiding them safely through the
    wilderness.
[53] He kept them safe so they were
    not afraid;

but the sea covered their enemies.
⁵⁴ He brought them to the border of
his holy land,
to this land of hills he had won
for them.
⁵⁵ He drove out the nations before
them;
he gave them their inheritance
by lot.
He settled the tribes of Israel into
their homes.

78:35 Hebrew *El-Elyon.* **78:51** Hebrew *in the tents of Ham.*

PROVERBS 24:27
Do your planning and prepare your
fields before building your house.

OCTOBER
8

JEREMIAH 10:1–11:23
Hear the word that the LORD speaks to
you, O Israel! ² This is what the LORD says:

"Do not act like the other nations,
who try to read their future
in the stars.
Do not be afraid of their predictions,
even though other nations are
terrified by them.
³ Their ways are futile and foolish.
They cut down a tree, and a
craftsman carves an idol.
⁴ They decorate it with gold and silver
and then fasten it securely with
hammer and nails
so it won't fall over.
⁵ Their gods are like
helpless scarecrows in a
cucumber field!
They cannot speak,
and they need to be carried
because they cannot walk.
Do not be afraid of such gods,
for they can neither harm you nor
do you any good."

⁶ LORD, there is no one like you!
For you are great, and your name
is full of power.
⁷ Who would not fear you, O King
of nations?
That title belongs to you alone!
Among all the wise people of
the earth
and in all the kingdoms of the world,
there is no one like you.

⁸ People who worship idols are stupid
and foolish.
The things they worship are made
of wood!
⁹ They bring beaten sheets of silver
from Tarshish
and gold from Uphaz,
and they give these materials to
skillful craftsmen
who make their idols.
Then they dress these gods in royal
blue and purple robes
made by expert tailors.
¹⁰ But the LORD is the only true God.
He is the living God and the
everlasting King!
The whole earth trembles at his anger.
The nations cannot stand up to
his wrath.

¹¹Say this to those who worship other
gods: "Your so-called gods, who did not
make the heavens and earth, will vanish
from the earth and from under the
heavens."*

¹² But God made the earth by his power,
and he preserves it by his wisdom.
With his own understanding
he stretched out the heavens.
¹³ When he speaks in the thunder,
the heavens roar with rain.
He causes the clouds to rise over
the earth.
He sends the lightning with the rain
and releases the wind from his
storehouses.
¹⁴ The whole human race is foolish
and has no knowledge!
The craftsmen are disgraced by
the idols they make,

for their carefully shaped works are
a fraud.
These idols have no breath
or power.
15 Idols are worthless; they are
ridiculous lies!
On the day of reckoning they will
all be destroyed.
16 But the God of Israel* is no idol!
He is the Creator of everything
that exists,
including Israel, his own special
possession.
The LORD of Heaven's Armies is
his name!

17 Pack your bags and prepare to leave;
the siege is about to begin.
18 For this is what the LORD says:
"Suddenly, I will fling out
all you who live in this land.
I will pour great troubles upon you,
and at last you will feel my anger."

19 My wound is severe,
and my grief is great.
My sickness is incurable,
but I must bear it.
20 My home is gone,
and no one is left to help me
rebuild it.
My children have been taken away,
and I will never see them again.
21 The shepherds of my people have
lost their senses.
They no longer seek wisdom from
the LORD.
Therefore, they fail completely,
and their flocks are scattered.
22 Listen! Hear the terrifying roar of
great armies
as they roll down from the north.
The towns of Judah will be
destroyed
and become a haunt for jackals.

23 I know, LORD, that our lives are not
our own.
We are not able to plan our
own course.
24 So correct me, LORD, but please
be gentle.

Do not correct me in anger,
for I would die.
25 Pour out your wrath on the nations
that refuse to acknowledge
you—
on the peoples that do not call
upon your name.
For they have devoured your people
Israel*;
they have devoured and
consumed them,
making the land a desolate
wilderness.

11:1THE LORD gave another message to
Jeremiah. He said, 2"Remind the people
of Judah and Jerusalem about the terms
of my covenant with them. 3 Say to them,
'This is what the LORD, the God of Israel,
says: Cursed is anyone who does not
obey the terms of my covenant! 4For I
said to your ancestors when I brought
them out of the iron-smelting furnace of
Egypt, "If you obey me and do whatever I
command you, then you will be my people, and I will be your God." 5 I said this so
I could keep my promise to your ancestors to give you a land flowing with milk
and honey—the land you live in today.'"

Then I replied, "Amen, LORD! May it
be so."

6Then the LORD said, "Broadcast this
message in the streets of Jerusalem. Go
from town to town throughout the land
and say, 'Remember the ancient covenant, and do everything it requires. 7 For
I solemnly warned your ancestors when I
brought them out of Egypt, "Obey me!" I
have repeated this warning over and
over to this day, 8 but your ancestors did
not listen or even pay attention. Instead,
they stubbornly followed their own evil
desires. And because they refused to
obey, I brought upon them all the curses
described in this covenant.'"

9Again the LORD spoke to me and said,
"I have discovered a conspiracy against
me among the people of Judah and Jerusalem. 10They have returned to the sins
of their forefathers. They have refused
to listen to me and are worshiping other
gods. Israel and Judah have both broken

the covenant I made with their ancestors. [11]Therefore, this is what the LORD says: I am going to bring calamity upon them, and they will not escape. Though they beg for mercy, I will not listen to their cries. [12]Then the people of Judah and Jerusalem will pray to their idols and burn incense before them. But the idols will not save them when disaster strikes! [13]Look now, people of Judah; you have as many gods as you have towns. You have as many altars of shame—altars for burning incense to your god Baal—as there are streets in Jerusalem.

[14]"Pray no more for these people, Jeremiah. Do not weep or pray for them, for I will not listen to them when they cry out to me in distress.

[15] "What right do my beloved people
    have to come to my Temple,
    when they have done so many
    immoral things?
Can their vows and sacrifices
    prevent their destruction?
They actually rejoice in doing
    evil!
[16] I, the LORD, once called them a
    thriving olive tree,
    beautiful to see and full
    of good fruit.
But now I have sent the fury of
    their enemies
    to burn them with fire,
    leaving them charred and broken.

[17]"I, the LORD of Heaven's Armies, who planted this olive tree, have ordered it destroyed. For the people of Israel and Judah have done evil, arousing my anger by burning incense to Baal."

[18]Then the LORD told me about the plots my enemies were making against me. [19]I was like a lamb being led to the slaughter. I had no idea that they were planning to kill me! "Let's destroy this man and all his words," they said. "Let's cut him down, so his name will be forgotten forever."

[20] O LORD of Heaven's Armies,
    you make righteous judgments,

and you examine the deepest
    thoughts and secrets.
Let me see your vengeance
    against them,
    for I have committed my cause
    to you.

[21]This is what the LORD says about the men of Anathoth who wanted me dead. They had said, "We will kill you if you do not stop prophesying in the LORD's name." [22]So this is what the LORD of Heaven's Armies says about them: "I will punish them! Their young men will die in battle, and their boys and girls will starve to death. [23]Not one of these plotters from Anathoth will survive, for I will bring disaster upon them when their time of punishment comes."

10:11 The original text of this verse is in Aramaic.
10:16 Hebrew *the Portion of Jacob.* See note on 5:20.
10:25 Hebrew *devoured Jacob.* See note on 5:20.

COLOSSIANS 3:18–4:18

Wives, submit to your husbands, as is fitting for those who belong to the Lord.

[19]Husbands, love your wives and never treat them harshly.

[20]Children, always obey your parents, for this pleases the Lord. [21]Fathers, do not aggravate your children, or they will become discouraged.

[22]Slaves, obey your earthly masters in everything you do. Try to please them all the time, not just when they are watching you. Serve them sincerely because of your reverent fear of the Lord. [23]**Work willingly at whatever you do, as though you were working for the Lord rather than for people.** [24]**Remember that the Lord will give you an inheritance as your reward, and that the Master you are serving is Christ.*** [25]But if you do what is wrong, you will be paid back for the wrong you have done. For God has no favorites.

[4:1]MASTERS, be just and fair to your slaves. Remember that you also have a Master—in heaven.

[2]Devote yourselves to prayer with an alert mind and a thankful heart. [3]Pray for us, too, that God will give us many op-

portunities to speak about his mysterious plan concerning Christ. That is why I am here in chains. [4]Pray that I will proclaim this message as clearly as I should.

[5]Live wisely among those who are not believers, and make the most of every opportunity. [6]Let your conversation be gracious and attractive* so that you will have the right response for everyone.

[7]Tychicus will give you a full report about how I am getting along. He is a beloved brother and faithful helper who serves with me in the Lord's work. [8]I have sent him to you for this very purpose—to let you know how we are doing and to encourage you. [9]I am also sending Onesimus, a faithful and beloved brother, one of your own people. He and Tychicus will tell you everything that's happening here.

[10]Aristarchus, who is in prison with me, sends you his greetings, and so does Mark, Barnabas's cousin. As you were instructed before, make Mark welcome if he comes your way. [11]Jesus (the one we call Justus) also sends his greetings. These are the only Jewish believers among my co-workers; they are working with me here for the Kingdom of God. And what a comfort they have been!

[12]Epaphras, a member of your own fellowship and a servant of Christ Jesus, sends you his greetings. He always prays earnestly for you, asking God to make you strong and perfect, fully confident that you are following the whole will of God. [13]I can assure you that he prays hard for you and also for the believers in Laodicea and Hierapolis.

[14]Luke, the beloved doctor, sends his greetings, and so does Demas. [15]Please give my greetings to our brothers and sisters* at Laodicea, and to Nympha and the church that meets in her house.

[16]After you have read this letter, pass it on to the church at Laodicea so they can read it, too. And you should read the letter I wrote to them.

[17]And say to Archippus, "Be sure to carry out the ministry the Lord gave you."

[18]HERE IS MY GREETING IN MY OWN HANDWRITING—PAUL.

Remember my chains.
May God's grace be with you.

3:24 Or *and serve Christ as your Master.* 4:6 Greek *and seasoned with salt.* 4:15 Greek *brothers.*

PSALM 78:56-72

But they kept testing and rebelling
     against God Most High.
They did not obey his laws.
[57] They turned back and were as
     faithless as their parents.
They were as undependable as
     a crooked bow.
[58] They angered God by building
     shrines to other gods;
they made him jealous with
     their idols.
[59] When God heard them, he was
     very angry,
and he completely rejected
     Israel.
[60] Then he abandoned his dwelling
     at Shiloh,
the Tabernacle where he had
     lived among the people.
[61] He allowed the Ark of his might to
     be captured;
he surrendered his glory into
     enemy hands.
[62] He gave his people over to be
     butchered by the sword,
because he was so angry with
     his own people—his special
     possession.
[63] Their young men were killed by fire;
     their young women died before
     singing their wedding songs.
[64] Their priests were slaughtered,
     and their widows could not
     mourn their deaths.

[65] Then the Lord rose up as though
     waking from sleep,
like a warrior aroused from a
     drunken stupor.
[66] He routed his enemies
     and sent them to eternal shame.
[67] But he rejected Joseph's descendants;
     he did not choose the tribe of
     Ephraim.
[68] He chose instead the tribe of Judah,
     and Mount Zion, which he loved.

⁶⁹ There he built his sanctuary as high
    as the heavens,
      as solid and enduring as the earth.
⁷⁰ He chose his servant David,
      calling him from the sheep pens.
⁷¹ He took David from tending the
    ewes and lambs
      and made him the shepherd of
      Jacob's descendants—
        God's own people, Israel.
⁷² He cared for them with a true heart
      and led them with skillful hands.

PROVERBS 24:28-29
Don't testify against your neighbors
without cause; don't lie about them. And
don't say, "Now I can pay them back for
what they've done to me! I'll get even with
them!"

OCTOBER
9

JEREMIAH 12:1–14:10
Lᴏʀᴅ, you always give me justice
      when I bring a case before you.
So let me bring you this complaint:
Why are the wicked so prosperous?
    Why are evil people so happy?
² You have planted them,
      and they have taken root and
      prospered.
Your name is on their lips,
      but you are far from their hearts.
³ But as for me, Lᴏʀᴅ, you know
    my heart.
You see me and test my thoughts.
Drag these people away like sheep
    to be butchered!
    Set them aside to be slaughtered!

⁴ How long must this land mourn?
      Even the grass in the fields has
      withered.
The wild animals and birds have
    disappeared
      because of the evil in the land.

For the people have said,
    "The Lᴏʀᴅ doesn't see what's
    ahead for us!"

⁵ "If racing against mere men makes
    you tired,
      how will you race against horses?
If you stumble and fall on open
    ground,
      what will you do in the thickets
      near the Jordan?
⁶ Even your brothers, members of
    your own family,
      have turned against you.
They plot and raise complaints
    against you.
Do not trust them,
      no matter how pleasantly they
      speak.

⁷ "I have abandoned my people, my
    special possession.
    I have surrendered my dearest
    ones to their enemies.
⁸ My chosen people have roared at me
    like a lion of the forest,
      so I have treated them with
      contempt.
⁹ My chosen people act like speckled
    vultures,*
      but they themselves are
      surrounded by vultures.
Bring on the wild animals to pick
    their corpses clean!

¹⁰ "Many rulers have ravaged my
    vineyard,
      trampling down the vines
      and turning all its beauty into
      a barren wilderness.
¹¹ They have made it an empty
    wasteland;
      I hear its mournful cry.
The whole land is desolate,
      and no one even cares.
¹² On all the bare hilltops,
      destroying armies can be seen.
The sword of the Lᴏʀᴅ devours
    people
      from one end of the nation
      to the other.
    No one will escape!
¹³ My people have planted wheat

but are harvesting thorns.
They have worn themselves out,
but it has done them no good.
They will harvest a crop of shame
because of the fierce anger
of the LORD."

¹⁴Now this is what the LORD says: "I will uproot from their land all the evil nations reaching out for the possession I gave my people Israel. And I will uproot Judah from among them. ¹⁵But afterward I will return and have compassion on all of them. I will bring them home to their own lands again, each nation to its own possession. ¹⁶And if these nations truly learn the ways of my people, and if they learn to swear by my name, saying, 'As surely as the LORD lives' (just as they taught my people to swear by the name of Baal), then they will be given a place among my people. ¹⁷But any nation who refuses to obey me will be uprooted and destroyed. I, the LORD, have spoken!"

^{13:1}THIS is what the LORD said to me: "Go and buy a linen loincloth and put it on, but do not wash it." ²So I bought the loincloth as the LORD directed me, and I put it on.

³Then the LORD gave me another message: ⁴"Take the linen loincloth you are wearing, and go to the Euphrates River.* Hide it there in a hole in the rocks." ⁵So I went and hid it by the Euphrates as the LORD had instructed me.

⁶A long time afterward the LORD said to me, "Go back to the Euphrates and get the loincloth I told you to hide there." ⁷So I went to the Euphrates and dug it out of the hole where I had hidden it. But now it was rotting and falling apart. The loincloth was good for nothing.

⁸Then I received this message from the LORD: ⁹"This is what the LORD says: This shows how I will rot away the pride of Judah and Jerusalem. ¹⁰These wicked people refuse to listen to me. They stubbornly follow their own desires and worship other gods. Therefore, they will become like this loincloth—good for nothing! ¹¹As a loincloth clings to a man's waist, so I created Judah and Israel to cling to me, says the LORD. They were to be my people, my pride, my glory—an honor to my name. But they would not listen to me.

¹²"So tell them, 'This is what the LORD, the God of Israel, says: May all your jars be filled with wine.' And they will reply, 'Of course! Jars are made to be filled with wine!'

¹³"Then tell them, 'No, this is what the LORD means: I will fill everyone in this land with drunkenness—from the king sitting on David's throne to the priests and the prophets, right down to the common people of Jerusalem. ¹⁴I will smash them against each other, even parents against children, says the LORD. I will not let my pity or mercy or compassion keep me from destroying them.'"

¹⁵ Listen and pay attention!
    Do not be arrogant, for the LORD
        has spoken.
¹⁶ Give glory to the LORD your God
        before it is too late.
    Acknowledge him before he brings
        darkness upon you,
    causing you to stumble and fall on
        the darkening mountains.
    For then, when you look for light,
        you will find only terrible
        darkness and gloom.
¹⁷ And if you still refuse to listen,
    I will weep alone because of
        your pride.
    My eyes will overflow with tears,
        because the LORD's flock will be
        led away into exile.

¹⁸ Say to the king and his mother,
    "Come down from your thrones
        and sit in the dust,
    for your glorious crowns
        will soon be snatched from your
        heads."
¹⁹ The towns of the Negev will close
        their gates,
    and no one will be able to open
        them.
    The people of Judah will be taken
        away as captives.
    All will be carried into exile.

20 Open up your eyes and see
  the armies marching down from
  the north!
Where is your flock—
  your beautiful flock—
  that he gave you to care for?
21 What will you say when the LORD
  takes the allies you have
  cultivated
  and appoints them as your rulers?
Pangs of anguish will grip you,
  like those of a woman in labor!
22 You may ask yourself,
  "Why is all this happening to me?"
  It is because of your many sins!
That is why you have been stripped
  and raped by invading armies.
23 Can an Ethiopian* change the color
  of his skin?
  Can a leopard take away its spots?
Neither can you start doing good,
  for you have always done evil.

24 "I will scatter you like chaff
  that is blown away by the desert
  winds.
25 This is your allotment,
  the portion I have assigned to you,"
  says the LORD,
"for you have forgotten me,
  putting your trust in false gods.
26 I myself will strip you
  and expose you to shame.
27 I have seen your adultery and lust,
  and your disgusting idol worship
  out in the fields and on the hills.
What sorrow awaits you, Jerusalem!
  How long before you are pure?"

14:1THIS message came to Jeremiah
from the LORD, explaining why he was
holding back the rain:

2 "Judah wilts;
  commerce at the city gates grinds
  to a halt.
All the people sit on the ground
  in mourning,
  and a great cry rises from
  Jerusalem.
3 The nobles send servants to get water,
  but all the wells are dry.
The servants return with empty
  pitchers,
  confused and desperate,
  covering their heads in grief.
4 The ground is parched
  and cracked for lack of rain.
The farmers are deeply troubled;
  they, too, cover their heads.
5 Even the doe abandons her
  newborn fawn
  because there is no grass in
  the field.
6 The wild donkeys stand on the
  bare hills
  panting like thirsty jackals.
They strain their eyes looking for
  grass,
  but there is none to be found."

7 The people say, "Our wickedness
  has caught up with us, LORD,
  but help us for the sake of your
  own reputation.
We have turned away from you
  and sinned against you again
  and again.
8 O Hope of Israel, our Savior in times
  of trouble,
  why are you like a stranger to us?
Why are you like a traveler passing
  through the land,
  stopping only for the night?
9 Are you also confused?
  Is our champion helpless to
  save us?
You are right here among
  us, LORD.
  We are known as your people.
  Please don't abandon us now!"

10 So this is what the LORD says to his
  people:
"You love to wander far from me
  and do not restrain yourselves.
Therefore, I will no longer accept
  you as my people.
Now I will remember all your
  wickedness
  and will punish you for
  your sins."

12:9 Or *speckled hyenas.*   13:4 Hebrew *Perath;* also in
13:5, 6, 7.   13:23 Hebrew *a Cushite.*

1 THESSALONIANS 1:1–2:8

This letter is from Paul, Silas,* and Timothy.

We are writing to the church in Thessalonica, to you who belong to God the Father and the Lord Jesus Christ.

May God give you grace and peace.

[2] We always thank God for all of you and pray for you constantly. [3] As we pray to our God and Father about you, we think of your faithful work, your loving deeds, and the enduring hope you have because of our Lord Jesus Christ.

[4] We know, dear brothers and sisters,* that God loves you and has chosen you to be his own people. [5] For when we brought you the Good News, it was not only with words but also with power, for the Holy Spirit gave you full assurance* that what we said was true. And you know of our concern for you from the way we lived when we were with you. [6] So you received the message with joy from the Holy Spirit in spite of the severe suffering it brought you. In this way, you imitated both us and the Lord. [7] As a result, you have become an example to all the believers in Greece—throughout both Macedonia and Achaia.*

[8] And now the word of the Lord is ringing out from you to people everywhere, even beyond Macedonia and Achaia, for wherever we go we find people telling us about your faith in God. We don't need to tell them about it, [9] for they keep talking about the wonderful welcome you gave us and how you turned away from idols to serve the living and true God. [10] And they speak of how you are looking forward to the coming of God's Son from heaven—Jesus, whom God raised from the dead. He is the one who has rescued us from the terrors of the coming judgment.

[2:1] You yourselves know, dear brothers and sisters,* that our visit to you was not a failure. [2] You know how badly we had been treated at Philippi just before we came to you and how much we suffered there. Yet our God gave us the courage to declare his Good News to you boldly, in spite of great opposition. [3] So you can see we were not preaching with any deceit or impure motives or trickery.

[4] For we speak as messengers approved by God to be entrusted with the Good News. Our purpose is to please God, not people. He alone examines the motives of our hearts. [5] Never once did we try to win you with flattery, as you well know. And God is our witness that we were not pretending to be your friends just to get your money! [6] As for human praise, we have never sought it from you or anyone else.

[7] As apostles of Christ we certainly had a right to make some demands of you, but instead we were like children* among you. Or we were like a mother feeding and caring for her own children. [8] We loved you so much that we shared with you not only God's Good News but our own lives, too.

1:1 Greek *Silvanus*, the Greek form of the name.
1:4 Greek *brothers*.   1:5 Or *with the power of the Holy Spirit, so you can have full assurance*.   1:7 *Macedonia* and *Achaia* were the northern and southern regions of Greece.
2:1 Greek *brothers*; also in 2:9, 14, 17.   2:7 Some manuscripts read *we were gentle*.

PSALM 79:1–13
A psalm of Asaph.

[1] ⬤ God, pagan nations have
        conquered your land,
        your special possession.
They have defiled your holy
        Temple
        and made Jerusalem a heap
        of ruins.
[2] They have left the bodies of your
        servants
        as food for the birds of heaven.
The flesh of your godly ones
        has become food for the wild
        animals.
[3] Blood has flowed like water all
        around Jerusalem;
        no one is left to bury the dead.
[4] We are mocked by our neighbors,
        an object of scorn and derision to
        those around us.

[5] O LORD, how long will you be angry
        with us? Forever?

How long will your jealousy burn
like fire?
6 Pour out your wrath on the nations
that refuse to acknowledge
you—
on kingdoms that do not call
upon your name.
7 For they have devoured your
people Israel,*
making the land a desolate
wilderness.
8 Do not hold us guilty for the sins of
our ancestors!
Let your compassion quickly
meet our needs,
for we are on the brink of despair.

9 **Help us, O God of our salvation!
Help us for the glory of your
name.**

**Save us and forgive our sins
for the honor of your name.**
10 Why should pagan nations be
allowed to scoff,
asking, "Where is their God?"
Show us your vengeance against the
nations,
for they have spilled the blood of
your servants.
11 Listen to the moaning of the
prisoners.
Demonstrate your great power
by saving those condemned
to die.
12 O Lord, pay back our neighbors
seven times
for the scorn they have hurled
at you.
13 Then we your people, the sheep of
your pasture,
will thank you forever and ever,
praising your greatness from
generation to generation.

79:7 Hebrew *devoured Jacob.* See note on 44:4.

PROVERBS 24:30-34

I walked by the field of a lazy person, the
vineyard of one with no common sense. I
saw that it was overgrown with nettles. It
was covered with weeds, and its walls
were broken down. Then, as I looked and

thought about it, I learned this lesson: A
little extra sleep, a little more slumber, a
little folding of the hands to rest—then
poverty will pounce on you like a bandit;
scarcity will attack you like an armed
robber.

OCTOBER
10

JEREMIAH 14:11–16:15

Then the LORD said to me [Jeremiah],
"Do not pray for these people anymore.
12When they fast, I will pay no attention. When they present their burnt offerings and grain offerings to me, I will
not accept them. Instead, I will devour
them with war, famine, and disease."

13Then I said, "O Sovereign LORD,
their prophets are telling them, 'All is
well—no war or famine will come. The
LORD will surely send you peace.'"

14Then the LORD said, "These prophets are telling lies in my name. I did not
send them or tell them to speak. I did not
give them any messages. They prophesy
of visions and revelations they have
never seen or heard. They speak foolishness made up in their own lying hearts.
15Therefore, this is what the LORD says: I
will punish these lying prophets, for they
have spoken in my name even though I
never sent them. They say that no war or
famine will come, but they themselves
will die by war and famine! 16As for the
people to whom they prophesy—their
bodies will be thrown out into the streets
of Jerusalem, victims of famine and war.
There will be no one left to bury them.
Husbands, wives, sons, and daughters—
all will be gone. For I will pour out their
own wickedness on them. 17Now, Jeremiah, say this to them:

"Night and day my eyes overflow
with tears.
I cannot stop weeping,

for my virgin daughter—my
  precious people—
has been struck down
and lies mortally wounded.
18 If I go out into the fields,
  I see the bodies of people
    slaughtered by the enemy.
If I walk the city streets,
  I see people who have died of
    starvation.
The prophets and priests continue
  with their work,
  but they don't know what
    they're doing."

19 Lord, have you completely
  rejected Judah?
  Do you really hate Jerusalem?*
Why have you wounded us past all
  hope of healing?
  We hoped for peace, but no
    peace came.
  We hoped for a time of healing,
    but found only terror.
20 Lord, we confess our wickedness
    and that of our ancestors, too.
  We all have sinned against you.
21 For the sake of your reputation,
    Lord, do not abandon us.
  Do not disgrace your own
    glorious throne.
  Please remember us,
    and do not break your covenant
      with us.

22 Can any of the worthless foreign
    gods send us rain?
  Does it fall from the sky by
    itself?
No, you are the one, O Lord our God!
  Only you can do such things.
  So we will wait for you to help us.

15:1 Then the Lord said to me, "Even if
Moses and Samuel stood before me
pleading for these people, I wouldn't
help them. Away with them! Get them
out of my sight! 2And if they say to you,
'But where can we go?' tell them, 'This is
what the Lord says:

"'Those who are destined for death,
  to death;

those who are destined for war,
  to war;
those who are destined for famine,
  to famine;
those who are destined for
  captivity, to captivity.'

3"I will send four kinds of destroyers
against them," says the Lord. "I will send
the sword to kill, the dogs to drag away,
the vultures to devour, and the wild animals to finish up what is left. 4Because of
the wicked things Manasseh son of Hezekiah, king of Judah, did in Jerusalem, I
will make my people an object of horror
to all the kingdoms of the earth.

5 "Who will feel sorry for you,
  Jerusalem?
  Who will weep for you?
  Who will even bother to ask how
    you are?
6 You have abandoned me
    and turned your back on me,"
  says the Lord.
"Therefore, I will raise my fist to
    destroy you.
  I am tired of always giving you
    another chance.
7 I will winnow you like grain at the
    gates of your cities
  and take away the children you
    hold dear.
I will destroy my own people,
  because they refuse to change
    their evil ways.
8 There will be more widows
    than the grains of sand on the
      seashore.
At noontime I will bring a destroyer
  against the mothers of young men.
I will cause anguish and terror
  to come upon them suddenly.
9 The mother of seven grows faint
    and gasps for breath;
  her sun has gone down while it is
    still day.
She sits childless now,
  disgraced and humiliated.
And I will hand over those who
    are left
  to be killed by the enemy.

I, the LORD, have spoken!"

¹⁰Then I said,

"What sorrow is mine, my mother.
　　Oh, that I had died at birth!
　　I am hated everywhere I go.
　I am neither a lender who threatens
　　　to foreclose
　　nor a borrower who refuses
　　　to pay—
　　yet they all curse me."

¹¹The LORD replied,

"I will take care of you, Jeremiah.
　　Your enemies will ask you to
　　　plead on their behalf
　　in times of trouble and distress.
¹² Can a man break a bar of iron from
　　　the north,
　　or a bar of bronze?
¹³ At no cost to them,
　　I will hand over your wealth and
　　　treasures
　as plunder to your enemies,
　　for sin runs rampant in your land.
¹⁴ I will tell your enemies to take you
　　as captives to a foreign land.
　For my anger blazes like a fire
　　that will burn forever.*"

¹⁵Then I said,

"LORD, you know what's happening
　　to me.
　　Please step in and help me.
　　Punish my persecutors!
　Please give me time; don't let me
　　die young.
　It's for your sake that I am
　　suffering.
¹⁶ When I discovered your words,
　　I devoured them.
　　They are my joy and my heart's
　　　delight,
　for I bear your name,
　　O LORD God of Heaven's Armies.
¹⁷ I never joined the people in their
　　merry feasts.
　　I sat alone because your hand
　　　was on me.
　　I was filled with indignation
　　　at their sins.

¹⁸ Why then does my suffering
　　continue?
　　Why is my wound so incurable?
　Your help seems as uncertain as a
　　seasonal brook,
　　like a spring that has gone dry."

¹⁹This is how the LORD responds:

"If you return to me, I will
　　restore you
　　so you can continue to serve me.
　If you speak good words rather than
　　worthless ones,
　　you will be my spokesman.
　You must influence them;
　　do not let them influence you!
²⁰ They will fight against you like an
　　attacking army,
　　but I will make you as secure
　　　as a fortified wall of bronze.
　They will not conquer you,
　　for I am with you to protect and
　　　rescue you.
　I, the LORD, have spoken!
²¹ Yes, I will certainly keep you safe
　　from these wicked men.
　　I will rescue you from their
　　　cruel hands."

16:1 THE LORD gave me another message. He said, ²"Do not get married or have children in this place. ³For this is what the LORD says about the children born here in this city and about their mothers and fathers: ⁴They will die from terrible diseases. No one will mourn for them or bury them, and they will lie scattered on the ground like manure. They will die from war and famine, and their bodies will be food for the vultures and wild animals."

⁵This is what the LORD says: "Do not go to funerals to mourn and show sympathy for these people, for I have removed my protection and peace from them. I have taken away my unfailing love and my mercy. ⁶Both the great and the lowly will die in this land. No one will bury them or mourn for them. Their friends will not cut themselves in sorrow or shave their heads in sadness. ⁷No one will offer a meal to comfort those who

mourn at the dead—not even at the death of a mother or father. No one will send a cup of wine to console them.

⁸"And do not go to their feasts and parties. Do not eat and drink with them at all. ⁹For this is what the LORD of Heaven's Armies, the God of Israel, says: In your own lifetime, before your very eyes, I will put an end to the happy singing and laughter in this land. The joyful voices of bridegrooms and brides will no longer be heard.

¹⁰"When you tell the people all these things, they will ask, 'Why has the LORD decreed such terrible things against us? What have we done to deserve such treatment? What is our sin against the LORD our God?'

¹¹"Then you will give them the LORD's reply: 'It is because your ancestors were unfaithful to me. They worshiped other gods and served them. They abandoned me and did not obey my word. ¹²And you are even worse than your ancestors! You stubbornly follow your own evil desires and refuse to listen to me. ¹³So I will throw you out of this land and send you into a foreign land where you and your ancestors have never been. There you can worship idols day and night—and I will grant you no favors!'

¹⁴"But the time is coming," says the LORD, "when people who are taking an oath will no longer say, 'As surely as the LORD lives, who rescued the people of Israel from the land of Egypt.' ¹⁵Instead, they will say, 'As surely as the LORD lives, who brought the people of Israel back to their own land from the land of the north and from all the countries to which he had exiled them.' For I will bring them back to this land that I gave their ancestors."

14:19 Hebrew *Zion?*   15:14 As in some Hebrew manuscripts (see also 17:4); most Hebrew manuscripts read *will burn against you.*

1 THESSALONIANS 2:9–3:13

Don't you remember, dear brothers and sisters, how hard we [Paul and his coworkers] worked among you? Night and day we toiled to earn a living so that we would not be a burden to any of you as we preached God's Good News to you. ¹⁰You yourselves are our witnesses—and so is God—that we were devout and honest and faultless toward all of you believers. ¹¹And you know that we treated each of you as a father treats his own children. ¹²We pleaded with you, encouraged you, and urged you to live your lives in a way that God would consider worthy. For he called you to share in his Kingdom and glory.

¹³Therefore, we never stop thanking God that when you received his message from us, you didn't think of our words as mere human ideas. You accepted what we said as the very word of God—which, of course, it is. And this word continues to work in you who believe.

¹⁴And then, dear brothers and sisters, you suffered persecution from your own countrymen. In this way, you imitated the believers in God's churches in Judea who, because of their belief in Christ Jesus, suffered from their own people, the Jews. ¹⁵For some of the Jews killed the prophets, and some even killed the Lord Jesus. Now they have persecuted us, too. They fail to please God and work against all humanity ¹⁶as they try to keep us from preaching the Good News of salvation to the Gentiles. By doing this, they continue to pile up their sins. But the anger of God has caught up with them at last.

¹⁷Dear brothers and sisters, after we were separated from you for a little while (though our hearts never left you), we tried very hard to come back because of our intense longing to see you again. ¹⁸We wanted very much to come to you, and I, Paul, tried again and again, but Satan prevented us. ¹⁹After all, what gives us hope and joy, and what will be our proud reward and crown as we stand before our Lord Jesus when he returns? It is you! ²⁰Yes, you are our pride and joy.

³:¹FINALLY, when we could stand it no longer, we decided to stay alone in Athens, ²and we sent Timothy to visit you. He is our brother and God's co-worker*

in proclaiming the Good News of Christ. We sent him to strengthen you, to encourage you in your faith, [3]and to keep you from being shaken by the troubles you were going through. But you know that we are destined for such troubles. [4]Even while we were with you, we warned you that troubles would soon come—and they did, as you well know. [5]That is why, when I could bear it no longer, I sent Timothy to find out whether your faith was still strong. I was afraid that the tempter had gotten the best of you and that our work had been useless.

[6]But now Timothy has just returned, bringing us good news about your faith and love. He reports that you always remember our visit with joy and that you want to see us as much as we want to see you. [7]So we have been greatly encouraged in the midst of our troubles and suffering, dear brothers and sisters,* because you have remained strong in your faith. [8]It gives us new life to know that you are standing firm in the Lord.

[9]How we thank God for you! Because of you we have great joy as we enter God's presence. [10]Night and day we pray earnestly for you, asking God to let us see you again to fill the gaps in your faith.

[11]May God our Father and our Lord Jesus bring us to you very soon. [12]**And may the Lord make your love for one another and for all people grow and overflow, just as our love for you overflows.** [13]May he, as a result, make your hearts strong, blameless, and holy as you stand before God our Father when our Lord Jesus comes again with all his holy people. Amen.

3:2 Other manuscripts read *and God's servant;* still others read *and a co-worker,* or *and a servant and co-worker for God,* or *and God's servant and our co-worker.*   3:7 Greek *brothers.*

PSALM 80:1-19

For the choir director: A psalm of Asaph, to be sung to the tune "Lilies of the Covenant."

   [1] **P**lease listen, O Shepherd of Israel,
       you who lead Joseph's
       descendants like a flock.

O God, enthroned above the
   cherubim,
   display your radiant glory
[2]   to Ephraim, Benjamin, and
       Manasseh.
Show us your mighty power.
   Come to rescue us!

[3] Turn us again to yourself, O God.
   Make your face shine down
       upon us.
   Only then will we be saved.
[4] O LORD God of Heaven's Armies,
   how long will you be angry with
       our prayers?
[5] You have fed us with sorrow
   and made us drink tears by the
       bucketful.
[6] You have made us the scorn* of
   neighboring nations.
   Our enemies treat us as a joke.

[7] Turn us again to yourself, O God
   of Heaven's Armies.
   Make your face shine down
       upon us.
   Only then will we be saved.
[8] You brought us from Egypt like
   a grapevine;
   you drove away the pagan nations
   and transplanted us into
   your land.
[9] You cleared the ground for us,
   and we took root and filled the
       land.
[10] Our shade covered the mountains;
   our branches covered the mighty
       cedars.
[11] We spread our branches west to the
   Mediterranean Sea;
   our shoots spread east to the
       Euphrates River.*
[12] But now, why have you broken down
   our walls
   so that all who pass by may steal
       our fruit?
[13] The wild boar from the forest
   devours it,
   and the wild animals feed on it.

[14] Come back, we beg you, O God of
   Heaven's Armies.

Look down from heaven and see
our plight.
Take care of this grapevine
15 that you yourself have planted,
this son you have raised for
yourself.
16 For we are chopped up and burned
by our enemies.
May they perish at the sight
of your frown.
17 Strengthen the man you love,
the son of your choice.
18 Then we will never abandon
you again.
Revive us so we can call on your
name once more.

19 Turn us again to yourself, O Lord
God of Heaven's Armies.
Make your face shine down
upon us.
Only then will we be saved.

80:6 As in Syriac version; Hebrew reads *the strife.*
80:11 Hebrew *west to the sea, . . . east to the river.*

PROVERBS 25:1-5
These are more proverbs of Solomon,
collected by the advisers of King Hezekiah of Judah. □ It is God's privilege to
conceal things and the king's privilege
to discover them. □ No one can comprehend the height of heaven, the depth of
the earth, or all that goes on in the king's
mind! □ Remove the impurities from
silver, and the sterling will be ready for
the silversmith. Remove the wicked
from the king's court, and his reign will
be made secure by justice.

OCTOBER
11

JEREMIAH 16:16–18:23
"But now I am sending for many fishermen who will catch them," says the Lord.
"I am sending for hunters who will hunt
them down in the mountains, hills, and
caves. 17 I am watching them closely, and
I see every sin. They cannot hope to hide
from me. 18 I will double their punishment for all their sins, because they have
defiled my land with lifeless images of
their detestable gods and have filled my
territory with their evil deeds."

19 Lord, you are my strength
and fortress,
my refuge in the day of trouble!
Nations from around the world
will come to you and say,
"Our ancestors left us a foolish
heritage,
for they worshiped worthless
idols.
20 Can people make their own gods?
These are not real gods at all!"

21 The Lord says,
"Now I will show them my power;
now I will show them my might.
At last they will know and understand
that I am the Lord.

17:1 "The sin of Judah
is inscribed with an iron chisel—
engraved with a diamond point on
their stony hearts
and on the corners of their
altars.
2 Even their children go to worship
at their pagan altars and
Asherah poles,
beneath every green tree
and on every high hill.
3 So I will hand over my holy
mountain—
along with all your wealth
and treasures
and your pagan shrines—
as plunder to your enemies,
for sin runs rampant in
your land.
4 The wonderful possession I have
reserved for you
will slip from your hands.
I will tell your enemies to take you
as captives to a foreign land.
For my anger blazes like a fire
that will burn forever."

5 This is what the LORD says:
"Cursed are those who put their
     trust in mere humans,
     who rely on human strength
     and turn their hearts away from
          the LORD.
6 They are like stunted shrubs in
     the desert,
     with no hope for the future.
     They will live in the barren wilderness,
     in an uninhabited salty land.

7 "But blessed are those who trust in
     the LORD
     and have made the LORD their
          hope and confidence.
8 They are like trees planted along a
     riverbank,
     with roots that reach deep into
          the water.
     Such trees are not bothered by
          the heat
     or worried by long months
          of drought.
     Their leaves stay green,
     and they never stop producing
          fruit.

9 "The human heart is the most
     deceitful of all things,
     and desperately wicked.
     Who really knows how bad it is?
10 But I, the LORD, search all hearts
     and examine secret motives.
     I give all people their due rewards,
     according to what their actions
          deserve."

11 Like a partridge that hatches eggs
     she has not laid,
     so are those who get their wealth
          by unjust means.
     At midlife they will lose their riches;
     in the end, they will become poor
          old fools.
12 But we worship at your throne—
     eternal, high, and glorious!
13 O LORD, the hope of Israel,
     all who turn away from you will
          be disgraced.
     They will be buried in the dust of
          the earth,

for they have abandoned the LORD,
     the fountain of living water.

14 O LORD, if you heal me, I will be truly
     healed;
     if you save me, I will be truly saved.
     My praises are for you alone!
15 People scoff at me and say,
     "What is this 'message from the
          LORD' you talk about?
     Why don't your predictions
          come true?"

16 LORD, I have not abandoned my job
     as a shepherd for your people.
     I have not urged you to send disaster.
     You have heard everything
          I've said.
17 LORD, don't terrorize me!
     You alone are my hope in the day
          of disaster.
18 Bring shame and dismay on all who
     persecute me,
     but don't let me experience
          shame and dismay.
     Bring a day of terror on them.
     Yes, bring double destruction
          upon them!

19 This is what the LORD said to me:
"Go and stand in the gates of Jerusalem,
first in the gate where the king goes in
and out, and then in each of the other
gates. 20 Say to all the people, 'Listen to
this message from the LORD, you kings
of Judah and all you people of Judah and
everyone living in Jerusalem. 21 This is
what the LORD says: Listen to my warning! Stop carrying on your trade at Jerusalem's gates on the Sabbath day. 22 Do
not do your work on the Sabbath, but
make it a holy day. I gave this command
to your ancestors, 23 but they did not listen or obey. They stubbornly refused to
pay attention or accept my discipline.

24 "'But if you obey me, says the LORD,
and do not carry on your trade at the
gates or work on the Sabbath day, and if
you keep it holy, 25 then kings and their
officials will go in and out of these gates
forever. There will always be a descendant of David sitting on the throne here
in Jerusalem. Kings and their officials

will always ride in and out among the people of Judah in chariots and on horses, and this city will remain forever. ²⁶And from all around Jerusalem, from the towns of Judah and Benjamin, from the western foothills* and the hill country and the Negev, the people will come with their burnt offerings and sacrifices. They will bring their grain offerings, frankincense, and thanksgiving offerings to the LORD's Temple.

²⁷"'But if you do not listen to me and refuse to keep the Sabbath holy, and if on the Sabbath day you bring loads of merchandise through the gates of Jerusalem just as on other days, then I will set fire to these gates. The fire will spread to the palaces, and no one will be able to put out the roaring flames.'"

¹⁸:¹THE LORD gave another message to Jeremiah. He said, ²"Go down to the potter's shop, and I will speak to you there." ³So I did as he told me and found the potter working at his wheel. ⁴But the jar he was making did not turn out as he had hoped, so he crushed it into a lump of clay again and started over.

⁵Then the LORD gave me this message: ⁶"O Israel, can I not do to you as this potter has done to his clay? As the clay is in the potter's hand, so are you in my hand. ⁷If I announce that a certain nation or kingdom is to be uprooted, torn down, and destroyed, ⁸but then that nation renounces its evil ways, I will not destroy it as I had planned. ⁹And if I announce that I will plant and build up a certain nation or kingdom, ¹⁰but then that nation turns to evil and refuses to obey me, I will not bless it as I said I would.

¹¹"Therefore, Jeremiah, go and warn all Judah and Jerusalem. Say to them, 'This is what the LORD says: I am planning disaster for you instead of good. So turn from your evil ways, each of you, and do what is right.'"

¹²But the people replied, "Don't waste your breath. We will continue to live as we want to, stubbornly following our own evil desires."

¹³So this is what the LORD says:

"Has anyone ever heard of such a thing,
    even among the pagan nations?
My virgin daughter Israel
    has done something terrible!
¹⁴ Does the snow ever disappear
        from the mountaintops of
        Lebanon?
    Do the cold streams flowing from
        those distant mountains ever
        run dry?
¹⁵ But my people are not so reliable,
        for they have deserted me;
    they burn incense to worthless
        idols.
They have stumbled off the ancient
        highways
    and walk in muddy paths.
¹⁶ Therefore, their land will become
        desolate,
    a monument to their stupidity.
All who pass by will be astonished
    and will shake their heads in
        amazement.
¹⁷ I will scatter my people before their
        enemies
    as the east wind scatters dust.
And in all their trouble I will turn my
        back on them
    and refuse to notice their
        distress."

¹⁸Then the people said, "Come on, let's plot a way to stop Jeremiah. We have plenty of priests and wise men and prophets. We don't need him to teach the word and give us advice and prophecies. Let's spread rumors about him and ignore what he says."

¹⁹ LORD, hear me and help me!
    Listen to what my enemies are
        saying.
²⁰ Should they repay evil for good?
    They have dug a pit to kill me,
    though I pleaded for them
        and tried to protect them from
        your anger.
²¹ So let their children starve!
    Let them die by the sword!
    Let their wives become childless
        widows.

Let their old men die in a plague,
and let their young men be killed
in battle!
²² Let screaming be heard from
their homes
as warriors come suddenly upon
them.
For they have dug a pit for me
and have hidden traps along my
path.
²³ LORD, you know all about their
murderous plots against me.
Don't forgive their crimes and
blot out their sins.
Let them die before you.
Deal with them in your anger.

17:26 Hebrew *the Shephelah.*

1 THESSALONIANS 4:1–5:3

Finally, dear brothers and sisters,* we
[Paul and his co-workers] urge you in
the name of the Lord Jesus to live in a
way that pleases God, as we have taught
you. You live this way already, and we
encourage you to do so even more. ²For
you remember what we taught you by
the authority of the Lord Jesus.

³God's will is for you to be holy, so stay
away from all sexual sin. ⁴Then each of
you will control his own body* and live
in holiness and honor—⁵not in lustful
passion like the pagans who do not know
God and his ways. ⁶Never harm or cheat
a Christian brother in this matter by violating his wife,* for the Lord avenges all
such sins, as we have solemnly warned
you before. ⁷God has called us to live
holy lives, not impure lives. ⁸Therefore,
anyone who refuses to live by these rules
is not disobeying human teaching but is
rejecting God, who gives his Holy Spirit
to you.

⁹But we don't need to write to you
about the importance of loving each
other,* for God himself has taught you
to love one another. ¹⁰Indeed, you already show your love for all the believers* throughout Macedonia. Even so,
dear brothers and sisters, we urge you
to love them even more.

¹¹Make it your goal to live a quiet life,
minding your own business and work-
ing with your hands, just as we instructed you before. ¹²Then people
who are not Christians will respect the
way you live, and you will not need to
depend on others.

¹³**And now, dear brothers and sis-
ters, we want you to know what will
happen to the believers who have
died* so you will not grieve like people who have no hope. ¹⁴For since we
believe that Jesus died and was
raised to life again, we also believe
that when Jesus returns, God will
bring back with him the believers
who have died.**

¹⁵We tell you this directly from the
Lord: We who are still living when the
Lord returns will not meet him ahead of
those who have died.* ¹⁶For the Lord
himself will come down from heaven
with a commanding shout, with the
voice of the archangel, and with the
trumpet call of God. First, the Christians
who have died* will rise from their
graves. ¹⁷Then, together with them, we
who are still alive and remain on the
earth will be caught up in the clouds to
meet the Lord in the air. Then we will be
with the Lord forever. ¹⁸So encourage
each other with these words.

^{5:1}Now concerning how and when all
this will happen, dear brothers and sisters,* we don't really need to write you.
²For you know quite well that the day of
the Lord's return will come unexpect-
edly, like a thief in the night. ³When people are saying, "Everything is peaceful
and secure," then disaster will fall on
them as suddenly as a pregnant woman's
labor pains begin. And there will be no
escape.

4:1 Greek *brothers;* also in 4:10, 13.   4:4 Or *will know
how to take a wife for himself;* or *will learn to live with his
own wife;* Greek reads *will know how to possess his own
vessel.*   4:6 Greek *Never harm or cheat a brother in this
matter.*   4:9 Greek *about brotherly love.*   4:10 Greek *the
brothers.*   4:13 Greek *those who have fallen asleep;* also
in 4:14.   4:15 Greek *those who have fallen asleep.*
4:16 Greek *the dead in Christ.*   5:1 Greek *brothers;*
also in 5:4, 12, 14, 25, 26, 27.

PSALM 81:1-16
*For the choir director: A psalm of Asaph, to be accompanied by a stringed instrument.**

¹ **S**ing praises to God, our strength.
  Sing to the God of Jacob.
² Sing! Beat the tambourine.
  Play the sweet lyre and the harp.
³ Blow the ram's horn at new moon,
  and again at full moon to call a
  festival!
⁴ For this is required by the decrees
  of Israel;
  it is a regulation of the God
  of Jacob.
⁵ He made it a law for Israel*
  when he attacked Egypt to set
  us free.

  I heard an unknown voice say,
⁶ "Now I will take the load from your
  shoulders;
  I will free your hands from their
  heavy tasks.
⁷ You cried to me in trouble, and
  I saved you;
  I answered out of the thundercloud
  and tested your faith when there
  was no water at Meribah.
                                    Interlude

⁸ "Listen to me, O my people, while
  I give you stern warnings.
  O Israel, if you would only listen
  to me!
⁹ You must never have a foreign god;
  you must not bow down before a
  false god.
¹⁰ For it was I, the LORD your God,
  who rescued you from the land
  of Egypt.
  Open your mouth wide, and I will
  fill it with good things.

¹¹ "But no, my people wouldn't listen.
  Israel did not want me around.
¹² So I let them follow their own
  stubborn desires,
  living according to their own ideas.
¹³ Oh, that my people would listen
  to me!
  Oh, that Israel would follow me,
  walking in my paths!

¹⁴ How quickly I would then subdue
  their enemies!
  How soon my hands would be
  upon their foes!
¹⁵ Those who hate the LORD would
  cringe before him;
  they would be doomed forever.
¹⁶ But I would feed you with the
  finest wheat.
  I would satisfy you with wild
  honey from the rock."

81:TITLE Hebrew *according to the gittith.*   **81:5** Hebrew *for Joseph.*

PROVERBS 25:6-8
Don't demand an audience with the king or push for a place among the great. It's better to wait for an invitation to the head table than to be sent away in public disgrace. □ Just because you've seen something, don't be in a hurry to go to court. For what will you do in the end if your neighbor deals you a shameful defeat?

OCTOBER 12

JEREMIAH 19:1–21:14
This is what the LORD said to me [Jeremiah]: "Go and buy a clay jar. Then ask some of the leaders of the people and of the priests to follow you. ²Go out through the Gate of Broken Pots to the garbage dump in the valley of Ben-Hinnom, and give them this message. ³Say to them, 'Listen to this message from the LORD, you kings of Judah and citizens of Jerusalem! This is what the LORD of Heaven's Armies, the God of Israel, says: I will bring a terrible disaster on this place, and the ears of those who hear about it will ring!

⁴" 'For Israel has forsaken me and turned this valley into a place of wickedness. The people burn incense to foreign gods—idols never before acknowledged

by this generation, by their ancestors, or by the kings of Judah. And they have filled this place with the blood of innocent children. 5They have built pagan shrines to Baal, and there they burn their sons as sacrifices to Baal. I have never commanded such a horrible deed; it never even crossed my mind to command such a thing! 6So beware, for the time is coming, says the LORD, when this garbage dump will no longer be called Topheth or the valley of Ben-Hinnom, but the Valley of Slaughter.

7"'For I will upset the careful plans of Judah and Jerusalem. I will allow the people to be slaughtered by invading armies, and I will leave their dead bodies as food for the vultures and wild animals. 8I will reduce Jerusalem to ruins, making it a monument to their stupidity. All who pass by will be astonished and will gasp at the destruction they see there. 9I will see to it that your enemies lay siege to the city until all the food is gone. Then those trapped inside will eat their own sons and daughters and friends. They will be driven to utter despair.'

10"As these men watch you, Jeremiah, smash the jar you brought. 11Then say to them, 'This is what the LORD of Heaven's Armies says: As this jar lies shattered, so I will shatter the people of Judah and Jerusalem beyond all hope of repair. They will bury the bodies here in Topheth, the garbage dump, until there is no more room for them. 12This is what I will do to this place and its people, says the LORD. I will cause this city to become defiled like Topheth. 13Yes, all the houses in Jerusalem, including the palace of Judah's kings, will become like Topheth—all the houses where you burned incense on the rooftops to your star gods, and where liquid offerings were poured out to your idols.'"

14Then Jeremiah returned from Topheth, the garbage dump where he had delivered this message, and he stopped in front of the Temple of the LORD. He said to the people there, 15"This is what the LORD of Heaven's Armies, the God of Israel, says: 'I will bring disaster upon this city and its surrounding towns as I promised, because you have stubbornly refused to listen to me.'"

20:1Now Pashhur son of Immer, the priest in charge of the Temple of the LORD, heard what Jeremiah was prophesying. 2So he arrested Jeremiah the prophet and had him whipped and put in stocks at the Benjamin Gate of the LORD's Temple.

3The next day, when Pashhur finally released him, Jeremiah said, "Pashhur, the LORD has changed your name. From now on you are to be called 'The Man Who Lives in Terror.'* 4For this is what the LORD says: 'I will send terror upon you and all your friends, and you will watch as they are slaughtered by the swords of the enemy. I will hand the people of Judah over to the king of Babylon. He will take them captive to Babylon or run them through with the sword. 5And I will let your enemies plunder Jerusalem. All the famed treasures of the city—the precious jewels and gold and silver of your kings—will be carried off to Babylon. 6As for you, Pashhur, you and all your household will go as captives to Babylon. There you will die and be buried, you and all your friends to whom you prophesied that everything would be all right.'"

7 O LORD, you misled me,
    and I allowed myself to be misled.
  You are stronger than I am,
    and you overpowered me.
  Now I am mocked every day;
    everyone laughs at me.
8 When I speak, the words burst out.
    "Violence and destruction!"
      I shout.
  So these messages from the LORD
    have made me a household joke.
9 But if I say I'll never mention the
      LORD
    or speak in his name,
  his word burns in my heart like
      a fire.
  It's like a fire in my bones!
  I am worn out trying to hold it in!
    I can't do it!

¹⁰ I have heard the many rumors
about me.
They call me "The Man Who
Lives in Terror."
They threaten, "If you say anything,
we will report it."
Even my old friends are
watching me,
waiting for a fatal slip.
"He will trap himself," they say,
"and then we will get our revenge
on him."

¹¹ But the LORD stands beside me like
a great warrior.
Before him my persecutors will
stumble.
They cannot defeat me.
They will fail and be thoroughly
humiliated.
Their dishonor will never be
forgotten.

¹² O LORD of Heaven's Armies,
you test those who are righteous,
and you examine the deepest
thoughts and secrets.
Let me see your vengeance
against them,
for I have committed my cause
to you.

¹³ Sing to the LORD!
Praise the LORD!
For though I was poor and needy,
he rescued me from my
oppressors.

¹⁴ Yet I curse the day I was born!
May no one celebrate the day
of my birth.

¹⁵ I curse the messenger who told
my father,
"Good news—you have a son!"

¹⁶ Let him be destroyed like the cities
of old
that the LORD overthrew without
mercy.
Terrify him all day long with battle
shouts,

¹⁷ because he did not kill me at birth.
Oh, that I had died in my mother's
womb,
that her body had been my grave!

¹⁸ Why was I ever born?
My entire life has been filled
with trouble, sorrow, and shame.

^{21:1}THE LORD spoke through Jeremiah
when King Zedekiah sent Pashhur son
of Malkijah and Zephaniah son of Maaseiah, the priest, to speak with him.
They begged Jeremiah, ²"Please speak
to the LORD for us and ask him to help
us. King Nebuchadnezzar* of Babylon
is attacking Judah. Perhaps the LORD
will be gracious and do a mighty miracle as he has done in the past. Perhaps
he will force Nebuchadnezzar to withdraw his armies."

³Jeremiah replied, "Go back to King
Zedekiah and tell him, ⁴'This is what the
LORD, the God of Israel, says: I will make
your weapons useless against the king of
Babylon and the Babylonians* who are
outside your walls attacking you. In fact,
I will bring your enemies right into the
heart of this city. ⁵I myself will fight
against you with a strong hand and a
powerful arm, for I am very angry. You
have made me furious! ⁶I will send a terrible plague upon this city, and both people and animals will die. ⁷And after all
that, says the LORD, I will hand over King
Zedekiah, his staff, and everyone else in
the city who survives the disease, war,
and famine. I will hand them over to
King Nebuchadnezzar of Babylon and to
their other enemies. He will slaughter
them and show them no mercy, pity, or
compassion.'

⁸"Tell all the people, 'This is what the
LORD says: Take your choice of life or
death! ⁹Everyone who stays in Jerusalem
will die from war, famine, or disease, but
those who go out and surrender to the
Babylonians will live. Their reward will
be life! ¹⁰For I have decided to bring disaster and not good upon this city, says
the LORD. It will be handed over to the
king of Babylon, and he will reduce it to
ashes.'

¹¹"Say to the royal family of Judah,
'Listen to this message from the LORD!
¹²This is what the LORD says to the dy-
nasty of David:

"'Give justice each morning to the
people you judge!
Help those who have been robbed;
rescue them from their oppressors.
Otherwise, my anger will burn like
an unquenchable fire
because of all your sins.
[13] I will personally fight against the
people in Jerusalem,
that mighty fortress—
the people who boast, "No one can
touch us here.
No one can break in here."
[14] And I myself will punish you for
your sinfulness,
says the LORD.
I will light a fire in your forests
that will burn up everything
around you.'"

20:3 Hebrew *Magor-missabib,* which means "surrounded
by terror"; also in 20:10.   21:2 Hebrew *Nebuchadrezzar,* a
variant spelling of Nebuchadnezzar; also in 21:7.   21:4 Or
Chaldeans; also in 21:9.

1 THESSALONIANS 5:4-28

But you aren't in the dark about these
things, dear brothers and sisters, and you
won't be surprised when the day of the
Lord comes like a thief.* [5]For you are all
children of the light and of the day; we
don't belong to darkness and night. [6]So
be on your guard, not asleep like the others. Stay alert and be clearheaded. [7]Night
is the time when people sleep and drinkers get drunk. [8]But let us who live in the
light be clearheaded, protected by the armor of faith and love, and wearing as our
helmet the confidence of our salvation.

[9]**For God chose to save us through
our Lord Jesus Christ, not to pour out
his anger on us.** [10]**Christ died for us
so that, whether we are dead or alive
when he returns, we can live with
him forever.** [11]So encourage each
other and build each other up, just as
you are already doing.

[12]Dear brothers and sisters, honor
those who are your leaders in the Lord's
work. They work hard among you and
give you spiritual guidance. [13]Show
them great respect and wholehearted
love because of their work. And live
peacefully with each other.

[14]Brothers and sisters, we urge you to
warn those who are lazy. Encourage
those who are timid. Take tender care
of those who are weak. Be patient with
everyone.

[15]See that no one pays back evil for
evil, but always try to do good to each
other and to all people.

[16]Always be joyful. [17]Never stop praying. [18]Be thankful in all circumstances,
for this is God's will for you who belong
to Christ Jesus.

[19]Do not stifle the Holy Spirit. [20]Do not
scoff at prophecies, [21]but test everything
that is said. Hold on to what is good.
[22]Stay away from every kind of evil.

[23]Now may the God of peace make
you holy in every way, and may your
whole spirit and soul and body be kept
blameless until our Lord Jesus Christ
comes again. [24]God will make this happen, for he who calls you is faithful.

[25]Dear brothers and sisters, pray for us.
[26]Greet all the brothers and sisters
with Christian love.*

[27]I command you in the name of the
Lord to read this letter to all the brothers and sisters.

[28]May the grace of our Lord Jesus
Christ be with you.

5:4 Some manuscripts read *comes upon you as if you were
thieves.*   5:26 Greek *with a holy kiss.*

PSALM 82:1-8

A psalm of Asaph.

[1] **G**od presides over heaven's court;
he pronounces judgment on the
heavenly beings:
[2] "How long will you hand down
unjust decisions
by favoring the wicked? *Interlude*

[3] "Give justice to the poor and the
orphan;
uphold the rights of the
oppressed and the destitute.
[4] Rescue the poor and helpless;
deliver them from the grasp of
evil people.
[5] But these oppressors know nothing;
they are so ignorant!
They wander about in darkness,

while the whole world is shaken
  to the core.
⁶ I say, 'You are gods;
  you are all children of the
    Most High.
⁷ But you will die like mere mortals
  and fall like every other ruler.'"

⁸ Rise up, O God, and judge the earth,
  for all the nations belong to you.

PROVERBS 25:9-10
When arguing with your neighbor, don't
betray another person's secret. Others
may accuse you of gossip, and you will
never regain your good reputation.

OCTOBER
13

JEREMIAH 22:1–23:20
This is what the LORD said to me [Jere-
miah]: "Go over and speak directly to the
king of Judah. Say to him, ²'Listen to this
message from the LORD, you king of Judah, sitting on David's throne. Let your
attendants and your people listen, too.
³This is what the LORD says: Be fair-
minded and just. Do what is right! Help
those who have been robbed; rescue
them from their oppressors. Quit your
evil deeds! Do not mistreat foreigners, orphans, and widows. Stop murdering the
innocent! ⁴If you obey me, there will always be a descendant of David sitting on
the throne here in Jerusalem. The king
will ride through the palace gates in chariots and on horses, with his parade of attendants and subjects. ⁵But if you refuse
to pay attention to this warning, I swear
by my own name, says the LORD, that this
palace will become a pile of rubble.'"

⁶Now this is what the LORD says concerning Judah's royal palace:

"I love you as much as fruitful Gilead
  and the green forests of Lebanon.
But I will turn you into a desert,

with no one living within your walls.
⁷ I will call for wreckers,
  who will bring out their tools to
    dismantle you.
They will tear out all your fine
    cedar beams
  and throw them on the fire.

⁸"People from many nations will pass
by the ruins of this city and say to one
another, 'Why did the LORD destroy
such a great city?' ⁹And the answer will
be, 'Because they violated their covenant with the LORD their God by worshiping other gods.'"

¹⁰ Do not weep for the dead king or
    mourn his loss.
  Instead, weep for the captive king
    being led away!
  For he will never return to see his
    native land again.

¹¹For this is what the LORD says about
Jehoahaz,* who succeeded his father,
King Josiah, and was taken away as a
captive: "He will never return. ¹²He will
die in a distant land and will never again
see his own country."

¹³ And the LORD says, "What sorrow
    awaits Jehoiakim,*
  who builds his palace with forced
    labor.*
  He builds injustice into its walls,
    for he makes his neighbors work
      for nothing.
  He does not pay them for their
    labor.
¹⁴ He says, 'I will build a magnificent
      palace
    with huge rooms and many
      windows.
  I will panel it throughout with
    fragrant cedar
  and paint it a lovely red.'
¹⁵ But a beautiful cedar palace does
    not make a great king!
  Your father, Josiah, also had
    plenty to eat and drink.
  But he was just and right in all his
    dealings.
  That is why God blessed him.

¹⁶ He gave justice and help to the poor
    and needy,
        and everything went well for him.
    Isn't that what it means to know me?"
    says the LORD.
¹⁷ "But you! You have eyes only for
        greed and dishonesty!
    You murder the innocent,
    oppress the poor, and reign
        ruthlessly."

¹⁸Therefore, this is what the LORD says
about Jehoiakim, son of King Josiah:

    "The people will not mourn for him,
        crying to one another,
        'Alas, my brother! Alas, my sister!'
    His subjects will not mourn
        for him, crying,
        'Alas, our master is dead! Alas, his
            splendor is gone!'
¹⁹ He will be buried like a dead donkey—
        dragged out of Jerusalem and
            dumped outside the gates!
²⁰ Weep for your allies in Lebanon.
    Shout for them in Bashan.
    Search for them in the regions east
        of the river.*
    See, they are all destroyed.
    Not one is left to help you.
²¹ I warned you when you were
        prosperous,
    but you replied, 'Don't bother me.'
    You have been that way since
        childhood—
    you simply will not obey me!
²² And now the wind will blow away
        your allies.
    All your friends will be taken
        away as captives.
    Surely then you will see your
        wickedness and be ashamed.
²³ It may be nice to live in a beautiful
        palace
    paneled with wood from the
        cedars of Lebanon,
    but soon you will groan with pangs
        of anguish—
    anguish like that of a woman
        in labor.

²⁴"As surely as I live," says the LORD, "I
will abandon you, Jehoiachin* son of Jehoiakim, king of Judah. Even if you were
the signet ring on my right hand, I
would pull you off. ²⁵I will hand you
over to those who seek to kill you, those
you so desperately fear—to King Nebuchadnezzar* of Babylon and the mighty
Babylonian* army. ²⁶I will expel you
and your mother from this land, and
you will die in a foreign country, not in
your native land. ²⁷You will never again
return to the land you yearn for.

²⁸ "Why is this man Jehoiachin like a
        discarded, broken jar?
    Why are he and his children
        to be exiled to a foreign land?
²⁹ O earth, earth, earth!
    Listen to this message from
        the LORD!
³⁰ This is what the LORD says:
    'Let the record show that this man
        Jehoiachin was childless.
    He is a failure,
    for none of his children will
        succeed him on the throne
            of David
    to rule over Judah.'

^{23:1}"WHAT sorrow awaits the leaders of
my people—the shepherds of my sheep—
for they have destroyed and scattered
the very ones they were expected to care
for," says the LORD.

²Therefore, this is what the LORD, the
God of Israel, says to these shepherds:
"Instead of caring for my flock and leading them to safety, you have deserted
them and driven them to destruction.
Now I will pour out judgment on you for
the evil you have done to them. ³But I will
gather together the remnant of my flock
from the countries where I have driven
them. I will bring them back to their own
sheepfold, and they will be fruitful and
increase in number. ⁴Then I will appoint
responsible shepherds who will care for
them, and they will never be afraid again.
Not a single one will be lost or missing. I,
the LORD have spoken!

⁵ "For the time is coming,"
    says the LORD,

"when I will raise up a righteous
   descendant*
from King David's line.
He will be a King who rules with
   wisdom.
   He will do what is just and right
      throughout the land.
⁶ And this will be his name:
   'The LORD Is Our Righteousness.'*
In that day Judah will be saved,
   and Israel will live in safety.

⁷"In that day," says the LORD, "when
people are taking an oath, they will no
longer say, 'As surely as the LORD lives,
who rescued the people of Israel from
the land of Egypt.' ⁸Instead, they will say,
'As surely as the LORD lives, who brought
the people of Israel back to their own
land from the land of the north and from
all the countries to which he had exiled
them.' Then they will live in their own
land."

⁹ My heart is broken because of the
      false prophets,
   and my bones tremble.
I stagger like a drunkard,
   like someone overcome by wine,
because of the holy words
   the LORD has spoken against them.
¹⁰ For the land is full of adultery,
   and it lies under a curse.
The land itself is in mourning—
   its wilderness pastures are
      dried up.
For they all do evil
   and abuse what power they have.

¹¹ "Even the priests and prophets
      are ungodly, wicked men.
   I have seen their despicable acts
      right here in my own Temple,"
   says the LORD.
¹² "Therefore, the paths they take
      will become slippery.
   They will be chased through the dark,
      and there they will fall.
   For I will bring disaster upon them
      at the time fixed for their
         punishment.
   I, the LORD, have spoken!

¹³ "I saw that the prophets of Samaria
      were terribly evil,
   for they prophesied in the name
      of Baal
   and led my people of Israel
      into sin.
¹⁴ But now I see that the prophets of
      Jerusalem are even worse!
   They commit adultery and love
      dishonesty.
   They encourage those who are
      doing evil
   so that no one turns away from
      their sins.
   These prophets are as wicked
      as the people of Sodom and
         Gomorrah once were."

¹⁵Therefore, this is what the LORD of
Heaven's Armies says concerning the
prophets:

"I will feed them with bitterness
   and give them poison to drink.
For it is because of Jerusalem's
   prophets
that wickedness has filled
   this land."

¹⁶This is what the LORD of Heaven's Armies says to his people:

"Do not listen to these prophets
   when they prophesy to you,
filling you with futile hopes.
They are making up everything
   they say.
   They do not speak for the LORD!
¹⁷ They keep saying to those who
      despise my word,
   'Don't worry! The LORD says you
      will have peace!'
And to those who stubbornly follow
   their own desires,
   they say, 'No harm will come
      your way!'

¹⁸ "Have any of these prophets been in
      the LORD's presence
   to hear what he is really saying?
   Has even one of them cared
      enough to listen?
¹⁹ Look! The LORD's anger bursts out
      like a storm,

a whirlwind that swirls down on
the heads of the wicked.
²⁰ The anger of the LORD will not
diminish
until it has finished all he
has planned.
In the days to come
you will understand all this
very clearly."

22:11 Hebrew *Shallum*, another name for Jehoahaz.
22:13a The brother and successor of the exiled Jehoahaz.
See 22:18. 22:13b Hebrew *by unrighteousness.*
22:20 Or *in Abarim.* 22:24 Hebrew *Coniah*, a variant
spelling of Jehoiachin; also 22:28. 22:25a Hebrew
Nebuchadrezzar, a variant spelling of Nebuchadnezzar.
22:25b Or *Chaldean.* 23:5 Hebrew *a righteous branch.*
23:6 Hebrew *Yahweh Tsidqenu.*

2 THESSALONIANS 1:1-12

This letter is from Paul, Silas,* and Timothy.

We are writing to the church in Thessalonica, to you who belong to God our Father and the Lord Jesus Christ.

²May God our Father* and the Lord Jesus Christ give you grace and peace.

³Dear brothers and sisters,* we can't help but thank God for you, because your faith is flourishing and your love for one another is growing. ⁴We proudly tell God's other churches about your endurance and faithfulness in all the persecutions and hardships you are suffering. ⁵And God will use this persecution to show his justice and to make you worthy of his Kingdom, for which you are suffering. ⁶In his justice he will pay back those who persecute you.

⁷And God will provide rest for you who are being persecuted and also for us when the Lord Jesus appears from heaven. He will come with his mighty angels, ⁸in flaming fire, bringing judgment on those who don't know God and on those who refuse to obey the Good News of our Lord Jesus. ⁹They will be punished with eternal destruction, forever separated from the Lord and from his glorious power. ¹⁰When he comes on that day, he will receive glory from his holy people—praise from all who believe. And this includes you, for you believed what we told you about him. ¹¹**So we keep on praying for you,**
asking our God to enable you to **live a**
life worthy of his call. May **he give**
you the power to accomplish all the
good things your faith prompts **you**
to do. ¹²Then the name of our Lord
Jesus will be honored because of the
way you live, and you will be honored
along with him. This is all made possible because of the grace of our God and
our Lord Jesus Christ.*

1:1 Greek *Silvanus*, the Greek form of the name.
1:2 Some manuscripts read *God the Father.* 1:3 Greek
Brothers. 1:12 Or *of our God and Lord, Jesus Christ.*

PSALM 83:1-18

A song. A psalm of Asaph.

¹ **O** God, do not be silent!
Do not be deaf.
Do not be quiet, O God.
² Don't you hear the uproar
of your enemies?
Don't you see that your arrogant
enemies are rising up?
³ They devise crafty schemes against
your people;
they conspire against your
precious ones.
⁴ "Come," they say, "let us wipe out
Israel as a nation.
We will destroy the very memory
of its existence."
⁵ Yes, this was their unanimous
decision.
They signed a treaty as allies
against you—
⁶ these Edomites and Ishmaelites;
Moabites and Hagrites;
⁷ Gebalites, Ammonites, and
Amalekites;
and people from Philistia and
Tyre.
⁸ Assyria has joined them, too,
and is allied with the descendants
of Lot.   *Interlude*

⁹ Do to them as you did to the
Midianites
and as you did to Sisera and Jabin
at the Kishon River.
¹⁰ They were destroyed at Endor,
and their decaying corpses
fertilized the soil.

¹¹ Let their mighty nobles die as Oreb
  and Zeeb did.
  Let all their princes die like Zebah
  and Zalmunna,
¹² for they said, "Let us seize for our
  own use
  these pasturelands of God!"
¹³ O my God, scatter them like
  tumbleweed,
  like chaff before the wind!
¹⁴ As a fire burns a forest
  and as a flame sets mountains
  ablaze,
¹⁵ chase them with your fierce storm;
  terrify them with your tempest.
¹⁶ Utterly disgrace them
  until they submit to your name,
  O Lᴏʀᴅ.
¹⁷ Let them be ashamed and terrified
  forever.
  Let them die in disgrace.
¹⁸ Then they will learn that you alone
  are called the Lᴏʀᴅ,
  that you alone are the Most High,
  supreme over all the earth.

PROVERBS 25:11-14
Timely advice is lovely, like golden ap-
ples in a silver basket. □ To one who listens, valid criticism is like a gold earring
or other gold jewelry. □ Trustworthy
messengers refresh like snow in summer. They revive the spirit of their employer. □ A person who promises a gift
but doesn't give it is like clouds and
wind that bring no rain.

OCTOBER
14

JEREMIAH 23:21–25:38
  "I [the Lᴏʀᴅ] have not sent these
  prophets,
  yet they run around claiming to
  speak for me.
  I have given them no message,
  yet they go on prophesying.

²² If they had stood before me and
  listened to me,
  they would have spoken my words,
  and they would have turned
  my people
  from their evil ways and
  deeds.
²³ Am I a God who is only close at
  hand?" says the Lᴏʀᴅ.
  "No, I am far away at the same
  time.
²⁴ Can anyone hide from me in a
  secret place?
  Am I not everywhere in all the
  heavens and earth?"
  says the Lᴏʀᴅ.

²⁵"I have heard these prophets say,
'Listen to the dream I had from God last
night.' And then they proceed to tell lies
in my name. ²⁶How long will this go on?
If they are prophets, they are prophets
of deceit, inventing everything they say.
²⁷By telling these false dreams, they are
trying to get my people to forget me,
just as their ancestors did by worshiping the idols of Baal.

²⁸ "Let these false prophets tell
  their dreams,
  but let my true messengers
  faithfully proclaim my
  every word.
  There is a difference between
  straw and grain!
²⁹ Does not my word burn like fire?"
  says the Lᴏʀᴅ.
  "Is it not like a mighty hammer
  that smashes a rock to pieces?

³⁰"Therefore," says the Lᴏʀᴅ, "I am
against these prophets who steal messages from each other and claim they
are from me. ³¹I am against these
smooth-tongued prophets who say,
'This prophecy is from the Lᴏʀᴅ!' ³²I am
against these false prophets. Their
imaginary dreams are flagrant lies that
lead my people into sin. I did not send
or appoint them, and they have no message at all for my people. I, the Lᴏʀᴅ
have spoken!
³³"Suppose one of the people or one

of the prophets or priests asks you, 'What prophecy has the LORD burdened you with now?' You must reply, 'You are the burden!* The LORD says he will abandon you!'

34"If any prophet, priest, or anyone else says, 'I have a prophecy from the LORD,' I will punish that person along with his entire family. 35You should keep asking each other, 'What is the LORD's answer?' or 'What is the LORD saying?' 36But stop using this phrase, 'prophecy from the LORD.' For people are using it to give authority to their own ideas, turning upside down the words of our God, the living God, the LORD of Heaven's Armies.

37"This is what you should say to the prophets: 'What is the LORD's answer?' or 'What is the LORD saying?' 38But suppose they respond, 'This is a prophecy from the LORD!' Then you should say, 'This is what the LORD says: Because you have used this phrase, "prophecy from the LORD," even though I warned you not to use it, 39I will forget you completely. I will expel you from my presence, along with this city that I gave to you and your ancestors. 40And I will make you an object of ridicule, and your name will be infamous throughout the ages.'"

24:1AFTER King Nebuchadnezzar* of Babylon exiled Jehoiachin* son of Jehoiakim, king of Judah, to Babylon along with the officials of Judah and all the craftsmen and artisans, the LORD gave me this vision. I saw two baskets of figs placed in front of the LORD's Temple in Jerusalem. 2One basket was filled with fresh, ripe figs, while the other was filled with bad figs that were too rotten to eat.

3Then the LORD said to me, "What do you see, Jeremiah?"

I replied, "Figs, some very good and some very bad, too rotten to eat."

4Then the LORD gave me this message: 5"This is what the LORD, the God of Israel, says: The good figs represent the exiles I sent from Judah to the land of the Babylonians.* 6I will watch over and care for them, and I will bring them back here again. I will build them up and not tear them down. I will plant them and not uproot them. 7I will give them hearts that recognize me as the LORD. They will be my people, and I will be their God, for they will return to me wholeheartedly.

8"But the bad figs," the LORD said, "represent King Zedekiah of Judah, his officials, all the people left in Jerusalem, and those who live in Egypt. I will treat them like bad figs, too rotten to eat. 9I will make them an object of horror and a symbol of evil to every nation on earth. They will be disgraced and mocked, taunted and cursed, wherever I scatter them. 10And I will send war, famine, and disease until they have vanished from the land of Israel, which I gave to them and their ancestors."

25:1THIS message for all the people of Judah came to Jeremiah from the LORD during the fourth year of Jehoiakim's reign over Judah.* This was the year when King Nebuchadnezzar* of Babylon began his reign.

2Jeremiah the prophet said to all the people in Judah and Jerusalem, 3"For the past twenty-three years—from the thirteenth year of the reign of Josiah son of Amon,* king of Judah, until now—the LORD has been giving me his messages. I have faithfully passed them on to you, but you have not listened.

4"Again and again the LORD has sent you his servants, the prophets, but you have not listened or even paid attention. 5Each time the message was this: 'Turn from the evil road you are traveling and from the evil things you are doing. Only then will I let you live in this land that the LORD gave to you and your ancestors forever. 6Do not provoke my anger by worshiping idols you made with your own hands. Then I will not harm you.'

7"But you would not listen to me," says the LORD. "You made me furious by worshiping idols you made with your own hands, bringing on yourselves all the disasters you now suffer. 8And now the

Lord of Heaven's Armies says: Because you have not listened to me, 9I will gather together all the armies of the north under King Nebuchadnezzar of Babylon, whom I have appointed as my deputy. I will bring them all against this land and its people and against the surrounding nations. I will completely destroy* you and make you an object of horror and contempt and a ruin forever. 10I will take away your happy singing and laughter. The joyful voices of bridegrooms and brides will no longer be heard. Your millstones will fall silent, and the lights in your homes will go out. 11This entire land will become a desolate wasteland. Israel and her neighboring lands will serve the king of Babylon for seventy years.

12"Then, after the seventy years of captivity are over, I will punish the king of Babylon and his people for their sins," says the Lord. "I will make the country of the Babylonians* a wasteland forever. 13I will bring upon them all the terrors I have promised in this book—all the penalties announced by Jeremiah against the nations. 14Many nations and great kings will enslave the Babylonians, just as they enslaved my people. I will punish them in proportion to the suffering they cause my people."

15This is what the Lord, the God of Israel, said to me: "Take from my hand this cup filled to the brim with my anger, and make all the nations to whom I send you drink from it. 16When they drink from it, they will stagger, crazed by the warfare I will send against them."

17So I took the cup of anger from the Lord and made all the nations drink from it—every nation to which the Lord sent me. 18I went to Jerusalem and the other towns of Judah, and their kings and officials drank from the cup. From that day until this, they have been a desolate ruin, an object of horror, contempt, and cursing. 19I gave the cup to Pharaoh, king of Egypt, his attendants, his officials, and all his people, 20along with all the foreigners living in that land. I also gave it to all the kings of the land of Uz and the kings of the Philistine cities of Ashkelon, Gaza, Ekron, and what remains of Ashdod. 21Then I gave the cup to the nations of Edom, Moab, and Ammon, 22and the kings of Tyre and Sidon, and the kings of the regions across the sea. 23I gave it to Dedan, Tema, and Buz, and to the people who live in distant places.* 24I gave it to the kings of Arabia, the kings of the nomadic tribes of the desert, 25and to the kings of Zimri, Elam, and Media. 26And I gave it to the kings of the northern countries, far and near, one after the other—all the kingdoms of the world. And finally, the king of Babylon* himself drank from the cup of the Lord's anger.

27Then the Lord said to me, "Now tell them, 'This is what the Lord of Heaven's Armies, the God of Israel, says: Drink from this cup of my anger. Get drunk and vomit; fall to rise no more, for I am sending terrible wars against you.' 28And if they refuse to accept the cup, tell them, 'The Lord of Heaven's Armies says: You have no choice but to drink from it. 29I have begun to punish Jerusalem, the city that bears my name. Now should I let you go unpunished? No, you will not escape disaster. I will call for war against all the nations of the earth. I, the Lord of Heaven's Armies, have spoken!'

30"Now prophesy all these things, and say to them,

"'The Lord will roar against his
    own land
  from his holy dwelling in heaven.
He will shout like those who tread
    grapes;
  he will shout against everyone
    on earth.
31 His cry of judgment will reach the
    ends of the earth,
  for the Lord will bring his case
    against all the nations.
He will judge all the people of the
    earth,
  slaughtering the wicked with the
    sword.
I, the Lord, have spoken!'"

32 This is what the Lord of Heaven's Armies says:

"Look! Disaster will fall upon
nation after nation!
A great whirlwind of fury is rising
from the most distant corners of
the earth!"

33In that day those the LORD has slaughtered will fill the earth from one end to the other. No one will mourn for them or gather up their bodies to bury them. They will be scattered on the ground like manure.

34 Weep and moan, you evil shepherds!
Roll in the dust, you leaders
of the flock!
The time of your slaughter has
arrived;
you will fall and shatter like a
fragile vase.
35 You will find no place to hide;
there will be no way to escape.
36 Listen to the frantic cries of the
shepherds.
The leaders of the flock are
wailing in despair,
for the LORD is ruining their
pastures.
37 Peaceful meadows will be turned
into a wasteland
by the LORD's fierce anger.
38 He has left his den like a strong lion
seeking its prey,
and their land will be made desolate
by the sword of the enemy
and the LORD's fierce anger.

23:33 As in Greek version and Latin Vulgate; Hebrew reads *What burden?*   24:1a Hebrew *Nebuchadrezzar*, a variant spelling of Nebuchadnezzar.   24:1b Hebrew *Jeconiah*, a variant spelling of Jehoiachin.   24:5 Or *Chaldeans*.   25:1a The fourth year of Jehoiakim's reign and the accession year of Nebuchadnezzar's reign was 605 B.C.   25:1b Hebrew *Nebuchadrezzar*, a variant spelling of Nebuchadnezzar; also in 25:9.   25:3 The thirteenth year of Josiah's reign was 627 B.C.   25:9 The Hebrew term used here refers to the complete consecration of things or people to the LORD, either by destroying them or by giving them as an offering.   25:12 Or *Chaldeans*.   25:23 Or *who clip the corners of their hair*.   25:26 Hebrew *of Sheshach*, a code name for Babylon.

2 THESSALONIANS 2:1-17

Now, dear brothers and sisters,* let us [Paul and his co-workers] clarify some things about the coming of our Lord Jesus Christ and how we will be gathered to meet him. 2Don't be so easily shaken or alarmed by those who say that the day of the Lord has already begun. Don't believe them, even if they claim to have had a spiritual vision, a revelation, or a letter supposedly from us. 3Don't be fooled by what they say. For that day will not come until there is a great rebellion against God and the man of lawlessness* is revealed—the one who brings destruction.* 4He will exalt himself and defy everything that people call god and every object of worship. He will even sit in the temple of God, claiming that he himself is God.

5Don't you remember that I told you about all this when I was with you? 6And you know what is holding him back, for he can be revealed only when his time comes. 7For this lawlessness is already at work secretly, and it will remain secret until the one who is holding it back steps out of the way. 8Then the man of lawlessness will be revealed, but the Lord Jesus will kill him with the breath of his mouth and destroy him by the splendor of his coming.

9This man will come to do the work of Satan with counterfeit power and signs and miracles. 10He will use every kind of evil deception to fool those on their way to destruction, because they refuse to love and accept the truth that would save them. 11So God will cause them to be greatly deceived, and they will believe these lies. 12Then they will be condemned for enjoying evil rather than believing the truth.

13As for us, we can't help but thank God for you, dear brothers and sisters loved by the Lord. We are always thankful that God chose you to be among the first* to experience salvation—a salvation that came through the Spirit who makes you holy and through your belief in the truth. 14He called you to salvation when we told you the Good News; now you can share in the glory of our Lord Jesus Christ.

15With all these things in mind, dear brothers and sisters, stand firm and keep a strong grip on the teaching we passed on to you both in person and by letter.

[16]Now may our Lord Jesus Christ himself and God our Father, who loved us and by his grace gave us eternal comfort and a wonderful hope, [17]comfort you and strengthen you in every good thing you do and say.

2:1 Greek *brothers;* also in 2:13, 15.   2:3a Some manuscripts read *the man of sin.*   2:3b Greek *the son of destruction.*   2:13 Some manuscripts read *chose you from the very beginning.*

PSALM 84:1-12

*For the choir director: A psalm of the descendants of Korah, to be accompanied by a stringed instrument.**

[1] How lovely is your dwelling place,
    O LORD of Heaven's Armies.
[2] I long, yes, I faint with longing
    to enter the courts of the LORD.
  With my whole being, body
      and soul,
    I will shout joyfully to the living
        God.
[3] Even the sparrow finds a home,
    and the swallow builds her nest
      and raises her young
  at a place near your altar,
    O LORD of Heaven's Armies,
      my King and my God!
[4] What joy for those who can live in
      your house,
    always singing your praises.
                        Interlude

[5] What joy for those whose strength
      comes from the LORD,
    who have set their minds on a
      pilgrimage to Jerusalem.
[6] When they walk through the Valley
      of Weeping,*
    it will become a place of
      refreshing springs.
  The autumn rains will clothe it
      with blessings.
[7] They will continue to grow stronger,
    and each of them will appear
      before God in Jerusalem.*

[8] O LORD God of Heaven's Armies,
    hear my prayer.
  Listen, O God of Jacob.
                        Interlude

[9] O God, look with favor upon the
      king, our shield!
  Show favor to the one you
      have anointed.

[10] A single day in your courts
    is better than a thousand
      anywhere else!
  I would rather be a gatekeeper
    in the house of my God
  than live the good life in the
      homes of the wicked.
[11] For the LORD God is our sun and
      our shield.
  He gives us grace and glory.
  The LORD will withhold no good
      thing
    from those who do what is right.
[12] O LORD of Heaven's Armies,
    what joy for those who trust
      in you.

84:TITLE Hebrew *according to the gittith.*   84:6 Or *Valley of Poplars;* Hebrew reads *valley of Baca.*   84:7 Hebrew *Zion.*

PROVERBS 25:15

[P]atience can persuade a prince, and soft speech can break bones.

OCTOBER 15

JEREMIAH 26:1–27:22

This message came to Jeremiah from the LORD early in the reign of Jehoiakim son of Josiah,* king of Judah. [2]"This is what the LORD says: Stand in the courtyard in front of the Temple of the LORD, and make an announcement to the people who have come there to worship from all over Judah. Give them my entire message; include every word. [3]Perhaps they will listen and turn from their evil ways. Then I will change my mind about the disaster I am ready to pour out on them because of their sins.

[4]"Say to them, 'This is what the LORD says: If you will not listen to me and

obey my word I have given you, [5]and if you will not listen to my servants, the prophets—for I sent them again and again to warn you, but you would not listen to them—[6]then I will destroy this Temple as I destroyed Shiloh, the place where the Tabernacle was located. And I will make Jerusalem an object of cursing in every nation on earth.'"

[7]The priests, the prophets, and all the people listened to Jeremiah as he spoke in front of the LORD's Temple. [8]But when Jeremiah had finished his message, saying everything the LORD had told him to say, the priests and prophets and all the people at the Temple mobbed him. "Kill him!" they shouted. [9]"What right do you have to prophesy in the LORD's name that this Temple will be destroyed like Shiloh? What do you mean, saying that Jerusalem will be destroyed and left with no inhabitants?" And all the people threatened him as he stood in front of the Temple.

[10]When the officials of Judah heard what was happening, they rushed over from the palace and sat down at the New Gate of the Temple to hold court. [11]The priests and prophets presented their accusations to the officials and the people. "This man should die!" they said. "You have heard with your own ears what a traitor he is, for he has prophesied against this city."

[12]Then Jeremiah spoke to the officials and the people in his own defense. "The LORD sent me to prophesy against this Temple and this city," he said. "The LORD gave me every word that I have spoken. [13]But if you stop your sinning and begin to obey the LORD your God, he will change his mind about this disaster that he has announced against you. [14]As for me, I am in your hands—do with me as you think best. [15]But if you kill me, rest assured that you will be killing an innocent man! The responsibility for such a deed will lie on you, on this city, and on every person living in it. For it is absolutely true that the LORD sent me to speak every word you have heard."

[16]Then the officials and the people said to the priests and prophets, "This man does not deserve the death sentence, for he has spoken to us in the name of the LORD our God."

[17]Then some of the wise old men stood and spoke to all the people assembled there. [18]They said, "Remember when Micah of Moresheth prophesied during the reign of King Hezekiah of Judah. He told the people of Judah,

'This is what the LORD of Heaven's
    Armies says:
Mount Zion will be plowed like an
    open field;
Jerusalem will be reduced
    to ruins!
A thicket will grow on the heights
    where the Temple now stands.'*

[19]But did King Hezekiah and the people kill him for saying this? No, they turned from their sins and worshiped the LORD. They begged him for mercy. Then the LORD changed his mind about the terrible disaster he had pronounced against them. So we are about to do ourselves great harm."

[20]At this time Uriah son of Shemaiah from Kiriath-jearim was also prophesying for the LORD. And he predicted the same terrible disaster against the city and nation as Jeremiah did. [21]When King Jehoiakim and the army officers and officials heard what he was saying, the king sent someone to kill him. But Uriah heard about the plan and escaped in fear to Egypt. [22]Then King Jehoiakim sent Elnathan son of Acbor to Egypt along with several other men to capture Uriah. [23]They took him prisoner and brought him back to King Jehoiakim. The king then killed Uriah with a sword and had him buried in an unmarked grave.

[24]Nevertheless, Ahikam son of Shaphan stood up for Jeremiah and persuaded the court not to turn him over to the mob to be killed.

27:1THIS message came to Jeremiah from the LORD early in the reign of Zedekiah* son of Josiah, king of Judah. [2]This is what the LORD said to me:

"Make a yoke, and fasten it on your neck with leather thongs. ³Then send messages to the kings of Edom, Moab, Ammon, Tyre, and Sidon through their ambassadors who have come to see King Zedekiah in Jerusalem. ⁴Give them this message for their masters: 'This is what the Lord of Heaven's Armies, the God of Israel, says: ⁵With my great strength and powerful arm I made the earth and all its people and every animal. I can give these things of mine to anyone I choose. ⁶Now I will give your countries to King Nebuchadnezzar of Babylon, who is my servant. I have put everything, even the wild animals, under his control. ⁷All the nations will serve him, his son, and his grandson until his time is up. Then many nations and great kings will conquer and rule over Babylon. ⁸So you must submit to Babylon's king and serve him; put your neck under Babylon's yoke! I will punish any nation that refuses to be his slave, says the Lord. I will send war, famine, and disease upon that nation until Babylon has conquered it.

⁹'Do not listen to your false prophets, fortune-tellers, interpreters of dreams, mediums, and sorcerers who say, "The king of Babylon will not conquer you." ¹⁰They are all liars, and their lies will lead to your being driven out of your land. I will drive you out and send you far away to die. ¹¹But the people of any nation that submits to the king of Babylon will be allowed to stay in their own country to farm the land as usual. I, the Lord, have spoken!'"

¹²Then I repeated this same message to King Zedekiah of Judah. "If you want to live, submit to the yoke of the king of Babylon and his people. ¹³Why do you insist on dying—you and your people? Why should you choose war, famine, and disease, which the Lord will bring against every nation that refuses to submit to Babylon's king? ¹⁴Do not listen to the false prophets who keep telling you, 'The king of Babylon will not conquer you.' They are liars. ¹⁵This is what the Lord says: 'I have not sent these proph-

ets! They are telling you lies in my name, so I will drive you from this land. You will all die—you and all these prophets, too.'"

¹⁶Then I spoke to the priests and the people and said, "This is what the Lord says: 'Do not listen to your prophets who claim that soon the gold articles taken from my Temple will be returned from Babylon. It is all a lie! ¹⁷Do not listen to them. Surrender to the king of Babylon, and you will live. Why should this whole city be destroyed? ¹⁸If they really are prophets and speak the Lord's messages, let them pray to the Lord of Heaven's Armies. Let them pray that the articles remaining in the Lord's Temple and in the king's palace and in the palaces of Jerusalem will not be carried away to Babylon!'

¹⁹"For the Lord of Heaven's Armies has spoken about the pillars in front of the Temple, the great bronze basin called the Sea, the water carts, and all the other ceremonial articles. ²⁰King Nebuchadnezzar of Babylon left them here when he exiled Jehoiachin* son of Jehoiakim, king of Judah, to Babylon, along with all the other nobles of Judah and Jerusalem. ²¹Yes, this is what the Lord of Heaven's Armies, the God of Israel, says about the precious things still in the Temple and in the palace of Judah's king: ²²'They will all be carried away to Babylon and will stay there until I send for them,' says the Lord. 'Then I will bring them back to Jerusalem again.'"

26:1 The first year of Jehoiakim's reign was 608 B.C. 26:18 Mic 3:12. 27:1 As in some Hebrew manuscripts and Syriac version (see also 27:3, 12); most Hebrew manuscripts read *Jehoiakim*. 27:20 Hebrew *Jeconiah*, a variant spelling of Jehoiachin.

2 THESSALONIANS 3:1-18

Finally, dear brothers and sisters,* we [Paul and his co-workers] ask you to pray for us. Pray that the Lord's message will spread rapidly and be honored wherever it goes, just as when it came to you. ²Pray, too, that we will be rescued from wicked and evil people, for not everyone is a believer. ³But the Lord is faithful; he will strengthen you and guard you from the evil one.* ⁴And we are confident in the Lord that you are doing and will continue to do the things we commanded you. ⁵May the Lord lead your hearts into a full understanding and expression of the love of God and the patient endurance that comes from Christ.

⁶And now, dear brothers and sisters, we give you this command in the name of our Lord Jesus Christ: Stay away from all believers* who live idle lives and don't follow the tradition they received* from us. ⁷For you know that you ought to imitate us. We were not idle when we were with you. ⁸We never accepted food from anyone without paying for it. We worked hard day and night so we would not be a burden to any of you. ⁹We certainly had the right to ask you to feed us, but we wanted to give you an example to follow. ¹⁰Even while we were with you, we gave you this command: "Those unwilling to work will not get to eat."

¹¹Yet we hear that some of you are living idle lives, refusing to work and meddling in other people's business. ¹²We command such people and urge them in the name of the Lord Jesus Christ to settle down and work to earn their own living. ¹³As for the rest of you, dear brothers and sisters, never get tired of doing good.

¹⁴Take note of those who refuse to obey what we say in this letter. Stay away from them so they will be ashamed. ¹⁵Don't think of them as enemies, but warn them as you would a brother or sister.*

¹⁶Now may the Lord of peace himself give you his peace at all times and in every situation. The Lord be with you all.

¹⁷HERE IS MY GREETING IN MY OWN HANDWRITING—PAUL. I DO THIS IN ALL MY LETTERS TO PROVE THEY ARE FROM ME.

¹⁸May the grace of our Lord Jesus Christ be with you all.

3:1 Greek *brothers;* also in 3:6, 13. **3:3** Or *from evil.*
3:6a Greek *from every brother.* **3:6b** Some manuscripts read *you received.* **3:15** Greek *as a brother.*

PSALM 85:1-13

For the choir director: A psalm of the descendants of Korah.

¹ LORD, you poured out blessings on your land!
You restored the fortunes of Israel.*
² You forgave the guilt of your people—
yes, you covered all their sins.
Interlude
³ You held back your fury.
You kept back your blazing anger.

⁴ Now restore us again, O God of our salvation.
Put aside your anger against us once more.
⁵ Will you be angry with us always?
Will you prolong your wrath to all generations?
⁶ Won't you revive us again,
so your people can rejoice in you?
⁷ Show us your unfailing love, O LORD,
and grant us your salvation.

⁸ I listen carefully to what God the LORD is saying,
for he speaks peace to his faithful people.
But let them not return to their foolish ways.
⁹ Surely his salvation is near to those who fear him,
so our land will be filled with his glory.

¹⁰ **Unfailing love and truth have met together.**
Righteousness and peace have kissed!
¹¹ **Truth springs up from the earth,**
and righteousness smiles down from heaven.
¹² Yes, the LORD pours down his blessings.
Our land will yield its bountiful harvest.
¹³ Righteousness goes as a herald before him,
preparing the way for his steps.

85:1 Hebrew *of Jacob.* See note on 44:4.

PROVERBS 25:16
Do you like honey? Don't eat too much, or it will make you sick!

OCTOBER 16

JEREMIAH 28:1–29:32
One day in late summer* of that same year—the fourth year of the reign of Zedekiah, king of Judah—Hananiah son of Azzur, a prophet from Gibeon, addressed me publicly in the Temple while all the priests and people listened. He said, ²"This is what the LORD of Heaven's Armies, the God of Israel, says: 'I will remove the yoke of the king of Babylon from your necks. ³Within two years I will bring back all the Temple treasures that King Nebuchadnezzar carried off to Babylon. ⁴And I will bring back Jehoiachin* son of Jehoiakim, king of Judah, and all the other captives that were taken to Babylon. I will surely break the yoke that the king of Babylon has put on your necks. I, the LORD, have spoken!'"

⁵Jeremiah responded to Hananiah as they stood in front of all the priests and people at the Temple. ⁶He said, "Amen! May your prophecies come true! I hope the LORD does everything you say. I hope he does bring back from Babylon the treasures of this Temple and all the captives. ⁷But listen now to the solemn words I speak to you in the presence of all these people. ⁸The ancient prophets who preceded you and me spoke against many nations, always warning of war, disaster, and disease. ⁹So a prophet who predicts peace must show he is right. Only when his predictions come true can we know that he is really from the LORD."

¹⁰Then Hananiah the prophet took the yoke off Jeremiah's neck and broke it in pieces. ¹¹And Hananiah said again to the crowd that had gathered, "This is what the LORD says: 'Just as this yoke has been broken, within two years I will break the yoke of oppression from all the nations now subject to King Nebuchadnezzar of Babylon.'" With that, Jeremiah left the Temple area.

¹²Soon after this confrontation with Hananiah, the LORD gave this message to Jeremiah: ¹³"Go and tell Hananiah, 'This is what the LORD says: You have broken a wooden yoke, but you have replaced it with a yoke of iron. ¹⁴The LORD of Heaven's Armies, the God of Israel, says: I have put a yoke of iron on the necks of all these nations, forcing them into slavery under King Nebuchadnezzar of Babylon. I have put everything, even the wild animals, under his control.'"

¹⁵Then Jeremiah the prophet said to Hananiah, "Listen, Hananiah! The LORD has not sent you, but the people believe your lies. ¹⁶Therefore, this is what the LORD says: 'You must die. Your life will end this very year because you have rebelled against the LORD.'"

¹⁷Two months later* the prophet Hananiah died.

²⁹:¹JEREMIAH wrote a letter from Jerusalem to the elders, priests, prophets, and all the people who had been exiled to Babylon by King Nebuchadnezzar. ²This was after King Jehoiachin,* the queen mother, the court officials, the other officials of Judah, and all the craftsmen and artisans had been deported from Jerusalem. ³He sent the letter with Elasah son of Shaphan and Gemariah son of Hilkiah when they went to Babylon as King Zedekiah's ambassadors to Nebuchadnezzar. This is what Jeremiah's letter said:

⁴This is what the LORD of Heaven's Armies, the God of Israel, says to all the captives he has exiled to Babylon from Jerusalem: ⁵"Build homes, and plan to stay. Plant gardens, and eat the food they produce. ⁶Marry and

have children. Then find spouses for them so that you may have many grandchildren. Multiply! Do not dwindle away! 7And work for the peace and prosperity of the city where I sent you into exile. Pray to the LORD for it, for its welfare will determine your welfare."

8This is what the LORD of Heaven's Armies, the God of Israel, says: "Do not let your prophets and fortune-tellers who are with you in the land of Babylon trick you. Do not listen to their dreams, 9because they are telling you lies in my name. I have not sent them," says the LORD.

10This is what the LORD says: "You will be in Babylon for seventy years. But then I will come and do for you all the good things I have promised, and I will bring you home again. 11For I know the plans I have for you," says the LORD. "They are plans for good and not for disaster, to give you a future and a hope. 12In those days when you pray, I will listen. 13If you look for me wholeheartedly, you will find me. 14I will be found by you," says the LORD. "I will end your captivity and restore your fortunes. I will gather you out of the nations where I sent you and will bring you home again to your own land."

15You claim that the LORD has raised up prophets for you in Babylon. 16But this is what the LORD says about the king who sits on David's throne and all those still living here in Jerusalem—your relatives who were not exiled to Babylon. 17This is what the LORD of Heaven's Armies says: "I will send war, famine, and disease upon them and make them like bad figs, too rotten to eat. 18Yes, I will pursue them with war, famine, and disease, and I will scatter them around the world. In every nation where I send them, I will make them an object of damnation, horror, contempt, and mockery. 19For they refuse to listen

to me, though I have spoken to them repeatedly through the prophets I sent. And you who are in exile have not listened either," says the LORD.

20Therefore, listen to this message from the LORD, all you captives there in Babylon. 21This is what the LORD of Heaven's Armies, the God of Israel, says about your prophets— Ahab son of Kolaiah and Zedekiah son of Maaseiah—who are telling you lies in my name: "I will turn them over to Nebuchadnezzar* for execution before your eyes. 22Their terrible fate will become proverbial, so that the Judean exiles will curse someone by saying, 'May the LORD make you like Zedekiah and Ahab, whom the king of Babylon burned alive!' 23For these men have done terrible things among my people. They have committed adultery with their neighbors' wives and have lied in my name, saying things I did not command. I am a witness to this. I, the LORD, have spoken."

24The LORD sent this message to Shemaiah the Nehelamite in Babylon: 25"This is what the LORD of Heaven's Armies, the God of Israel, says: You wrote a letter on your own authority to Zephaniah son of Maaseiah, the priest, and you sent copies to the other priests and people in Jerusalem. You wrote to Zephaniah,

26"The LORD has appointed you to replace Jehoiada as the priest in charge of the house of the LORD. You are responsible to put into stocks and neck irons any crazy man who claims to be a prophet. 27So why have you done nothing to stop Jeremiah from Anathoth, who pretends to be a prophet among you? 28Jeremiah sent a letter here to Babylon, predicting that our captivity will be a long one. He said, 'Build homes, and plan to stay. Plant gardens, and eat the food they produce.'"

²⁹But when Zephaniah the priest received Shemaiah's letter, he took it to Jeremiah and read it to him. ³⁰Then the LORD gave this message to Jeremiah: ³¹"Send an open letter to all the exiles in Babylon. Tell them, 'This is what the LORD says concerning Shemaiah the Nehelamite: Since he has prophesied to you when I did not send him and has tricked you into believing his lies, ³²I will punish him and his family. None of his descendants will see the good things I will do for my people, for he has incited you to rebel against me. I, the LORD, have spoken!'"

28:1 Hebrew *In the fifth month,* of the ancient Hebrew lunar calendar. The fifth month in the fourth year of Zedekiah's reign occurred within the months of August and September 593 B.C. Also see note on 1:3. 28:4 Hebrew *Jeconiah,* a variant spelling of Jehoiachin. 28:17 Hebrew *In the seventh month of that same year.* See 28:1 and the note there. 29:2 Hebrew *Jeconiah,* a variant spelling of Jehoiachin. 29:21 Hebrew *Nebuchadrezzar,* a variant spelling of Nebuchadnezzar.

1 TIMOTHY 1:1-20

This letter is from Paul, an apostle of Christ Jesus, appointed by the command of God our Savior and Christ Jesus, who gives us hope.

²I am writing to Timothy, my true son in the faith.

May God the Father and Christ Jesus our Lord give you grace, mercy, and peace.

³When I left for Macedonia, I urged you to stay there in Ephesus and stop those whose teaching is contrary to the truth. ⁴Don't let them waste their time in endless discussion of myths and spiritual pedigrees. These things only lead to meaningless speculations,* which don't help people live a life of faith in God.*

⁵The purpose of my instruction is that all believers would be filled with love that comes from a pure heart, a clear conscience, and genuine faith. ⁶But some people have missed this whole point. They have turned away from these things and spend their time in meaningless discussions. ⁷They want to be known as teachers of the law of Moses, but they don't know what they are talking about, even though they speak so confidently.

⁸We know that the law is good when used correctly. ⁹For the law was not intended for people who do what is right. It is for people who are lawless and rebellious, who are ungodly and sinful, who consider nothing sacred and defile what is holy, who kill their father or mother or commit other murders. ¹⁰The law is for people who are sexually immoral, or who practice homosexuality, or are slave traders,* liars, promise breakers, or who do anything else that contradicts the wholesome teaching ¹¹that comes from the glorious Good News entrusted to me by our blessed God.

¹²I thank Christ Jesus our Lord, who has given me strength to do his work. He considered me trustworthy and appointed me to serve him, ¹³even though I used to blaspheme the name of Christ. In my insolence, I persecuted his people. But God had mercy on me because I did it in ignorance and unbelief. ¹⁴Oh, how generous and gracious our Lord was! He filled me with the faith and love that come from Christ Jesus.

¹⁵This is a trustworthy saying, and everyone should accept it: "Christ Jesus came into the world to save sinners"— and I am the worst of them all. ¹⁶But God had mercy on me so that Christ Jesus could use me as a prime example of his great patience with even the worst sinners. Then others will realize that they, too, can believe in him and receive eternal life. ¹⁷All honor and glory to God forever and ever! He is the eternal King, the unseen one who never dies; he alone is God. Amen.

¹⁸Timothy, my son, here are my instructions for you, based on the prophetic words spoken about you earlier. May they help you fight well in the Lord's battles. ¹⁹Cling to your faith in Christ, and keep your conscience clear. For some people have deliberately violated their consciences; as a result, their faith has been shipwrecked. ²⁰Hymenaeus and Alexander are two examples. I threw them out and handed them over

to Satan so they might learn not to blaspheme God.

1:4a Greek *in myths and endless genealogies, which cause speculation.*   1:4b Greek *a stewardship of God in faith.* 1:10 Or *kidnappers.*

PSALM 86:1-17
A prayer of David.

1 **B**end down, O Lᴏʀᴅ, and hear
    my prayer;
    answer me, for I need your help.
2 Protect me, for I am devoted to you.
    Save me, for I serve you and
      trust you.
    You are my God.
3 Be merciful to me, O Lord,
    for I am calling on you constantly.
4 Give me happiness, O Lord,
    for I give myself to you.
5 **O Lord, you are so good, so ready**
    to forgive,
    so full of unfailing love for all
      who ask for your help.
6 **Listen closely to my prayer,**
    O Lᴏʀᴅ;
    hear my urgent cry.
7 **I will call to you whenever I'm in**
    trouble,
    and you will answer me.

8 No pagan god is like you, O Lord.
    None can do what you do!
9 All the nations you made
    will come and bow before you,
    Lord;
    they will praise your holy name.
10 For you are great and perform
    wonderful deeds.
    You alone are God.

11 Teach me your ways, O Lᴏʀᴅ,
    that I may live according to
    your truth!
    Grant me purity of heart,
    so that I may honor you.
12 With all my heart I will praise you,
    O Lord my God.
    I will give glory to your name
    forever.
13 for your love for me is very great.
    You have rescued me from the
    depths of death.*

14 O God, insolent people rise up
    against me;
    a violent gang is trying to kill me.
    You mean nothing to them.
15 But you, O Lord,
    are a God of compassion
    and mercy,
    slow to get angry
    and filled with unfailing love and
      faithfulness.
16 Look down and have mercy on me.
    Give your strength to your servant;
    save me, the son of your servant.
17 Send me a sign of your favor.
    Then those who hate me will be
    put to shame,
    for you, O Lᴏʀᴅ, help and
    comfort me.

86:13 Hebrew *of Sheol.*

PROVERBS 25:17
Don't visit your neighbors too often, or you will wear out your welcome.

OCTOBER 17

JEREMIAH 30:1–31:26
The Lᴏʀᴅ gave another message to Jeremiah. He said, 2"This is what the Lᴏʀᴅ, the God of Israel, says: Write down for the record everything I have said to you, Jeremiah. 3For the time is coming when I will restore the fortunes of my people of Israel and Judah. I will bring them home to this land that I gave to their ancestors, and they will possess it again. I, the Lᴏʀᴅ, have spoken!"

4This is the message the Lᴏʀᴅ gave concerning Israel and Judah. 5This is what the Lᴏʀᴅ says:

"I hear cries of fear;
    there is terror and no peace.
6 Now let me ask you a question:
    Do men give birth to babies?

Then why do they stand there,
    ashen-faced,
        hands pressed against their sides
        like a woman in labor?
7 In all history there has never been
        such a time of terror.
    It will be a time of trouble for my
        people Israel.*
    Yet in the end they will be saved!
8 For in that day,"
    says the LORD of Heaven's Armies,
    "I will break the yoke from their
        necks
    and snap their chains.
    Foreigners will no longer be
        their masters.
9   For my people will serve the LORD
        their God
    and their king descended from
        David—
        the king I will raise up for them.

10 "So do not be afraid, Jacob, my
        servant;
    do not be dismayed, Israel,"
    says the LORD.
    "For I will bring you home again
        from distant lands,
    and your children will return
        from their exile.
    Israel will return to a life of peace
        and quiet,
    and no one will terrorize them.
11 For I am with you and will
        save you,"
    says the LORD.
    "I will completely destroy the
        nations where I have
        scattered you,
    but I will not completely
        destroy you.
    I will discipline you, but
        with justice;
    I cannot let you go
        unpunished."

12 This is what the LORD says:
    "Your injury is incurable—
        a terrible wound.
13 There is no one to help you
        or to bind up your injury.
    No medicine can heal you.

14 All your lovers—your allies—have
        left you
    and do not care about you
        anymore.
    I have wounded you cruelly,
        as though I were your enemy.
    For your sins are many,
        and your guilt is great.
15 Why do you protest your
        punishment—
        this wound that has no cure?
    I have had to punish you
        because your sins are many
        and your guilt is great.

16 "But all who devour you will be
        devoured,
    and all your enemies will be sent
        into exile.
    All who plunder you will be
        plundered,
    and all who attack you will
        be attacked.
17 I will give you back your health
    and heal your wounds," says
        the LORD.
    "For you are called an outcast—
        'Jerusalem* for whom no
        one cares.'"

18 This is what the LORD says:
    "When I bring Israel home again
        from captivity
    and restore their fortunes,
    Jerusalem will be rebuilt on
        its ruins,
    and the palace reconstructed
        as before.
19 There will be joy and songs of
        thanksgiving,
    and I will multiply my people, not
        diminish them;
    I will honor them, not despise them.
20   Their children will prosper as
        they did long ago.
    I will establish them as a nation
        before me,
    and I will punish anyone who
        hurts them.
21 They will have their own ruler again,
    and he will come from their
        own people.

I will invite him to approach me,"
  says the LORD,
    "for who would dare to come
      unless invited?
²² You will be my people,
  and I will be your God."

²³ Look! The LORD's anger bursts out
    like a storm,
  a driving wind that swirls down
    on the heads of the wicked.
²⁴ The fierce anger of the LORD will
    not diminish
  until it has finished all he has
    planned.
In the days to come
  you will understand all this.

³¹:¹"IN that day," says the LORD, "I will be the God of all the families of Israel, and they will be my people. ²This is what the LORD says:

"Those who survive the coming
    destruction
  will find blessings even in the
    barren land,
  for I will give rest to the people
    of Israel."

³ Long ago the LORD said to Israel:
"I have loved you, my people, with
    an everlasting love.
  With unfailing love I have drawn
    you to myself.
⁴ I will rebuild you, my virgin Israel.
  You will again be happy
  and dance merrily with your
    tambourines.
⁵ Again you will plant your vineyards
    on the mountains of Samaria
  and eat from your own gardens
    there.
⁶ The day will come when watchmen
    will shout
  from the hill country of Ephraim,
'Come, let us go up to Jerusalem*
  to worship the LORD our God.'"

⁷ Now this is what the LORD says:
"Sing with joy for Israel.*
  Shout for the greatest of nations!
  Shout out with praise and joy:
'Save your people, O LORD,

the remnant of Israel!'
⁸ For I will bring them from the north
  and from the distant corners of
    the earth.
I will not forget the blind and lame,
  the expectant mothers and
    women in labor.
A great company will return!
⁹ Tears of joy will stream down their
    faces,
  and I will lead them home with
    great care.
They will walk beside quiet streams
  and on smooth paths where they
    will not stumble.
For I am Israel's father,
  and Ephraim is my oldest child.

¹⁰ "Listen to this message from the LORD,
  you nations of the world;
  proclaim it in distant coastlands:
The LORD, who scattered his people,
  will gather them and watch
    over them
  as a shepherd does his flock.
¹¹ For the LORD has redeemed Israel
  from those too strong for them.
¹² They will come home and sing songs
    of joy on the heights of Jerusalem.
  They will be radiant because of
    the LORD's good gifts—
the abundant crops of grain, new
    wine, and olive oil,
  and the healthy flocks and herds.
Their life will be like a watered
    garden,
  and all their sorrows will be gone.
¹³ The young women will dance for joy,
  and the men—old and young—will
    join in the celebration.
I will turn their mourning into joy.
  I will comfort them and exchange
    their sorrow for rejoicing.
¹⁴ The priests will enjoy abundance,
  and my people will feast on my
    good gifts.
  I, the LORD, have spoken!"

¹⁵This is what the LORD says:

"A cry is heard in Ramah—
  deep anguish and bitter
    weeping.

Rachel weeps for her children,
refusing to be comforted—
for her children are gone."

16 But now this is what the LORD says:
"Do not weep any longer,
for I will reward you," says the
LORD.
"Your children will come back
to you
from the distant land of the
enemy.
17 There is hope for your future," says
the LORD.
"Your children will come again to
their own land.
18 I have heard Israel* saying,
'You disciplined me severely,
like a calf that needs training for
the yoke.
Turn me again to you and
restore me,
for you alone are the LORD
my God.
19 I turned away from God,
but then I was sorry.
I kicked myself for my stupidity!
I was thoroughly ashamed
of all I did in my younger days.'
20 "Is not Israel still my son,
my darling child?" says the LORD.
"I often have to punish him,
but I still love him.
That's why I long for him
and surely will have mercy
on him.
21 Set up road signs;
put up guideposts.
Mark well the path
by which you came.
Come back again, my virgin Israel;
return to your towns here.
22 How long will you wander,
my wayward daughter?
For the LORD will cause something
new to happen—
Israel will embrace her God.*"

23 This is what the LORD of Heaven's
Armies, the God of Israel, says: "When I
bring them back from captivity, the people of Judah and its towns will again say,

'The LORD bless you, O righteous home,
O holy mountain!' 24 Townspeople and
farmers and shepherds alike will live
together in peace and happiness. 25 For I
have given rest to the weary and joy to
the sorrowing."

26 At this, I woke up and looked
around. My sleep had been very sweet.

30:7 Hebrew *Jacob;* also in 30:10b, 18. See note on 5:20.
30:17 Hebrew *Zion.*   **31:6** Hebrew *Zion;* also in 31:12.
31:7 Hebrew *Jacob;* also in 31:11. See note on 5:20.
31:18 Hebrew *Ephraim,* referring to the northern kingdom
of Israel; also in 31:20.   **31:22** Hebrew *a woman will court
a suitor.*

1 TIMOTHY 2:1-15

❚ [Paul] urge you [Timothy], first of all, to
pray for all people. Ask God to help them;
intercede on their behalf, and give
thanks for them. 2 Pray this way for kings
and all who are in authority so that we
can live peaceful and quiet lives marked
by godliness and dignity. 3 This is good
and pleases God our Savior, 4 who wants
everyone to be saved and to understand
the truth. 5 **For there is only one God
and one Mediator who can reconcile
God and humanity—the man Christ
Jesus. 6 He gave his life to purchase
freedom for everyone. This is the
message God gave to the world at just
the right time.** 7 And I have been chosen
as a preacher and apostle to teach the
Gentiles this message about faith and
truth. I'm not exaggerating—just telling
the truth.

8 In every place of worship, I want
men to pray with holy hands lifted up to
God, free from anger and controversy.

9 And I want women to be modest in
their appearance.* They should wear
decent and appropriate clothing and
not draw attention to themselves by the
way they fix their hair or by wearing
gold or pearls or expensive clothes.
10 For women who claim to be devoted to
God should make themselves attractive
by the good things they do.

11 Women should learn quietly and
submissively. 12 I do not let women teach
men or have authority over them.* Let
them listen quietly. 13 For God made
Adam first, and afterward he made Eve.

[14]And it was not Adam who was deceived by Satan. The woman was deceived, and sin was the result. [15]But women will be saved through childbearing,* assuming they continue to live in faith, love, holiness, and modesty.

2:9 Or *to pray in modest apparel.*   2:12 Or *teach men or usurp their authority.*   2:15 Or *will be saved by accepting their role as mothers,* or *will be saved by the birth of the Child.*

PSALM 87:1-7
A song. A psalm of the descendants of Korah.

[1] **O**n the holy mountain
   stands the city founded
      by the LORD.
[2] He loves the city of Jerusalem
      more than any other city in Israel.*
[3] O city of God,
   what glorious things are
      said of you!   *Interlude*

[4] I will count Egypt* and Babylon
      among those who know me—
   also Philistia and Tyre, and even
      distant Ethiopia.*
   They have all become citizens
      of Jerusalem!
[5] Regarding Jerusalem* it will
      be said,
   "Everyone enjoys the rights of
      citizenship there."
   And the Most High will personally
      bless this city.
[6] When the LORD registers the
      nations, he will say,
   "They have all become citizens
      of Jerusalem."   *Interlude*

[7] The people will play flutes*
      and sing,
   "The source of my life springs
      from Jerusalem!"

87:2 Hebrew *He loves the gates of Zion more than all the dwellings of Jacob.* See note on 44:4.   87:4a Hebrew *Rahab,* the name of a mythical sea monster that represents chaos in ancient literature. The name is used here as a poetic name for Egypt.   87:4b Hebrew *Cush.* 87:5 Hebrew *Zion.*   87:7 Or *will dance.*

PROVERBS 25:18-19
Telling lies about others is as harmful as hitting them with an ax, wounding them with a sword, or shooting them with a sharp arrow. □Putting confidence in an unreliable person in times of trouble is like chewing with a broken tooth or walking on a lame foot.

OCTOBER 18

JEREMIAH 31:27–32:44
"**T**he day is coming," says the LORD, "when I will greatly increase the human population and the number of animals here in Israel and Judah. [28]In the past I deliberately uprooted and tore down this nation. I overthrew it, destroyed it, and brought disaster upon it. But in the future I will just as deliberately plant it and build it up. I, the LORD, have spoken!

[29]"The people will no longer quote this proverb:

'The parents have eaten
   sour grapes,
but their children's mouths
   pucker at the taste.'

[30]All people will die for their own sins— those who eat the sour grapes will be the ones whose mouths will pucker.

[31]"The day is coming," says the LORD, "when I will make a new covenant with the people of Israel and Judah. [32]This covenant will not be like the one I made with their ancestors when I took them by the hand and brought them out of the land of Egypt. They broke that covenant, though I loved them as a husband loves his wife," says the LORD.

[33]**"But this is the new covenant I will make with the people of Israel on that day," says the LORD. "I will put my instructions deep within them, and I will write them on their hearts. I will be their God, and they will be my people.** [34]And they will not need to teach their neighbors, nor will they need to teach their relatives, saying,

'You should know the LORD.' For everyone, from the least to the greatest, will know me already," says the LORD. "And I will forgive their wickedness, and I will never again remember their sins."

35 It is the LORD who provides the sun
    to light the day
  and the moon and stars to light
    the night,
  and who stirs the sea into
    roaring waves.
  His name is the LORD of Heaven's
    Armies,
  and this is what he says:
36 "I am as likely to reject my
    people Israel
  as I am to abolish the laws
    of nature!"
37 This is what the LORD says:
  "Just as the heavens cannot be
    measured
  and the foundations of the earth
    cannot be explored,
  so I will not consider casting
    them away
  for the evil they have done.
  I, the LORD, have spoken!

38"The day is coming," says the LORD, "when all Jerusalem will be rebuilt for me, from the Tower of Hananel to the Corner Gate. 39A measuring line will be stretched out over the hill of Gareb and across to Goah. 40And the entire area—including the graveyard and ash dump in the valley, and all the fields out to the Kidron Valley on the east as far as the Horse Gate—will be holy to the LORD. The city will never again be captured or destroyed."

32:1THE following message came to Jeremiah from the LORD in the tenth year of the reign of Zedekiah,* king of Judah. This was also the eighteenth year of the reign of King Nebuchadnezzar.* 2Jerusalem was then under siege from the Babylonian army, and Jeremiah was imprisoned in the courtyard of the guard in the royal palace. 3King Zedekiah had put him there, asking why he kept giving this prophecy: "This is what the LORD says: 'I am about to hand this city over to the king of Babylon, and he will take it. 4King Zedekiah will be captured by the Babylonians* and taken to meet the king of Babylon face to face. 5He will take Zedekiah to Babylon, and I will deal with him there,' says the LORD. 'If you fight against the Babylonians, you will never succeed.'"

6At that time the LORD sent me a message. He said, 7"Your cousin Hanamel son of Shallum will come and say to you, 'Buy my field at Anathoth. By law you have the right to buy it before it is offered to anyone else.'"

8Then, just as the LORD had said he would, my cousin Hanamel came and visited me in the prison. He said, "Please buy my field at Anathoth in the land of Benjamin. By law you have the right to buy it before it is offered to anyone else, so buy it for yourself." Then I knew that the message I had heard was from the LORD.

9So I bought the field at Anathoth, paying Hanamel seventeen pieces* of silver for it. 10I signed and sealed the deed of purchase before witnesses, weighed out the silver, and paid him. 11Then I took the sealed deed and an unsealed copy of the deed, which contained the terms and conditions of the purchase, 12and I handed them to Baruch son of Neriah and grandson of Mahseiah. I did all this in the presence of my cousin Hanamel, the witnesses who had signed the deed, and all the men of Judah who were there in the courtyard of the guardhouse.

13Then I said to Baruch as they all listened, 14"This is what the LORD of Heaven's Armies, the God of Israel, says: 'Take both this sealed deed and the unsealed copy, and put them into a pottery jar to preserve them for a long time.' 15For this is what the LORD of Heaven's Armies, the God of Israel, says: 'Someday people will again own property here in this land and will buy and sell houses and vineyards and fields.'"

16Then after I had given the papers to Baruch, I prayed to the LORD:

¹⁷"O Sovereign Lord! You made the heavens and earth by your strong hand and powerful arm. Nothing is too hard for you! ¹⁸You show unfailing love to thousands, but you also bring the consequences of one generation's sin upon the next. You are the great and powerful God, the Lord of Heaven's Armies. ¹⁹You have all wisdom and do great and mighty miracles. You see the conduct of all people, and you give them what they deserve. ²⁰You performed miraculous signs and wonders in the land of Egypt— things still remembered to this day! And you have continued to do great miracles in Israel and all around the world. You have made your name famous to this day.

²¹"You brought Israel out of Egypt with mighty signs and wonders, with a strong hand and powerful arm, and with overwhelming terror. ²²You gave the people of Israel this land that you had promised their ancestors long before—a land flowing with milk and honey. ²³Our ancestors came and conquered it and lived in it, but they refused to obey you or follow your word. They have not done anything you commanded. That is why you have sent this terrible disaster upon them.

²⁴"See how the siege ramps have been built against the city walls! Through war, famine, and disease, the city will be handed over to the Babylonians, who will conquer it. Everything has happened just as you said. ²⁵And yet, O Sovereign Lord, you have told me to buy the field— paying good money for it before these witnesses—even though the city will soon be handed over to the Babylonians."

²⁶Then this message came to Jeremiah from the Lord: ²⁷"I am the Lord, the God of all the peoples of the world. Is anything too hard for me? ²⁸Therefore, this is what the Lord says: I will hand this city over to the Babylonians and to Nebuchadnezzar, king of Babylon, and he will capture it. ²⁹The Babylonians outside the walls will come in and set fire to the city. They will burn down all these houses where the people provoked my anger by burning incense to Baal on the rooftops and by pouring out liquid offerings to other gods. ³⁰Israel and Judah have done nothing but wrong since their earliest days. They have infuriated me with all their evil deeds," says the Lord. ³¹"From the time this city was built until now, it has done nothing but anger me, so I am determined to get rid of it.

³²"The sins of Israel and Judah—the sins of the people of Jerusalem, the kings, the officials, the priests, and the prophets—have stirred up my anger. ³³My people have turned their backs on me and have refused to return. Even though I diligently taught them, they would not receive instruction or obey. ³⁴They have set up their abominable idols right in my own Temple, defiling it. ³⁵They have built pagan shrines to Baal in the valley of Ben-Hinnom, and there they sacrifice their sons and daughters to Molech. I have never commanded such a horrible deed; it never even crossed my mind to command such a thing. What an incredible evil, causing Judah to sin so greatly!

³⁶"Now I want to say something more about this city. You have been saying, 'It will fall to the king of Babylon through war, famine, and disease.' But this is what the Lord, the God of Israel, says: ³⁷I will certainly bring my people back again from all the countries where I will scatter them in my fury. I will bring them back to this very city and let them live in peace and safety. ³⁸They will be my people, and I will be their God. ³⁹And I will give them one heart and one purpose: to worship me forever, for their own good and for the good of all their descendants. ⁴⁰And I will make an everlasting covenant with them: I will never stop doing good for them. I will put a desire in their hearts to worship me, and they will never leave me. ⁴¹I will

find joy doing good for them and will faithfully and wholeheartedly replant them in this land.

42"This is what the LORD says: Just as I have brought all these calamities on them, so I will do all the good I have promised them. 43Fields will again be bought and sold in this land about which you now say, 'It has been ravaged by the Babylonians, a desolate land where people and animals have all disappeared.' 44Yes, fields will once again be bought and sold—deeds signed and sealed and witnessed—in the land of Benjamin and here in Jerusalem, in the towns of Judah and in the hill country, in the foothills of Judah* and in the Negev, too. For someday I will restore prosperity to them. I, the LORD, have spoken!"

32:1a The tenth year of Zedekiah's reign and the eighteenth year of Nebuchadnezzar's reign was 587 B.C. 32:1b Hebrew *Nebuchadrezzar*, a variant spelling of Nebuchadnezzar; also in 32:28. 32:4 Or *Chaldeans;* also in 32:5, 24, 25, 28, 29, 43. 32:9 Hebrew *17 shekels,* about 7 ounces or 194 grams in weight. 32:44 Hebrew *the Shephelah.*

1 TIMOTHY 3:1-16

This is a trustworthy saying: "If someone aspires to be an elder,* he desires an honorable position." 2So an elder must be a man whose life is above reproach. He must be faithful to his wife.* He must exercise self-control, live wisely, and have a good reputation. He must enjoy having guests in his home, and he must be able to teach. 3He must not be a heavy drinker* or be violent. He must be gentle, not quarrelsome, and not love money. 4He must manage his own family well, having children who respect and obey him. 5For if a man cannot manage his own household, how can he take care of God's church?

6An elder must not be a new believer, because he might become proud, and the devil would cause him to fall.* 7Also, people outside the church must speak well of him so that he will not be disgraced and fall into the devil's trap.

8In the same way, deacons must be well respected and have integrity. They must not be heavy drinkers or dishonest with money. 9They must be committed to the mystery of the faith now revealed and must live with a clear conscience. 10Before they are appointed as deacons, let them be closely examined. If they pass the test, then let them serve as deacons.

11In the same way, their wives* must be respected and must not slander others. They must exercise self-control and be faithful in everything they do.

12A deacon must be faithful to his wife, and he must manage his children and household well. 13Those who do well as deacons will be rewarded with respect from others and will have increased confidence in their faith in Christ Jesus.

14I am writing these things to you now, even though I hope to be with you soon, 15so that if I am delayed, you will know how people must conduct themselves in the household of God. This is the church of the living God, which is the pillar and foundation of the truth.

16Without question, this is the great mystery of our faith*:

Christ* was revealed in a
    human body
and vindicated by the Spirit.*
He was seen by angels
    and announced to the nations.
He was believed in throughout
    the world
and taken to heaven in glory.

3:1 Or *an overseer*, or *a bishop*; also in 3:2, 6. 3:2 Or *must have only one wife*, or *must be married only once;* Greek reads *must be the husband of one wife;* also in 3:12. 3:3 Greek *must not drink too much wine;* similarly in 3:8. 3:6 Or *he might fall into the same judgment as the devil.* 3:11 Or *the women deacons.* The Greek word can be translated *women* or *wives.* 3:16a Or *of godliness.* 3:16b Greek *He who;* other manuscripts read *God.* 3:16c Or *in his spirit.*

PSALM 88:1-18

For the choir director: A psalm of the descendants of Korah. A song to be sung to the tune "The Suffering of Affliction." A psalm of Heman the Ezrahite.*

1 ○ LORD, God of my salvation,
    I cry out to you by day.
    I come to you at night.
2 Now hear my prayer;
    listen to my cry.

3 For my life is full of troubles,
and death* draws near.
4 I am as good as dead,
like a strong man with no
strength left.
5 They have left me among the dead,
and I lie like a corpse in a grave.
I am forgotten,
cut off from your care.
6 You have thrown me into the
lowest pit,
into the darkest depths.
7 Your anger weighs me down;
with wave after wave you have
engulfed me.   *Interlude*

8 You have driven my friends away
by making me repulsive to them.
I am in a trap with no way of escape.
9 My eyes are blinded by my tears.
Each day I beg for your help, O LORD;
I lift my hands to you for mercy.
10 Are your wonderful deeds of
any use to the dead?
Do the dead rise up and
praise you?   *Interlude*

11 Can those in the grave declare your
unfailing love?
Can they proclaim your
faithfulness in the place
of destruction?*
12 Can the darkness speak of your
wonderful deeds?
Can anyone in the land of
forgetfulness talk about your
righteousness?
13 O LORD, I cry out to you.
I will keep on pleading day
by day.
14 O LORD, why do you reject me?
Why do you turn your face
from me?
15 I have been sick and close to death
since my youth.
I stand helpless and desperate
before your terrors.
16 Your fierce anger has
overwhelmed me.
Your terrors have paralyzed me.
17 They swirl around me like
floodwaters all day long.

They have engulfed me completely.
18 You have taken away my
companions and loved ones.
Darkness is my closest friend.

88:TITLE Hebrew *maskil*. This may be a literary or musical
term. 88:3 Hebrew *Sheol*. 88:11 Hebrew *in Abaddon?*

PROVERBS 25:20-22
Singing cheerful songs to a person with
a heavy heart is like taking someone's
coat in cold weather or pouring vinegar
in a wound. □If your enemies are hungry, give them food to eat. If they are
thirsty, give them water to drink. You will
heap burning coals of shame on their
heads, and the LORD will reward you.

OCTOBER 19

JEREMIAH 33:1–34:22
While Jeremiah was still confined in the
courtyard of the guard, the LORD gave
him this second message: 2"This is what
the LORD says—the LORD who made the
earth, who formed and established it,
whose name is the LORD: 3Ask me and I
will tell you remarkable secrets you do
not know about things to come. 4For this
is what the LORD, the God of Israel, says:
You have torn down the houses of this
city and even the king's palace to get materials to strengthen the walls against the
siege ramps and swords of the enemy.
5You expect to fight the Babylonians,*
but the men of this city are already as
good as dead, for I have determined to
destroy them in my terrible anger. I have
abandoned them because of all their
wickedness.

6"Nevertheless, the time will come
when I will heal Jerusalem's wounds
and give it prosperity and true peace. 7I
will restore the fortunes of Judah and
Israel and rebuild their towns. 8I will
cleanse them of their sins against me
and forgive all their sins of rebellion.

⁹Then this city will bring me joy, glory, and honor before all the nations of the earth! The people of the world will see all the good I do for my people, and they will tremble with awe at the peace and prosperity I provide for them.

¹⁰"This is what the LORD says: You have said, 'This is a desolate land where people and animals have all disappeared.' Yet in the empty streets of Jerusalem and Judah's other towns, there will be heard once more ¹¹the sounds of joy and laughter. The joyful voices of bridegrooms and brides will be heard again, along with the joyous songs of people bringing thanksgiving offerings to the LORD. They will sing,

'Give thanks to the LORD of
　Heaven's Armies,
　for the LORD is good.
His faithful love endures forever!'

For I will restore the prosperity of this land to what it was in the past, says the LORD.

¹²"This is what the LORD of Heaven's Armies says: This land—though it is now desolate and has no people and animals—will once more have pastures where shepherds can lead their flocks. ¹³Once again shepherds will count their flocks in the towns of the hill country, the foothills of Judah,* the Negev, the land of Benjamin, the vicinity of Jerusalem, and all the towns of Judah. I, the LORD, have spoken!

¹⁴"The day will come, says the LORD, when I will do for Israel and Judah all the good things I have promised them.

¹⁵ "In those days and at that time
　I will raise up a righteous
　　descendant* from King
　　David's line.
He will do what is just and right
　throughout the land.
¹⁶ In that day Judah will be saved,
　and Jerusalem will live
　　in safety.
And this will be its name:
　'The LORD Is Our Righteousness.'*

¹⁷For this is what the LORD says: David will have a descendant sitting on the throne of Israel forever. ¹⁸And there will always be Levitical priests to offer burnt offerings and grain offerings and sacrifices to me."

¹⁹Then this message came to Jeremiah from the LORD: ²⁰"This is what the LORD says: If you can break my covenant with the day and the night so that one does not follow the other, ²¹only then will my covenant with my servant David be broken. Only then will he no longer have a descendant to reign on his throne. The same is true for my covenant with the Levitical priests who minister before me. ²²And as the stars of the sky cannot be counted and the sand on the seashore cannot be measured, so I will multiply the descendants of my servant David and the Levites who minister before me."

²³The LORD gave another message to Jeremiah. He said, ²⁴"Have you noticed what people are saying?—'The LORD chose Judah and Israel and then abandoned them!' They are sneering and saying that Israel is not worthy to be counted as a nation. ²⁵But this is what the LORD says: I would no more reject my people than I would change my laws that govern night and day, earth and sky. ²⁶I will never abandon the descendants of Jacob or David, my servant, or change the plan that David's descendants will rule the descendants of Abraham, Isaac, and Jacob. Instead, I will restore them to their land and have mercy on them."

³⁴:¹KING Nebuchadnezzar of Babylon came with all the armies from the kingdoms he ruled, and he fought against Jerusalem and the towns of Judah. At that time this message came to Jeremiah from the LORD: ²"Go to King Zedekiah of Judah, and tell him, 'This is what the LORD, the God of Israel, says: I am about to hand this city over to the king of Babylon, and he will burn it down. ³You will not escape his grasp but will be captured and taken to meet the king of Babylon face to face. Then you will be exiled to Babylon.

4"'But listen to this promise from the Lord, O Zedekiah, king of Judah. This is what the Lord says: You will not be killed in war 5but will die peacefully. People will burn incense in your memory, just as they did for your ancestors, the kings who preceded you. They will mourn for you, crying, "Alas, our master is dead!" This I have decreed, says the Lord.'"

6So Jeremiah the prophet delivered the message to King Zedekiah of Judah. 7At this time the Babylonian army was besieging Jerusalem, Lachish, and Azekah—the only fortified cities of Judah not yet captured.

8This message came to Jeremiah from the Lord after King Zedekiah made a covenant with the people, proclaiming freedom for the slaves. 9He had ordered all the people to free their Hebrew slaves—both men and women. No one was to keep a fellow Judean in bondage. 10The officials and all the people had obeyed the king's command, 11but later they changed their minds. They took back the men and women they had freed, forcing them to be slaves again.

12So the Lord gave them this message through Jeremiah: 13"This is what the Lord, the God of Israel, says: I made a covenant with your ancestors long ago when I rescued them from their slavery in Egypt. 14I told them that every Hebrew slave must be freed after serving six years. But your ancestors paid no attention to me. 15Recently you repented and did what was right, following my command. You freed your slaves and made a solemn covenant with me in the Temple that bears my name. 16But now you have shrugged off your oath and defiled my name by taking back the men and women you had freed, forcing them to be slaves once again.

17"Therefore, this is what the Lord says: Since you have not obeyed me by setting your countrymen free, I will set you free to be destroyed by war, disease, and famine. You will be an object of horror to all the nations of the earth. 18Because you have broken the terms of our covenant, I will cut you apart just

as you cut apart the calf when you walked between its halves to solemnize your vows. 19Yes, I will cut you apart, whether you are officials of Judah or Jerusalem, court officials, priests, or common people—for you have broken your oath. 20I will give you to your enemies, and they will kill you. Your bodies will be food for the vultures and wild animals.

21"I will hand over King Zedekiah of Judah and his officials to the army of the king of Babylon. And although Babylon's king has left Jerusalem for a while, 22I will call the Babylonian armies back again. They will fight against this city and will capture it and burn it down. I will see to it that all the towns of Judah are destroyed, with no one living there."

33:5 Or *Chaldeans.*   33:13 Hebrew *the Shephelah.*
33:15 Hebrew *a righteous branch.*   33:16 Hebrew
Yahweh Tsidqenu.

1 TIMOTHY 4:1-16

Now the Holy Spirit tells us clearly that in the last times some will turn away from the true faith; they will follow deceptive spirits and teachings that come from demons. 2These people are hypocrites and liars, and their consciences are dead.*

3They will say it is wrong to be married and wrong to eat certain foods. But God created those foods to be eaten with thanks by faithful people who know the truth. 4Since everything God created is good, we should not reject any of it but receive it with thanks. 5For we know it is made acceptable* by the word of God and prayer.

6If you explain these things to the brothers and sisters,* Timothy, you will be a worthy servant of Christ Jesus, one who is nourished by the message of faith and the good teaching you have followed. 7Do not waste time arguing over godless ideas and old wives' tales. Instead, train yourself to be godly. 8"Physical training is good, but training for godliness is much better, promising benefits in this life and in the life to come." 9This is a trustworthy saying, and everyone should accept it. [10]This is why we work hard and continue to struggle,* for our hope is in the living God, who is the Savior of all people and particularly of all believers.

[11]Teach these things and insist that everyone learn them. [12]**Don't let anyone think less of you because you are young. Be an example to all believers in what you say, in the way you live, in your love, your faith, and your purity.** [13]Until I get there, focus on reading the Scriptures to the church, encouraging the believers, and teaching them.

[14]Do not neglect the spiritual gift you received through the prophecy spoken over you when the elders of the church laid their hands on you. [15]Give your complete attention to these matters. Throw yourself into your tasks so that everyone will see your progress. [16]Keep a close watch on how you live and on your teaching. Stay true to what is right for the sake of your own salvation and the salvation of those who hear you.

4:2 Greek *are seared.*   4:5 Or *made holy.*   4:6 Greek *brothers.*   4:10 Some manuscripts read *continue to suffer.*

PSALM 89:1-13
A psalm* of Ethan the Ezrahite.

[1] I will sing of the LORD's unfailing
      love forever!
   Young and old will hear of
      your faithfulness.
[2] Your unfailing love will last forever.
   Your faithfulness is as enduring
      as the heavens.

[3] The LORD said, "I have made a
      covenant with David, my
      chosen servant.
   I have sworn this oath to him:
[4] 'I will establish your descendants as
      kings forever;
   they will sit on your throne from
      now until eternity.'"   *Interlude*
[5] All heaven will praise your great
      wonders, LORD;
   myriads of angels will praise you
      for your faithfulness.
[6] For who in all of heaven can
      compare with the LORD?

What mightiest angel is anything
      like the LORD?
[7] The highest angelic powers stand in
      awe of God.
   He is far more awesome than all
      who surround his throne.
[8] O LORD God of Heaven's Armies!
   Where is there anyone as mighty
      as you, O LORD?
   You are entirely faithful.
[9] You rule the oceans.
   You subdue their storm-tossed
      waves.
[10] You crushed the great sea monster.*
   You scattered your enemies with
      your mighty arm.
[11] The heavens are yours, and the earth
      is yours;
   everything in the world is yours—
      you created it all.
[12] You created north and south.
   Mount Tabor and Mount Hermon
      praise your name.
[13] Powerful is your arm!
   Strong is your hand!
   Your right hand is lifted high in
      glorious strength.

89:TITLE Hebrew *maskil.* This may be a literary or musical term.   89:10 Hebrew *Rahab,* the name of a mythical sea monster that represents chaos in ancient literature.

PROVERBS 25:23-24
As surely as a north wind brings rain, so a gossiping tongue causes anger! □ It's better to live alone in the corner of an attic than with a quarrelsome wife in a lovely home.

OCTOBER
20

JEREMIAH 35:1-36:32
This is the message the LORD gave Jeremiah when Jehoiakim son of Josiah was king of Judah: [2]"Go to the settlement where the families of the Recabites live,

and invite them to the LORD's Temple. Take them into one of the inner rooms, and offer them some wine."

³So I went to see Jaazaniah son of Jeremiah and grandson of Habazziniah and all his brothers and sons—representing all the Recabite families. ⁴I took them to the Temple, and we went into the room assigned to the sons of Hanan son of Igdaliah, a man of God. This room was located next to the one used by the Temple officials, directly above the room of Maaseiah son of Shallum, the Temple gatekeeper.

⁵I set cups and jugs of wine before them and invited them to have a drink, ⁶but they refused. "No," they said, "we don't drink wine, because our ancestor Jehonadab* son of Recab gave us this command: 'You and your descendants must never drink wine. ⁷And do not build houses or plant crops or vineyards, but always live in tents. If you follow these commands, you will live long, good lives in the land.' ⁸So we have obeyed him in all these things. We have never had a drink of wine to this day, nor have our wives, our sons, or our daughters. ⁹We haven't built houses or owned vineyards or farms or planted crops. ¹⁰We have lived in tents and have fully obeyed all the commands of Jehonadab, our ancestor. ¹¹But when King Nebuchadnezzar* of Babylon attacked this country, we were afraid of the Babylonian and Syrian* armies. So we decided to move to Jerusalem. That is why we are here."

¹²Then the LORD gave this message to Jeremiah: ¹³"This is what the LORD of Heaven's Armies, the God of Israel, says: Go and say to the people in Judah and Jerusalem, 'Come and learn a lesson about how to obey me. ¹⁴The Recabites do not drink wine to this day because their ancestor Jehonadab told them not to. But I have spoken to you again and again, and you refuse to obey me. ¹⁵Time after time I sent you prophets, who told you, "Turn from your wicked ways, and start doing things right. Stop worshiping other gods so that you might live in peace here in the land I have given to you and your an-

cestors." But you would not listen to me or obey me. ¹⁶The descendants of Jehonadab son of Recab have obeyed their ancestor completely, but you have refused to listen to me.'

¹⁷"Therefore, this is what the LORD God of Heaven's Armies, the God of Israel, says: 'Because you refuse to listen or answer when I call, I will send upon Judah and Jerusalem all the disasters I have threatened.'"

¹⁸Then Jeremiah turned to the Recabites and said, "This is what the LORD of Heaven's Armies, the God of Israel, says: 'You have obeyed your ancestor Jehonadab in every respect, following all his instructions.' ¹⁹Therefore, this is what the LORD of Heaven's Armies, the God of Israel, says: 'Jehonadab son of Recab will always have descendants who serve me.'"

36:1DURING the fourth year that Jehoiakim son of Josiah was king in Judah,* the LORD gave this message to Jeremiah: ²"Get a scroll, and write down all my messages against Israel, Judah, and the other nations. Begin with the first message back in the days of Josiah, and write down every message, right up to the present time. ³Perhaps the people of Judah will repent when they hear again all the terrible things I have planned for them. Then I will be able to forgive their sins and wrongdoings."

⁴So Jeremiah sent for Baruch son of Neriah, and as Jeremiah dictated all the prophecies that the LORD had given him, Baruch wrote them on a scroll. ⁵Then Jeremiah said to Baruch, "I am a prisoner here and unable to go to the Temple. ⁶So you go to the Temple on the next day of fasting, and read the messages from the LORD that I have had you write on this scroll. Read them so the people who are there from all over Judah will hear them. ⁷Perhaps even yet they will turn from their evil ways and ask the LORD's forgiveness before it is too late. For the LORD has threatened them with his terrible anger."

⁸Baruch did as Jeremiah told him and read these messages from the LORD to

the people at the Temple. 9He did this on a day of sacred fasting held in late autumn,* during the fifth year of the reign of Jehoiakim son of Josiah. People from all over Judah had come to Jerusalem to attend the services at the Temple on that day. 10Baruch read Jeremiah's words on the scroll to all the people. He stood in front of the Temple room of Gemariah, son of Shaphan the secretary. This room was just off the upper courtyard of the Temple, near the New Gate entrance.

11When Micaiah son of Gemariah and grandson of Shaphan heard the messages from the LORD, 12he went down to the secretary's room in the palace where the administrative officials were meeting. Elishama the secretary was there, along with Delaiah son of Shemaiah, Elnathan son of Acbor, Gemariah son of Shaphan, Zedekiah son of Hananiah, and all the other officials. 13When Micaiah told them about the messages Baruch was reading to the people, 14the officials sent Jehudi son of Nethaniah, grandson of Shelemiah and great-grandson of Cushi, to ask Baruch to come and read the messages to them, too. So Baruch took the scroll and went to them. 15"Sit down and read the scroll to us," the officials said, and Baruch did as they requested.

16When they heard all the messages, they looked at one another in alarm. "We must tell the king what we have heard," they said to Baruch. 17"But first, tell us how you got these messages. Did they come directly from Jeremiah?"

18So Baruch explained, "Jeremiah dictated them, and I wrote them down in ink, word for word, on this scroll."

19"You and Jeremiah should both hide," the officials told Baruch. "Don't tell anyone where you are!" 20Then the officials left the scroll for safekeeping in the room of Elishama the secretary and went to tell the king what had happened.

21The king sent Jehudi to get the scroll. Jehudi brought it from Elishama's room and read it to the king as all his officials stood by. 22It was late autumn, and the king was in a winterized part of the palace, sitting in front of a fire to keep warm. 23Each time Jehudi finished reading three or four columns, the king took a knife and cut off that section of the scroll. He then threw it into the fire, section by section, until the whole scroll was burned up. 24Neither the king nor his attendants showed any signs of fear or repentance at what they heard. 25Even when Elnathan, Delaiah, and Gemariah begged the king not to burn the scroll, he wouldn't listen.

26Then the king commanded his son Jerahmeel, Seraiah son of Azriel, and Shelemiah son of Abdeel to arrest Baruch and Jeremiah. But the LORD had hidden them.

27After the king had burned the scroll on which Baruch had written Jeremiah's words, the LORD gave Jeremiah another message. He said, 28"Get another scroll, and write everything again just as you did on the scroll King Jehoiakim burned. 29Then say to the king, 'This is what the LORD says: You burned the scroll because it said the king of Babylon would destroy this land and empty it of people and animals. 30Now this is what the LORD says about King Jehoiakim of Judah: He will have no heirs to sit on the throne of David. His dead body will be thrown out to lie unburied—exposed to the heat of the day and the frost of the night. 31I will punish him and his family and his attendants for their sins. I will pour out on them and on all the people of Jerusalem and Judah all the disasters I promised, for they would not listen to my warnings.'"

32So Jeremiah took another scroll and dictated again to his secretary, Baruch. He wrote everything that had been on the scroll King Jehoiakim had burned in the fire. Only this time he added much more!

35:6 Hebrew *Jonadab,* a variant spelling of Jehonadab; also in 35:10, 14, 16, 18, 19. See 2 Kgs 10:15.   35:11a Hebrew *Nebuchadrezzar,* a variant spelling of Nebuchadnezzar.   35:11b Or *Chaldean and Aramean.*   36:1 The fourth year of Jehoiakim's reign was 605 B.C.   36:9 Hebrew *in the ninth month,* of the ancient Hebrew lunar calendar (also in 36:22). The ninth month in the fifth year of Jehoiakim's reign occurred within the months of November and December 604 B.C. Also see note on 1:3.

1 TIMOTHY 5:1-25

Never speak harshly to an older man,* but appeal to him respectfully as you would to your own father. Talk to younger men as you would to your own brothers. ²Treat older women as you would your mother, and treat younger women with all purity as you would your own sisters.

³Take care of* any widow who has no one else to care for her. ⁴But if she has children or grandchildren, their first responsibility is to show godliness at home and repay their parents by taking care of them. This is something that pleases God.

⁵Now a true widow, a woman who is truly alone in this world, has placed her hope in God. She prays night and day, asking God for his help. ⁶But the widow who lives only for pleasure is spiritually dead even while she lives. ⁷Give these instructions to the church so that no one will be open to criticism.

⁸But those who won't care for their relatives, especially those in their own household, have denied the true faith. Such people are worse than unbelievers.

⁹A widow who is put on the list for support must be a woman who is at least sixty years old and was faithful to her husband.* ¹⁰She must be well respected by everyone because of the good she has done. Has she brought up her children well? Has she been kind to strangers and served other believers humbly?* Has she helped those who are in trouble? Has she always been ready to do good?

¹¹The younger widows should not be on the list, because their physical desires will overpower their devotion to Christ and they will want to remarry. ¹²Then they would be guilty of breaking their previous pledge. ¹³And if they are on the list, they will learn to be lazy and will spend their time gossiping from house to house, meddling in other people's business and talking about things they shouldn't. ¹⁴So I advise these younger widows to marry again, have children, and take care of their own homes. Then the enemy will not be able to say anything against them. ¹⁵For I am afraid that some of them have already gone astray and now follow Satan.

¹⁶If a woman who is a believer has relatives who are widows, she must take care of them and not put the responsibility on the church. Then the church can care for the widows who are truly alone.

¹⁷Elders who do their work well should be respected and paid well,* especially those who work hard at both preaching and teaching. ¹⁸For the Scripture says, "You must not muzzle an ox to keep it from eating as it treads out the grain." And in another place, "Those who work deserve their pay!"*

¹⁹Do not listen to an accusation against an elder unless it is confirmed by two or three witnesses. ²⁰Those who sin should be reprimanded in front of the whole church; this will serve as a strong warning to others.

²¹I solemnly command you in the presence of God and Christ Jesus and the holy angels to obey these instructions without taking sides or showing favoritism to anyone.

²²Never be in a hurry about appointing a church leader.* Do not share in the sins of others. Keep yourself pure.

²³Don't drink only water. You ought to drink a little wine for the sake of your stomach because you are sick so often.

²⁴**Remember, the sins of some people are obvious, leading them to certain judgment. But there are others whose sins will not be revealed until later. ²⁵In the same way, the good deeds of some people are obvious. And the good deeds done in secret will someday come to light.**

5:1 Or *an elder.*   5:3 Or *Honor.*   5:9 Greek *was the wife of one husband.*   5:10 Greek *and washed the feet of saints?*
5:17 Greek *should be worthy of double honor.*   5:18 Deut 25:4; Luke 10:7.   5:22 Greek *about the laying on of hands.*

PSALM 89:14-37

Righteousness and justice are the
foundation of your throne.
Unfailing love and truth walk
before you as attendants.

¹⁵ Happy are those who hear the joyful
call to worship,
for they will walk in the light of
your presence, LORD.
¹⁶ They rejoice all day long in your
wonderful reputation.
They exult in your righteousness.
¹⁷ You are their glorious strength.
It pleases you to make us strong.
¹⁸ Yes, our protection comes from
the LORD,
and he, the Holy One of Israel, has
given us our king.

¹⁹ Long ago you spoke in a vision to
your faithful people.
You said, "I have raised up a warrior.
I have selected him from the
common people to be king.
²⁰ I have found my servant David.
I have anointed him with my
holy oil.
²¹ I will steady him with my hand;
with my powerful arm I will make
him strong.
²² His enemies will not defeat him,
nor will the wicked overpower
him.
²³ I will beat down his adversaries
before him
and destroy those who hate him.
²⁴ My faithfulness and unfailing love
will be with him,
and by my authority he will grow
in power.
²⁵ I will extend his rule over the sea,
his dominion over the rivers.
²⁶ And he will call out to me, 'You are
my Father,
my God, and the Rock of my
salvation.'
²⁷ I will make him my firstborn son,
the mightiest king on earth.
²⁸ I will love him and be kind to
him forever;
my covenant with him will
never end.
²⁹ I will preserve an heir for him;
his throne will be as endless as
the days of heaven.
³⁰ But if his descendants forsake
my instructions

and fail to obey my regulations,
³¹ if they do not obey my decrees
and fail to keep my commands,
³² then I will punish their sin with
the rod,
and their disobedience with
beating.
³³ But I will never stop loving him
nor fail to keep my promise to him.
³⁴ No, I will not break my covenant;
I will not take back a single
word I said.
³⁵ I have sworn an oath to David,
and in my holiness I cannot lie:
³⁶ His dynasty will go on forever;
his kingdom will endure as the sun.
³⁷ It will be as eternal as the moon,
my faithful witness in the sky!"

Interlude

PROVERBS 25:25-27

Good news from far away is like cold water to the thirsty. ☐ If the godly give in to the wicked, it's like polluting a fountain or muddying a spring. ☐ It's not good to eat too much honey, and it's not good to seek honors for yourself.

OCTOBER 21

JEREMIAH 37:1–38:28

Zedekiah son of Josiah succeeded Jehoiachin* son of Jehoiakim as the king of Judah. He was appointed by King Nebuchadnezzar* of Babylon. ²But neither King Zedekiah nor his attendants nor the people who were left in the land listened to what the LORD said through Jeremiah.

³Nevertheless, King Zedekiah sent Jehucal son of Shelemiah, and Zephaniah the priest, son of Maaseiah, to ask Jeremiah, "Please pray to the LORD our God for us." ⁴Jeremiah had not yet been imprisoned, so he could come and go among the people as he pleased.

⁵At this time the army of Pharaoh Hophra* of Egypt appeared at the southern border of Judah. When the Babylonian* army heard about it, they withdrew from their siege of Jerusalem.

⁶Then the LORD gave this message to Jeremiah: ⁷"This is what the LORD, the God of Israel, says: The king of Judah sent you to ask me what is going to happen. Tell him, 'Pharaoh's army is about to return to Egypt, though he came here to help you. ⁸Then the Babylonians* will come back and capture this city and burn it to the ground.'

⁹"This is what the LORD says: Do not fool yourselves into thinking that the Babylonians are gone for good. They aren't! ¹⁰Even if you were to destroy the entire Babylonian army, leaving only a handful of wounded survivors, they would still stagger from their tents and burn this city to the ground!"

¹¹When the Babylonian army left Jerusalem because of Pharaoh's approaching army, ¹²Jeremiah started to leave the city on his way to the territory of Benjamin, to claim his share of the property among his relatives there.* ¹³But as he was walking through the Benjamin Gate, a sentry arrested him and said, "You are defecting to the Babylonians!" The sentry making the arrest was Irijah son of Shelemiah, grandson of Hananiah.

¹⁴"That's not true!" Jeremiah protested. "I had no intention of doing any such thing." But Irijah wouldn't listen, and he took Jeremiah before the officials. ¹⁵They were furious with Jeremiah and had him flogged and imprisoned in the house of Jonathan the secretary. Jonathan's house had been converted into a prison. ¹⁶Jeremiah was put into a dungeon cell, where he remained for many days.

¹⁷Later King Zedekiah secretly requested that Jeremiah come to the palace, where the king asked him, "Do you have any messages from the LORD?"

"Yes, I do!" said Jeremiah. "You will be defeated by the king of Babylon."

¹⁸Then Jeremiah asked the king, "What crime have I committed? What have I done against you, your attendants, or the people that I should be imprisoned like this? ¹⁹Where are your prophets now who told you the king of Babylon would not attack you or this land? ²⁰Listen, my lord the king, I beg you. Don't send me back to the dungeon in the house of Jonathan the secretary, for I will die there."

²¹So King Zedekiah commanded that Jeremiah not be returned to the dungeon. Instead, he was imprisoned in the courtyard of the guard in the royal palace. The king also commanded that Jeremiah be given a loaf of fresh bread every day as long as there was any left in the city. So Jeremiah was put in the palace prison.

38:1Now Shephatiah son of Mattan, Gedaliah son of Pashhur, Jehucal* son of Shelemiah, and Pashhur son of Malkijah heard what Jeremiah had been telling the people. He had been saying, ²"This is what the LORD says: 'Everyone who stays in Jerusalem will die from war, famine, or disease, but those who surrender to the Babylonians* will live. Their reward will be life. They will live!' ³The LORD also says: 'The city of Jerusalem will certainly be handed over to the army of the king of Babylon, who will capture it.'"

⁴So these officials went to the king and said, "Sir, this man must die! That kind of talk will undermine the morale of the few fighting men we have left, as well as that of all the people. This man is a traitor!"

⁵King Zedekiah agreed. "All right," he said. "Do as you like. I can't stop you."

⁶So the officials took Jeremiah from his cell and lowered him by ropes into an empty cistern in the prison yard. It belonged to Malkijah, a member of the royal family. There was no water in the cistern, but there was a thick layer of mud at the bottom, and Jeremiah sank down into it.

⁷But Ebed-melech the Ethiopian,* an important court official, heard that Jeremiah was in the cistern. At that time

the king was holding court at the Benjamin Gate, [8] so Ebed-melech rushed from the palace to speak with him. [9] "My lord the king," he said, "these men have done a very evil thing in putting Jeremiah the prophet into the cistern. He will soon die of hunger, for almost all the bread in the city is gone."

[10] So the king told Ebed-melech, "Take thirty of my men with you, and pull Jeremiah out of the cistern before he dies."

[11] So Ebed-melech took the men with him and went to a room in the palace beneath the treasury, where he found some old rags and discarded clothing. He carried these to the cistern and lowered them to Jeremiah on a rope. [12] Ebed-melech called down to Jeremiah, "Put these rags under your armpits to protect you from the ropes." Then when Jeremiah was ready, [13] they pulled him out. So Jeremiah was returned to the courtyard of the guard—the palace prison—where he remained.

[14] One day King Zedekiah sent for Jeremiah and had him brought to the third entrance of the LORD's Temple. "I want to ask you something," the king said. "And don't try to hide the truth."

[15] Jeremiah said, "If I tell you the truth, you will kill me. And if I give you advice, you won't listen to me anyway."

[16] So King Zedekiah secretly promised him, "As surely as the LORD our Creator lives, I will not kill you or hand you over to the men who want you dead."

[17] Then Jeremiah said to Zedekiah, "This is what the LORD God of Heaven's Armies, the God of Israel, says: 'If you surrender to the Babylonian officers, you and your family will live, and the city will not be burned down. [18] But if you refuse to surrender, you will not escape! This city will be handed over to the Babylonians, and they will burn it to the ground.'"

[19] "But I am afraid to surrender," the king said, "for the Babylonians may hand me over to the Judeans who have defected to them. And who knows what they will do to me!"

[20] Jeremiah replied, "You won't be handed over to them if you choose to obey the LORD. Your life will be spared, and all will go well for you. [21] But if you refuse to surrender, this is what the LORD has revealed to me: [22] All the women left in your palace will be brought out and given to the officers of the Babylonian army. Then the women will taunt you, saying,

'What fine friends you have!
    They have betrayed and misled you.
When your feet sank in the mud,
    they left you to your fate!'

[23] All your wives and children will be led out to the Babylonians, and you will not escape. You will be seized by the king of Babylon, and this city will be burned down."

[24] Then Zedekiah said to Jeremiah, "Don't tell anyone you told me this, or you will die! [25] My officials may hear that I spoke to you, and they may say, 'Tell us what you and the king were talking about. If you don't tell us, we will kill you.' [26] If this happens, just tell them you begged me not to send you back to Jonathan's dungeon, for fear you would die there."

[27] Sure enough, it wasn't long before the king's officials came to Jeremiah and asked him why the king had called for him. But Jeremiah followed the king's instructions, and they left without finding out the truth. No one had overheard the conversation between Jeremiah and the king. [28] And Jeremiah remained a prisoner in the courtyard of the guard until the day Jerusalem was captured.

37:1a Hebrew *Coniah,* a variant spelling of Jehoiachin. 37:1b Hebrew *Nebuchadrezzar,* a variant spelling of Nebuchadnezzar. 37:5a Hebrew *army of Pharaoh;* see 44:30. 37:5b Or *Chaldean;* also in 37:10, 11. 37:8 Or *Chaldeans;* also in 37:9, 13. 37:12 Hebrew *to separate from there in the midst of the people.* 38:1 Hebrew *Jucal,* a variant spelling of Jehucal; see 37:3. 38:2 Or *Chaldeans;* also in 38:18, 19, 23. 38:7 Hebrew *the Cushite.*

1 TIMOTHY 6:1-21

All slaves should show full respect for their masters so they will not bring shame on the name of God and his teaching. [2] If the masters are believers, that is no excuse for being disrespectful. Those slaves should work all the harder because their efforts are helping other believers* who are well loved.

Teach these things, Timothy, and encourage everyone to obey them. ³Some people may contradict our teaching, but these are the wholesome teachings of the Lord Jesus Christ. These teachings promote a godly life. ⁴Anyone who teaches something different is arrogant and lacks understanding. Such a person has an unhealthy desire to quibble over the meaning of words. This stirs up arguments ending in jealousy, division, slander, and evil suspicions. ⁵These people always cause trouble. Their minds are corrupt, and they have turned their backs on the truth. To them, a show of godliness is just a way to become wealthy.

⁶Yet true godliness with contentment is itself great wealth. ⁷After all, we brought nothing with us when we came into the world, and we can't take anything with us when we leave it. ⁸So if we have enough food and clothing, let us be content.

⁹But people who long to be rich fall into temptation and are trapped by many foolish and harmful desires that plunge them into ruin and destruction. ¹⁰For the love of money is the root of all kinds of evil. And some people, craving money, have wandered from the true faith and pierced themselves with many sorrows.

¹¹But you, Timothy, are a man of God; so run from all these evil things. Pursue righteousness and a godly life, along with faith, love, perseverance, and gentleness. ¹²Fight the good fight for the true faith. Hold tightly to the eternal life to which God has called you, which you have confessed so well before many witnesses. ¹³And I charge you before God, who gives life to all, and before Christ Jesus, who gave a good testimony before Pontius Pilate, ¹⁴that you obey this command without wavering. Then no one can find fault with you from now until our Lord Jesus Christ comes again. ¹⁵For at just the right time Christ will be

revealed from heaven by the blessed and only almighty God, the King of all kings and Lord of all lords. ¹⁶He alone can never die, and he lives in light so brilliant that no human can approach him. No human eye has ever seen him, nor ever will. All honor and power to him forever! Amen.

¹⁷Teach those who are rich in this world not to be proud and not to trust in their money, which is so unreliable. Their trust should be in God, who richly gives us all we need for our enjoyment. ¹⁸Tell them to use their money to do good. They should be rich in good works and generous to those in need, always being ready to share with others. ¹⁹By doing this they will be storing up their treasure as a good foundation for the future so that they may experience true life.

²⁰Timothy, guard what God has entrusted to you. Avoid godless, foolish discussions with those who oppose you with their so-called knowledge. ²¹Some people have wandered from the faith by following such foolishness.

May God's grace be with you all.

6:2 Greek *brothers.*

PSALM 89:38-52

But now you [the Lord] have
rejected him [David] and cast
him off.
You are angry with your
anointed king.
³⁹ You have renounced your covenant
with him;
you have thrown his crown
in the dust.
⁴⁰ You have broken down the walls
protecting him
and ruined every fort
defending him.
⁴¹ Everyone who comes along has
robbed him,
and he has become a joke
to his neighbors.
⁴² You have strengthened his enemies
and made them all rejoice.
⁴³ You have made his sword useless
and refused to help him in battle.
⁴⁴ You have ended his splendor

and overturned his throne.
⁴⁵ You have made him old before
    his time
    and publicly disgraced him.

Interlude

⁴⁶ O LORD, how long will this go on?
    Will you hide yourself forever?
    How long will your anger burn
    like fire?
⁴⁷ Remember how short my life is,
    how empty and futile this human
    existence!
⁴⁸ No one can live forever; all will die.
    No one can escape the power
    of the grave.*   *Interlude*

⁴⁹ Lord, where is your unfailing love?
    You promised it to David with a
    faithful pledge.
⁵⁰ Consider, Lord, how your servants
    are disgraced!
    I carry in my heart the insults of
    so many people.
⁵¹ Your enemies have mocked me,
    O LORD;
    they mock your anointed king
    wherever he goes.

⁵² Praise the LORD forever!
    Amen and amen!

89:48 Hebrew *of Sheol.*

PROVERBS 25:28
A person without self-control is like a
city with broken-down walls.

OCTOBER 22

JEREMIAH 39:1–41:18
In January* of the ninth year of King
Zedekiah's reign, King Nebuchadnezzar* came with his army to besiege Jerusalem. ²Two and a half years later, on
July 18* in the eleventh year of Zedekiah's reign, the Babylonians broke
through the wall, and the city fell. ³All the
officers of the Babylonian army came
in and sat in triumph at the Middle Gate:
Nergal-sharezer of Samgar, and Nebo-
sarsekim,* a chief officer, and Nergal-
sharezer, the king's adviser, and all the
other officers.

⁴When King Zedekiah and all the soldiers saw that the Babylonians had
broken into the city, they fled. They
waited for nightfall and then slipped
through the gate between the two walls
behind the king's garden and headed
toward the Jordan Valley.*

⁵But the Babylonian* troops chased
the king and caught him on the plains of
Jericho. They took him to King Nebuchadnezzar of Babylon, who was at Riblah in the land of Hamath. There the king
of Babylon pronounced judgment upon
Zedekiah. ⁶He made Zedekiah watch as
they slaughtered his sons and all the nobles of Judah. ⁷Then they gouged out
Zedekiah's eyes, bound him in bronze
chains, and led him away to Babylon.

⁸Meanwhile, the Babylonians burned
Jerusalem, including the palace, and tore
down the walls of the city. ⁹Then Nebuzaradan, the captain of the guard, sent to
Babylon the rest of the people who remained in the city as well as those who
had defected to him. ¹⁰But Nebuzaradan
left a few of the poorest people in Judah,
and he assigned them vineyards and
fields to care for.

¹¹King Nebuchadnezzar had told Nebuzaradan, the captain of the guard, to
find Jeremiah. ¹²"See that he isn't hurt,"
he said. "Look after him well, and give
him anything he wants." ¹³So Nebuzaradan, the captain of the guard; Nebushaz-
ban, a chief officer; Nergal-sharezer, the
king's adviser; and the other officers of
Babylon's king ¹⁴sent messengers to
bring Jeremiah out of the prison. They
put him under the care of Gedaliah son
of Ahikam and grandson of Shaphan, who
took him back to his home. So Jeremiah
stayed in Judah among his own people.

¹⁵The LORD had given the following
message to Jeremiah while he was still in
prison: ¹⁶"Say to Ebed-melech the Ethiopian,* 'This is what the LORD of Heaven's

Armies, the God of Israel, says: I will do to this city everything I have threatened. I will send disaster, not prosperity. You will see its destruction, ¹⁷but I will rescue you from those you fear so much. ¹⁸Because you trusted me, I will give you your life as a reward. I will rescue you and keep you safe. I, the LORD, have spoken!'"

^{40:1}THE LORD gave a message to Jeremiah after Nebuzaradan, the captain of the guard, had released him at Ramah. He had found Jeremiah bound in chains among all the other captives of Jerusalem and Judah who were being sent to exile in Babylon.

²The captain of the guard called for Jeremiah and said, "The LORD your God has brought this disaster on this land, ³just as he said he would. For these people have sinned against the LORD and disobeyed him. That is why it happened. ⁴But I am going to take off your chains and let you go. If you want to come with me to Babylon, you are welcome. I will see that you are well cared for. But if you don't want to come, you may stay here. The whole land is before you—go wherever you like. ⁵If you decide to stay, then return to Gedaliah son of Ahikam and grandson of Shaphan. He has been appointed governor of Judah by the king of Babylon. Stay there with the people he rules. But it's up to you; go wherever you like."

Then Nebuzaradan, the captain of the guard, gave Jeremiah some food and money and let him go. ⁶So Jeremiah returned to Gedaliah son of Ahikam at Mizpah, and he lived in Judah with the few who were still left in the land.

⁷The leaders of the Judean guerrilla bands in the countryside heard that the king of Babylon had appointed Gedaliah son of Ahikam as governor over the poor people who were left behind in Judah—the men, women, and children who hadn't been exiled to Babylon. ⁸So they went to see Gedaliah at Mizpah. These included: Ishmael son of Nethaniah, Johanan and Jonathan sons of Kareah, Seraiah son of Tanhumeth, the sons of

Ephai the Netophathite, Jezaniah son of the Maacathite, and all their men.

⁹Gedaliah vowed to them that the Babylonians* meant them no harm. "Don't be afraid to serve them. Live in the land and serve the king of Babylon, and all will go well for you," he promised. ¹⁰"As for me, I will stay at Mizpah to represent you before the Babylonians who come to meet with us. Settle in the towns you have taken, and live off the land. Harvest the grapes and summer fruits and olives, and store them away."

¹¹When the Judeans in Moab, Ammon, Edom, and the other nearby countries heard that the king of Babylon had left a few people in Judah and that Gedaliah was the governor, ¹²they began to return to Judah from the places to which they had fled. They stopped at Mizpah to meet with Gedaliah and then went into the Judean countryside to gather a great harvest of grapes and other crops.

¹³Soon after this, Johanan son of Kareah and the other guerrilla leaders came to Gedaliah at Mizpah. ¹⁴They said to him, "Did you know that Baalis, king of Ammon, has sent Ishmael son of Nethaniah to assassinate you?" But Gedaliah refused to believe them.

¹⁵Later Johanan had a private conference with Gedaliah and volunteered to kill Ishmael secretly. "Why should we let him come and murder you?" Johanan asked. "What will happen then to the Judeans who have returned? Why should the few of us who are still left be scattered and lost?"

¹⁶But Gedaliah said to Johanan, "I forbid you to do any such thing, for you are lying about Ishmael."

^{41:1}BUT in midautumn,* Ishmael son of Nethaniah and grandson of Elishama, who was a member of the royal family and had been one of the king's high officials, went to Mizpah with ten men to meet Gedaliah. While they were eating together, ²Ishmael and his ten men suddenly jumped up, drew their swords, and killed Gedaliah, whom the king of Bab-

ylon had appointed governor. ³Ishmael also killed all the Judeans and the Babylonian* soldiers who were with Gedaliah at Mizpah.

⁴The next day, before anyone had heard about Gedaliah's murder, ⁵eighty men arrived from Shechem, Shiloh, and Samaria to worship at the Temple of the LORD. They had shaved off their beards, torn their clothes, and cut themselves, and had brought along grain offerings and frankincense. ⁶Ishmael left Mizpah to meet them, weeping as he went. When he reached them, he said, "Oh, come and see what has happened to Gedaliah!"

⁷But as soon as they were all inside the town, Ishmael and his men killed all but ten of them and threw their bodies into a cistern. ⁸The other ten had talked Ishmael into letting them go by promising to bring him their stores of wheat, barley, olive oil, and honey that they had hidden away. ⁹The cistern where Ishmael dumped the bodies of the men he murdered was the large one dug by King Asa when he fortified Mizpah to protect himself against King Baasha of Israel. Ishmael son of Nethaniah filled it with corpses.

¹⁰Then Ishmael made captives of the king's daughters and the other people who had been left under Gedaliah's care in Mizpah by Nebuzaradan, the captain of the guard. Taking them with him, he started back toward the land of Ammon.

¹¹But when Johanan son of Kareah and the other guerrilla leaders heard about Ishmael's crimes, ¹²they took all their men and set out to stop him. They caught up with him at the large pool near Gibeon. ¹³The people Ishmael had captured shouted for joy when they saw Johanan and the other guerrilla leaders. ¹⁴And all the captives from Mizpah escaped and began to help Johanan. ¹⁵Meanwhile, Ishmael and eight of his men escaped from Johanan into the land of Ammon.

¹⁶Then Johanan son of Kareah and the other guerrilla leaders took all the people they had rescued in Gibeon—the soldiers, women, children, and court officials* whom Ishmael had captured

after he killed Gedaliah. ¹⁷They took them all to the village of Geruth-kimham near Bethlehem, where they prepared to leave for Egypt. ¹⁸They were afraid of what the Babylonians* would do when they heard that Ishmael had killed Gedaliah, the governor appointed by the Babylonian king.

39:1a Hebrew *in the tenth month,* of the ancient Hebrew lunar calendar. A number of events in Jeremiah can be cross-checked with dates in surviving Babylonian records and related accurately to our modern calendar. This event occurred on January 15, 588 B.C.; see 52:4a and the note there. **39:1b** Hebrew *Nebuchadrezzar,* a variant spelling of Nebuchadnezzar; also in 39:11. **39:2** Hebrew *On the ninth day of the fourth month.* This day was July 18, 586 B.C.; also see note on 39:1a. **39:3** Or *Nergal-sharezer, Samgar-nebo, Sarsekim.* **39:4** Hebrew *the Arabah.* **39:5** Or *Chaldean;* similarly in 39:8. **39:16** Hebrew *the Cushite.* **40:9** Or *Chaldeans;* also in 40:10. **41:1** Hebrew *in the seventh month,* of the ancient Hebrew lunar calendar. This month occurred within the months of October and November 586 B.C.; also see note on 39:1a. **41:3** Or *Chaldean.* **41:16** Or *eunuchs.* **41:18** Or *Chaldeans.*

2 TIMOTHY 1:1-18

This letter is from Paul, chosen by the will of God to be an apostle of Christ Jesus. I have been sent out to tell others about the life he has promised through faith in Christ Jesus.

²I am writing to Timothy, my dear son.

May God the Father and Christ Jesus our Lord give you grace, mercy, and peace.

³Timothy, I thank God for you—the God I serve with a clear conscience, just as my ancestors did. Night and day I constantly remember you in my prayers. ⁴I long to see you again, for I remember your tears as we parted. And I will be filled with joy when we are together again.

⁵I remember your genuine faith, for you share the faith that first filled your grandmother Lois and your mother, Eunice. And I know that same faith continues strong in you. ⁶This is why I remind you to fan into flames the spiritual gift God gave you when I laid my hands on you. ⁷For God has not given us a spirit of fear and timidity, but of power, love, and self-discipline.

⁸So never be ashamed to tell others about our Lord. And don't be ashamed of me, either, even though I'm in prison for him. With the strength God gives you, be ready to suffer with me for the sake of the Good News. ⁹For God saved

us and called us to live a holy life. He did this, not because we deserved it, but because that was his plan from before the beginning of time—to show us his grace through Christ Jesus. [10]And now he has made all of this plain to us by the appearing of Christ Jesus, our Savior. He broke the power of death and illuminated the way to life and immortality through the Good News. [11]And God chose me to be a preacher, an apostle, and a teacher of this Good News.

[12]That is why I am suffering here in prison. But I am not ashamed of it, for I know the one in whom I trust, and I am sure that he is able to guard what I have entrusted to him* until the day of his return.

[13]Hold on to the pattern of wholesome teaching you learned from me—a pattern shaped by the faith and love that you have in Christ Jesus. [14]Through the power of the Holy Spirit who lives within us, carefully guard the precious truth that has been entrusted to you.

[15]As you know, everyone from the province of Asia has deserted me—even Phygelus and Hermogenes.

[16]May the Lord show special kindness to Onesiphorus and all his family because he often visited and encouraged me. He was never ashamed of me because I was in chains. [17]When he came to Rome, he searched everywhere until he found me. [18]May the Lord show him special kindness on the day of Christ's return. And you know very well how helpful he was in Ephesus.

1:12 Or *what has been entrusted to me.*

PSALM 90:1–91:16
A prayer of Moses, the man of God.

[1] Lord, through all the
        generations
        you have been our home!
[2] Before the mountains were
        born,
        before you gave birth to the earth
        and the world,
        from beginning to end, you
        are God.

[3] You turn people back to dust, saying,
        "Return to dust, you mortals!"
[4] For you, a thousand years are as a
        passing day,
        as brief as a few night hours.
[5] You sweep people away like dreams
        that disappear.
        They are like grass that springs
        up in the morning.
[6] In the morning it blooms and
        flourishes,
        but by evening it is dry and
        withered.
[7] We wither beneath your anger;
        we are overwhelmed by your fury.
[8] You spread out our sins before you—
        our secret sins—and you see
        them all.
[9] We live our lives beneath your wrath,
        ending our years with a groan.

[10] Seventy years are given to us!
        Some even live to eighty.
     But even the best years are filled
        with pain and trouble;
        soon they disappear, and we
        fly away.
[11] Who can comprehend the power
        of your anger?
        Your wrath is as awesome as the
        fear you deserve.
[12] Teach us to realize the brevity
        of life,
        so that we may grow in wisdom.
[13] O Lord, come back to us!
        How long will you delay?
        Take pity on your servants!
[14] Satisfy us each morning with your
        unfailing love,
        so we may sing for joy to the end
        of our lives.
[15] Give us gladness in proportion to
        our former misery!
        Replace the evil years with good.
[16] Let us, your servants, see you
        work again;
        let our children see your glory.
[17] And may the Lord our God show us
        his approval
        and make our efforts successful.
        Yes, make our efforts successful!

91:1 THOSE who live in the shelter
of the Most High
will find rest in the shadow
of the Almighty.
2 This I declare about the LORD:
He alone is my refuge, my place
of safety;
he is my God, and I trust him.
3 For he will rescue you from
every trap
and protect you from deadly
disease.
4 He will cover you with his
feathers.
He will shelter you with his wings.
His faithful promises are your
armor and protection.
5 Do not be afraid of the terrors
of the night,
nor the arrow that flies in
the day.
6 Do not dread the disease that stalks
in darkness,
nor the disaster that strikes
at midday.
7 Though a thousand fall at your side,
though ten thousand are dying
around you,
these evils will not touch you.
8 Just open your eyes,
and see how the wicked are
punished.

9 If you make the LORD your refuge,
if you make the Most High
your shelter,
10 no evil will conquer you;
no plague will come near
your home.
11 For he will order his angels
to protect you wherever you go.
12 They will hold you up with
their hands
so you won't even hurt your foot
on a stone.
13 You will trample upon lions
and cobras;
you will crush fierce lions and
serpents under your feet!

14 The LORD says, "I will rescue those
who love me.
I will protect those who trust in
my name.
15 When they call on me, I will answer;
I will be with them in trouble.
I will rescue and honor them.
16 I will reward them with a long life
and give them my salvation."

PROVERBS 26:1-2

Honor is no more associated with fools
than snow with summer or rain with
harvest. □ Like a fluttering sparrow or a
darting swallow, an undeserved curse
will not land on its intended victim.

OCTOBER 23

JEREMIAH 42:1–44:23

Then all the guerrilla leaders, including
Johanan son of Kareah and Jezaniah*
son of Hoshaiah, and all the people,
from the least to the greatest, approached 2 Jeremiah the prophet. They
said, "Please pray to the LORD your God
for us. As you can see, we are only a tiny
remnant compared to what we were before. 3 Pray that the LORD your God will
show us what to do and where to go."

4 "All right," Jeremiah replied. "I will
pray to the LORD your God, as you have
asked, and I will tell you everything he
says. I will hide nothing from you."

5 Then they said to Jeremiah, "May
the LORD your God be a faithful witness
against us if we refuse to obey whatever
he tells us to do! 6 Whether we like it or
not, we will obey the LORD our God to
whom we are sending you with our plea.
For if we obey him, everything will turn
out well for us."

7 Ten days later the LORD gave his
reply to Jeremiah. 8 So he called for Johanan son of Kareah and the other
guerrilla leaders, and for all the people,
from the least to the greatest. 9 He said

to them, "You sent me to the LORD, the God of Israel, with your request, and this is his reply: [10]'Stay here in this land. If you do, I will build you up and not tear you down; I will plant you and not uproot you. For I am sorry about all the punishment I have had to bring upon you. [11]Do not fear the king of Babylon anymore,' says the LORD. 'For I am with you and will save you and rescue you from his power. [12]I will be merciful to you by making him kind, so he will let you stay here in your land.'

[13]"But if you refuse to obey the LORD your God, and if you say, 'We will not stay here; [14]instead, we will go to Egypt where we will be free from war, the call to arms, and hunger,' [15]then hear the LORD's message to the remnant of Judah. This is what the LORD of Heaven's Armies, the God of Israel, says: 'If you are determined to go to Egypt and live there, [16]the very war and famine you fear will catch up to you, and you will die there. [17]That is the fate awaiting every one of you who insists on going to live in Egypt. Yes, you will die from war, famine, and disease. None of you will escape the disaster I will bring upon you there.'

[18]"This is what the LORD of Heaven's Armies, the God of Israel, says: 'Just as my anger and fury have been poured out on the people of Jerusalem, so they will be poured out on you when you enter Egypt. You will be an object of damnation, horror, cursing, and mockery. And you will never see your homeland again.'

[19]"Listen, you remnant of Judah. The LORD has told you: 'Do not go to Egypt!' Don't forget this warning I have given you today. [20]For you were not being honest when you sent me to pray to the LORD your God for you. You said, 'Just tell us what the LORD our God says, and we will do it!' [21]And today I have told you exactly what he said, but you will not obey the LORD your God any better now than you have in the past. [22]So you can be sure that you will die from war, famine, and disease in Egypt, where you insist on going."

[43:1]WHEN Jeremiah had finished giving this message from the LORD their God to all the people, [2]Azariah son of Hoshaiah and Johanan son of Kareah and all the other proud men said to Jeremiah, "You lie! The LORD our God hasn't forbidden us to go to Egypt! [3]Baruch son of Neriah has convinced you to say this, because he wants us to stay here and be killed by the Babylonians* or be carried off into exile."

[4]So Johanan and the other guerrilla leaders and all the people refused to obey the LORD's command to stay in Judah. [5]Johanan and the other leaders took with them all the people who had returned from the nearby countries to which they had fled. [6]In the crowd were men, women, and children, the king's daughters, and all those whom Nebuzaradan, the captain of the guard, had left with Gedaliah. The prophet Jeremiah and Baruch were also included. [7]The people refused to obey the voice of the LORD and went to Egypt, going as far as the city of Tahpanhes.

[8]Then at Tahpanhes, the LORD gave another message to Jeremiah. He said, [9]"While the people of Judah are watching, take some large rocks and bury them under the pavement stones at the entrance of Pharaoh's palace here in Tahpanhes. [10]Then say to the people of Judah, 'This is what the LORD of Heaven's Armies, the God of Israel, says: I will certainly bring my servant Nebuchadnezzar,* king of Babylon, here to Egypt. I will set his throne over these stones that I have hidden. He will spread his royal canopy over them. [11]And when he comes, he will destroy the land of Egypt. He will bring death to those destined for death, captivity to those destined for captivity, and war to those destined for war. [12]He will set fire to the temples of Egypt's gods; he will burn the temples and carry the idols away as plunder. He will pick clean the land of Egypt as a shepherd picks fleas from his cloak. And he himself will leave unharmed. [13]He will break down the sacred pillars standing in the temple of the sun* in Egypt,

and he will burn down the temples of Egypt's gods.'"

44:1THIS is the message Jeremiah received concerning the Judeans living in northern Egypt in the cities of Migdol, Tahpanhes, and Memphis,* and in southern Egypt* as well: 2"This is what the LORD of Heaven's Armies, the God of Israel, says: You saw the calamity I brought on Jerusalem and all the towns of Judah. They now lie deserted and in ruins. 3 They provoked my anger with all their wickedness. They burned incense and worshiped other gods—gods that neither they nor you nor any of your ancestors had ever even known.

4"Again and again I sent my servants, the prophets, to plead with them, 'Don't do these horrible things that I hate so much.' 5 But my people would not listen or turn back from their wicked ways. They kept on burning incense to these gods. 6And so my fury boiled over and fell like fire on the towns of Judah and into the streets of Jerusalem, and they are still a desolate ruin today.

7"And now the LORD God of Heaven's Armies, the God of Israel, asks you: Why are you destroying yourselves? For not one of you will survive—not a man, woman, or child among you who has come here from Judah, not even the babies in your arms. 8Why provoke my anger by burning incense to the idols you have made here in Egypt? You will only destroy yourselves and make yourselves an object of cursing and mockery for all the nations of the earth. 9Have you forgotten the sins of your ancestors, the sins of the kings and queens of Judah, and the sins you and your wives committed in Judah and Jerusalem? 10To this very hour you have shown no remorse or reverence. No one has chosen to follow my word and the decrees I gave to you and your ancestors before you.

11"Therefore, this is what the LORD of Heaven's Armies, the God of Israel, says: I am determined to destroy every one of you! 12I will take this remnant of Judah—those who were determined to come

here and live in Egypt—and I will consume them. They will fall here in Egypt, killed by war and famine. All will die, from the least to the greatest. They will be an object of damnation, horror, cursing, and mockery. 13I will punish them in Egypt just as I punished them in Jerusalem, by war, famine, and disease. 14Of that remnant who fled to Egypt, hoping someday to return to Judah, there will be no survivors. Even though they long to return home, only a handful will do so."

15Then all the women present and all the men who knew that their wives had burned incense to idols—a great crowd of all the Judeans living in northern Egypt and southern Egypt*—answered Jeremiah, 16"We will not listen to your messages from the LORD! 17We will do whatever we want. We will burn incense and pour out liquid offerings to the Queen of Heaven just as much as we like—just as we, and our ancestors, and our kings and officials have always done in the towns of Judah and in the streets of Jerusalem. For in those days we had plenty to eat, and we were well off and had no troubles! 18But ever since we quit burning incense to the Queen of Heaven and stopped worshiping her with liquid offerings, we have been in great trouble and have been dying from war and famine."

19"Besides," the women added, "do you suppose that we were burning incense and pouring out liquid offerings to the Queen of Heaven, and making cakes marked with her image, without our husbands knowing it and helping us? Of course not!"

20Then Jeremiah said to all of them, men and women alike, who had given him that answer, 21"Do you think the LORD did not know that you and your ancestors, your kings and officials, and all the people were burning incense to idols in the towns of Judah and in the streets of Jerusalem? 22It was because the LORD could no longer bear all the disgusting things you were doing that he made your land an object of cursing—a desolate ruin without inhabitants—as it is today. 23All these terrible things happened to you because you have burned incense to idols and sinned against the LORD. You have refused to obey him and have not followed his instructions, his decrees, and his laws."

42:1 Greek version reads *Azariah;* compare 43:2.   43:3 Or *Chaldeans.*   43:10 Hebrew *Nebuchadrezzar,* a variant spelling of Nebuchadnezzar.   43:13 Or *in Heliopolis.*
44:1a Hebrew *Noph.*   44:1b Hebrew *in Pathros.*
44:15 Hebrew *in Egypt, in Pathros.*

2 TIMOTHY 2:1-21

Timothy, my dear son, be strong through the grace that God gives you in Christ Jesus. ²You have heard me teach things that have been confirmed by many reliable witnesses. Now teach these truths to other trustworthy people who will be able to pass them on to others.

³Endure suffering along with me, as a good soldier of Christ Jesus. ⁴Soldiers don't get tied up in the affairs of civilian life, for then they cannot please the officer who enlisted them. ⁵And athletes cannot win the prize unless they follow the rules. ⁶And hardworking farmers should be the first to enjoy the fruit of their labor. ⁷Think about what I am saying. The Lord will help you understand all these things.

⁸Always remember that Jesus Christ, a descendant of King David, was raised from the dead. This is the Good News I preach. ⁹And because I preach this Good News, I am suffering and have been chained like a criminal. But the word of God cannot be chained. ¹⁰So I am willing to endure anything if it will bring salvation and eternal glory in Christ Jesus to those God has chosen.

¹¹This is a trustworthy saying:

If we die with him,
    we will also live with him.
¹² If we endure hardship,
    we will reign with him.
If we deny him,
    he will deny us.
¹³ If we are unfaithful,
    he remains faithful,
    for he cannot deny who he is.

¹⁴Remind everyone about these things, and command them in God's presence to stop fighting over words. Such arguments are useless, and they can ruin those who hear them.

¹⁵**Work hard so you can present yourself to God and receive his approval. Be a good worker, one who does not need to be ashamed and who correctly explains the word of truth.** ¹⁶Avoid worthless, foolish talk that only leads to more godless behavior. ¹⁷This kind of talk spreads like cancer, as in the case of Hymenaeus and Philetus. ¹⁸They have left the path of truth, claiming that the resurrection of the dead has already occurred; in this way, they have turned some people away from the faith.

¹⁹But God's truth stands firm like a foundation stone with this inscription: "The LORD knows those who are his,"* and "All who belong to the LORD must turn away from evil."*

²⁰In a wealthy home some utensils are made of gold and silver, and some are made of wood and clay. The expensive utensils are used for special occasions, and the cheap ones are for everyday use. ²¹If you keep yourself pure, you will be a special utensil for honorable use. Your life will be clean, and you will be ready for the Master to use you for every good work.

2:19a Num 16:5.   2:19b See Isa 52:11.

PSALM 92:1-93:5

A psalm. A song to be sung on the Sabbath Day.

¹ It is good to give thanks to
        the LORD,
    to sing praises to the
        Most High.
² It is good to proclaim your unfailing
        love in the morning,
    your faithfulness in the evening,
³ accompanied by the ten-stringed
        harp
    and the melody of the lyre.

⁴ You thrill me, LORD, with all you
        have done for me!
    I sing for joy because of what you
        have done.

5 O LORD, what great works you do!
   And how deep are your
      thoughts.
6 Only a simpleton would not know,
   and only a fool would not
      understand this:
7 Though the wicked sprout
      like weeds
   and evildoers flourish,
   they will be destroyed forever.

8 But you, O LORD, will be exalted
      forever.
9 Your enemies, LORD, will surely
      perish;
   all evildoers will be scattered.
10 But you have made me as strong
      as a wild ox.
   You have anointed me with the
      finest oil.
11 My eyes have seen the downfall of
      my enemies;
   my ears have heard the defeat
      of my wicked opponents.
12 But the godly will flourish like
      palm trees
   and grow strong like the
      cedars of Lebanon.
13 For they are transplanted to the
      LORD's own house.
   They flourish in the courts
      of our God.
14 Even in old age they will still
      produce fruit;
   they will remain vital and green.
15 They will declare, "The LORD is just!
   He is my rock!
   There is no evil in him!"

93:1 THE LORD is king! He is robed
      in majesty.
   Indeed, the LORD is robed in
      majesty and armed with
      strength.
   The world stands firm
      and cannot be shaken.

2 Your throne, O LORD, has stood from
      time immemorial.
   You yourself are from the
      everlasting past.
3 The floods have risen up, O LORD.

The floods have roared like
      thunder;
   the floods have lifted their
      pounding waves.
4 But mightier than the violent raging
      of the seas,
   mightier than the breakers on the
      shore—
   the LORD above is mightier
      than these!
5 Your royal laws cannot be changed.
   Your reign, O LORD, is holy
      forever and ever.

PROVERBS 26:3-5
Guide a horse with a whip, a donkey
with a bridle, and a fool with a rod to his
back! □ Don't answer the foolish arguments of fools, or you will become as
foolish as they are. □ Be sure to answer
the foolish arguments of fools, or they
will become wise in their own estima-
tion.

OCTOBER 24

JEREMIAH 44:24–47:7
Then Jeremiah said to them all, including the women, "Listen to this message
from the LORD, all you citizens of Judah
who live in Egypt. 25 This is what the
LORD of Heaven's Armies, the God of Israel, says: 'You and your wives have said,
"We will keep our promises to burn incense and pour out liquid offerings to
the Queen of Heaven," and you have
proved by your actions that you meant
it. So go ahead and carry out your promises and vows to her!'
26 "But listen to this message from the
LORD, all you Judeans now living in
Egypt: 'I have sworn by my great name,'
says the LORD, 'that my name will no
longer be spoken by any of the Judeans
in the land of Egypt. None of you may
invoke my name or use this oath: "As

surely as the Sovereign LORD lives." ²⁷For I will watch over you to bring you disaster and not good. Everyone from Judah who is now living in Egypt will suffer war and famine until all of you are dead. ²⁸Only a small number will escape death and return to Judah from Egypt. Then all those who came to Egypt will find out whose words are true—mine or theirs!

²⁹"'And this is the proof I give you,' says the LORD, 'that all I have threatened will happen to you and that I will punish you here.' ³⁰This is what the LORD says: 'I will turn Pharaoh Hophra, king of Egypt, over to his enemies who want to kill him, just as I turned King Zedekiah of Judah over to King Nebuchadnezzar* of Babylon.'"

45:1THE prophet Jeremiah gave a message to Baruch son of Neriah in the fourth year of the reign of Jehoiakim son of Josiah,* after Baruch had written down everything Jeremiah had dictated to him. He said, ²"This is what the LORD, the God of Israel, says to you, Baruch: ³You have said, 'I am overwhelmed with trouble! Haven't I had enough pain already? And now the LORD has added more! I am worn out from sighing and can find no rest.'

⁴"Baruch, this is what the LORD says: 'I will destroy this nation that I built. I will uproot what I planted. ⁵Are you seeking great things for yourself? Don't do it! I will bring great disaster upon all these people; but I will give you your life as a reward wherever you go. I, the LORD, have spoken!'"

46:1THE following messages were given to Jeremiah the prophet from the LORD concerning foreign nations.

²This message concerning Egypt was given in the fourth year of the reign of Jehoiakim son of Josiah, the king of Judah, on the occasion of the battle of Carchemish* when Pharaoh Neco, king of Egypt, and his army were defeated beside the Euphrates River by King Nebuchadnezzar* of Babylon.

³ "Prepare your shields,
and advance into battle!
⁴ Harness the horses,
and mount the stallions.
Take your positions.
Put on your helmets.
Sharpen your spears,
and prepare your armor.
⁵ But what do I see?
The Egyptian army flees in terror.
The bravest of its fighting men run
without a backward glance.
They are terrorized at every turn,"
says the LORD.
⁶ "The swiftest runners cannot flee;
the mightiest warriors cannot
escape.
By the Euphrates River to the north,
they stumble and fall.

⁷ "Who is this, rising like the Nile at
floodtime,
overflowing all the land?
⁸ It is the Egyptian army,
overflowing all the land,
boasting that it will cover the earth
like a flood,
destroying cities and their
people.
⁹ Charge, you horses and chariots;
attack, you mighty warriors
of Egypt!
Come, all you allies from Ethiopia,
Libya, and Lydia*
who are skilled with the shield
and bow!
¹⁰ For this is the day of the Lord, the
LORD of Heaven's Armies,
a day of vengeance on his
enemies.
The sword will devour until
it is satisfied,
yes, until it is drunk with
your blood!
The Lord, the LORD of Heaven's
Armies, will receive a
sacrifice today
in the north country beside the
Euphrates River.

¹¹ "Go up to Gilead to get medicine,
O virgin daughter of Egypt!

But your many treatments
    will bring you no healing.
[12] The nations have heard of your
    shame.
    The earth is filled with your cries
      of despair.
    Your mightiest warriors will run into
      each other
    and fall down together."

[13] Then the LORD gave the prophet Jeremiah this message about King Nebuchadnezzar's plans to attack Egypt.

[14] "Shout it out in Egypt!
    Publish it in the cities of Migdol,
      Memphis,* and Tahpanhes!
    Mobilize for battle,
      for the sword will devour
        everyone around you.
[15] Why have your warriors fallen?
    They cannot stand, for
      the LORD has knocked them
      down.
[16] They stumble and fall over each
      other
    and say among themselves,
    'Come, let's go back to our people,
      to the land of our birth.
    Let's get away from the sword
      of the enemy!'
[17] There they will say,
    'Pharaoh, the king of Egypt, is a
      loudmouth
    who missed his opportunity!'

[18] "As surely as I live," says the King,
      whose name is the LORD of
      Heaven's Armies,
    "one is coming against Egypt
      who is as tall as Mount Tabor,
      or as Mount Carmel by the sea!
[19] Pack up! Get ready to leave for exile,
    you citizens of Egypt!
    The city of Memphis will be
      destroyed,
    without a single inhabitant.
[20] Egypt is as sleek as a beautiful
      young cow,
    but a horsefly from the north is
      on its way!
[21] Egypt's mercenaries have become
      like fattened calves.

They, too, will turn and run,
    for it is a day of great disaster
      for Egypt,
    a time of great punishment.
[22] Egypt flees, silent as a serpent
      gliding away.
    The invading army marches in;
    they come against her with axes
      like woodsmen.
[23] They will cut down her people like
      trees," says the LORD,
    "for they are more numerous
      than locusts.
[24] Egypt will be humiliated;
    she will be handed over to people
      from the north."

[25] The LORD of Heaven's Armies, the God of Israel, says: "I will punish Amon, the god of Thebes,* and all the other gods of Egypt. I will punish its rulers and Pharaoh, too, and all who trust in him. [26] I will hand them over to those who want them killed—to King Nebuchadnezzar of Babylon and his army. But afterward the land will recover from the ravages of war. I, the LORD, have spoken!

[27] "But do not be afraid, Jacob,
      my servant;
    do not be dismayed, Israel.
    For I will bring you home again
      from distant lands,
    and your children will return
      from their exile.
    Israel* will return to a life of peace
      and quiet,
    and no one will terrorize them.
[28] Do not be afraid, Jacob, my servant,
    for I am with you," says
      the LORD.
    "I will completely destroy the
      nations to which I have
      exiled you,
    but I will not completely
      destroy you.
    I will discipline you, but with
      justice;
    I cannot let you go unpunished."

47:1 THIS is the LORD's message to the prophet Jeremiah concerning the Philistines of Gaza, before it was captured by the Egyptian army. ²This is what the Lord says:

"A flood is coming from the north
  to overflow the land.
It will destroy the land and
  everything in it—
  cities and people alike.
People will scream in terror,
  and everyone in the land
  will wail.
³ Hear the clatter of stallions'
  hooves
  and the rumble of wheels as the
  chariots rush by.
Terrified fathers run madly,
  without a backward glance at
  their helpless children.

⁴ "The time has come for the
  Philistines to be destroyed,
  along with their allies from Tyre
  and Sidon.
Yes, the Lord is destroying the
  remnant of the Philistines,
  those colonists from the island
  of Crete.*
⁵ Gaza will be humiliated, its head
  shaved bald;
  Ashkelon will lie silent.
You remnant from the
  Mediterranean coast,*
  how long will you lament
  and mourn?

⁶ "Now, O sword of the Lord,
  when will you be at rest again?
Go back into your sheath;
  rest and be still.

⁷ "But how can it be still
  when the Lord has sent it on a
  mission?
For the city of Ashkelon
  and the people living along the sea
  must be destroyed."

44:30 Hebrew *Nebuchadrezzar*, a variant spelling of
Nebuchadnezzar.   45:1 The fourth year of Jehoiakim's
reign was 605 B.C.   46:2a This event occurred in 605 B.C.,
during the fourth year of Jehoiakim's reign (according
to the calendar system in which the new year begins in the
spring).   46:2b Hebrew *Nebuchadrezzar*, a variant spelling
of Nebuchadnezzar; also in 46:13, 26.   46:9 Hebrew *from
Cush, Put, and Lud.*   46:14 Hebrew *Noph;* also in 46:19.
46:25 Hebrew *of No.*   46:27 Hebrew *Jacob.* See note on
5:20.   47:4 Hebrew *from Caphtor.*   47:5 Hebrew *the
plain.*

2 TIMOTHY 2:22–3:17

Run from anything that stimulates youthful lusts. Instead, pursue righteous living, faithfulness, love, and peace. Enjoy the companionship of those who call on the Lord with pure hearts.

²³Again I say, don't get involved in foolish, ignorant arguments that only start fights. ²⁴A servant of the Lord must not quarrel but must be kind to everyone, be able to teach, and be patient with difficult people. ²⁵Gently instruct those who oppose the truth. Perhaps God will change those people's hearts, and they will learn the truth. ²⁶Then they will come to their senses and escape from the devil's trap. For they have been held captive by him to do whatever he wants.

³:¹You should know this, Timothy, that in the last days there will be very difficult times. ²For people will love only themselves and their money. They will be boastful and proud, scoffing at God, disobedient to their parents, and ungrateful. They will consider nothing sacred. ³They will be unloving and unforgiving; they will slander others and have no self-control. They will be cruel and hate what is good. ⁴They will betray their friends, be reckless, be puffed up with pride, and love pleasure rather than God. ⁵They will act religious, but they will reject the power that could make them godly. Stay away from people like that!

⁶They are the kind who work their way into people's homes and win the confidence of* vulnerable women who are burdened with the guilt of sin and controlled by various desires. ⁷(Such women are forever following new teachings, but they are never able to understand the truth.) ⁸These teachers oppose the truth just as Jannes and Jambres opposed Moses. They have depraved minds and a counterfeit faith. ⁹But they won't get away with this for long. Someday everyone will recognize what fools they are, just as with Jannes and Jambres.

¹⁰But you, Timothy, certainly know what I teach, and how I live, and what

my purpose in life is. You know my faith, my patience, my love, and my endurance. [11]You know how much persecution and suffering I have endured. You know all about how I was persecuted in Antioch, Iconium, and Lystra—but the Lord rescued me from all of it. [12]Yes, and everyone who wants to live a godly life in Christ Jesus will suffer persecution. [13]But evil people and impostors will flourish. They will deceive others and will themselves be deceived.

[14]But you must remain faithful to the things you have been taught. You know they are true, for you know you can trust those who taught you. [15]You have been taught the holy Scriptures from childhood, and they have given you the wisdom to receive the salvation that comes by trusting in Christ Jesus. [16]**All Scripture is inspired by God and is useful to teach us what is true and to make us realize what is wrong in our lives. It corrects us when we are wrong and teaches us to do what is right. [17]God uses it to prepare and equip his people to do every good work.**

3:6 Greek *and take captive.*

PSALM 94:1-23

O LORD, the God of vengeance,
O God of vengeance, let your
    glorious justice shine forth!
[2] Arise, O judge of the earth.
    Give the proud what
        they deserve.
[3] How long, O LORD?
    How long will the wicked be
        allowed to gloat?
[4] How long will they speak with
        arrogance?
    How long will these evil
        people boast?
[5] They crush your people, LORD,
    hurting those you claim as
        your own.
[6] They kill widows and foreigners
    and murder orphans.
[7] "The LORD isn't looking," they say,
    "and besides, the God of Israel*
        doesn't care."

[8] Think again, you fools!
    When will you finally catch on?
[9] Is he deaf—the one who made
        your ears?
    Is he blind—the one who formed
        your eyes?
[10] He punishes the nations—won't he
        also punish you?
    He knows everything—doesn't he
        also know what you are doing?
[11] The LORD knows people's thoughts;
    he knows they are worthless!

[12] Joyful are those you discipline, LORD,
    those you teach with your
        instructions.
[13] You give them relief from
        troubled times
    until a pit is dug to capture
        the wicked.
[14] The LORD will not reject his people;
    he will not abandon his special
        possession.
[15] Judgment will again be founded
        on justice,
    and those with virtuous hearts
        will pursue it.

[16] Who will protect me from the
        wicked?
    Who will stand up for me against
        evildoers?
[17] Unless the LORD had helped me,
    I would soon have settled in the
        silence of the grave.
[18] I cried out, "I am slipping!"
    but your unfailing love, O LORD,
        supported me.
[19] When doubts filled my mind,
    your comfort gave me renewed
        hope and cheer.

[20] Can unjust leaders claim that God is
        on their side—
    leaders whose decrees permit
        injustice?
[21] They gang up against the righteous
    and condemn the innocent to
        death.
[22] But the LORD is my fortress;
    my God is the mighty rock
        where I hide.

23 God will turn the sins of evil people
back on them.
He will destroy them for
their sins.
The LORD our God will
destroy them.

94:7 Hebrew *of Jacob*. See note on 44:4.

PROVERBS 26:6-8

Trusting a fool to convey a message is like cutting off one's feet or drinking poison! □ A proverb in the mouth of a fool is as useless as a paralyzed leg. □ Honoring a fool is as foolish as tying a stone to a slingshot.

OCTOBER
25

JEREMIAH 48:1–49:22

This message was given concerning Moab. This is what the LORD of Heaven's Armies, the God of Israel, says:

"What sorrow awaits the city
of Nebo;
it will soon lie in ruins.
The city of Kiriathaim will be
humiliated and captured;
the fortress will be humiliated
and broken down.
2 No one will ever brag about Moab
again,
for in Heshbon there is a plot
to destroy her.
'Come,' they say, 'we will cut her off
from being a nation.'
The town of Madmen,* too, will
be silenced;
the sword will follow you there.
3 Listen to the cries from Horonaim,
cries of devastation and great
destruction.
4 All Moab is destroyed.
Her little ones will cry out.*
5 Her refugees weep bitterly,
climbing the slope to Luhith.

They cry out in terror,
descending the slope to Horonaim.
6 Flee for your lives!
Hide* in the wilderness!
7 Because you have trusted in your
wealth and skill,
you will be taken captive.
Your god Chemosh, with his priests
and officials,
will be hauled off to distant lands!

8 "All the towns will be destroyed,
and no one will escape—
either on the plateaus or in
the valleys,
for the LORD has spoken.
9 Oh, that Moab had wings
so she could fly away,*
for her towns will be left empty,
with no one living in them.
10 Cursed are those who refuse to do
the LORD's work,
who hold back their swords from
shedding blood!

11 "From his earliest history, Moab has
lived in peace,
never going into exile.
He is like wine that has been allowed
to settle.
He has not been poured from
flask to flask,
and he is now fragrant and
smooth.
12 But the time is coming soon," says
the LORD,
"when I will send men to pour
him from his jar.
They will pour him out,
then shatter the jar!
13 At last Moab will be ashamed of his
idol Chemosh,
as the people of Israel were
ashamed of their gold calf
at Bethel.*

14 "You used to boast, 'We are heroes,
mighty men of war.'
15 But now Moab and his towns will be
destroyed.
His most promising youth are
doomed to slaughter,"

says the King, whose name is the
LORD of Heaven's Armies.

16 "Destruction is coming fast for Moab;
calamity threatens ominously.
17 You friends of Moab,
weep for him and cry!
See how the strong scepter is
broken,
how the beautiful staff is
shattered!

18 "Come down from your glory
and sit in the dust, you people
of Dibon,
for those who destroy Moab will
shatter Dibon, too.
They will tear down all your towers.
19 You people of Aroer,
stand beside the road and watch.
Shout to those who flee from Moab,
'What has happened there?'

20 "And the reply comes back,
'Moab lies in ruins, disgraced;
weep and wail!
Tell it by the banks of the Arnon River:
Moab has been destroyed!'
21 Judgment has been poured out on
the towns of the plateau—
on Holon and Jahaz* and
Mephaath,
22 on Dibon and Nebo and Beth-
diblathaim,
23   on Kiriathaim and Beth-gamul
and Beth-meon,
24 on Kerioth and Bozrah—
all the towns of Moab, far and near.

25 "The strength of Moab has ended.
His arm has been broken," says
the LORD.
26 "Let him stagger and fall like a
drunkard,
for he has rebelled against the LORD.
Moab will wallow in his own vomit,
ridiculed by all.
27 Did you not ridicule the people of
Israel?
Were they caught in the company
of thieves
that you should despise them as
you do?

28 "You people of Moab,
flee from your towns and live in
the caves.
Hide like doves that nest
in the clefts of the rocks.
29 We have all heard of the pride
of Moab,
for his pride is very great.
We know of his lofty pride,
his arrogance, and his haughty
heart.
30 I know about his insolence,"
says the LORD,
"but his boasts are empty—
as empty as his deeds.
31 So now I wail for Moab;
yes, I will mourn for Moab.
My heart is broken for the men
of Kir-hareseth.*

32 "You people of Sibmah, rich in
vineyards,
I will weep for you even more
than I did for Jazer.
Your spreading vines once reached
as far as the Dead Sea,*
but the destroyer has stripped
you bare!
He has harvested your grapes and
summer fruits.
33 Joy and gladness are gone from
fruitful Moab.
The presses yield no wine.
No one treads the grapes with
shouts of joy.
There is shouting, yes, but
not of joy.

34"Instead, their awful cries of terror
can be heard from Heshbon clear
across to Elealeh and Jahaz; from Zoar
all the way to Horonaim and Eglath-
shelishiyah. Even the waters of Nimrim
are dried up now.

35"I will put an end to Moab," says the
LORD, "for the people offer sacrifices at
the pagan shrines and burn incense to
their false gods. 36My heart moans like
a flute for Moab and Kir-hareseth, for
all their wealth has disappeared. 37The
people shave their heads and beards in
mourning. They slash their hands and

put on clothes made of burlap. [38]There is crying and sorrow in every Moabite home and on every street. For I have smashed Moab like an old, unwanted jar. [39]How it is shattered! Hear the wailing! See the shame of Moab! It has become an object of ridicule, an example of ruin to all its neighbors."

[40]This is what the LORD says:

"Look! The enemy swoops down like
     an eagle,
   spreading his wings over Moab.
[41] Its cities will fall,
   and its strongholds will be seized.
Even the mightiest warriors will be
     in anguish
   like a woman in labor.
[42] Moab will no longer be a nation,
   for it has boasted against
     the LORD.

[43] "Terror and traps and snares will be
     your lot,
   O Moab," says the LORD.
[44] "Those who flee in terror will fall
     into a trap,
   and those who escape the trap
     will step into a snare.
I will see to it that you do not
     get away,
   for the time of your judgment
     has come,"
   says the LORD.
[45] "The people flee as far as Heshbon
     but are unable to go on.
For a fire comes from Heshbon,
     King Sihon's ancient home,
to devour the entire land
   with all its rebellious people.

[46] "O Moab, they weep for you!
   The people of the god Chemosh
     are destroyed!
Your sons and your daughters
   have been taken away as captives.
[47] But I will restore the fortunes
     of Moab
   in days to come.
   I, the LORD, have spoken!"

This is the end of Jeremiah's prophecy concerning Moab.

[49:1]THIS message was given concerning the Ammonites. This is what the LORD says:

"Are there no descendants of Israel
     to inherit the land of Gad?
Why are you, who worship Molech,*
     living in its towns?
[2] In the days to come," says the LORD,
   "I will sound the battle cry against
     your city of Rabbah.
It will become a desolate heap
     of ruins,
   and the neighboring towns will
     be burned.
Then Israel will take back the land
   you took from her," says the LORD.

[3] "Cry out, O Heshbon,
   for the town of Ai is destroyed.
Weep, O people of Rabbah!
   Put on your clothes of mourning.
Weep and wail, hiding in the hedges,
   for your god Molech, with his
     priests and officials,
   will be hauled off to distant
     lands.
[4] You are proud of your fertile valleys,
   but they will soon be ruined.
You trusted in your wealth,
   you rebellious daughter,
   and thought no one could ever
     harm you.
[5] But look! I will bring terror
     upon you,"
   says the Lord, the LORD of
     Heaven's Armies.
   "Your neighbors will chase you
     from your land,
   and no one will help your
     exiles as they flee.
[6] But I will restore the fortunes of the
     Ammonites
   in days to come.
   I, the LORD, have spoken."

[7]This message was given concerning Edom. This is what the LORD of Heaven's Armies says:

"Is there no wisdom in Teman?
   Is no one left to give wise
     counsel?

⁸ Turn and flee!
  Hide in deep caves, you people
    of Dedan!
  For when I bring disaster on Edom,*
    I will punish you, too!
⁹ Those who harvest grapes
    always leave a few for the poor.
  If thieves came at night,
    they would not take everything.
¹⁰ But I will strip bare the land of
      Edom,
    and there will be no place left
      to hide.
  Its children, its brothers, and its
      neighbors
    will all be destroyed,
    and Edom itself will be no more.
¹¹ But I will protect the orphans who
      remain among you.
    Your widows, too, can depend on
      me for help."

¹²And this is what the LORD says:
"If the innocent must suffer, how much
more must you! You will not go unpunished! You must drink this cup of
judgment! ¹³For I have sworn by my
own name," says the LORD, "that Bozrah
will become an object of horror and a
heap of ruins; it will be mocked and
cursed. All its towns and villages will be
desolate forever."

¹⁴ I have heard a message from
      the LORD
    that an ambassador was sent to
      the nations to say,
  "Form a coalition against Edom,
    and prepare for battle!"

¹⁵ The LORD says to Edom,
  "I will cut you down to size among
      the nations.
    You will be despised by all.
¹⁶ You have been deceived
    by the fear you inspire in others
    and by your own pride.
  You live in a rock fortress
    and control the mountain
      heights.
  But even if you make your nest
    among the peaks with
      the eagles,

  I will bring you crashing down,"
    says the LORD.

¹⁷ "Edom will be an object of horror.
    All who pass by will be appalled
    and will gasp at the destruction
      they see there.
¹⁸ It will be like the destruction of
      Sodom and Gomorrah
    and their neighboring towns,"
      says the LORD.
  "No one will live there;
    no one will inhabit it.
¹⁹ I will come like a lion from the
      thickets of the Jordan,
    leaping on the sheep in the pasture.
  I will chase Edom from its land,
    and I will appoint the leader
      of my choice.
  For who is like me, and who can
      challenge me?
    What ruler can oppose my will?"

²⁰ Listen to the LORD's plans against
      Edom
    and the people of Teman.
  Even the little children will be
    dragged off like sheep,
    and their homes will be destroyed.
²¹ The earth will shake with the noise
      of Edom's fall,
    and its cry of despair will be heard
      all the way to the Red Sea.*
²² Look! The enemy swoops down like
      an eagle,
    spreading his wings over Bozrah.
  Even the mightiest warriors will be
      in anguish
    like a woman in labor.

48:2 *Madmen* sounds like the Hebrew word for "silence";
it should not be confused with the English word *madmen*.
48:4 Greek version reads *Her cries are heard as far away
as Zoar.* **48:6** Or *Hide like a wild donkey;* or *Hide like a
juniper shrub;* or *Be like* (the town of) *Aroer.* The meaning of
the Hebrew is uncertain. **48:9** Or *Put salt on Moab, / for
she will be laid waste.* **48:13** Hebrew *ashamed when they
trusted in Bethel.* **48:21** Hebrew *Jahzah,* a variant spelling
of Jahaz. **48:31** Hebrew *Kir-heres,* a variant spelling of
Kir-hareseth; also in 48:36. **48:32** Hebrew *the sea of
Jazer.* **49:1** Hebrew *Malcam,* a variant spelling of Molech;
also in 49:3. **49:8** Hebrew *Esau;* also in 49:10.
49:21 Hebrew *sea of reeds.*

2 TIMOTHY 4:1-22

❚ [Paul] solemnly urge you [Timothy] in
the presence of God and Christ Jesus,
who will someday judge the living and

the dead when he appears to set up his Kingdom: ²**Preach the word of God. Be prepared, whether the time is favorable or not. Patiently correct, rebuke, and encourage your people with good teaching.**

³For a time is coming when people will no longer listen to sound and wholesome teaching. They will follow their own desires and will look for teachers who will tell them whatever their itching ears want to hear. ⁴They will reject the truth and chase after myths.

⁵But you should keep a clear mind in every situation. Don't be afraid of suffering for the Lord. Work at telling others the Good News, and fully carry out the ministry God has given you.

⁶As for me, my life has already been poured out as an offering to God. The time of my death is near. ⁷I have fought the good fight, I have finished the race, and I have remained faithful. ⁸And now the prize awaits me—the crown of righteousness, which the Lord, the righteous Judge, will give me on the day of his return. And the prize is not just for me but for all who eagerly look forward to his appearing.

⁹Timothy, please come as soon as you can. ¹⁰Demas has deserted me because he loves the things of this life and has gone to Thessalonica. Crescens has gone to Galatia, and Titus has gone to Dalmatia. ¹¹Only Luke is with me. Bring Mark with you when you come, for he will be helpful to me in my ministry. ¹²I sent Tychicus to Ephesus. ¹³When you come, be sure to bring the coat I left with Carpus at Troas. Also bring my books, and especially my papers.*

¹⁴Alexander the copper-smith did me much harm, but the Lord will judge him for what he has done. ¹⁵Be careful of him, for he fought against everything we said.

¹⁶The first time I was brought before the judge, no one came with me. Everyone abandoned me. May it not be counted against them. ¹⁷But the Lord stood with me and gave me strength so that I might preach the Good News in its entirety for all the Gentiles to hear. And he rescued me from certain death.*

¹⁸Yes, and the Lord will deliver me from every evil attack and will bring me safely into his heavenly Kingdom. All glory to God forever and ever! Amen.

¹⁹Give my greetings to Priscilla and Aquila and those living in the household of Onesiphorus. ²⁰Erastus stayed at Corinth, and I left Trophimus sick at Miletus.

²¹Do your best to get here before winter. Eubulus sends you greetings, and so do Pudens, Linus, Claudia, and all the brothers and sisters.*

²²May the Lord be with your spirit. And may his grace be with all of you.

4:13 Greek *especially the parchments.*   **4:17** Greek *from the mouth of a lion.*   **4:21** Greek *brothers.*

PSALM 95:1–96:13

Come, let us sing to the LORD!
Let us shout joyfully to the Rock
of our salvation.
² Let us come to him with thanksgiving.
Let us sing psalms of praise
to him.
³ For the LORD is a great God,
a great King above all gods.
⁴ He holds in his hands the depths of
the earth
and the mightiest mountains.
⁵ The sea belongs to him, for he
made it.
His hands formed the dry
land, too.

⁶ Come, let us worship and bow down.
Let us kneel before the LORD our
maker,
⁷   for he is our God.
We are the people he watches over,
the flock under his care.

If only you would listen to his
voice today!
⁸ The LORD says, "Don't harden
your hearts as Israel did
at Meribah,
as they did at Massah in the
wilderness.
⁹ For there your ancestors tested and
tried my patience,

even though they saw everything
I did.

¹⁰ For forty years I was angry with
them, and I said,
'They are a people whose hearts turn
away from me.
They refuse to do what I
tell them.'

¹¹ So in my anger I took an oath:
'They will never enter my place
of rest.'"

⁹⁶:¹ SING a new song to the LORD!
Let the whole earth sing to the
LORD!

² Sing to the LORD; praise his name.
Each day proclaim the good news
that he saves.

³ Publish his glorious deeds among
the nations.
Tell everyone about the amazing
things he does.

⁴ Great is the LORD! He is most
worthy of praise!
He is to be feared above all gods.

⁵ The gods of other nations are mere
idols,
but the LORD made the heavens!

⁶ Honor and majesty surround him;
strength and beauty fill his
sanctuary.

⁷ O nations of the world, recognize
the LORD;
recognize that the LORD is
glorious and strong.

⁸ Give to the LORD the glory he deserves!
Bring your offering and come into
his courts.

⁹ Worship the LORD in all his holy
splendor.
Let all the earth tremble
before him.

¹⁰ Tell all the nations, "The LORD
reigns!"
The world stands firm and cannot
be shaken.
He will judge all peoples fairly.

¹¹ Let the heavens be glad, and the
earth rejoice!
Let the sea and everything in it
shout his praise!

¹² Let the fields and their crops burst
out with joy!
Let the trees of the forest rustle
with praise

¹³ before the LORD, for he is coming!
He is coming to judge the earth.
He will judge the world with justice,
and the nations with his truth.

PROVERBS 26:9-12

A proverb in the mouth of a fool is like a
thorny branch brandished by a drunk.
□ An employer who hires a fool or a by-
stander is like an archer who shoots at
random. □ As a dog returns to its vomit,
so a fool repeats his foolishness. □ There
is more hope for fools than for people
who think they are wise.

OCTOBER
26

JEREMIAH 49:23–50:46

This message was given concerning Damascus. This is what the LORD says:

"The towns of Hamath and Arpad
are struck with fear,
for they have heard the news of
their destruction.
Their hearts are troubled
like a wild sea in a raging storm.

²⁴ Damascus has become feeble,
and all her people turn to flee.
Fear, anguish, and pain have
gripped her
as they grip a woman in labor.

²⁵ That famous city, a city of joy,
will be forsaken!

²⁶ Her young men will fall in the
streets and die.
Her soldiers will all be killed,"
says the LORD of Heaven's Armies.

²⁷ "And I will set fire to the walls of
Damascus
that will burn up the palaces of
Ben-hadad."

²⁸This message was given concerning Kedar and the kingdoms of Hazor, which were attacked by King Nebuchadnezzar* of Babylon. This is what the LORD says:

"Advance against Kedar!
  Destroy the warriors from
    the East!
²⁹ Their flocks and tents will be
    captured,
  and their household goods and
    camels will be taken away.
  Everywhere shouts of panic will
    be heard:
  'We are terrorized at every turn!'
³⁰ Run for your lives," says the LORD.
  "Hide yourselves in deep caves,
    you people of Hazor,
  for King Nebuchadnezzar of
    Babylon has plotted against you
    and is preparing to destroy you.

³¹ "Go up and attack that complacent
    nation,"
  says the LORD.
  "Its people live alone in the desert
    without walls or gates.
³² Their camels and other livestock
    will all be yours.
  I will scatter to the winds these
    people
  who live in remote places.*
  I will bring calamity upon them
    from every direction," says the
    LORD.
³³ "Hazor will be inhabited by jackals,
  and it will be desolate forever.
  No one will live there;
    no one will inhabit it."

³⁴This message concerning Elam came to the prophet Jeremiah from the LORD at the beginning of the reign of King Zedekiah of Judah. ³⁵This is what the LORD of Heaven's Armies says:

"I will destroy the archers of Elam—
    the best of their forces.
³⁶ I will bring enemies from all
    directions,
  and I will scatter the people of
    Elam to the four winds.

They will be exiled to countries
    around the world.
³⁷ I myself will go with Elam's enemies
    to shatter it.
  In my fierce anger, I will bring
    great disaster
  upon the people of Elam," says
    the LORD.
  "Their enemies will chase them with
    the sword
  until I have destroyed them
    completely.
³⁸ I will set my throne in Elam," says
    the LORD,
  "and I will destroy its king and
    officials.
³⁹ But I will restore the fortunes of
    Elam
  in days to come.
  I, the LORD, have spoken!"

⁵⁰:¹THE LORD gave Jeremiah the prophet this message concerning Babylon and the land of the Babylonians.* ²This is what the LORD says:

"Tell the whole world,
  and keep nothing back.
Raise a signal flag
  to tell everyone that Babylon will
    fall!
Her images and idols* will be
    shattered.
  Her gods Bel and Marduk will be
    utterly disgraced.
³ For a nation will attack her from
    the north
  and bring such destruction that
    no one will live there again.
Everything will be gone;
  both people and animals will flee.

⁴ "In those coming days,"
    says the LORD,
  "the people of Israel will return
    home
  together with the people of Judah.
They will come weeping
  and seeking the LORD their God.
⁵ They will ask the way to Jerusalem*
  and will start back home again.
They will bind themselves to
    the LORD

with an eternal covenant that will
never be forgotten.

6 "My people have been lost sheep.
   Their shepherds have led
      them astray
   and turned them loose in the
      mountains.
   They have lost their way
      and can't remember how to get
      back to the sheepfold.
7 All who found them devoured them.
   Their enemies said,
   'We did nothing wrong in attacking
      them,
      for they sinned against the LORD,
   their true place of rest,
      and the hope of their ancestors.'

8 "But now, flee from Babylon!
   Leave the land of the Babylonians.
   Like male goats at the head of the
      flock,
      lead my people home again.
9 For I am raising up an army
      of great nations from the north.
   They will join forces to attack
      Babylon,
      and she will be captured.
   The enemies' arrows will go straight
      to the mark;
      they will not miss!
10 Babylonia* will be looted
      until the attackers are glutted
      with loot.
   I, the LORD, have spoken!

11 "You rejoice and are glad,
      you who plundered my chosen
      people.
   You frisk about like a calf in a
      meadow
      and neigh like a stallion.
12 But your homeland* will be
      overwhelmed
      with shame and disgrace.
   You will become the least of
      nations—
      a wilderness, a dry and desolate
      land.
13 Because of the LORD's anger,
      Babylon will become a deserted
      wasteland.

All who pass by will be horrified
   and will gasp at the destruction
   they see there.

14 "Yes, prepare to attack Babylon,
      all you surrounding nations.
   Let your archers shoot at her; spare
      no arrows.
   For she has sinned against
      the LORD.
15 Shout war cries against her from
      every side.
   Look! She surrenders!
   Her walls have fallen.
   It is the LORD's vengeance,
      so take vengeance on her.
   Do to her as she has done to
      others!
16 Take from Babylon all those who
      plant crops;
      send all the harvesters away.
   Because of the sword of the enemy,
      everyone will run away and rush
      back to their own lands.

17 "The Israelites are like sheep
      that have been scattered by lions.
   First the king of Assyria ate them up.
      Then King Nebuchadnezzar* of
      Babylon cracked their bones."
18 Therefore, this is what the LORD of
      Heaven's Armies,
      the God of Israel, says:
   "Now I will punish the king of
      Babylon and his land,
      just as I punished the king
      of Assyria.
19 And I will bring Israel home again to
      its own land,
      to feed in the fields of Carmel and
      Bashan,
   and to be satisfied once more
      in the hill country of Ephraim and
      Gilead.
20 In those days," says the LORD,
      "no sin will be found in Israel or
      in Judah,
      for I will forgive the remnant I
      preserve.

21 "Go up, my warriors, against the land
      of Merathaim
      and against the people of Pekod.

Pursue, kill, and completely destroy*
    them,
    as I have commanded you," says
        the LORD.
22 "Let the battle cry be heard in the
    land,
    a shout of great destruction.
23 Babylon, the mightiest hammer in
    all the earth,
    lies broken and shattered.
    Babylon is desolate among
        the nations!
24 Listen, Babylon, for I have set a trap
    for you.
    You are caught, for you have
        fought against the LORD.
25 The LORD has opened his armory
    and brought out weapons to vent
        his fury.
    The terror that falls upon the
        Babylonians
    will be the work of the
        Sovereign LORD of Heaven's
        Armies.
26 Yes, come against her from distant
    lands.
    Break open her granaries.
    Crush her walls and houses into
        heaps of rubble.
    Destroy her completely,
        and leave nothing!
27 Destroy even her young bulls—
    it will be terrible for them, too!
    Slaughter them all!
    For Babylon's day of reckoning
        has come.
28 Listen to the people who have
        escaped from Babylon,
    as they tell in Jerusalem
    how the LORD our God has taken
        vengeance
        against those who destroyed
        his Temple.

29 "Send out a call for archers to come
    to Babylon.
    Surround the city so none
        can escape.
    Do to her as she has done
        to others,
    for she has defied the LORD, the
        Holy One of Israel.

30 Her young men will fall in the
    streets and die.
    Her soldiers will all be killed,"
        says the LORD.

31 "See, I am your enemy, you arrogant
    people,"
    says the Lord, the LORD of
        Heaven's Armies.
    "Your day of reckoning has arrived—
        the day when I will punish you.
32 O land of arrogance, you will
    stumble and fall,
    and no one will raise you up.
    For I will light a fire in the cities of
        Babylon
    that will burn up everything
        around them."

33 This is what the LORD of Heaven's
    Armies says:
    "The people of Israel and Judah have
        been wronged.
    Their captors hold them and
        refuse to let them go.
34 But the one who redeems them
    is strong.
    His name is the LORD of Heaven's
        Armies.
    He will defend them
        and give them rest again in Israel.
    But for the people of Babylon
        there will be no rest!

35 "The sword of destruction will strike
    the Babylonians,"
    says the LORD.
    "It will strike the people of
        Babylon—
        her officials and wise men, too.
36 The sword will strike her wise
    counselors,
        and they will become fools.
    The sword will strike her mightiest
        warriors,
        and panic will seize them.
37 The sword will strike her horses
    and chariots
        and her allies from other lands,
        and they will all become like
            women.
    The sword will strike her treasures,
        and they all will be plundered.

38 The sword will even strike her water
        supply,
    causing it to dry up.
And why? Because the whole land is
        filled with idols,
    and the people are madly in love
        with them.

39 "Soon Babylon will be inhabited by
        desert animals and hyenas.
    It will be a home for owls.
Never again will people live there;
    it will lie desolate forever.

40 I will destroy it as I* destroyed
        Sodom and Gomorrah
    and their neighboring towns,"
        says the LORD.
"No one will live there;
    no one will inhabit it.

41 "Look! A great army is coming from
        the north.
    A great nation and many kings
    are rising against you from far-off
        lands.

42 They are armed with bows and
        spears.
    They are cruel and show no
        mercy.
As they ride forward on horses,
    they sound like a roaring sea.
They are coming in battle formation,
    planning to destroy you, Babylon.

43 The king of Babylon has heard
        reports about the enemy,
    and he is weak with fright.
Pangs of anguish have gripped him,
    like those of a woman in labor.

44 "I will come like a lion from the
        thickets of the Jordan,
    leaping on the sheep in the
        pasture.
I will chase Babylon from its land,
    and I will appoint the leader
        of my choice.
For who is like me, and who can
        challenge me?
    What ruler can oppose my will?"

45 Listen to the LORD's plans against
        Babylon
    and the land of the Babylonians.

Even the little children will be
        dragged off like sheep,
    and their homes will be
        destroyed.
46 The earth will shake with the shout,
        "Babylon has been taken!"
    and its cry of despair will be
        heard around the world.

49:28 Hebrew *Nebuchadrezzar*, a variant spelling of
Nebuchadnezzar; also in 49:30.   49:32 Or *who clip the
corners of their hair.*   50:1 Or *Chaldeans;* also in 50:8, 25,
35, 45.   50:2 The Hebrew term (literally *round things*)
probably alludes to dung.   50:5 Hebrew *Zion;* also in
50:28.   50:10 Or *Chaldea.*   50:12 Hebrew *your mother.*
50:17 Hebrew *Nebuchadrezzar,* a variant spelling of
Nebuchadnezzar.   50:21 The Hebrew term used here
refers to the complete consecration of things or people to
the LORD, either by destroying them or by giving them as an
offering.   50:40 Hebrew *as God.*

TITUS 1:1-16

This letter is from Paul, a slave of God
and an apostle of Jesus Christ. I have
been sent to proclaim faith to* those
God has chosen and to teach them to
know the truth that shows them how to
live godly lives. 2 This truth gives them
confidence that they have eternal life,
which God—who does not lie—promised them before the world began. 3 And
now at just the right time he has revealed
this message, which we announce to
everyone. It is by the command of God
our Savior that I have been entrusted
with this work for him.

4 I am writing to Titus, my true son in
the faith that we share.

May God the Father and Christ Jesus
our Savior give you grace and peace.

5 I left you on the island of Crete so
you could complete our work there and
appoint elders in each town as I instructed you. 6 An elder must live a
blameless life. He must be faithful to
his wife,* and his children must be believers who don't have a reputation for
being wild or rebellious. 7 For an elder*
must live a blameless life. He must not
be arrogant or quick-tempered; he
must not be a heavy drinker,* violent, or
dishonest with money.

8 Rather, he must enjoy having guests
in his home, and he must love what is
good. He must live wisely and be just. He
must live a devout and disciplined life.

⁹He must have a strong belief in the trustworthy message he was taught; then he will be able to encourage others with wholesome teaching and show those who oppose it where they are wrong.

¹⁰For there are many rebellious people who engage in useless talk and deceive others. This is especially true of those who insist on circumcision for salvation. ¹¹They must be silenced, because they are turning whole families away from the truth by their false teaching. And they do it only for money. ¹²Even one of their own men, a prophet from Crete, has said about them, "The people of Crete are all liars, cruel animals, and lazy gluttons."* ¹³This is true. So reprimand them sternly to make them strong in the faith. ¹⁴They must stop listening to Jewish myths and the commands of people who have turned away from the truth.

¹⁵Everything is pure to those whose hearts are pure. But nothing is pure to those who are corrupt and unbelieving, because their minds and consciences are corrupted. ¹⁶Such people claim they know God, but they deny him by the way they live. They are detestable and disobedient, worthless for doing anything good.

1:1 Or *to strengthen the faith of.* 1:6 Or *must have only one wife,* or *must be married only once;* Greek reads *must be the husband of one wife.* 1:7a Or *an overseer,* or *a bishop.* 1:7b Greek *must not drink too much wine.* 1:12 This quotation is from Epimenides of Knossos.

PSALM 97:1–98:9

The LORD is king!
  Let the earth rejoice!
  Let the farthest coastlands
    be glad.
² Dark clouds surround him.
  Righteousness and justice are the
    foundation of his throne.
³ Fire spreads ahead of him
  and burns up all his foes.
⁴ His lightning flashes out across
    the world.
  The earth sees and trembles.
⁵ The mountains melt like wax before
    the LORD,
  before the Lord of all the earth.

⁶ The heavens proclaim his
    righteousness;
  every nation sees his glory.
⁷ Those who worship idols are
    disgraced—
  all who brag about their
    worthless gods—
  for every god must bow to him.
⁸ Jerusalem* has heard and rejoiced,
  and all the towns of Judah
    are glad
  because of your justice, O LORD!
⁹ For you, O LORD, are supreme over
    all the earth;
  you are exalted far above all gods.

¹⁰ You who love the LORD, hate evil!
  He protects the lives of his
    godly people
  and rescues them from the power
    of the wicked.
¹¹ Light shines on the godly,
  and joy on those whose hearts
    are right.
¹² May all who are godly rejoice
    in the LORD
  and praise his holy name!

98:1 SING a new song to the LORD,
  for he has done wonderful deeds.
  His right hand has won a mighty
    victory;
  his holy arm has shown his
    saving power!
² The LORD has announced
    his victory
  and has revealed his
    righteousness to every nation!
³ He has remembered his promise to
    love and be faithful to Israel.
  The ends of the earth have seen
    the victory of our God.

⁴ Shout to the LORD, all the earth;
  break out in praise and sing for joy!
⁵ Sing your praise to the LORD with
    the harp,
  with the harp and melodious song,
⁶ with trumpets and the sound of the
    ram's horn.
  Make a joyful symphony before
    the LORD, the King!

⁷ Let the sea and everything in it shout
    his praise!
    Let the earth and all living things
        join in.
⁸ Let the rivers clap their hands
        in glee!
    Let the hills sing out their songs
        of joy
⁹ before the LORD.
    For the LORD is coming to judge
        the earth.
    He will judge the world with justice,
        and the nations with fairness.

97:8 Hebrew *Zion*.

PROVERBS 26:13-16

The lazy person claims, "There's a lion on the road! Yes, I'm sure there's a lion out there!" □ As a door swings back and forth on its hinges, so the lazy person turns over in bed. □ Lazy people take food in their hand but don't even lift it to their mouth. □ Lazy people consider themselves smarter than seven wise counselors.

OCTOBER 27

JEREMIAH 51:1-53

This is what the LORD says:
"I will stir up a destroyer against
    Babylon
    and the people of Babylonia.*
² Foreigners will come and
        winnow her,
    blowing her away as chaff.
    They will come from every side
        to rise against her in her
            day of trouble.
³ Don't let the archers put on their
        armor
    or draw their bows.
    Don't spare even her best soldiers!
    Let her army be completely
        destroyed.*

⁴ They will fall dead in the land of the
        Babylonians,*
    slashed to death in her streets.
⁵ For the LORD of Heaven's Armies
    has not abandoned Israel and
        Judah.
    He is still their God,
        even though their land was filled
            with sin
    against the Holy One of Israel."

⁶ Flee from Babylon! Save yourselves!
    Don't get trapped in her
        punishment!
    It is the LORD's time for vengeance;
        he will repay her in full.
⁷ Babylon has been a gold cup in
        the LORD's hands,
    a cup that made the whole earth
        drunk.
    The nations drank Babylon's wine,
        and it drove them all mad.
⁸ But suddenly Babylon, too, has fallen.
    Weep for her.
    Give her medicine.
        Perhaps she can yet be healed.
⁹ We would have helped her
        if we could,
    but nothing can save her now.
    Let her go; abandon her.
    Return now to your own land.
    For her punishment reaches to the
        heavens;
        it is so great it cannot be
            measured.
¹⁰ The LORD has vindicated us.
    Come, let us announce in
        Jerusalem*
    everything the LORD our God
        has done.

¹¹ Sharpen the arrows!
    Lift up the shields!*
    For the LORD has inspired the kings
        of the Medes
    to march against Babylon and
        destroy her.
    This is his vengeance against those
        who desecrated his Temple.
¹² Raise the battle flag against Babylon!
    Reinforce the guard and station
        the watchmen.

Prepare an ambush,
  for the LORD will fulfill all his
    plans against Babylon.
¹³ You are a city by a great river,
  a great center of commerce,
  but your end has come.
  The thread of your life is cut.
¹⁴ The LORD of Heaven's Armies has
    taken this vow
  and has sworn to it by his
    own name:
  "Your cities will be filled with
    enemies,
  like fields swarming with locusts,
  and they will shout in triumph
    over you."

¹⁵ The LORD made the earth by
    his power,
  and he preserves it by his wisdom.
  With his own understanding
    he stretched out the heavens.
¹⁶ When he speaks in the thunder,
  the heavens are filled with water.
  He causes the clouds to rise over
    the earth.
  He sends the lightning with
    the rain
  and releases the wind from
    his storehouses.

¹⁷ The whole human race is foolish
    and has no knowledge!
  The craftsmen are disgraced by
    the idols they make,
  for their carefully shaped works are
    a fraud.
  These idols have no breath
    or power.
¹⁸ Idols are worthless; they are
    ridiculous lies!
  On the day of reckoning they will
    all be destroyed.
¹⁹ But the God of Israel* is no idol!
  He is the Creator of everything
    that exists,
  including his people, his own special
    possession.
  The LORD of Heaven's Armies is
    his name!

²⁰ "You* are my battle-ax and sword,"
  says the LORD.

"With you I will shatter nations
    and destroy many kingdoms.
²¹ With you I will shatter armies—
  destroying the horse and rider,
    the chariot and charioteer.
²² With you I will shatter men
    and women,
  old people and children,
  young men and maidens.
²³ With you I will shatter shepherds
    and flocks,
  farmers and oxen,
  captains and officers.

²⁴ "I will repay Babylon
    and the people of Babylonia*
  for all the wrong they have done
    to my people in Jerusalem," says
      the LORD.

²⁵ "Look, O mighty mountain,
    destroyer of the earth!
  I am your enemy," says the LORD.
  "I will raise my fist against you,
    to knock you down from the
      heights.
  When I am finished,
    you will be nothing but a heap of
      burnt rubble.
²⁶ You will be desolate forever.
  Even your stones will never again
    be used for building.
  You will be completely wiped out,"
    says the LORD.

²⁷ Raise a signal flag to the nations.
  Sound the battle cry!
  Mobilize them all against Babylon.
    Prepare them to fight
      against her!
  Bring out the armies of Ararat,
    Minni, and Ashkenaz.
  Appoint a commander,
    and bring a multitude of horses
      like swarming locusts!
²⁸ Bring against her the armies of the
    nations—
  led by the kings of the Medes
    and all their captains and officers.

²⁹ The earth trembles and writhes
    in pain,
  for everything the LORD has

planned against Babylon stands
unchanged.
Babylon will be left desolate without
a single inhabitant.
30   Her mightiest warriors no
longer fight.
They stay in their barracks, their
courage gone.
They have become like women.
The invaders have burned the houses
and broken down the city gates.
31 The news is passed from one runner
to the next
as the messengers hurry to tell
the king
that his city has been captured.
32 All the escape routes are blocked.
The marshes have been set
aflame,
and the army is in a panic.

33 This is what the LORD of Heaven's
Armies,
the God of Israel, says:
"Babylon is like wheat on a
threshing floor,
about to be trampled.
In just a little while
her harvest will begin."

34 "King Nebuchadnezzar* of Babylon
has eaten and crushed us
and drained us of strength.
He has swallowed us like a great
monster
and filled his belly with our
riches.
He has thrown us out of our own
country.
35 Make Babylon suffer as she made
us suffer,"
say the people of Zion.
"Make the people of Babylonia pay
for spilling our blood,"
says Jerusalem.

36This is what the LORD says to Jerusalem:

"I will be your lawyer to plead
your case,
and I will avenge you.
I will dry up her river,

as well as her springs,
37 and Babylon will become a heap
of ruins,
haunted by jackals.
She will be an object of horror
and contempt,
a place where no one lives.
38 Her people will roar together like
strong lions.
They will growl like lion cubs.
39 And while they lie inflamed with all
their wine,
I will prepare a different kind of
feast for them.
I will make them drink until they
fall asleep,
and they will never wake up again,"
says the LORD.
40 "I will bring them down
like lambs to the slaughter,
like rams and goats to be sacrificed.

41 "How Babylon* is fallen—
great Babylon, praised throughout
the earth!
Now she has become an object
of horror
among the nations.
42 The sea has risen over Babylon;
she is covered by its crashing
waves.
43 Her cities now lie in ruins;
she is a dry wasteland
where no one lives or even
passes by.
44 And I will punish Bel, the god of
Babylon,
and make him vomit up all he
has eaten.
The nations will no longer come and
worship him.
The wall of Babylon has fallen!

45 "Come out, my people, flee
from Babylon.
Save yourselves! Run from the
LORD's fierce anger.
46 But do not panic; don't be afraid
when you hear the first rumor of
approaching forces.
For rumors will keep coming year
by year.

Violence will erupt in the land
    as the leaders fight against
    each other.
[47] For the time is surely coming
    when I will punish this great city
    and all her idols.
Her whole land will be disgraced,
    and her dead will lie in
    the streets.
[48] Then the heavens and earth
    will rejoice,
    for out of the north will come
      destroying armies
    against Babylon," says the LORD.
[49] "Just as Babylon killed the people
    of Israel
    and others throughout
      the world,
    so must her people be killed.
[50] Get out, all you who have escaped
    the sword!
Do not stand and watch—flee
    while you can!
Remember the LORD, though
    you are in a far-off land,
    and think about your home
    in Jerusalem."

[51] "We are ashamed," the people say.
    "We are insulted and
      disgraced
because the LORD's Temple
    has been defiled by foreigners."

[52] "Yes," says the LORD, "but the time
    is coming
    when I will destroy Babylon's idols.
The groans of her wounded people
    will be heard throughout
    the land.
[53] Though Babylon reaches as high as
    the heavens
    and makes her fortifications
      incredibly strong,
I will still send enemies to
      plunder her.
I, the LORD, have spoken!"

51:1 Hebrew *of Leb-kamai*, a code name for Babylonia.
51:3 The Hebrew term used here refers to the complete consecration of things or people to the LORD, either by destroying them or by giving them as an offering.   51:4 Or *Chaldeans;* also in 51:54.   51:10 Hebrew *Zion;* also in 51:24.   51:11 Greek version reads *Fill up the quivers.* 51:19 Hebrew *the Portion of Jacob.* See note on 5:20.

51:20 Possibly Cyrus, whom God used to conquer Babylon. Compare Isa 44:28; 45:1.   51:24 Or *Chaldea;* also in 51:35.   51:34 Hebrew *Nebuchadrezzar,* a variant spelling of Nebuchadnezzar.   51:41 Hebrew *Sheshach,* a code name for Babylon.

TITUS 2:1-15

As for you, Titus, promote the kind of living that reflects wholesome teaching. [2] Teach the older men to exercise self-control, to be worthy of respect, and to live wisely. They must have sound faith and be filled with love and patience.

[3] Similarly, teach the older women to live in a way that honors God. They must not slander others or be heavy drinkers.* Instead, they should teach others what is good. [4] These older women must train the younger women to love their husbands and their children, [5] to live wisely and be pure, to work in their homes,* to do good, and to be submissive to their husbands. Then they will not bring shame on the word of God.

[6] In the same way, encourage the young men to live wisely. [7] And you yourself must be an example to them by doing good works of every kind. Let everything you do reflect the integrity and seriousness of your teaching. [8] Teach the truth so that your teaching can't be criticized. Then those who oppose us will be ashamed and have nothing bad to say about us.

[9] Slaves must always obey their masters and do their best to please them. They must not talk back [10] or steal, but must show themselves to be entirely trustworthy and good. Then they will make the teaching about God our Savior attractive in every way.

[11] For the grace of God has been revealed, bringing salvation to all people. [12] And we are instructed to turn from godless living and sinful pleasures. We should live in this evil world with wisdom, righteousness, and devotion to God, [13] while we look forward with hope to that wonderful day when the glory of our great God and Savior, Jesus Christ, will be revealed. [14] He gave his life to free us from every kind of sin, to cleanse us, and

to make us his very own people, totally committed to doing good deeds.

¹⁵You must teach these things and encourage the believers to do them. You have the authority to correct them when necessary, so don't let anyone disregard what you say.

2:3 Greek *be enslaved to much wine.*   2:5 Some manuscripts read *to care for their homes.*

PSALM 99:1-9
The Lord is king!
    Let the nations tremble!
He sits on his throne between
        the cherubim.
    Let the whole earth quake!
² The Lord sits in majesty in
        Jerusalem,*
    exalted above all the nations.
³ Let them praise your great and
        awesome name.
    Your name is holy!
⁴ **Mighty King, lover of justice,**
    you have established fairness.
You have acted with justice
    and righteousness throughout
    Israel.*
⁵ **Exalt the Lord our God!**
    Bow low before his feet, for
    he is holy!

⁶ Moses and Aaron were among
        his priests;
    Samuel also called on
        his name.
They cried to the Lord for help,
    and he answered them.
⁷ He spoke to Israel from the pillar
        of cloud,
    and they followed the laws and
        decrees he gave them.
⁸ O Lord our God, you answered
        them.
    You were a forgiving God
        to them,
    but you punished them when
        they went wrong.

⁹ Exalt the Lord our God,
    and worship at his holy mountain
        in Jerusalem,
    for the Lord our God is holy!

99:2 Hebrew *Zion.*   99:4 Hebrew *Jacob.* See note on 44:4.

PROVERBS 26:17
Interfering in someone else's argument is as foolish as yanking a dog's ears.

OCTOBER
28

JEREMIAH 51:54–52:34
"Listen! Hear the cry of Babylon,
    the sound of great destruction
        from the land of the
        Babylonians.
⁵⁵ For the Lord is destroying
        Babylon.
    He will silence her loud voice.
Waves of enemies pound against
        her;
    the noise of battle rings through
        the city.
⁵⁶ Destroying armies come against
        Babylon.
    Her mighty men are captured,
    and their weapons break
        in their hands.
For the Lord is a God who gives
        just punishment;
    he always repays in full.
⁵⁷ I will make her officials and wise
        men drunk,
    along with her captains, officers,
        and warriors.
They will fall asleep
    and never wake up again!"
says the King, whose name is
    the Lord of Heaven's Armies.

⁵⁸ This is what the Lord of Heaven's
        Armies says:
"The thick walls of Babylon will be
        leveled to the ground,
    and her massive gates will
        be burned.
The builders from many lands have
        worked in vain,
    for their work will be destroyed
        by fire!"

59 The prophet Jeremiah gave this message to Seraiah son of Neriah and grandson of Mahseiah, a staff officer, when Seraiah went to Babylon with King Zedekiah of Judah. This was during the fourth year of Zedekiah's reign.* 60 Jeremiah had recorded on a scroll all the terrible disasters that would soon come upon Babylon—all the words written here. 61 He said to Seraiah, "When you get to Babylon, read aloud everything on this scroll. 62 Then say, 'LORD, you have said that you will destroy Babylon so that neither people nor animals will remain here. She will lie empty and abandoned forever.' 63 When you have finished reading the scroll, tie it to a stone and throw it into the Euphrates River. 64 Then say, 'In this same way Babylon and her people will sink, never again to rise, because of the disasters I will bring upon her.'"

This is the end of Jeremiah's messages.

52:1 ZEDEKIAH was twenty-one years old when he became king, and he reigned in Jerusalem eleven years. His mother was Hamutal, the daughter of Jeremiah from Libnah. 2 But Zedekiah did what was evil in the LORD's sight, just as Jehoiakim had done. 3 These things happened because of the LORD's anger against the people of Jerusalem and Judah, until he finally banished them from his presence and sent them into exile.

Zedekiah rebelled against the king of Babylon. 4 So on January 15,* during the ninth year of Zedekiah's reign, King Nebuchadnezzar* of Babylon led his entire army against Jerusalem. They surrounded the city and built siege ramps against its walls. 5 Jerusalem was kept under siege until the eleventh year of King Zedekiah's reign.

6 By July 18 in the eleventh year of Zedekiah's reign,* the famine in the city had become very severe, and the last of the food was entirely gone. 7 Then a section of the city wall was broken down, and all the soldiers fled. Since the city was surrounded by the Babylonians,* they waited for nightfall. Then they slipped through the gate between the two walls behind the king's garden and headed toward the Jordan Valley.*

8 But the Babylonian troops chased King Zedekiah and caught him on the plains of Jericho, for his men had all deserted him and scattered. 9 They took him to the king of Babylon at Riblah in the land of Hamath. There the king of Babylon pronounced judgment upon Zedekiah. 10 He made Zedekiah watch as they slaughtered his sons and all the other officials of Judah. 11 Then they gouged out Zedekiah's eyes, bound him in bronze chains, and led him away to Babylon. Zedekiah remained there in prison until the day of his death.

12 On August 17 of that year,* which was the nineteenth year of King Nebuchadnezzar's reign, Nebuzaradan, the captain of the guard and an official of the Babylonian king, arrived in Jerusalem. 13 He burned down the Temple of the LORD, the royal palace, and all the houses of Jerusalem. He destroyed all the important buildings* in the city. 14 Then he supervised the entire Babylonian* army as they tore down the walls of Jerusalem on every side. 15 Nebuzaradan, the captain of the guard, then took as exiles some of the poorest of the people, the rest of the people who remained in the city, the defectors who had declared their allegiance to the king of Babylon, and the rest of the craftsmen. 16 But Nebuzaradan allowed some of the poorest people to stay behind in Judah to care for the vineyards and fields.

17 The Babylonians broke up the bronze pillars in front of the LORD's Temple, the bronze water carts, and the great bronze basin called the Sea, and they carried all the bronze away to Babylon. 18 They also took all the ash buckets, shovels, lamp snuffers, basins, dishes, and all the other bronze articles used for making sacrifices at the Temple. 19 Nebuzaradan, the captain of the guard, also took the small bowls, incense burners, basins, pots, lampstands,

dishes, bowls used for liquid offerings, and all the other articles made of pure gold or silver.

20The weight of the bronze from the two pillars, the Sea with the twelve bronze oxen beneath it, and the water carts was too great to be measured. These things had been made for the LORD's Temple in the days of King Solomon. 21Each of the pillars was 27 feet tall and 18 feet in circumference.* They were hollow, with walls 3 inches thick.* 22The bronze capital on top of each pillar was 7½ feet* high and was decorated with a network of bronze pomegranates all the way around. 23There were 96 pomegranates on the sides, and a total of 100 on the network around the top.

24Nebuzaradan, the captain of the guard, took with him as prisoners Seraiah the high priest, Zephaniah the priest of the second rank, and the three chief gatekeepers. 25And from among the people still hiding in the city, he took an officer who had been in charge of the Judean army; seven of the king's personal advisers; the army commander's chief secretary, who was in charge of recruitment; and sixty other citizens. 26Nebuzaradan, the captain of the guard, took them all to the king of Babylon at Riblah. 27And there at Riblah, in the land of Hamath, the king of Babylon had them all put to death. So the people of Judah were sent into exile from their land.

28The number of captives taken to Babylon in the seventh year of Nebuchadnezzar's reign* was 3,023. 29Then in Nebuchadnezzar's eighteenth year* he took 832 more. 30In Nebuchadnezzar's twenty-third year* he sent Nebuzaradan, the captain of the guard, who took 745 more—a total of 4,600 captives in all.

31In the thirty-seventh year of the exile of King Jehoiachin of Judah, Evilmerodach ascended to the Babylonian throne. He was kind to* Jehoiachin and released him from prison on March 31 of that year.* 32He spoke kindly to Je-

hoiachin and gave him a higher place than all the other exiled kings in Babylon. 33He supplied Jehoiachin with new clothes to replace his prison garb and allowed him to dine in the king's presence for the rest of his life. 34So the Babylonian king gave him a regular food allowance as long as he lived. This continued until the day of his death.

51:59 The fourth year of Zedekiah's reign was 593 B.C. 52:4a Hebrew *on the tenth day of the tenth month,* of the ancient Hebrew lunar calendar. A number of events in Jeremiah can be cross-checked with dates in surviving Babylonian records and related accurately to our modern calendar. This day was January 15, 588 B.C. 52:4b Hebrew *Nebuchadrezzar,* a variant spelling of Nebuchadnezzar; also in 52:12, 28, 29, 30. 52:6 Hebrew *By the ninth day of the fourth month* [in the eleventh year of Zedekiah's reign]. This day was July 18, 586 B.C.; also see note on 52:4a. 52:7a Or *the Chaldeans;* similarly in 52:8, 17. 52:7b Hebrew *the Arabah.* 52:12 Hebrew *On the tenth day of the fifth month,* of the ancient Hebrew lunar calendar. This day was August 17, 586 B.C.; also see note on 52:4a. 52:13 Or *destroyed the houses of all the important people.* 52:14 Or *Chaldean.* 52:21a Hebrew *18 cubits* [8.1 meters] *tall and 12 cubits* [5.4 meters] *in circumference.* 52:21b Hebrew *4 fingers thick* [8 centimeters]. 52:22 Hebrew *5 cubits* [2.3 meters]. 52:28 This exile in the seventh year of Nebuchadnezzar's reign occurred in 597 B.C. 52:29 This exile in the eighteenth year of Nebuchadnezzar's reign occurred in 586 B.C. 52:30 This exile in the twenty-third year of Nebuchadnezzar's reign occurred in 581 B.C. 52:31a Hebrew *He raised the head of.* 52:31b Hebrew *on the twenty-fifth day of the twelfth month,* of the ancient lunar Hebrew calendar. This day was March 31, 561 B.C.; also see note on 52:4a.

TITUS 3:1-15

Remind the believers to submit to the government and its officers. They should be obedient, always ready to do what is good. 2They must not slander anyone and must avoid quarreling. Instead, they should be gentle and show true humility to everyone.

3Once we, too, were foolish and disobedient. We were misled and became slaves to many lusts and pleasures. Our lives were full of evil and envy, and we hated each other.

4But—"When God our Savior revealed his kindness and love, 5he saved us, not because of the righteous things we had done, but because of his mercy. He washed away our sins, giving us a new birth and new life through the Holy Spirit.* 6He generously poured out the Spirit upon us through Jesus Christ our Savior. 7Because of his grace he declared us righteous and gave us confidence that we will inherit eternal life." ⁸This is a trustworthy saying, and I want you to insist on these teachings so that all who trust in God will devote themselves to doing good. These teachings are good and beneficial for everyone.

⁹Do not get involved in foolish discussions about spiritual pedigrees* or in quarrels and fights about obedience to Jewish laws. These things are useless and a waste of time. ¹⁰If people are causing divisions among you, give a first and second warning. After that, have nothing more to do with them. ¹¹For people like that have turned away from the truth, and their own sins condemn them.

¹²I am planning to send either Artemas or Tychicus to you. As soon as one of them arrives, do your best to meet me at Nicopolis, for I have decided to stay there for the winter. ¹³Do everything you can to help Zenas the lawyer and Apollos with their trip. See that they are given everything they need. ¹⁴Our people must learn to do good by meeting the urgent needs of others; then they will not be unproductive.

¹⁵Everybody here sends greetings. Please give my greetings to the believers—all who love us.

May God's grace be with you all.

3:5 Greek *He saved us through the washing of regeneration and renewing of the Holy Spirit.* 3:9 Or *spiritual genealogies.*

PSALM 100:1-5
A psalm of thanksgiving.

¹ **S**hout with joy to the LORD, all
    the earth!
² 	Worship the LORD with
        gladness.
    Come before him, singing
        with joy.
³ Acknowledge that the LORD is God!
    He made us, and we are his.
    We are his people, the sheep of
        his pasture.
⁴ **Enter his gates with thanksgiving;**
    go into his courts with praise.
    Give thanks to him and praise
        his name.
⁵ **For the LORD is good.**

His unfailing love continues
    forever,
and his faithfulness continues
    to each generation.

PROVERBS 26:18-19
Just as damaging as a madman shooting a deadly weapon is someone who lies to a friend and then says, "I was only joking."

OCTOBER 29

*LAMENTATIONS 1:1-2:22
Jerusalem, once so full of people,
    is now deserted.
She who was once great among
        the nations
    now sits alone like a widow.
Once the queen of all the earth,
    she is now a slave.

² She sobs through the night;
    tears stream down her cheeks.
Among all her lovers,
    there is no one left to comfort her.
All her friends have betrayed her
    and become her enemies.

³ Judah has been led away into
        captivity,
    oppressed with cruel slavery.
She lives among foreign nations
    and has no place of rest.
Her enemies have chased her down,
    and she has nowhere to turn.

⁴ The roads to Jerusalem* are
        in mourning,
    for crowds no longer come to
        celebrate the festivals.
The city gates are silent,
    her priests groan,
her young women are crying—
    how bitter is her fate!

⁵ Her oppressors have become
    her masters,

and her enemies prosper,
for the LORD has punished
    Jerusalem
    for her many sins.
Her children have been captured
    and taken away to distant lands.

6 All the majesty of beautiful
    Jerusalem*
    has been stripped away.
Her princes are like starving deer
    searching for pasture.
They are too weak to run
    from the pursuing enemy.

7 In the midst of her sadness and
    wandering,
    Jerusalem remembers her
    ancient splendor.
But now she has fallen to her enemy,
    and there is no one to help her.
Her enemy struck her down
    and laughed as she fell.

8 Jerusalem has sinned greatly,
    so she has been tossed away
    like a filthy rag.
All who once honored her now
    despise her,
    for they have seen her stripped
    naked and humiliated.
All she can do is groan
    and hide her face.

9 She defiled herself with immorality
    and gave no thought to her future.
Now she lies in the gutter
    with no one to lift her out.
"LORD, see my misery," she cries.
    "The enemy has triumphed."

10 The enemy has plundered her
    completely,
    taking every precious thing
    she owns.
She has seen foreigners violate her
    sacred Temple,
    the place the LORD had forbidden
    them to enter.

11 Her people groan as they search
    for bread.
    They have sold their treasures for
    food to stay alive.

"O LORD, look," she mourns,
    "and see how I am despised.

12 "Does it mean nothing to you, all you
    who pass by?
    Look around and see if there is
    any suffering like mine,
which the LORD brought on me
    when he erupted in fierce anger.

13 "He has sent fire from heaven that
    burns in my bones.
He has placed a trap in my path
    and turned me back.
He has left me devastated,
    racked with sickness all day long.

14 "He wove my sins into ropes
    to hitch me to a yoke of captivity.
The Lord sapped my strength and
    turned me over to my enemies;
    I am helpless in their hands.

15 "The Lord has treated my
    mighty men
    with contempt.
At his command a great army
    has come
    to crush my young warriors.
The Lord has trampled his
    beloved city*
    like grapes are trampled in
    a winepress.

16 "For all these things I weep;
    tears flow down my cheeks.
No one is here to comfort me;
    any who might encourage me are
    far away.
My children have no future,
    for the enemy has conquered us."

17 Jerusalem reaches out for help,
    but no one comforts her.
Regarding his people Israel,*
    the LORD has said,
"Let their neighbors be their
    enemies!
Let them be thrown away like
    a filthy rag!"

18 "The LORD is right," Jerusalem says,
    "for I rebelled against him.
Listen, people everywhere;
    look upon my anguish and despair,

for my sons and daughters
   have been taken captive to
   distant lands.

¹⁹ "I begged my allies for help,
   but they betrayed me.
My priests and leaders
   starved to death in the city,
even as they searched for food
   to save their lives.

²⁰ "LORD, see my anguish!
   My heart is broken
and my soul despairs,
   for I have rebelled against you.
In the streets the sword kills,
   and at home there is only death.

²¹ "Others heard my groans,
   but no one turned to comfort me.
When my enemies heard about
     my troubles,
   they were happy to see what you
   had done.
Oh, bring the day you promised,
   when they will suffer as I have
   suffered.

²² "Look at all their evil deeds,
   LORD.
   Punish them,
as you have punished me
   for all my sins.
My groans are many,
   and I am sick at heart."

²:¹ THE Lord in his anger
   has cast a dark shadow over
   beautiful Jerusalem.*
The fairest of Israel's cities lies in
   the dust,
   thrown down from the heights
   of heaven.
In his day of great anger,
   the Lord has shown no mercy
   even to his Temple.*

² Without mercy the Lord has
   destroyed
   every home in Israel.*
In his anger he has broken down
   the fortress walls of beautiful
   Jerusalem.*
He has brought them to the ground,

dishonoring the kingdom and
   its rulers.

³ All the strength of Israel
   vanishes beneath his fierce anger.
The Lord has withdrawn his
   protection
   as the enemy attacks.
He consumes the whole land
   of Israel
   like a raging fire.

⁴ He bends his bow against his people,
   as though he were their enemy.
His strength is used against them
   to kill their finest youth.
His fury is poured out like fire
   on beautiful Jerusalem.*

⁵ Yes, the Lord has vanquished Israel
   like an enemy.
He has destroyed her palaces
   and demolished her fortresses.
He has brought unending sorrow
   and tears
   upon beautiful Jerusalem.

⁶ He has broken down his Temple
   as though it were merely a garden
   shelter.
The LORD has blotted out all memory
   of the holy festivals and
   Sabbath days.
Kings and priests fall together
   before his fierce anger.

⁷ The Lord has rejected his own altar;
   he despises his own sanctuary.
He has given Jerusalem's palaces
   to her enemies.
They shout in the LORD's Temple
   as though it were a day
   of celebration.

⁸ The LORD was determined
   to destroy the walls of beautiful
   Jerusalem.
He made careful plans for their
   destruction,
   then did what he had planned.
Therefore, the ramparts and walls
   have fallen down before him.

⁹ Jerusalem's gates have sunk into
   the ground.

He has smashed their locks
    and bars.
Her kings and princes have been
    exiled to distant lands;
    her law has ceased to exist.
Her prophets receive
    no more visions from the LORD.

¹⁰ The leaders of beautiful Jerusalem
    sit on the ground in silence.
They are clothed in burlap
    and throw dust on their heads.
The young women of Jerusalem
    hang their heads in shame.

¹¹ I have cried until the tears no
    longer come;
    my heart is broken.
My spirit is poured out in agony
    as I see the desperate plight
    of my people.
Little children and tiny babies
    are fainting and dying in the
    streets.

¹² They cry out to their mothers,
    "We need food and drink!"
Their lives ebb away in the streets
    like the life of a warrior wounded
    in battle.
They gasp for life
    as they collapse in their
    mothers' arms.

¹³ What can I say about you?
    Who has ever seen such sorrow?
O daughter of Jerusalem,
    to what can I compare your anguish?
O virgin daughter of Zion,
    how can I comfort you?
For your wound is as deep as the sea.
    Who can heal you?

¹⁴ Your prophets have said
    so many foolish things, false
    to the core.
They did not save you from exile
    by pointing out your sins.
Instead, they painted false pictures,
    filling you with false hope.

¹⁵ All who pass by jeer at you.
    They scoff and insult beautiful
    Jerusalem,* saying,

"Is this the city called 'Most
    Beautiful in All the World'
    and 'Joy of All the Earth'?"

¹⁶ All your enemies mock you.
    They scoff and snarl and say,
    "We have destroyed her at last!
We have long waited for
    this day,
    and it is finally here!"

¹⁷ But it is the LORD who did just
    as he planned.
He has fulfilled the promises
    of disaster
    he made long ago.
He has destroyed Jerusalem
    without mercy.
He has caused her enemies to
    gloat over her
    and has given them power
    over her.

¹⁸ Cry aloud* before the Lord,
    O walls of beautiful Jerusalem!
Let your tears flow like a river
    day and night.
Give yourselves no rest;
    give your eyes no relief.

¹⁹ Rise during the night and cry out.
    Pour out your hearts like water
    to the Lord.
Lift up your hands to him
    in prayer,
    pleading for your children,
for in every street
    they are faint with hunger.

²⁰ "O LORD, think about this!
    Should you treat your own
    people this way?
Should mothers eat their own
    children,
    those they once bounced on
    their knees?
Should priests and prophets
    be killed
    within the Lord's Temple?

²¹ "See them lying in the streets—
    young and old,
boys and girls,
    killed by the swords of the enemy.

You have killed them in your anger,
   slaughtering them without mercy.

22 "You have invited terrors from
   all around,
   as though you were calling them
     to a day of feasting.
In the day of the Lord's anger,
   no one has escaped or survived.
The enemy has killed all the
   children
   whom I carried and raised."

1 Each of the first four chapters of this book is an acrostic, laid out in the order of the Hebrew alphabet. The first word of each verse begins with a successive Hebrew letter. Chapters 1, 2, and 4 have one verse for each of the 22 Hebrew letters. Chapter 3 contains 22 stanzas of three verses each. Though chapter 5 has 22 verses, it is not an acrostic. **1:4** Hebrew *Zion;* also in 1:17. **1:6** Hebrew *of the daughter of Zion.* **1:15** Hebrew *the virgin daughter of Judah.* **1:17** Hebrew *Jacob.* The names "Jacob" and "Israel" are often interchanged throughout the Old Testament, referring sometimes to the individual patriarch and sometimes to the nation. **2:1a** Hebrew *the daughter of Zion;* also in 2:8, 10, 18. **2:1b** Hebrew *his footstool.* **2:2a** Hebrew *Jacob;* also in 2:3b. See note on 1:17. **2:2b** Hebrew *the daughter of Judah;* also in 2:5. **2:4** Hebrew *on the tent of the daughter of Zion.* **2:15** Hebrew *the daughter of Jerusalem.* **2:18** Hebrew *Their heart cried.*

PHILEMON 1:1-25

This letter is from Paul, a prisoner for preaching the Good News about Christ Jesus, and from our brother Timothy.

I am writing to Philemon, our beloved co-worker, ²and to our sister Apphia, and to our fellow soldier Archippus, and to the church that meets in your* house.

³May God our Father and the Lord Jesus Christ give you grace and peace.

⁴I always thank my God when I pray for you, Philemon, ⁵because I keep hearing about your faith in the Lord Jesus and your love for all of God's people. ⁶And I am praying that you will put into action the generosity that comes from your faith as you understand and experience all the good things we have in Christ. ⁷Your love has given me much joy and comfort, my brother, for your kindness has often refreshed the hearts of God's people.

⁸That is why I am boldly asking a favor of you. I could demand it in the name of Christ because it is the right thing for you to do. ⁹But because of our love, I prefer simply to ask you. Con-sider this as a request from me—Paul, an old man and now also a prisoner for the sake of Christ Jesus.*

¹⁰I appeal to you to show kindness to my child, Onesimus. I became his father in the faith while here in prison. ¹¹Onesimus* hasn't been of much use to you in the past, but now he is very useful to both of us. ¹²I am sending him back to you, and with him comes my own heart.

¹³I wanted to keep him here with me while I am in these chains for preaching the Good News, and he would have helped me on your behalf. ¹⁴But I didn't want to do anything without your consent. I wanted you to help because you were willing, not because you were forced. ¹⁵It seems Onesimus ran away* for a little while so that you could have him back forever. ¹⁶He is no longer like a slave to you. He is more than a slave, for he is a beloved brother, especially to me. Now he will mean much more to you, both as a man and as a brother in the Lord.

¹⁷So if you consider me your partner, welcome him as you would welcome me. ¹⁸If he has wronged you in any way or owes you anything, charge it to me. ¹⁹I, Paul, write this with my own hand: I will repay it. And I won't mention that you owe me your very soul!

²⁰Yes, my brother, please do me this favor* for the Lord's sake. Give me this encouragement in Christ.

²¹I am confident as I write this letter that you will do what I ask and even more! ²²One more thing—please prepare a guest room for me, for I am hoping that God will answer your prayers and let me return to you soon.

²³Epaphras, my fellow prisoner in Christ Jesus, sends you his greetings. ²⁴So do Mark, Aristarchus, Demas, and Luke, my co-workers.

²⁵May the grace of the Lord Jesus Christ be with your spirit.

2 Throughout this letter, *you* and *your* are singular except in verses 3, 22, and 25. 9 Or *a prisoner of Christ Jesus.* 11 *Onesimus* means "useful." 15 Greek *Onesimus was separated from you.* 20 Greek *onaimen,* a play on the name Onesimus.

PSALM 101:1-8
A psalm of David.

1 **I will sing of your love and**
    justice, Lord.
    I will praise you with songs.
2 **I will be careful to live a**
    blameless life—
    when will you come to help me?
    I will lead a life of integrity
    in my own home.
3 I will refuse to look at
    anything vile and vulgar.
    I hate all who deal crookedly;
    I will have nothing to do
    with them.
4 I will reject perverse ideas
    and stay away from every evil.
5 I will not tolerate people who
    slander their neighbors.
    I will not endure conceit
    and pride.

6 I will search for faithful people
    to be my companions.
    Only those who are above reproach
    will be allowed to serve me.
7 I will not allow deceivers to serve in
    my house,
    and liars will not stay in
    my presence.
8 My daily task will be to ferret out
    the wicked
    and free the city of the Lord
    from their grip.

PROVERBS 26:20
Fire goes out without wood, and quarrels disappear when gossip stops.

OCTOBER 30

LAMENTATIONS 3:1-66
I am the one who has seen
    the afflictions
    that come from the rod of the
    Lord's anger.

2 He has led me into darkness,
    shutting out all light.
3 He has turned his hand against me
    again and again, all day long.

4 He has made my skin and flesh
    grow old.
    He has broken my bones.
5 He has besieged and surrounded me
    with anguish and distress.
6 He has buried me in a dark place,
    like those long dead.

7 He has walled me in, and I cannot
    escape.
    He has bound me in heavy chains.
8 And though I cry and shout,
    he has shut out my prayers.
9 He has blocked my way with a high
    stone wall;
    he has made my road crooked.

10 He has hidden like a bear or a lion,
    waiting to attack me.
11 He has dragged me off the path and
    torn me in pieces,
    leaving me helpless and
    devastated.
12 He has drawn his bow
    and made me the target for
    his arrows.

13 He shot his arrows
    deep into my heart.
14 My own people laugh at me.
    All day long they sing their
    mocking songs.
15 He has filled me with bitterness
    and given me a bitter cup of
    sorrow to drink.

16 He has made me chew on gravel.
    He has rolled me in the dust.
17 Peace has been stripped away,
    and I have forgotten what
    prosperity is.
18 I cry out, "My splendor is gone!
    Everything I had hoped for from
    the Lord is lost!"

19 The thought of my suffering and
    homelessness
    is bitter beyond words.*
20 I will never forget this awful time,

as I grieve over my loss.
²¹ Yet I still dare to hope
    when I remember this:

²² The faithful love of the LORD
        never ends!*
    His mercies never cease.
²³ Great is his faithfulness;
        his mercies begin afresh each
        morning.
²⁴ I say to myself, "The LORD is my
        inheritance;
    therefore, I will hope in him!"

²⁵ The LORD is good to those who
        depend on him,
    to those who search for him.
²⁶ So it is good to wait quietly
    for salvation from the LORD.
²⁷ And it is good for people to submit
        at an early age
    to the yoke of his discipline:

²⁸ Let them sit alone in silence
    beneath the LORD's demands.
²⁹ Let them lie face down in the dust,
    for there may be hope at last.
³⁰ Let them turn the other cheek to
        those who strike them
    and accept the insults of their
        enemies.

³¹ For no one is abandoned
    by the Lord forever.
³² Though he brings grief, he also
        shows compassion
    because of the greatness of his
        unfailing love.
³³ For he does not enjoy hurting people
    or causing them sorrow.

³⁴ If people crush underfoot
    all the prisoners of the land,
³⁵ if they deprive others of their rights
    in defiance of the Most High,
³⁶ if they twist justice in the courts—
    doesn't the Lord see all these
        things?

³⁷ Who can command things
        to happen
    without the Lord's permission?
³⁸ Does not the Most High
    send both calamity and good?

³⁹ Then why should we, mere humans,
        complain
    when we are punished for our sins?

⁴⁰ Instead, let us test and examine our
        ways.
    Let us turn back to the LORD.
⁴¹ Let us lift our hearts and hands
    to God in heaven and say,
⁴² "We have sinned and rebelled,
    and you have not forgiven us.

⁴³ "You have engulfed us with your
        anger, chased us down,
    and slaughtered us without
        mercy.
⁴⁴ You have hidden yourself in a cloud
    so our prayers cannot reach you.
⁴⁵ You have discarded us as refuse
        and garbage
    among the nations.

⁴⁶ "All our enemies
    have spoken out against us.
⁴⁷ We are filled with fear,
    for we are trapped, devastated,
        and ruined."
⁴⁸ Tears stream from my eyes
    because of the destruction
        of my people!

⁴⁹ My tears flow endlessly;
    they will not stop
⁵⁰ until the LORD looks down
    from heaven and sees.
⁵¹ My heart is breaking
    over the fate of all the women
        of Jerusalem.

⁵² My enemies, whom I have
        never harmed,
    hunted me down like a bird.
⁵³ They threw me into a pit
    and dropped stones on me.
⁵⁴ The water rose over my head,
    and I cried out, "This is the end!"

⁵⁵ But I called on your name, LORD,
    from deep within the pit.
⁵⁶ You heard me when I cried, "Listen
        to my pleading!
    Hear my cry for help!"
⁵⁷ Yes, you came when I called;
    you told me, "Do not fear."

⁵⁸ Lord, you are my lawyer! Plead
my case!
For you have redeemed my life.
⁵⁹ You have seen the wrong they have
done to me, LORD.
Be my judge, and prove me right.
⁶⁰ You have seen the vengeful plots
my enemies have laid against
me.

⁶¹ LORD, you have heard the vile names
they call me.
You know all about the plans they
have made.
⁶² My enemies whisper and mutter
as they plot against me all
day long.
⁶³ Look at them! Whether they sit
or stand,
I am the object of their mocking
songs.

⁶⁴ Pay them back, LORD,
for all the evil they have done.
⁶⁵ Give them hard and stubborn
hearts,
and then let your curse fall on
them!
⁶⁶ Chase them down in your anger,
destroying them beneath the
LORD's heavens.

3:19 Or is *wormwood and gall.*   3:22 As in Syriac version;
Hebrew reads *of the LORD keeps us from destruction.*

HEBREWS 1:1-14

Long ago God spoke many times and in
many ways to our ancestors through the
prophets. ²And now in these final days,
he has spoken to us through his Son.
God promised everything to the Son as
an inheritance, and through the Son he
created the universe. ³**The Son radi-
ates God's own glory and expresses
the very character of God, and he sus-
tains everything by the mighty power
of his command. When he had
cleansed us from our sins, he sat
down in the place of honor at the
right hand of the majestic God in
heaven.** ⁴This shows that the Son is far
greater than the angels, just as the name
God gave him is greater than their
names.

⁵For God never said to any angel what
he said to Jesus:

"You are my Son.
Today I have become
your Father.*"

God also said,

"I will be his Father,
and he will be my Son."*

⁶And when he brought his firstborn Son
into the world, God said,*

"Let all of God's angels
worship him."*

⁷Regarding the angels, he says,

"He sends his angels like the winds,
his servants like flames of fire."*

⁸But to the Son he says,

"Your throne, O God, endures
forever and ever.
You rule with a scepter of justice.
⁹ You love justice and hate evil.
Therefore, O God, your God has
anointed you,
pouring out the oil of joy on you
more than on anyone else."*

¹⁰He also says to the Son,

"In the beginning, Lord, you laid the
foundation of the earth
and made the heavens with your
hands.
¹¹ They will perish, but you remain
forever.
They will wear out like old
clothing.
¹² You will fold them up like a cloak
and discard them like old
clothing.
But you are always the same;
you will live forever."*

¹³And God never said to any of the angels,

"Sit in the place of honor at my
right hand
until I humble your enemies,
making them a footstool under
your feet."*

14Therefore, angels are only servants—spirits sent to care for people who will inherit salvation.

1:5a Or *Today I reveal you as my Son.* Ps 2:7.   **1:5b** 2 Sam 7:14.   **1:6a** Or *when he again brings his firstborn son into the world, God will say.*   **1:6b** Deut 32:43.   **1:7** Ps 104:4 (Greek version).   **1:8-9** Ps 45:6-7.   **1:10-12** Ps 102:25-27.   **1:13** Ps 110:1.

PSALM 102:1-28

A prayer of one overwhelmed with trouble, pouring out problems before the LORD.

1 LORD, hear my prayer!
    Listen to my plea!
2 Don't turn away from me
    in my time of distress.
  Bend down to listen,
    and answer me quickly when I call
      to you.
3 For my days disappear like smoke,
    and my bones burn like red-hot
      coals.
4 My heart is sick, withered like grass,
    and I have lost my appetite.
5 Because of my groaning,
    I am reduced to skin and bones.
6 I am like an owl in the desert,
    like a little owl in a far-off
      wilderness.
7 I lie awake,
    lonely as a solitary bird
      on the roof.
8 My enemies taunt me day after day.
    They mock and curse me.
9 I eat ashes for food.
    My tears run down into my drink
10 because of your anger and wrath.
    For you have picked me up and
      thrown me out.
11 My life passes as swiftly as the
      evening shadows.
    I am withering away like grass.

12 But you, O LORD, will sit on your
      throne forever.
    Your fame will endure to every
      generation.
13 You will arise and have mercy
      on Jerusalem*—
    and now is the time to pity her,
    now is the time you promised
      to help.

14 For your people love every stone
      in her walls
    and cherish even the dust
      in her streets.
15 Then the nations will tremble
      before the LORD.
    The kings of the earth will
      tremble before his glory.
16 For the LORD will rebuild Jerusalem.
    He will appear in his glory.
17 He will listen to the prayers of
      the destitute.
    He will not reject their pleas.

18 Let this be recorded for future
      generations,
    so that a people not yet born will
      praise the LORD.
19 Tell them the LORD looked down
      from his heavenly sanctuary.
    He looked down to earth from
      heaven
20   to hear the groans of the
      prisoners,
    to release those condemned
      to die.
21 And so the LORD's fame will be
      celebrated in Zion,
    his praises in Jerusalem,
22 when multitudes gather together
    and kingdoms come to worship
      the LORD.

23 He broke my strength in midlife,
    cutting short my days.
24 But I cried to him, "O my God, who
      lives forever,
    don't take my life while I am
      so young!
25 Long ago you laid the foundation
      of the earth
    and made the heavens with
      your hands.
26 They will perish, but you
      remain forever;
    they will wear out like old
      clothing.
    You will change them like a garment
      and discard them.
27 But you are always the same;
    you will live forever.
28 The children of your people

will live in security.
Their children's children
  will thrive in your presence."
102:13 Hebrew *Zion;* also in 102:16.

PROVERBS 26:21-22
A quarrelsome person starts fights as easily as hot embers light charcoal or fire lights wood. ☐Rumors are dainty morsels that sink deep into one's heart.

OCTOBER 31

LAMENTATIONS 4:1–5:22
How the gold has lost its luster!
Even the finest gold has
  become dull.
The sacred gemstones
  lie scattered in the streets!

2 See how the precious children
    of Jerusalem,*
  worth their weight in
    fine gold,
are now treated like pots of clay
  made by a common potter.

3 Even the jackals feed their young,
    but not my people Israel.
They ignore their children's cries,
    like ostriches in the desert.

4 The parched tongues of their
    little ones
  stick to the roofs of their mouths
    in thirst.
The children cry for bread,
  but no one has any to give them.

5 The people who once ate the
    richest foods
  now beg in the streets for
    anything they can get.
Those who once wore the finest
    clothes
  now search the garbage dumps
    for food.

6 The guilt* of my people
    is greater than that of Sodom,
where utter disaster struck
    in a moment
  and no hand offered help.

7 Our princes once glowed
    with health—
  brighter than snow, whiter
    than milk.
Their faces were as ruddy as rubies,
    their appearance like fine jewels.*

8 But now their faces are blacker
    than soot.
  No one recognizes them in the
    streets.
Their skin sticks to their bones;
    it is as dry and hard as wood.

9 Those killed by the sword are
    better off
    than those who die of hunger.
Starving, they waste away
    for lack of food from the fields.

10 Tenderhearted women
    have cooked their own children.
  They have eaten them
    to survive the siege.

11 But now the anger of the LORD
    is satisfied.
  His fierce anger has been
    poured out.
He started a fire in Jerusalem*
    that burned the city to its
      foundations.

12 Not a king in all the earth—
    no one in all the world—
  would have believed that an enemy
    could march through the gates
      of Jerusalem.

13 Yet it happened because of the sins
    of her prophets
    and the sins of her priests,
  who defiled the city
    by shedding innocent blood.

14 They wandered blindly
    through the streets,
  so defiled by blood
    that no one dared touch them.

¹⁵ "Get away!" the people shouted
    at them.
    "You're defiled! Don't touch us!"
So they fled to distant lands
    and wandered among foreign
      nations,
    but none would let them stay.

¹⁶ The LORD himself has
      scattered them,
    and he no longer helps them.
People show no respect for the
      priests
    and no longer honor the leaders.

¹⁷ We looked in vain for our allies
    to come and save us,
but we were looking to nations
    that could not help us.

¹⁸ We couldn't go into the streets
    without danger to our lives.
Our end was near; our days were
      numbered.
    We were doomed!

¹⁹ Our enemies were swifter than
      eagles in flight.
    If we fled to the mountains, they
      found us.
If we hid in the wilderness,
    they were waiting for us there.

²⁰ Our king—the LORD's anointed, the
      very life of our nation—
    was caught in their snares.
We had thought that his shadow
    would protect us against any
      nation on earth!

²¹ Are you rejoicing in the land
      of Uz,
    O people of Edom?
But you, too, must drink from the
    cup of the LORD's anger.
You, too, will be stripped naked in
    your drunkenness.

²² O beautiful Jerusalem,* your
      punishment will end;
    you will soon return from exile.
But Edom, your punishment is just
      beginning;
    soon your many sins will be
      exposed.

⁵:¹ LORD, remember what has hap-
      pened to us.
    See how we have been disgraced!
² Our inheritance has been turned
      over to strangers,
    our homes to foreigners.
³ We are orphaned and fatherless.
    Our mothers are widowed.
⁴ We have to pay for water to drink,
    and even firewood is expensive.
⁵ Those who pursue us are at our heels;
    we are exhausted but are
      given no rest.
⁶ We submitted to Egypt and Assyria
    to get enough food to survive.
⁷ Our ancestors sinned, but they have
      died—
    and we are suffering the
      punishment they deserved!

⁸ Slaves have now become
      our masters;
    there is no one left to rescue us.
⁹ We hunt for food at the risk
      of our lives,
    for violence rules the countryside.
¹⁰ The famine has blackened our skin
    as though baked in an oven.
¹¹ Our enemies rape the women in
      Jerusalem*
    and the young girls in all the
      towns of Judah.
¹² Our princes are being hanged by
      their thumbs,
    and our elders are treated
      with contempt.
¹³ Young men are led away to work
      at millstones,
    and boys stagger under heavy
      loads of wood.
¹⁴ The elders no longer sit in the
      city gates;
    the young men no longer dance
      and sing.
¹⁵ Joy has left our hearts;
    our dancing has turned to
      mourning.
¹⁶ The garlands have* fallen from
      our heads.
    Weep for us because we have
      sinned.
¹⁷ Our hearts are sick and weary,

and our eyes grow dim with tears.
18 For Jerusalem* is empty and
    desolate,
  a place haunted by jackals.

19 But LORD, you remain the same
    forever!
  Your throne continues from
    generation to generation.
20 Why do you continue to forget us?
  Why have you abandoned
    us for so long?
21 Restore us, O LORD, and bring us
    back to you again!
  Give us back the joys we once had!
22 Or have you utterly rejected us?
  Are you angry with us still?

4:2 Hebrew *precious sons of Zion.*   4:6 Or *punishment.*
4:7 Hebrew *like lapis lazuli.*   4:11 Hebrew *in Zion.*
4:22 Hebrew *O daughter of Zion.*   5:11 Hebrew *in Zion.*
5:16 Or *The crown has.*   5:18 Hebrew *Mount Zion.*

HEBREWS 2:1-18

So we must listen very carefully to the truth we have heard, or we may drift away from it. 2For the message God delivered through angels has always stood firm, and every violation of the law and every act of disobedience was punished. 3So what makes us think we can escape if we ignore this great salvation that was first announced by the Lord Jesus himself and then delivered to us by those who heard him speak? 4And God confirmed the message by giving signs and wonders and various miracles and gifts of the Holy Spirit whenever he chose.

5And furthermore, it is not angels who will control the future world we are talking about. 6For in one place the Scriptures say,

"What are people that you should
    think of them,
  or a son of man* that you should
    care for him?
7 Yet you made them only a little
    lower than the angels
  and crowned them with glory
    and honor.*
8 You gave them authority over
    all things."*

Now when it says "all things," it means nothing is left out. But we have not yet seen all things put under their authority. 9**What we do see is Jesus, who was given a position "a little lower than the angels"; and because he suffered death for us, he is now "crowned with glory and honor." Yes, by God's grace, Jesus tasted death for everyone.** 10God, for whom and through whom everything was made, chose to bring many children into glory. And it was only right that he should make Jesus, through his suffering, a perfect leader, fit to bring them into their salvation.

11So now Jesus and the ones he makes holy have the same Father. That is why Jesus is not ashamed to call them his brothers and sisters.* 12For he said to God,

"I will proclaim your name to my
    brothers and sisters.
  I will praise you among your
    assembled people."*

13He also said,

"I will put my trust in him,"
  that is, "I and the children God
    has given me."*

14Because God's children are human beings—made of flesh and blood—the Son also became flesh and blood. For only as a human being could he die, and only by dying could he break the power of the devil, who had* the power of death. 15Only in this way could he set free all who have lived their lives as slaves to the fear of dying.

16We also know that the Son did not come to help angels; he came to help the descendants of Abraham. 17Therefore, it was necessary for him to be made in every respect like us, his brothers and sisters,* so that he could be our merciful and faithful High Priest before God. Then he could offer a sacrifice that would take away the sins of the people. 18Since he himself has gone through suffering and testing, he is able to help us when we are being tested.

2:6 Or *the Son of Man.*   2:7 Some manuscripts add *You put them in charge of everything you made.*   2:6-8 Ps 8:4-6 (Greek version).   2:11 Greek *brothers;* also in 2:12.   2:12 Ps 22:22.   2:13 Isa 8:17-18.   2:14 Or *has.* 2:17 Greek *like the brothers.*

PSALM 103:1-22
A psalm of David.

1   Let all that I am praise the LORD;
    with my whole heart, I will praise
      his holy name.
2   Let all that I am praise the LORD;
    may I never forget the good things
      he does for me.
3   He forgives all my sins
    and heals all my diseases.
4   He redeems me from death
    and crowns me with love and
      tender mercies.
5   He fills my life with good things.
    My youth is renewed like
      the eagle's!

6   The LORD gives righteousness
    and justice to all who are
      treated unfairly.

7   He revealed his character to Moses
    and his deeds to the people
      of Israel.
8   The LORD is compassionate and
      merciful,
    slow to get angry and filled with
      unfailing love.
9   He will not constantly accuse us,
    nor remain angry forever.
10 He does not punish us for all
      our sins;
    he does not deal harshly with us,
      as we deserve.
11 For his unfailing love toward those
      who fear him
    is as great as the height of the
      heavens above the earth.
12 He has removed our sins as far
      from us

as the east is from the west.
13 The LORD is like a father to
      his children,
    tender and compassionate to
      those who fear him.
14 For he knows how weak we are;
    he remembers we are only dust.
15 Our days on earth are like grass;
    like wildflowers, we bloom
      and die.
16 The wind blows, and we are gone—
    as though we had never
      been here.
17 But the love of the LORD remains
      forever
    with those who fear him.
His salvation extends to the
      children's children
18 of those who are faithful
      to his covenant,
    of those who obey his
      commandments!

19 The LORD has made the heavens
      his throne;
    from there he rules over
      everything.

20 Praise the LORD, you angels,
    you mighty ones who carry
      out his plans,
    listening for each of his
      commands.
21 Yes, praise the LORD, you armies
      of angels
    who serve him and do his will!
22 Praise the LORD, everything he
      has created,
    everything in all his kingdom.

    Let all that I am praise the LORD.

PROVERBS 26:23
Smooth* words may hide a wicked heart, just as a pretty glaze covers a clay pot.

26:23 As in Greek version; Hebrew reads *Burning.*

NOVEMBER

1

EZEKIEL 1:1–3:15

On July 31* of my thirtieth year,* while I [Ezekiel] was with the Judean exiles beside the Kebar River in Babylon, the heavens were opened and I saw visions of God. ²This happened during the fifth year of King Jehoiachin's captivity. ³(The LORD gave this message to Ezekiel son of Buzi, a priest, beside the Kebar River in the land of the Babylonians,* and he felt the hand of the LORD take hold of him.)

⁴As I looked, I saw a great storm coming from the north, driving before it a huge cloud that flashed with lightning and shone with brilliant light. There was fire inside the cloud, and in the middle of the fire glowed something like gleaming amber.* ⁵From the center of the cloud came four living beings that looked human, ⁶except that each had four faces and four wings. ⁷Their legs were straight, and their feet had hooves like those of a calf and shone like burnished bronze. ⁸Under each of their four wings I could see human hands. So each of the four beings had four faces and four wings. ⁹The wings of each living being touched the wings of the beings beside it. Each one moved straight forward in any direction without turning around.

¹⁰Each had a human face in the front, the face of a lion on the right side, the face of an ox on the left side, and the face of an eagle at the back. ¹¹Each had two pairs of outstretched wings—one pair stretched out to touch the wings of the living beings on either side of it, and the other pair covered its body. ¹²They went in whatever direction the spirit chose, and they moved straight forward in any direction without turning around.

¹³The living beings looked like bright coals of fire or brilliant torches, and lightning seemed to flash back and forth among them. ¹⁴And the living beings darted to and fro like flashes of lightning.

¹⁵As I looked at these beings, I saw four wheels touching the ground beside them, one wheel belonging to each. ¹⁶The wheels sparkled as if made of beryl. All four wheels looked alike and were made the same; each wheel had a second wheel turning crosswise within it. ¹⁷The beings could move in any of the four directions they faced, without turning as they moved. ¹⁸The rims of the four wheels were tall and frightening, and they were covered with eyes all around.

¹⁹When the living beings moved, the wheels moved with them. When they flew upward, the wheels went up, too. ²⁰The spirit of the living beings was in the wheels. So wherever the spirit went, the wheels and the living beings also went. ²¹When the beings moved, the wheels moved. When the beings stopped, the wheels stopped. When the beings flew upward, the wheels rose up, for the spirit of the living beings was in the wheels.

²²Spread out above them was a surface like the sky, glittering like crystal. ²³Beneath this surface the wings of each living being stretched out to touch the others' wings, and each had two wings covering its body. ²⁴As they flew, their wings sounded to me like waves crashing against the shore or like the voice of the Almighty* or like the shouting of a mighty army. When they stopped, they let down their wings. ²⁵As they stood with wings lowered, a voice spoke from beyond the crystal surface above them.

²⁶Above this surface was something that looked like a throne made of blue lapis lazuli. And on this throne high

above was a figure whose appearance resembled a man. [27] From what appeared to be his waist up, he looked like gleaming amber, flickering like a fire. And from his waist down, he looked like a burning flame, shining with splendor. [28] All around him was a glowing halo, like a rainbow shining in the clouds on a rainy day. This is what the glory of the LORD looked like to me. When I saw it, I fell face down on the ground, and I heard someone's voice speaking to me.

[2:1] "STAND up, son of man," said the voice. "I want to speak with you." [2] The Spirit came into me as he spoke, and he set me on my feet. I listened carefully to his words. [3] "Son of man," he said, "I am sending you to the nation of Israel, a rebellious nation that has rebelled against me. They and their ancestors have been rebelling against me to this very day. [4] They are a stubborn and hard-hearted people. But I am sending you to say to them, 'This is what the Sovereign LORD says!' [5] And whether they listen or refuse to listen—for remember, they are rebels—at least they will know they have had a prophet among them.

[6] "Son of man, do not fear them or their words. Don't be afraid even though their threats surround you like nettles and briers and stinging scorpions. Do not be dismayed by their dark scowls, even though they are rebels. [7] You must give them my messages whether they listen or not. But they won't listen, for they are completely rebellious! [8] Son of man, listen to what I say to you. Do not join them in their rebellion. Open your mouth, and eat what I give you."

[9] Then I looked and saw a hand reaching out to me. It held a scroll, [10] which he unrolled. And I saw that both sides were covered with funeral songs, words of sorrow, and pronouncements of doom.

[3:1] THE voice said to me, "Son of man, eat what I am giving you—eat this scroll! Then go and give its message to the people of Israel." [2] So I opened my mouth, and he fed me the scroll. [3] "Fill your stom-

ach with this," he said. And when I ate it, it tasted as sweet as honey in my mouth.

[4] Then he said, "Son of man, go to the people of Israel and give them my messages. [5] I am not sending you to a foreign people whose language you cannot understand. [6] No, I am not sending you to people with strange and difficult speech. If I did, they would listen! [7] But the people of Israel won't listen to you any more than they listen to me! For the whole lot of them are hard-hearted and stubborn. [8] But look, I have made you as obstinate and hard-hearted as they are. [9] I have made your forehead as hard as the hardest rock! So don't be afraid of them or fear their angry looks, even though they are rebels."

[10] Then he added, "Son of man, let all my words sink deep into your own heart first. Listen to them carefully for yourself. [11] Then go to your people in exile and say to them, 'This is what the Sovereign LORD says!' Do this whether they listen to you or not."

[12] Then the Spirit lifted me up, and I heard a loud rumbling sound behind me. (May the glory of the LORD be praised in his place!)* [13] It was the sound of the wings of the living beings as they brushed against each other and the rumbling of their wheels beneath them.

[14] The Spirit lifted me up and took me away. I went in bitterness and turmoil, but the LORD's hold on me was strong. [15] Then I came to the colony of Judean exiles in Tel-abib, beside the Kebar River. I was overwhelmed and sat among them for seven days.

1:1a Hebrew *On the fifth day of the fourth month,* of the ancient Hebrew lunar calendar. A number of dates in Ezekiel can be cross-checked with dates in surviving Babylonian records and related accurately to our modern calendar. This event occurred on July 31, 593 B.C.   **1:1b** Or *in the thirtieth year.*   **1:3** Or *Chaldeans.*   **1:4** Or *like burnished metal;* also in 1:27.   **1:24** Hebrew *Shaddai.*   **3:12** A possible reading for this verse is *Then the Spirit lifted me up, and as the glory of the LORD rose from its place, I heard a loud rumbling sound behind me.*

HEBREWS 3:1-19

And so, dear brothers and sisters who belong to God and* are partners with those called to heaven, think carefully about this Jesus whom we declare to be

God's messenger* and High Priest. [2]For he was faithful to God, who appointed him, just as Moses served faithfully when he was entrusted with God's entire* house.

[3]But Jesus deserves far more glory than Moses, just as a person who builds a house deserves more praise than the house itself. [4]For every house has a builder, but the one who built everything is God.

[5]Moses was certainly faithful in God's house as a servant. His work was an illustration of the truths God would reveal later. [6]But Christ, as the Son, is in charge of God's entire house. And we are God's house, if we keep our courage and remain confident in our hope in Christ.*

[7]That is why the Holy Spirit says,

"Today when you hear his voice,
[8]   don't harden your hearts
as Israel did when they rebelled,
    when they tested me in the
        wilderness.
[9] There your ancestors tested and
        tried my patience,
    even though they saw my miracles
        for forty years.
[10] So I was angry with them, and I said,
    'Their hearts always turn away
        from me.
    They refuse to do what I tell them.'
[11] So in my anger I took an oath:
    'They will never enter my
        place of rest.'"*

[12]**Be careful then, dear brothers and sisters.* Make sure that your own hearts are not evil and unbelieving, turning you away from the living God. [13]You must warn each other every day, while it is still "today," so that none of you will be deceived by sin and hardened against God.** [14]For if we are faithful to the end, trusting God just as firmly as when we first believed, we will share in all that belongs to Christ. [15]Remember what it says:

"Today when you hear his voice,
    don't harden your hearts
    as Israel did when they rebelled."*

[16]And who was it who rebelled against God, even though they heard his voice? Wasn't it the people Moses led out of Egypt? [17]And who made God angry for forty years? Wasn't it the people who sinned, whose corpses lay in the wilderness? [18]And to whom was God speaking when he took an oath that they would never enter his rest? Wasn't it the people who disobeyed him? [19]So we see that because of their unbelief they were not able to enter his rest.

3:1a Greek *And so, holy brothers who.*   3:1b Greek *God's apostle.*   3:2 Some manuscripts omit *entire.*   3:6 Some manuscripts add *to the end.*   3:7-11 Ps 95:7-11.   3:12 Greek *brothers.*   3:15 Ps 95:7-8.

PSALM 104:1-23
Let all that I am praise the LORD.

O LORD my God, how great you are!
    You are robed with honor
        and majesty.
[2]   You are dressed in a robe
        of light.
You stretch out the starry curtain
    of the heavens;
[3]   you lay out the rafters of your
        home in the rain clouds.
You make the clouds your chariot;
    you ride upon the wings of
        the wind.
[4] The winds are your messengers;
    flames of fire are your servants.*

[5] You placed the world on its
        foundation
    so it would never be moved.
[6] You clothed the earth with floods
        of water,
    water that covered even the
        mountains.
[7] At your command, the water fled;
    at the sound of your thunder,
        it hurried away.
[8] Mountains rose and valleys sank
    to the levels you decreed.
[9] Then you set a firm boundary for
        the seas,
    so they would never again cover
        the earth.

[10] You make springs pour water into
        the ravines,

so streams gush down from the
mountains.
¹¹ They provide water for all the
animals,
and the wild donkeys quench
their thirst.
¹² The birds nest beside the streams
and sing among the branches
of the trees.
¹³ You send rain on the mountains
from your heavenly home,
and you fill the earth with the
fruit of your labor.
¹⁴ You cause grass to grow for the
livestock
and plants for people to use.
You allow them to produce food
from the earth—
¹⁵   wine to make them glad,
olive oil to soothe their skin,
and bread to give them
strength.
¹⁶ The trees of the LORD are well cared
for—
the cedars of Lebanon that he
planted.
¹⁷ There the birds make their
nests,
and the storks make their homes
in the cypresses.
¹⁸ High in the mountains live the
wild goats,
and the rocks form a refuge for
the hyraxes.*

¹⁹ You made the moon to mark the
seasons,
and the sun knows when to set.
²⁰ You send the darkness, and it
becomes night,
when all the forest animals
prowl about.
²¹ Then the young lions roar for
their prey,
stalking the food provided by God.
²² At dawn they slink back
into their dens to rest.
²³ Then people go off to their work,
where they labor until evening.

104:4 Greek version reads *He sends his angels like the
winds, / his servants like flames of fire.* Compare Heb 1:7.
104:18 Or *coneys,* or *rock badgers.*

PROVERBS 26:24-26

People may cover their hatred with
pleasant words, but they're deceiving
you. They pretend to be kind, but don't
believe them. Their hearts are full of
many evils.* While their hatred may be
concealed by trickery, their wrong-
doing will be exposed in public.

26:25 Hebrew *seven evils.*

NOVEMBER 2

EZEKIEL 3:16-6:14

After seven days the LORD gave me
[Ezekiel] a message. He said, ¹⁷"Son of
man, I have appointed you as a watch-
man for Israel. Whenever you receive a
message from me, warn people imme-
diately. ¹⁸If I warn the wicked, saying,
'You are under the penalty of death,' but
you fail to deliver the warning, they will
die in their sins. And I will hold you responsible for their deaths. ¹⁹If you
warn them and they refuse to repent
and keep on sinning, they will die in
their sins. But you will have saved yourself because you obeyed me.

²⁰"If righteous people turn away
from their righteous behavior and ignore the obstacles I put in their way,
they will die. And if you do not warn
them, they will die in their sins. None of
their righteous acts will be remembered, and I will hold you responsible
for their deaths. ²¹But if you warn righteous people not to sin and they listen to
you and do not sin, they will live, and
you will have saved yourself, too."

²²Then the LORD took hold of me and
said, "Get up and go out into the valley,
and I will speak to you there." ²³So I got
up and went, and there I saw the glory of
the LORD, just as I had seen in my first
vision by the Kebar River. And I fell face
down on the ground.

²⁴Then the Spirit came into me and set me on my feet. He spoke to me and said, "Go to your house and shut yourself in. ²⁵There, son of man, you will be tied with ropes so you cannot go out among the people. ²⁶And I will make your tongue stick to the roof of your mouth so that you will be speechless and unable to rebuke them, for they are rebels. ²⁷But when I give you a message, I will loosen your tongue and let you speak. Then you will say to them, 'This is what the Sovereign LORD says!' Those who choose to listen will listen, but those who refuse will refuse, for they are rebels.

⁴:¹"AND now, son of man, take a large clay brick and set it down in front of you. Then draw a map of the city of Jerusalem on it. ²Show the city under siege. Build a wall around it so no one can escape. Set up the enemy camp, and surround the city with siege ramps and battering rams. ³Then take an iron griddle and place it between you and the city. Turn toward the city and demonstrate how harsh the siege will be against Jerusalem. This will be a warning to the people of Israel.

⁴"Now lie on your left side and place the sins of Israel on yourself. You are to bear their sins for the number of days you lie there on your side. ⁵I am requiring you to bear Israel's sins for 390 days— one day for each year of their sin. ⁶After that, turn over and lie on your right side for 40 days—one day for each year of Judah's sin.

⁷"Meanwhile, keep staring at the siege of Jerusalem. Lie there with your arm bared and prophesy her destruction. ⁸I will tie you up with ropes so you won't be able to turn from side to side until the days of your siege have been completed.

⁹"Now go and get some wheat, barley, beans, lentils, millet, and emmer wheat, and mix them together in a storage jar. Use them to make bread for yourself during the 390 days you will be lying on your side. ¹⁰Ration this out to yourself,

eight ounces* of food for each day, and eat it at set times. ¹¹Then measure out a jar* of water for each day, and drink it at set times. ¹²Prepare and eat this food as you would barley cakes. While all the people are watching, bake it over a fire using dried human dung as fuel and then eat the bread." ¹³Then the LORD said, "This is how Israel will eat defiled bread in the Gentile lands to which I will banish them!"

¹⁴Then I said, "O Sovereign LORD, must I be defiled by using human dung? For I have never been defiled before. From the time I was a child until now I have never eaten any animal that died of sickness or was killed by other animals. I have never eaten any meat forbidden by the law."

¹⁵"All right," the LORD said. "You may bake your bread with cow dung instead of human dung." ¹⁶Then he told me, "Son of man, I will make food very scarce in Jerusalem. It will be weighed out with great care and eaten fearfully. The water will be rationed out drop by drop, and the people will drink it with dismay. ¹⁷Lacking food and water, people will look at one another in terror, and they will waste away under their punishment.

⁵:¹"SON of man, take a sharp sword and use it as a razor to shave your head and beard. Use a scale to weigh the hair into three equal parts. ²Place a third of it at the center of your map of Jerusalem. After acting out the siege, burn it there. Scatter another third across your map and chop it with a sword. Scatter the last third to the wind, for I will scatter my people with the sword. ³Keep just a bit of the hair and tie it up in your robe. ⁴Then take some of these hairs out and throw them into the fire, burning them up. A fire will then spread from this remnant and destroy all of Israel.

⁵"This is what the Sovereign LORD says: This is an illustration of what will happen to Jerusalem. I placed her at the center of the nations, ⁶but she has rebelled against my regulations and decrees

and has been even more wicked than the surrounding nations. She has refused to obey the regulations and decrees I gave her to follow.

⁷"Therefore, this is what the Sovereign LORD says: You people have behaved worse than your neighbors and have refused to obey my decrees and regulations. You have not even lived up to the standards of the nations around you. ⁸Therefore, I myself, the Sovereign LORD, am now your enemy. I will punish you publicly while all the nations watch. ⁹Because of your detestable idols, I will punish you like I have never punished anyone before or ever will again. ¹⁰Parents will eat their own children, and children will eat their parents. I will punish you and scatter to the winds the few who survive.

¹¹"As surely as I live, says the Sovereign LORD, I will cut you off completely. I will show you no pity at all because you have defiled my Temple with your vile images and detestable sins. ¹²A third of your people will die in the city from disease and famine. A third of them will be slaughtered by the enemy outside the city walls. And I will scatter a third to the winds, chasing them with my sword. ¹³Then at last my anger will be spent, and I will be satisfied. And when my fury against them has subsided, all Israel will know that I, the LORD, have spoken to them in my jealous anger.

¹⁴"So I will turn you into a ruin, a mockery in the eyes of the surrounding nations and to all who pass by. ¹⁵You will become an object of mockery and taunting and horror. You will be a warning to all the nations around you. They will see what happens when the LORD punishes a nation in anger and rebukes it, says the LORD.

¹⁶"I will shower you with the deadly arrows of famine to destroy you. The famine will become more and more severe until every crumb of food is gone. ¹⁷And along with the famine, wild animals will attack you and rob you of your children. Disease and war will stalk your land, and I will bring the sword of the enemy against you. I, the LORD, have spoken!"

⁶:¹AGAIN a message came to me from the LORD: ²"Son of man, turn and face the mountains of Israel and prophesy against them. ³Proclaim this message from the Sovereign LORD against the mountains of Israel. This is what the Sovereign LORD says to the mountains and hills and to the ravines and valleys: I am about to bring war upon you, and I will smash your pagan shrines. ⁴All your altars will be demolished, and your places of worship will be destroyed. I will kill your people in front of your idols.* ⁵I will lay your corpses in front of your idols and scatter your bones around your altars. ⁶Wherever you live there will be desolation, and I will destroy your pagan shrines. Your altars will be demolished, your idols will be smashed, your places of worship will be torn down, and all the religious objects you have made will be destroyed. ⁷The place will be littered with corpses, and you will know that I alone am the LORD.

⁸"But I will let a few of my people escape destruction, and they will be scattered among the nations of the world. ⁹Then when they are exiled among the nations, they will remember me. They will recognize how hurt I am by their unfaithful hearts and lustful eyes that long for their idols. Then at last they will hate themselves for all their detestable sins. ¹⁰They will know that I alone am the LORD and that I was serious when I said I would bring this calamity on them.

¹¹"This is what the Sovereign LORD says: Clap your hands in horror, and stamp your feet. Cry out because of all the detestable sins the people of Israel have committed. Now they are going to die from war and famine and disease. ¹²Disease will strike down those who are far away in exile. War will destroy those who are nearby. And anyone who survives will be killed by famine. So at last I will spend my fury on them. ¹³They will know that I am the LORD when their dead lie scattered among their idols and altars

on every hill and mountain and under every green tree and every great shade tree—the places where they offered sacrifices to their idols. ¹⁴I will crush them and make their cities desolate from the wilderness in the south to Riblah* in the north. Then they will know that I am the LORD."

4:10 Hebrew *20 shekels* [228 grams].   4:11 Hebrew ⅙ *of a hin* [about 1 pint or 0.6 liters].   6:4 The Hebrew term (literally *round things*) probably alludes to dung; also in 6:5, 6, 9, 13.   6:14 As in some Hebrew manuscripts; most Hebrew manuscripts read *Diblah*.

HEBREWS 4:1-16

God's promise of entering his rest still stands, so we ought to tremble with fear that some of you might fail to experience it. ²For this good news—that God has prepared this rest—has been announced to us just as it was to them. But it did them no good because they didn't share the faith of those who listened to God.* ³For only we who believe can enter his rest. As for the others, God said,

"In my anger I took an oath:
    'They will never enter my place
        of rest,'"*

even though this rest has been ready since he made the world. ⁴We know it is ready because of the place in the Scriptures where it mentions the seventh day: "On the seventh day God rested from all his work."* ⁵But in the other passage God said, "They will never enter my place of rest."*

⁶So God's rest is there for people to enter, but those who first heard this good news failed to enter because they disobeyed God. ⁷So God set another time for entering his rest, and that time is today. God announced this through David much later in the words already quoted:

"Today when you hear his voice,
    don't harden your hearts."*

⁸Now if Joshua had succeeded in giving them this rest, God would not have spoken about another day of rest still to come. ⁹So there is a special rest* still waiting for the people of God. ¹⁰For all who have entered into God's rest have

rested from their labors, just as God did after creating the world. ¹¹So let us do our best to enter that rest. But if we disobey God, as the people of Israel did, we will fall.

¹²**For the word of God is alive and powerful. It is sharper than the sharpest two-edged sword, cutting between soul and spirit, between joint and marrow. It exposes our innermost thoughts and desires.** ¹³Nothing in all creation is hidden from God. Everything is naked and exposed before his eyes, and he is the one to whom we are accountable.

¹⁴So then, since we have a great High Priest who has entered heaven, Jesus the Son of God, let us hold firmly to what we believe. ¹⁵This High Priest of ours understands our weaknesses, for he faced all of the same testings we do, yet he did not sin. ¹⁶So let us come boldly to the throne of our gracious God. There we will receive his mercy, and we will find grace to help us when we need it most.

4:2 Some manuscripts read *they didn't combine what they heard with faith.*   4:3 Ps 95:11.   4:4 Gen 2:2.   4:5 Ps 95:11.   4:7 Ps 95:7-8.   4:9 Or *a Sabbath rest.*

PSALM 104:24-35

O LORD, what a variety of things
        you have made!
    In wisdom you have made
        them all.
    The earth is full of your
        creatures.
²⁵ Here is the ocean, vast and wide,
        teeming with life of every kind,
        both large and small.
²⁶ See the ships sailing along,
        and Leviathan,* which you made
            to play in the sea.

²⁷ They all depend on you
        to give them food as they need it.
²⁸ When you supply it, they gather it.
        You open your hand to feed them,
        and they are richly satisfied.
²⁹ But if you turn away from them,
        they panic.
    When you take away their breath,
        they die and turn again to dust.

³⁰ When you give them your breath,*
　　life is created,
　　and you renew the face
　　of the earth.

³¹ May the glory of the Lᴏʀᴅ continue
　　forever!
　　The Lᴏʀᴅ takes pleasure in all
　　he has made!

³² The earth trembles at his glance;
　　the mountains smoke at
　　his touch.

³³ I will sing to the Lᴏʀᴅ as long
　　as I live.
　　I will praise my God to my last
　　breath!

³⁴ May all my thoughts be pleasing
　　to him,
　　for I rejoice in the Lᴏʀᴅ.

³⁵ Let all sinners vanish from the face
　　of the earth;
　　let the wicked disappear forever.

　Let all that I am praise the Lᴏʀᴅ.

　Praise the Lᴏʀᴅ!

104:26 The identification of Leviathan is disputed, ranging
from an earthly creature to a mythical sea monster in
ancient literature.   **104:30** Or *When you send your Spirit.*

PROVERBS 26:27

If you set a trap for others, you will get
caught in it yourself. If you roll a boulder down on others, it will crush you instead.

NOVEMBER 3

EZEKIEL 7:1–9:11

Then this message came to me [Ezekiel]
from the Lᴏʀᴅ: ²"Son of man, this is
what the Sovereign Lᴏʀᴅ says to Israel:

　"The end is here!
　　Wherever you look—
　east, west, north, or south—
　　your land is finished.

³ No hope remains,
　　for I will unleash my anger
　　against you.
　I will call you to account
　　for all your detestable sins.

⁴ I will turn my eyes away and show
　　no pity.
　I will repay you for all your
　　detestable sins.
　Then you will know that I am
　　the Lᴏʀᴅ.

⁵ "This is what the Sovereign
　　Lᴏʀᴅ says:
　Disaster after disaster
　　is coming your way!

⁶ The end has come.
　　It has finally arrived.
　Your final doom is waiting!

⁷ O people of Israel, the day of your
　　destruction is dawning.
　The time has come; the day
　　of trouble is near.
　Shouts of anguish will be heard
　　on the mountains,
　　not shouts of joy.

⁸ Soon I will pour out my fury on you
　　and unleash my anger
　　against you.
　I will call you to account
　　for all your detestable sins.

⁹ I will turn my eyes away and
　　show no pity.
　I will repay you for all your
　　detestable sins.
　Then you will know that it is I,
　　the Lᴏʀᴅ,
　　who is striking the blow.

¹⁰ "The day of judgment is here;
　　your destruction awaits!
　The people's wickedness and pride
　　have blossomed to full flower.

¹¹ Their violence has grown into a rod
　　that will beat them for their
　　wickedness.
　None of these proud and wicked
　　people will survive.
　　All their wealth and prestige will
　　be swept away.

¹² Yes, the time has come;
　　the day is here!

Buyers should not rejoice
　　over bargains,
　　nor sellers grieve over losses,
for all of them will fall
　　under my terrible anger.
13 Even if the merchants survive,
　　they will never return to their
　　　business.
For what God has said applies to
　　everyone—
　　it will not be changed!
Not one person whose life is
　　twisted by sin
　　will ever recover.

14 "The trumpet calls Israel's army
　　to mobilize,
　　but no one listens,
　　for my fury is against them all.
15 There is war outside the city
　　and disease and famine within.
Those outside the city walls
　　will be killed by enemy swords.
Those inside the city
　　will die of famine and disease.
16 The survivors who escape to the
　　mountains
　　will moan like doves, weeping
　　for their sins.
17 Their hands will hang limp,
　　their knees will be weak as water.
18 They will dress themselves in burlap;
　　horror and shame will
　　cover them.
They will shave their heads
　　in sorrow and remorse.

19 "They will throw their money
　　in the streets,
　　tossing it out like worthless trash.
Their silver and gold won't save
　　them
　　on that day of the LORD's anger.
It will neither satisfy nor feed them,
　　for their greed can only trip
　　them up.
20 They were proud of their beautiful
　　jewelry
　　and used it to make detestable
　　idols and vile images.
Therefore, I will make all their wealth
　　disgusting to them.

21 I will give it as plunder to foreigners,
　　to the most wicked of nations,
　　and they will defile it.
22 I will turn my eyes from them
　　as these robbers invade and
　　defile my treasured land.

23 "Prepare chains for my people,
　　for the land is bloodied by terrible
　　　crimes.
Jerusalem is filled with violence.
24 I will bring the most ruthless
　　of nations
　　to occupy their homes.
I will break down their proud
　　fortresses
　　and defile their sanctuaries.
25 Terror and trembling will overcome
　　my people.
They will look for peace but
　　not find it.
26 Calamity will follow calamity;
　　rumor will follow rumor.
They will look in vain
　　for a vision from the prophets.
They will receive no teaching
　　from the priests
　　and no counsel from the
　　leaders.
27 The king and the prince will
　　stand helpless,
　　weeping in despair,
and the people's hands
　　will tremble with fear.
I will bring on them
　　the evil they have done to others,
and they will receive the
　　punishment
　　they so richly deserve.
Then they will know that I am
　　the LORD."

8:1 THEN on September 17,* during the sixth year of King Jehoiachin's captivity, while the leaders of Judah were in my home, the Sovereign LORD took hold of me. 2 I saw a figure that appeared to be a man. From what appeared to be his waist down, he looked like a burning flame. From the waist up he looked like gleaming amber.* 3 He reached out what seemed to be a hand and took me by the hair. Then the Spirit lifted me up into the sky and transported me to Jerusalem in a vision from God. I was taken to the north gate of the inner courtyard of the Temple, where there is a large idol that has made the LORD very jealous. ⁴Suddenly, the glory of the God of Israel was there, just as I had seen it before in the valley.

⁵Then the LORD said to me, "Son of man, look toward the north." So I looked, and there to the north, beside the entrance to the gate near the altar, stood the idol that had made the LORD so jealous.

⁶"Son of man," he said, "do you see what they are doing? Do you see the detestable sins the people of Israel are committing to drive me from my Temple? But come, and you will see even more detestable sins than these!" ⁷Then he brought me to the door of the Temple courtyard, where I could see a hole in the wall. ⁸He said to me, "Now, son of man, dig into the wall." So I dug into the wall and found a hidden doorway.

⁹"Go in," he said, "and see the wicked and detestable sins they are committing in there!" ¹⁰So I went in and saw the walls engraved with all kinds of crawling animals and detestable creatures. I also saw the various idols* worshiped by the people of Israel. ¹¹Seventy leaders of Israel were standing there with Jaazaniah son of Shaphan in the center. Each of them held an incense burner, from which a cloud of incense rose above their heads.

¹²Then the LORD said to me, "Son of man, have you seen what the leaders of Israel are doing with their idols in dark rooms? They are saying, 'The LORD doesn't see us; he has deserted our land!'" ¹³Then the LORD added, "Come, and I will show you even more detestable sins than these!"

¹⁴He brought me to the north gate of the LORD's Temple, and some women were sitting there, weeping for the god Tammuz. ¹⁵"Have you seen this?" he asked. "But I will show you even more detestable sins than these!"

¹⁶Then he brought me into the inner courtyard of the LORD's Temple. At the entrance to the sanctuary, between the entry room and the bronze altar, there were about twenty-five men with their backs to the sanctuary of the LORD. They were facing east, bowing low to the ground, worshiping the sun!

¹⁷"Have you seen this, son of man?" he asked. "Is it nothing to the people of Judah that they commit these detestable sins, leading the whole nation into violence, thumbing their noses at me, and provoking my anger? ¹⁸Therefore, I will respond in fury. I will neither pity nor spare them. And though they cry for mercy, I will not listen."

⁹:¹THEN the LORD thundered, "Bring on the men appointed to punish the city! Tell them to bring their weapons with them!" ²Six men soon appeared from the upper gate that faces north, each carrying a deadly weapon in his hand. With them was a man dressed in linen, who carried a writer's case at his side. They all went into the Temple courtyard and stood beside the bronze altar.

³Then the glory of the God of Israel rose up from between the cherubim, where it had rested, and moved to the entrance of the Temple. And the LORD called to the man dressed in linen who was carrying the writer's case. ⁴He said to him, "Walk through the streets of Jerusalem and put a mark on the foreheads of all who weep and sigh because of the detestable sins being committed in their city."

⁵Then I heard the LORD say to the other men, "Follow him through the city and kill everyone whose forehead is not marked. Show no mercy; have no pity! ⁶Kill them all—old and young, girls and women and little children. But do not touch anyone with the mark. Begin right here at the Temple." So they began by killing the seventy leaders.

⁷"Defile the Temple!" the LORD commanded. "Fill its courtyards with corpses. Go!" So they went and began killing throughout the city.

[8]While they were out killing, I was all alone. I fell face down on the ground and cried out, "O Sovereign LORD! Will your fury against Jerusalem wipe out everyone left in Israel?"

[9]Then he said to me, "The sins of the people of Israel and Judah are very, very great. The entire land is full of murder; the city is filled with injustice. They are saying, 'The LORD doesn't see it! The LORD has abandoned the land!' [10]So I will not spare them or have any pity on them. I will fully repay them for all they have done."

[11]Then the man in linen clothing, who carried the writer's case, reported back and said, "I have done as you commanded."

8:1 Hebrew *on the fifth day of the sixth month,* of the ancient Hebrew lunar calendar. This event occurred on September 17, 592 B.C.; also see note on 1:1.   8:2 Or *like burnished metal.*   8:10 The Hebrew term (literally *round things*) probably alludes to dung.

HEBREWS 5:1-14

Every high priest is a man chosen to represent other people in their dealings with God. He presents their gifts to God and offers sacrifices for their sins. [2]And he is able to deal gently with ignorant and wayward people because he himself is subject to the same weaknesses. [3]That is why he must offer sacrifices for his own sins as well as theirs.

[4]And no one can become a high priest simply because he wants such an honor. He must be called by God for this work, just as Aaron was. [5]That is why Christ did not honor himself by assuming he could become High Priest. No, he was chosen by God, who said to him,

"You are my Son.
    Today I have become your Father.*"

[6]And in another passage God said to him,

"You are a priest forever in the
    order of Melchizedek."*

[7]While Jesus was here on earth, he offered prayers and pleadings, with a loud cry and tears, to the one who could rescue him from death. And God heard his prayers because of his deep reverence for God. **[8]Even though Jesus was God's Son, he learned obedience from the things he suffered. [9]In this way, God qualified him as a perfect High Priest, and he became the source of eternal salvation for all those who obey him.** [10]And God designated him to be a High Priest in the order of Melchizedek.

[11]There is much more we would like to say about this, but it is difficult to explain, especially since you are spiritually dull and don't seem to listen. [12]You have been believers so long now that you ought to be teaching others. Instead, you need someone to teach you again the basic things about God's word.* You are like babies who need milk and cannot eat solid food. [13]For someone who lives on milk is still an infant and doesn't know how to do what is right. [14]Solid food is for those who are mature, who through training have the skill to recognize the difference between right and wrong.

5:5 Or *Today I reveal you as my Son.* Ps 2:7.   5:6 Ps 110:4.
5:12 Or *about the oracles of God.*

PSALM 105:1-15

Give thanks to the LORD and
    proclaim his greatness.
Let the whole world know what
    he has done.
[2] Sing to him; yes, sing his praises.
    Tell everyone about his
        wonderful deeds.
[3] Exult in his holy name;
    rejoice, you who worship
        the LORD.
[4] Search for the LORD and for
        his strength;
    continually seek him.
[5] Remember the wonders he has
        performed,
    his miracles, and the rulings
        he has given,
[6] you children of his servant
        Abraham,
    you descendants of Jacob,
        his chosen ones.

⁷ He is the LORD our God.
His justice is seen throughout
the land.
⁸ He always stands by his covenant—
the commitment he made to a
thousand generations.
⁹ This is the covenant he made with
Abraham
and the oath he swore to Isaac.
¹⁰ He confirmed it to Jacob as a decree,
and to the people of Israel as a
never-ending covenant:
¹¹ "I will give you the land of Canaan
as your special possession."

¹² He said this when they were few in
number,
a tiny group of strangers in
Canaan.
¹³ They wandered from nation to
nation,
from one kingdom to another.
¹⁴ Yet he did not let anyone oppress
them.
He warned kings on their behalf:
¹⁵ "Do not touch my chosen people,
and do not hurt my prophets."

PROVERBS 26:28
A lying tongue hates its victims, and
flattering words cause ruin.

NOVEMBER 4

EZEKIEL 10:1–11:25
In my [Ezekiel's] vision I saw what appeared to be a throne of blue lapis lazuli
above the crystal surface over the heads
of the cherubim. ²Then the LORD spoke
to the man in linen clothing and said, "Go
between the whirling wheels beneath
the cherubim, and take a handful of
burning coals and scatter them over the
city." He did this as I watched.
³The cherubim were standing at the
south end of the Temple when the man
went in, and the cloud of glory filled the
inner courtyard. ⁴Then the glory of the
LORD rose up from above the cherubim
and went over to the door of the Temple.
The Temple was filled with this cloud of
glory, and the courtyard glowed brightly
with the glory of the LORD. ⁵The moving
wings of the cherubim sounded like the
voice of God Almighty* and could be
heard even in the outer courtyard.
⁶The LORD said to the man in linen
clothing, "Go between the cherubim and
take some burning coals from between
the wheels." So the man went in and
stood beside one of the wheels. ⁷Then
one of the cherubim reached out his
hand and took some live coals from the
fire burning among them. He put the
coals into the hands of the man in linen
clothing, and the man took them and
went out. ⁸(All the cherubim had what
looked like human hands under their
wings.)
⁹I looked, and each of the four cherubim had a wheel beside him, and the
wheels sparkled like beryl. ¹⁰All four
wheels looked alike and were made the
same; each wheel had a second wheel
turning crosswise within it. ¹¹The cherubim could move in any of the four directions they faced, without turning as
they moved. They went straight in the
direction they faced, never turning
aside. ¹²Both the cherubim and the
wheels were covered with eyes. The
cherubim had eyes all over their bodies,
including their hands, their backs, and
their wings. ¹³I heard someone refer to
the wheels as "the whirling wheels."
¹⁴Each of the four cherubim had four
faces: the first was the face of an ox,* the
second was a human face, the third was
the face of a lion, and the fourth was the
face of an eagle.
¹⁵Then the cherubim rose upward.
These were the same living beings I had
seen beside the Kebar River. ¹⁶When
the cherubim moved, the wheels moved
with them. When they lifted their wings
to fly, the wheels stayed beside them.
¹⁷When the cherubim stopped, the
wheels stopped. When they flew up-

ward, the wheels rose up, for the spirit of the living beings was in the wheels.

[18]Then the glory of the LORD moved out from the door of the Temple and hovered above the cherubim. [19]And as I watched, the cherubim flew with their wheels to the east gate of the LORD's Temple. And the glory of the God of Israel hovered above them.

[20]These were the same living beings I had seen beneath the God of Israel when I was by the Kebar River. I knew they were cherubim, [21]for each had four faces and four wings and what looked like human hands under their wings. [22]And their faces were just like the faces of the beings I had seen at the Kebar, and they traveled straight ahead, just as the others had.

[11:1]THEN the Spirit lifted me and brought me to the east gateway of the LORD's Temple, where I saw twenty-five prominent men of the city. Among them were Jaazaniah son of Azzur and Pelatiah son of Benaiah, who were leaders among the people.

[2]The Spirit said to me, "Son of man, these are the men who are planning evil and giving wicked counsel in this city. [3]They say to the people, 'Is it not a good time to build houses? This city is like an iron pot. We are safe inside it like meat in a pot.*' [4]Therefore, son of man, prophesy against them loudly and clearly."

[5]Then the Spirit of the LORD came upon me, and he told me to say, "This is what the LORD says to the people of Israel: I know what you are saying, for I know every thought that comes into your minds. [6]You have murdered many in this city and filled its streets with the dead.

[7]"Therefore, this is what the Sovereign LORD says: This city is an iron pot all right, but the pieces of meat are the victims of your injustice. As for you, I will soon drag you from this pot. [8]I will bring on you the sword of war you so greatly fear, says the Sovereign LORD. [9]I will drive you out of Jerusalem and hand you over to foreigners, who will carry out my judgments against you. [10]You will be slaughtered all the way to the borders of Israel. I will execute judgment on you, and you will know that I am the LORD. [11]No, this city will not be an iron pot for you, and you will not be like meat safe inside it. I will judge you even to the borders of Israel, [12]and you will know that I am the LORD. For you have refused to obey my decrees and regulations; instead, you have copied the standards of the nations around you."

[13]While I was still prophesying, Pelatiah son of Benaiah suddenly died. Then I fell face down on the ground and cried out, "O Sovereign LORD, are you going to kill everyone in Israel?"

[14]Then this message came to me from the LORD: [15]"Son of man, the people still left in Jerusalem are talking about you and your relatives and all the people of Israel who are in exile. They are saying, 'Those people are far away from the LORD, so now he has given their land to us!'

[16]"Therefore, tell the exiles, 'This is what the Sovereign LORD says: Although I have scattered you in the countries of the world, I will be a sanctuary to you during your time in exile. [17]I, the Sovereign LORD, will gather you back from the nations where you have been scattered, and I will give you the land of Israel once again.'

[18]"When the people return to their homeland, they will remove every trace of their vile images and detestable idols. [19]And I will give them singleness of heart and put a new spirit within them. I will take away their stony, stubborn heart and give them a tender, responsive heart,* [20]so they will obey my decrees and regulations. Then they will truly be my people, and I will be their God. [21]But as for those who long for vile images and detestable idols, I will repay them fully for their sins. I, the Sovereign LORD, have spoken!"

[22]Then the cherubim lifted their wings and rose into the air with their wheels beside them, and the glory of the God of Israel hovered above them. [23]Then the glory of the LORD went up

from the city and stopped above the mountain to the east.

²⁴Afterward the Spirit of God carried me back again to Babylonia,* to the people in exile there. And so ended the vision of my visit to Jerusalem. ²⁵And I told the exiles everything the LORD had shown me.

10:5 Hebrew *El-Shaddai.* 10:14 Hebrew *the face of a cherub;* compare 1:10. 11:3 Hebrew *This city is the pot, and we are the meat.* 11:19 Hebrew *a heart of flesh.* 11:24 Or *Chaldea.*

HEBREWS 6:1-20

So let us stop going over the basic teachings about Christ again and again. Let us go on instead and become mature in our understanding. Surely we don't need to start again with the fundamental importance of repenting from evil deeds and placing our faith in God. ²You don't need further instruction about baptisms, the laying on of hands, the resurrection of the dead, and eternal judgment. ³And so, God willing, we will move forward to further understanding.

⁴For it is impossible to bring back to repentance those who were once enlightened—those who have experienced the good things of heaven and shared in the Holy Spirit, ⁵who have tasted the goodness of the word of God and the power of the age to come—⁶and who then turn away from God. It is impossible to bring such people back to repentance; by rejecting the Son of God, they themselves are nailing him to the cross once again and holding him up to public shame.

⁷When the ground soaks up the falling rain and bears a good crop for the farmer, it has God's blessing. ⁸But if a field bears thorns and thistles, it is useless. The farmer will soon condemn that field and burn it.

⁹Dear friends, even though we are talking this way, we really don't believe it applies to you. We are confident that you are meant for better things, things that come with salvation. **¹⁰For God is not unjust. He will not forget how hard you have worked for him and how you have shown your love to him**

by caring for other believers,* as you still do. **¹¹**Our great desire is that you will keep on loving others as long as life lasts, in order to make certain that what you hope for will come true. ¹²Then you will not become spiritually dull and indifferent. Instead, you will follow the example of those who are going to inherit God's promises because of their faith and endurance.

¹³For example, there was God's promise to Abraham. Since there was no one greater to swear by, God took an oath in his own name, saying:

¹⁴ "I will certainly bless you,
    and I will multiply your
        descendants beyond
        number."*

¹⁵Then Abraham waited patiently, and he received what God had promised.

¹⁶Now when people take an oath, they call on someone greater than themselves to hold them to it. And without any question that oath is binding. ¹⁷God also bound himself with an oath, so that those who received the promise could be perfectly sure that he would never change his mind. ¹⁸So God has given both his promise and his oath. These two things are unchangeable because it is impossible for God to lie. Therefore, we who have fled to him for refuge can have great confidence as we hold to the hope that lies before us. ¹⁹This hope is a strong and trustworthy anchor for our souls. It leads us through the curtain into God's inner sanctuary. ²⁰Jesus has already gone in there for us. He has become our eternal High Priest in the order of Melchizedek.

6:10 Greek *the saints.* 6:14 Gen 22:17.

PSALM 105:16-36

He [the LORD] called for a famine on
    the land of Canaan,
    cutting off its food supply.
¹⁷ Then he sent someone to Egypt
    ahead of them—
    Joseph, who was sold as a slave.
¹⁸ They bruised his feet with fetters

and placed his neck in an
iron collar.
¹⁹ Until the time came to fulfill
his dreams,*
the LORD tested Joseph's
character.
²⁰ Then Pharaoh sent for him and
set him free;
the ruler of the nation opened
his prison door.
²¹ Joseph was put in charge of all the
king's household;
he became ruler over all the king's
possessions.
²² He could instruct the king's aides as
he pleased
and teach the king's advisers.

²³ Then Israel arrived in Egypt;
Jacob lived as a foreigner in the
land of Ham.
²⁴ And the LORD multiplied the people
of Israel
until they became too mighty
for their enemies.
²⁵ Then he turned the Egyptians
against the Israelites,
and they plotted against the
LORD's servants.

²⁶ But the LORD sent his servant Moses,
along with Aaron, whom he
had chosen.
²⁷ They performed miraculous signs
among the Egyptians,
and wonders in the land of Ham.
²⁸ The LORD blanketed Egypt in
darkness,
for they had defied his
commands to let his
people go.
²⁹ He turned their water into blood,
poisoning all the fish.
³⁰ Then frogs overran the land
and even invaded the king's
bedrooms.
³¹ When the LORD spoke, flies
descended on the Egyptians,
and gnats swarmed across Egypt.
³² He sent them hail instead of rain,
and lightning flashed over
the land.

³³ He ruined their grapevines and
fig trees
and shattered all the trees.
³⁴ He spoke, and hordes of locusts
came—
young locusts beyond number.
³⁵ They ate up everything green in
the land,
destroying all the crops in
their fields.
³⁶ Then he killed the oldest son in
each Egyptian home,
the pride and joy of each family.

105:19 Hebrew *his word.*

PROVERBS 27:1-2
Don't brag about tomorrow, since you
don't know what the day will bring.
□ Let someone else praise you, not your
own mouth—a stranger, not your own
lips.

NOVEMBER 5

EZEKIEL 12:1–14:11
Again a message came to me [Ezekiel]
from the LORD: ²"Son of man, you live
among rebels who have eyes but refuse
to see. They have ears but refuse to
hear. For they are a rebellious people.

³"So now, son of man, pretend you
are being sent into exile. Pack the few
items an exile could carry, and leave
your home to go somewhere else. Do
this right in front of the people so they
can see you. For perhaps they will pay
attention to this, even though they are
such rebels. ⁴Bring your baggage outside during the day so they can watch
you. Then in the evening, as they are
watching, leave your house as captives
do when they begin a long march to distant lands. ⁵Dig a hole through the wall
while they are watching and go out
through it. ⁶As they watch, lift your

pack to your shoulders and walk away into the night. Cover your face so you cannot see the land you are leaving. For I have made you a sign for the people of Israel."

[7]So I did as I was told. In broad daylight I brought my pack outside, filled with the things I might carry into exile. Then in the evening while the people looked on, I dug through the wall with my hands and went out into the night with my pack on my shoulder.

[8]The next morning this message came to me from the LORD: [9]"Son of man, these rebels, the people of Israel, have asked you what all this means. [10]Say to them, 'This is what the Sovereign LORD says: These actions contain a message for King Zedekiah in Jerusalem* and for all the people of Israel.' [11]Explain that your actions are a sign to show what will soon happen to them, for they will be driven into exile as captives.

[12]"Even Zedekiah will leave Jerusalem at night through a hole in the wall, taking only what he can carry with him. He will cover his face, and his eyes will not see the land he is leaving. [13]Then I will throw my net over him and capture him in my snare. I will bring him to Babylon, the land of the Babylonians,* though he will never see it, and he will die there. [14]I will scatter his servants and warriors to the four winds and send the sword after them. [15]And when I scatter them among the nations, they will know that I am the LORD. [16]But I will spare a few of them from death by war, famine, or disease, so they can confess all their detestable sins to their captors. Then they will know that I am the LORD."

[17]Then this message came to me from the LORD: [18]"Son of man, tremble as you eat your food. Shake with fear as you drink your water. [19]Tell the people, 'This is what the Sovereign LORD says concerning those living in Israel and Jerusalem: They will eat their food with trembling and sip their water in despair, for their land will be stripped bare because of their violence. [20]The cities will be destroyed and the farm-

land made desolate. Then you will know that I am the LORD.'"

[21]Again a message came to me from the LORD: [22]"Son of man, you've heard that proverb they quote in Israel: 'Time passes, and prophecies come to nothing.' [23]Tell the people, 'This is what the Sovereign LORD says: I will put an end to this proverb, and you will soon stop quoting it.' Now give them this new proverb to replace the old one: 'The time has come for every prophecy to be fulfilled!'

[24]"There will be no more false visions and flattering predictions in Israel. [25]For I am the LORD! If I say it, it will happen. There will be no more delays, you rebels of Israel. I will fulfill my threat of destruction in your own lifetime. I, the Sovereign LORD, have spoken!"

[26]Then this message came to me from the LORD: [27]"Son of man, the people of Israel are saying, 'He's talking about the distant future. His visions won't come true for a long, long time.' [28]Therefore, tell them, 'This is what the Sovereign LORD says: No more delay! I will now do everything I have threatened. I, the Sovereign LORD, have spoken!'"

[13:1]THEN this message came to me from the LORD: [2]"Son of man, prophesy against the false prophets of Israel who are inventing their own prophecies. Say to them, 'Listen to the word of the LORD. [3]This is what the Sovereign LORD says: What sorrow awaits the false prophets who are following their own imaginations and have seen nothing at all!'

[4]"O people of Israel, these prophets of yours are like jackals digging in the ruins. [5]They have done nothing to repair the breaks in the walls around the nation. They have not helped it to stand firm in battle on the day of the LORD. [6]Instead, they have told lies and made false predictions. They say, 'This message is from the LORD,' even though the LORD never sent them. And yet they expect him to fulfill their prophecies! [7]Can your visions be anything but false if you claim, 'This message is from the LORD,' when I have not even spoken to you?

8"Therefore, this is what the Sovereign LORD says: Because what you say is false and your visions are a lie, I will stand against you, says the Sovereign LORD. 9 I will raise my fist against all the prophets who see false visions and make lying predictions, and they will be banished from the community of Israel. I will blot their names from Israel's record books, and they will never again set foot in their own land. Then you will know that I am the Sovereign LORD.

10"This will happen because these evil prophets deceive my people by saying, 'All is peaceful' when there is no peace at all! It's as if the people have built a flimsy wall, and these prophets are trying to reinforce it by covering it with whitewash! 11 Tell these whitewashers that their wall will soon fall down. A heavy rainstorm will undermine it; great hailstones and mighty winds will knock it down. 12 And when the wall falls, the people will cry out, 'What happened to your whitewash?'

13"Therefore, this is what the Sovereign LORD says: I will sweep away your whitewashed wall with a storm of indignation, with a great flood of anger, and with hailstones of fury. 14 I will break down your wall right to its foundation, and when it falls, it will crush you. Then you will know that I am the LORD. 15 At last my anger against the wall and those who covered it with whitewash will be satisfied. Then I will say to you: 'The wall and those who whitewashed it are both gone. 16 They were lying prophets who claimed peace would come to Jerusalem when there was no peace. I, the Sovereign LORD, have spoken!'

17"Now, son of man, speak out against the women who prophesy from their own imaginations. 18 This is what the Sovereign LORD says: What sorrow awaits you women who are ensnaring the souls of my people, young and old alike. You tie magic charms on their wrists and furnish them with magic veils. Do you think you can trap others without bringing destruction on yourselves? 19 You bring shame on me among my people for a few handfuls of barley or a piece of bread. By lying to my people who love to listen to lies, you kill those who should not die, and you promise life to those who should not live.

20"This is what the Sovereign LORD says: I am against all your magic charms, which you use to ensnare my people like birds. I will tear them from your arms, setting my people free like birds set free from a cage. 21 I will tear off the magic veils and save my people from your grasp. They will no longer be your victims. Then you will know that I am the LORD. 22 You have discouraged the righteous with your lies, but I didn't want them to be sad. And you have encouraged the wicked by promising them life, even though they continue in their sins. 23 Because of all this, you will no longer talk of seeing visions that you never saw, nor will you make predictions. For I will rescue my people from your grasp. Then you will know that I am the LORD."

14:1 THEN some of the leaders of Israel visited me, and while they were sitting with me, 2 this message came to me from the LORD: 3"Son of man, these leaders have set up idols* in their hearts. They have embraced things that will make them fall into sin. Why should I listen to their requests? 4 Tell them, 'This is what the Sovereign LORD says: The people of Israel have set up idols in their hearts and fallen into sin, and then they go to a prophet asking for a message. So I, the LORD, will give them the kind of answer their great idolatry deserves. 5 I will do this to capture the minds and hearts of all my people who have turned from me to worship their detestable idols.'

6"Therefore, tell the people of Israel, 'This is what the Sovereign LORD says: Repent and turn away from your idols, and stop all your detestable sins. 7 I, the LORD, will answer all those, both Israelites and foreigners, who reject me and set up idols in their hearts and so fall into sin, and who then come to a prophet asking for my advice. 8 I will turn against such people and make a terrible example of them, eliminating them from among my people. Then you will know that I am the LORD.

9"'And if a prophet is deceived into giving a message, it is because I, the LORD, have deceived that prophet. I will lift my fist against such prophets and cut them off from the community of Israel. ¹⁰False prophets and those who seek their guidance will all be punished for their sins. ¹¹In this way, the people of Israel will learn not to stray from me, polluting themselves with sin. They will be my people, and I will be their God. I, the Sovereign LORD, have spoken!'"

12:10 Hebrew *the prince in Jerusalem;* similarly in 12:12. 12:13 Or *Chaldeans.*   14:3 The Hebrew term (literally *round things*) probably alludes to dung; also in 14:4, 5, 6, 7.

HEBREWS 7:1-17

This Melchizedek was king of the city of Salem and also a priest of God Most High. When Abraham was returning home after winning a great battle against the kings, Melchizedek met him and blessed him. ²Then Abraham took a tenth of all he had captured in battle and gave it to Melchizedek. The name Melchizedek means "king of justice," and king of Salem means "king of peace." ³There is no record of his father or mother or any of his ancestors—no beginning or end to his life. He remains a priest forever, resembling the Son of God.

⁴Consider then how great this Melchizedek was. Even Abraham, the great patriarch of Israel, recognized this by giving him a tenth of what he had taken in battle. ⁵Now the law of Moses required that the priests, who are descendants of Levi, must collect a tithe from the rest of the people of Israel,* who are also descendants of Abraham. ⁶But Melchizedek, who was not a descendant of Levi, collected a tenth from Abraham. And Melchizedek placed a blessing upon Abraham, the one who had already received the promises of God. ⁷And without question, the person who has the power to give a blessing is greater than the one who is blessed.

⁸The priests who collect tithes are men who die, so Melchizedek is greater than they are, because we are told that he lives on. ⁹In addition, we might even say that these Levites—the ones who collect the tithe—paid a tithe to Melchizedek when their ancestor Abraham paid a tithe to him. ¹⁰For although Levi wasn't born yet, the seed from which he came was in Abraham's body when Melchizedek collected the tithe from him.

¹¹So if the priesthood of Levi, on which the law was based, could have achieved the perfection God intended, why did God need to establish a different priesthood, with a priest in the order of Melchizedek instead of the order of Levi and Aaron?*

¹²And if the priesthood is changed, the law must also be changed to permit it. ¹³For the priest we are talking about belongs to a different tribe, whose members have never served at the altar as priests. ¹⁴What I mean is, our Lord came from the tribe of Judah, and Moses never mentioned priests coming from that tribe.

¹⁵This change has been made very clear since a different priest, who is like Melchizedek, has appeared. ¹⁶Jesus became a priest, not by meeting the physical requirement of belonging to the tribe of Levi, but by the power of a life that cannot be destroyed. ¹⁷And the psalmist pointed this out when he prophesied,

"You are a priest forever in the order of Melchizedek."*

7:5 Greek *from their brothers.*   7:11 Greek *the order of Aaron?*   7:17 Ps 110:4.

PSALM 105:37-45

The LORD brought his people
    out of Egypt, loaded with
    silver and gold;
and not one among the tribes
    of Israel even stumbled.
³⁸ Egypt was glad when they
    were gone,
for they feared them greatly.
³⁹ **The LORD spread a cloud above
    them as a covering**

and gave them a great fire
  to light the darkness.
40 They asked for meat, and he
    sent them quail;
  he satisfied their hunger with
    manna—bread from heaven.
41 He split open a rock, and water
    gushed out
  to form a river through the
    dry wasteland.
42 For he remembered his sacred
    promise
  to his servant Abraham.
43 So he brought his people out
    of Egypt with joy,
  his chosen ones with rejoicing.
44 He gave his people the lands of
    pagan nations,
  and they harvested crops that
    others had planted.
45 All this happened so they would
    follow his decrees
  and obey his instructions.

Praise the LORD!

PROVERBS 27:3
A stone is heavy and sand is weighty,
but the resentment caused by a fool is
even heavier.

NOVEMBER
6

EZEKIEL 14:12–16:41
Then this message came to me [Ezekiel]
from the LORD: 13"Son of man, suppose
the people of a country were to sin
against me, and I lifted my fist to crush
them, cutting off their food supply and
sending a famine to destroy both people and animals. 14Even if Noah, Daniel,
and Job were there, their righteousness
would save no one but themselves, says
the Sovereign LORD.

15"Or suppose I were to send wild animals to invade the country, kill the peo-

ple, and make the land too desolate and
dangerous to pass through. 16As surely
as I live, says the Sovereign LORD, even
if those three men were there, they
wouldn't be able to save their own sons
or daughters. They alone would be saved,
but the land would be made desolate.

17"Or suppose I were to bring war
against the land, and I sent enemy armies
to destroy both people and animals. 18As
surely as I live, says the Sovereign LORD,
even if those three men were there, they
wouldn't be able to save their own sons or
daughters. They alone would be saved.

19"Or suppose I were to pour out my
fury by sending an epidemic into the
land, and the disease killed people and
animals alike. 20As surely as I live, says
the Sovereign LORD, even if Noah, Daniel, and Job were there, they wouldn't be
able to save their own sons or daughters. They alone would be saved by their
righteousness.

21"Now this is what the Sovereign
LORD says: How terrible it will be when
all four of these dreadful punishments
fall upon Jerusalem—war, famine, wild
animals, and disease—destroying all her
people and animals. 22Yet there will be
survivors, and they will come here to join
you as exiles in Babylon. You will see
with your own eyes how wicked they are,
and then you will feel better about what I
have done to Jerusalem. 23When you
meet them and see their behavior, you
will understand that these things are not
being done to Israel without cause. I, the
Sovereign LORD, have spoken!"

15:1Then this message came to me from
the LORD: 2"Son of man, how does a
grapevine compare to a tree? Is a vine's
wood as useful as the wood of a tree?
3Can its wood be used for making
things, like pegs to hang up pots and
pans? 4No, it can only be used for fuel,
and even as fuel, it burns too quickly.
5Vines are useless both before and after
being put into the fire!

6"And this is what the Sovereign
LORD says: The people of Jerusalem are
like grapevines growing among the

trees of the forest. Since they are useless, I have thrown them on the fire to be burned. ⁷And I will see to it that if they escape from one fire, they will fall into another. When I turn against them, you will know that I am the LORD. ⁸And I will make the land desolate because my people have been unfaithful to me. I, the Sovereign LORD, have spoken!"

¹⁶:¹THEN another message came to me from the LORD: ²"Son of man, confront Jerusalem with her detestable sins. ³Give her this message from the Sovereign LORD: You are nothing but a Canaanite! Your father was an Amorite and your mother a Hittite. ⁴On the day you were born, no one cared about you. Your umbilical cord was not cut, and you were never washed, rubbed with salt, and wrapped in cloth. ⁵No one had the slightest interest in you; no one pitied you or cared for you. On the day you were born, you were unwanted, dumped in a field and left to die.

⁶"But I came by and saw you there, helplessly kicking about in your own blood. As you lay there, I said, 'Live!' ⁷And I helped you to thrive like a plant in the field. You grew up and became a beautiful jewel. Your breasts became full, and your body hair grew, but you were still naked. ⁸And when I passed by again, I saw that you were old enough for love. So I wrapped my cloak around you to cover your nakedness and declared my marriage vows. I made a covenant with you, says the Sovereign LORD, and you became mine.

⁹"Then I bathed you and washed off your blood, and I rubbed fragrant oils into your skin. ¹⁰I gave you expensive clothing of fine linen and silk, beautifully embroidered, and sandals made of fine goatskin leather. ¹¹I gave you lovely jewelry, bracelets, beautiful necklaces, ¹²a ring for your nose, earrings for your ears, and a lovely crown for your head. ¹³And so you were adorned with gold and silver. Your clothes were made of fine linen and were beautifully embroidered. You ate the finest foods—choice

flour, honey, and olive oil—and became more beautiful than ever. You looked like a queen, and so you were! ¹⁴Your fame soon spread throughout the world because of your beauty. I dressed you in my splendor and perfected your beauty, says the Sovereign LORD.

¹⁵"But you thought your fame and beauty were your own. So you gave yourself as a prostitute to every man who came along. Your beauty was theirs for the asking. ¹⁶You used the lovely things I gave you to make shrines for idols, where you played the prostitute. Unbelievable! How could such a thing ever happen? ¹⁷You took the very jewels and gold and silver ornaments I had given you and made statues of men and worshiped them. This is adultery against me! ¹⁸You used the beautifully embroidered clothes I gave you to dress your idols. Then you used my special oil and my incense to worship them. ¹⁹Imagine it! You set before them as a sacrifice the choice flour, olive oil, and honey I had given you, says the Sovereign LORD.

²⁰"Then you took your sons and daughters—the children you had borne to me—and sacrificed them to your gods. Was your prostitution not enough? ²¹Must you also slaughter my children by sacrificing them to idols? ²²In all your years of adultery and detestable sin, you have not once remembered the days long ago when you lay naked in a field, kicking about in your own blood.

²³"What sorrow awaits you, says the Sovereign LORD. In addition to all your other wickedness, ²⁴you built a pagan shrine and put altars to idols in every town square. ²⁵On every street corner you defiled your beauty, offering your body to every passerby in an endless stream of prostitution. ²⁶Then you added lustful Egypt to your lovers, provoking my anger with your increasing promiscuity. ²⁷That is why I struck you with my fist and reduced your boundaries. I handed you over to your enemies, the Philistines, and even they were shocked by your lewd conduct. ²⁸You have prostituted yourself with the Assyr-

ians, too. It seems you can never find enough new lovers! And after your prostitution there, you still were not satisfied. [29]You added to your lovers by embracing Babylonia,* the land of merchants, but you still weren't satisfied.

[30]"What a sick heart you have, says the Sovereign LORD, to do such things as these, acting like a shameless prostitute. [31]You build your pagan shrines on every street corner and your altars to idols in every square. In fact, you have been worse than a prostitute, so eager for sin that you have not even demanded payment. [32]Yes, you are an adulterous wife who takes in strangers instead of her own husband. [33]Prostitutes charge for their services—but not you! You give gifts to your lovers, bribing them to come and have sex with you. [34]So you are the opposite of other prostitutes. You pay your lovers instead of their paying you!

[35]"Therefore, you prostitute, listen to this message from the LORD! [36]This is what the Sovereign LORD says: Because you have poured out your lust and exposed yourself in prostitution to all your lovers, and because you have worshiped detestable idols,* and because you have slaughtered your children as sacrifices to your gods, [37]this is what I am going to do. I will gather together all your allies—the lovers with whom you have sinned, both those you loved and those you hated—and I will strip you naked in front of them so they can stare at you. [38]I will punish you for your murder and adultery. I will cover you with blood in my jealous fury. [39]Then I will give you to these many nations who are your lovers, and they will destroy you. They will knock down your pagan shrines and the altars to your idols. They will strip you and take your beautiful jewels, leaving you stark naked. [40]They will band together in a mob to stone you and cut you up with swords. [41]They will burn your homes and punish you in front of many women. I will stop your prostitution and end your payments to your many lovers."

16:29 Or *Chaldea.*   **16:36** The Hebrew term (literally *round things*) probably alludes to dung.

HEBREWS 7:18-28

Yes, the old requirement about the priesthood was set aside because it was weak and useless. [19]For the law never made anything perfect. But now we have confidence in a better hope, through which we draw near to God.

[20]This new system was established with a solemn oath. Aaron's descendants became priests without such an oath, [21]but there was an oath regarding Jesus. For God said to him,

> "The LORD has taken an oath and
>   will not break his vow:
>   'You are a priest forever.'"*

[22]Because of this oath, Jesus is the one who guarantees this better covenant with God.

[23]There were many priests under the old system, for death prevented them from remaining in office. [24]But because Jesus lives forever, his priesthood lasts forever. [25]Therefore he is able, once and forever, to save* those who come to God through him. He lives forever to intercede with God on their behalf. [26]He is the kind of High Priest we need because He is holy and blameless, unstained by sin. He has been set apart from sinners and has been given the highest place of honor in heaven.* [27]Unlike those other high priests, he does not need to offer sacrifices every day. They did this for their own sins first and then for the sins of the people. But Jesus did this once for all when He offered Himself as the sacrifice for the people's sins. [28]**The law appointed high priests who were limited by human weakness. But after the law was given, God appointed His Son with an oath, and His Son has been made the perfect High Priest forever.**

7:21 Ps 110:4.   **7:25** Or *is able to save completely.*
7:26 Or *has been exalted higher than the heavens.*

PSALM 106:1-12

Praise the LORD!

Give thanks to the LORD, for he
    is good!

His faithful love endures forever.
² Who can list the glorious miracles
   of the Lord?
   Who can ever praise Him
      enough?
³ There is joy for those who deal
      justly with others
   and always do what is right.
⁴ Remember me, Lord, when you
      show favor to your people;
   come near and rescue me.
⁵ Let me share in the prosperity of
      your chosen ones.
   Let me rejoice in the joy
      of your people;
   let me praise you with those who
      are your heritage.

⁶ Like our ancestors, we have sinned.
   We have done wrong! We have
      acted wickedly!
⁷ Our ancestors in Egypt
   were not impressed by the Lord's
      miraculous deeds.
   They soon forgot his many acts of
      kindness to them.
   Instead, they rebelled against
      him at the Red Sea.*
⁸ Even so, he saved them—
   to defend the honor of his name
   and to demonstrate his
      mighty power.
⁹ He commanded the Red Sea*
      to dry up.
   He led Israel across the sea
      as if it were a desert.
¹⁰ So he rescued them from their
      enemies
   and redeemed them from
      their foes.
¹¹ Then the water returned and
      covered their enemies;
   not one of them survived.
¹² Then his people believed his
      promises.
   Then they sang his praise.

106:7 Hebrew *at the sea, the sea of reeds.*   **106:9** Hebrew
sea of reeds; also in 106:22.

PROVERBS 27:4-6
Anger is cruel, and wrath is like a flood,
but jealousy is even more dangerous.

□ An open rebuke is better than hidden
love! □ Wounds from a sincere friend
are better than many kisses from an enemy.

NOVEMBER 7

EZEKIEL 16:42–17:24
"**T**hen at last my [Lord's] fury against you
will be spent, and my jealous anger will
subside. I will be calm and will not be angry with you anymore. ⁴³But first, because you have not remembered your
youth but have angered me by doing all
these evil things, I will fully repay you for
all of your sins, says the Sovereign Lord.
For you have added lewd acts to all your
detestable sins. ⁴⁴Everyone who makes
up proverbs will say of you, 'Like mother,
like daughter.' ⁴⁵For your mother loathed
her husband and her children, and so do
you. And you are exactly like your sisters,
for they despised their husbands and
their children. Truly your mother was a
Hittite and your father an Amorite.

⁴⁶"Your older sister was Samaria, who
lived with her daughters in the north.
Your younger sister was Sodom, who
lived with her daughters in the south.
⁴⁷But you have not merely sinned as
they did. You quickly surpassed them in
corruption. ⁴⁸As surely as I live, says the
Sovereign Lord, Sodom and her daughters were never as wicked as you and
your daughters. ⁴⁹Sodom's sins were
pride, gluttony, and laziness, while the
poor and needy suffered outside her
door. ⁵⁰She was proud and committed
detestable sins, so I wiped her out, as you
have seen.*

⁵¹"Even Samaria did not commit half
your sins. You have done far more detestable things than your sisters ever
did. They seem righteous compared to
you. ⁵²Shame on you! Your sins are so

terrible that you make your sisters seem righteous, even virtuous.

⁵³"But someday I will restore the fortunes of Sodom and Samaria, and I will restore you, too. ⁵⁴Then you will be truly ashamed of everything you have done, for your sins make them feel good in comparison. ⁵⁵Yes, your sisters, Sodom and Samaria, and all their people will be restored, and at that time you also will be restored. ⁵⁶In your proud days you held Sodom in contempt. ⁵⁷But now your greater wickedness has been exposed to all the world, and you are the one who is scorned—by Edom* and all her neighbors and by Philistia. ⁵⁸This is your punishment for all your lewdness and detestable sins, says the LORD.

⁵⁹"Now this is what the Sovereign LORD says: I will give you what you deserve, for you have taken your solemn vows lightly by breaking your covenant. ⁶⁰Yet I will remember the covenant I made with you when you were young, and I will establish an everlasting covenant with you. ⁶¹Then you will remember with shame all the evil you have done. I will make your sisters, Samaria and Sodom, to be your daughters, even though they are not part of our covenant. ⁶²And I will reaffirm my covenant with you, and you will know that I am the LORD. ⁶³You will remember your sins and cover your mouth in silent shame when I forgive you of all that you have done. I, the Sovereign LORD, have spoken!"

¹⁷:¹THEN this message came to me from the LORD: ²"Son of man, give this riddle, and tell this story to the people of Israel. ³Give them this message from the Sovereign LORD:

"A great eagle with broad wings
    and long feathers,
  covered with many-colored
    plumage, came to Lebanon.
He seized the top of a cedar tree
⁴   and plucked off its highest branch.
He carried it away to a city filled
    with merchants.
  He planted it in a city of traders.

⁵ He also took a seedling from
    the land
  and planted it in fertile soil.
He placed it beside a broad river,
    where it could grow like a
    willow tree.
⁶ It took root there and
  grew into a low, spreading vine.
  Its branches turned up toward
    the eagle,
  and its roots grew down into
    the ground.
It produced strong branches
  and put out shoots.
⁷ But then another great eagle came
  with broad wings and full
    plumage.
So the vine now sent its roots and
    branches
  toward him for water,
⁸ even though it was already planted
    in good soil
  and had plenty of water
so it could grow into a splendid
    vine
  and produce rich leaves and
    luscious fruit.

⁹ "So now the Sovereign LORD asks:
  Will this vine grow and prosper?
  No! I will pull it up, roots
    and all!
I will cut off its fruit
  and let its leaves wither and die.
I will pull it up easily
  without a strong arm or
    a large army.
¹⁰ But when the vine is transplanted,
    will it thrive?
No, it will wither away
  when the east wind blows
    against it.
It will die in the same good soil
  where it had grown so well."

¹¹Then this message came to me from the LORD: ¹²"Say to these rebels of Israel: Don't you understand the meaning of this riddle of the eagles? The king of Babylon came to Jerusalem, took away her king and princes, and brought them to Babylon. ¹³He made a treaty with a

member of the royal family and forced him to take an oath of loyalty. He also exiled Israel's most influential leaders, [14]so Israel would not become strong again and revolt. Only by keeping her treaty with Babylon could Israel survive.

[15]"Nevertheless, this man of Israel's royal family rebelled against Babylon, sending ambassadors to Egypt to request a great army and many horses. Can Israel break her sworn treaties like that and get away with it? [16]No! For as surely as I live, says the Sovereign LORD, the king of Israel will die in Babylon, the land of the king who put him in power and whose treaty he disregarded and broke. [17]Pharaoh and all his mighty army will fail to help Israel when the king of Babylon lays siege to Jerusalem again and destroys many lives. [18]For the king of Israel disregarded his treaty and broke it after swearing to obey; therefore, he will not escape.

[19]"So this is what the Sovereign LORD says: As surely as I live, I will punish him for breaking my covenant and disregarding the solemn oath he made in my name. [20]I will throw my net over him and capture him in my snare. I will bring him to Babylon and put him on trial for this treason against me. [21]And all his best warriors* will be killed in battle, and those who survive will be scattered to the four winds. Then you will know that I, the LORD, have spoken.

[22]"This is what the Sovereign LORD says: I will take a branch from the top of a tall cedar, and I will plant it on the top of Israel's highest mountain. [23]It will become a majestic cedar, sending forth its branches and producing seed. Birds of every sort will nest in it, finding shelter in the shade of its branches. [24]**And all the trees will know that it is I, the LORD, who cuts the tall tree down and makes the short tree grow tall. It is I who makes the green tree wither and gives the dead tree new life. I, the LORD, have spoken, and I will do what I said!"**

16:50 As in a few Hebrew manuscripts and Greek version; Masoretic Text reads *as I have seen.* 16:57 Many ancient manuscripts read *Aram.* 17:21 Or *his fleeing warriors.* The meaning of the Hebrew is uncertain.

HEBREWS 8:1-13

Here is the main point: We have a High Priest who sat down in the place of honor beside the throne of the majestic God in heaven. [2]There he ministers in the heavenly Tabernacle,* the true place of worship that was built by the Lord and not by human hands.

[3]And since every high priest is required to offer gifts and sacrifices, our High Priest must make an offering, too. [4]If he were here on earth, he would not even be a priest, since there already are priests who offer the gifts required by the law. [5]They serve in a system of worship that is only a copy, a shadow of the real one in heaven. For when Moses was getting ready to build the Tabernacle, God gave him this warning: "Be sure that you make everything according to the pattern I have shown you here on the mountain."*

[6]But now Jesus, our High Priest, has been given a ministry that is far superior to the old priesthood, for he is the one who mediates for us a far better covenant with God, based on better promises.

[7]If the first covenant had been faultless, there would have been no need for a second covenant to replace it. [8]But when God found fault with the people, he said:

"The day is coming, says the LORD,
    when I will make a new covenant
    with the people of Israel and
        Judah.
[9] This covenant will not be like
        the one
    I made with their ancestors
when I took them by the hand
    and led them out of the land
        of Egypt.
They did not remain faithful to
        my covenant,
    so I turned my back on them, says
        the LORD.
[10] But this is the new covenant I
        will make
    with the people of Israel on that
        day,* says the LORD:

I will put my laws in their minds,
and I will write them on their hearts.
I will be their God,
and they will be my people.
¹¹ And they will not need to teach
their neighbors,
nor will they need to teach their
relatives,*
saying, 'You should know the
LORD.'
For everyone, from the least to the
greatest,
will know me already.
¹² And I will forgive their wickedness,
and I will never again remember
their sins."*

¹³ When God speaks of a "new" covenant, it means he has made the first
one obsolete. It is now out of date and
will soon disappear.

8:2 Or *tent;* also in 8:5.   **8:5** Exod 25:40; 26:30.
8:10 Greek *after those days.*   **8:11** Greek *their brother.*
8:8-12 Jer 31:31-34.

PSALM 106:13-31
Yet how quickly they [the Israelites]
forgot what he had done!
They wouldn't wait for his
counsel!
¹⁴ In the wilderness their desires ran
wild,
testing God's patience in that dry
wasteland.
¹⁵ So he gave them what they asked for,
but he sent a plague along with it.
¹⁶ The people in the camp were jealous
of Moses
and envious of Aaron, the LORD's
holy priest.
¹⁷ Because of this, the earth opened up;
it swallowed Dathan
and buried Abiram and the
other rebels.
¹⁸ Fire fell upon their followers;
a flame consumed the wicked.

¹⁹ The people made a calf at
Mount Sinai*;
they bowed before an image
made of gold.
²⁰ They traded their glorious God
for a statue of a grass-eating bull.

²¹ They forgot God, their savior,
who had done such great things
in Egypt—
²² such wonderful things in the
land of Ham,
such awesome deeds at the Red
Sea.
²³ So he declared he would destroy
them.
But Moses, his chosen one,
stepped between the LORD
and the people.
He begged him to turn from his
anger and not destroy them.

²⁴ The people refused to enter the
pleasant land,
for they wouldn't believe his
promise to care for them.
²⁵ Instead, they grumbled in their tents
and refused to obey the LORD.
²⁶ Therefore, he solemnly swore
that he would kill them in the
wilderness,
²⁷ that he would scatter their
descendants among the
nations,
exiling them to distant lands.

²⁸ Then our ancestors joined in the
worship of Baal at Peor;
they even ate sacrifices offered
to the dead!
²⁹ They angered the LORD with all
these things,
so a plague broke out among
them.
³⁰ But Phinehas had the courage
to intervene,
and the plague was stopped.
³¹ So he has been regarded as a
righteous man
ever since that time.

106:19 Hebrew *at Horeb,* another name for Sinai.

PROVERBS 27:7-9
A person who is full refuses honey, but
even bitter food tastes sweet to the hungry. □ A person who strays from home
is like a bird that strays from its nest.
□ The heartfelt counsel of a friend is as
sweet as perfume and incense.

NOVEMBER 8

EZEKIEL 18:1–19:14

Then another message came to me [Ezekiel] from the LORD: ²"Why do you quote this proverb concerning the land of Israel: 'The parents have eaten sour grapes, but their children's mouths pucker at the taste'? ³As surely as I live, says the Sovereign LORD, you will not quote this proverb anymore in Israel. ⁴For all people are mine to judge—both parents and children alike. And this is my rule: The person who sins is the one who will die.

⁵"Suppose a certain man is righteous and does what is just and right. ⁶He does not feast in the mountains before Israel's idols* or worship them. He does not commit adultery or have intercourse with a woman during her menstrual period. ⁷He is a merciful creditor, not keeping the items given as security by poor debtors. He does not rob the poor but instead gives food to the hungry and provides clothes for the needy. ⁸He grants loans without interest, stays away from injustice, is honest and fair when judging others, ⁹and faithfully obeys my decrees and regulations. Anyone who does these things is just and will surely live, says the Sovereign LORD.

¹⁰"But suppose that man has a son who grows up to be a robber or murderer and refuses to do what is right. ¹¹And that son does all the evil things his father would never do—he worships idols on the mountains, commits adultery, ¹²oppresses the poor and helpless, steals from debtors by refusing to let them redeem their security, worships idols, commits detestable sins, ¹³and lends money at excessive interest. Should such a sinful person live? No! He must die and must take full blame.

¹⁴"But suppose that sinful son, in turn, has a son who sees his father's wickedness and decides against that kind of life. ¹⁵This son refuses to worship idols on the mountains and does not commit adultery. ¹⁶He does not exploit the poor, but instead is fair to debtors and does not rob them. He gives food to the hungry and provides clothes for the needy. ¹⁷He helps the poor, does not lend money at interest, and obeys all my regulations and decrees. Such a person will not die because of his father's sins; he will surely live. ¹⁸But the father will die for his many sins—for being cruel, robbing people, and doing what was clearly wrong among his people.

¹⁹"'What?' you ask. 'Doesn't the child pay for the parent's sins?' No! For if the child does what is just and right and keeps my decrees, that child will surely live. ²⁰The person who sins is the one who will die. The child will not be punished for the parent's sins, and the parent will not be punished for the child's sins. Righteous people will be rewarded for their own righteous behavior, and wicked people will be punished for their own wickedness. ²¹But if wicked people turn away from all their sins and begin to obey my decrees and do what is just and right, they will surely live and not die. ²²All their past sins will be forgotten, and they will live because of the righteous things they have done.

²³"Do you think that I like to see wicked people die? says the Sovereign LORD. Of course not! I want them to turn from their wicked ways and live. ²⁴However, if righteous people turn from their righteous behavior and start doing sinful things and act like other sinners, should they be allowed to live? No, of course not! All their righteous acts will be forgotten, and they will die for their sins.

²⁵"Yet you say, 'The Lord isn't doing what's right!' Listen to me, O people of Israel. Am I the one not doing what's right, or is it you? ²⁶When righteous people turn from their righteous behavior and start doing sinful things, they will die for it. Yes, they will die because of their sinful deeds. ²⁷And if wicked people turn from their wickedness, obey the law, and do what is just and right, they will save

their lives. [28]They will live because they thought it over and decided to turn from their sins. Such people will not die. [29]And yet the people of Israel keep saying, 'The Lord isn't doing what's right!' O people of Israel, it is you who are not doing what's right, not I.

[30]"Therefore, I will judge each of you, O people of Israel, according to your actions, says the Sovereign LORD. Repent, and turn from your sins. Don't let them destroy you! [31]**Put all your rebellion behind you, and find yourselves a new heart and a new spirit. For why should you die, O people of Israel?** [32]**I don't want you to die, says the Sovereign LORD. Turn back and live!**

[19:1]"SING this funeral song for the princes of Israel:

[2] "What is your mother?
    A lioness among lions!
She lay down among the young lions
    and reared her cubs.
[3] She raised one of her cubs
    to become a strong young lion.
He learned to hunt and devour prey,
    and he became a man-eater.
[4] Then the nations heard about him,
    and he was trapped in their pit.
They led him away with hooks
    to the land of Egypt.

[5] "When the lioness saw
    that her hopes for him were gone,
she took another of her cubs
    and taught him to be a strong
        young lion.
[6] He prowled among the other lions
    and stood out among them
        in his strength.
He learned to hunt and devour prey,
    and he, too, became a man-eater.
[7] He demolished fortresses*
    and destroyed their towns and
        cities.
Their farms were desolated,
    and their crops were destroyed.
The land and its people trembled
        in fear
    when they heard him roar.
[8] Then the armies of the nations
    attacked him,

surrounding him from every
    direction.
They threw a net over him
    and captured him in their pit.
[9] With hooks, they dragged him
        into a cage
    and brought him before the king
        of Babylon.
They held him in captivity,
    so his voice could never again
        be heard
    on the mountains of Israel.

[10] "Your mother was like a vine
    planted by the water's edge.
It had lush, green foliage
    because of the abundant water.
[11] Its branches became strong—
    strong enough to be a ruler's
        scepter.
It grew very tall,
    towering above all others.
It stood out because of its height
    and its many lush branches.
[12] But the vine was uprooted in fury
    and thrown down to the ground.
The desert wind dried up its fruit
    and tore off its strong branches,
so that it withered
    and was destroyed by fire.
[13] Now the vine is transplanted to the
        wilderness,
    where the ground is hard and dry.
[14] A fire has burst out from its branches
    and devoured its fruit.
Its remaining limbs are not
    strong enough to be a ruler's
        scepter.

"This is a funeral song, and it will be used in a funeral."

18:6 The Hebrew term (literally *round things*) probably alludes to dung; also in 18:12, 15. **19:7** As in Greek version; Hebrew reads *He knew widows.*

HEBREWS 9:1-10

That first covenant between God and Israel had regulations for worship and a place of worship here on earth. [2]There were two rooms in that Tabernacle.* In the first room were a lampstand, a table, and sacred loaves of bread on the table. This room was called the Holy Place.

³Then there was a curtain, and behind the curtain was the second room* called the Most Holy Place. ⁴In that room were a gold incense altar and a wooden chest called the Ark of the Covenant, which was covered with gold on all sides. Inside the Ark were a gold jar containing manna, Aaron's staff that sprouted leaves, and the stone tablets of the covenant. ⁵Above the Ark were the cherubim of divine glory, whose wings stretched out over the Ark's cover, the place of atonement. But we cannot explain these things in detail now.

⁶When these things were all in place, the priests regularly entered the first room* as they performed their religious duties. ⁷But only the high priest ever entered the Most Holy Place, and only once a year. And he always offered blood for his own sins and for the sins the people had committed in ignorance. ⁸By these regulations the Holy Spirit revealed that the entrance to the Most Holy Place was not freely open as long as the Tabernacle* and the system it represented were still in use.

⁹This is an illustration pointing to the present time. For the gifts and sacrifices that the priests offer are not able to cleanse the consciences of the people who bring them. ¹⁰For that old system deals only with food and drink and various cleansing ceremonies—physical regulations that were in effect only until a better system could be established.

9:2 Or *tent;* also in 9:11, 21.   9:3 Greek *second tent.*
9:6 Greek *first tent.*   9:8 Or *the first room;* Greek reads *the first tent.*

PSALM 106:32-48
At Meribah, too, they [the Israelites] angered the Lᴏʀᴅ,
    causing Moses serious trouble.
³³ They made Moses angry,*
    and he spoke foolishly.

³⁴ Israel failed to destroy the nations in the land,
    as the Lᴏʀᴅ had commanded them.
³⁵ Instead, they mingled among the pagans
    and adopted their evil customs.

³⁶ They worshiped their idols,
    which led to their downfall.
³⁷ They even sacrificed their sons
    and their daughters to the demons.
³⁸ They shed innocent blood,
    the blood of their sons and daughters.
By sacrificing them to the idols of Canaan,
    they polluted the land with murder.
³⁹ They defiled themselves by their evil deeds,
    and their love of idols was adultery in the Lᴏʀᴅ's sight.

⁴⁰ That is why the Lᴏʀᴅ's anger burned against his people,
    and he abhorred his own special possession.
⁴¹ He handed them over to pagan nations,
    and they were ruled by those who hated them.
⁴² Their enemies crushed them
    and brought them under their cruel power.
⁴³ Again and again he rescued them,
    but they chose to rebel against him,
    and they were finally destroyed by their sin.
⁴⁴ Even so, he pitied them in their distress
    and listened to their cries.
⁴⁵ He remembered his covenant with them
    and relented because of his unfailing love.
⁴⁶ He even caused their captors
    to treat them with kindness.

⁴⁷ Save us, O Lᴏʀᴅ our God!
    Gather us back from among the nations,
    so we can thank your holy name
    and rejoice and praise you.

⁴⁸ Praise the Lᴏʀᴅ, the God of Israel,
    who lives from everlasting to everlasting!
    Let all the people say, "Amen!"

Praise the Lᴏʀᴅ!

106:33 Hebrew *They embittered his spirit.*

PROVERBS 27:10

Never abandon a friend—either yours or your father's. When disaster strikes, you won't have to ask your brother for assistance. It's better to go to a neighbor than to a brother who lives far away.

NOVEMBER 9

EZEKIEL 20:1-49

On August 14,* during the seventh year of King Jehoiachin's captivity, some of the leaders of Israel came to request a message from the LORD. They sat down in front of me to wait for his reply. ²Then this message came to me from the LORD: ³"Son of man, tell the leaders of Israel, 'This is what the Sovereign LORD says: How dare you come to ask me for a message? As surely as I live, says the Sovereign LORD, I will tell you nothing!'

⁴"Son of man, bring charges against them and condemn them. Make them realize how detestable the sins of their ancestors really were. ⁵Give them this message from the Sovereign LORD: When I chose Israel—when I revealed myself to the descendants of Jacob in Egypt—I took a solemn oath that I, the LORD, would be their God. ⁶I took a solemn oath that day that I would bring them out of Egypt to a land I had discovered and explored for them—a good land, a land flowing with milk and honey, the best of all lands anywhere. ⁷Then I said to them, 'Each of you, get rid of the vile images you are so obsessed with. Do not defile yourselves with the idols* of Egypt, for I am the LORD your God.'

⁸"But they rebelled against me and would not listen. They did not get rid of the vile images they were obsessed with, or forsake the idols of Egypt. Then I threatened to pour out my fury on them

to satisfy my anger while they were still in Egypt. ⁹But I didn't do it, for I acted to protect the honor of my name. I would not allow shame to be brought on my name among the surrounding nations who saw me reveal myself by bringing the Israelites out of Egypt. ¹⁰So I brought them out of Egypt and led them into the wilderness. ¹¹There I gave them my decrees and regulations so they could find life by keeping them. ¹²And I gave them my Sabbath days of rest as a sign between them and me. It was to remind them that I am the LORD, who had set them apart to be holy.

¹³"But the people of Israel rebelled against me, and they refused to obey my decrees there in the wilderness. They wouldn't obey my regulations even though obedience would have given them life. They also violated my Sabbath days. So I threatened to pour out my fury on them, and I made plans to utterly consume them in the wilderness. ¹⁴But again I held back in order to protect the honor of my name before the nations who had seen my power in bringing Israel out of Egypt. ¹⁵But I took a solemn oath against them in the wilderness. I swore I would not bring them into the land I had given them, a land flowing with milk and honey, the most beautiful place on earth. ¹⁶For they had rejected my regulations, refused to follow my decrees, and violated my Sabbath days. Their hearts were given to their idols. ¹⁷Nevertheless, I took pity on them and held back from destroying them in the wilderness.

¹⁸"Then I warned their children not to follow in their parents' footsteps, defiling themselves with their idols. ¹⁹'I am the LORD your God,' I told them. 'Follow my decrees, pay attention to my regulations, ²⁰and keep my Sabbath days holy, for they are a sign to remind you that I am the LORD your God.'

²¹"But their children, too, rebelled against me. They refused to keep my decrees and follow my regulations, even though obedience would have given them life. And they also violated

my Sabbath days. So again I threatened to pour out my fury on them in the wilderness. 22Nevertheless, I withdrew my judgment against them to protect the honor of my name before the nations that had seen my power in bringing them out of Egypt. 23But I took a solemn oath against them in the wilderness. I swore I would scatter them among all the nations 24because they did not obey my regulations. They scorned my decrees by violating my Sabbath days and longing for the idols of their ancestors. 25I gave them over to worthless decrees and regulations that would not lead to life. 26I let them pollute themselves* with the very gifts I had given them, and I allowed them to give their firstborn children as offerings to their gods—so I might devastate them and remind them that I alone am the LORD.

27"Therefore, son of man, give the people of Israel this message from the Sovereign LORD: Your ancestors continued to blaspheme and betray me, 28for when I brought them into the land I had promised them, they offered sacrifices on every high hill and under every green tree they saw! They roused my fury as they offered up sacrifices to their gods. They brought their perfumes and incense and poured out their liquid offerings to them. 29I said to them, 'What is this high place where you are going?' (This kind of pagan shrine has been called Bamah—'high place'—ever since.)

30"Therefore, give the people of Israel this message from the Sovereign LORD: Do you plan to pollute yourselves just as your ancestors did? Do you intend to keep prostituting yourselves by worshiping vile images? 31For when you offer gifts to them and give your little children to be burned as sacrifices,* you continue to pollute yourselves with idols to this day. Should I allow you to ask for a message from me, O people of Israel? As surely as I live, says the Sovereign LORD, I will tell you nothing.

32"You say, 'We want to be like the nations all around us, who serve idols of wood and stone.' But what you have in mind will never happen. 33As surely as I live, says the Sovereign LORD, I will rule over you with an iron fist in great anger and with awesome power. 34And in anger I will reach out with my strong hand and powerful arm, and I will bring you back* from the lands where you are scattered. 35I will bring you into the wilderness of the nations, and there I will judge you face to face. 36I will judge you there just as I did your ancestors in the wilderness after bringing them out of Egypt, says the Sovereign LORD. 37I will examine you carefully and hold you to the terms of the covenant. 38I will purge you of all those who rebel and revolt against me. I will bring them out of the countries where they are in exile, but they will never enter the land of Israel. Then you will know that I am the LORD.

39"As for you, O people of Israel, this is what the Sovereign LORD says: Go right ahead and worship your idols, but sooner or later you will obey me and will stop bringing shame on my holy name by worshiping idols. 40For on my holy mountain, the great mountain of Israel, says the Sovereign LORD, the people of Israel will someday worship me, and I will accept them. There I will require that you bring me all your offerings and choice gifts and sacrifices. 41When I bring you home from exile, you will be like a pleasing sacrifice to me. And I will display my holiness through you as all the nations watch. 42Then when I have brought you home to the land I promised with a solemn oath to give to your ancestors, you will know that I am the LORD. 43You will look back on all the ways you defiled yourselves and will hate yourselves because of the evil you have done. 44You will know that I am the LORD, O people of Israel, when I have honored my name by treating you mercifully in spite of your wickedness. I, the Sovereign LORD, have spoken!"

45*Then this message came to me from the LORD: 46"Son of man, turn and face the south* and speak out against it;

prophesy against the brushlands of the Negev. [47]Tell the southern wilderness, 'This is what the Sovereign LORD says: Hear the word of the LORD! I will set you on fire, and every tree, both green and dry, will be burned. The terrible flames will not be quenched and will scorch everything from south to north. [48]And everyone in the world will see that I, the LORD, have set this fire. It will not be put out.'"

[49]Then I said, "O Sovereign LORD, they are saying of me, 'He only talks in riddles!'"

20:1 Hebrew *In the fifth month, on the tenth day,* of the ancient Hebrew lunar calendar. This day was August 14, 591 B.C.; also see note on 1:1.   20:7 The Hebrew term (literally *round things*) probably alludes to dung; also in 20:8, 16, 18, 24, 31, 39.   20:25-26 Or *I gave them worthless decrees and regulations. . . . I polluted them.*   20:31 Or *and make your little children pass through the fire.*
20:34 Greek version reads *I will welcome you.* Compare 2 Cor 6:17.   20:45 Verses 20:45-49 are numbered 21:1-5 in Hebrew text.   20:46 Hebrew *toward Teman.*

HEBREWS 9:11-28

So Christ has now become the High Priest over all the good things that have come.* He has entered that greater, more perfect Tabernacle in heaven, which was not made by human hands and is not part of this created world. [12]With his own blood—not the blood of goats and calves—he entered the Most Holy Place once for all time and secured our redemption forever.

[13]Under the old system, the blood of goats and bulls and the ashes of a young cow could cleanse people's bodies from ceremonial impurity. [14]Just think how much more the blood of Christ will purify our consciences from sinful deeds* so that we can worship the living God. For by the power of the eternal Spirit, Christ offered himself to God as a perfect sacrifice for our sins. [15]That is why he is the one who mediates a new covenant between God and people, so that all who are called can receive the eternal inheritance God has promised them. For Christ died to set them free from the penalty of the sins they had committed under that first covenant.

[16]Now when someone leaves a will,* it is necessary to prove that the person who made it is dead.* [17]The will goes into effect only after the person's death. While the person who made it is still alive, the will cannot be put into effect.

[18]That is why even the first covenant was put into effect with the blood of an animal. [19]For after Moses had read each of God's commandments to all the people, he took the blood of calves and goats,* along with water, and sprinkled both the book of God's law and all the people, using hyssop branches and scarlet wool. [20]Then he said, "This blood confirms the covenant God has made with you."* [21]And in the same way, he sprinkled blood on the Tabernacle and on everything used for worship. [22]In fact, according to the law of Moses, nearly everything was purified with blood. For without the shedding of blood, there is no forgiveness.

[23]That is why the Tabernacle and everything in it, which were copies of things in heaven, had to be purified by the blood of animals. But the real things in heaven had to be purified with far better sacrifices than the blood of animals.

[24]For Christ did not enter into a holy place made with human hands, which was only a copy of the true one in heaven. He entered into heaven itself to appear now before God on our behalf. [25]And he did not enter heaven to offer himself again and again, like the high priest here on earth who enters the Most Holy Place year after year with the blood of an animal. [26]If that had been necessary, Christ would have had to die again and again, ever since the world began. But now, once for all time, he has appeared at the end of the age* to remove sin by his own death as a sacrifice.

[27]**And just as each person is destined to die once and after that comes judgment, [28]so also Christ died once for all time as a sacrifice to take away the sins of many people. He will come again, not to deal with our sins, but to bring salvation to all who are eagerly waiting for him.**

9:11 Some manuscripts read *that are about to come.*
9:14 Greek *from dead works.*   9:16a Or *covenant;* also

in 9:17.   **9:16b** Or *Now when someone makes a covenant,*
it is necessary to ratify it with the death of a sacrifice.
9:19 Some manuscripts omit *and goats.*   **9:20** Exod 24:8.
9:26 Greek *the ages.*

PSALM 107:1-43

Give thanks to the LORD, for
    he is good!
    His faithful love endures forever.
2 Has the LORD redeemed you? Then
    speak out!
    Tell others he has redeemed you
    from your enemies.
3 For he has gathered the exiles from
    many lands,
    from east and west,
    from north and south.

4 Some wandered in the wilderness,
    lost and homeless.
5 Hungry and thirsty,
    they nearly died.
6 "LORD, help!" they cried in
    their trouble,
    and he rescued them from their
    distress.
7 He led them straight to safety,
    to a city where they could live.
8 Let them praise the LORD for his
    great love
    and for the wonderful things he
    has done for them.
9 For he satisfies the thirsty
    and fills the hungry with
    good things.

10 Some sat in darkness and deepest
    gloom,
    imprisoned in iron chains of misery.
11 They rebelled against the words
    of God,
    scorning the counsel of the
    Most High.
12 That is why he broke them with
    hard labor;
    they fell, and no one was there to
    help them.
13 "LORD, help!" they cried in their
    trouble,
    and he saved them from their
    distress.
14 He led them from the darkness and
    deepest gloom;

    he snapped their chains.
15 Let them praise the LORD for his
    great love
    and for the wonderful things he
    has done for them.
16 For he broke down their prison
    gates of bronze;
    he cut apart their bars of iron.

17 Some were fools; they rebelled
    and suffered for their sins.
18 They couldn't stand the thought
    of food,
    and they were knocking on
    death's door.
19 "LORD, help!" they cried in their
    trouble,
    and he saved them from their
    distress.
20 He sent out his word and healed
    them,
    snatching them from the door
    of death.
21 Let them praise the LORD for his
    great love
    and for the wonderful things
    he has done for them.
22 Let them offer sacrifices of
    thanksgiving
    and sing joyfully about his
    glorious acts.

23 Some went off to sea in ships,
    plying the trade routes of the
    world.
24 They, too, observed the LORD's
    power in action,
    his impressive works on the
    deepest seas.
25 He spoke, and the winds rose,
    stirring up the waves.
26 Their ships were tossed to the
    heavens
    and plunged again to the depths;
    the sailors cringed in terror.
27 They reeled and staggered like
    drunkards
    and were at their wits' end.
28 "LORD, help!" they cried in their
    trouble,
    and he saved them from their
    distress.

²⁹ He calmed the storm to a whisper
and stilled the waves.
³⁰ What a blessing was that stillness
as he brought them safely into
harbor!
³¹ Let them praise the LORD for his
great love
and for the wonderful things he
has done for them.
³² Let them exalt him publicly before
the congregation
and before the leaders of
the nation.

³³ He changes rivers into deserts,
and springs of water into dry,
thirsty land.
³⁴ He turns the fruitful land into salty
wastelands,
because of the wickedness of
those who live there.
³⁵ But he also turns deserts into pools
of water,
the dry land into springs of water.
³⁶ He brings the hungry to settle there
and to build their cities.
³⁷ They sow their fields, plant their
vineyards,
and harvest their bumper crops.
³⁸ How he blesses them!
They raise large families there,
and their herds of livestock
increase.

³⁹ When they decrease in number and
become impoverished
through oppression, trouble,
and sorrow,
⁴⁰ the LORD pours contempt on their
princes,
causing them to wander in
trackless wastelands.
⁴¹ But he rescues the poor from trouble
and increases their families like
flocks of sheep.
⁴² The godly will see these things and
be glad,
while the wicked are struck
silent.
⁴³ Those who are wise will take all this
to heart;
they will see in our history the
faithful love of the LORD.

PROVERBS 27:11
Be wise, my child,* and make my heart
glad. Then I will be able to answer my
critics.

27:11 Hebrew *my son.*

NOVEMBER
10

EZEKIEL 21:1–22:31
¹***T**hen this message came to me
[Ezekiel] from the LORD: ²"Son of man,
turn and face Jerusalem and prophesy
against Israel and her sanctuaries. ³Tell
her, 'This is what the LORD says: I am
your enemy, O Israel, and I am about to
unsheath my sword to destroy your people—the righteous and the wicked alike.
⁴Yes, I will cut off both the righteous and
the wicked! I will draw my sword against
everyone in the land from south to
north. ⁵Everyone in the world will know
that I am the LORD. My sword is in my
hand, and it will not return to its sheath
until its work is finished.'

⁶"Son of man, groan before the peo-
ple! Groan before them with bitter anguish and a broken heart. ⁷When they
ask why you are groaning, tell them, 'I
groan because of the terrifying news I
have heard. When it comes true, the
boldest heart will melt with fear; all
strength will disappear. Every spirit will
faint; strong knees will become as weak
as water. And the Sovereign LORD says:
It is coming! It's on its way!'"

⁸Then the LORD said to me, ⁹"Son of
man, give the people this message from
the LORD:

"A sword, a sword
is being sharpened and polished.
¹⁰ It is sharpened for terrible slaughter
and polished to flash like
lightning!
Now will you laugh?

Those far stronger than you have
fallen beneath its power!*
[11] Yes, the sword is now being
sharpened and polished;
it is being prepared for the
executioner.

[12] "Son of man, cry out and wail;
pound your thighs in anguish,
for that sword will slaughter my
people and their leaders—
everyone will die!
[13] It will put them all to the test.
What chance do they have?*
says the Sovereign LORD.

[14] "Son of man, prophesy to them
and clap your hands.
Then take the sword and brandish
it twice,
even three times,
to symbolize the great massacre,
the great massacre facing them
on every side.
[15] Let their hearts melt with terror,
for the sword glitters at every gate.
It flashes like lightning
and is polished for slaughter!
[16] O sword, slash to the right,
then slash to the left,
wherever you will,
wherever you want.
[17] I, too, will clap my hands,
and I will satisfy my fury.
I, the LORD, have spoken!"

[18] Then this message came to me
from the LORD: [19] "Son of man, make a
map and trace two routes on it for the
sword of Babylon's king to follow. Put a
signpost on the road that comes out of
Babylon where the road forks into
two—[20] one road going to Ammon and
its capital, Rabbah, and the other to Judah and fortified Jerusalem. [21] The king
of Babylon now stands at the fork, uncertain whether to attack Jerusalem or
Rabbah. He calls his magicians to look
for omens. They cast lots by shaking arrows from the quiver. They inspect the
livers of animal sacrifices. [22] The omen
in his right hand says, 'Jerusalem!' With
battering rams his soldiers will go

against the gates, shouting for the kill.
They will put up siege towers and build
ramps against the walls. [23] The people
of Jerusalem will think it is a false omen,
because of their treaty with the Babylonians. But the king of Babylon will remind the people of their rebellion.
Then he will attack and capture them.

[24] "Therefore, this is what the Sovereign LORD says: Again and again you remind me of your sin and your guilt. You
don't even try to hide it! In everything
you do, your sins are obvious for all to
see. So now the time of your punishment has come!

[25] "O you corrupt and wicked prince
of Israel, your final day of reckoning is
here! [26] This is what the Sovereign LORD
says:

"Take off your jeweled crown,
for the old order changes.
Now the lowly will be exalted,
and the mighty will be brought
down.
[27] Destruction! Destruction!
I will surely destroy the kingdom.
And it will not be restored until the
one appears
who has the right to judge it.
Then I will hand it over to him.

[28] "And now, son of man, prophesy
concerning the Ammonites and their
mockery. Give them this message from
the Sovereign LORD:

"A sword, a sword
is drawn for your slaughter.
It is polished to destroy,
flashing like lightning!
[29] Your prophets have given false
visions,
and your fortune-tellers have
told lies.
The sword will fall on the necks of
the wicked
for whom the day of final
reckoning has come.

[30] "Now return the sword to its sheath,
for in your own country,
the land of your birth,

I will pass judgment upon you.
³¹ I will pour out my fury on you
and blow on you with the fire of
my anger.
I will hand you over to cruel men
who are skilled in destruction.
³² You will be fuel for the fire,
and your blood will be spilled in
your own land.
You will be utterly wiped out,
your memory lost to history,
for I, the LORD, have spoken!"

^{22:1}Now this message came to me from
the LORD: ²"Son of man, are you ready
to judge Jerusalem? Are you ready to
judge this city of murderers? Publicly
denounce her detestable sins, ³ and give
her this message from the Sovereign
LORD: O city of murderers, doomed and
damned—city of idols,* filthy and
foul—⁴you are guilty because of the
blood you have shed. You are defiled
because of the idols you have made.
Your day of destruction has come! You
have reached the end of your years. I
will make you an object of mockery
throughout the world. ⁵O infamous city,
filled with confusion, you will be
mocked by people far and near.

⁶"Every leader in Israel who lives
within your walls is bent on murder. ⁷Fa-
thers and mothers are treated with contempt. Foreigners are forced to pay for
protection. Orphans and widows are
wronged and oppressed among you.
⁸You despise my holy things and violate
my Sabbath days of rest. ⁹People accuse
others falsely and send them to their
death. You are filled with idol worshipers and people who do obscene things.
¹⁰Men sleep with their fathers' wives and
have intercourse with women who are
menstruating. ¹¹Within your walls live
men who commit adultery with their
neighbors' wives, who defile their
daughters-in-law, or who rape their own
sisters. ¹²There are hired murderers,
loan racketeers, and extortioners everywhere. They never even think of me and
my commands, says the Sovereign LORD.
¹³"But now I clap my hands in indig-

nation over your dishonest gain and
bloodshed. ¹⁴How strong and courageous will you be in my day of reckoning? I, the LORD, have spoken, and I will
do what I said. ¹⁵I will scatter you among
the nations and purge you of your wickedness. ¹⁶And when I have been dishonored among the nations because of
you,* you will know that I am the LORD."

¹⁷Then this message came to me
from the LORD: ¹⁸"Son of man, the people of Israel are the worthless slag that
remains after silver is smelted. They
are the dross that is left over—a useless
mixture of copper, tin, iron, and lead.
¹⁹So tell them, 'This is what the Sover-
eign LORD says: Because you are all
worthless slag, I will bring you to my
crucible in Jerusalem. ²⁰Just as copper,
iron, lead, and tin are melted down in a
furnace, I will melt you down in the
heat of my fury. ²¹I will gather you together and blow the fire of my anger
upon you, ²²and you will melt like silver
in fierce heat. Then you will know that
I, the LORD, have poured out my fury on
you.'"

²³Again a message came to me from
the LORD: ²⁴"Son of man, give the people of Israel this message: In the day of
my indignation, you will be like a polluted land, a land without rain. ²⁵Your
princes* plot conspiracies just as lions
stalk their prey. They devour innocent
people, seizing treasures and extorting
wealth. They make many widows in the
land. ²⁶Your priests have violated my instructions and defiled my holy things.
They make no distinction between
what is holy and what is not. And they
do not teach my people the difference
between what is ceremonially clean and
unclean. They disregard my Sabbath
days so that I am dishonored among
them. ²⁷Your leaders are like wolves
who tear apart their victims. They actually destroy people's lives for money!
²⁸And your prophets cover up for them
by announcing false visions and mak-
ing lying predictions. They say, 'My
message is from the Sovereign LORD,'
when the LORD hasn't spoken a single

word to them. [29]Even common people oppress the poor, rob the needy, and deprive foreigners of justice.

[30]"I looked for someone who might rebuild the wall of righteousness that guards the land. I searched for someone to stand in the gap in the wall so I wouldn't have to destroy the land, but I found no one. [31]So now I will pour out my fury on them, consuming them with the fire of my anger. I will heap on their heads the full penalty for all their sins. I, the Sovereign LORD, have spoken!"

21:1 Verses 21:1-32 are numbered 21:6-37 in Hebrew text.   21:10 The meaning of the Hebrew is uncertain.   21:13 The meaning of the Hebrew is uncertain.   22:3 The Hebrew term (literally *round things*) probably alludes to dung; also in 22:4.   22:16 Or *when you have been dishonored among the nations.*   22:25 As in Greek version; Hebrew reads *prophets.*

HEBREWS 10:1-17

The old system under the law of Moses was only a shadow, a dim preview of the good things to come, not the good things themselves. The sacrifices under that system were repeated again and again, year after year, but they were never able to provide perfect cleansing for those who came to worship. [2]If they could have provided perfect cleansing, the sacrifices would have stopped, for the worshipers would have been purified once for all time, and their feelings of guilt would have disappeared.

[3]But instead, those sacrifices actually reminded them of their sins year after year. [4]For it is not possible for the blood of bulls and goats to take away sins. [5]That is why, when Christ* came into the world, he said to God,

"You did not want animal sacrifices
      or sin offerings.
   But you have given me a body
      to offer.
[6] You were not pleased with burnt
      offerings
   or other offerings for sin.
[7] Then I said, 'Look, I have come
      to do your will, O God—
   as is written about me in the
      Scriptures.'"*

[8]First, Christ said, "You did not want animal sacrifices or sin offerings or burnt offerings or other offerings for sin, nor were you pleased with them" (though they are required by the law of Moses). [9]Then he said, "Look, I have come to do your will." He cancels the first covenant in order to put the second into effect. [10]For God's will was for us to be made holy by the sacrifice of the body of Jesus Christ, once for all time.

[11]Under the old covenant, the priest stands and ministers before the altar day after day, offering the same sacrifices again and again, which can never take away sins. [12]**But our High Priest offered himself to God as a single sacrifice for sins, good for all time. Then he sat down in the place of hon**or at **God's right hand.** [13]There he waits until his enemies are humbled and made a footstool under his feet. [14]For by that one offering he forever made perfect those who are being made holy.

[15]And the Holy Spirit also testifies that this is so. For he says,

[16] "This is the new covenant I
      will make
   with my people on that day,*
      says the LORD:
   I will put my laws in their hearts,
      and I will write them on their
         minds."*

[17]Then he says,

   "I will never again remember
      their sins and lawless deeds."*

10:5 Greek *he;* also in 10:8.   10:5-7 Ps 40:6-8 (Greek version).   10:16a Greek *after those days.*   10:16b Jer 31:33a.   10:17 Jer 31:34b.

PSALM 108:1-13

A song. A psalm of David.

[1] **M**y heart is confident in you,
      O God;
   no wonder I can sing your praises
      with all my heart!
[2] Wake up, lyre and harp!
   I will wake the dawn with my
      song.

³ I will thank you, LORD, among all
    the people.
  I will sing your praises among
    the nations.
⁴ For your unfailing love is higher
    than the heavens.
  Your faithfulness reaches to
    the clouds.
⁵ Be exalted, O God, above the
    highest heavens.
  May your glory shine over all
    the earth.

⁶ Now rescue your beloved people.
  Answer and save us by your power.
⁷ God has promised this by his
    holiness*:
  "I will divide up Shechem with joy.
  I will measure out the valley
    of Succoth.
⁸ Gilead is mine,
    and Manasseh, too.
  Ephraim, my helmet, will produce
    my warriors,
    and Judah, my scepter, will
    produce my kings.
⁹ But Moab, my washbasin, will
    become my servant,
    and I will wipe my feet on Edom
    and shout in triumph over
    Philistia."

¹⁰ Who will bring me into the fortified
    city?
  Who will bring me victory over
    Edom?
¹¹ Have you rejected us, O God?
  Will you no longer march with
    our armies?
¹² Oh, please help us against our
    enemies,
  for all human help is useless.
¹³ With God's help we will
    do mighty things,
  for he will trample down
    our foes.

108:7 Or *in his sanctuary.*

PROVERBS 27:12

A prudent person foresees danger and takes precautions. The simpleton goes blindly on and suffers the consequences.

NOVEMBER
11

EZEKIEL 23:1-49

This message came to me [Ezekiel] from the LORD: ²"Son of man, once there were two sisters who were daughters of the same mother. ³They became prostitutes in Egypt. Even as young girls, they allowed men to fondle their breasts. ⁴The older girl was named Oholah, and her sister was Oholibah. I married them, and they bore me sons and daughters. I am speaking of Samaria and Jerusalem, for Oholah is Samaria and Oholibah is Jerusalem.

⁵"Then Oholah lusted after other lovers instead of me, and she gave her love to the Assyrian officers. ⁶They were all attractive young men, captains and commanders dressed in handsome blue, charioteers driving their horses. ⁷And so she prostituted herself with the most desirable men of Assyria, worshiping their idols* and defiling herself. ⁸For when she left Egypt, she did not leave her spirit of prostitution behind. She was still as lewd as in her youth, when the Egyptians slept with her, fondled her breasts, and used her as a prostitute.

⁹"And so I handed her over to her Assyrian lovers, whom she desired so much. ¹⁰They stripped her, took away her children as their slaves, and then killed her. After she received her punishment, her reputation was known to every woman in the land.

¹¹"Yet even though Oholibah saw what had happened to Oholah, her sister, she followed right in her footsteps. And she was even more depraved, abandoning herself to her lust and prostitution. ¹²She fawned over all the Assyrian officers—those captains and commanders in handsome uniforms, those charioteers driving their horses—all of them attractive young men. ¹³I saw the way she was going, defiling herself just like her older sister.

¹⁴"Then she carried her prostitution even further. She fell in love with pictures that were painted on a wall—pictures of Babylonian* military officers, outfitted in striking red uniforms. ¹⁵Handsome belts encircled their waists, and flowing turbans crowned their heads. They were dressed like chariot officers from the land of Babylonia.* ¹⁶When she saw these paintings, she longed to give herself to them, so she sent messengers to Babylonia to invite them to come to her. ¹⁷So they came and committed adultery with her, defiling her in the bed of love. After being defiled, however, she rejected them in disgust.

¹⁸"In the same way, I became disgusted with Oholibah and rejected her, just as I had rejected her sister, because she flaunted herself before them and gave herself to satisfy their lusts. ¹⁹Yet she turned to even greater prostitution, remembering her youth when she was a prostitute in Egypt. ²⁰She lusted after lovers with genitals as large as a donkey's and emissions like those of a horse. ²¹And so, Oholibah, you relived your former days as a young girl in Egypt, when you first allowed your breasts to be fondled.

²²"Therefore, Oholibah, this is what the Sovereign LORD says: I will send your lovers against you from every direction—those very nations from which you turned away in disgust. ²³For the Babylonians will come with all the Chaldeans from Pekod and Shoa and Koa. And all the Assyrians will come with them—handsome young captains, commanders, chariot officers, and other high-ranking officers, all riding their horses. ²⁴They will all come against you from the north* with chariots, wagons, and a great army prepared for attack. They will take up positions on every side, surrounding you with men armed with shields and helmets. And I will hand you over to them for punishment so they can do with you as they please. ²⁵I will turn my jealous anger against you, and they will deal harshly with you. They will cut off your nose and ears, and

any survivors will then be slaughtered by the sword. Your children will be taken away as captives, and everything that is left will be burned. ²⁶They will strip you of your beautiful clothes and jewels. ²⁷In this way, I will put a stop to the lewdness and prostitution you brought from Egypt. You will never again cast longing eyes on those things or fondly remember your time in Egypt.

²⁸"For this is what the Sovereign LORD says: I will surely hand you over to your enemies, to those you loathe, those you rejected. ²⁹They will treat you with hatred and rob you of all you own, leaving you stark naked. The shame of your prostitution will be exposed to all the world. ³⁰You brought all this on yourself by prostituting yourself to other nations, defiling yourself with all their idols. ³¹Because you have followed in your sister's footsteps, I will force you to drink the same cup of terror she drank.

³²"Yes, this is what the Sovereign LORD says:

"You will drink from your sister's
     cup of terror,
     a cup that is large and deep.
It is filled to the brim
     with scorn and derision.
³³ Drunkenness and anguish will
     fill you,
     for your cup is filled to the brim
     with distress and desolation,
     the same cup your sister Samaria
     drank.
³⁴ You will drain that cup of terror
     to the very bottom.
Then you will smash it to pieces
     and beat your breast in anguish.
     I, the Sovereign LORD, have
     spoken!

³⁵"And because you have forgotten me and turned your back on me, this is what the Sovereign LORD says: You must bear the consequences of all your lewdness and prostitution."

³⁶The LORD said to me, "Son of man, you must accuse Oholah and Oholibah of all their detestable sins. ³⁷They have committed both adultery and murder—

adultery by worshiping idols and murder by burning as sacrifices the children they bore to me. [38]Furthermore, they have defiled my Temple and violated my Sabbath day! [39]On the very day that they sacrificed their children to their idols, they boldly came into my Temple to worship! They came in and defiled my house.

[40]"You sisters sent messengers to distant lands to get men. Then when they arrived, you bathed yourselves, painted your eyelids, and put on your finest jewels for them. [41]You sat with them on a beautifully embroidered couch and put my incense and my special oil on a table that was spread before you. [42]From your room came the sound of many men carousing. They were lustful men and drunkards* from the wilderness, who put bracelets on your wrists and beautiful crowns on your heads. [43]Then I said, 'If they really want to have sex with old worn-out prostitutes like these, let them!' [44]And that is what they did. They had sex with Oholah and Oholibah, these shameless prostitutes. [45]But righteous people will judge these sister cities for what they really are—adulterers and murderers.

[46]"Now this is what the Sovereign LORD says: Bring an army against them and hand them over to be terrorized and plundered. [47]For their enemies will stone them and kill them with swords. They will butcher their sons and daughters and burn their homes. [48]In this way, I will put an end to lewdness and idolatry in the land, and my judgment will be a warning to others not to follow their wicked example. [49]You will be fully repaid for all your prostitution—your worship of idols. Yes, you will suffer the full penalty. Then you will know that I am the Sovereign LORD."

23:7 The Hebrew term (literally *round things*) probably alludes to dung; also in 23:30, 37, 39, 49.   23:14 Or *Chaldean*.   23:15 Or *Chaldea;* also in 23:16.   23:24 As in Greek version; the meaning of the Hebrew is uncertain. 23:42 Or *Sabeans*.

HEBREWS 10:18-39

[A]nd when sins have been forgiven, there is no need to offer any more sacrifices.

[19]And so, dear brothers and sisters,* we can boldly enter heaven's Most Holy Place because of the blood of Jesus. [20]By his death,* Jesus opened a new and life-giving way through the curtain into the Most Holy Place. [21]And since we have a great High Priest who rules over God's house, [22]let us go right into the presence of God with sincere hearts fully trusting him. For our guilty consciences have been sprinkled with Christ's blood to make us clean, and our bodies have been washed with pure water.

[23]**Let us hold tightly without wavering to the hope we affirm, for God can be trusted to keep his promise. [24]Let us think of ways to motivate one another to acts of love and good works.** [25]And let us not neglect our meeting together, as some people do, but encourage one another, especially now that the day of his return is drawing near.

[26]Dear friends, if we deliberately continue sinning after we have received knowledge of the truth, there is no longer any sacrifice that will cover these sins. [27]There is only the terrible expectation of God's judgment and the raging fire that will consume his enemies. [28]For anyone who refused to obey the law of Moses was put to death without mercy on the testimony of two or three witnesses. [29]Just think how much worse the punishment will be for those who have trampled on the Son of God, and have treated the blood of the covenant, which made us holy, as if it were common and unholy, and have insulted and disdained the Holy Spirit who brings God's mercy to us. [30]For we know the one who said,

"I will take revenge.
　 I will pay them back."*

He also said,

"The LORD will judge his own
　 people."*

[31]It is a terrible thing to fall into the hands of the living God.

[32]Think back on those early days when you first learned about Christ.* Remember how you remained faithful

even though it meant terrible suffering. [33]Sometimes you were exposed to public ridicule and were beaten, and sometimes you helped others who were suffering the same things. [34]You suffered along with those who were thrown into jail, and when all you owned was taken from you, you accepted it with joy. You knew there were better things waiting for you that will last forever.

[35]So do not throw away this confident trust in the Lord. Remember the great reward it brings you! [36]Patient endurance is what you need now, so that you will continue to do God's will. Then you will receive all that he has promised.

[37] "For in just a little while,
the Coming One will come and
not delay.
[38] And my righteous ones will live
by faith.*
But I will take no pleasure in
anyone who turns away."*

[39]But we are not like those who turn away from God to their own destruction. We are the faithful ones, whose souls will be saved.

10:19 Greek *brothers.*   10:20 Greek *Through his flesh.* 10:30a Deut 32:35.   10:30b Deut 32:36.   10:32 Greek *when you were first enlightened.*   10:38 Or *my righteous ones will live by their faithfulness;* Greek reads *my righteous one will live by faith.*   10:37-38 Hab 2:3-4.

PSALM 109:1-31
For the choir director: A psalm of David.

[1] O God, whom I praise,
don't stand silent and aloof
[2] while the wicked slander me
and tell lies about me.
[3] They surround me with hateful
words
and fight against me for no
reason.
[4] I love them, but they try to destroy
me with accusations
even as I am praying for them!
[5] They repay evil for good,
and hatred for my love.

[6] They say,* "Get an evil person to
turn against him.

Send an accuser to bring him
to trial.
[7] When his case comes up for
judgment,
let him be pronounced guilty.
Count his prayers as sins.
[8] Let his years be few;
let someone else take his
position.
[9] May his children become fatherless,
and his wife a widow.
[10] May his children wander as beggars
and be driven from their ruined
homes.
[11] May creditors seize his entire estate,
and strangers take all he has
earned.
[12] Let no one be kind to him;
let no one pity his fatherless
children.
[13] May all his offspring die.
May his family name be blotted
out in a single generation.
[14] May the LORD never forget the sins
of his fathers;
may his mother's sins never be
erased from the record.
[15] May the LORD always remember
these sins,
and may his name disappear from
human memory.
[16] For he refused all kindness to others;
he persecuted the poor and needy,
and he hounded the
brokenhearted to death.
[17] He loved to curse others;
now you curse him.
He never blessed others;
now don't you bless him.
[18] Cursing is as natural to him as his
clothing,
or the water he drinks,
or the rich food he eats.
[19] Now may his curses return and
cling to him like clothing;
may they be tied around him
like a belt."

[20] May those curses become the
LORD's punishment
for my accusers who speak evil
of me.

21 But deal well with me, O Sovereign
    Lord,
    for the sake of your own reputation!
Rescue me
    because you are so faithful
        and good.
22 For I am poor and needy,
    and my heart is full of pain.
23 I am fading like a shadow at dusk;
    I am brushed off like a locust.
24 My knees are weak from fasting,
    and I am skin and bones.
25 I am a joke to people everywhere;
    when they see me, they shake
        their heads in scorn.

26 Help me, O Lord my God!
    Save me because of your
        unfailing love.
27 Let them see that this is your doing,
    that you yourself have done it,
    Lord.
28 Then let them curse me if they like,
    but you will bless me!
When they attack me, they will
        be disgraced!
    But I, your servant, will go right
        on rejoicing!
29 May my accusers be clothed with
        disgrace;
    may their humiliation cover them
        like a cloak.
30 But I will give repeated thanks
        to the Lord,
    praising him to everyone.
31 For he stands beside the needy,
    ready to save them from those
        who condemn them.

109:6 Hebrew lacks *They say.*

PROVERBS 27:13

Get security from someone who guarantees a stranger's debt. Get a deposit if he does it for foreigners.*

27:13 As in Greek and Latin versions (see also 20:16); Hebrew reads *for a promiscuous woman.*

NOVEMBER 12

EZEKIEL 24:1–26:21

On January 15,* during the ninth year of King Jehoiachin's captivity, this message came to me [Ezekiel] from the Lord: 2"Son of man, write down today's date, because on this very day the king of Babylon is beginning his attack against Jerusalem. 3 Then give these rebels an illustration with this message from the Sovereign Lord:

"Put a pot on the fire,
    and pour in some water.
4 Fill it with choice pieces of meat—
    the rump and the shoulder
    and all the most tender cuts.
5 Use only the best sheep from the
        flock,
    and heap fuel on the fire beneath
        the pot.
Bring the pot to a boil,
    and cook the bones along with
        the meat.

6 "Now this is what the Sovereign
        Lord says:
What sorrow awaits Jerusalem,
    the city of murderers!
She is a cooking pot
    whose corruption can't be
        cleaned out.
Take the meat out in random order,
    for no piece is better than
        another.
7 For the blood of her murders
    is splashed on the rocks.
It isn't even spilled on the ground,
    where the dust could cover it!
8 So I will splash her blood on a rock
        for all to see,
    an expression of my anger
        and vengeance against her.

9 "This is what the Sovereign
        Lord says:
What sorrow awaits Jerusalem,
    the city of murderers!

I myself will pile up the fuel
    beneath her.
[10] Yes, heap on the wood!
    Let the fire roar to make the
      pot boil.
Cook the meat with many spices,
    and afterward burn the bones.
[11] Now set the empty pot on the coals.
    Heat it red hot!
    Burn away the filth and corruption.
[12] But it's hopeless;
    the corruption can't be
      cleaned out.
    So throw it into the fire.
[13] Your impurity is your lewdness
    and the corruption of your
      idolatry.
    I tried to cleanse you,
    but you refused.
    So now you will remain in your filth
    until my fury against you has been
      satisfied.

[14]"I, the LORD, have spoken! The time has come, and I won't hold back. I will not change my mind, and I will have no pity on you. You will be judged on the basis of all your wicked actions, says the Sovereign LORD."

[15]Then this message came to me from the LORD: [16]"Son of man, with one blow I will take away your dearest treasure. Yet you must not show any sorrow at her death. Do not weep; let there be no tears. [17]Groan silently, but let there be no wailing at her grave. Do not uncover your head or take off your sandals. Do not perform the usual rituals of mourning or accept any food brought to you by consoling friends."

[18]So I proclaimed this to the people the next morning, and in the evening my wife died. The next morning I did everything I had been told to do. [19]Then the people asked, "What does all this mean? What are you trying to tell us?"

[20]So I said to them, "A message came to me from the LORD, [21]and I was told to give this message to the people of Israel. This is what the Sovereign LORD says: I will defile my Temple, the source of your security and pride, the place your heart delights in. Your sons and daughters whom you left behind in Judea will be slaughtered by the sword. [22]Then you will do as Ezekiel has done. You will not mourn in public or console yourselves by eating the food brought by friends. [23]Your heads will remain covered, and your sandals will not be taken off. You will not mourn or weep, but you will waste away because of your sins. You will mourn privately for all the evil you have done. [24]Ezekiel is an example for you; you will do just as he has done. And when that time comes, you will know that I am the LORD."

[25]Then the LORD said to me, "Son of man, on the day I take away their stronghold—their joy and glory, their heart's desire, their dearest treasure—I will also take away their sons and daughters. [26]And on that day a survivor from Jerusalem will come to you in Babylon and tell you what has happened. [27]And when he arrives, your voice will suddenly return so you can talk to him, and you will be a symbol for these people. Then they will know that I am the LORD."

[25:1]THEN this message came to me from the LORD: [2]"Son of man, turn and face the land of Ammon and prophesy against its people. [3]Give the Ammonites this message from the Sovereign LORD: Hear the word of the Sovereign LORD! Because you cheered when my Temple was defiled, mocked Israel in her desolation, and laughed at Judah as she went away into exile, [4]I will allow nomads from the eastern deserts to overrun your country. They will set up their camps among you and pitch their tents on your land. They will harvest all your fruit and drink the milk from your livestock. [5]And I will turn the city of Rabbah into a pasture for camels, and all the land of the Ammonites into a resting place for sheep and goats. Then you will know that I am the LORD.

[6]"This is what the Sovereign LORD says: Because you clapped and danced and cheered with glee at the destruction of my people, [7]I will raise my fist of

judgment against you. I will give you as plunder to many nations. I will cut you off from being a nation and destroy you completely. Then you will know that I am the LORD.

8"This is what the Sovereign LORD says: Because the people of Moab have said that Judah is just like all the other nations, 9I will open up their eastern flank and wipe out their glorious frontier towns—Beth-jeshimoth, Baal-meon, and Kiriathaim. 10And I will hand Moab over to nomads from the eastern deserts, just as I handed over Ammon. Yes, the Ammonites will no longer be counted among the nations. 11In the same way, I will bring my judgment down on the Moabites. Then they will know that I am the LORD.

12"This is what the Sovereign LORD says: The people of Edom have sinned greatly by avenging themselves against the people of Judah. 13Therefore, says the Sovereign LORD, I will raise my fist of judgment against Edom. I will wipe out its people and animals with the sword. I will make a wasteland of everything from Teman to Dedan. 14I will accomplish this by the hand of my people of Israel. They will carry out my vengeance with anger, and Edom will know that this vengeance is from me. I, the Sovereign LORD, have spoken!

15"This is what the Sovereign LORD says: The people of Philistia have acted against Judah out of bitter revenge and long-standing contempt. 16Therefore, this is what the Sovereign LORD says: I will raise my fist of judgment against the land of the Philistines. I will wipe out the Kerethites and utterly destroy the people who live by the sea. 17I will execute terrible vengeance against them to punish them for what they have done. And when I have inflicted my revenge, they will know that I am the LORD."

26:1On February 3, during the twelfth year of King Jehoiachin's captivity,* this message came to me from the LORD: 2"Son of man, Tyre has rejoiced over the fall of Jerusalem, saying, 'Ha! She who

was the gateway to the rich trade routes to the east has been broken, and I am the heir! Because she has been made desolate, I will become wealthy!'

3"Therefore, this is what the Sovereign LORD says: I am your enemy, O Tyre, and I will bring many nations against you, like the waves of the sea crashing against your shoreline. 4They will destroy the walls of Tyre and tear down its towers. I will scrape away its soil and make it a bare rock! 5It will be just a rock in the sea, a place for fishermen to spread their nets, for I have spoken, says the Sovereign LORD. Tyre will become the prey of many nations, 6and its mainland villages will be destroyed by the sword. Then they will know that I am the LORD.

7"This is what the Sovereign LORD says: From the north I will bring King Nebuchadnezzar* of Babylon against Tyre. He is king of kings and brings his horses, chariots, charioteers, and great army. 8First he will destroy your mainland villages. Then he will attack you by building a siege wall, constructing a ramp, and raising a roof of shields against you. 9He will pound your walls with battering rams and demolish your towers with sledgehammers. 10The hooves of his horses will choke the city with dust, and the noise of the charioteers and chariot wheels will shake your walls as they storm through your broken gates. 11His horsemen will trample through every street in the city. They will butcher your people, and your strong pillars will topple.

12"They will plunder all your riches and merchandise and break down your walls. They will destroy your lovely homes and dump your stones and timbers and even your dust into the sea. 13I will stop the music of your songs. No more will the sound of harps be heard among your people. 14I will make your island a bare rock, a place for fishermen to spread their nets. You will never be rebuilt, for I, the LORD, have spoken. Yes, the Sovereign LORD has spoken!

15"This is what the Sovereign LORD says to Tyre: The whole coastline will tremble at the sound of your fall, as the screams of the wounded echo in the continuing slaughter. [16]All the seaport rulers will step down from their thrones and take off their royal robes and beautiful clothing. They will sit on the ground trembling with horror at your destruction. [17]Then they will wail for you, singing this funeral song:

"O famous island city,
    once ruler of the sea,
    how you have been destroyed!
Your people, with their naval power,
    once spread fear around the world.
[18] Now the coastlands tremble
    at your fall.
    The islands are dismayed as you
    disappear.

[19]"This is what the Sovereign LORD says: I will make Tyre an uninhabited ruin, like many others. I will bury you beneath the terrible waves of enemy attack. Great seas will swallow you. [20]I will send you to the pit to join those who descended there long ago. Your city will lie in ruins, buried beneath the earth, like those in the pit who have entered the world of the dead. You will have no place of respect here in the land of the living. [21]I will bring you to a terrible end, and you will exist no more. You will be looked for, but you will never again be found. I, the Sovereign LORD, have spoken!"

24:1 Hebrew *On the tenth day of the tenth month,* of the ancient Hebrew lunar calendar. This event occurred on January 15, 588 B.C.; also see note on 1:1.   26:1 Hebrew *In the eleventh year, on the first day of the month,* of the ancient Hebrew lunar calendar year. Since an element is missing in the date formula here, scholars have reconstructed this probable reading: *In the eleventh [month of the twelfth] year, on the first day of the month.* This reading would put this message on February 3, 585 B.C.; also see note on 1:1.   26:7 Hebrew *Nebuchadrezzar,* a variant spelling of Nebuchadnezzar.

HEBREWS 11:1-16

Faith is the confidence that what we hope for will actually happen; it gives us assurance about things we cannot see. [2]Through their faith, the people in days of old earned a good reputation.

[3]By faith we understand that the entire universe was formed at God's command, that what we now see did not come from anything that can be seen.

[4]It was by faith that Abel brought a more acceptable offering to God than Cain did. Abel's offering gave evidence that he was a righteous man, and God showed his approval of his gifts. Although Abel is long dead, he still speaks to us by his example of faith.

[5]It was by faith that Enoch was taken up to heaven without dying—"he disappeared, because God took him."* For before he was taken up, he was known as a person who pleased God. [6]And it is impossible to please God without faith. Anyone who wants to come to him must believe that God exists and that he rewards those who sincerely seek him.

[7]It was by faith that Noah built a large boat to save his family from the flood. He obeyed God, who warned him about things that had never happened before. By his faith Noah condemned the rest of the world, and he received the righteousness that comes by faith.

[8]It was by faith that Abraham obeyed when God called him to leave home and go to another land that God would give him as his inheritance. He went without knowing where he was going. [9]And even when he reached the land God promised him, he lived there by faith—for he was like a foreigner, living in tents. And so did Isaac and Jacob, who inherited the same promise. [10]Abraham was confidently looking forward to a city with eternal foundations, a city designed and built by God.

[11]It was by faith that even Sarah was able to have a child, though she was barren and was too old. She believed* that God would keep his promise. [12]And so a whole nation came from this one man who was as good as dead—a nation with so many people that, like the stars in the sky and the sand on the seashore, there is no way to count them.

[13]All these people died still believing what God had promised them. They did not receive what was promised, but they saw it all from a distance and welcomed it. They agreed that they were foreigners

and nomads here on earth. [14]Obviously people who say such things are looking forward to a country they can call their own. [15]If they had longed for the country they came from, they could have gone back. [16]But they were looking for a better place, a heavenly homeland. That is why God is not ashamed to be called their God, for he has prepared a city for them.

11:5 Gen 5:24.   11:11 Or *It was by faith that he [Abraham] was able to have a child, even though Sarah was barren and he was too old. He believed.*

PSALM 110:1-7
A psalm of David.

[1] The LORD said to my Lord,
    "Sit in the place of honor at my
        right hand
until I humble your enemies,
    making them a footstool under
        your feet."

[2] The LORD will extend your
        powerful kingdom from
        Jerusalem*;
    you will rule over your enemies.
[3] When you go to war,
    your people will serve you
        willingly.
You are arrayed in holy garments,
    and your strength will be
        renewed each day like the
        morning dew.

[4] The LORD has taken an oath and will
        not break his vow:
    "You are a priest forever in the
        order of Melchizedek."

[5] The Lord stands at your right hand
        to protect you.
    He will strike down many kings
        when his anger erupts.
[6] He will punish the nations
    and fill their lands with
        corpses;
    he will shatter heads over the
        whole earth.
[7] But he himself will be refreshed
        from brooks along the way.
    He will be victorious.

110:2 Hebrew *Zion.*

PROVERBS 27:14
A loud and cheerful greeting early in the morning will be taken as a curse!

NOVEMBER 13

EZEKIEL 27:1–28:26
Then this message came to me [Ezekiel] from the LORD: [2]"Son of man, sing a funeral song for Tyre, [3]that mighty gateway to the sea, the trading center of the world. Give Tyre this message from the Sovereign LORD:

"You boasted, O Tyre,
    'My beauty is perfect!'
[4] You extended your boundaries
        into the sea.
    Your builders made your beauty
        perfect.
[5] You were like a great ship
        built of the finest cypress from
        Senir.*
    They took a cedar from Lebanon
        to make a mast for you.
[6] They carved your oars
        from the oaks of Bashan.
    Your deck of pine from the coasts
        of Cyprus*
        was inlaid with ivory.
[7] Your sails were made of Egypt's
        finest linen,
    and they flew as a banner
        above you.
You stood beneath blue and purple
        awnings
    made bright with dyes from the
        coasts of Elishah.
[8] Your oarsmen came from Sidon
        and Arvad;
    your helmsmen were skilled men
        from Tyre itself.
[9] Wise old craftsmen from Gebal did
        the caulking.
    Ships from every land came

with goods to barter for your trade.

10"Men from distant Persia, Lydia, and Libya* served in your great army. They hung their shields and helmets on your walls, giving you great honor. 11Men from Arvad and Helech stood on your walls. Your towers were manned by men from Gammad. Their shields hung on your walls, completing your beauty.

12"Tarshish sent merchants to buy your wares in exchange for silver, iron, tin, and lead. 13Merchants from Greece,* Tubal, and Meshech brought slaves and articles of bronze to trade with you.

14"From Togarmah came riding horses, chariot horses, and mules, all in exchange for your goods. 15Merchants came to you from Dedan.* Numerous coastlands were your captive markets; they brought payment in ivory tusks and ebony wood.

16"Syria* sent merchants to buy your rich variety of goods. They traded turquoise, purple dyes, embroidery, fine linen, and jewelry of coral and rubies. 17Judah and Israel traded for your wares, offering wheat from Minnith, figs,* honey, olive oil, and balm.

18"Damascus sent merchants to buy your rich variety of goods, bringing wine from Helbon and white wool from Zahar. 19Greeks from Uzal* came to trade for your merchandise. Wrought iron, cassia, and fragrant calamus were bartered for your wares.

20"Dedan sent merchants to trade their expensive saddle blankets with you. 21The Arabians and the princes of Kedar sent merchants to trade lambs and rams and male goats in exchange for your goods. 22The merchants of Sheba and Raamah came with all kinds of spices, jewels, and gold in exchange for your wares.

23"Haran, Canneh, Eden, Sheba, Asshur, and Kilmad came with their merchandise, too. 24They brought choice fabrics to trade—blue cloth, embroidery, and multicolored carpets rolled up and bound with cords. 25The ships of Tarshish were your ocean caravans. Your island warehouse was filled to the brim!

26 "But look! Your oarsmen
have taken you into stormy
seas!
A mighty eastern gale
has wrecked you in the heart
of the sea!
27 Everything is lost—
your riches and wares,
your sailors and pilots,
your ship builders, merchants,
and warriors.
On the day of your ruin,
everyone on board sinks into the
depths of the sea.
28 Your cities by the sea tremble
as your pilots cry out in terror.
29 All the oarsmen abandon
their ships;
the sailors and pilots on shore
come to stand on the beach.
30 They cry aloud over you
and weep bitterly.
They throw dust on their heads
and roll in ashes.
31 They shave their heads in grief
for you
and dress themselves in burlap.
They weep for you with bitter
anguish
and deep mourning.
32 As they wail and mourn over you,
they sing this sad funeral song:
'Was there ever such a city as Tyre,
now silent at the bottom
of the sea?
33 The merchandise you traded
satisfied the desires of many
nations.
Kings at the ends of the earth
were enriched by your trade.
34 Now you are a wrecked ship,
broken at the bottom of the sea.
All your merchandise and crew
have gone down with you.
35 All who live along the coastlands
are appalled at your terrible fate.
Their kings are filled with horror
and look on with twisted faces.
36 The merchants among the nations

shake their heads at the sight
of you,*
for you have come to a horrible end
and will exist no more.'"

28:1THEN this message came to me from
the LORD: 2"Son of man, give the prince
of Tyre this message from the Sovereign LORD:

"In your great pride you claim,
'I am a god!
I sit on a divine throne in the
heart of the sea.'
But you are only a man and
not a god,
though you boast that you are
a god.
3 You regard yourself as wiser than
Daniel
and think no secret is hidden
from you.
4 With your wisdom and
understanding you have
amassed great wealth—
gold and silver for your treasuries.
5 Yes, your wisdom has made you
very rich,
and your riches have made you
very proud.

6 "Therefore, this is what the
Sovereign LORD says:
Because you think you are as wise
as a god,
7   I will now bring against you a
foreign army,
the terror of the nations.
They will draw their swords against
your marvelous wisdom
and defile your splendor!
8 They will bring you down to the pit,
and you will die in the heart
of the sea,
pierced with many wounds.
9 Will you then boast, 'I am a god!'
to those who kill you?
To them you will be no god
but merely a man!
10 You will die like an outcast*
at the hands of foreigners.
I, the Sovereign LORD, have
spoken!"

11Then this further message came to
me from the LORD: 12"Son of man, sing
this funeral song for the king of Tyre.
Give him this message from the Sovereign LORD:

"You were the model of perfection,
full of wisdom and exquisite in
beauty.
13 You were in Eden,
the garden of God.
Your clothing was adorned with
every precious stone*—
red carnelian, pale-green peridot,
white moonstone,
blue-green beryl, onyx, green
jasper,
blue lapis lazuli, turquoise, and
emerald—
all beautifully crafted for you
and set in the finest gold.
They were given to you
on the day you were created.
14 I ordained and anointed you
as the mighty angelic guardian.*
You had access to the holy mountain
of God
and walked among the stones
of fire.

15 "You were blameless in all you did
from the day you were created
until the day evil was found
in you.
16 Your rich commerce led you
to violence,
and you sinned.
So I banished you in disgrace
from the mountain of God.
I expelled you, O mighty guardian,
from your place among the
stones of fire.
17 Your heart was filled with pride
because of all your beauty.
Your wisdom was corrupted
by your love of splendor.
So I threw you to the ground
and exposed you to the curious
gaze of kings.
18 You defiled your sanctuaries
with your many sins and your
dishonest trade.

So I brought fire out from
  within you,
  and it consumed you.
I reduced you to ashes on the
  ground
  in the sight of all who were
  watching.
19 All who knew you are appalled
  at your fate.
  You have come to a terrible end,
  and you will exist no more."

20Then another message came to me
from the LORD: 21"Son of man, turn and
face the city of Sidon and prophesy
against it. 22Give the people of Sidon
this message from the Sovereign LORD:

"I am your enemy, O Sidon,
  and I will reveal my glory by what
  I do to you.
When I bring judgment against you
  and reveal my holiness among
  you,
everyone watching will know
  that I am the LORD.
23 I will send a plague against you,
  and blood will be spilled in your
  streets.
The attack will come from every
  direction,
  and your people will lie
  slaughtered within your walls.
Then everyone will know
  that I am the LORD.
24 No longer will Israel's scornful
  neighbors
  prick and tear at her like briers
  and thorns.
For then they will know
  that I am the Sovereign LORD.

25"This is what the Sovereign LORD
says: The people of Israel will again live
in their own land, the land I gave my servant Jacob. For I will gather them from
the distant lands where I have scattered
them. I will reveal to the nations of the
world my holiness among my people.
26They will live safely in Israel and build
homes and plant vineyards. And when I
punish the neighboring nations that

treated them with contempt, they will
know that I am the LORD their God."

27:5 Or *Hermon.*   27:6 Hebrew *Kittim.*   27:10 Hebrew
Paras, Lud, and Put.   27:13 Hebrew *Javan.*   27:15 Greek
version reads *Rhodes.*   27:16 Hebrew *Aram;* some
manuscripts read *Edom.*   27:17 The meaning of the
Hebrew is uncertain.   27:19 Hebrew *Vedan and Javan
from Uzal.* The meaning of the Hebrew is uncertain.
27:36 Hebrew *hiss at you.*   28:10 Hebrew *will die the
death of the uncircumcised.*   28:13 The identification of
some of these gemstones is uncertain.   28:14 Hebrew
guardian cherub; similarly in 28:16.

HEBREWS 11:17-31

It was by faith that Abraham offered
Isaac as a sacrifice when God was testing him. Abraham, who had received
God's promises, was ready to sacrifice
his only son, Isaac, 18even though God
had told him, "Isaac is the son through
whom your descendants will be counted."*
19Abraham reasoned that if Isaac died,
God was able to bring him back to life
again. And in a sense, Abraham did receive his son back from the dead.

20It was by faith that Isaac promised
blessings for the future to his sons, Jacob and Esau.

21It was by faith that Jacob, when he
was old and dying, blessed each of Joseph's sons and bowed in worship as he
leaned on his staff.

22It was by faith that Joseph, when he
was about to die, said confidently that
the people of Israel would leave Egypt.
He even commanded them to take his
bones with them when they left.

23It was by faith that Moses' parents
hid him for three months when he was
born. They saw that God had given them
an unusual child, and they were not
afraid to disobey the king's command.

24It was by faith that Moses, when he
grew up, refused to be called the son of
Pharaoh's daughter. 25He chose to share
the oppression of God's people instead
of enjoying the fleeting pleasures of sin.
26He thought it was better to suffer for
the sake of Christ than to own the treasures of Egypt, for he was looking ahead
to his great reward. 27It was by faith that
Moses left the land of Egypt, not fearing
the king's anger. He kept right on going
because he kept his eyes on the one who
is invisible. 28It was by faith that Moses

commanded the people of Israel to keep the Passover and to sprinkle blood on the doorposts so that the angel of death would not kill their firstborn sons.

²⁹It was by faith that the people of Israel went right through the Red Sea as though they were on dry ground. But when the Egyptians tried to follow, they were all drowned.

³⁰It was by faith that the people of Israel marched around Jericho for seven days, and the walls came crashing down.

³¹It was by faith that Rahab the prostitute was not destroyed with the people in her city who refused to obey God. For she had given a friendly welcome to the spies.

11:18 Gen 21:12.

PSALM 111:1-10*
Praise the LORD!

I will thank the LORD with all
        my heart
    as I meet with his godly people.
² **How amazing are the deeds
        of the LORD!
    All who delight in him should
        ponder them.**
³ **Everything he does reveals his
        glory and majesty.
    His righteousness never fails.**
⁴ He causes us to remember his
        wonderful works.
    How gracious and merciful is
        our LORD!
⁵ He gives food to those who fear him;
    he always remembers his
        covenant.
⁶ He has shown his great power
        to his people
    by giving them the lands of other
        nations.
⁷ All he does is just and good,
    and all his commandments are
        trustworthy.
⁸ They are forever true,
    to be obeyed faithfully and
        with integrity.
⁹ He has paid a full ransom for
        his people.

He has guaranteed his covenant
        with them forever.
    What a holy, awe-inspiring name
        he has!
¹⁰ Fear of the LORD is the foundation
        of true wisdom.
    All who obey his commandments
        will grow in wisdom.

Praise him forever!

111 This psalm is a Hebrew acrostic poem; after the introductory note of praise, each line begins with a successive letter of the Hebrew alphabet.

PROVERBS 27:15-16
A quarrelsome wife is as annoying as constant dripping on a rainy day. Stopping her complaints is like trying to stop the wind or trying to hold something with greased hands.

NOVEMBER 14

EZEKIEL 29:1–30:26
On January 7,* during the tenth year of King Jehoiachin's captivity, this message came to me [Ezekiel] from the LORD: ²"Son of man, turn and face Egypt and prophesy against Pharaoh the king and all the people of Egypt. ³Give them this message from the Sovereign LORD:

"I am your enemy, O Pharaoh,
        king of Egypt—
    you great monster, lurking in the
        streams of the Nile.
    For you have said, 'The Nile River
        is mine;
    I made it for myself.'
⁴ I will put hooks in your jaws
    and drag you out on the land
    with fish sticking to your scales.
⁵ I will leave you and all your fish
    stranded in the wilderness to die.
    You will lie unburied on the open
        ground,

for I have given you as food to the
wild animals and birds.
6 All the people of Egypt will know
that I am the LORD,
for to Israel you were just a staff
made of reeds.
7 When Israel leaned on you,
you splintered and broke
and stabbed her in the armpit.
When she put her weight on you,
you gave way,
and her back was thrown out
of joint.

8"Therefore, this is what the Sovereign LORD says: I will bring an army against you, O Egypt, and destroy both people and animals. 9 The land of Egypt will become a desolate wasteland, and the Egyptians will know that I am the LORD.

"Because you said, 'The Nile River is mine; I made it,' 10 I am now the enemy of both you and your river. I will make the land of Egypt a totally desolate wasteland, from Migdol to Aswan, as far south as the border of Ethiopia.* 11 For forty years not a soul will pass that way, neither people nor animals. It will be completely uninhabited. 12 I will make Egypt desolate, and it will be surrounded by other desolate nations. Its cities will be empty and desolate for forty years, surrounded by other ruined cities. I will scatter the Egyptians to distant lands.

13"But this is what the Sovereign LORD also says: At the end of the forty years I will bring the Egyptians home again from the nations to which they have been scattered. 14 I will restore the prosperity of Egypt and bring its people back to the land of Pathros in southern Egypt from which they came. But Egypt will remain an unimportant, minor kingdom. 15 It will be the lowliest of all the nations, never again great enough to rise above its neighbors.

16"Then Israel will no longer be tempted to trust in Egypt for help. Egypt's shattered condition will remind Israel of how sinful she was to trust Egypt in ear-

lier days. Then Israel will know that I am the Sovereign LORD."

17 On April 26, the first day of the new year,* during the twenty-seventh year of King Jehoiachin's captivity, this message came to me from the LORD: 18 "Son of man, the army of King Nebuchadnezzar* of Babylon fought so hard against Tyre that the warriors' heads were rubbed bare and their shoulders were raw and blistered. Yet Nebuchadnezzar and his army won no plunder to compensate them for all their work. 19 Therefore, this is what the Sovereign LORD says: I will give the land of Egypt to Nebuchadnezzar, king of Babylon. He will carry off its wealth, plundering everything it has so he can pay his army. 20 Yes, I have given him the land of Egypt as a reward for his work, says the Sovereign LORD, because he was working for me when he destroyed Tyre.

21 "And the day will come when I will cause the ancient glory of Israel to revive,* and then, Ezekiel, your words will be respected. Then they will know that I am the LORD."

30:1 THIS is another message that came to me from the LORD: 2 "Son of man, prophesy and give this message from the Sovereign LORD:

"Weep and wail
for that day,
3 for the terrible day is almost here—
the day of the LORD!
It is a day of clouds and gloom,
a day of despair for the nations.
4 A sword will come against Egypt,
and those who are slaughtered
will cover the ground.
Its wealth will be carried away
and its foundations destroyed.
The land of Ethiopia* will be
ravished.
5   Ethiopia, Libya, Lydia, all Arabia,*
and all their other allies
will be destroyed in that war.

6 "For this is what the LORD says:
All of Egypt's allies will fall,

and the pride of her power will
    end.
From Migdol to Aswan*
    they will be slaughtered by the
    sword,
    says the Sovereign Lord.
7 Egypt will be desolate,
    surrounded by desolate nations,
    and its cities will be in ruins,
    surrounded by other ruined
    cities.
8 And the people of Egypt will know
    that I am the Lord
    when I have set Egypt on fire
    and destroyed all their allies.
9 At that time I will send swift
    messengers in ships
    to terrify the complacent
    Ethiopians.
Great panic will come upon them
    on that day of Egypt's certain
    destruction.
Watch for it!
    It is sure to come!

10 "For this is what the Sovereign Lord
    says:
By the power of King
    Nebuchadnezzar* of Babylon,
    I will destroy the hordes of Egypt.
11 He and his armies—the most
    ruthless of all—
    will be sent to demolish the land.
They will make war against Egypt
    until slaughtered Egyptians cover
    the ground.
12 I will dry up the Nile River
    and sell the land to wicked men.
I will destroy the land of Egypt and
    everything in it
    by the hands of foreigners.
    I, the Lord, have spoken!

13 "This is what the Sovereign Lord
    says:
I will smash the idols* of Egypt
    and the images at Memphis.*
There will be no rulers left in Egypt;
    terror will sweep the land.
14 I will destroy southern Egypt,*
    set fire to Zoan,

    and bring judgment against
    Thebes.*
15 I will pour out my fury on
    Pelusium,*
    the strongest fortress of Egypt,
    and I will stamp out
    the hordes of Thebes.
16 Yes, I will set fire to all Egypt!
    Pelusium will be racked with pain;
Thebes will be torn apart;
    Memphis will live in constant
    terror.
17 The young men of Heliopolis and
    Bubastis* will die in battle,
    and the women* will be taken
    away as slaves.
18 When I come to break the proud
    strength of Egypt,
    it will be a dark day for
    Tahpanhes, too.
A dark cloud will cover Tahpanhes,
    and its daughters will be led away
    as captives.
19 And so I will greatly punish Egypt,
    and they will know that I am the
    Lord."

20On April 29,* during the eleventh
year of King Jehoiachin's captivity, this
message came to me from the Lord:
21"Son of man, I have broken the arm of
Pharaoh, the king of Egypt. His arm has
not been put in a cast so that it may heal.
Neither has it been bound up with a
splint to make it strong enough to hold a
sword. 22 Therefore, this is what the Sovereign Lord says: I am the enemy of Pharaoh, the king of Egypt! I will break both
of his arms—the good arm along with
the broken one—and I will make his
sword clatter to the ground. 23I will scatter the Egyptians to many lands throughout the world. 24I will strengthen the
arms of Babylon's king and put my
sword in his hand. But I will break the
arms of Pharaoh, king of Egypt, and he
will lie there mortally wounded, groaning in pain. 25I will strengthen the arms
of the king of Babylon, while the arms of
Pharaoh fall useless to his sides. And
when I put my sword in the hand of Babylon's king and he brings it against the

land of Egypt, Egypt will know that I am the LORD. ²⁶I will scatter the Egyptians among the nations, dispersing them throughout the earth. Then they will know that I am the LORD."

29:1 Hebrew *On the twelfth day of the tenth month*, of the ancient Hebrew lunar calendar. This event occurred on January 7, 587 B.C.; also see note on 1:1. **29:10** Hebrew *from Migdol to Syene as far as the border of Cush.*
29:17 Hebrew *On the first day of the first month*, of the ancient Hebrew lunar calendar. This event occurred on April 26, 571 B.C.; also see note on 1:1. **29:18** Hebrew *Nebuchadrezzar*, a variant spelling of Nebuchadnezzar; also in 29:19. **29:21** Hebrew *I will cause a horn to sprout for the house of Israel.* **30:4** Hebrew *Cush;* similarly in 30:9. **30:5** Hebrew *Cush, Put, Lud, all Arabia, Cub. Cub* is otherwise unknown and may be another spelling for *Lub* (Libya). **30:6** Hebrew *to Syene.* **30:10** Hebrew *Nebuchadrezzar*, a variant spelling of Nebuchadnezzar. **30:13a** The Hebrew term (literally *round things*) probably alludes to dung. **30:13b** Hebrew *Noph;* also in 30:16. **30:14a** Hebrew *Pathros.* **30:14b** Hebrew *No;* also in 30:15, 16. **30:15** Hebrew *Sin;* also in 30:16. **30:17a** Hebrew *of Awen and Pi-beseth.* **30:17b** Or *and her cities.* **30:20** Hebrew *On the seventh day of the first month*, of the ancient Hebrew lunar calendar. This event occurred on April 29, 587 B.C.; also see note on 1:1.

HEBREWS 11:32–12:13

How much more do I need to say? It would take too long to recount the stories of the faith of Gideon, Barak, Samson, Jephthah, David, Samuel, and all the prophets. ³³By faith these people overthrew kingdoms, ruled with justice, and received what God had promised them. They shut the mouths of lions, ³⁴quenched the flames of fire, and escaped death by the edge of the sword. Their weakness was turned to strength. They became strong in battle and put whole armies to flight. ³⁵Women received their loved ones back again from death.

But others were tortured, refusing to turn from God in order to be set free. They placed their hope in a better life after the resurrection. ³⁶Some were jeered at, and their backs were cut open with whips. Others were chained in prisons. ³⁷Some died by stoning, some were sawed in half,* and others were killed with the sword. Some went about wearing skins of sheep and goats, destitute and oppressed and mistreated. ³⁸They were too good for this world, wandering over deserts and mountains, hiding in caves and holes in the ground. ³⁹All these people earned a good rep-

utation because of their faith, yet none of them received all that God had promised. ⁴⁰For God had something better in mind for us, so that they would not reach perfection without us.

¹²:¹THEREFORE, since we are surrounded by such a huge crowd of witnesses to the life of faith, let us strip off every weight that slows us down, especially the sin that so easily trips us up. And let us run with endurance the race God has set before us. ²We do this by keeping our eyes on Jesus, the champion who initiates and perfects our faith.* Because of the joy* awaiting him, he endured the cross, disregarding its shame. Now he is seated in the place of honor beside God's throne. ³Think of all the hostility he endured from sinful people;* then you won't become weary and give up. ⁴After all, you have not yet given your lives in your struggle against sin.

⁵And have you forgotten the encouraging words God spoke to you as his children?* He said,

"My child,* don't make light of the
LORD's discipline,
and don't give up when
he corrects you.
⁶ For the LORD disciplines those
he loves,
and he punishes each one he
accepts as his child."*

⁷As you endure this divine discipline, remember that God is treating you as his own children. Who ever heard of a child who is never disciplined by its father? ⁸If God doesn't discipline you as he does all of his children, it means that you are illegitimate and are not really his children at all. ⁹Since we respected our earthly fathers who disciplined us, shouldn't we submit even more to the discipline of the Father of our spirits, and live forever?*

¹⁰For our earthly fathers disciplined us for a few years, doing the best they knew how. But God's discipline is always good for us, so that we might share

in his holiness. [11]No discipline is enjoyable while it is happening—it's painful! But afterward there will be a peaceful harvest of right living for those who are trained in this way.

[12]So take a new grip with your tired hands and strengthen your weak knees. [13]Mark out a straight path for your feet so that those who are weak and lame will not fall but become strong.

11:37 Some manuscripts add *some were tested.*   **12:2a** Or *Jesus, the originator and perfecter of our faith.*   **12:2b** Or *Instead of the joy.*   **12:3** Some manuscripts read *Think of how people hurt themselves by opposing him.*   **12:5a** Greek *sons;* also in 12:7, 8.   **12:5b** Greek *son;* also in 12:6, 7.   **12:5-6** Prov 3:11-12 (Greek version).   **12:9** Or *and really live?*

PSALM 112:1-10*
Praise the LORD!

How joyful are those who fear
    the LORD
    and delight in obeying his
        commands.
[2] Their children will be successful
        everywhere;
    an entire generation of godly
        people will be blessed.
[3] They themselves will be wealthy,
    and their good deeds will last
        forever.
[4] Light shines in the darkness
    for the godly.
    They are generous,
        compassionate, and righteous.
[5] Good comes to those who lend
        money generously
    and conduct their business fairly.
[6] Such people will not be overcome
        by evil.
    Those who are righteous will be
        long remembered.
[7] They do not fear bad news;
    they confidently trust the LORD
        to care for them.
[8] They are confident and fearless
    and can face their foes
        triumphantly.
[9] They share freely and give
        generously to those in need.
    Their good deeds will be
        remembered forever.
    They will have influence and honor.

[10] The wicked will see this and
        be infuriated.
    They will grind their teeth
        in anger;
    they will slink away, their hopes
        thwarted.

112 This psalm is a Hebrew acrostic poem; after the introductory note of praise, each line begins with a successive letter of the Hebrew alphabet.

PROVERBS 27:17
As iron sharpens iron, so a friend sharpens a friend.

NOVEMBER
15

EZEKIEL 31:1–32:32
On June 21,* during the eleventh year of King Jehoiachin's captivity, this message came to me [Ezekiel] from the LORD: [2]"Son of man, give this message to Pharaoh, king of Egypt, and all his hordes:

"To whom would you compare your
        greatness?
[3] You are like mighty Assyria,
    which was once like a cedar
        of Lebanon,
    with beautiful branches that cast
        deep forest shade
    and with its top high among
        the clouds.
[4] Deep springs watered it
    and helped it to grow tall and
        luxuriant.
    The water flowed around it like
        a river,
        streaming to all the trees
            nearby.
[5] This great tree towered high,
        higher than all the other trees
            around it.
    It prospered and grew long thick
        branches
        because of all the water at
            its roots.

⁶ The birds nested in its branches,
and in its shade all the wild
animals gave birth.
All the great nations of the world
lived in its shadow.
⁷ It was strong and beautiful,
with wide-spreading branches,
for its roots went deep
into abundant water.
⁸ No other cedar in the garden
of God
could rival it.
No cypress had branches to
equal it;
no plane tree had boughs to
compare.
No tree in the garden of God
came close to it in beauty.
⁹ Because I made this tree so beautiful,
and gave it such magnificent
foliage,
it was the envy of all the other trees
of Eden,
the garden of God.

¹⁰"Therefore, this is what the Sovereign LORD says: Because Egypt* became proud and arrogant, and because it set itself so high above the others, with its top reaching to the clouds, ¹¹I will hand it over to a mighty nation that will destroy it as its wickedness deserves. I have already discarded it. ¹²A foreign army— the terror of the nations—has cut it down and left it fallen on the ground. Its branches are scattered across the mountains and valleys and ravines of the land. All those who lived in its shadow have gone away and left it lying there.

¹³ "The birds roost on its fallen trunk,
and the wild animals lie among
its branches.
¹⁴ Let the tree of no other nation
proudly exult in its own
prosperity,
though it be higher than
the clouds
and it be watered from the depths.
For all are doomed to die,
to go down to the depths of the
earth.

They will land in the pit
along with everyone else on earth.

¹⁵"This is what the Sovereign LORD says: When Assyria went down to the grave,* I made the deep springs mourn. I stopped its rivers and dried up its abundant water. I clothed Lebanon in black and caused the trees of the field to wilt. ¹⁶I made the nations shake with fear at the sound of its fall, for I sent it down to the grave with all the others who descend to the pit. And all the other proud trees of Eden, the most beautiful and the best of Lebanon, the ones whose roots went deep into the water, took comfort to find it there with them in the depths of the earth. ¹⁷Its allies, too, were all destroyed and had passed away. They had gone down to the grave—all those nations that had lived in its shade.

¹⁸"O Egypt, to which of the trees of Eden will you compare your strength and glory? You, too, will be brought down to the depths with all these other nations. You will lie there among the outcasts* who have died by the sword. This will be the fate of Pharaoh and all his hordes. I, the Sovereign LORD, have spoken!"

³²:¹On March 3,* during the twelfth year of King Jehoiachin's captivity, this message came to me from the LORD: ²"Son of man, mourn for Pharaoh, king of Egypt, and give him this message:

"You think of yourself as a strong
young lion among the nations,
but you are really just a sea
monster,
heaving around in your own rivers,
stirring up mud with your feet.
³ Therefore, this is what the Sovereign
LORD says:
I will send many people
to catch you in my net
and haul you out of the water.
⁴ I will leave you stranded on the land
to die.
All the birds of the heavens will
land on you,
and the wild animals of the whole
earth

will gorge themselves on you.
⁵ I will scatter your flesh on the hills
and fill the valleys with your
bones.
⁶ I will drench the earth with your
gushing blood
all the way to the mountains,
filling the ravines to the brim.
⁷ When I blot you out,
I will veil the heavens and darken
the stars.
I will cover the sun with a cloud,
and the moon will not give you its
light.
⁸ I will darken the bright stars
overhead
and cover your land in darkness.
I, the Sovereign LORD, have spoken!

⁹"I will disturb many hearts when I
bring news of your downfall to distant
nations you have never seen. ¹⁰Yes, I will
shock many lands, and their kings will
be terrified at your fate. They will shud-
der in fear for their lives as I brandish
my sword before them on the day of
your fall. ¹¹For this is what the Sovereign LORD says:

"The sword of the king of Babylon
will come against you.
¹² I will destroy your hordes with the
swords of mighty warriors—
the terror of the nations.
They will shatter the pride of Egypt,
and all its hordes will be
destroyed.
¹³ I will destroy all your flocks and
herds
that graze beside the streams.
Never again will people or animals
muddy those waters with their
feet.
¹⁴ Then I will let the waters of Egypt
become calm again,
and they will flow as smoothly
as olive oil,
says the Sovereign LORD.
¹⁵ And when I destroy Egypt
and strip you of everything
you own
and strike down all your people,

then you will know that I am the
LORD.
¹⁶ Yes, this is the funeral song
they will sing for Egypt.
Let all the nations mourn.
Let them mourn for Egypt and
its hordes.
I, the Sovereign LORD, have
spoken!"

¹⁷On March 17,* during the twelfth
year, another message came to me from
the LORD: ¹⁸"Son of man, weep for the
hordes of Egypt and for the other mighty
nations.* For I will send them down to
the world below in company with those
who descend to the pit. ¹⁹Say to them,

'O Egypt, are you lovelier than the
other nations?
No! So go down to the pit and lie
there among the outcasts.*'

²⁰The Egyptians will fall with the many
who have died by the sword, for the
sword is drawn against them. Egypt and
its hordes will be dragged away to their
judgment. ²¹Down in the grave* mighty
leaders will mockingly welcome Egypt
and its allies, saying, 'They have come
down; they lie among the outcasts,
hordes slaughtered by the sword.'

²²"Assyria lies there surrounded by
the graves of its army, those who were
slaughtered by the sword. ²³Their
graves are in the depths of the pit, and
they are surrounded by their allies.
They struck terror in the hearts of people everywhere, but now they have been
slaughtered by the sword.

²⁴"Elam lies there surrounded by the
graves of all its hordes, those who were
slaughtered by the sword. They struck
terror in the hearts of people everywhere, but now they have descended as
outcasts to the world below. Now they
lie in the pit and share the shame of
those who have gone before them.
²⁵They have a resting place among the
slaughtered, surrounded by the graves
of all their hordes. Yes, they terrorized
the nations while they lived, but now
they lie in shame with others in the pit,

all of them outcasts, slaughtered by the sword.

26"Meshech and Tubal are there, surrounded by the graves of all their hordes. They once struck terror in the hearts of people everywhere. But now they are outcasts, all slaughtered by the sword. 27 They are not buried in honor like their fallen heroes, who went down to the grave* with their weapons—their shields covering their bodies* and their swords beneath their heads. Their guilt rests upon them because they brought terror to everyone while they were still alive.

28"You too, Egypt, will lie crushed and broken among the outcasts, all slaughtered by the sword.

29"Edom is there with its kings and princes. Mighty as they were, they also lie among those slaughtered by the sword, with the outcasts who have gone down to the pit.

30"All the princes of the north and the Sidonians are there with others who have died. Once a terror, they have been put to shame. They lie there as outcasts with others who were slaughtered by the sword. They share the shame of all who have descended to the pit.

31"When Pharaoh and his entire army arrive, he will take comfort that he is not alone in having his hordes killed, says the Sovereign LORD. 32Although I have caused his terror to fall upon all the living, Pharaoh and his hordes will lie there among the outcasts who were slaughtered by the sword. I, the Sovereign LORD, have spoken!"

31:1 Hebrew *On the first day of the third month,* of the ancient Hebrew lunar calendar. This event occurred on June 21, 587 B.C.; also see note on 1:1.   31:10 Hebrew *you.*   31:15 Hebrew *to Sheol;* also in 31:16, 17.   31:18 Hebrew *among the uncircumcised.*   32:1 Hebrew *On the first day of the twelfth month,* of the ancient Hebrew lunar calendar. This event occurred on March 3, 585 B.C.; also see note on 1:1.   32:17 Hebrew *On the fifteenth day of the month,* presumably in the twelfth month of the ancient Hebrew lunar calendar (see 32:1). This would put this message at the end of King Jehoiachin's twelfth year of captivity, on March 17, 585 B.C.; also see note on 1:1. Greek version reads *On the fifteenth day of the first month,* which would put this message on April 27, 586 B.C., at the beginning of Jehoiachin's twelfth year.   32:18 The meaning of the Hebrew is uncertain.   32:19 Hebrew *the uncircumcised;* also in 32:21, 24, 25, 26, 28, 29, 30, 32.   32:21 Hebrew *in Sheol.*   32:27a Hebrew *to Sheol.*   32:27b The meaning of the Hebrew is uncertain.

HEBREWS 12:14-29

Work at living in peace with everyone, and work at living a holy life, for those who are not holy will not see the Lord. 15Look after each other so that none of you fails to receive the grace of God. Watch out that no poisonous root of bitterness grows up to trouble you, corrupting many. 16Make sure that no one is immoral or godless like Esau, who traded his birthright as the firstborn son for a single meal. 17 You know that afterward, when he wanted his father's blessing, he was rejected. It was too late for repentance, even though he begged with bitter tears.

18You have not come to a physical mountain,* to a place of flaming fire, darkness, gloom, and whirlwind, as the Israelites did at Mount Sinai. 19For they heard an awesome trumpet blast and a voice so terrible that they begged God to stop speaking. 20They staggered back under God's command: "If even an animal touches the mountain, it must be stoned to death."* 21Moses himself was so frightened at the sight that he said, "I am terrified and trembling."*

22No, you have come to Mount Zion, to the city of the living God, the heavenly Jerusalem, and to countless thousands of angels in a joyful gathering. 23 You have come to the assembly of God's firstborn children, whose names are written in heaven. You have come to God himself, who is the judge over all things. You have come to the spirits of the righteous ones in heaven who have now been made perfect. 24You have come to Jesus, the one who mediates the new covenant between God and people, and to the sprinkled blood, which speaks of forgiveness instead of crying out for vengeance like the blood of Abel.

25Be careful that you do not refuse to listen to the One who is speaking. For if the people of Israel did not escape when they refused to listen to Moses, the earthly messenger, we will certainly not escape if we reject the One who speaks to us from heaven! 26When God spoke from Mount Sinai his voice shook the earth, but now he makes another promise: "Once again I will shake not only the earth but the heavens also."* 27 This means that all of creation will be shaken and removed, so that only unshakable things will remain.

28Since we are receiving a Kingdom that is unshakable, let us be thankful and please God by worshiping him with holy fear and awe. 29For our God is a devouring fire.

12:18 Greek *to something that can be touched.*
12:20 Exod 19:13.   12:21 Deut 9:19.   12:26 Hag 2:6.

PSALM 113:1–114:8

Praise the LORD!

Yes, give praise, O servants
of the LORD.
Praise the name of the LORD!
2 Blessed be the name of the LORD
now and forever.
3 Everywhere—from east to west—
praise the name of the LORD.
4 For the LORD is high above
the nations;
his glory is higher than the
heavens.

5 Who can be compared with the
LORD our God,
who is enthroned on high?
6 He stoops to look down
on heaven and on earth.
7 He lifts the poor from the dust
and the needy from the garbage
dump.
8 He sets them among princes,
even the princes of his own people!
9 He gives the childless woman
a family,
making her a happy mother.

Praise the LORD!

114:1WHEN the Israelites escaped from
Egypt—
when the family of Jacob left that
foreign land—
2 the land of Judah became God's
sanctuary,
and Israel became his kingdom.

3 The Red Sea* saw them coming and
hurried out of their way!

The water of the Jordan River
turned away.
4 The mountains skipped like rams,
the hills like lambs!
5 What's wrong, Red Sea, that made
you hurry out of their way?
What happened, Jordan River,
that you turned away?
6 Why, mountains, did you skip
like rams?
Why, hills, like lambs?

7 Tremble, O earth, at the presence
of the Lord,
at the presence of the God of Jacob.
8 He turned the rock into a pool
of water;
yes, a spring of water flowed from
solid rock.

114:3 Hebrew *the sea;* also in 114:5.

PROVERBS 27:18-20

As workers who tend a fig tree are allowed to eat the fruit, so workers who protect their employer's interests will be rewarded. □ As a face is reflected in water, so the heart reflects the real person. □ Just as Death and Destruction* are never satisfied, so human desire is never satisfied.

27:20 Hebrew *Sheol and Abaddon.*

NOVEMBER 16

EZEKIEL 33:1–34:31

Once again a message came to me [Ezekiel] from the LORD: 2"Son of man, give your people this message: 'When I bring an army against a country, the people of that land choose one of their own to be a watchman. 3When the watchman sees the enemy coming, he sounds the alarm to warn the people. 4Then if those who hear the alarm refuse to take action, it is their own fault if they die. 5They heard the alarm but ignored it, so the responsibility is theirs. If they had listened to the warning, they could have saved their lives. ⁶But if the watchman sees the enemy coming and doesn't sound the alarm to warn the people, he is responsible for their captivity. They will die in their sins, but I will hold the watchman responsible for their deaths.'

⁷"Now, son of man, I am making you a watchman for the people of Israel. Therefore, listen to what I say and warn them for me. ⁸If I announce that some wicked people are sure to die and you fail to tell them to change their ways, then they will die in their sins, and I will hold you responsible for their deaths. ⁹But if you warn them to repent and they don't repent, they will die in their sins, but you will have saved yourself.

¹⁰"Son of man, give the people of Israel this message: You are saying, 'Our sins are heavy upon us; we are wasting away! How can we survive?' ¹¹As surely as I live, says the Sovereign LORD, I take no pleasure in the death of wicked people. I only want them to turn from their wicked ways so they can live. Turn! Turn from your wickedness, O people of Israel! Why should you die?

¹²"Son of man, give your people this message: The righteous behavior of righteous people will not save them if they turn to sin, nor will the wicked behavior of wicked people destroy them if they repent and turn from their sins. ¹³When I tell righteous people that they will live, but then they sin, expecting their past righteousness to save them, then none of their righteous acts will be remembered. I will destroy them for their sins. ¹⁴And suppose I tell some wicked people that they will surely die, but then they turn from their sins and do what is just and right. ¹⁵For instance, they might give back a debtor's security, return what they have stolen, and obey my life-giving laws, no longer doing what is evil. If they do this, then they will surely live and not die. ¹⁶None of their past sins will be brought up again, for

they have done what is just and right, and they will surely live.

¹⁷"Your people are saying, 'The Lord isn't doing what's right,' but it is they who are not doing what's right. ¹⁸For again I say, when righteous people turn away from their righteous behavior and turn to evil, they will die. ¹⁹But if wicked people turn from their wickedness and do what is just and right, they will live. ²⁰O people of Israel, you are saying, 'The Lord isn't doing what's right.' But I judge each of you according to your deeds."

²¹On January 8,* during the twelfth year of our captivity, a survivor from Jerusalem came to me and said, "The city has fallen!" ²²The previous evening the LORD had taken hold of me and given me back my voice. So I was able to speak when this man arrived the next morning.

²³Then this message came to me from the LORD: ²⁴"Son of man, the scattered remnants of Judah living among the ruined cities keep saying, 'Abraham was only one man, yet he gained possession of the entire land. We are many; surely the land has been given to us as a possession.' ²⁵So tell these people, 'This is what the Sovereign LORD says: You eat meat with blood in it, you worship idols,* and you murder the innocent. Do you really think the land should be yours? ²⁶Murderers! Idolaters! Adulterers! Should the land belong to you?'

²⁷"Say to them, 'This is what the Sovereign LORD says: As surely as I live, those living in the ruins will die by the sword. And I will send wild animals to eat those living in the open fields. Those hiding in the forts and caves will die of disease. ²⁸I will completely destroy the land and demolish her pride. Her arrogant power will come to an end. The mountains of Israel will be so desolate that no one will even travel through them. ²⁹When I have completely destroyed the land because of their detestable sins, then they will know that I am the LORD.'

³⁰"Son of man, your people talk about you in their houses and whisper about

you at the doors. They say to each other, 'Come on, let's go hear the prophet tell us what the LORD is saying!' 31So my people come pretending to be sincere and sit before you. They listen to your words, but they have no intention of doing what you say. Their mouths are full of lustful words, and their hearts seek only after money. 32You are very entertaining to them, like someone who sings love songs with a beautiful voice or plays fine music on an instrument. They hear what you say, but they don't act on it! 33But when all these terrible things happen to them—as they certainly will—then they will know a prophet has been among them."

34:1THEN this message came to me from the LORD: 2"Son of man, prophesy against the shepherds, the leaders of Israel. Give them this message from the Sovereign LORD: What sorrow awaits you shepherds who feed yourselves instead of your flocks. Shouldn't shepherds feed their sheep? 3You drink the milk, wear the wool, and butcher the best animals, but you let your flocks starve. 4You have not taken care of the weak. You have not tended the sick or bound up the injured. You have not gone looking for those who have wandered away and are lost. Instead, you have ruled them with harshness and cruelty. 5So my sheep have been scattered without a shepherd, and they are easy prey for any wild animal. 6They have wandered through all the mountains and all the hills, across the face of the earth, yet no one has gone to search for them.

7"Therefore, you shepherds, hear the word of the LORD: 8As surely as I live, says the Sovereign LORD, you abandoned my flock and left them to be attacked by every wild animal. And though you were my shepherds, you didn't search for my sheep when they were lost. You took care of yourselves and left the sheep to starve. 9Therefore, you shepherds, hear the word of the LORD. 10This is what the Sovereign LORD says: I now consider these shepherds my enemies, and I will hold them responsible for what has happened to my flock. I will take away their right to feed the flock, and I will stop them from feeding themselves. I will rescue my flock from their mouths; the sheep will no longer be their prey.

11"For this is what the Sovereign LORD says: I myself will search and find my sheep. 12I will be like a shepherd looking for his scattered flock. I will find my sheep and rescue them from all the places where they were scattered on that dark and cloudy day. 13I will bring them back home to their own land of Israel from among the peoples and nations. I will feed them on the mountains of Israel and by the rivers and in all the places where people live. 14Yes, I will give them good pastureland on the high hills of Israel. There they will lie down in pleasant places and feed in the lush pastures of the hills. 15I myself will tend my sheep and give them a place to lie down in peace, says the Sovereign LORD. 16I will search for my lost ones who strayed away, and I will bring them safely home again. I will bandage the injured and strengthen the weak. But I will destroy those who are fat and powerful. I will feed them, yes—feed them justice!

17"And as for you, my flock, this is what the Sovereign LORD says to his people: I will judge between one animal of the flock and another, separating the sheep from the goats. 18Isn't it enough for you to keep the best of the pastures for yourselves? Must you also trample down the rest? Isn't it enough for you to drink clear water for yourselves? Must you also muddy the rest with your feet? 19Why must my flock eat what you have trampled down and drink water you have fouled?

20"Therefore, this is what the Sovereign LORD says: I will surely judge between the fat sheep and the scrawny sheep. 21For you fat sheep pushed and butted and crowded my sick and hungry flock until you scattered them to distant lands. 22So I will rescue my flock, and they will no longer be abused.

I will judge between one animal of the flock and another. ²³And I will set over them one shepherd, my servant David. He will feed them and be a shepherd to them. ²⁴And I, the LORD, will be their God, and my servant David will be a prince among my people. I, the LORD, have spoken!

²⁵"I will make a covenant of peace with my people and drive away the dangerous animals from the land. Then they will be able to camp safely in the wildest places and sleep in the woods without fear. ²⁶I will bless my people and their homes around my holy hill. And in the proper season I will send the showers they need. There will be showers of blessing. ²⁷The orchards and fields of my people will yield bumper crops, and everyone will live in safety. When I have broken their chains of slavery and rescued them from those who enslaved them, then they will know that I am the LORD. ²⁸They will no longer be prey for other nations, and wild animals will no longer devour them. They will live in safety, and no one will frighten them.

²⁹"And I will make their land famous for its crops, so my people will never again suffer from famines or the insults of foreign nations. ³⁰In this way, they will know that I, the LORD their God, am with them. And they will know that they, the people of Israel, are my people, says the Sovereign LORD. ³¹You are my flock, the sheep of my pasture. You are my people, and I am your God. I, the Sovereign LORD, have spoken!"

33:21 Hebrew *On the fifth day of the tenth month,* of the ancient Hebrew lunar calendar. This event occurred on January 8, 585 B.C.; also see note on 1:1.   33:25 The Hebrew term (literally *round things*) probably alludes to dung.

HEBREWS 13:1-25

Keep on loving each other as brothers and sisters.* ²Don't forget to show hospitality to strangers, for some who have done this have entertained angels without realizing it! ³Remember those in prison, as if you were there yourself. Remember also those being mistreated, as if you felt their pain in your own bodies.

⁴Give honor to marriage, and remain faithful to one another in marriage. God will surely judge people who are immoral and those who commit adultery.

⁵Don't love money; be satisfied with what you have. For God has said,

"I will never fail you.
    I will never abandon you."*

⁶So we can say with confidence,

"The LORD is my helper,
    so I will have no fear.
What can mere people do
    to me?"*

⁷Remember your leaders who taught you the word of God. Think of all the good that has come from their lives, and follow the example of their faith.

⁸Jesus Christ is the same yesterday, today, and forever. ⁹So do not be attracted by strange, new ideas. Your strength comes from God's grace, not from rules about food, which don't help those who follow them.

¹⁰We have an altar from which the priests in the Tabernacle* have no right to eat. ¹¹Under the old system, the high priest brought the blood of animals into the Holy Place as a sacrifice for sin, and the bodies of the animals were burned outside the camp. ¹²So also Jesus suffered and died outside the city gates to make his people holy by means of his own blood. ¹³So let us go out to him, outside the camp, and bear the disgrace he bore. ¹⁴For this world is not our permanent home; we are looking forward to a home yet to come.

¹⁵**Therefore, let us offer through Jesus a continual sacrifice of praise to God, proclaiming our allegiance to his name. ¹⁶And don't forget to do good and to share with those in need. These are the sacrifices that please God.**

¹⁷Obey your spiritual leaders, and do what they say. Their work is to watch over your souls, and they are accountable to God. Give them reason to do this

with joy and not with sorrow. That would certainly not be for your benefit.

18Pray for us, for our conscience is clear and we want to live honorably in everything we do. 19And especially pray that I will be able to come back to you soon.

20 Now may the God of peace—
who brought up from the dead
our Lord Jesus,
the great Shepherd of the sheep,
and ratified an eternal covenant
with his blood—
21 may he equip you with all you need
for doing his will.
May he produce in you,*
through the power of Jesus Christ,
every good thing that is pleasing
to him.
All glory to him forever and ever!
Amen.

22I urge you, dear brothers and sisters,* to pay attention to what I have written in this brief exhortation.

23I want you to know that our brother Timothy has been released from jail. If he comes here soon, I will bring him with me to see you.

24Greet all your leaders and all the believers there. The believers from Italy send you their greetings.

25May God's grace be with you all.

13:1 Greek *Continue in brotherly love.*　13:5 Deut 31:6, 8. 13:6 Ps 118:6.　13:10 Or *tent.*　13:21 Some manuscripts read *in us.*　13:22 Greek *brothers.*

PSALM 115:1-18

Not to us, O Lord, not to us,
but to your name goes all
the glory
for your unfailing love and
faithfulness.
2 Why let the nations say,
"Where is their God?"
3 Our God is in the heavens,
and he does as he wishes.
4 Their idols are merely things of
silver and gold,
shaped by human hands.
5 They have mouths but cannot speak,
and eyes but cannot see.

6 They have ears but cannot hear,
and noses but cannot smell.
7 They have hands but cannot feel,
and feet but cannot walk,
and throats but cannot make
a sound.
8 And those who make idols are just
like them,
as are all who trust in them.

9 O Israel, trust the Lord!
He is your helper and your shield.
10 O priests, descendants of Aaron,
trust the Lord!
He is your helper and your shield.
11 All you who fear the Lord, trust
the Lord!
He is your helper and your shield.

12 The Lord remembers us and will
bless us.
He will bless the people of Israel
and bless the priests, the
descendants of Aaron.
13 He will bless those who fear
the Lord,
both great and lowly.

14 May the Lord richly bless
both you and your children.
15 May you be blessed by the Lord,
who made heaven and earth.
16 The heavens belong to the Lord,
but he has given the earth to all
humanity.
17 The dead cannot sing praises
to the Lord,
for they have gone into the silence
of the grave.
18 But we can praise the Lord
both now and forever!

Praise the Lord!

PROVERBS 27:21-22

Fire tests the purity of silver and gold, but a person is tested by being praised.* □ You cannot separate fools from their foolishness, even though you grind them like grain with mortar and pestle.

27:21 Or *by flattery.*

NOVEMBER
17

EZEKIEL 35:1–36:38

Again a message came to me [Ezekiel] from the LORD: ²"Son of man, turn and face Mount Seir, and prophesy against its people. ³Give them this message from the Sovereign LORD:

"I am your enemy, O Mount Seir,
and I will raise my fist against you
to destroy you completely.
⁴ I will demolish your cities
and make you desolate.
Then you will know that I am
the LORD.

⁵"Your eternal hatred for the people of Israel led you to butcher them when they were helpless, when I had already punished them for all their sins. ⁶As surely as I live, says the Sovereign LORD, since you show no distaste for blood, I will give you a bloodbath of your own. Your turn has come! ⁷I will make Mount Seir utterly desolate, killing off all who try to escape and any who return. ⁸I will fill your mountains with the dead. Your hills, your valleys, and your ravines will be filled with people slaughtered by the sword. ⁹I will make you desolate forever. Your cities will never be rebuilt. Then you will know that I am the LORD.

¹⁰"For you said, 'The lands of Israel and Judah will be ours. We will take possession of them. What do we care that the LORD is there!' ¹¹Therefore, as surely as I live, says the Sovereign LORD, I will pay back your angry deeds with my own. I will punish you for all your acts of anger, envy, and hatred. And I will make myself known to Israel* by what I do to you. ¹²Then you will know that I, the LORD, have heard every contemptuous word you spoke against the mountains of Israel. For you said, 'They are desolate; they have been given to us as food to eat!' ¹³In saying that, you boasted proudly against me, and I have heard it all!

¹⁴"This is what the Sovereign LORD says: The whole world will rejoice when I make you desolate. ¹⁵You rejoiced at the desolation of Israel's territory. Now I will rejoice at yours! You will be wiped out, you people of Mount Seir and all who live in Edom! Then you will know that I am the LORD.

36:1"SON of man, prophesy to Israel's mountains. Give them this message: O mountains of Israel, hear the word of the LORD! ²This is what the Sovereign LORD says: Your enemies have taunted you, saying, 'Aha! Now the ancient heights belong to us!' ³Therefore, son of man, give the mountains of Israel this message from the Sovereign LORD: Your enemies have attacked you from all directions, making you the property of many nations and the object of much mocking and slander. ⁴Therefore, O mountains of Israel, hear the word of the Sovereign LORD. He speaks to the hills and mountains, ravines and valleys, and to ruined wastes and long-deserted cities that have been destroyed and mocked by the surrounding nations. ⁵This is what the Sovereign LORD says: My jealous anger burns against these nations, especially Edom, because they have shown utter contempt for me by gleefully taking my land for themselves as plunder.

⁶"Therefore, prophesy to the hills and mountains, the ravines and valleys of Israel. This is what the Sovereign LORD says: I am furious that you have suffered shame before the surrounding nations. ⁷Therefore, this is what the Sovereign LORD says: I have taken a solemn oath that those nations will soon have their own shame to endure.

⁸"But the mountains of Israel will produce heavy crops of fruit for my people—for they will be coming home again soon! ⁹See, I care about you, and I will pay attention to you. Your ground will be plowed and your crops planted. ¹⁰I will greatly increase the population of Israel, and the ruined cities will be rebuilt and filled with people. ¹¹I will in-

crease not only the people, but also your animals. O mountains of Israel, I will bring people to live on you once again. I will make you even more prosperous than you were before. Then you will know that I am the LORD. ¹²I will cause my people to walk on you once again, and you will be their territory. You will never again rob them of their children.

¹³"This is what the Sovereign LORD says: The other nations taunt you, saying, 'Israel is a land that devours its own people and robs them of their children!' ¹⁴But you will never again devour your people or rob them of their children, says the Sovereign LORD. ¹⁵I will not let you hear those other nations insult you, and you will no longer be mocked by them. You will not be a land that causes its nation to fall, says the Sovereign LORD."

¹⁶Then this further message came to me from the LORD: ¹⁷"Son of man, when the people of Israel were living in their own land, they defiled it by the evil way they lived. To me their conduct was as unclean as a woman's menstrual cloth. ¹⁸They polluted the land with murder and the worship of idols,* so I poured out my fury on them. ¹⁹I scattered them to many lands to punish them for the evil way they had lived. ²⁰But when they were scattered among the nations, they brought shame on my holy name. For the nations said, 'These are the people of the LORD, but he couldn't keep them safe in his own land!' ²¹Then I was concerned for my holy name, on which my people brought shame among the nations.

²²"Therefore, give the people of Israel this message from the Sovereign LORD: I am bringing you back, but not because you deserve it. I am doing it to protect my holy name, on which you brought shame while you were scattered among the nations. ²³I will show how holy my great name is—the name on which you brought shame among the nations. And when I reveal my holiness through you before their very eyes, says the Sovereign LORD, then the nations will know

that I am the LORD. ²⁴For I will gather you up from all the nations and bring you home again to your land.

²⁵"Then I will sprinkle clean water on you, and you will be clean. Your filth will be washed away, and you will no longer worship idols. ²⁶And I will give you a new heart, and I will put a new spirit in you. I will take out your stony, stubborn heart and give you a tender, responsive heart.* ²⁷And I will put my Spirit in you so that you will follow my decrees and be careful to obey my regulations.

²⁸"And you will live in Israel, the land I gave your ancestors long ago. You will be my people, and I will be your God. ²⁹I will cleanse you of your filthy behavior. I will give you good crops of grain, and I will send no more famines on the land. ³⁰I will give you great harvests from your fruit trees and fields, and never again will the surrounding nations be able to scoff at your land for its famines. ³¹Then you will remember your past sins and despise yourselves for all the detestable things you did. ³²But remember, says the Sovereign LORD, I am not doing this because you deserve it. O my people of Israel, you should be utterly ashamed of all you have done!

³³"This is what the Sovereign LORD says: When I cleanse you from your sins, I will repopulate your cities, and the ruins will be rebuilt. ³⁴The fields that used to lie empty and desolate in plain view of everyone will again be farmed. ³⁵And when I bring you back, people will say, 'This former wasteland is now like the Garden of Eden! The abandoned and ruined cities now have strong walls and are filled with people!' ³⁶Then the surrounding nations that survive will know that I, the LORD, have rebuilt the ruins and replanted the wasteland. For I, the LORD, have spoken, and I will do what I say.

³⁷"This is what the Sovereign LORD says: I am ready to hear Israel's prayers and to increase their numbers like a flock. ³⁸They will be as numerous as the sacred flocks that fill Jerusalem's streets at the time of her festivals. The

ruined cities will be crowded with people once more, and everyone will know that I am the LORD."

35:11 Hebrew *to them*; Greek version reads *to you.*
36:18 The Hebrew term (literally *round things*) probably alludes to dung; also in 36:25. **36:26** Hebrew *a heart of flesh.*

JAMES 1:1-18

This letter is from James, a slave of God and of the Lord Jesus Christ.

I am writing to the "twelve tribes"— Jewish believers scattered abroad. Greetings!

2Dear brothers and sisters,* when troubles come your way, consider it an opportunity for great joy. 3For you know that when your faith is tested, your endurance has a chance to grow. 4So let it grow, for when your endurance is fully developed, you will be perfect and complete, needing nothing.

5If you need wisdom, ask our generous God, and he will give it to you. He will not rebuke you for asking. 6But when you ask him, be sure that your faith is in God alone. Do not waver, for a person with divided loyalty is as unsettled as a wave of the sea that is blown and tossed by the wind. 7Such people should not expect to receive anything from the Lord. 8Their loyalty is divided between God and the world, and they are unstable in everything they do.

9Believers who are* poor have something to boast about, for God has honored them. 10And those who are rich should boast that God has humbled them. They will fade away like a little flower in the field. 11The hot sun rises and the grass withers; the little flower droops and falls, and its beauty fades away. In the same way, the rich will fade away with all of their achievements.

12**God blesses those who patiently endure testing and temptation. Afterward they will receive the crown of life that God has promised to those who love him.** 13And remember, when you are being tempted, do not say, "God is tempting me." God is never tempted to do wrong,* and he never tempts anyone else. 14Temptation comes from our own

desires, which entice us and drag us away. 15These desires give birth to sinful actions. And when sin is allowed to grow, it gives birth to death.

16So don't be misled, my dear brothers and sisters. 17Whatever is good and perfect comes down to us from God our Father, who created all the lights in the heavens.* He never changes or casts a shifting shadow.* 18He chose to give birth to us by giving us his true word. And we, out of all creation, became his prized possession.*

1:2 Greek *brothers*; also in 1:16, 19. **1:9** Greek *The brother who is.* **1:13** Or *God should not be put to a test by evil people.* **1:17a** Greek *from above, from the Father of lights.* **1:17b** Some manuscripts read *He never changes, as a shifting shadow does.* **1:18** Greek *we became a kind of firstfruit of his creatures.*

PSALM 116:1-19

I love the LORD because he hears
    my voice
and my prayer for mercy.
2 Because he bends down to listen,
    I will pray as long as I have breath!
3 Death wrapped its ropes around me;
    the terrors of the grave*
    overtook me.
I saw only trouble and sorrow.
4 Then I called on the name of the
    LORD:
    "Please, LORD, save me!"
5 How kind the LORD is! How good
    he is!
So merciful, this God of ours!
6 The LORD protects those of
    childlike faith;
    I was facing death, and he
    saved me.
7 Let my soul be at rest again,
    for the LORD has been good to me.
8 He has saved me from death,
    my eyes from tears,
    my feet from stumbling.
9 And so I walk in the LORD's presence
    as I live here on earth!
10 I believed in you, so I said,
    "I am deeply troubled, LORD."
11 In my anxiety I cried out to you,
    "These people are all liars!"
12 What can I offer the LORD
    for all he has done for me?

¹³ I will lift up the cup of salvation
and praise the LORD's name for
saving me.
¹⁴ I will keep my promises to the LORD
in the presence of all his people.

¹⁵ The LORD cares deeply
when his loved ones die.
¹⁶ O LORD, I am your servant;
yes, I am your servant, born into
your household;
you have freed me from my chains.
¹⁷ I will offer you a sacrifice of
thanksgiving
and call on the name of the LORD.
¹⁸ I will fulfill my vows to the LORD
in the presence of all his people—
¹⁹ in the house of the LORD
in the heart of Jerusalem.

Praise the LORD!

116:3 Hebrew *of Sheol.*

PROVERBS 27:23-27

Know the state of your flocks, and put your heart into caring for your herds, for riches don't last forever, and the crown might not be passed to the next generation. After the hay is harvested and the new crop appears and the mountain grasses are gathered in, your sheep will provide wool for clothing, and your goats will provide the price of a field. And you will have enough goats' milk for yourself, your family, and your servant girls.

NOVEMBER
18

EZEKIEL 37:1–38:23

The LORD took hold of me [Ezekiel], and I was carried away by the Spirit of the LORD to a valley filled with bones. ²He led me all around among the bones that covered the valley floor. They were scattered everywhere across the ground and were completely dried out. ³Then

he asked me, "Son of man, can these bones become living people again?"

"O Sovereign LORD," I replied, "you alone know the answer to that."

⁴Then he said to me, "Speak a prophetic message to these bones and say, 'Dry bones, listen to the word of the LORD! ⁵This is what the Sovereign LORD says: Look! I am going to put breath into you and make you live again! ⁶I will put flesh and muscles on you and cover you with skin. I will put breath into you, and you will come to life. Then you will know that I am the LORD.'"

⁷So I spoke this message, just as he told me. Suddenly as I spoke, there was a rattling noise all across the valley. The bones of each body came together and attached themselves as complete skeletons. ⁸Then as I watched, muscles and flesh formed over the bones. Then skin formed to cover their bodies, but they still had no breath in them.

⁹Then he said to me, "Speak a prophetic message to the winds, son of man. Speak a prophetic message and say, 'This is what the Sovereign LORD says: Come, O breath, from the four winds! Breathe into these dead bodies so they may live again.'"

¹⁰So I spoke the message as he commanded me, and breath came into their bodies. They all came to life and stood up on their feet—a great army.

¹¹Then he said to me, "Son of man, these bones represent the people of Israel. They are saying, 'We have become old, dry bones—all hope is gone. Our nation is finished.' ¹²Therefore, prophesy to them and say, 'This is what the Sovereign LORD says: O my people, I will open your graves of exile and cause you to rise again. Then I will bring you back to the land of Israel. ¹³When this happens, O my people, you will know that I am the LORD. ¹⁴I will put my Spirit in you, and you will live again and return home to your own land. Then you will know that I, the LORD, have spoken, and I have done what I said. Yes, the LORD has spoken!'"

¹⁵Again a message came to me from the LORD: ¹⁶"Son of man, take a piece of

wood and carve on it these words: 'This represents Judah and its allied tribes.' Then take another piece and carve these words on it: 'This represents Ephraim and the northern tribes of Israel.'* [17]Now hold them together in your hand as if they were one piece of wood. [18]When your people ask you what your actions mean, [19]say to them, 'This is what the Sovereign LORD says: I will take Ephraim and the northern tribes and join them to Judah. I will make them one piece of wood in my hand.'

[20]"Then hold out the pieces of wood you have inscribed, so the people can see them. [21]And give them this message from the Sovereign LORD: I will gather the people of Israel from among the nations. I will bring them home to their own land from the places where they have been scattered. [22]I will unify them into one nation on the mountains of Israel. One king will rule them all; no longer will they be divided into two nations or into two kingdoms. [23]They will never again pollute themselves with their idols* and vile images and rebellion, for I will save them from their sinful backsliding. I will cleanse them. Then they will truly be my people, and I will be their God.

[24]"My servant David will be their king, and they will have only one shepherd. They will obey my regulations and be careful to keep my decrees. [25]They will live in the land I gave my servant Jacob, the land where their ancestors lived. They and their children and their grandchildren after them will live there forever, generation after generation. And my servant David will be their prince forever. [26]And I will make a covenant of peace with them, an everlasting covenant. I will give them their land and increase their numbers,* and I will put my Temple among them forever. [27]I will make my home among them. I will be their God, and they will be my people. [28]And when my Temple is among them forever, the nations will know that I am the LORD, who makes Israel holy."

[38:1]THIS is another message that came to me from the LORD: [2]"Son of man, turn and face Gog of the land of Magog, the prince who rules over the nations of Meshech and Tubal, and prophesy against him. [3]Give him this message from the Sovereign LORD: Gog, I am your enemy! [4]I will turn you around and put hooks in your jaws to lead you out with your whole army—your horses and charioteers in full armor and a great horde armed with shields and swords. [5]Persia, Ethiopia, and Libya* will join you, too, with all their weapons. [6]Gomer and all its armies will also join you, along with the armies of Beth-togarmah from the distant north, and many others.

[7]"Get ready; be prepared! Keep all the armies around you mobilized, and take command of them. [8]A long time from now you will be called into action. In the distant future you will swoop down on the land of Israel, which will be enjoying peace after recovering from war and after its people have returned from many lands to the mountains of Israel. [9]You and all your allies—a vast and awesome army—will roll down on them like a storm and cover the land like a cloud.

[10]"This is what the Sovereign LORD says: At that time evil thoughts will come to your mind, and you will devise a wicked scheme. [11]You will say, 'Israel is an unprotected land filled with unwalled villages! I will march against her and destroy these people who live in such confidence! [12]I will go to those formerly desolate cities that are now filled with people who have returned from exile in many nations. I will capture vast amounts of plunder, for the people are rich with livestock and other possessions now. They think the whole world revolves around them!' [13]But Sheba and Dedan and the merchants of Tarshish will ask, 'Do you really think the armies you have gathered can rob them of silver and gold? Do you think you can drive away their livestock and seize their goods and carry off plunder?'

[14]"Therefore, son of man, prophesy against Gog. Give him this message

from the Sovereign LORD: When my people are living in peace in their land, then you will rouse yourself.* [15]You will come from your homeland in the distant north with your vast cavalry and your mighty army, [16]and you will attack my people Israel, covering their land like a cloud. At that time in the distant future, I will bring you against my land as everyone watches, and my holiness will be displayed by what happens to you, Gog. Then all the nations will know that I am the LORD.

[17]"This is what the Sovereign LORD asks: Are you the one I was talking about long ago, when I announced through Israel's prophets that in the future I would bring you against my people? [18]But this is what the Sovereign LORD says: When Gog invades the land of Israel, my fury will boil over! [19]In my jealousy and blazing anger, I promise a mighty shaking in the land of Israel on that day. [20]All living things—the fish in the sea, the birds of the sky, the animals of the field, the small animals that scurry along the ground, and all the people on earth—will quake in terror at my presence. Mountains will be thrown down; cliffs will crumble; walls will fall to the earth. [21]I will summon the sword against you on all the hills of Israel, says the Sovereign LORD. Your men will turn their swords against each other. [22]I will punish you and your armies with disease and bloodshed; I will send torrential rain, hailstones, fire, and burning sulfur! [23]In this way, I will show my greatness and holiness, and I will make myself known to all the nations of the world. Then they will know that I am the LORD."

37:16 Hebrew *This is Ephraim's wood, representing Joseph and all the house of Israel.*   37:23 The Hebrew term (literally *round things*) probably alludes to dung.
37:26 Hebrew reads *I will give them and increase their numbers;* Greek version omits the entire phrase.
38:5 Hebrew *Paras, Cush, and Put.*   38:14 As in Greek version; Hebrew reads *then you will know.*

JAMES 1:19–2:17
Understand this, my dear brothers and sisters: You must all be quick to listen, slow to speak, and slow to get angry.

[20]Human anger* does not produce the righteousness* God desires. [21]So get rid of all the filth and evil in your lives, and humbly accept the word God has planted in your hearts, for it has the power to save your souls.

[22]But don't just listen to God's word. You must do what it says. Otherwise, you are only fooling yourselves. [23]For if you listen to the word and don't obey, it is like glancing at your face in a mirror. [24]You see yourself, walk away, and forget what you look like. [25]But if you look carefully into the perfect law that sets you free, and if you do what it says and don't forget what you heard, then God will bless you for doing it.

[26]If you claim to be religious but don't control your tongue, you are fooling yourself, and your religion is worthless. [27]**Pure and genuine religion in the sight of God the Father means caring for orphans and widows in their distress and refusing to let the world corrupt you.**

[2:1]MY dear brothers and sisters,* how can you claim to have faith in our glorious Lord Jesus Christ if you favor some people over others?

[2]For example, suppose someone comes into your meeting* dressed in fancy clothes and expensive jewelry, and another comes in who is poor and dressed in dirty clothes. [3]If you give special attention and a good seat to the rich person, but you say to the poor one, "You can stand over there, or else sit on the floor"—well, [4]doesn't this discrimination show that your judgments are guided by evil motives?

[5]Listen to me, dear brothers and sisters. Hasn't God chosen the poor in this world to be rich in faith? Aren't they the ones who will inherit the Kingdom he promised to those who love him? [6]But you dishonor the poor! Isn't it the rich who oppress you and drag you into court? [7]Aren't they the ones who slander Jesus Christ, whose noble name* you bear?

[8]Yes indeed, it is good when you obey

the royal law as found in the Scriptures: "Love your neighbor as yourself."* ⁹But if you favor some people over others, you are committing a sin. You are guilty of breaking the law.

¹⁰For the person who keeps all of the laws except one is as guilty as a person who has broken all of God's laws. ¹¹For the same God who said, "You must not commit adultery," also said, "You must not murder."* So if you murder someone but do not commit adultery, you have still broken the law.

¹²So whatever you say or whatever you do, remember that you will be judged by the law that sets you free. ¹³There will be no mercy for those who have not shown mercy to others. But if you have been merciful, God will be merciful when he judges you.

¹⁴What good is it, dear brothers and sisters, if you say you have faith but don't show it by your actions? Can that kind of faith save anyone? ¹⁵Suppose you see a brother or sister who has no food or clothing, ¹⁶and you say, "Goodbye and have a good day; stay warm and eat well"—but then you don't give that person any food or clothing. What good does that do?

¹⁷So you see, faith by itself isn't enough. Unless it produces good deeds, it is dead and useless.

1:20a Greek *A man's anger.*   1:20b Or *the justice.*
2:1 Greek *brothers;* also in 2:5, 14.   2:2 Greek *your synagogue.*   2:7 Greek *slander the noble name.*   2:8 Lev 19:18.   2:11 Exod 20:13-14; Deut 5:17-18.

PSALM 117:1-2

Praise the LORD, all you nations.
　Praise him, all you people
　　of the earth.
² For he loves us with unfailing love;
　the LORD's faithfulness
　　endures forever.

Praise the LORD!

PROVERBS 28:1

The wicked run away when no one is chasing them, but the godly are as bold as lions.

NOVEMBER 19

EZEKIEL 39:1–40:27

"Son of man, prophesy against Gog. Give him this message from the Sovereign LORD: I am your enemy, O Gog, ruler of the nations of Meshech and Tubal. ²I will turn you around and drive you toward the mountains of Israel, bringing you from the distant north. ³I will knock the bow from your left hand and the arrows from your right hand, and I will leave you helpless. ⁴You and your army and your allies will all die on the mountains. I will feed you to the vultures and wild animals. ⁵You will fall in the open fields, for I have spoken, says the Sovereign LORD. ⁶And I will rain down fire on Magog and on all your allies who live safely on the coasts. Then they will know that I am the LORD.

⁷"In this way, I will make known my holy name among my people of Israel. I will not let anyone bring shame on it. And the nations, too, will know that I am the LORD, the Holy One of Israel. ⁸That day of judgment will come, says the Sovereign LORD. Everything will happen just as I have declared it.

⁹"Then the people in the towns of Israel will go out and pick up your small and large shields, bows and arrows, javelins and spears, and they will use them for fuel. There will be enough to last them seven years! ¹⁰They won't need to cut wood from the fields or forests, for these weapons will give them all the fuel they need. They will plunder those who planned to plunder them, and they will rob those who planned to rob them, says the Sovereign LORD.

¹¹"And I will make a vast graveyard for Gog and his hordes in the Valley of the Travelers, east of the Dead Sea.* It will block the way of those who travel there, and they will change the name of the place to the Valley of Gog's Hordes. ¹²It will take seven months for the peo-

ple of Israel to bury the bodies and cleanse the land. ¹³Everyone in Israel will help, for it will be a glorious victory for Israel when I demonstrate my glory on that day, says the Sovereign LORD.

¹⁴"After seven months, teams of men will be appointed to search the land for skeletons to bury, so the land will be made clean again. ¹⁵Whenever bones are found, a marker will be set up so the burial crews will take them to be buried in the Valley of Gog's Hordes. ¹⁶(There will be a town there named Hamonah, which means 'horde.') And so the land will finally be cleansed.

¹⁷"And now, son of man, this is what the Sovereign LORD says: Call all the birds and wild animals. Say to them: Gather together for my great sacrificial feast. Come from far and near to the mountains of Israel, and there eat flesh and drink blood! ¹⁸Eat the flesh of mighty men and drink the blood of princes as though they were rams, lambs, goats, and bulls—all fattened animals from Bashan! ¹⁹Gorge yourselves with flesh until you are glutted; drink blood until you are drunk. This is the sacrificial feast I have prepared for you. ²⁰Feast at my banquet table—feast on horses and charioteers, on mighty men and all kinds of valiant warriors, says the Sovereign LORD.

²¹"In this way, I will demonstrate my glory to the nations. Everyone will see the punishment I have inflicted on them and the power of my fist when I strike. ²²And from that time on the people of Israel will know that I am the LORD their God. ²³The nations will then know why Israel was sent away to exile—it was punishment for sin, for they were unfaithful to their God. Therefore, I turned away from them and let their enemies destroy them. ²⁴I turned my face away and punished them because of their defilement and their sins.

²⁵"So now, this is what the Sovereign LORD says: I will end the captivity of my people*; I will have mercy on all Israel, for I jealously guard my holy reputation!

²⁶They will accept responsibility for their past shame and unfaithfulness after they come home to live in peace in their own land, with no one to bother them. ²⁷When I bring them home from the lands of their enemies, I will display my holiness among them for all the nations to see. ²⁸Then my people will know that I am the LORD their God, because I sent them away to exile and brought them home again. I will leave none of my people behind. ²⁹And I will never again turn my face from them, for I will pour out my Spirit upon the people of Israel. I, the Sovereign LORD, have spoken!"

^{40:1}ON April 28,* during the twenty-fifth year of our captivity—fourteen years after the fall of Jerusalem—the LORD took hold of me. ²In a vision from God he took me to the land of Israel and set me down on a very high mountain. From there I could see toward the south what appeared to be a city. ³As he brought me nearer, I saw a man whose face shone like bronze standing beside a gateway entrance. He was holding in his hand a linen measuring cord and a measuring rod.

⁴He said to me, "Son of man, watch and listen. Pay close attention to everything I show you. You have been brought here so I can show you many things. Then you will return to the people of Israel and tell them everything you have seen."

⁵I could see a wall completely surrounding the Temple area. The man took a measuring rod that was 10½ feet* long and measured the wall, and the wall was 10½ feet* thick and 10½ feet high.

⁶Then he went over to the eastern gateway. He climbed the steps and measured the threshold of the gateway; it was 10½ feet front to back.* ⁷There were guard alcoves on each side built into the gateway passage. Each of these alcoves was 10½ feet square, with a distance between them of 8¾ feet* along the passage wall. The gateway's inner threshold, which led to the entry room at the inner

end of the gateway passage, was 10½ feet front to back. 8He also measured the entry room of the gateway.* 9It was 14 feet* across, with supporting columns 3½ feet* thick. This entry room was at the inner end of the gateway structure, facing toward the Temple.

10There were three guard alcoves on each side of the gateway passage. Each had the same measurements, and the dividing walls separating them were also identical. 11The man measured the gateway entrance, which was 17½ feet* wide at the opening and 22¾ feet* wide in the gateway passage. 12In front of each of the guard alcoves was a 21-inch* curb. The alcoves themselves were 10½ feet* on each side.

13Then he measured the entire width of the gateway, measuring the distance between the back walls of facing guard alcoves; this distance was 43¾ feet.* 14He measured the dividing walls all along the inside of the gateway up to the entry room of the gateway; this distance was 105 feet.* 15The full length of the gateway passage was 87½ feet* from one end to the other. 16There were recessed windows that narrowed inward through the walls of the guard alcoves and their dividing walls. There were also windows in the entry room. The surfaces of the dividing walls were decorated with carved palm trees.

17Then the man brought me through the gateway into the outer courtyard of the Temple. A stone pavement ran along the walls of the courtyard, and thirty rooms were built against the walls, opening onto the pavement. 18This pavement flanked the gates and extended out from the walls into the courtyard the same distance as the gateway entrance. This was the lower pavement. 19Then the man measured across the Temple's outer courtyard between the outer and inner gateways; the distance was 175 feet.*

20The man measured the gateway on the north just like the one on the east. 21Here, too, there were three guard alcoves on each side, with dividing walls

and an entry room. All the measurements matched those of the east gateway. The gateway passage was 87½ feet long and 43¾ feet wide between the back walls of facing guard alcoves. 22The windows, the entry room, and the palm tree decorations were identical to those in the east gateway. There were seven steps leading up to the gateway entrance, and the entry room was at the inner end of the gateway passage. 23Here on the north side, just as on the east, there was another gateway leading to the Temple's inner courtyard directly opposite this outer gateway. The distance between the two gateways was 175 feet.

24Then the man took me around to the south gateway and measured its various parts, and they were exactly the same as in the others. 25It had windows along the walls as the others did, and there was an entry room where the gateway passage opened into the outer courtyard. And like the others, the gateway passage was 87½ feet long and 43¾ feet wide between the back walls of facing guard alcoves. 26This gateway also had a stairway of seven steps leading up to it, and an entry room at the inner end, and palm tree decorations along the dividing walls. 27And here again, directly opposite the outer gateway, was another gateway that led into the inner courtyard. The distance between the two gateways was 175 feet.

39:11 Hebrew *the sea.*   **39:25** Hebrew *of Jacob.*
40:1 Hebrew *At the beginning of the year, on the tenth day of the month,* of the ancient Hebrew lunar calendar. This event occurred on April 28, 573 B.C.; also see note on 1:1.
40:5a Hebrew *6 long cubits* [3.2 meters], *each being a cubit* [18 inches or 45 centimeters] *and a handbreadth* [3 inches or 8 centimeters] *in length.*   **40:5b** Hebrew *1 rod* [3.2 meters]; also in 40:5c, 7.   **40:6** As in Greek version, which reads *1 rod* [3.2 meters] *deep;* Hebrew reads *1 rod deep, and 1 threshold, 1 rod deep.*   **40:7** Hebrew *5 cubits* [2.7 meters]; also in 40:48.   **40:8** Many Hebrew manuscripts add *which faced inward toward the Temple; it was 1 rod* [10.5 feet or 3.2 meters] *deep. 9Then he measured the entry room of the gateway.*   **40:9a** Hebrew *8 cubits* [4.2 meters].   **40:9b** Hebrew *2 cubits* [1.1 meters].
40:11a Hebrew *10 cubits* [5.3 meters].   **40:11b** Hebrew *13 cubits* [6.9 meters].   **40:12a** Hebrew *1 cubit* [53 centimeters].   **40:12b** Hebrew *6 cubits* [3.2 meters].
40:13 Hebrew *25 cubits* [13.3 meters]; also in 40:21, 25, 29, 30, 33, 36.   **40:14** Hebrew *60 cubits* [31.8 meters]. The meaning of the Hebrew in this verse is uncertain.
40:15 Hebrew *50 cubits* [26.5 meters]; also in 40:21, 25, 29, 33, 36.   **40:19** Hebrew *100 cubits* [53 meters]; also in 40:23, 27, 47.

JAMES 2:18–3:18

Now someone may argue, "Some people have faith; others have good deeds." But I [James] say, "How can you show me your faith if you don't have good deeds? I will show you my faith by my good deeds."

[19] You say you have faith, for you believe that there is one God.* Good for you! Even the demons believe this, and they tremble in terror. [20] How foolish! Can't you see that faith without good deeds is useless?

[21] Don't you remember that our ancestor Abraham was shown to be right with God by his actions when he offered his son Isaac on the altar? [22] You see, his faith and his actions worked together. His actions made his faith complete. [23] And so it happened just as the Scriptures say: "Abraham believed God, and God counted him as righteous because of his faith."* He was even called the friend of God.* [24] So you see, we are shown to be right with God by what we do, not by faith alone.

[25] Rahab the prostitute is another example. She was shown to be right with God by her actions when she hid those messengers and sent them safely away by a different road. [26] Just as the body is dead without breath,* so also faith is dead without good works.

[3:1] DEAR brothers and sisters,* not many of you should become teachers in the church, for we who teach will be judged more strictly. [2] Indeed, we all make many mistakes. For if we could control our tongues, we would be perfect and could also control ourselves in every other way.

[3] We can make a large horse go wherever we want by means of a small bit in its mouth. [4] And a small rudder makes a huge ship turn wherever the pilot chooses to go, even though the winds are strong. [5] In the same way, the tongue is a small thing that makes grand speeches.

But a tiny spark can set a great forest on fire. [6] And the tongue is a flame of fire. It is a whole world of wickedness, corrupting your entire body. It can set your whole life on fire, for it is set on fire by hell itself.*

[7] People can tame all kinds of animals, birds, reptiles, and fish, [8] but no one can tame the tongue. It is restless and evil, full of deadly poison. [9] Sometimes it praises our Lord and Father, and sometimes it curses those who have been made in the image of God. [10] And so blessing and cursing come pouring out of the same mouth. Surely, my brothers and sisters, this is not right! [11] Does a spring of water bubble out with both fresh water and bitter water? [12] Does a fig tree produce olives, or a grapevine produce figs? No, and you can't draw fresh water from a salty spring.*

[13] If you are wise and understand God's ways, prove it by living an honorable life, doing good works with the humility that comes from wisdom. [14] But if you are bitterly jealous and there is selfish ambition in your heart, don't cover up the truth with boasting and lying. [15] For jealousy and selfishness are not God's kind of wisdom. Such things are earthly, unspiritual, and demonic. [16] For wherever there is jealousy and selfish ambition, there you will find disorder and evil of every kind.

[17] **But the wisdom from above is first of all pure. It is also peace loving, gentle at all times, and willing to yield to others. It is full of mercy and good deeds. It shows no favoritism and is always sincere.** [18] And those who are peacemakers will plant seeds of peace and reap a harvest of righteousness.*

2:19 Some manuscripts read *that God is one;* see Deut 6:4. 2:23a Gen 15:6. 2:23b See Isa 41:8. 2:26 Or *without spirit.* 3:1 Greek *brothers;* also in 3:10. 3:6 Or *for it will burn in hell.* 3:12 Greek *from salt.* 3:18 Or *of good things,* or *of justice.*

PSALM 118:1-18

Give thanks to the LORD, for
　　he is good!
　　His faithful love endures forever.

[2] Let all Israel repeat:
　　"His faithful love endures
　　　forever."

³ Let Aaron's descendants, the
    priests, repeat:
  "His faithful love endures
    forever."
⁴ Let all who fear the LORD repeat:
  "His faithful love endures forever."

⁵ In my distress I prayed to the LORD,
    and the LORD answered me and
    set me free.
⁶ The LORD is for me, so I will have
    no fear.
  What can mere people do to me?
⁷ Yes, the LORD is for me; he will
    help me.
  I will look in triumph at those
    who hate me.
⁸ It is better to take refuge in the LORD
    than to trust in people.
⁹ It is better to take refuge in the LORD
    than to trust in princes.

¹⁰ Though hostile nations
    surrounded me,
  I destroyed them all with the
    authority of the LORD.
¹¹ Yes, they surrounded and
    attacked me,
  but I destroyed them all with the
    authority of the LORD.
¹² They swarmed around me like bees;
    they blazed against me like a
    crackling fire.
  But I destroyed them all with the
    authority of the LORD.
¹³ My enemies did their best to kill me,
    but the LORD rescued me.
¹⁴ The LORD is my strength and
    my song;
  he has given me victory.
¹⁵ Songs of joy and victory are sung in
    the camp of the godly.
  The strong right arm of the LORD
    has done glorious things!
¹⁶ The strong right arm of the LORD is
    raised in triumph.
  The strong right arm of the LORD
    has done glorious things!
¹⁷ I will not die; instead, I will live
    to tell what the LORD has done.
¹⁸ The LORD has punished me severely,
    but he did not let me die.

PROVERBS 28:2
When there is moral rot within a nation, its government topples easily. But wise and knowledgeable leaders bring stability.

NOVEMBER 20

EZEKIEL 40:28–41:26
Then the man took me [Ezekiel] to the south gateway leading into the inner courtyard. He measured it, and it had the same measurements as the other gateways. ²⁹Its guard alcoves, dividing walls, and entry room were the same size as those in the others. It also had windows along its walls and in the entry room. And like the others, the gateway passage was 87½ feet long and 43¾ feet wide. ³⁰(The entry rooms of the gateways leading into the inner courtyard were 14 feet* across and 43¾ feet wide.) ³¹The entry room to the south gateway faced into the outer courtyard. It had palm tree decorations on its columns, and there were eight steps leading to its entrance.

³²Then he took me to the east gateway leading to the inner courtyard. He measured it, and it had the same measurements as the other gateways. ³³Its guard alcoves, dividing walls, and entry room were the same size as those of the others, and there were windows along the walls and in the entry room. The gateway passage measured 87½ feet long and 43¾ feet wide. ³⁴Its entry room faced into the outer courtyard. It had palm tree decorations on its columns, and there were eight steps leading to its entrance.

³⁵Then he took me around to the north gateway leading to the inner courtyard. He measured it, and it had the same measurements as the other gateways. ³⁶The guard alcoves, dividing

walls, and entry room of this gateway had the same measurements as in the others and the same window arrangements. The gateway passage measured 87½ feet long and 43¾ feet wide. [37] Its entry room faced into the outer courtyard, and it had palm tree decorations on the columns. There were eight steps leading to its entrance.

[38] A door led from the entry room of one of the inner gateways into a side room, where the meat for sacrifices was washed. [39] On each side of this entry room were two tables, where the sacrificial animals were slaughtered for the burnt offerings, sin offerings, and guilt offerings. [40] Outside the entry room, on each side of the stairs going up to the north entrance, were two more tables. [41] So there were eight tables in all—four inside and four outside—where the sacrifices were cut up and prepared. [42] There were also four tables of finished stone for preparation of the burnt offerings, each 31½ inches square and 21 inches high.* On these tables were placed the butchering knives and other implements for slaughtering the sacrificial animals. [43] There were hooks, each 3 inches* long, fastened to the foyer walls. The sacrificial meat was laid on the tables.

[44] Inside the inner courtyard were two rooms,* one beside the north gateway, facing south, and the other beside the south* gateway, facing north. [45] And the man said to me, "The room beside the north inner gate is for the priests who supervise the Temple maintenance. [46] The room beside the south inner gate is for the priests in charge of the altar—the descendants of Zadok—for they alone of all the Levites may approach the LORD to minister to him."

[47] Then the man measured the inner courtyard, and it was a square, 175 feet wide and 175 feet across. The altar stood in the courtyard in front of the Temple. [48] Then he brought me to the entry room of the Temple. He measured the walls on either side of the opening to the entry room, and they were 8¾ feet thick. The entrance itself was 24½ feet* wide, and the walls on each side of the entrance were an additional 5¼ feet* long. [49] The entry room was 35 feet* wide and 21 feet* deep. There were ten steps leading up to it, with a column on each side.

[41:1] AFTER that, the man brought me into the sanctuary of the Temple. He measured the walls on either side of its doorway, and they were 10½ feet* thick. [2] The doorway was 17½ feet* wide, and the walls on each side of it were 8¾ feet* long. The sanctuary itself was 70 feet long and 35 feet wide.*

[3] Then he went beyond the sanctuary into the inner room. He measured the walls on either side of its entrance, and they were 3½ feet* thick. The entrance was 10½ feet wide, and the walls on each side of the entrance were 12¼ feet* long. [4] The inner room of the sanctuary was 35 feet* long and 35 feet wide. "This," he told me, "is the Most Holy Place."

[5] Then he measured the wall of the Temple, and it was 10½ feet thick. There was a row of rooms along the outside wall; each room was 7 feet* wide. [6] These side rooms were built in three levels, one above the other, with thirty rooms on each level. The supports for these side rooms rested on exterior ledges on the Temple wall; they did not extend into the wall. [7] Each level was wider than the one below it, corresponding to the narrowing of the Temple wall as it rose higher. A stairway led up from the bottom level through the middle level to the top level.

[8] I saw that the Temple was built on a terrace, which provided a foundation for the side rooms. This terrace was 10½ feet* high. [9] The outer wall of the Temple's side rooms was 8¾ feet thick. This left an open area between these side rooms [10] and the row of rooms along the outer wall of the inner courtyard. This open area was 35 feet wide, and it went all the way around the

Temple. [11]Two doors opened from the side rooms into the terrace yard, which was 8¾ feet wide. One door faced north and the other south.

[12]A large building stood on the west, facing the Temple courtyard. It was 122½ feet wide and 157½ feet long, and its walls were 8¾ feet* thick. [13]Then the man measured the Temple, and it was 175 feet* long. The courtyard around the building, including its walls, was an additional 175 feet in length. [14]The inner courtyard to the east of the Temple was also 175 feet wide. [15]The building to the west, including its two walls, was also 175 feet wide.

The sanctuary, the inner room, and the entry room of the Temple [16]were all paneled with wood, as were the frames of the recessed windows. The inner walls of the Temple were paneled with wood above and below the windows. [17]The space above the door leading into the inner room, and its walls inside and out, were also paneled. [18]All the walls were decorated with carvings of cherubim, each with two faces, and there was a carving of a palm tree between each of the cherubim. [19]One face—that of a man—looked toward the palm tree on one side. The other face—that of a young lion—looked toward the palm tree on the other side. The figures were carved all along the inside of the Temple, [20]from the floor to the top of the walls, including the outer wall of the sanctuary.

[21]There were square columns at the entrance to the sanctuary, and the ones at the entrance of the Most Holy Place were similar. [22]There was an altar made of wood, 5¼ feet high and 3½ feet across.* Its corners, base, and sides were all made of wood. "This," the man told me, "is the table that stands in the LORD's presence."

[23]Both the sanctuary and the Most Holy Place had double doorways, [24]each with two swinging doors. [25]The doors leading into the sanctuary were decorated with carved cherubim and palm trees, just as on the walls. And there was

a wooden roof at the front of the entry room to the Temple. [26]On both sides of the entry room were recessed windows decorated with carved palm trees. The side rooms along the outside wall also had roofs.

40:30 As in 40:9, which reads 8 *cubits* [14 feet or 4.2 meters]; here the Hebrew reads 5 *cubits* [8¼ feet or 2.7 meters]. Some Hebrew manuscripts and the Greek version omit this entire verse.   **40:42** Hebrew 1½ *cubits* [80 centimeters] *long and* 1½ *cubits wide and* 1 *cubit* [53 centimeters] *high.*   **40:43** Hebrew *a handbreadth* [8 centimeters].   **40:44a** As in Greek version; Hebrew reads *rooms for singers.*   **40:44b** As in Greek version; Hebrew reads *east.*   **40:48a** Hebrew 14 *cubits* [7.4 meters]. **40:48b** Hebrew 3 *cubits* [1.6 meters].   **40:49a** Hebrew 20 *cubits* [10.6 meters].   **40:49b** As in Greek version, which reads 12 *cubits* [21 feet or 6.4 meters]; Hebrew reads 11 *cubits* [19¼ feet or 5.8 meters].   **41:1** Hebrew 6 *cubits* [3.2 meters]; also in 41:3, 5.   **41:2a** Hebrew 10 *cubits* [5.3 meters].   **41:2b** Hebrew 5 *cubits* [2.7 meters]; also in 41:9, 11.   **41:2c** Hebrew 40 *cubits* [21.2 meters] *long and* 20 *cubits* [10.6 meters] *wide.*   **41:3a** Hebrew 2 *cubits* [1.1 meters].   **41:3b** Hebrew 7 *cubits* [3.7 meters]. **41:4** Hebrew 20 *cubits* [10.6 meters]; also in 41:4b, 10. **41:5** Hebrew 4 *cubits* [2.1 meters].   **41:8** Hebrew 1 *rod,* 6 *cubits* [3.2 meters].   **41:12** Hebrew 70 *cubits* [37.1 meters] *wide and* 90 *cubits* [47.7 meters] *long, and its walls were* 5 *cubits* [2.7 meters] *thick.*   **41:13** Hebrew 100 *cubits* [53 meters]; also in 41:13b, 14, 15. **41:22** Hebrew 3 *cubits* [1.6 meters] *high and* 2 *cubits* [1.1 meters] *across.*

JAMES 4:1-17

What is causing the quarrels and fights among you? Don't they come from the evil desires at war within you? [2]You want what you don't have, so you scheme and kill to get it. You are jealous of what others have, but you can't get it, so you fight and wage war to take it away from them. Yet you don't have what you want because you don't ask God for it. [3]And even when you ask, you don't get it because your motives are all wrong—you want only what will give you pleasure.

[4]You adulterers!* Don't you realize that friendship with the world makes you an enemy of God? I say it again: If you want to be a friend of the world, you make yourself an enemy of God. [5]What do you think the Scriptures mean when they say that the spirit God has placed within us is filled with envy?* [6]But he gives us even more grace to stand against such evil desires. As the Scriptures say,

"God opposes the proud
    but favors the humble."*

7So humble yourselves before God. Resist the devil, and he will flee from you. 8Come close to God, and God will come close to you. Wash your hands, you sinners; purify your hearts, for your loyalty is divided between God and the world. 9Let there be tears for what you have done. Let there be sorrow and deep grief. Let there be sadness instead of laughter, and gloom instead of joy. 10Humble yourselves before the Lord, and he will lift you up in honor.

11Don't speak evil against each other, dear brothers and sisters.* If you criticize and judge each other, then you are criticizing and judging God's law. But your job is to obey the law, not to judge whether it applies to you. 12God alone, who gave the law, is the Judge. He alone has the power to save or to destroy. So what right do you have to judge your neighbor?

13Look here, you who say, "Today or tomorrow we are going to a certain town and will stay there a year. We will do business there and make a profit." 14How do you know what your life will be like tomorrow? Your life is like the morning fog—it's here a little while, then it's gone. 15What you ought to say is, "If the Lord wants us to, we will live and do this or that." 16Otherwise you are boasting about your own plans, and all such boasting is evil.

17Remember, it is sin to know what you ought to do and then not do it.

4:4 Greek *You adulteresses!*   4:5 Or *that God longs jealously for the human spirit he has placed within us?* or *that the Holy Spirit, whom God has placed within us, opposes our envy?* 4:6 Prov 3:34 (Greek version).   4:11 Greek *brothers.*

PSALM 118:19-29

Open for me the gates where the
  righteous enter,
  and I will go in and thank the Lord.
20 These gates lead to the presence
  of the Lord,
  and the godly enter there.
21 I thank you for answering my prayer
  and giving me victory!

22 The stone that the builders rejected
  has now become the cornerstone.
23 This is the Lord's doing,
  and it is wonderful to see.
24 This is the day the Lord has made.
  We will rejoice and be glad in it.
25 Please, Lord, please save us.
  Please, Lord, please give
  us success.
26 Bless the one who comes in the
  name of the Lord.
  We bless you from the house of
  the Lord.
27 The Lord is God, shining upon us.
  Take the sacrifice and bind it with
  cords on the altar.
28 You are my God, and I will
  praise you!
  You are my God, and I will
  exalt you!

29 Give thanks to the Lord, for
  he is good!
  His faithful love endures forever.

PROVERBS 28:3-5

A poor person who oppresses the poor is like a pounding rain that destroys the crops. □ To reject the law is to praise the wicked; to obey the law is to fight them. □ Evil people don't understand justice, but those who follow the Lord understand completely.

NOVEMBER 21

EZEKIEL 42:1–43:27

Then the man led me [Ezekiel] out of the Temple courtyard by way of the north gateway. We entered the outer courtyard and came to a group of rooms against the north wall of the inner courtyard. 2This structure, whose entrance opened toward the north, was 175 feet long and 87½ feet wide.* 3One block of rooms overlooked the 35-foot* width of the inner courtyard. Another block of rooms looked out onto the pavement of the outer courtyard. The two blocks were built three levels high and stood across from each other. [4]Between the two blocks of rooms ran a walkway 17½ feet* wide. It extended the entire 175 feet* of the complex, and all the doors faced north. [5]Each of the two upper levels of rooms was narrower than the one beneath it because the upper levels had to allow space for walkways in front of them. [6]Since there were three levels and they did not have supporting columns as in the courtyards, each of the upper levels was set back from the level beneath it. [7]There was an outer wall that separated the rooms from the outer courtyard; it was 87½ feet* long. [8]This wall added length to the outer block of rooms, which extended for only 87½ feet, while the inner block— the rooms toward the Temple— extended for 175 feet. [9]There was an eastern entrance from the outer courtyard to these rooms.

[10]On the south* side of the Temple there were two blocks of rooms just south of the inner courtyard between the Temple and the outer courtyard. These rooms were arranged just like the rooms on the north. [11]There was a walkway between the two blocks of rooms just like the complex on the north side of the Temple. This complex of rooms was the same length and width as the other one, and it had the same entrances and doors. The dimensions of each were identical. [12]So there was an entrance in the wall facing the doors of the inner block of rooms, and another on the east at the end of the interior walkway.

[13]Then the man told me, "These rooms that overlook the Temple from the north and south are holy. Here the priests who offer sacrifices to the Lord will eat the most holy offerings. And because these rooms are holy, they will be used to store the sacred offerings—the grain offerings, sin offerings, and guilt offerings. [14]When the priests leave the sanctuary, they must not go directly to the outer courtyard. They must first take off the clothes they wore while ministering, because these clothes are holy. They must put on other clothes before entering the parts of the building complex open to the public."

[15]When the man had finished measuring the inside of the Temple area, he led me out through the east gateway to measure the entire perimeter. [16]He measured the east side with his measuring rod, and it was 875 feet long.* [17]Then he measured the north side, and it was also 875 feet. [18]The south side was also 875 feet, [19]and the west side was also 875 feet. [20]So the area was 875 feet on each side with a wall all around it to separate what was holy from what was common.

43:1AFTER this, the man brought me back around to the east gateway. [2]Suddenly, the glory of the God of Israel appeared from the east. The sound of his coming was like the roar of rushing waters, and the whole landscape shone with his glory. [3]This vision was just like the others I had seen, first by the Kebar River and then when he came to destroy Jerusalem. I fell face down on the ground. [4]And the glory of the Lord came into the Temple through the east gateway.

[5]Then the Spirit took me up and brought me into the inner courtyard, and the glory of the Lord filled the Temple. [6]And I heard someone speaking to me from within the Temple, while the man who had been measuring stood beside me. [7]The Lord said to me, "Son of man, this is the place of my throne and the place where I will rest my feet. I will live here forever among the people of Israel. They and their kings will not defile my holy name any longer by their adulterous worship of other gods or by honoring the relics of their kings who have died. [8]They put their idol altars right next to mine with only a wall between them and me. They defiled my holy name by such detestable sin, so I consumed them in my anger. [9]Now let them stop worshiping other gods and honoring the relics of their kings, and I will live among them forever.

[10]"Son of man, describe to the people of Israel the Temple I have shown you, so they will be ashamed of all their sins. Let them study its plan, [11] and they will be ashamed* of what they have done. Describe to them all the specifications of the Temple—including its entrances and exits—and everything else about it. Tell them about its decrees and laws. Write down all these specifications and decrees as they watch so they will be sure to remember and follow them. [12] And this is the basic law of the Temple: absolute holiness! The entire top of the mountain where the Temple is built is holy. Yes, this is the basic law of the Temple.

[13]"These are the measurements of the altar*: There is a gutter all around the altar 21 inches deep and 21 inches wide,* with a curb 9 inches* wide around its edge. And this is the height* of the altar: [14]From the gutter the altar rises 3½ feet* to a lower ledge that surrounds the altar and is 21 inches* wide. From the lower ledge the altar rises 7 feet* to the upper ledge that is also 21 inches wide. [15]The top of the altar, the hearth, rises another 7 feet higher, with a horn rising up from each of the four corners. [16]The top of the altar is square, measuring 21 feet by 21 feet.* [17]The upper ledge also forms a square, measuring 24½ feet by 24½ feet,* with a 21-inch gutter and a 10½-inch curb* all around the edge. There are steps going up the east side of the altar."

[18]Then he said to me, "Son of man, this is what the Sovereign LORD says: These will be the regulations for the burning of offerings and the sprinkling of blood when the altar is built. [19]At that time, the Levitical priests of the family of Zadok, who minister before me, are to be given a young bull for a sin offering, says the Sovereign LORD. [20]You will take some of its blood and smear it on the four horns of the altar, the four corners of the upper ledge, and the curb that runs around that ledge. This will cleanse and make atonement for the altar. [21]Then take the young bull for the

sin offering and burn it at the appointed place outside the Temple area.

[22]"On the second day, sacrifice as a sin offering a young male goat that has no physical defects. Then cleanse and make atonement for the altar again, just as you did with the young bull. [23]When you have finished the cleansing ceremony, offer another young bull that has no defects and a perfect ram from the flock. [24]You are to present them to the LORD, and the priests are to sprinkle salt on them and offer them as a burnt offering to the LORD.

[25]"Every day for seven days a male goat, a young bull, and a ram from the flock will be sacrificed as a sin offering. None of these animals may have physical defects of any kind. [26]Do this each day for seven days to cleanse and make atonement for the altar, thus setting it apart for holy use. [27]On the eighth day, and on each day afterward, the priests will sacrifice on the altar the burnt offerings and peace offerings of the people. Then I will accept you. I, the Sovereign LORD, have spoken!"

42:2 Hebrew *100 cubits* [53 meters] *long and 50 cubits* [26.5 meters] *wide.*   **42:3** Hebrew *20 cubits* [10.6 meters].   **42:4a** Hebrew *10 cubits* [5.3 meters].   **42:4b** Hebrew *100 cubits* [53 meters]; also in 42:8.   **42:7** Hebrew *50 cubits* [26.5 meters]; also in 42:8.   **42:10** As in Greek version; Hebrew reads *east.*   **42:16** As in 45:2 and in Greek version at 42:17, which reads *500 cubits* [265 meters]; Hebrew reads *500 rods* [5,250 feet or 1,590 meters]; similarly in 42:17, 18, 19, 20.   **43:11** As in Greek version; Hebrew reads *if they are ashamed.*   **43:13a** Hebrew *measurements of the altar in long cubits, each being a cubit* [18 inches or 45 centimeters] *and a handbreadth* [3 inches or 8 centimeters] *in length.*   **43:13b** Hebrew *a cubit* [53 centimeters] *deep and a cubit wide.*   **43:13c** Hebrew *1 span* [23 centimeters].   **43:13d** As in Greek version; Hebrew reads *base.*   **43:14a** Hebrew *2 cubits* [1.1 meters].   **43:14b** Hebrew *1 cubit* [53 centimeters]; also in 43:14d.   **43:14c** Hebrew *4 cubits* [2.1 meters]; also in 43:15.   **43:16** Hebrew *12 cubits* [6.4 meters] *long and 12 cubits wide.*   **43:17a** Hebrew *14 cubits* [7.4 meters] *long and 14 cubits wide.*   **43:17b** Hebrew *a gutter of 1 cubit* [53 centimeters] *and a curb of ½ a cubit* [27 centimeters].

JAMES 5:1-20

Look here, you rich people: Weep and groan with anguish because of all the terrible troubles ahead of you. [2]Your wealth is rotting away, and your fine clothes are moth-eaten rags. [3]Your gold and silver have become worthless. The very wealth you were counting on will eat away your flesh like fire. This treasure you have accumulated will stand as evidence against you on the day of judgment. [4]For listen! Hear the cries of the field workers whom you have cheated of their pay. The wages you held back cry out against you. The cries of those who harvest your fields have reached the ears of the Lord of Heaven's Armies.

[5]You have spent your years on earth in luxury, satisfying your every desire. You have fattened yourselves for the day of slaughter. [6]You have condemned and killed innocent people,* who do not resist you.*

[7]Dear brothers and sisters,* be patient as you wait for the Lord's return. Consider the farmers who patiently wait for the rains in the fall and in the spring. They eagerly look for the valuable harvest to ripen. [8]You, too, must be patient. Take courage, for the coming of the Lord is near.

[9]Don't grumble about each other, brothers and sisters, or you will be judged. For look—the Judge is standing at the door!

[10]For examples of patience in suffering, dear brothers and sisters, look at the prophets who spoke in the name of the Lord. [11]We give great honor to those who endure under suffering. For instance, you know about Job, a man of great endurance. You can see how the Lord was kind to him at the end, for the Lord is full of tenderness and mercy.

[12]But most of all, my brothers and sisters, never take an oath, by heaven or earth or anything else. Just say a simple yes or no, so that you will not sin and be condemned.

[13]Are any of you suffering hardships? You should pray. Are any of you happy? You should sing praises. [14]Are any of you sick? You should call for the elders of the church to come and pray over you, anointing you with oil in the name of the Lord. [15]Such a prayer offered in faith will heal the sick, and the Lord will make you well. And if you have committed any sins, you will be forgiven.

[16]Confess your sins to each other and pray for each other so that you may be healed. The earnest prayer of a righteous person has great power and produces wonderful results. [17]Elijah was as human as we are, and yet when he prayed earnestly that no rain would fall, none fell for three and a half years! [18]Then, when he prayed again, the sky sent down rain and the earth began to yield its crops.

[19]My dear brothers and sisters, if someone among you wanders away from the truth and is brought back, [20]you can be sure that whoever brings the sinner back will save that person from death and bring about the forgiveness of many sins.

5:6a Or *killed the Righteous One.*   **5:6b** Or *Don't they resist you?* or *Doesn't God oppose you?* or *Aren't they now accusing you before God?*   **5:7** Greek *brothers;* also in 5:9, 10, 12, 19.

PSALM 119:1-16

*Aleph**

[1] **J**oyful are people of integrity,
    who follow the instructions
        of the Lord.
[2] Joyful are those who obey
        his laws
    and search for him with all
        their hearts.
[3] They do not compromise
        with evil,
    and they walk only in his paths.
[4] You have charged us
    to keep your commandments
        carefully.
[5] Oh, that my actions would
        consistently
    reflect your decrees!
[6] Then I will not be ashamed
    when I compare my life with
        your commands.
[7] As I learn your righteous
        regulations,
    I will thank you by living as
        I should!
[8] I will obey your decrees.
    Please don't give up on me!

Beth

[9] How can a young person stay pure?
    By obeying your word.

¹⁰ **I have tried hard to find you—**
   don't let me wander from
   your commands.
¹¹ **I have hidden your word**
   in my heart,
   that I might not sin against you.
¹² I praise you, O LORD;
   teach me your decrees.
¹³ I have recited aloud
   all the regulations you have
   given us.
¹⁴ I have rejoiced in your laws
   as much as in riches.
¹⁵ I will study your commandments
   and reflect on your ways.
¹⁶ I will delight in your decrees
   and not forget your word.

119 This psalm is a Hebrew acrostic poem; there are twenty-two stanzas, one for each successive letter of the Hebrew alphabet. Each of the eight verses within each stanza begins with the Hebrew letter named in its heading.

PROVERBS 28:6-7
Better to be poor and honest than to be dishonest and rich. ☐ Young people who obey the law are wise; those with wild friends bring shame to their parents.*

28:7 Hebrew *their father.*

NOVEMBER
22

EZEKIEL 44:1–45:12
Then the man brought me [Ezekiel] back to the east gateway in the outer wall of the Temple area, but it was closed. ²And the LORD said to me, "This gate must remain closed; it will never again be opened. No one will ever open it and pass through, for the LORD, the God of Israel, has entered here. Therefore, it must always remain shut. ³Only the prince himself may sit inside this gateway to feast in the LORD's presence. But he may come and go only through the entry room of the gateway."

⁴Then the man brought me through the north gateway to the front of the Temple. I looked and saw that the glory of the LORD filled the Temple of the LORD, and I fell face down on the ground.

⁵And the LORD said to me, "Son of man, take careful notice. Use your eyes and ears, and listen to everything I tell you about the regulations concerning the LORD's Temple. Take careful note of the procedures for using the Temple's entrances and exits. ⁶And give these rebels, the people of Israel, this message from the Sovereign LORD: O people of Israel, enough of your detestable sins! ⁷You have brought uncircumcised foreigners into my sanctuary—people who have no heart for God. In this way, you defiled my Temple even as you offered me my food, the fat and blood of sacrifices. In addition to all your other detestable sins, you have broken my covenant. ⁸Instead of safeguarding my sacred rituals, you have hired foreigners to take charge of my sanctuary.

⁹"So this is what the Sovereign LORD says: No foreigners, including those who live among the people of Israel, will enter my sanctuary if they have not been circumcised and have not surrendered themselves to the LORD. ¹⁰And the men of the tribe of Levi who abandoned me when Israel strayed away from me to worship idols* must bear the consequences of their unfaithfulness. ¹¹They may still be Temple guards and gatekeepers, and they may slaughter the animals brought for burnt offerings and be present to help the people. ¹²But they encouraged my people to worship idols, causing Israel to fall into deep sin. So I have taken a solemn oath that they must bear the consequences for their sins, says the Sovereign LORD. ¹³They may not approach me to minister as priests. They may not touch any of my holy things or the holy offerings, for they must bear the shame of all the detestable sins they have committed. ¹⁴They are to serve as the Temple caretakers, taking charge of the maintenance work and performing general duties.

¹⁵"However, the Levitical priests of

the family of Zadok continued to minister faithfully in the Temple when Israel abandoned me for idols. These men will serve as my ministers. They will stand in my presence and offer the fat and blood of the sacrifices, says the Sovereign LORD. 16They alone will enter my sanctuary and approach my table to serve me. They will fulfill all my requirements.

17"When they enter the gateway to the inner courtyard, they must wear only linen clothing. They must wear no wool while on duty in the inner courtyard or in the Temple itself. 18They must wear linen turbans and linen undergarments. They must not wear anything that would cause them to perspire. 19When they return to the outer courtyard where the people are, they must take off the clothes they wear while ministering to me. They must leave them in the sacred rooms and put on other clothes so they do not endanger anyone by transmitting holiness to them through this clothing.

20"They must neither shave their heads nor let their hair grow too long. Instead, they must trim it regularly. 21The priests must not drink wine before entering the inner courtyard. 22They may choose their wives only from among the virgins of Israel or the widows of the priests. They may not marry other widows or divorced women. 23They will teach my people the difference between what is holy and what is common, what is ceremonially clean and unclean.

24"They will serve as judges to resolve any disagreements among my people. Their decisions must be based on my regulations. And the priests themselves must obey my instructions and decrees at all the sacred festivals, and see to it that the Sabbaths are set apart as holy days.

25"A priest must not defile himself by being in the presence of a dead person unless it is his father, mother, child, brother, or unmarried sister. In such cases it is permitted. 26 Even then, he can return to his Temple duties only after being ceremonially cleansed and then waiting for seven days. 27The first day he returns to work and enters the inner courtyard and the sanctuary, he must offer a sin offering for himself, says the Sovereign LORD.

28"The priests will not have any property or possession of land, for I alone am their special possession. 29Their food will come from the gifts and sacrifices brought to the Temple by the people—the grain offerings, the sin offerings, and the guilt offerings. Whatever anyone sets apart* for the LORD will belong to the priests. 30The first of the ripe fruits and all the gifts brought to the LORD will go to the priests. The first samples of each grain harvest and the first of your flour must also be given to the priests so the LORD will bless your homes. 31The priests may not eat meat from any bird or animal that dies a natural death or that dies after being attacked by another animal.

45:1"WHEN you divide the land among the tribes of Israel, you must set aside a section for the LORD as his holy portion. This piece of land will be 8⅓ miles long and 6⅔ miles wide.* The entire area will be holy. 2A section of this land, measuring 875 feet by 875 feet,* will be set aside for the Temple. An additional strip of land 87½ feet* wide is to be left empty all around it. 3Within the larger sacred area, measure out a portion of land 8⅓ miles long and 3⅓ miles wide.* Within it the sanctuary of the Most Holy Place will be located. 4This area will be holy, set aside for the priests who minister to the LORD in the sanctuary. They will use it for their homes, and my Temple will be located within it. 5The strip of sacred land next to it, also 8⅓ miles long and 3⅓ miles wide, will be a living area for the Levites who work at the Temple. It will be their possession and a place for their towns.*

6"Adjacent to the larger sacred area will be a section of land 8⅓ miles long and 1⅔ miles wide.* This will be set aside for a city where anyone in Israel can live.

7"Two special sections of land will be

set apart for the prince. One section will share a border with the east side of the sacred lands and city, and the second section will share a border on the west side. Then the far eastern and western borders of the prince's lands will line up with the eastern and western boundaries of the tribal areas. ⁸These sections of land will be the prince's allotment. Then my princes will no longer oppress and rob my people; they will assign the rest of the land to the people, giving an allotment to each tribe.

⁹"For this is what the Sovereign LORD says: Enough, you princes of Israel! Stop your violence and oppression and do what is just and right. Quit robbing and cheating my people out of their land. Stop expelling them from their homes, says the Sovereign LORD. ¹⁰Use only honest weights and scales and honest measures, both dry and liquid.* ¹¹The homer* will be your standard unit for measuring volume. The ephah and the bath* will each measure one-tenth of a homer. ¹²The standard unit for weight will be the silver shekel.* One shekel will consist of twenty gerahs, and sixty shekels will be equal to one mina.*"

44:10 The Hebrew term (literally *round things*) probably alludes to dung; also in 44:12.   44:29 The Hebrew term used here refers to the complete consecration of things or people to the LORD, either by destroying them or by giving them as an offering.   45:1 Reflecting the Greek version, which reads *25,000 cubits* [13.3 kilometers] *long and 20,000 cubits* [10.6 kilometers] *wide;* Hebrew reads *25,000 cubits long and 10,000 cubits* [3½ miles or 5.3 kilometers] *wide.* Compare 45:3, 5; 48:9. 45:2a Hebrew *500 cubits* [265 meters] *by 500 cubits, a square.*   45:2b Hebrew *50 cubits* [26.5 meters]. 45:3 Hebrew *25,000 cubits* [13.3 kilometers] *long and 10,000 cubits* [5.3 kilometers] *wide;* also in 45:5. 45:5 As in Greek version; Hebrew reads *They will have as their possession 20 rooms.*   45:6 Hebrew *25,000 cubits* [13.3 kilometers] *long and 5,000 cubits* [2.65 kilometers] *wide.*   45:10 Hebrew *use honest scales, an honest ephah, and an honest bath.*   45:11a The *homer* measures about 40 gallons or 182 liters.   45:11b The *ephah* is a dry measure; the *bath* is a liquid measure.   45:12a The *shekel* weighs about 0.4 ounces or 11 grams.   45:12b Elsewhere the *mina* is equated to 50 shekels.

1 PETER 1:1-12

This letter is from Peter, an apostle of Jesus Christ.

I am writing to God's chosen people who are living as foreigners in the provinces of Pontus, Galatia, Cappadocia, Asia, and Bithynia.* ²God the Father knew you and chose you long ago, and his Spirit has made you holy. As a result, you have obeyed him and have been cleansed by the blood of Jesus Christ.

May God give you more and more grace and peace.

³All praise to God, the Father of our Lord Jesus Christ. It is by his great mercy that we have been born again, because God raised Jesus Christ from the dead. Now we live with great expectation, ⁴and we have a priceless inheritance—an inheritance that is kept in heaven for you, pure and undefiled, beyond the reach of change and decay. ⁵And through your faith, God is protecting you by his power until you receive this salvation, which is ready to be revealed on the last day for all to see.

⁶So be truly glad.* There is wonderful joy ahead, even though you have to endure many trials for a little while. ⁷These trials will show that your faith is genuine. It is being tested as fire tests and purifies gold—though your faith is far more precious than mere gold. So when your faith remains strong through many trials, it will bring you much praise and glory and honor on the day when Jesus Christ is revealed to the whole world.

⁸You love him even though you have never seen him. Though you do not see him now, you trust him; and you rejoice with a glorious, inexpressible joy. ⁹The reward for trusting him will be the salvation of your souls.

¹⁰This salvation was something even the prophets wanted to know more about when they prophesied about this gracious salvation prepared for you. ¹¹They wondered what time or situation the Spirit of Christ within them was talking about when he told them in advance about Christ's suffering and his great glory afterward.

¹²They were told that their messages were not for themselves, but for you. And now this Good News has been announced to you by those who preached in the power of the Holy Spirit sent

from heaven. It is all so wonderful that even the angels are eagerly watching these things happen.

1:1 *Pontus, Galatia, Cappadocia, Asia,* and *Bithynia* were Roman provinces in what is now Turkey.   1:6 Or *So you are truly glad.*

PSALM 119:17-32

Gimel

¹⁷ **B**e good to your servant,
that I may live and obey
your word.
¹⁸ Open my eyes to see
the wonderful truths in your
instructions.
¹⁹ I am only a foreigner in the land.
Don't hide your commands
from me!
²⁰ I am always overwhelmed
with a desire for your regulations.
²¹ You rebuke the arrogant;
those who wander from your
commands are cursed.
²² Don't let them scorn and insult me,
for I have obeyed your laws.
²³ Even princes sit and speak
against me,
but I will meditate on your decrees.
²⁴ Your laws please me;
they give me wise advice.

Daleth

²⁵ I lie in the dust;
revive me by your word.
²⁶ I told you my plans, and you
answered.
Now teach me your decrees.
²⁷ Help me understand the meaning
of your commandments,
and I will meditate on your
wonderful deeds.
²⁸ I weep with sorrow;
encourage me by your word.
²⁹ Keep me from lying to myself;
give me the privilege of knowing
your instructions.
³⁰ **I have chosen to be faithful;
I have determined to live by
your regulations.**
³¹ **I cling to your laws.
Lord, don't let me be put
to shame!**

³² **I will pursue your commands,
for you expand my
understanding.**

PROVERBS 28:8-10

Income from charging high interest rates will end up in the pocket of someone who is kind to the poor. □ God detests the prayers of a person who ignores the law. □ Those who lead good people along an evil path will fall into their own trap, but the honest will inherit good things.

NOVEMBER
23

EZEKIEL 45:13–46:24

"**Y**ou must give this tax to the prince: one bushel of wheat or barley for every 60* you harvest, ¹⁴one percent of your olive oil,* ¹⁵and one sheep or goat for every 200 in your flocks in Israel. These will be the grain offerings, burnt offerings, and peace offerings that will make atonement for the people who bring them, says the Sovereign Lord. ¹⁶All the people of Israel must join in bringing these offerings to the prince. ¹⁷The prince will be required to provide offerings that are given at the religious festivals, the new moon celebrations, the Sabbath days, and all other similar occasions. He will provide the sin offerings, burnt offerings, grain offerings, liquid offerings, and peace offerings to purify the people of Israel, making them right with the Lord.*

¹⁸"This is what the Sovereign Lord says: In early spring, on the first day of each new year,* sacrifice a young bull with no defects to purify the Temple. ¹⁹The priest will take blood from this sin offering and put it on the doorposts of the Temple, the four corners of the upper ledge of the altar, and the gateposts at the entrance to the inner court-

yard. [20]Do this also on the seventh day of the new year for anyone who has sinned through error or ignorance. In this way, you will purify* the Temple.

[21]"On the fourteenth day of the first month,* you must celebrate the Passover. This festival will last for seven days. The bread you eat during that time must be made without yeast. [22]On the day of Passover the prince will provide a young bull as a sin offering for himself and the people of Israel. [23]On each of the seven days of the feast he will prepare a burnt offering to the LORD, consisting of seven young bulls and seven rams without defects. A male goat will also be given each day for a sin offering. [24]The prince will provide a basket of flour as a grain offering and a gallon of olive oil* with each young bull and ram.

[25]"During the seven days of the Festival of Shelters, which occurs every year in early autumn,* the prince will provide these same sacrifices for the sin offering, the burnt offering, and the grain offering, along with the required olive oil.

[46:1]"THIS is what the Sovereign LORD says: The east gateway of the inner courtyard will be closed during the six workdays each week, but it will be open on Sabbath days and the days of new moon celebrations. [2]The prince will enter the entry room of the gateway from the outside. Then he will stand by the gatepost while the priest offers his burnt offering and peace offering. He will bow down in worship inside the gateway passage and then go back out the way he came. The gateway will not be closed until evening. [3]The common people will bow down and worship the LORD in front of this gateway on Sabbath days and the days of new moon celebrations.

[4]"Each Sabbath day the prince will present to the LORD a burnt offering of six lambs and one ram, all with no defects. [5]He will present a grain offering of a basket of choice flour to go with the ram and whatever amount of flour he chooses to go with each lamb, and he is to offer one gallon of olive oil* for each

basket of flour. [6]At the new moon celebrations, he will bring one young bull, six lambs, and one ram, all with no defects. [7]With the young bull he must bring a basket of choice flour for a grain offering. With the ram he must bring another basket of flour. And with each lamb he is to bring whatever amount of flour he chooses to give. With each basket of flour he must offer one gallon of olive oil.

[8]"The prince must enter the gateway through the entry room, and he must leave the same way. [9]But when the people come in through the north gateway to worship the LORD during the religious festivals, they must leave by the south gateway. And those who entered through the south gateway must leave by the north gateway. They must never leave by the same gateway they came in, but must always use the opposite gateway. [10]The prince will enter and leave with the people on these occasions.

[11]"So at the special feasts and sacred festivals, the grain offering will be a basket of choice flour with each young bull, another basket of flour with each ram, and as much flour as the prince chooses to give with each lamb. Give one gallon of olive oil with each basket of flour. [12]When the prince offers a voluntary burnt offering or peace offering to the LORD, the east gateway to the inner courtyard will be opened for him, and he will offer his sacrifices as he does on Sabbath days. Then he will leave, and the gateway will be shut behind him.

[13]"Each morning you must sacrifice a one-year-old lamb with no defects as a burnt offering to the LORD. [14]With the lamb, a grain offering must also be given to the LORD—about three quarts of flour with a third of a gallon of olive oil* to moisten the choice flour. This will be a permanent law for you. [15]The lamb, the grain offering, and the olive oil must be given as a daily sacrifice every morning without fail.

[16]"This is what the Sovereign LORD says: If the prince gives a gift of land to one of his sons as his inheritance, it will

belong to him and his descendants forever. ¹⁷But if the prince gives a gift of land from his inheritance to one of his servants, the servant may keep it only until the Year of Jubilee, which comes every fiftieth year.* At that time the land will return to the prince. But when the prince gives gifts to his sons, those gifts will be permanent. ¹⁸And the prince may never take anyone's property by force. If he gives property to his sons, it must be from his own land, for I do not want any of my people unjustly evicted from their property."

¹⁹In my vision, the man brought me through the entrance beside the gateway and led me to the sacred rooms assigned to the priests, which faced toward the north. He showed me a place at the extreme west end of these rooms. ²⁰He explained, "This is where the priests will cook the meat from the guilt offerings and sin offerings and bake the flour from the grain offerings into bread. They will do it here to avoid carrying the sacrifices through the outer courtyard and endangering the people by transmitting holiness to them."

²¹Then he brought me back to the outer courtyard and led me to each of its four corners. In each corner I saw an enclosure. ²²Each of these enclosures was 70 feet long and 52½ feet wide,* surrounded by walls. ²³Along the inside of these walls was a ledge of stone with fireplaces under the ledge all the way around. ²⁴The man said to me, "These are the kitchens to be used by the Temple assistants to boil the sacrifices offered by the people."

45:13 Hebrew ⅙ of an ephah from each homer of wheat and ⅙ of an ephah from each homer of barley. 45:14 Hebrew the portion of oil, measured by the bath, is ¹⁄₁₀ of a bath from each cor, which consists of 10 baths or 1 homer, for 10 baths are equivalent to a homer. 45:17 Or to make atonement for the people of Israel. 45:18 Hebrew On the first day of the first month, of the Hebrew calendar. This day in the ancient Hebrew lunar calendar occurred in March or April. 45:20 Or will make atonement for. 45:21 This day in the ancient Hebrew lunar calendar occurred in late March, April, or early May. 45:24 Hebrew an ephah [20 quarts or 22 liters] of flour ... and a hin [3.8 liters] of olive oil. 45:25 Hebrew the festival which begins on the fifteenth day of the seventh month (see Lev 23:33). This day in the ancient Hebrew lunar calendar occurred in late September, October, or early November.

46:5 Hebrew an ephah [20 quarts or 22 liters] of choice flour ... a hin [3.8 liters] of olive oil; similarly in 46:7, 11. 46:14 Hebrew ⅙ of an ephah [3.7 liters] of flour with ⅓ of a hin [1.3 liters] of olive oil. 46:17 Hebrew until the Year of Release; see Lev 25:8-17. 46:22 Hebrew 40 cubits [21.2 meters] long and 30 cubits [15.9 meters] wide.

1 PETER 1:13–2:10

So think clearly and exercise self-control. Look forward to the gracious salvation that will come to you when Jesus Christ is revealed to the world. ¹⁴So you must live as God's obedient children. Don't slip back into your old ways of living to satisfy your own desires. You didn't know any better then. ¹⁵But now you must be holy in everything you do, just as God who chose you is holy. ¹⁶For the Scriptures say, "You must be holy because I am holy."*

¹⁷And remember that the heavenly Father to whom you pray has no favorites. He will judge or reward you according to what you do. So you must live in reverent fear of him during your time as "foreigners in the land." ¹⁸For you know that God paid a ransom to save you from the empty life you inherited from your ancestors. And the ransom he paid was not mere gold or silver. ¹⁹It was the precious blood of Christ, the sinless, spotless Lamb of God. ²⁰God chose him as your ransom long before the world began, but he has now revealed him to you in these last days.

²¹Through Christ you have come to trust in God. And you have placed your faith and hope in God because he raised Christ from the dead and gave him great glory.

²²You were cleansed from your sins when you obeyed the truth, so now you must show sincere love to each other as brothers and sisters.* Love each other deeply with all your heart.*

²³For you have been born again, but not to a life that will quickly end. Your new life will last forever because it comes from the eternal, living word of God. ²⁴As the Scriptures say,

"People are like grass;
    their beauty is like a flower in
    the field.

The grass withers and the flower fades.
²⁵   But the word of the Lord remains
        forever."*

And that word is the Good News that was preached to you.

^{2:1}So get rid of all evil behavior. Be done with all deceit, hypocrisy, jealousy, and all unkind speech. ²Like newborn babies, you must crave pure spiritual milk so that you will grow into a full experience of salvation. Cry out for this nourishment, ³now that you have had a taste of the Lord's kindness.

⁴You are coming to Christ, who is the living cornerstone of God's temple. He was rejected by people, but he was chosen by God for great honor.

⁵And you are living stones that God is building into his spiritual temple. What's more, you are his holy priests.* Through the mediation of Jesus Christ, you offer spiritual sacrifices that please God. ⁶As the Scriptures say,

"I am placing a cornerstone
    in Jerusalem,*
    chosen for great honor,
and anyone who trusts in him
    will never be disgraced."*

⁷Yes, you who trust him recognize the honor God has given him. But for those who reject him,

"The stone that the builders rejected
    has now become the
        cornerstone."*

⁸And,

"He is the stone that makes people
    stumble,
    the rock that makes them fall."*

They stumble because they do not obey God's word, and so they meet the fate that was planned for them.

⁹**But you are not like that, for you are a chosen people. You are royal priests,* a holy nation, God's very own possession. As a result, you can show others the goodness of God, for**

he called you out of the darkness into his wonderful light.

¹⁰ "Once you had no identity as
        a people;
    now you are God's people.
Once you received no mercy;
    now you have received
        God's mercy."*

1:16 Lev 11:44-45; 19:2; 20:7.   1:22a Greek *must have brotherly love.*   1:22b Some manuscripts read *with a pure heart.*   1:24-25 Isa 40:6-8.   2:5 Greek *holy priesthood.* 2:6a Greek *in Zion.*   2:6b Isa 28:16 (Greek version). 2:7 Ps 118:22.   2:8 Isa 8:14.   2:9 Greek *a royal priesthood.*   2:10 Hos 1:6, 9; 2:23.

PSALM 119:33-48

He

³³ **T**each me your decrees, O LORD;
    I will keep them to the end.
³⁴ Give me understanding and I will
        obey your instructions;
    I will put them into practice with
        all my heart.
³⁵ Make me walk along the path of
        your commands,
    for that is where my happiness is
        found.
³⁶ Give me an eagerness for your laws
    rather than a love for money!
³⁷ Turn my eyes from worthless things,
    and give me life through
        your word.*
³⁸ Reassure me of your promise,
    made to those who fear you.
³⁹ Help me abandon my shameful ways;
    for your regulations are good.
⁴⁰ I long to obey your commandments!
    Renew my life with your goodness.

Waw
⁴¹ LORD, give me your unfailing love,
    the salvation that you promised me.
⁴² Then I can answer those who
        taunt me,
    for I trust in your word.
⁴³ Do not snatch your word of truth
        from me,
    for your regulations are my
        only hope.
⁴⁴ I will keep on obeying your
        instructions
    forever and ever.
⁴⁵ I will walk in freedom,

for I have devoted myself to your
commandments.
⁴⁶ I will speak to kings about your laws,
and I will not be ashamed.
⁴⁷ How I delight in your commands!
How I love them!
⁴⁸ I honor and love your commands.
I meditate on your decrees.

119:37 Some manuscripts read *in your ways.*

PROVERBS 28:11
Rich people may think they are wise,
but a poor person with discernment can
see right through them.

NOVEMBER
24

EZEKIEL 47:1–48:35
In my vision, the man brought me
[Ezekiel] back to the entrance of the
Temple. There I saw a stream flowing
east from beneath the door of the Temple and passing to the right of the altar
on its south side. ²The man brought me
outside the wall through the north gateway and led me around to the eastern
entrance. There I could see the water
flowing out through the south side of
the east gateway.

³Measuring as he went, he took me
along the stream for 1,750 feet* and
then led me across. The water was up to
my ankles. ⁴He measured off another
1,750 feet and led me across again.
This time the water was up to my knees.
After another 1,750 feet, it was up to
my waist. ⁵Then he measured another
1,750 feet, and the river was too deep to
walk across. It was deep enough to
swim in, but too deep to walk through.
⁶He asked me, "Have you been watching, son of man?" Then he led me back
along the riverbank. ⁷When I returned, I
was surprised by the sight of many trees
growing on both sides of the river. ⁸Then

he said to me, "This river flows east
through the desert into the valley of the
Dead Sea.* The waters of this stream will
make the salty waters of the Dead Sea
fresh and pure. ⁹There will be swarms of
living things wherever the water of this
river flows. Fish will abound in the Dead
Sea, for its waters will become fresh. Life
will flourish wherever this water flows.
¹⁰Fishermen will stand along the shores
of the Dead Sea. All the way from En-
gedi to En-eglaim, the shores will be covered with nets drying in the sun. Fish of
every kind will fill the Dead Sea, just as
they fill the Mediterranean.* ¹¹But the
marshes and swamps will not be purified; they will still be salty. ¹²Fruit trees
of all kinds will grow along both sides of
the river. The leaves of these trees will
never turn brown and fall, and there will
always be fruit on their branches. There
will be a new crop every month, for they
are watered by the river flowing from
the Temple. The fruit will be for food
and the leaves for healing."

¹³This is what the Sovereign LORD
says: "Divide the land in this way for the
twelve tribes of Israel: The descendants
of Joseph will be given two shares of
land.* ¹⁴Otherwise each tribe will receive an equal share. I took a solemn
oath and swore that I would give this
land to your ancestors, and it will now
come to you as your possession.

¹⁵"These are the boundaries of the
land: The northern border will run
from the Mediterranean toward
Hethlon, then on through Lebo-
hamath to Zedad; ¹⁶then it will run
to Berothah and Sibraim, which are
on the border between Damascus
and Hamath, and finally to Hazer-
hatticon, on the border of Hauran.
¹⁷So the northern border will run
from the Mediterranean to Hazar-
enan, on the border between
Hamath to the north and Damascus
to the south.
¹⁸"The eastern border starts
at a point between Hauran and
Damascus and runs south along the

Jordan River between Israel and Gilead, past the Dead Sea* and as far south as Tamar.* This will be the eastern border.

¹⁹"The southern border will go west from Tamar to the waters of Meribah at Kadesh* and then follow the course of the Brook of Egypt to the Mediterranean. This will be the southern border.

²⁰"On the west side, the Mediterranean itself will be your border from the southern border to the point where the northern border begins, opposite Lebo-hamath.

²¹"Divide the land within these boundaries among the tribes of Israel. ²²Distribute the land as an allotment for yourselves and for the foreigners who have joined you and are raising their families among you. They will be like native-born Israelites to you and will receive an allotment among the tribes. ²³These foreigners are to be given land within the territory of the tribe with whom they now live. I, the Sovereign LORD, have spoken!

⁴⁸:¹"HERE is the list of the tribes of Israel and the territory each is to receive. The territory of Dan is in the extreme north. Its boundary line follows the Hethlon road to Lebo-hamath and then runs on to Hazar-enan on the border of Damascus, with Hamath to the north. Dan's territory extends all the way across the land of Israel from east to west.

²"Asher's territory lies south of Dan's and also extends from east to west. ³Naphtali's land lies south of Asher's, also extending from east to west. ⁴Then comes Manasseh south of Naphtali, and its territory also extends from east to west. ⁵South of Manasseh is Ephraim, ⁶and then Reuben, ⁷and then Judah, all of whose boundaries extend from east to west.

⁸"South of Judah is the land set aside for a special purpose. It will be 8⅓ miles* wide and will extend as far east and west as the tribal territories, with the Temple at the center.

⁹"The area set aside for the LORD's Temple will be 8⅓ miles long and 6⅔ miles wide.* ¹⁰For the priests there will be a strip of land measuring 8⅓ miles long by 3⅓ miles wide,* with the LORD's Temple at the center. ¹¹This area is set aside for the ordained priests, the descendants of Zadok who served me faithfully and did not go astray with the people of Israel and the rest of the Levites. ¹²It will be their special portion when the land is distributed, the most sacred land of all. Next to the priests' territory will lie the land where the other Levites will live.

¹³"The land allotted to the Levites will be the same size and shape as that belonging to the priests—8⅓ miles long and 3⅓ miles wide. Together these portions of land will measure 8⅓ miles long by 6⅔ miles wide.* ¹⁴None of this special land may ever be sold or traded or used by others, for it belongs to the LORD; it is set apart as holy.

¹⁵"An additional strip of land 8⅓ miles long by 1⅔ miles wide,* south of the sacred Temple area, will be allotted for public use—homes, pasturelands, and common lands, with a city at the center. ¹⁶The city will measure 1½ miles* on each side—north, south, east, and west. ¹⁷Open lands will surround the city for 150 yards* in every direction. ¹⁸Outside the city there will be a farming area that stretches 3⅓ miles to the east and 3⅓ miles to the west* along the border of the sacred area. This farmland will produce food for the people working in the city. ¹⁹Those who come from the various tribes to work in the city may farm it. ²⁰This entire area—including the sacred lands and the city—is a square that measures 8⅓ miles* on each side.

²¹"The areas that remain, to the east and to the west of the sacred lands and the city, will belong to the prince. Each of these areas will be 8⅓ miles wide, extending in opposite directions to the eastern and western borders of Israel, with the sacred lands and the sanctuary of the Temple in the center. ²²So the prince's land will include everything

between the territories allotted to Judah and Benjamin, except for the areas set aside for the sacred lands and the city.

²³"These are the territories allotted to the rest of the tribes. Benjamin's territory lies just south of the prince's lands, and it extends across the entire land of Israel from east to west. ²⁴South of Benjamin's territory lies that of Simeon, also extending across the land from east to west. ²⁵Next is the territory of Issachar with the same eastern and western boundaries.

²⁶"Then comes the territory of Zebulun, which also extends across the land from east to west. ²⁷The territory of Gad is just south of Zebulun with the same borders to the east and west. ²⁸The southern border of Gad runs from Tamar to the waters of Meribah at Kadesh* and then follows the Brook of Egypt to the Mediterranean.*

²⁹"These are the allotments that will be set aside for each tribe's exclusive possession. I, the Sovereign LORD, have spoken!

³⁰"These will be the exits to the city: On the north wall, which is 1½ miles long, ³¹there will be three gates, each one named after a tribe of Israel. The first will be named for Reuben, the second for Judah, and the third for Levi. ³²On the east wall, also 1½ miles long, the gates will be named for Joseph, Benjamin, and Dan. ³³The south wall, also 1½ miles long, will have gates named for Simeon, Issachar, and Zebulun. ³⁴And on the west wall, also 1½ miles long, the gates will be named for Gad, Asher, and Naphtali.

³⁵"The distance around the entire city will be 6 miles.* And from that day the name of the city will be 'The LORD Is There.'*"

47:3 Hebrew *1,000 cubits* [530 meters]; also in 47:4, 5.
47:8 Hebrew *the sea*.   47:10 Hebrew *the great sea;* also in 47:15, 17, 19, 20.   47:13 It was important to retain twelve portions of land. Since Levi had no portion, the descendants of Joseph's sons, Ephraim and Manasseh, received land as two tribes.   47:18a Hebrew *the eastern sea*.   47:18b As in Greek version; Hebrew reads *you will measure*.
47:19 Hebrew *waters of Meribath-kadesh*.   48:8 Hebrew *25,000 cubits* [13.3 kilometers].   48:9 Reflecting one Greek manuscript and the Greek reading in 45:1: *25,000 cubits* [13.3 kilometers] *long and 20,000 cubits* [10.6 kilometers] *wide;* Hebrew reads *25,000 cubits long*

and 10,000 cubits [3⅓ miles or 5.3 kilometers] *wide*. Similarly in 48:13b. Compare 45:1-5; 48:10-13.
48:10 Hebrew *25,000 cubits* [13.3 kilometers] *long by 10,000 cubits* [5.3 kilometers] *wide;* also in 48:13a.
48:13 See note on 48:9.   48:15 Hebrew *25,000 cubits* [13.3 kilometers] *long by 5,000 cubits* [2.65 kilometers] *wide*.   48:16 Hebrew *4,500 cubits* [2.4 kilometers]; also in 48:30, 32, 33, 34.   48:17 Hebrew *250 cubits* [133 meters].   48:18 Hebrew *10,000 cubits* [5.3 kilometers] *to the east and 10,000 cubits to the west*.
48:20 Hebrew *25,000 cubits* [13.3 kilometers]; also in 48:21.   48:28a Hebrew *waters of Meribath-kadesh*.
48:28b Hebrew *the great sea*.   48:35a Hebrew *18,000 cubits* [9.6 kilometers].   48:35b Hebrew *Yahweh Shammah*.

1 PETER 2:11–3:7

Dear friends, I warn you as "temporary residents and foreigners" to keep away from worldly desires that wage war against your very souls. ¹²Be careful to live properly among your unbelieving neighbors. Then even if they accuse you of doing wrong, they will see your honorable behavior, and they will give honor to God when he judges the world.*

¹³For the Lord's sake, respect all human authority—whether the king as head of state, ¹⁴or the officials he has appointed. For the king has sent them to punish those who do wrong and to honor those who do right.

¹⁵It is God's will that your honorable lives should silence those ignorant people who make foolish accusations against you. ¹⁶For you are free, yet you are God's slaves, so don't use your freedom as an excuse to do evil. ¹⁷Respect everyone, and love your Christian brothers and sisters.* Fear God, and respect the king.

¹⁸You who are slaves must accept the authority of your masters with all respect.* Do what they tell you—not only if they are kind and reasonable, but even if they are cruel. ¹⁹For God is pleased with you when you do what you know is right and patiently endure unfair treatment. ²⁰Of course, you get no credit for being patient if you are beaten for doing wrong. But if you suffer for doing good and endure it patiently, God is pleased with you.

²¹For God called you to do good, even if it means suffering, just as Christ suffered* for you. He is your example, and you must follow in his steps.

[22] He never sinned,
nor ever deceived anyone.*
[23] He did not retaliate when he
was insulted,
nor threaten revenge when
he suffered.
He left his case in the hands of God,
who always judges fairly.
[24] He personally carried our sins
in his body on the cross
so that we can be dead to sin
and live for what is right.
By his wounds
you are healed.
[25] Once you were like sheep
who wandered away.
But now you have turned to your
Shepherd,
the Guardian of your souls.

3:1IN the same way, you wives must accept the authority of your husbands. Then, even if some refuse to obey the Good News, your godly lives will speak to them without any words. They will be won over [2]by observing your pure and reverent lives.

[3]Don't be concerned about the outward beauty of fancy hairstyles, expensive jewelry, or beautiful clothes. [4]You should clothe yourselves instead with the beauty that comes from within, the unfading beauty of a gentle and quiet spirit, which is so precious to God. [5]This is how the holy women of old made themselves beautiful. They trusted God and accepted the authority of their husbands. [6]For instance, Sarah obeyed her husband, Abraham, and called him her master. You are her daughters when you do what is right without fear of what your husbands might do.

[7]In the same way, you husbands must give honor to your wives. Treat your wife with understanding as you live together. She may be weaker than you are, but she is your equal partner in God's gift of new life. Treat her as you should so your prayers will not be hindered.

2:12 Or *on the day of visitation.*   2:17 Greek *love the brotherhood.*   2:18 Or *because you fear God.*   2:21 Some manuscripts read *died.*   2:22 Isa 53:9.

PSALM 119:49-64

Zayin

[49] **R**emember your promise to me;
it is my only hope.
[50] Your promise revives me;
it comforts me in all my troubles.
[51] The proud hold me in utter contempt,
but I do not turn away from your
instructions.
[52] I meditate on your age-old
regulations;
O Lord, they comfort me.
[53] I become furious with the wicked,
because they reject your
instructions.
[54] **Your decrees have been the theme
of my songs
wherever I have lived.**
[55] **I reflect at night on who you are,
O Lord;
therefore, I obey your
instructions.**
[56] **This is how I spend my life:
obeying your commandments.**

Heth

[57] Lord, you are mine!
I promise to obey your words!
[58] With all my heart I want your
blessings.
Be merciful as you promised.
[59] I pondered the direction of
my life,
and I turned to follow your laws.
[60] I will hurry, without delay,
to obey your commands.
[61] Evil people try to drag me into sin,
but I am firmly anchored to your
instructions.
[62] I rise at midnight to thank you
for your just regulations.
[63] I am a friend to anyone who fears
you—
anyone who obeys your
commandments.
[64] O Lord, your unfailing love fills
the earth;
teach me your decrees.

PROVERBS 28:12-13

When the godly succeed, everyone is glad. When the wicked take charge, people go into hiding. □People who conceal their sins will not prosper, but if they confess and turn from them, they will receive mercy.

NOVEMBER
25

DANIEL 1:1–2:23

During the third year of King Jehoia-kim's reign in Judah,* King Nebuchad-nezzar of Babylon came to Jerusalem and besieged it. ²The LORD gave him victory over King Jehoiakim of Judah and permitted him to take some of the sacred objects from the Temple of God. So Nebuchadnezzar took them back to the land of Babylonia* and placed them in the treasure-house of his god.

³Then the king ordered Ashpenaz, his chief of staff, to bring to the palace some of the young men of Judah's royal family and other noble families, who had been brought to Babylon as captives. ⁴"Select only strong, healthy, and good-looking young men," he said. "Make sure they are well versed in every branch of learning, are gifted with knowledge and good judgment, and are suited to serve in the royal palace. Train these young men in the language and literature of Babylon.*" ⁵The king assigned them a daily ration of food and wine from his own kitchens. They were to be trained for three years, and then they would enter the royal service.

⁶Daniel, Hananiah, Mishael, and Aza-riah were four of the young men chosen, all from the tribe of Judah. ⁷The chief of staff renamed them with these Babylonian names:

Daniel was called Belteshazzar.
Hananiah was called Shadrach.
Mishael was called Meshach.
Azariah was called Abednego.

⁸But Daniel was determined not to defile himself by eating the food and wine given to them by the king. He asked the chief of staff for permission not to eat these unacceptable foods. ⁹Now God had given the chief of staff both respect and affection for Daniel. ¹⁰But he responded, "I am afraid of my lord the king, who has ordered that you eat this food and wine. If you become pale and thin compared to the other youths your age, I am afraid the king will have me beheaded."

¹¹Daniel spoke with the attendant who had been appointed by the chief of staff to look after Daniel, Hananiah, Mishael, and Azariah. ¹²"Please test us for ten days on a diet of vegetables and water," Daniel said. ¹³"At the end of the ten days, see how we look compared to the other young men who are eating the king's food. Then make your decision in light of what you see." ¹⁴The attendant agreed to Daniel's suggestion and tested them for ten days.

¹⁵At the end of the ten days, Daniel and his three friends looked healthier and better nourished than the young men who had been eating the food assigned by the king. ¹⁶So after that, the attendant fed them only vegetables instead of the food and wine provided for the others.

¹⁷God gave these four young men an unusual aptitude for understanding every aspect of literature and wisdom. And God gave Daniel the special ability to interpret the meanings of visions and dreams.

¹⁸When the training period ordered by the king was completed, the chief of staff brought all the young men to King Nebuchadnezzar. ¹⁹The king talked with them, and no one impressed him as much as Daniel, Hananiah, Mishael, and Azariah. So they entered the royal service. ²⁰Whenever the king consulted them in any matter requiring wisdom and balanced judgment, he found them ten times more capable than any of the magicians and enchanters in his entire kingdom.

²¹Daniel remained in the royal ser-

vice until the first year of the reign of King Cyrus.*

2:1One night during the second year of his reign,* Nebuchadnezzar had such disturbing dreams that he couldn't sleep. 2He called in his magicians, enchanters, sorcerers, and astrologers,* and he demanded that they tell him what he had dreamed. As they stood before the king, 3he said, "I have had a dream that deeply troubles me, and I must know what it means."

4Then the astrologers answered the king in Aramaic,* "Long live the king! Tell us the dream, and we will tell you what it means."

5But the king said to the astrologers, "I am serious about this. If you don't tell me what my dream was and what it means, you will be torn limb from limb, and your houses will be turned into heaps of rubble! 6But if you tell me what I dreamed and what the dream means, I will give you many wonderful gifts and honors. Just tell me the dream and what it means!"

7They said again, "Please, Your Majesty. Tell us the dream, and we will tell you what it means."

8The king replied, "I know what you are doing! You're stalling for time because you know I am serious when I say, 9'If you don't tell me the dream, you are doomed.' So you have conspired to tell me lies, hoping I will change my mind. But tell me the dream, and then I'll know that you can tell me what it means."

10The astrologers replied to the king, "No one on earth can tell the king his dream! And no king, however great and powerful, has ever asked such a thing of any magician, enchanter, or astrologer! 11The king's demand is impossible. No one except the gods can tell you your dream, and they do not live here among people."

12The king was furious when he heard this, and he ordered that all the wise men of Babylon be executed. 13And because of the king's decree, men were sent to find and kill Daniel and his friends.

14When Arioch, the commander of the king's guard, came to kill them, Daniel handled the situation with wisdom and discretion. 15He asked Arioch, "Why has the king issued such a harsh decree?" So Arioch told him all that had happened. 16Daniel went at once to see the king and requested more time to tell the king what the dream meant.

17Then Daniel went home and told his friends Hananiah, Mishael, and Azariah what had happened. 18He urged them to ask the God of heaven to show them his mercy by telling them the secret, so they would not be executed along with the other wise men of Babylon. 19That night the secret was revealed to Daniel in a vision. Then Daniel praised the God of heaven. 20He said,

"Praise the name of God forever
    and ever,
  for he has all wisdom
    and power.
21 He controls the course of world
    events;
  he removes kings and sets up
    other kings.
He gives wisdom to the wise
  and knowledge to the scholars.
22 He reveals deep and mysterious
    things
  and knows what lies hidden in
    darkness,
  though he is surrounded by light.
23 I thank and praise you, God of my
    ancestors,
  for you have given me wisdom
    and strength.
You have told me what we asked
    of you
  and revealed to us what the king
    demanded."

1:1 This event occurred in 605 B.C., during the third year of Jehoiakim's reign (according to the calendar system in which the new year begins in the spring).   1:2 Hebrew the land of Shinar.   1:4 Or of the Chaldeans.   1:21 Cyrus began his reign (over Babylon) in 539 B.C.   2:1 The second year of Nebuchadnezzar's reign was 603 B.C.   2:2 Or Chaldeans; also in 2:4, 5, 10.   2:4 The original text from this point through chapter 7 is in Aramaic.

1 PETER 3:8–4:6

Finally, all of you should be of one mind. Sympathize with each other. Love each other as brothers and sisters.* Be tenderhearted, and keep a humble attitude. 9Don't repay evil for evil. Don't retaliate with insults when people insult you. Instead, pay them back with a blessing. That is what God has called you to do, and he will bless you for it. 10For the Scriptures say,

"If you want to enjoy life
    and see many happy days,
keep your tongue from speaking evil
    and your lips from telling lies.
11 Turn away from evil and do good.
    Search for peace, and work to
        maintain it.
12 The eyes of the Lord watch over
        those who do right,
    and his ears are open to their
        prayers.
But the Lord turns his face
    against those who do evil."*

13Now, who will want to harm you if you are eager to do good? 14But even if you suffer for doing what is right, God will reward you for it. So don't worry or be afraid of their threats. 15**Instead, you must worship Christ as Lord of your life. And if someone asks about your Christian hope, always be ready to explain it.** 16But do this in a gentle and respectful way.* Keep your conscience clear. Then if people speak against you, they will be ashamed when they see what a good life you live because you belong to Christ. 17Remember, it is better to suffer for doing good, if that is what God wants, than to suffer for doing wrong!

18Christ suffered* for our sins once for all time. He never sinned, but he died for sinners to bring you safely home to God. He suffered physical death, but he was raised to life in the Spirit.* 19So he went and preached to the spirits in prison—20those who disobeyed God long ago when God waited patiently while Noah was building his boat. Only eight people were saved from drowning in that terrible flood.* 21And that water is a picture of baptism, which now saves you, not by removing dirt from your body, but as a response to God from* a clean conscience. It is effective because of the resurrection of Jesus Christ.

22Now Christ has gone to heaven. He is seated in the place of honor next to God, and all the angels and authorities and powers accept his authority.

4:1So then, since Christ suffered physical pain, you must arm yourselves with the same attitude he had, and be ready to suffer, too. For if you have suffered physically for Christ, you have finished with sin.* 2You won't spend the rest of your lives chasing your own desires, but you will be anxious to do the will of God. 3You have had enough in the past of the evil things that godless people enjoy—their immorality and lust, their feasting and drunkenness and wild parties, and their terrible worship of idols.

4Of course, your former friends are surprised when you no longer plunge into the flood of wild and destructive things they do. So they slander you. 5But remember that they will have to face God, who will judge everyone, both the living and the dead. 6That is why the Good News was preached to those who are now dead*—so although they were destined to die like all people,* they now live forever with God in the Spirit.*

3:8 Greek Show brotherly love.   3:10-12 Ps 34:12-16.   3:16 Some English translations put this sentence in verse 15.   3:18a Some manuscripts read died.   3:18b Or in spirit.   3:20 Greek saved through water.   3:21 Or as an appeal to God for.   4:1 Or For the one [or One] who has suffered physically has finished with sin.   4:6a Greek preached even to the dead.   4:6b Or so although people had judged them worthy of death.   4:6c Or in spirit.

PSALM 119:65–80

Teth
65 **Y**ou have done many good things
        for me, LORD,
    just as you promised.
66 I believe in your commands;
    now teach me good judgment
        and knowledge.

⁶⁷ I used to wander off until you
  disciplined me;
    but now I closely follow
    your word.
⁶⁸ You are good and do only good;
    teach me your decrees.
⁶⁹ Arrogant people smear me with lies,
    but in truth I obey your
    commandments with all
    my heart.
⁷⁰ Their hearts are dull and stupid,
    but I delight in your instructions.
⁷¹ My suffering was good for me,
    for it taught me to pay attention
    to your decrees.
⁷² Your instructions are more valuable
    to me
    than millions in gold and silver.

Yodh

⁷³ You made me; you created me.
    Now give me the sense to follow
    your commands.
⁷⁴ May all who fear you find in me a
    cause for joy,
    for I have put my hope in
    your word.
⁷⁵ I know, O LORD, that your
    regulations are fair;
    you disciplined me because
    I needed it.
⁷⁶ Now let your unfailing love
    comfort me,
    just as you promised me, your
    servant.
⁷⁷ Surround me with your tender
    mercies so I may live,
    for your instructions are my
    delight.
⁷⁸ Bring disgrace upon the arrogant
    people who lied about me;
    meanwhile, I will concentrate on
    your commandments.
⁷⁹ Let me be united with all who
    fear you,
    with those who know your laws.
⁸⁰ May I be blameless in keeping your
    decrees;
    then I will never be ashamed.

PROVERBS 28:14

Blessed are those who fear to do wrong,* but the stubborn are headed for serious trouble.

28:14 Or *those who fear the LORD;* Hebrew reads *those who fear.*

NOVEMBER
26

DANIEL 2:24–3:30

Then Daniel went in to see Arioch, whom the king had ordered to execute the wise men of Babylon. Daniel said to him, "Don't kill the wise men. Take me to the king, and I will tell him the meaning of his dream."

²⁵Arioch quickly took Daniel to the king and said, "I have found one of the captives from Judah who will tell the king the meaning of his dream!"

²⁶The king said to Daniel (also known as Belteshazzar), "Is this true? Can you tell me what my dream was and what it means?"

²⁷Daniel replied, "There are no wise men, enchanters, magicians, or fortune-tellers who can reveal the king's secret. ²⁸But there is a God in heaven who reveals secrets, and he has shown King Nebuchadnezzar what will happen in the future. Now I will tell you your dream and the visions you saw as you lay on your bed.

²⁹"While Your Majesty was sleeping, you dreamed about coming events. He who reveals secrets has shown you what is going to happen. ³⁰And it is not because I am wiser than anyone else that I know the secret of your dream, but because God wants you to understand what was in your heart.

³¹"In your vision, Your Majesty, you saw standing before you a huge, shining statue of a man. It was a frightening sight. ³²The head of the statue was made of fine gold. Its chest and arms

were silver, its belly and thighs were bronze, [33] its legs were iron, and its feet were a combination of iron and baked clay. [34] As you watched, a rock was cut from a mountain, but not by human hands. It struck the feet of iron and clay, smashing them to bits. [35] The whole statue was crushed into small pieces of iron, clay, bronze, silver, and gold. Then the wind blew them away without a trace, like chaff on a threshing floor. But the rock that knocked the statue down became a great mountain that covered the whole earth.

[36] "That was the dream. Now we will tell the king what it means. [37] Your Majesty, you are the greatest of kings. The God of heaven has given you sovereignty, power, strength, and honor. [38] He has made you the ruler over all the inhabited world and has put even the wild animals and birds under your control. You are the head of gold.

[39] "But after your kingdom comes to an end, another kingdom, inferior to yours, will rise to take your place. After that kingdom has fallen, yet a third kingdom, represented by bronze, will rise to rule the world. [40] Following that kingdom, there will be a fourth one, as strong as iron. That kingdom will smash and crush all previous empires, just as iron smashes and crushes everything it strikes. [41] The feet and toes you saw were a combination of iron and baked clay, showing that this kingdom will be divided. Like iron mixed with clay, it will have some of the strength of iron. [42] But while some parts of it will be as strong as iron, other parts will be as weak as clay. [43] This mixture of iron and clay also shows that these kingdoms will try to strengthen themselves by forming alliances with each other through intermarriage. But they will not hold together, just as iron and clay do not mix.

[44] "During the reigns of those kings, the God of heaven will set up a kingdom that will never be destroyed or conquered. It will crush all these kingdoms into nothingness, and it will stand forever. [45] That is the meaning of the rock cut from the mountain, though not by human hands, that crushed to pieces the statue of iron, bronze, clay, silver, and gold. The great God was showing the king what will happen in the future. The dream is true, and its meaning is certain."

[46] Then King Nebuchadnezzar threw himself down before Daniel and worshiped him, and he commanded his people to offer sacrifices and burn sweet incense before him. [47] The king said to Daniel, "Truly, your God is the greatest of gods, the LORD over kings, a revealer of mysteries, for you have been able to reveal this secret."

[48] Then the king appointed Daniel to a high position and gave him many valuable gifts. He made Daniel ruler over the whole province of Babylon, as well as chief over all his wise men. [49] At Daniel's request, the king appointed Shadrach, Meshach, and Abednego to be in charge of all the affairs of the province of Babylon, while Daniel remained in the king's court.

[3:1] KING Nebuchadnezzar made a gold statue ninety feet tall and nine feet wide* and set it up on the plain of Dura in the province of Babylon. [2] Then he sent messages to the high officers, officials, governors, advisers, treasurers, judges, magistrates, and all the provincial officials to come to the dedication of the statue he had set up. [3] So all these officials* came and stood before the statue King Nebuchadnezzar had set up.

[4] Then a herald shouted out, "People of all races and nations and languages, listen to the king's command! [5] When you hear the sound of the horn, flute, zither, lyre, harp, pipes, and other musical instruments,* bow to the ground to worship King Nebuchadnezzar's gold statue. [6] Anyone who refuses to obey will immediately be thrown into a blazing furnace."

[7] So at the sound of the musical instruments,* all the people, whatever their race or nation or language, bowed to the ground and worshiped the gold

statue that King Nebuchadnezzar had set up.

[8]But some of the astrologers* went to the king and informed on the Jews. [9]They said to King Nebuchadnezzar, "Long live the king! [10]You issued a decree requiring all the people to bow down and worship the gold statue when they hear the sound of the horn, flute, zither, lyre, harp, pipes, and other musical instruments. [11]That decree also states that those who refuse to obey must be thrown into a blazing furnace. [12]But there are some Jews—Shadrach, Meshach, and Abednego—whom you have put in charge of the province of Babylon. They pay no attention to you, Your Majesty. They refuse to serve your gods and do not worship the gold statue you have set up."

[13]Then Nebuchadnezzar flew into a rage and ordered that Shadrach, Meshach, and Abednego be brought before him. When they were brought in, [14]Nebuchadnezzar said to them, "Is it true, Shadrach, Meshach, and Abednego, that you refuse to serve my gods or to worship the gold statue I have set up? [15]I will give you one more chance to bow down and worship the statue I have made when you hear the sound of the musical instruments.* But if you refuse, you will be thrown immediately into the blazing furnace. And then what god will be able to rescue you from my power?"

[16]Shadrach, Meshach, and Abednego replied, "O Nebuchadnezzar, we do not need to defend ourselves before you. [17]If we are thrown into the blazing furnace, the God whom we serve is able to save us. He will rescue us from your power, Your Majesty. [18]But even if he doesn't, we want to make it clear to you, Your Majesty, that we will never serve your gods or worship the gold statue you have set up."

[19]Nebuchadnezzar was so furious with Shadrach, Meshach, and Abednego that his face became distorted with rage. He commanded that the furnace be heated seven times hotter than usual. [20]Then he ordered some of the strongest men of his army to bind Shadrach, Meshach, and Abednego and throw them into the blazing furnace. [21]So they tied them up and threw them into the furnace, fully dressed in their pants, turbans, robes, and other garments. [22]And because the king, in his anger, had demanded such a hot fire in the furnace, the flames killed the soldiers as they threw the three men in. [23]So Shadrach, Meshach, and Abednego, securely tied, fell into the roaring flames.

[24]But suddenly, Nebuchadnezzar jumped up in amazement and exclaimed to his advisers, "Didn't we tie up three men and throw them into the furnace?"

"Yes, Your Majesty, we certainly did," they replied.

[25]"Look!" Nebuchadnezzar shouted. "I see four men, unbound, walking around in the fire unharmed! And the fourth looks like a god*!"

[26]Then Nebuchadnezzar came as close as he could to the door of the flaming furnace and shouted: "Shadrach, Meshach, and Abednego, servants of the Most High God, come out! Come here!"

So Shadrach, Meshach, and Abednego stepped out of the fire. [27]Then the high officers, officials, governors, and advisers crowded around them and saw that the fire had not touched them. Not a hair on their heads was singed, and their clothing was not scorched. They didn't even smell of smoke!

[28]Then Nebuchadnezzar said, "Praise to the God of Shadrach, Meshach, and Abednego! He sent his angel to rescue his servants who trusted in him. They defied the king's command and were willing to die rather than serve or worship any god except their own God. [29]Therefore, I make this decree: If any people, whatever their race or nation or language, speak a word against the God of Shadrach, Meshach, and Abednego, they will be torn limb from limb, and their houses will be turned into heaps of rubble. There is no other god who can rescue like this!"

[30]Then the king promoted Shadrach,

Meshach, and Abednego to even higher positions in the province of Babylon.

3:1 Aramaic *60 cubits* [27 meters] *tall and 6 cubits* [2.7 meters] *wide.* 3:3 Aramaic *the high officers, officials, governors, advisers, treasurers, judges, magistrates, and all the provincial officials.* 3:5 The identification of some of these musical instruments is uncertain. 3:7 Aramaic *the horn, flute, zither, lyre, harp, and other musical instruments.* 3:8 Aramaic *Chaldeans.* 3:15 Aramaic *the horn, flute, zither, lyre, harp, pipes, and other musical instruments.* 3:25 Aramaic *like a son of the gods.*

1 PETER 4:7–5:14

The end of the world is coming soon. Therefore, be earnest and disciplined in your prayers. ⁸Most important of all, continue to show deep love for each other, for love covers a multitude of sins. ⁹Cheerfully share your home with those who need a meal or a place to stay.

¹⁰God has given each of you a gift from his great variety of spiritual gifts. Use them well to serve one another. ¹¹Do you have the gift of speaking? Then speak as though God himself were speaking through you. Do you have the gift of helping others? Do it with all the strength and energy that God supplies. Then everything you do will bring glory to God through Jesus Christ. All glory and power to him forever and ever! Amen.

¹²Dear friends, don't be surprised at the fiery trials you are going through, as if something strange were happening to you. ¹³Instead, be very glad—for these trials make you partners with Christ in his suffering, so that you will have the wonderful joy of seeing his glory when it is revealed to all the world.

¹⁴So be happy when you are insulted for being a Christian,* for then the glorious Spirit of God* rests upon you.* ¹⁵If you suffer, however, it must not be for murder, stealing, making trouble, or prying into other people's affairs. ¹⁶But it is no shame to suffer for being a Christian. Praise God for the privilege of being called by his name! ¹⁷For the time has come for judgment, and it must begin with God's household. And if judgment begins with us, what terrible fate awaits those who have never obeyed God's Good News? ¹⁸And also,

"If the righteous are barely saved,
    what will happen to godless
    sinners?"*

¹⁹So if you are suffering in a manner that pleases God, keep on doing what is right, and trust your lives to the God who created you, for he will never fail you.

5:1AND now, a word to you who are elders in the churches. I, too, am an elder and a witness to the sufferings of Christ. And I, too, will share in his glory when he is revealed to the whole world. As a fellow elder, I appeal to you: ²Care for the flock that God has entrusted to you. Watch over it willingly, not grudgingly—not for what you will get out of it, but because you are eager to serve God. ³Don't lord it over the people assigned to your care, but lead them by your own good example. ⁴And when the Great Shepherd appears, you will receive a crown of never-ending glory and honor.

⁵In the same way, you younger men must accept the authority of the elders. And all of you, serve each other in humility, for

"God opposes the proud
    but favors the humble."*

⁶**So humble yourselves under the mighty power of God, and at the right time he will lift you up in honor. ⁷Give all your worries and cares to God, for he cares about you.**

⁸Stay alert! Watch out for your great enemy, the devil. He prowls around like a roaring lion, looking for someone to devour. ⁹Stand firm against him, and be strong in your faith. Remember that your Christian brothers and sisters* all over the world are going through the same kind of suffering you are.

¹⁰In his kindness God called you to share in his eternal glory by means of Christ Jesus. So after you have suffered a little while, he will restore, support, and strengthen you, and he will place you on a firm foundation. ¹¹All power to him forever! Amen.

¹²I have written and sent this short let-

ter to you with the help of Silas,* whom I commend to you as a faithful brother. My purpose in writing is to encourage you and assure you that what you are experiencing is truly part of God's grace for you. Stand firm in this grace.

13 Your sister church here in Babylon* sends you greetings, and so does my son Mark. 14Greet each other with Christian love.*

Peace be with all of you who are in Christ.

4:14a Greek *for the name of Christ.*   4:14b Or *for the glory of God, which is his Spirit.*   4:14c Some manuscripts add *On their part he is blasphemed, but on your part he is glorified.*   4:18 Prov 11:31 (Greek version).   5:5 Prov 3:34 (Greek version).   5:9 Greek *your brothers.*   5:12 Greek *Silvanus.*   5:13 Greek *The elect one in Babylon.* Babylon was probably symbolic for Rome.   5:14 Greek *with a kiss of love.*

PSALM 119:81-96

Kaph

81 I am worn out waiting for
    your [the LORD's] rescue,
    but I have put my hope in your word.
82 My eyes are straining to see your
    promises come true.
    When will you comfort me?
83 I am shriveled like a wineskin
    in the smoke,
    but I have not forgotten to obey
    your decrees.
84 How long must I wait?
    When will you punish those who
    persecute me?
85 These arrogant people who hate
    your instructions
    have dug deep pits to trap me.
86 All your commands are trustworthy.
    Protect me from those who hunt
    me down without cause.
87 They almost finished me off,
    but I refused to abandon your
    commandments.
88 In your unfailing love, spare my life;
    then I can continue to obey
    your laws.

Lamedh

89 Your eternal word, O LORD,
    stands firm in heaven.
90 Your faithfulness extends to every
    generation,

    as enduring as the earth you
    created.
91 Your regulations remain true
    to this day,
    for everything serves your plans.
92 If your instructions hadn't sustained
    me with joy,
    I would have died in my misery.
93 I will never forget your
    commandments,
    for by them you give me life.
94 I am yours; rescue me!
    For I have worked hard at obeying
    your commandments.
95 Though the wicked hide along the
    way to kill me,
    I will quietly keep my mind on
    your laws.
96 Even perfection has its limits,
    but your commands have no limit.

PROVERBS 28:15-16

A wicked ruler is as dangerous to the poor as a roaring lion or an attacking bear. □ A ruler with no understanding will oppress his people, but one who hates corruption will have a long life.

NOVEMBER 27

DANIEL 4:1-37

1*King Nebuchadnezzar sent this message to the people of every race and nation and language throughout the world:

"Peace and prosperity to you!
    2"I want you all to know about the miraculous signs and wonders the Most High God has performed for me.

3 How great are his signs,
    how powerful his wonders!
    His kingdom will last forever,
    his rule through all
    generations.

⁴*"I, Nebuchadnezzar, was living in my palace in comfort and prosperity. ⁵But one night I had a dream that frightened me; I saw visions that terrified me as I lay in my bed. ⁶So I issued an order calling in all the wise men of Babylon, so they could tell me what my dream meant. ⁷When all the magicians, enchanters, astrologers,* and fortune-tellers came in, I told them the dream, but they could not tell me what it meant. ⁸At last Daniel came in before me, and I told him the dream. (He was named Belteshazzar after my god, and the spirit of the holy gods is in him.)

⁹"I said to him, 'Belteshazzar, chief of the magicians, I know that the spirit of the holy gods is in you and that no mystery is too great for you to solve. Now tell me what my dream means.

¹⁰"'While I was lying in my bed, this is what I dreamed. I saw a large tree in the middle of the earth. ¹¹The tree grew very tall and strong, reaching high into the heavens for all the world to see. ¹²It had fresh green leaves, and it was loaded with fruit for all to eat. Wild animals lived in its shade, and birds nested in its branches. All the world was fed from this tree.

¹³"'Then as I lay there dreaming, I saw a messenger,* a holy one, coming down from heaven. ¹⁴The messenger shouted,

"Cut down the tree and lop off
    its branches!
    Shake off its leaves and scatter
        its fruit!
Chase the wild animals from
    its shade
    and the birds from its branches.
¹⁵ But leave the stump and the roots
    in the ground,
    bound with a band of iron
        and bronze
    and surrounded by tender
        grass.

Now let him be drenched with the
    dew of heaven,
    and let him live with the wild
        animals among the plants
        of the field.
¹⁶ For seven periods of time,
    let him have the mind of
        a wild animal
    instead of the mind
        of a human.
¹⁷ For this has been decreed by the
        messengers*;
    it is commanded by the holy
        ones,
so that everyone may know
    that the Most High rules over
        the kingdoms of the world.
He gives them to anyone he
        chooses—
    even to the lowliest of people."

¹⁸"'Belteshazzar, that was the dream that I, King Nebuchadnezzar, had. Now tell me what it means, for none of the wise men of my kingdom can do so. But you can tell me because the spirit of the holy gods is in you.'

¹⁹"Upon hearing this, Daniel (also known as Belteshazzar) was overcome for a time, frightened by the meaning of the dream. Then the king said to him, 'Belteshazzar, don't be alarmed by the dream and what it means.'

"Belteshazzar replied, 'I wish the events foreshadowed in this dream would happen to your enemies, my lord, and not to you! ²⁰The tree you saw was growing very tall and strong, reaching high into the heavens for all the world to see. ²¹It had fresh green leaves and was loaded with fruit for all to eat. Wild animals lived in its shade, and birds nested in its branches. ²²That tree, Your Majesty, is you. For you have grown strong and great; your greatness reaches up to heaven, and your rule to the ends of the earth.

²³"'Then you saw a messenger, a

holy one, coming down from heaven and saying, "Cut down the tree and destroy it. But leave the stump and the roots in the ground, bound with a band of iron and bronze and surrounded by tender grass. Let him be drenched with the dew of heaven. Let him live with the animals of the field for seven periods of time."

24"'This is what the dream means, Your Majesty, and what the Most High has declared will happen to my lord the king. 25 You will be driven from human society, and you will live in the fields with the wild animals. You will eat grass like a cow, and you will be drenched with the dew of heaven. Seven periods of time will pass while you live this way, until you learn that the Most High rules over the kingdoms of the world and gives them to anyone he chooses. 26 But the stump and roots of the tree were left in the ground. This means that you will receive your kingdom back again when you have learned that heaven rules.

27"'King Nebuchadnezzar, please accept my advice. Stop sinning and do what is right. Break from your wicked past and be merciful to the poor. Perhaps then you will continue to prosper.'

28"But all these things did happen to King Nebuchadnezzar. 29 Twelve months later he was taking a walk on the flat roof of the royal palace in Babylon. 30 As he looked out across the city, he said, 'Look at this great city of Babylon! By my own mighty power, I have built this beautiful city as my royal residence to display my majestic splendor.'

31"While these words were still in his mouth, a voice called down from heaven, 'O King Nebuchadnezzar, this message is for you! You are no longer ruler of this kingdom. 32 You will be driven from human society. You will live in the fields with the

wild animals, and you will eat grass like a cow. Seven periods of time will pass while you live this way, until you learn that the Most High rules over the kingdoms of the world and gives them to anyone he chooses.'

33"That same hour the judgment was fulfilled, and Nebuchadnezzar was driven from human society. He ate grass like a cow, and he was drenched with the dew of heaven. He lived this way until his hair was as long as eagles' feathers and his nails were like birds' claws.

34"After this time had passed, I, Nebuchadnezzar, looked up to heaven. My sanity returned, and I praised and worshiped the Most High and honored the one who lives forever.

His rule is everlasting,
    and his kingdom is eternal.
35 All the people of the earth
    are nothing compared to him.
He does as he pleases
    among the angels of heaven
    and among the people
        of the earth.
No one can stop him or say to him,
    'What do you mean by doing
        these things?'

36"When my sanity returned to me, so did my honor and glory and kingdom. My advisers and nobles sought me out, and I was restored as head of my kingdom, with even greater honor than before. 37"Now I, Nebuchadnezzar, praise and glorify and honor the King of heaven. All his acts are just and true, and he is able to humble the proud."

4:1 Verses 4:1-3 are numbered 3:31-33 in Aramaic text. 4:4 Verses 4:4-37 are numbered 4:1-34 in Aramaic text. 4:7 Or Chaldeans. 4:13 Aramaic a watcher; also in 4:23. 4:17 Aramaic the watchers.

2 PETER 1:1-21

This letter is from Simon* Peter, a slave and apostle of Jesus Christ.

I am writing to you who share the

same precious faith we have. This faith was given to you because of the justice and fairness* of Jesus Christ, our God and Savior.

²May God give you more and more grace and peace as you grow in your knowledge of God and Jesus our Lord.

³By his divine power, God has given us everything we need for living a godly life. We have received all of this by coming to know him, the one who called us to himself by means of his marvelous glory and excellence. ⁴And because of his glory and excellence, he has given us great and precious promises. These are the promises that enable you to share his divine nature and escape the world's corruption caused by human desires.

⁵In view of all this, make every effort to respond to God's promises. Supplement your faith with a generous provision of moral excellence, and moral excellence with knowledge, ⁶and knowledge with self-control, and self-control with patient endurance, and patient endurance with godliness, ⁷and godliness with brotherly affection, and brotherly affection with love for everyone.

⁸The more you grow like this, the more productive and useful you will be in your knowledge of our Lord Jesus Christ. ⁹But those who fail to develop in this way are shortsighted or blind, forgetting that they have been cleansed from their old sins.

¹⁰So, dear brothers and sisters,* work hard to prove that you really are among those God has called and chosen. Do these things, and you will never fall away. ¹¹Then God will give you a grand entrance into the eternal Kingdom of our Lord and Savior Jesus Christ.

¹²Therefore, I will always remind you about these things—even though you already know them and are standing firm in the truth you have been taught. ¹³And it is only right that I should keep on reminding you as long as I live.* ¹⁴For our Lord Jesus Christ has shown me that I must soon leave this earthly life,* ¹⁵so I will work hard to make sure you always remember these things after I am gone.

¹⁶For we were not making up clever stories when we told you about the powerful coming of our Lord Jesus Christ. We saw his majestic splendor with our own eyes ¹⁷when he received honor and glory from God the Father. The voice from the majestic glory of God said to him, "This is my dearly loved Son, who brings me great joy."* ¹⁸We ourselves heard that voice from heaven when we were with him on the holy mountain.

¹⁹Because of that experience, we have even greater confidence in the message proclaimed by the prophets. You must pay close attention to what they wrote, for their words are like a lamp shining in a dark place—until the Day dawns, and Christ the Morning Star shines* in your hearts. **²⁰Above all, you must realize that no prophecy in Scripture ever came from the prophet's own understanding,* ²¹or from human initiative. No, those prophets were moved by the Holy Spirit, and they spoke from God.**

1:1a Greek *Symeon.*   **1:1b** Or *to you in the righteousness.*
1:10 Greek *brothers.*   **1:13** Greek *as long as I am in this tent* [or *tabernacle*].   **1:14** Greek *I must soon put off my tent* [or *tabernacle*].   **1:17** Matt 17:5; Mark 9:7; Luke 9:35.   **1:19** Or *rises.*   **1:20** Or *is a matter of one's own interpretation.*

PSALM 119:97-112

Mem

⁹⁷ **O**h, how I love your [the LORD's] instructions!
    I think about them all day long.
⁹⁸ Your commands make me wiser than my enemies,
    for they are my constant guide.
⁹⁹ Yes, I have more insight than my teachers,
    for I am always thinking of your laws.
¹⁰⁰ I am even wiser than my elders,
    for I have kept your commandments.
¹⁰¹ I have refused to walk on any evil path,
    so that I may remain obedient to your word.
¹⁰² I haven't turned away from your regulations,

for you have taught me well.
[103] How sweet your words taste to me;
they are sweeter than honey.
[104] Your commandments give me
understanding;
no wonder I hate every false way
of life.

Nun
[105] Your word is a lamp to guide my feet
and a light for my path.
[106] I've promised it once, and I'll
promise it again:
I will obey your righteous
regulations.
[107] I have suffered much, O LORD;
restore my life again as you
promised.
[108] LORD, accept my offering of praise,
and teach me your regulations.
[109] My life constantly hangs in the
balance,
but I will not stop obeying your
instructions.
[110] The wicked have set their traps
for me,
but I will not turn from your
commandments.
[111] Your laws are my treasure;
they are my heart's delight.
[112] I am determined to keep your decrees
to the very end.

PROVERBS 28:17-18
A murderer's tormented conscience will drive him into the grave. Don't protect him! □ The blameless will be rescued from harm, but the crooked will be suddenly destroyed.

NOVEMBER
28

DANIEL 5:1-31
Many years later King Belshazzar gave a great feast for 1,000 of his nobles, and he drank wine with them. [2] While Bel-

shazzar was drinking the wine, he gave orders to bring in the gold and silver cups that his predecessor,* Nebuchadnezzar, had taken from the Temple in Jerusalem. He wanted to drink from them with his nobles, his wives, and his concubines. [3] So they brought these gold cups taken from the Temple, the house of God in Jerusalem, and the king and his nobles, his wives, and his concubines drank from them. [4] While they drank from them they praised their idols made of gold, silver, bronze, iron, wood, and stone.

[5] Suddenly, they saw the fingers of a human hand writing on the plaster wall of the king's palace, near the lampstand. The king himself saw the hand as it wrote, [6] and his face turned pale with fright. His knees knocked together in fear and his legs gave way beneath him.

[7] The king shouted for the enchanters, astrologers,* and fortune-tellers to be brought before him. He said to these wise men of Babylon, "Whoever can read this writing and tell me what it means will be dressed in purple robes of royal honor and will have a gold chain placed around his neck. He will become the third highest ruler in the kingdom!"

[8] But when all the king's wise men had come in, none of them could read the writing or tell him what it meant. [9] So the king grew even more alarmed, and his face turned pale. His nobles, too, were shaken.

[10] But when the queen mother heard what was happening, she hurried to the banquet hall. She said to Belshazzar, "Long live the king! Don't be so pale and frightened. [11] There is a man in your kingdom who has within him the spirit of the holy gods. During Nebuchadnezzar's reign, this man was found to have insight, understanding, and wisdom like that of the gods. Your predecessor, the king—your predecessor King Nebuchadnezzar—made him chief over all the magicians, enchanters, astrologers, and fortune-tellers of Babylon. [12] This man Daniel, whom the

king named Belteshazzar, has exceptional ability and is filled with divine knowledge and understanding. He can interpret dreams, explain riddles, and solve difficult problems. Call for Daniel, and he will tell you what the writing means."

¹³So Daniel was brought in before the king. The king asked him, "Are you Daniel, one of the exiles brought from Judah by my predecessor, King Nebuchadnezzar? ¹⁴I have heard that you have the spirit of the gods within you and that you are filled with insight, understanding, and wisdom. ¹⁵My wise men and enchanters have tried to read the words on the wall and tell me their meaning, but they cannot do it. ¹⁶I am told that you can give interpretations and solve difficult problems. If you can read these words and tell me their meaning, you will be clothed in purple robes of royal honor, and you will have a gold chain placed around your neck. You will become the third highest ruler in the kingdom."

¹⁷Daniel answered the king, "Keep your gifts or give them to someone else, but I will tell you what the writing means. ¹⁸Your Majesty, the Most High God gave sovereignty, majesty, glory, and honor to your predecessor, Nebuchadnezzar. ¹⁹He made him so great that people of all races and nations and languages trembled before him in fear. He killed those he wanted to kill and spared those he wanted to spare. He honored those he wanted to honor and disgraced those he wanted to disgrace. ²⁰But when his heart and mind were puffed up with arrogance, he was brought down from his royal throne and stripped of his glory. ²¹He was driven from human society. He was given the mind of a wild animal, and he lived among the wild donkeys. He ate grass like a cow, and he was drenched with the dew of heaven, until he learned that the Most High God rules over the kingdoms of the world and appoints anyone he desires to rule over them. ²²"You are his successor,* O Belshaz-

zar, and you knew all this, yet you have not humbled yourself. ²³For you have proudly defied the LORD of heaven and have had these cups from his Temple brought before you. You and your nobles and your wives and concubines have been drinking wine from them while praising gods of silver, gold, bronze, iron, wood, and stone—gods that neither see nor hear nor know anything at all. But you have not honored the God who gives you the breath of life and controls your destiny! ²⁴So God has sent this hand to write this message.

²⁵"This is the message that was written: MENE, MENE, TEKEL, and PARSIN. ²⁶This is what these words mean:

Mene means 'numbered'—God has numbered the days of your reign and has brought it to an end.
²⁷ Tekel means 'weighed'—you have been weighed on the balances and have not measured up.
²⁸ Parsin* means 'divided'—your kingdom has been divided and given to the Medes and Persians."

²⁹Then at Belshazzar's command, Daniel was dressed in purple robes, a gold chain was hung around his neck, and he was proclaimed the third highest ruler in the kingdom.

³⁰That very night Belshazzar, the Babylonian* king, was killed.*

³¹*And Darius the Mede took over the kingdom at the age of sixty-two.

5:2 Aramaic father; also in 5:11, 13, 18.   5:7 Or Chaldeans; also in 5:11.   5:22 Aramaic son. 5:28 Aramaic Peres, the singular of Parsin.   5:30a Or Chaldean.   5:30b The Persians and Medes conquered Babylon in October 539 B.C.   5:31 Verse 5:31 is numbered 6:1 in Aramaic text.

2 PETER 2:1-22

But there were also false prophets in Israel, just as there will be false teachers among you. They will cleverly teach destructive heresies and even deny the Master who bought them. In this way, they will bring sudden destruction on themselves. ²Many will follow their evil teaching and shameful immorality. And because of these teachers, the way of truth will be slandered. ³In their greed they will make up clever lies to get hold of your money. But God condemned them long ago, and their destruction will not be delayed.

⁴For God did not spare even the angels who sinned. He threw them into hell,* in gloomy pits of darkness,* where they are being held until the day of judgment. ⁵And God did not spare the ancient world—except for Noah and the seven others in his family. Noah warned the world of God's righteous judgment. So God protected Noah when he destroyed the world of ungodly people with a vast flood. ⁶Later, God condemned the cities of Sodom and Gomorrah and turned them into heaps of ashes. He made them an example of what will happen to ungodly people. ⁷But God also rescued Lot out of Sodom because he was a righteous man who was sick of the shameful immorality of the wicked people around him. ⁸Yes, Lot was a righteous man who was tormented in his soul by the wickedness he saw and heard day after day. ⁹So you see, the Lord knows how to rescue godly people from their trials, even while keeping the wicked under punishment until the day of final judgment. ¹⁰He is especially hard on those who follow their own twisted sexual desire, and who despise authority.

These people are proud and arrogant, daring even to scoff at supernatural beings* without so much as trembling. ¹¹But the angels, who are far greater in power and strength, do not dare to bring from the Lord* a charge of blasphemy against those supernatural beings.

¹²These false teachers are like unthinking animals, creatures of instinct, born to be caught and destroyed. They scoff at things they do not understand, and like animals, they will be destroyed. ¹³Their destruction is their reward for the harm they have done. They love to indulge in evil pleasures in broad daylight. They are a disgrace and a stain among

you. They delight in deception* even as they eat with you in your fellowship meals. ¹⁴They commit adultery with their eyes, and their desire for sin is never satisfied. They lure unstable people into sin, and they are well trained in greed. They live under God's curse. ¹⁵They have wandered off the right road and followed the footsteps of Balaam son of Beor,* who loved to earn money by doing wrong. ¹⁶But Balaam was stopped from his mad course when his donkey rebuked him with a human voice.

¹⁷These people are as useless as dried-up springs or as mist blown away by the wind. They are doomed to blackest darkness. ¹⁸They brag about themselves with empty, foolish boasting. With an appeal to twisted sexual desires, they lure back into sin those who have barely escaped from a lifestyle of deception. ¹⁹They promise freedom, but they themselves are slaves of sin and corruption. For you are a slave to whatever controls you. ²⁰And when people escape from the wickedness of the world by knowing our Lord and Savior Jesus Christ and then get tangled up and enslaved by sin again, they are worse off than before. ²¹It would be better if they had never known the way to righteousness than to know it and then reject the command they were given to live a holy life. ²²They prove the truth of this proverb: "A dog returns to its vomit."* And another says, "A washed pig returns to the mud."

2:4a Greek *Tartarus.*   2:4b Some manuscripts read *in chains of gloom.*   2:10 Greek *at glorious ones,* which are probably evil angels.   2:11 Other manuscripts read *to the Lord;* still others omit this phrase.   2:13 Some manuscripts read *in fellowship meals.*   2:15 Some manuscripts read *Bosor.*   2:22 Prov 26:11.

PSALM 119:113-128

Samekh
¹¹³ ▌ [the Lord] hate those with
        divided loyalties,
    but I love your instructions.
¹¹⁴ You are my refuge and my shield;
    your word is my source of hope.
¹¹⁵ Get out of my life, you evil-minded
        people,

for I intend to obey the
commands of my God.
[116] LORD, sustain me as you promised,
that I may live!
Do not let my hope be crushed.
[117] Sustain me, and I will be rescued;
then I will meditate continually
on your decrees.
[118] But you have rejected all who stray
from your decrees.
They are only fooling themselves.
[119] You skim off the wicked of the
earth like scum;
no wonder I love to obey your
laws!
[120] I tremble in fear of you;
I stand in awe of your regulations.

Ayin

[121] Don't leave me to the mercy of my
enemies,
for I have done what is just and
right.
[122] Please guarantee a blessing
for me.
Don't let the arrogant oppress me!
[123] **My eyes strain to see your rescue,
to see the truth of your promise
fulfilled.**
[124] **I am your servant; deal with me in
unfailing love,
and teach me your decrees.**
[125] Give discernment to me, your
servant;
then I will understand your laws.
[126] LORD, it is time for you to act,
for these evil people have violated
your instructions.
[127] Truly, I love your commands
more than gold, even the
finest gold.
[128] Each of your commandments
is right.
That is why I hate every false way.

PROVERBS 28:19-20

A hard worker has plenty of food, but
a person who chases fantasies ends up
in poverty. □ The trustworthy person
will get a rich reward, but a person
who wants quick riches will get into
trouble.

NOVEMBER
29

DANIEL 6:1-28

[1] ***D**arius the Mede decided to divide
the kingdom into 120 provinces, and
he appointed a high officer to rule over
each province. [2] The king also chose
Daniel and two others as administrators
to supervise the high officers and protect the king's interests. [3] Daniel soon
proved himself more capable than all
the other administrators and high officers. Because of Daniel's great ability,
the king made plans to place him over
the entire empire.

[4] Then the other administrators and
high officers began searching for some
fault in the way Daniel was handling government affairs, but they couldn't find
anything to criticize or condemn. He was
faithful, always responsible, and completely trustworthy. [5] So they concluded,
"Our only chance of finding grounds for
accusing Daniel will be in connection
with the rules of his religion."

[6] So the administrators and high officers went to the king and said, "Long live
King Darius! [7] We are all in agreement—
we administrators, officials, high officers, advisers, and governors—that the
king should make a law that will be
strictly enforced. Give orders that for the
next thirty days any person who prays to
anyone, divine or human—except to you,
Your Majesty—will be thrown into the
den of lions. [8] And now, Your Majesty,
issue and sign this law so it cannot be
changed, an official law of the Medes and
Persians that cannot be revoked." [9] So
King Darius signed the law.

[10] But when Daniel learned that the
law had been signed, he went home and
knelt down as usual in his upstairs
room, with its windows open toward
Jerusalem. He prayed three times a day,
just as he had always done, giving
thanks to his God. [11] Then the officials
went together to Daniel's house and

found him praying and asking for God's help. [12] So they went straight to the king and reminded him about his law. "Did you not sign a law that for the next thirty days any person who prays to anyone, divine or human—except to you, Your Majesty—will be thrown into the den of lions?"

"Yes," the king replied, "that decision stands; it is an official law of the Medes and Persians that cannot be revoked."

[13] Then they told the king, "That man Daniel, one of the captives from Judah, is ignoring you and your law. He still prays to his God three times a day."

[14] Hearing this, the king was deeply troubled, and he tried to think of a way to save Daniel. He spent the rest of the day looking for a way to get Daniel out of this predicament.

[15] In the evening the men went together to the king and said, "Your Majesty, you know that according to the law of the Medes and the Persians, no law that the king signs can be changed."

[16] So at last the king gave orders for Daniel to be arrested and thrown into the den of lions. The king said to him, "May your God, whom you serve so faithfully, rescue you."

[17] A stone was brought and placed over the mouth of the den. The king sealed the stone with his own royal seal and the seals of his nobles, so that no one could rescue Daniel. [18] Then the king returned to his palace and spent the night fasting. He refused his usual entertainment and couldn't sleep at all that night.

[19] Very early the next morning, the king got up and hurried out to the lions' den. [20] When he got there, he called out in anguish, "Daniel, servant of the living God! Was your God, whom you serve so faithfully, able to rescue you from the lions?"

[21] Daniel answered, "Long live the king! [22] My God sent his angel to shut the lions' mouths so that they would not hurt me, for I have been found innocent in his sight. And I have not wronged you, Your Majesty."

[23] The king was overjoyed and or-dered that Daniel be lifted from the den. Not a scratch was found on him, for he had trusted in his God.

[24] Then the king gave orders to arrest the men who had maliciously accused Daniel. He had them thrown into the lions' den, along with their wives and children. The lions leaped on them and tore them apart before they even hit the floor of the den.

[25] Then King Darius sent this message to the people of every race and nation and language throughout the world:

"Peace and prosperity to you!

[26] "I decree that everyone throughout my kingdom should tremble with fear before the God of Daniel.

> For he is the living God,
>   and he will endure forever.
> His kingdom will never be
>   destroyed,
>   and his rule will never end.
> [27] He rescues and saves his people;
>   he performs miraculous signs
>   and wonders
>   in the heavens and on earth.
> He has rescued Daniel
>   from the power of the lions."

[28] So Daniel prospered during the reign of Darius and the reign of Cyrus the Persian.*

6:1 Verses 6:1-28 are numbered 6:2-29 in Aramaic text.
6:28 Or of Darius, that is, the reign of Cyrus the Persian.

2 PETER 3:1-18

This is my second letter to you, dear friends, and in both of them I [Peter] have tried to stimulate your wholesome thinking and refresh your memory. [2] I want you to remember what the holy prophets said long ago and what our Lord and Savior commanded through your apostles.

[3] Most importantly, I want to remind you that in the last days scoffers will come, mocking the truth and following their own desires. [4] They will say, "What happened to the promise that Jesus is coming again? From before the times of our ancestors, everything has remained

the same since the world was first created."

5 They deliberately forget that God made the heavens by the word of his command, and he brought the earth out from the water and surrounded it with water. 6 Then he used the water to destroy the ancient world with a mighty flood. 7 And by the same word, the present heavens and earth have been stored up for fire. They are being kept for the day of judgment, when ungodly people will be destroyed.

8 But you must not forget this one thing, dear friends: A day is like a thousand years to the Lord, and a thousand years is like a day. 9 **The Lord isn't really being slow about his promise, as some people think. No, he is being patient for your sake. He does not want anyone to be destroyed, but wants everyone to repent.** 10 But the day of the Lord will come as unexpectedly as a thief. Then the heavens will pass away with a terrible noise, and the very elements themselves will disappear in fire, and the earth and everything on it will be found to deserve judgment.*

11 Since everything around us is going to be destroyed like this, what holy and godly lives you should live, 12 looking forward to the day of God and hurrying it along. On that day, he will set the heavens on fire, and the elements will melt away in the flames. 13 But we are looking forward to the new heavens and new earth he has promised, a world filled with God's righteousness.

14 And so, dear friends, while you are waiting for these things to happen, make every effort to be found living peaceful lives that are pure and blameless in his sight.

15 And remember, the Lord's patience gives people time to be saved. This is what our beloved brother Paul also wrote to you with the wisdom God gave him— 16 speaking of these things in all of his letters. Some of his comments are hard to understand, and those who are ignorant and unstable have twisted his letters to mean something quite different, just as

they do with other parts of Scripture. And this will result in their destruction.

17 I am warning you ahead of time, dear friends. Be on guard so that you will not be carried away by the errors of these wicked people and lose your own secure footing. 18 Rather, you must grow in the grace and knowledge of our Lord and Savior Jesus Christ.

All glory to him, both now and forever! Amen.

3:10 Other manuscripts read *will be burned up;* still others read *will be found destroyed.*

PSALM 119:129-152

Pe

129 **Y**our [the LORD's] laws are wonderful.
No wonder I obey them!
130 The teaching of your word gives light,
so even the simple can understand.
131 I pant with expectation,
longing for your commands.
132 Come and show me your mercy,
as you do for all who love your name.
133 Guide my steps by your word,
so I will not be overcome by evil.
134 Ransom me from the oppression of evil people;
then I can obey your commandments.
135 Look upon me with love;
teach me your decrees.
136 Rivers of tears gush from my eyes
because people disobey your instructions.

Tsadhe

137 O LORD, you are righteous,
and your regulations are fair.
138 Your laws are perfect
and completely trustworthy.
139 I am overwhelmed with indignation,
for my enemies have disregarded your words.
140 Your promises have been thoroughly tested;
that is why I love them so much.
141 I am insignificant and despised,
but I don't forget your commandments.

¹⁴²Your justice is eternal,
   and your instructions are
     perfectly true.
¹⁴³As pressure and stress bear
   down on me,
   I find joy in your commands.
¹⁴⁴Your laws are always right;
   help me to understand them
     so I may live.

Qoph

¹⁴⁵I pray with all my heart; answer
   me, LORD!
   I will obey your decrees.
¹⁴⁶I cry out to you; rescue me,
   that I may obey your laws.
¹⁴⁷I rise early, before the sun is up;
   I cry out for help and put my hope
     in your words.
¹⁴⁸I stay awake through the night,
   thinking about your promise.
¹⁴⁹In your faithful love, O LORD, hear
   my cry;
   let me be revived by following
     your regulations.
¹⁵⁰Lawless people are coming to
   attack me;
   they live far from your
     instructions.
¹⁵¹But you are near, O LORD,
   and all your commands are true.
¹⁵²I have known from my earliest days
   that your laws will last forever.

PROVERBS 28:21-22

Showing partiality is never good, yet some will do wrong for a mere piece of bread. □ Greedy people try to get rich quick but don't realize they're headed for poverty.

NOVEMBER
30

DANIEL 7:1-28

Earlier, during the first year of King Belshazzar's reign in Babylon,* Daniel had a dream and saw visions as he lay in his bed. He wrote down the dream, and this is what he saw.

²In my vision that night, I, Daniel, saw a great storm churning the surface of a great sea, with strong winds blowing from every direction. ³Then four huge beasts came up out of the water, each different from the others.

⁴The first beast was like a lion with eagles' wings. As I watched, its wings were pulled off, and it was left standing with its two hind feet on the ground, like a human being. And it was given a human mind.

⁵Then I saw a second beast, and it looked like a bear. It was rearing up on one side, and it had three ribs in its mouth between its teeth. And I heard a voice saying to it, "Get up! Devour the flesh of many people!"

⁶Then the third of these strange beasts appeared, and it looked like a leopard. It had four bird's wings on its back, and it had four heads. Great authority was given to this beast.

⁷Then in my vision that night, I saw a fourth beast—terrifying, dreadful, and very strong. It devoured and crushed its victims with huge iron teeth and trampled their remains beneath its feet. It was different from any of the other beasts, and it had ten horns.

⁸As I was looking at the horns, suddenly another small horn appeared among them. Three of the first horns were torn out by the roots to make room for it. This little horn had eyes like human eyes and a mouth that was boasting arrogantly.

⁹ I watched as thrones were put
    in place
   and the Ancient One* sat down
    to judge.
His clothing was as white as snow,
   his hair like purest wool.
He sat on a fiery throne
   with wheels of blazing fire,
¹⁰ and a river of fire was pouring out,
   flowing from his presence.
Millions of angels ministered
   to him;
   many millions stood to attend him.

Then the court began its session,
and the books were opened.

¹¹I continued to watch because I could hear the little horn's boastful speech. I kept watching until the fourth beast was killed and its body was destroyed by fire. ¹²The other three beasts had their authority taken from them, but they were allowed to live a while longer.*

¹³As my vision continued that night, I saw someone like a son of man* coming with the clouds of heaven. He approached the Ancient One and was led into his presence. ¹⁴He was given authority, honor, and sovereignty over all the nations of the world, so that people of every race and nation and language would obey him. His rule is eternal—it will never end. His kingdom will never be destroyed.

¹⁵I, Daniel, was troubled by all I had seen, and my visions terrified me. ¹⁶So I approached one of those standing beside the throne and asked him what it all meant. He explained it to me like this: ¹⁷"These four huge beasts represent four kingdoms that will arise from the earth. ¹⁸But in the end, the holy people of the Most High will be given the kingdom, and they will rule forever and ever."

¹⁹Then I wanted to know the true meaning of the fourth beast, the one so different from the others and so terrifying. It had devoured and crushed its victims with iron teeth and bronze claws, trampling their remains beneath its feet. ²⁰I also asked about the ten horns on the fourth beast's head and the little horn that came up afterward and destroyed three of the other horns. This horn had seemed greater than the others, and it had human eyes and a mouth that was boasting arrogantly. ²¹As I watched, this horn was waging war against God's holy people and was defeating them, ²²until the Ancient One—the Most High—came and judged in favor of his holy people. Then the time

arrived for the holy people to take over the kingdom.

²³Then he said to me, "This fourth beast is the fourth world power that will rule the earth. It will be different from all the others. It will devour the whole world, trampling and crushing everything in its path. ²⁴Its ten horns are ten kings who will rule that empire. Then another king will arise, different from the other ten, who will subdue three of them. ²⁵He will defy the Most High and oppress the holy people of the Most High. He will try to change their sacred festivals and laws, and they will be placed under his control for a time, times, and half a time.

²⁶"But then the court will pass judgment, and all his power will be taken away and completely destroyed. ²⁷Then the sovereignty, power, and greatness of all the kingdoms under heaven will be given to the holy people of the Most High. His kingdom will last forever, and all rulers will serve and obey him."

²⁸That was the end of the vision. I, Daniel, was terrified by my thoughts and my face was pale with fear, but I kept these things to myself.

7:1 The first year of Belshazzar's reign (who was co-regent with his father, Nabonidus) was 556 B.C. (or perhaps as late as 553 B.C.). 7:9 Aramaic *an Ancient of Days;* also in 7:13, 22. 7:12 Aramaic *for a season and a time.* 7:13 Or *like a Son of Man.*

1 JOHN 1:1-10

We proclaim to you the one who existed from the beginning,* whom we have heard and seen. We saw him with our own eyes and touched him with our own hands. He is the Word of life. ²This one who is life itself was revealed to us, and we have seen him. And now we testify and proclaim to you that he is the one who is eternal life. He was with the Father, and then he was revealed to us. ³We proclaim to you what we ourselves have actually seen and heard so that you may have fellowship with us. And our fellowship is with the Father and with his Son, Jesus Christ. ⁴We are writing these things so that you may fully share our joy.*

⁵This is the message we heard from Jesus* and now declare to you: God is light, and there is no darkness in him at all. ⁶So we are lying if we say we have fellowship with God but go on living in spiritual darkness; we are not practicing the truth. ⁷**But if we are living in the light, as God is in the light, then we have fellowship with each other, and the blood of Jesus, his Son, cleanses us from all sin.**

⁸If we claim we have no sin, we are only fooling ourselves and not living in the truth. ⁹But if we confess our sins to him, he is faithful and just to forgive us our sins and to cleanse us from all wickedness. ¹⁰If we claim we have not sinned, we are calling God a liar and showing that his word has no place in our hearts.

1:1 Greek *What was from the beginning.*   1:4 Or *so that our joy may be complete;* some manuscripts read *your joy.* 1:5 Greek *from him.*

PSALM 119:153-176

Resh

¹⁵³ Look upon my suffering and
    rescue me,
      for I have not forgotten
        your [the LORD's]
        instructions.
¹⁵⁴ Argue my case; take my side!
      Protect my life as you
        promised.
¹⁵⁵ The wicked are far from rescue,
      for they do not bother with
        your decrees.
¹⁵⁶ LORD, how great is your mercy;
      let me be revived by following
        your regulations.
¹⁵⁷ Many persecute and trouble me,
      yet I have not swerved from
        your laws.
¹⁵⁸ Seeing these traitors makes me
        sick at heart,
      because they care nothing for
        your word.
¹⁵⁹ See how I love your
        commandments, LORD.
      Give back my life because of your
        unfailing love.

¹⁶⁰ The very essence of your words
        is truth;
      all your just regulations will
        stand forever.

Shin

¹⁶¹ Powerful people harass me
        without cause,
      but my heart trembles only at
        your word.
¹⁶² I rejoice in your word
      like one who discovers a great
        treasure.
¹⁶³ I hate and abhor all falsehood,
      but I love your instructions.
¹⁶⁴ I will praise you seven times
        a day
      because all your regulations are
        just.
¹⁶⁵ Those who love your instructions
        have great peace
      and do not stumble.
¹⁶⁶ I long for your rescue, LORD,
      so I have obeyed your commands.
¹⁶⁷ I have obeyed your laws,
      for I love them very much.
¹⁶⁸ Yes, I obey your commandments
        and laws
      because you know everything
        I do.

Taw

¹⁶⁹ O LORD, listen to my cry;
      give me the discerning mind you
        promised.
¹⁷⁰ Listen to my prayer;
      rescue me as you promised.
¹⁷¹ Let praise flow from my lips,
      for you have taught me your
        decrees.
¹⁷² Let my tongue sing about
        your word,
      for all your commands
        are right.
¹⁷³ Give me a helping hand,
      for I have chosen to follow your
        commandments.
¹⁷⁴ O LORD, I have longed for
        your rescue,
      and your instructions are my
        delight.
¹⁷⁵ Let me live so I can
        praise you,

and may your regulations help me.
¹⁷⁶ I have wandered away like
    a lost sheep;
    come and find me,
    for I have not forgotten your
        commands.

PROVERBS 28:23-24

In the end, people appreciate honest criticism far more than flattery. ☐ Anyone who steals from his father and mother and says, "What's wrong with that?" is no better than a murderer.

DECEMBER

1

DANIEL 8:1-27

1***D**uring the third year of King Belshazzar's reign, I, Daniel, saw another vision, following the one that had already appeared to me. 2In this vision I was at the fortress of Susa, in the province of Elam, standing beside the Ulai River.*

3As I looked up, I saw a ram with two long horns standing beside the river.* One of the horns was longer than the other, even though it had grown later than the other one. 4The ram butted everything out of his way to the west, to the north, and to the south, and no one could stand against him or help his victims. He did as he pleased and became very great.

5While I was watching, suddenly a male goat appeared from the west, crossing the land so swiftly that he didn't even touch the ground. This goat, which had one very large horn between its eyes, 6headed toward the two-horned ram that I had seen standing beside the river, rushing at him in a rage. 7The goat charged furiously at the ram and struck him, breaking off both his horns. Now the ram was helpless, and the goat knocked him down and trampled him. No one could rescue the ram from the goat's power.

8The goat became very powerful. But at the height of his power, his large horn was broken off. In the large horn's place grew four prominent horns pointing in the four directions of the earth. 9Then from one of the prominent horns came a small horn whose power grew very great. It extended toward the south and the east and toward the glorious land of Israel. 10Its power reached to the heavens, where it attacked the heavenly army, throwing some of the heavenly beings and some of the stars to the ground and trampling them. 11It even challenged the Commander of heaven's army by canceling the daily sacrifices offered to him and by destroying his Temple. 12The army of heaven was restrained from responding to this rebellion. So the daily sacrifice was halted, and truth was overthrown. The horn succeeded in everything it did.*

13Then I heard two holy ones talking to each other. One of them asked, "How long will the events of this vision last? How long will the rebellion that causes desecration stop the daily sacrifices? How long will the Temple and heaven's army be trampled on?"

14The other replied, "It will take 2,300 evenings and mornings; then the Temple will be made right again."

15As I, Daniel, was trying to understand the meaning of this vision, someone who looked like a man stood in front of me. 16And I heard a human voice calling out from the Ulai River, "Gabriel, tell this man the meaning of his vision."

17As Gabriel approached the place where I was standing, I became so terrified that I fell with my face to the ground. "Son of man," he said, "you must understand that the events you have seen in your vision relate to the time of the end."

18While he was speaking, I fainted and lay there with my face to the ground. But Gabriel roused me with a touch and helped me to my feet.

19Then he said, "I am here to tell you what will happen later in the time of wrath. What you have seen pertains to the very end of time. 20The two-horned ram represents the kings of Media and Persia. 21The shaggy male goat represents the king of Greece,* and the large horn between his eyes represents the first king of the Greek Empire. [22] The four prominent horns that replaced the one large horn show that the Greek Empire will break into four kingdoms, but none as great as the first.

[23] "At the end of their rule, when their sin is at its height, a fierce king, a master of intrigue, will rise to power. [24] He will become very strong, but not by his own power. He will cause a shocking amount of destruction and succeed in everything he does. He will destroy powerful leaders and devastate the holy people. [25] He will be a master of deception and will become arrogant; he will destroy many without warning. He will even take on the Prince of princes in battle, but he will be broken, though not by human power.

[26] "This vision about the 2,300 evenings and mornings* is true. But none of these things will happen for a long time, so keep this vision a secret."

[27] Then I, Daniel, was overcome and lay sick for several days. Afterward I got up and performed my duties for the king, but I was greatly troubled by the vision and could not understand it.

8:1 The original text from this point through chapter 12 is in Hebrew. See note at 2:4.   8:2 Or *the Ulai Gate;* also in 8:16.   8:3 Or *the gate;* also in 8:6.   8:11-12 The meaning of the Hebrew for these verses is uncertain.   8:21 Hebrew *of Javan.*   8:26 Hebrew *about the evenings and mornings;* compare 8:14.

1 JOHN 2:1-17

My dear children, I [John] am writing this to you so that you will not sin. But if anyone does sin, we have an advocate who pleads our case before the Father. He is Jesus Christ, the one who is truly righteous. [2] He himself is the sacrifice that atones for our sins—and not only our sins but the sins of all the world.

[3] And we can be sure that we know him if we obey his commandments. [4] If someone claims, "I know God," but doesn't obey God's commandments, that person is a liar and is not living in the truth. [5] But those who obey God's word truly show how completely they love him. That is how we know

we are living in him. [6] Those who say they live in God should live their lives as Jesus did.

[7] Dear friends, I am not writing a new commandment for you; rather it is an old one you have had from the very beginning. This old commandment—to love one another—is the same message you heard before. [8] Yet it is also new. Jesus lived the truth of this commandment, and you also are living it. For the darkness is disappearing, and the true light is already shining.

[9] If anyone claims, "I am living in the light," but hates a Christian brother or sister,* that person is still living in darkness. [10] Anyone who loves another brother or sister* is living in the light and does not cause others to stumble. [11] But anyone who hates another brother or sister is still living and walking in darkness. Such a person does not know the way to go, having been blinded by the darkness.

[12] I am writing to you who are
God's children
because your sins have been
forgiven through Jesus.*
[13] I am writing to you who are mature
in the faith*
because you know Christ, who
existed from the beginning.
I am writing to you who are young
in the faith
because you have won your battle
with the evil one.
[14] I have written to you who are
God's children
because you know the Father.
I have written to you who are
mature in the faith
because you know Christ,
who existed from the
beginning.
I have written to you who are
young in the faith
because you are strong.
God's word lives in your
hearts,
and you have won your battle
with the evil one.

[15]Do not love this world nor the things it offers you, for when you love the world, you do not have the love of the Father in you. [16]For the world offers only a craving for physical pleasure, a craving for everything we see, and pride in our achievements and possessions. These are not from the Father, but are from this world. [17]And this world is fading away, along with everything that people crave. But anyone who does what pleases God will live forever.

2:9 Greek *hates his brother;* similarly in 2:11.   **2:10** Greek *loves his brother.*   **2:12** Greek *through his name.*   **2:13** Or *to you fathers;* also in 2:14.

PSALM 120:1-7
A song for pilgrims ascending to Jerusalem.

[1] I took my troubles to the LORD;
    I cried out to him, and he
        answered my prayer.
[2] Rescue me, O LORD, from liars
    and from all deceitful people.
[3] O deceptive tongue, what will God
        do to you?
    How will he increase your
        punishment?
[4] You will be pierced with sharp
        arrows
    and burned with glowing coals.

[5] How I suffer in far-off Meshech.
    It pains me to live in
        distant Kedar.
[6] I am tired of living
    among people who hate peace.
[7] I search for peace;
    but when I speak of peace, they
        want war!

PROVERBS 28:25-26
Greed causes fighting; trusting the LORD leads to prosperity. □Those who trust their own insight are foolish, but anyone who walks in wisdom is safe.

DECEMBER 2

DANIEL 9:1–11:1
It was the first year of the reign of Darius the Mede, the son of Ahasuerus, who became king of the Babylonians.* [2]During the first year of his reign, I, Daniel, learned from reading the word of the LORD, as revealed to Jeremiah the prophet, that Jerusalem must lie desolate for seventy years.* [3]So I turned to the LORD God and pleaded with him in prayer and fasting. I also wore rough burlap and sprinkled myself with ashes.

[4]I prayed to the LORD my God and confessed:

"O Lord, you are a great and awesome God! You always fulfill your covenant and keep your promises of unfailing love to those who love you and obey your commands. [5]But we have sinned and done wrong. We have rebelled against you and scorned your commands and regulations. [6]We have refused to listen to your servants the prophets, who spoke on your authority to our kings and princes and ancestors and to all the people of the land.

[7]"Lord, you are in the right; but as you see, our faces are covered with shame. This is true of all of us, including the people of Judah and Jerusalem and all Israel, scattered near and far, wherever you have driven us because of our disloyalty to you. [8]O LORD, we and our kings, princes, and ancestors are covered with shame because we have sinned against you. [9]But the Lord our God is merciful and forgiving, even though we have rebelled against him. [10]We have not obeyed the LORD our God, for we have not followed the instructions he gave us through his servants the prophets. [11]All Israel has disobeyed your instruction and

turned away, refusing to listen to your voice.

"So now the solemn curses and judgments written in the Law of Moses, the servant of God, have been poured down on us because of our sin. 12 You have kept your word and done to us and our rulers exactly as you warned. Never has there been such a disaster as happened in Jerusalem. 13 Every curse written against us in the Law of Moses has come true. Yet we have refused to seek mercy from the LORD our God by turning from our sins and recognizing his truth. 14 Therefore, the LORD has brought upon us the disaster he prepared. The LORD our God was right to do all of these things, for we did not obey him.

15 "O Lord our God, you brought lasting honor to your name by rescuing your people from Egypt in a great display of power. But we have sinned and are full of wickedness. 16 In view of all your faithful mercies, Lord, please turn your furious anger away from your city Jerusalem, your holy mountain. All the neighboring nations mock Jerusalem and your people because of our sins and the sins of our ancestors.

17 "O our God, hear your servant's prayer! Listen as I plead. For your own sake, Lord, smile again on your desolate sanctuary.

18 "O my God, lean down and listen to me. Open your eyes and see our despair. See how your city—the city that bears your name—lies in ruins. We make this plea, not because we deserve help, but because of your mercy.

19 "O Lord, hear. O Lord, forgive. O Lord, listen and act! For your own sake, do not delay, O my God, for your people and your city bear your name."

20 I went on praying and confessing my sin and the sin of my people, pleading with the LORD my God for Jerusalem, his holy mountain. 21 As I was praying, Gabriel, whom I had seen in the earlier vision, came swiftly to me at the time of the evening sacrifice. 22 He explained to me, "Daniel, I have come here to give you insight and understanding. 23 The moment you began praying, a command was given. And now I am here to tell you what it was, for you are very precious to God. Listen carefully so that you can understand the meaning of your vision.

24 "A period of seventy sets of seven* has been decreed for your people and your holy city to finish their rebellion, to put an end to their sin, to atone for their guilt, to bring in everlasting righteousness, to confirm the prophetic vision, and to anoint the Most Holy Place.* 25 Now listen and understand! Seven sets of seven plus sixty-two sets of seven* will pass from the time the command is given to rebuild Jerusalem until a ruler—the Anointed One*—comes. Jerusalem will be rebuilt with streets and strong defenses,* despite the perilous times.

26 "After this period of sixty-two sets of seven,* the Anointed One will be killed, appearing to have accomplished nothing, and a ruler will arise whose armies will destroy the city and the Temple. The end will come with a flood, and war and its miseries are decreed from that time to the very end. 27 The ruler will make a treaty with the people for a period of one set of seven,* but after half this time, he will put an end to the sacrifices and offerings. And as a climax to all his terrible deeds,* he will set up a sacrilegious object that causes desecration,* until the fate decreed for this defiler is finally poured out on him."

10:1 In the third year of the reign of King Cyrus of Persia,* Daniel (also known as Belteshazzar) had another vision. He understood that the vision concerned events certain to happen in the future—times of war and great hardship.

2 When this vision came to me, I, Daniel, had been in mourning for three whole weeks. 3 All that time I had eaten no rich food. No meat or wine crossed

my lips, and I used no fragrant lotions until those three weeks had passed.

[4]On April 23,* as I was standing on the bank of the great Tigris River, [5]I looked up and saw a man dressed in linen clothing, with a belt of pure gold around his waist. [6]His body looked like a precious gem. His face flashed like lightning, and his eyes flamed like torches. His arms and feet shone like polished bronze, and his voice roared like a vast multitude of people.

[7]Only I, Daniel, saw this vision. The men with me saw nothing, but they were suddenly terrified and ran away to hide. [8]So I was left there all alone to see this amazing vision. My strength left me, my face grew deathly pale, and I felt very weak. [9]Then I heard the man speak, and when I heard the sound of his voice, I fainted and lay there with my face to the ground.

[10]Just then a hand touched me and lifted me, still trembling, to my hands and knees. [11]And the man said to me, "Daniel, you are very precious to God, so listen carefully to what I have to say to you. Stand up, for I have been sent to you." When he said this to me, I stood up, still trembling.

[12]Then he said, "Don't be afraid, Daniel. Since the first day you began to pray for understanding and to humble yourself before your God, your request has been heard in heaven. I have come in answer to your prayer. [13]But for twenty-one days the spirit prince* of the kingdom of Persia blocked my way. Then Michael, one of the archangels,* came to help me, and I left him there with the spirit prince of the kingdom of Persia.* [14]Now I am here to explain what will happen to your people in the future, for this vision concerns a time yet to come."

[15]While he was speaking to me, I looked down at the ground, unable to say a word. [16]Then the one who looked like a man* touched my lips, and I opened my mouth and began to speak. I said to the one standing in front of me, "I am filled with anguish because of the vision I have seen, my lord, and I am very weak. [17]How

can someone like me, your servant, talk to you, my lord? My strength is gone, and I can hardly breathe."

[18]Then the one who looked like a man touched me again, and I felt my strength returning. [19]"Don't be afraid," he said, "for you are very precious to God. Peace! Be encouraged! Be strong!"

As he spoke these words to me, I suddenly felt stronger and said to him, "Please speak to me, my lord, for you have strengthened me."

[20]He replied, "Do you know why I have come? Soon I must return to fight against the spirit prince of the kingdom of Persia, and after that the spirit prince of the kingdom of Greece* will come. [21]Meanwhile, I will tell you what is written in the Book of Truth. (No one helps me against these spirit princes except Michael, your spirit prince.* [11:1]I have been standing beside Michael* to support and strengthen him since the first year of the reign of Darius the Mede.)"

9:1 Or *the Chaldeans.*   9:2 See Jer 25:11-12; 29:10.
9:24a Hebrew *seventy sevens.*   9:24b Or *the Most Holy One.*   9:25a Hebrew *Seven sevens plus sixty-two sevens.*
9:25b Or *an anointed one;* similarly in 9:26. Hebrew reads *a messiah.*   9:25c Or *and a moat,* or *and trenches.*
9:26 Hebrew *After sixty-two sevens.*   9:27a Hebrew *for one seven.*   9:27b Hebrew *And on the wing of abominations;* the meaning of the Hebrew is uncertain.   9:27c Hebrew *an abomination of desolation.*   10:1 The third year of Cyrus's reign was 536 B.C.   10:4 Hebrew *On the twenty-fourth day of the first month,* of the ancient Hebrew lunar calendar. This date in the book of Daniel can be cross-checked with dates in surviving Persian records and can be related accurately to our modern calendar. This event occurred on April 23, 536 B.C.   10:13a Hebrew *the prince;* also in 10:13c, 20.   10:13b Hebrew *the chief princes.*
10:13c As in one Greek version; Hebrew reads *and I was left there with the kings of Persia.* The meaning of the Hebrew is uncertain.   10:16 As in most manuscripts of the Masoretic Text; one manuscript of the Masoretic Text and one Greek version read *Then something that looked like a human hand.*   10:20 Hebrew *of Javan.*   10:21 Hebrew *against these except Michael, your prince.*   11:1 Hebrew *him.*

1 JOHN 2:18–3:6

Dear children, the last hour is here. You have heard that the Antichrist is coming, and already many such antichrists have appeared. From this we know that the last hour has come. [19]These people left our churches, but they never really belonged with us; otherwise they would have stayed with us. When they left, it proved that they did not belong with us. [20]But you are not like that, for the Holy

One has given you his Spirit,* and all of you know the truth. ²¹So I am writing to you not because you don't know the truth but because you know the difference between truth and lies. ²²And who is a liar? Anyone who says that Jesus is not the Christ.* Anyone who denies the Father and the Son is an antichrist.* ²³Anyone who denies the Son doesn't have the Father, either. But anyone who acknowledges the Son has the Father also.

²⁴So you must remain faithful to what you have been taught from the beginning. If you do, you will remain in fellowship with the Son and with the Father. ²⁵And in this fellowship we enjoy the eternal life he promised us.

²⁶I am writing these things to warn you about those who want to lead you astray. ²⁷But you have received the Holy Spirit,* and he lives within you, so you don't need anyone to teach you what is true. For the Spirit* teaches you everything you need to know, and what he teaches is true—it is not a lie. So just as he has taught you, remain in fellowship with Christ.

²⁸And now, dear children, remain in fellowship with Christ so that when he returns, you will be full of courage and not shrink back from him in shame.

²⁹Since we know that Christ is righteous, we also know that all who do what is right are God's children.

3:1SEE how very much our Father loves us, for he calls us his children, and that is what we are! But the people who belong to this world don't recognize that we are God's children because they don't know him. ²Dear friends, we are already God's children, but he has not yet shown us what we will be like when Christ appears. But we do know that we will be like him, for we will see him as he really is. ³And all who have this eager expectation will keep themselves pure, just as he is pure.

⁴Everyone who sins is breaking God's law, for all sin is contrary to the law of God. ⁵And you know that Jesus came to take away our sins, and there is no sin in

him. ⁶Anyone who continues to live in him will not sin. But anyone who keeps on sinning does not know him or understand who he is.

2:20 Greek *But you have an anointing from the Holy One.*
2:22a Or *not the Messiah.*   2:22b Or *the antichrist.*
2:27a Greek *the anointing from him.*   2:27b Greek *the anointing.*

PSALM 121:1-8

A song for pilgrims ascending to Jerusalem.

¹ I look up to the mountains—
    does my help come from there?
² My help comes from the LORD,
    who made heaven and earth!

³ He will not let you stumble;
    the one who watches over you will
        not slumber.
⁴ Indeed, he who watches over Israel
    never slumbers or sleeps.

⁵ The LORD himself watches over you!
    The LORD stands beside you as
        your protective shade.
⁶ The sun will not harm you by day,
    nor the moon at night.

⁷ The LORD keeps you from all harm
    and watches over your life.
⁸ The LORD keeps watch over you as
    you come and go,
    both now and forever.

PROVERBS 28:27-28

Whoever gives to the poor will lack nothing, but those who close their eyes to poverty will be cursed. □ When the wicked take charge, people go into hiding. When the wicked meet disaster, the godly flourish.

DECEMBER 3

DANIEL 11:2-35

"Now then, I will reveal the truth to you. Three more Persian kings will reign, to be succeeded by a fourth, far richer than the others. He will use his wealth to stir up everyone to fight against the kingdom of Greece.*

³"Then a mighty king will rise to power who will rule with great authority and accomplish everything he sets out to do. ⁴But at the height of his power, his kingdom will be broken apart and divided into four parts. It will not be ruled by the king's descendants, nor will the kingdom hold the authority it once had. For his empire will be uprooted and given to others.

⁵"The king of the south will increase in power, but one of his own officials will become more powerful than he and will rule his kingdom with great strength.

⁶"Some years later an alliance will be formed between the king of the north and the king of the south. The daughter of the king of the south will be given in marriage to the king of the north to secure the alliance, but she will lose her influence over him, and so will her father. She will be abandoned along with her supporters. ⁷But when one of her relatives* becomes king of the south, he will raise an army and enter the fortress of the king of the north and defeat him. ⁸When he returns to Egypt, he will carry back their idols with him, along with priceless articles of gold and silver. For some years afterward he will leave the king of the north alone.

⁹"Later the king of the north will invade the realm of the king of the south but will soon return to his own land. ¹⁰However, the sons of the king of the north will assemble a mighty army that will advance like a flood and carry the battle as far as the enemy's fortress.

¹¹"Then, in a rage, the king of the south will rally against the vast forces assembled by the king of the north and will defeat them. ¹²After the enemy army is swept away, the king of the south will be filled with pride and will execute many thousands of his enemies. But his success will be short lived.

¹³"A few years later the king of the north will return with a fully equipped army far greater than before. ¹⁴At that time there will be a general uprising against the king of the south. Violent men among your own people will join them in fulfillment of this vision, but they will not succeed. ¹⁵Then the king of the north will come and lay siege to a fortified city and capture it. The best troops of the south will not be able to stand in the face of the onslaught.

¹⁶"The king of the north will march onward unopposed; none will be able to stop him. He will pause in the glorious land of Israel,* intent on destroying it. ¹⁷He will make plans to come with the might of his entire kingdom and will form an alliance with the king of the south. He will give him a daughter in marriage in order to overthrow the kingdom from within, but his plan will fail.

¹⁸"After this, he will turn his attention to the coastland and conquer many cities. But a commander from another land will put an end to his insolence and cause him to retreat in shame. ¹⁹He will take refuge in his own fortresses but will stumble and fall and be seen no more.

²⁰"His successor will send out a tax collector to maintain the royal splendor. But after a very brief reign, he will die, though not from anger or in battle.

²¹"The next to come to power will be a despicable man who is not in line for royal succession. He will slip in when least expected and take over the kingdom by flattery and intrigue. ²²Before him great armies will be swept away, including a covenant prince. ²³With deceitful promises, he will make various alliances. He will become strong despite having only a handful of followers. ²⁴Without warning he will enter the richest areas of the land. Then he will distribute among his followers the plunder and wealth of the rich—something his predecessors had never done. He will plot the overthrow of strongholds, but this will last for only a short while.

²⁵"Then he will stir up his courage and raise a great army against the king of the south. The king of the south will go to battle with a mighty army, but to no avail, for there will be plots against

him. [26]His own household will cause his downfall. His army will be swept away, and many will be killed. [27]Seeking nothing but each other's harm, these kings will plot against each other at the conference table, attempting to deceive each other. But it will make no difference, for the end will come at the appointed time.

[28]"The king of the north will then return home with great riches. On the way he will set himself against the people of the holy covenant, doing much damage before continuing his journey.

[29]"Then at the appointed time he will once again invade the south, but this time the result will be different. [30]For warships from western coastlands* will scare him off, and he will withdraw and return home. But he will vent his anger against the people of the holy covenant and reward those who forsake the covenant.

[31]"His army will take over the Temple fortress, pollute the sanctuary, put a stop to the daily sacrifices, and set up the sacrilegious object that causes desecration.* [32]He will flatter and win over those who have violated the covenant. But the people who know their God will be strong and will resist him.

[33]"Wise leaders will give instruction to many, but these teachers will die by fire and sword, or they will be jailed and robbed. [34]During these persecutions, little help will arrive, and many who join them will not be sincere. [35]And some of the wise will fall victim to persecution. In this way, they will be refined and cleansed and made pure until the time of the end, for the appointed time is still to come."

11:2 Hebrew *of Javan.*   11:7 Hebrew *a branch from her roots.*   11:16 Hebrew *the glorious land.*   11:30 Hebrew *from Kittim.*   11:31 Hebrew *the abomination of desolation.*

1 JOHN 3:7-24

Dear children, don't let anyone deceive you about this: When people do what is right, it shows that they are righteous, even as Christ is righteous. [8]But when people keep on sinning, it shows that they belong to the devil, who has been sinning since the beginning. But the Son of God came to destroy the works of the devil. [9]Those who have been born into God's family do not make a practice of sinning, because God's life* is in them. So they can't keep on sinning, because they are children of God. [10]So now we can tell who are children of God and who are children of the devil. Anyone who does not live righteously and does not love other believers* does not belong to God.

[11]This is the message you have heard from the beginning: We should love one another. [12]We must not be like Cain, who belonged to the evil one and killed his brother. And why did he kill him? Because Cain had been doing what was evil, and his brother had been doing what was righteous. [13]So don't be surprised, dear brothers and sisters,* if the world hates you.

[14]If we love our Christian brothers and sisters,* it proves that we have passed from death to life. But a person who has no love is still dead. [15]Anyone who hates another brother or sister* is really a murderer at heart. And you know that murderers don't have eternal life within them.

[16]**We know what real love is because Jesus gave up his life for us. So we also ought to give up our lives for our brothers and sisters.** [17]If someone has enough money to live well and sees a brother or sister* in need but shows no compassion—how can God's love be in that person?

[18]Dear children, let's not merely say that we love each other; let us show the truth by our actions. [19]Our actions will show that we belong to the truth, so we will be confident when we stand before God. [20]Even if we feel guilty, God is greater than our feelings, and he knows everything.

[21]Dear friends, if we don't feel guilty, we can come to God with bold confidence. [22]And we will receive from him whatever we ask because we obey him and do the things that please him.

23And this is his commandment: We must believe in the name of his Son, Jesus Christ, and love one another, just as he commanded us. 24Those who obey God's commandments remain in fellowship with him, and he with them. And we know he lives in us because the Spirit he gave us lives in us.

3:9 Greek *because his seed.*   3:10 Greek *does not love his brother.*   3:13 Greek *brothers.*   3:14 Greek *the brothers;* similarly in 3:16.   3:15 Greek *hates his brother.* 3:17 Greek *sees his brother.*

PSALM 122:1-9

A song for pilgrims ascending to Jerusalem. A psalm of David.

1 I was glad when they said to me,
    "Let us go to the house of
        the LORD."
2 And now here we are,
        standing inside your gates,
        O Jerusalem.
3 Jerusalem is a well-built city;
        its seamless walls cannot be
        breached.
4 All the tribes of Israel—the LORD's
        people—
    make their pilgrimage here.
    They come to give thanks to the
        name of the LORD,
        as the law requires of Israel.
5 Here stand the thrones where
        judgment is given,
        the thrones of the dynasty of David.

6 Pray for peace in Jerusalem.
    May all who love this city prosper.
7 O Jerusalem, may there be peace
        within your walls
    and prosperity in your palaces.
8 For the sake of my family and
        friends, I will say,
    "May you have peace."
9 For the sake of the house of the
        LORD our God,
    I will seek what is best for you,
        O Jerusalem.

PROVERBS 29:1

Whoever stubbornly refuses to accept criticism will suddenly be destroyed beyond recovery.

DECEMBER 4

DANIEL 11:36–12:13

"The king will do as he pleases, exalting himself and claiming to be greater than every god, even blaspheming the God of gods. He will succeed, but only until the time of wrath is completed. For what has been determined will surely take place. 37He will have no respect for the gods of his ancestors, or for the god loved by women, or for any other god, for he will boast that he is greater than them all. 38Instead of these, he will worship the god of fortresses—a god his ancestors never knew—and lavish on him gold, silver, precious stones, and expensive gifts. 39Claiming this foreign god's help, he will attack the strongest fortresses. He will honor those who submit to him, appointing them to positions of authority and dividing the land among them as their reward.*

40"Then at the time of the end, the king of the south will attack the king of the north. The king of the north will storm out with chariots, charioteers, and a vast navy. He will invade various lands and sweep through them like a flood. 41He will enter the glorious land of Israel,* and many nations will fall, but Moab, Edom, and the best part of Ammon will escape. 42He will conquer many countries, and even Egypt will not escape. 43He will gain control over the gold, silver, and treasures of Egypt, and the Libyans and Ethiopians* will be his servants.

44"But then news from the east and the north will alarm him, and he will set out in great anger to destroy and obliterate many. 45He will stop between the glorious holy mountain and the sea and will pitch his royal tents. But while he is there, his time will suddenly run out, and no one will help him.

12:1"At that time Michael, the archangel* who stands guard over your nation, will arise. Then there will be a time of anguish greater than any since nations first came into existence. But at that time every one of your people whose name is written in the book will be rescued. ²Many of those whose bodies lie dead and buried will rise up, some to everlasting life and some to shame and everlasting disgrace. ³Those who are wise will shine as bright as the sky, and those who lead many to righteousness will shine like the stars forever. ⁴But you, Daniel, keep this prophecy a secret; seal up the book until the time of the end, when many will rush here and there, and knowledge will increase."

⁵Then I, Daniel, looked and saw two others standing on opposite banks of the river. ⁶One of them asked the man dressed in linen, who was now standing above the river, "How long will it be until these shocking events are over?"

⁷The man dressed in linen, who was standing above the river, raised both his hands toward heaven and took a solemn oath by the One who lives forever, saying, "It will go on for a time, times, and half a time. When the shattering of the holy people has finally come to an end, all these things will have happened."

⁸I heard what he said, but I did not understand what he meant. So I asked, "How will all this finally end, my lord?"

⁹But he said, "Go now, Daniel, for what I have said is kept secret and sealed until the time of the end. ¹⁰Many will be purified, cleansed, and refined by these trials. But the wicked will continue in their wickedness, and none of them will understand. Only those who are wise will know what it means.

¹¹"From the time the daily sacrifice is stopped and the sacrilegious object that causes desecration* is set up to be worshiped, there will be 1,290 days. ¹²And blessed are those who wait and remain until the end of the 1,335 days!

¹³"As for you, go your way until the end. You will rest, and then at the end of the days, you will rise again to receive the inheritance set aside for you."

11:39 Or *at a price*. 11:41 Hebrew *the glorious land*.
11:43 Hebrew *Cushites*. 12:1 Hebrew *the great prince*.
12:11 Hebrew *the abomination of desolation*.

1 JOHN 4:1-21

Dear friends, do not believe everyone who claims to speak by the Spirit. You must test them to see if the spirit they have comes from God. For there are many false prophets in the world. ²This is how we know if they have the Spirit of God: If a person claiming to be a prophet* acknowledges that Jesus Christ came in a real body, that person has the Spirit of God. ³But if someone claims to be a prophet and does not acknowledge the truth about Jesus, that person is not from God. Such a person has the spirit of the Antichrist, which you heard is coming into the world and indeed is already here.

⁴But you belong to God, my dear children. You have already won a victory over those people, because the Spirit who lives in you is greater than the spirit who lives in the world. ⁵Those people belong to this world, so they speak from the world's viewpoint, and the world listens to them. ⁶But we belong to God, and those who know God listen to us. If they do not belong to God, they do not listen to us. That is how we know if someone has the Spirit of truth or the spirit of deception.

⁷Dear friends, let us continue to love one another, for love comes from God. Anyone who loves is a child of God and knows God. ⁸But anyone who does not love does not know God, for God is love.

⁹God showed how much he loved us by sending his one and only Son into the world so that we might have eternal life through him. ¹⁰**This is real love—not that we loved God, but that he loved us and sent his Son as a sacrifice to take away our sins.**

¹¹**Dear friends, since God loved us that much, we surely ought to love each other.** ¹²No one has ever seen God. But if we love each other, God lives in us, and his love is brought to full expression in us.

¹³And God has given us his Spirit as proof that we live in him and he in us. ¹⁴Furthermore, we have seen with our own eyes and now testify that the Father sent his Son to be the Savior of the world. ¹⁵All who confess that Jesus is the Son of God have God living in them, and they live in God. ¹⁶We know how much God loves us, and we have put our trust in his love.

God is love, and all who live in love live in God, and God lives in them. ¹⁷And as we live in God, our love grows more perfect. So we will not be afraid on the day of judgment, but we can face him with confidence because we live like Jesus here in this world.

¹⁸Such love has no fear, because perfect love expels all fear. If we are afraid, it is for fear of punishment, and this shows that we have not fully experienced his perfect love. ¹⁹We love each other* because he loved us first.

²⁰If someone says, "I love God," but hates a Christian brother or sister,* that person is a liar; for if we don't love people we can see, how can we love God, whom we cannot see? ²¹And he has given us this command: Those who love God must also love their Christian brothers and sisters.*

4:2 Greek *If a spirit;* similarly in 4:3. 4:19 Greek *We love.* Other manuscripts read *We love God;* still others read *We love him.* 4:20 Greek *hates his brother.* 4:21 Greek *The one who loves God must also love his brother.*

PSALM 123:1-4

A song for pilgrims ascending to Jerusalem.

¹ I lift my eyes to you,
        O God, enthroned in heaven.
² We keep looking to the LORD our
        God for his mercy,
    just as servants keep their eyes on
        their master,
    as a slave girl watches her
        mistress for the slightest signal.
³ Have mercy on us, LORD, have mercy,
        for we have had our fill of
        contempt.
⁴ We have had more than our fill of
        the scoffing of the proud
    and the contempt of the arrogant.

PROVERBS 29:2-4

When the godly are in authority, the people rejoice. But when the wicked are in power, they groan. □ The man who loves wisdom brings joy to his father, but if he hangs around with prostitutes, his wealth is wasted. □ A just king gives stability to his nation, but one who demands bribes destroys it.

DECEMBER
5

HOSEA 1:1–3:5

The LORD gave this message to Hosea son of Beeri during the years when Uzziah, Jotham, Ahaz, and Hezekiah were kings of Judah, and Jeroboam son of Jehoash* was king of Israel.

²When the LORD first began speaking to Israel through Hosea, he said to him, "Go and marry a prostitute,* so that some of her children will be conceived in prostitution. This will illustrate how Israel has acted like a prostitute by turning against the LORD and worshiping other gods."

³So Hosea married Gomer, the daughter of Diblaim, and she became pregnant and gave Hosea a son. ⁴And the LORD said, "Name the child Jezreel, for I am about to punish King Jehu's dynasty to avenge the murders he committed at Jezreel. In fact, I will bring an end to Israel's independence. ⁵I will break its military power in the Jezreel Valley."

⁶Soon Gomer became pregnant again and gave birth to a daughter. And the LORD said to Hosea, "Name your daughter Lo-ruhamah—'Not loved'—for I will no longer show love to the people of Israel or forgive them. ⁷But I will show love to the people of Judah. I will free them from their enemies—not with weapons and armies or horses and

charioteers, but by my power as the LORD their God."

⁸After Gomer had weaned Lo-ruhamah, she again became pregnant and gave birth to a second son. ⁹And the LORD said, "Name him Lo-ammi—'Not my people'—for Israel is not my people, and I am not their God.

¹⁰*"Yet the time will come when Israel's people will be like the sands of the seashore—too many to count! Then, at the place where they were told, 'You are not my people,' it will be said, 'You are children of the living God.' ¹¹Then the people of Judah and Israel will unite together. They will choose one leader for themselves, and they will return from exile together. What a day that will be—the day of Jezreel*—when God will again plant his people in his land.

²:¹*"In that day you will call your brothers Ammi—'My people.' And you will call your sisters Ruhamah—'The ones I love.'

²:² "BUT now bring charges against
    Israel—your mother—
  for she is no longer my wife,
    and I am no longer her husband.
  Tell her to remove the prostitute's
    makeup from her face
    and the clothing that exposes
    her breasts.
³ Otherwise, I will strip her as naked
    as she was on the day she was born.
  I will leave her to die of thirst,
    as in a dry and barren wilderness.
⁴ And I will not love her children,
    for they were conceived in
    prostitution.
⁵ Their mother is a shameless
    prostitute
    and became pregnant in a
    shameful way.
  She said, 'I'll run after other lovers
    and sell myself to them for food
    and water,
  for clothing of wool and linen,
    and for olive oil and drinks.'

⁶ "For this reason I will fence her in
    with thornbushes.

I will block her path with a wall
    to make her lose her way.
⁷ When she runs after her lovers,
    she won't be able to catch them.
  She will search for them
    but not find them.
  Then she will think,
  'I might as well return to my
    husband,
    for I was better off with him than
    I am now.'
⁸ She doesn't realize it was I who gave
    her everything she has—
    the grain, the new wine, the
    olive oil;
  I even gave her silver and gold.
    But she gave all my gifts to Baal.

⁹ "But now I will take back the
    ripened grain and new wine
  I generously provided each
    harvest season.
  I will take away the wool and linen
    clothing
  I gave her to cover her nakedness.
¹⁰ I will strip her naked in public,
    while all her lovers look on.
  No one will be able
    to rescue her from my hands.
¹¹ I will put an end to her annual
    festivals,
    her new moon celebrations, and
    her Sabbath days—
    all her appointed festivals.
¹² I will destroy her grapevines and
    fig trees,
    things she claims her lovers
    gave her.
  I will let them grow into tangled
    thickets,
    where only wild animals will eat
    the fruit.
¹³ I will punish her for all those times
    when she burned incense to her
    images of Baal,
  when she put on her earrings
    and jewels
    and went out to look for
    her lovers
  but forgot all about me,"
    says the LORD.

[14] "But then I will win her back
once again.
I will lead her into the desert
and speak tenderly to her there.
[15] I will return her vineyards to her
and transform the Valley of
Trouble* into a gateway
of hope.
She will give herself to me there,
as she did long ago when she
was young,
when I freed her from her
captivity in Egypt.
[16] When that day comes," says
the LORD,
"you will call me 'my husband'
instead of 'my master.'*
[17] O Israel, I will wipe the many names
of Baal from your lips,
and you will never mention them
again.
[18] On that day I will make a covenant
with all the wild animals and the
birds of the sky
and the animals that scurry along
the ground
so they will not harm you.
I will remove all weapons of war
from the land,
all swords and bows,
so you can live unafraid
in peace and safety.
[19] I will make you my wife forever,
showing you righteousness
and justice,
unfailing love and compassion.
[20] I will be faithful to you and make
you mine,
and you will finally know me as
the LORD.

[21] "In that day, I will answer,"
says the LORD.
"I will answer the sky as it pleads
for clouds.
And the sky will answer the earth
with rain.
[22] Then the earth will answer the
thirsty cries
of the grain, the grapevines, and
the olive trees.
And they in turn will answer,

'Jezreel'—'God plants!'
[23] At that time I will plant a crop
of Israelites
and raise them for myself.
I will show love
to those I called 'Not loved.'*
And to those I called 'Not
my people,'*
I will say, 'Now you are my people.'
And they will reply, 'You are
our God!'"

[3:1]THEN the LORD said to me, "Go and love your wife again, even though she* commits adultery with another lover. This will illustrate that the LORD still loves Israel, even though the people have turned to other gods and love to worship them.*"

[2]So I bought her back for fifteen pieces of silver* and five bushels of barley and a measure of wine.* [3]Then I said to her, "You must live in my house for many days and stop your prostitution. During this time, you will not have sexual relations with anyone, not even with me.*"

[4]This shows that Israel will go a long time without a king or prince, and without sacrifices, sacred pillars, priests,* or even idols! [5]But afterward the people will return and devote themselves to the LORD their God and to David's descendant, their king.* In the last days, they will tremble in awe of the LORD and of his goodness.

1:1 Hebrew *Joash*, a variant spelling of Jehoash.   1:2 Or *a promiscuous woman.*   1:10 Verses 1:10-11 are numbered 2:1-2 in Hebrew text.   1:11 *Jezreel* means "God plants."   2:1 Verses 2:1-23 are numbered 2:3-25 in Hebrew text.   2:15 Hebrew *valley of Achor.*   2:16 Hebrew *'my baal.'*   2:23a Hebrew *Lo-ruhamah;* see 1:6.   2:23b Hebrew *Lo-ammi;* see 1:9.   3:1a Or *Go and love a woman who.*   3:1b Hebrew *love their raisin cakes.*   3:2a Hebrew *15 shekels of silver,* about 6 ounces or 171 grams in weight.   3:2b As in Greek version, which reads *a homer of barley and a measure of wine;* Hebrew reads *a homer* (5 bushels or 182 liters) *of barley and a lethech* (2.5 bushels or 91 liters) *of barley.*   3:3 Or *and I will live with you.*   3:4 Hebrew *ephod,* the vest worn by the priest.   3:5 Hebrew *to David their king.*

1 JOHN 5:1-21

Everyone who believes that Jesus is the Christ* has become a child of God. And everyone who loves the Father loves his children, too. [2]We know we love God's children if we love God and obey his commandments. ³Loving God means keeping his commandments, and his commandments are not burdensome. ⁴For every child of God defeats this evil world, and we achieve this victory through our faith. ⁵And who can win this battle against the world? Only those who believe that Jesus is the Son of God.

⁶And Jesus Christ was revealed as God's Son by his baptism in water and by shedding his blood on the cross*— not by water only, but by water and blood. And the Spirit, who is truth, confirms it with his testimony. ⁷So we have these three witnesses*—⁸the Spirit, the water, and the blood—and all three agree. ⁹Since we believe human testimony, surely we can believe the greater testimony that comes from God. And God has testified about his Son. ¹⁰All who believe in the Son of God know in their hearts that this testimony is true. Those who don't believe this are actually calling God a liar because they don't believe what God has testified about his Son.

¹¹**And this is what God has testified: He has given us eternal life, and this life is in his Son. ¹²Whoever has the Son has life; whoever does not have God's Son does not have life.**

¹³I have written this to you who believe in the name of the Son of God, so that you may know you have eternal life. ¹⁴And we are confident that he hears us whenever we ask for anything that pleases him. ¹⁵And since we know he hears us when we make our requests, we also know that he will give us what we ask for.

¹⁶If you see a Christian brother or sister* sinning in a way that does not lead to death, you should pray, and God will give that person life. But there is a sin that leads to death, and I am not saying you should pray for those who commit it. ¹⁷All wicked actions are sin, but not every sin leads to death.

¹⁸We know that God's children do not make a practice of sinning, for God's Son holds them securely, and the

evil one cannot touch them. ¹⁹We know that we are children of God and that the world around us is under the control of the evil one.

²⁰And we know that the Son of God has come, and he has given us understanding so that we can know the true God.* And now we live in fellowship with the true God because we live in fellowship with his Son, Jesus Christ. He is the only true God, and he is eternal life.

²¹Dear children, keep away from anything that might take God's place in your hearts.*

5:1 Or *the Messiah.* 5:6 Greek *This is he who came by water and blood.* 5:7 A few very late manuscripts add *in heaven—the Father, the Word, and the Holy Spirit, and these three are one. And we have three witnesses on earth.* 5:16 Greek *a brother.* 5:20 Greek *the one who is true.* 5:21 Greek *keep yourselves from idols.*

PSALM 124:1-8

A song for pilgrims ascending to Jerusalem. A psalm of David.

¹ **W**hat if the LORD had not been on our side?
   Let all Israel repeat:
² What if the LORD had not been on our side
   when people attacked us?
³ They would have swallowed us alive in their burning anger.
⁴ The waters would have engulfed us;
   a torrent would have overwhelmed us.
⁵ Yes, the raging waters of their fury
   would have overwhelmed our very lives.

⁶ Praise the LORD,
   who did not let their teeth tear us apart!
⁷ We escaped like a bird from a hunter's trap.
   The trap is broken, and we are free!
⁸ Our help is from the LORD,
   who made heaven and earth.

PROVERBS 29:5-8

To flatter friends is to lay a trap for their feet. □ Evil people are trapped by sin, but the righteous escape, shouting for joy. □ The godly care about the rights of

the poor; the wicked don't care at all.
□Mockers can get a whole town agitated, but the wise will calm anger.

DECEMBER 6

HOSEA 4:1–5:15

Hear the word of the LORD,
O people of Israel!
The LORD has brought charges
against you, saying:
"There is no faithfulness,
no kindness,
no knowledge of God in your
land.

2 You make vows and break them;
you kill and steal and commit
adultery.
There is violence everywhere—
one murder after another.

3 That is why your land is in
mourning,
and everyone is wasting away.
Even the wild animals, the birds
of the sky,
and the fish of the sea are
disappearing.

4 "Don't point your finger at someone
else
and try to pass the blame!
My complaint, you priests,
is with you.*

5 So you will stumble in broad
daylight,
and your false prophets will fall
with you in the night.
And I will destroy Israel, your
mother.

6 My people are being destroyed
because they don't know me.
Since you priests refuse to know me,
I refuse to recognize you as
my priests.
Since you have forgotten the laws
of your God,

I will forget to bless your children.

7 The more priests there are,
the more they sin against me.
They have exchanged the glory
of God
for the shame of idols.*

8 "When the people bring their sin
offerings, the priests get fed.
So the priests are glad when the
people sin!

9 'And what the priests do, the people
also do.'
So now I will punish both priests
and people
for their wicked deeds.

10 They will eat and still be hungry.
They will play the prostitute and
gain nothing from it,
for they have deserted the LORD

11 to worship other gods.

"Wine has robbed my people
of their understanding.

12 They ask a piece of wood for advice!
They think a stick can tell them
the future!
Longing after idols
has made them foolish.
They have played the prostitute,
serving other gods and deserting
their God.

13 They offer sacrifices to idols on the
mountaintops.
They go up into the hills to burn
incense
in the pleasant shade of oaks,
poplars, and terebinth trees.

"That is why your daughters turn
to prostitution,
and your daughters-in-law
commit adultery.

14 But why should I punish them
for their prostitution and
adultery?
For your men are doing the same
thing,
sinning with whores and shrine
prostitutes.
O foolish people! You refuse to
understand,
so you will be destroyed.

15 "Though you, Israel, are a prostitute,
   may Judah avoid such guilt.
   Do not join the false worship at
      Gilgal or Beth-aven,*
   even though they take oaths there
      in the LORD's name.
16 Israel is stubborn,
   like a stubborn heifer.
   So should the LORD feed her
   like a lamb in a lush pasture?
17 Leave Israel* alone,
   because she is married to idolatry.
18 When the rulers of Israel finish
      their drinking,
   off they go to find some
      prostitutes.
   They love shame more than
      honor.*
19 So a mighty wind will sweep them
      away.
   Their sacrifices to idols will bring
      them shame.

5:1 "HEAR this, you priests.
   Pay attention, you leaders of
      Israel.
   Listen, you members of the royal
      family.
   Judgment has been handed down
      against you.
   For you have led the people into
      a snare
   by worshiping the idols at Mizpah
      and Tabor.
2 You have dug a deep pit to trap them
      at Acacia Grove.*
   But I will settle with you for what
      you have done.
3 I know what you are like, O Ephraim.
   You cannot hide yourself from
      me, O Israel.
   You have left me as a prostitute
      leaves her husband;
   you are utterly defiled.
4 Your deeds won't let you return to
      your God.
   You are a prostitute through and
      through,
   and you do not know the LORD.

5 "The arrogance of Israel testifies
      against her;

   Israel and Ephraim will stumble
      under their load of guilt.
   Judah, too, will fall with them.
6 When they come with their flocks
      and herds
   to offer sacrifices to the LORD,
   they will not find him,
   because he has withdrawn
      from them.
7 They have betrayed the honor of the
      LORD,
   bearing children that are not his.
   Now their false religion will devour
      them
   along with their wealth.*

8 "Sound the alarm in Gibeah!
   Blow the trumpet in Ramah!
   Raise the battle cry in Beth-aven*!
   Lead on into battle, O warriors of
      Benjamin!
9 One thing is certain, Israel*:
   On your day of punishment,
   you will become a heap of rubble.

10 "The leaders of Judah have become
      like thieves.*
   So I will pour my anger on them
      like a waterfall.
11 The people of Israel will be crushed
      and broken by my judgment
   because they are determined to
      worship idols.*
12 I will destroy Israel as a moth
      consumes wool.
   I will make Judah as weak as
      rotten wood.

13 "When Israel and Judah saw how
      sick they were,
   Israel turned to Assyria—
   to the great king there—
   but he could neither help nor
      cure them.
14 I will be like a lion to Israel,
   like a strong young lion to Judah.
   I will tear them to pieces!
   I will carry them off,
   and no one will be left to rescue
      them.
15 Then I will return to my place
   until they admit their guilt and
      turn to me.

For as soon as trouble comes,
they will earnestly search
for me."

4:4 Hebrew *Your people are like those with a complaint against the priests.* 4:7 As in Syriac version and an ancient Hebrew tradition; Masoretic Text reads *I will turn their glory into shame.* 4:15 *Beth-aven* means "house of wickedness"; it is being used as another name for Bethel, which means "house of God." 4:17 Hebrew *Ephraim,* referring to the northern kingdom of Israel. 4:18 As in Greek version; the meaning of the Hebrew is uncertain. 5:2 Hebrew *at Shittim.* The meaning of the Hebrew for this sentence is uncertain. 5:7 The meaning of the Hebrew is uncertain. 5:8 *Beth-aven* means "house of wickedness"; it is being used as another name for Bethel, which means "house of God." 5:9 Hebrew *Ephraim,* referring to the northern kingdom of Israel; also in 5:11, 12, 13, 14. 5:10 Hebrew *like those who move a boundary marker.* 5:11 Or *determined to follow human commands.* The meaning of the Hebrew is uncertain.

2 JOHN 1:1-13

This letter is from John, the elder.*

I am writing to the chosen lady and to her children,* whom I love in the truth—as does everyone else who knows the truth—²because the truth lives in us and will be with us forever.

³Grace, mercy, and peace, which come from God the Father and from Jesus Christ—the Son of the Father—will continue to be with us who live in truth and love.

⁴How happy I was to meet some of your children and find them living according to the truth, just as the Father commanded.

⁵I am writing to remind you, dear friends,* that we should love one another. This is not a new commandment, but one we have had from the beginning. ⁶Love means doing what God has commanded us, and he has commanded us to love one another, just as you heard from the beginning.

⁷I say this because many deceivers have gone out into the world. They deny that Jesus Christ came* in a real body. Such a person is a deceiver and an antichrist. ⁸Watch out that you do not lose what we* have worked so hard to achieve. Be diligent so that you receive your full reward. ⁹Anyone who wanders away from this teaching has no relationship with God. But anyone who remains in the teaching of Christ has a relationship with both the Father and the Son.

¹⁰If anyone comes to your meeting and does not teach the truth about Christ, don't invite that person into your home or give any kind of encouragement. ¹¹Anyone who encourages such people becomes a partner in their evil work.

¹²I have much more to say to you, but I don't want to do it with paper and ink. For I hope to visit you soon and talk with you face to face. Then our joy will be complete.

¹³Greetings from the children of your sister,* chosen by God.

1a Greek *From the elder.* 1b Or *the church God has chosen and its members.* 5 Greek *I urge you, lady.* 7 Or *will come.* 8 Some manuscripts read *you.* 13 Or *from the members of your sister church.*

PSALM 125:1-5

A song for pilgrims ascending to Jerusalem.

¹ **Those who trust in the LORD are as secure as Mount Zion;**
 they will not be defeated but will endure forever.
² **Just as the mountains surround Jerusalem,**
 so the LORD surrounds his people, both now and forever.
³ The wicked will not rule the land of the godly,
 for then the godly might be tempted to do wrong.
⁴ O LORD, do good to those who are good,
 whose hearts are in tune with you.
⁵ But banish those who turn to crooked ways, O LORD.
 Take them away with those who do evil.

May Israel have peace!

PROVERBS 29:9-11

If a wise person takes a fool to court, there will be ranting and ridicule but no satisfaction. ☐The bloodthirsty hate blameless people, but the upright seek to help them.* ☐Fools vent their anger, but the wise quietly hold it back.

29:10 Or *The bloodthirsty hate blameless people, / and they seek to kill the upright;* Hebrew reads *The bloodthirsty hate blameless people; / as for the upright, they seek their life.*

DECEMBER 7

HOSEA 6:1–9:17

"Come, let us return to the LORD.
He has torn us to pieces;
  now he will heal us.
He has injured us;
  now he will bandage our wounds.
2 In just a short time he will restore us,
  so that we may live in his
    presence.
3 Oh, that we might know the LORD!
  Let us press on to know him.
He will respond to us as surely as the
    arrival of dawn
  or the coming of rains in early
    spring."

4 "O Israel* and Judah,
  what should I do with you?" asks
    the LORD.
"For your love vanishes like the
    morning mist
  and disappears like dew in the
    sunlight.
5 I sent my prophets to cut you to
    pieces—
  to slaughter you with my words,
  with judgments as inescapable
    as light.
6 I want you to show love,*
  not offer sacrifices.
I want you to know me*
  more than I want burnt
    offerings.
7 But like Adam,* you broke my
    covenant
  and betrayed my trust.

8 "Gilead is a city of sinners,
  tracked with footprints of blood.
9 Priests form bands of robbers,
  waiting in ambush for their
    victims.
They murder travelers along the
    road to Shechem
  and practice every kind of sin.
10 Yes, I have seen something horrible
  in Ephraim and Israel:

My people are defiled by
  prostituting themselves with
  other gods!

11 "O Judah, a harvest of punishment is
    also waiting for you,
  though I wanted to restore the
    fortunes of my people.

7:1 "I WANT to heal Israel,* but its sins
    are too great.
  Samaria is filled with liars.
Thieves are on the inside
  and bandits on the outside!
2 Its people don't realize
  that I am watching them.
Their sinful deeds are all around
    them,
  and I see them all.

3 "The people entertain the king with
    their wickedness,
  and the princes laugh at their lies.
4 They are all adulterers,
  always aflame with lust.
They are like an oven that is kept hot
  while the baker is kneading
  the dough.
5 On royal holidays, the princes get
    drunk with wine,
  carousing with those who mock
    them.
6 Their hearts are like an oven
  blazing with intrigue.
Their plot smolders* through
    the night,
  and in the morning it breaks out
    like a raging fire.
7 Burning like an oven,
  they consume their leaders.
They kill their kings one after
    another,
  and no one cries to me for help.

8 "The people of Israel mingle with
    godless foreigners,
  making themselves as worthless
    as a half-baked cake!
9 Worshiping foreign gods has
  sapped their strength,
  but they don't even know it.
Their hair is gray,
  but they don't realize they're old
    and weak.

10 Their arrogance testifies against
   them,
       yet they don't return to the LORD
       their God
       or even try to find him.

11 "The people of Israel have become
   like silly, witless doves,
       first calling to Egypt, then flying
       to Assyria for help.
12 But as they fly about,
       I will throw my net over them
   and bring them down like a bird
       from the sky.
       I will punish them for all the evil
       they do.*

13 "What sorrow awaits those who
   have deserted me!
       Let them die, for they have
       rebelled against me.
   I wanted to redeem them,
       but they have told lies about me.
14 They do not cry out to me with
   sincere hearts.
       Instead, they sit on their couches
       and wail.
   They cut themselves,* begging
       foreign gods for grain and
       new wine,
       and they turn away from me.
15 I trained them and made them
   strong,
       yet now they plot evil against me.
16 They look everywhere except to the
   Most High.
       They are as useless as a
       crooked bow.
   Their leaders will be killed by their
       enemies
       because of their insolence
       toward me.
   Then the people of Egypt
       will laugh at them.

8:1 "SOUND the alarm!
       The enemy descends like
       an eagle on the people of
       the LORD,
   for they have broken my covenant
       and revolted against my law.
2 Now Israel pleads with me,
       'Help us, for you are our God!'

3 But it is too late.
   The people of Israel have rejected
       what is good,
       and now their enemies will chase
       after them.
4 The people have appointed kings
       without my consent,
       and princes without my
       knowledge.
   By making idols for themselves from
       their silver and gold,
       they have brought about their
       own destruction.

5 "O Samaria, I reject this calf—
       this idol you have made.
   My fury burns against you.
       How long will you be incapable of
       innocence?
6 This calf you worship, O Israel,
       was crafted by your own hands!
   It is not God!
       Therefore, it must be smashed
       to bits.

7 "They have planted the wind
       and will harvest the whirlwind.
   The stalks of grain wither
       and produce nothing to eat.
   And even if there is any grain,
       foreigners will eat it.
8 The people of Israel have been
   swallowed up;
       they lie among the nations like an
       old discarded pot.
9 Like a wild donkey looking for
   a mate,
       they have gone up to Assyria.
   The people of Israel* have sold
       themselves—
       sold themselves to many lovers.
10 But though they have sold
       themselves to many allies,
       I will now gather them together
       for judgment.
   Then they will writhe
       under the burden of the
       great king.

11 "Israel has built many altars to take
   away sin,
       but these very altars became
       places for sinning!

¹² Even though I gave them all my laws,
    they act as if those laws don't
      apply to them.
¹³ The people of Israel love their rituals
    of sacrifice,
      but to me their sacrifices are all
        meaningless.
  I will hold my people accountable
    for their sins,
      and I will punish them.
    They will return to Egypt.
¹⁴ Israel has forgotten its Maker and
    built great palaces,
      and Judah has fortified its cities.
  Therefore, I will send down fire on
    their cities
      and will burn up their fortresses."

^{9:1} O PEOPLE of Israel,
    do not rejoice as other nations do.
  For you have been unfaithful to
    your God,
      hiring yourselves out like
        prostitutes,
      worshiping other gods on every
        threshing floor.
² So now your harvests will be too
    small to feed you.
      There will be no grapes for
        making new wine.
³ You may no longer stay here in the
    LORD's land.
      Instead, you will return to Egypt,
    and in Assyria you will eat food
      that is ceremonially unclean.
⁴ There you will make no offerings of
    wine to the LORD.
      None of your sacrifices there will
        please him.
  They will be unclean, like food
    touched by a person in
      mourning.
    All who present such sacrifices
      will be defiled.
  They may eat this food themselves,
    but they may not offer it to the
      LORD.
⁵ What then will you do on festival
    days?
      How will you observe the LORD's
        festivals?

⁶ Even if you escape destruction
    from Assyria,
      Egypt will conquer you, and
        Memphis* will bury you.
  Nettles will take over your treasures
    of silver;
      thistles will invade your ruined
        homes.
⁷ The time of Israel's punishment
    has come;
      the day of payment is here.
    Soon Israel will know this all
      too well.
  Because of your great sin and
    hostility,
      you say, "The prophets are crazy
      and the inspired men are fools!"
⁸ The prophet is a watchman over
    Israel* for my God,
      yet traps are laid for him
        wherever he goes.
    He faces hostility even in the
      house of God.
⁹ The things my people do are as
    depraved
      as what they did in Gibeah
        long ago.
  God will not forget.
    He will surely punish them for
      their sins.

¹⁰ The LORD says, "O Israel, when I first
    found you,
      it was like finding fresh grapes in
        the desert.
  When I saw your ancestors,
    it was like seeing the first ripe figs
      of the season.
  But then they deserted me for
    Baal-peor,
      giving themselves to that
        shameful idol.
  Soon they became vile,
    as vile as the god they worshiped.
¹¹ The glory of Israel will fly away
    like a bird,
      for your children will not be born
  or grow in the womb
      or even be conceived.
¹² Even if you do have children who
    grow up,
      I will take them from you.

It will be a terrible day when
I turn away
and leave you alone.
[13] I have watched Israel become as
beautiful as Tyre.
But now Israel will bring out her
children for slaughter."

[14] O LORD, what should I request for
your people?
I will ask for wombs that don't
give birth
and breasts that give no milk.

[15] The LORD says, "All their wickedness
began at Gilgal;
there I began to hate them.
I will drive them from my land
because of their evil actions.
I will love them no more
because all their leaders
are rebels.
[16] The people of Israel are struck
down.
Their roots are dried up,
and they will bear no more fruit.
And if they give birth,
I will slaughter their beloved
children."

[17] My God will reject the people
of Israel
because they will not listen
or obey.
They will be wanderers,
homeless among the nations.

6:4 Hebrew *Ephraim*, referring to the northern kingdom
of Israel. **6:6a** Greek version reads *to show mercy.*
Compare Matt 9:13; 12:7. **6:6b** Hebrew *to know God.*
6:7 Or *But at Adam.* **7:1** Hebrew *Ephraim*, referring
to the northern kingdom of Israel; also in 7:8, 11.
7:6 Hebrew *Their baker sleeps.* **7:12** Hebrew *I will punish
them because of what was reported against them in the
assembly.* **7:14** As in Greek version; Hebrew reads *They
gather together.* **8:9** Hebrew *Ephraim*, referring to the
northern kingdom of Israel; also in 8:11. **9:6** Memphis
was the capital of northern Egypt. **9:8** Hebrew *Ephraim,*
referring to the northern kingdom of Israel; also in 9:11,
13, 16.

3 JOHN 1:1-15

This letter is from John, the elder.*

I am writing to Gaius, my dear friend,
whom I love in the truth.
[2] Dear friend, I hope all is well with
you and that you are as healthy in body
as you are strong in spirit. [3] Some of the
traveling teachers* recently returned
and made me very happy by telling me
about your faithfulness and that you are
living according to the truth. [4] I could
have no greater joy than to hear that my
children are following the truth.

[5] Dear friend, you are being faithful to
God when you care for the traveling
teachers who pass through, even
though they are strangers to you. [6] They
have told the church here of your loving
friendship. Please continue providing
for such teachers in a manner that
pleases God. [7] For they are traveling for
the Lord,* and they accept nothing
from people who are not believers.* [8] So
we ourselves should support them so
that we can be their partners as they
teach the truth.

[9] I wrote to the church about this, but
Diotrephes, who loves to be the leader,
refuses to have anything to do with us.
[10] When I come, I will report some of the
things he is doing and the evil accusations he is making against us. Not only
does he refuse to welcome the traveling
teachers, he also tells others not to help
them. And when they do help, he puts
them out of the church.

[11] Dear friend, don't let this bad example influence you. Follow only what
is good. Remember that those who do
good prove that they are God's children,
and those who do evil prove that they do
not know God.*

[12] Everyone speaks highly of De-
metrius, as does the truth itself. We
ourselves can say the same for him, and
you know we speak the truth.

[13] I have much more to say to you, but
I don't want to write it with pen and ink.
[14] For I hope to see you soon, and then
we will talk face to face.

[15] *Peace be with you.
Your friends here send you their
greetings. Please give my personal
greetings to each of our friends there.

1 Greek *From the elder.* **3** Greek *the brothers;* also in
verses 5 and 10. **7a** Greek *They went out on behalf of the
Name.* **7b** Greek *from Gentiles.* **11** Greek *they have not
seen God.* **15** Some English translations combine
verses 14 and 15 into verse 14.

PSALM 126:1-6
A song for pilgrims ascending to Jerusalem.

¹ **W**hen the Lord brought back his
    exiles to Jerusalem,*
    it was like a dream!
² We were filled with laughter,
    and we sang for joy.
And the other nations said,
    "What amazing things the Lord
        has done for them."
³ Yes, the Lord has done amazing
    things for us!
    What joy!

⁴ **Restore our fortunes, Lord,**
    as streams renew the desert.
⁵ **Those who plant in tears**
    will harvest with shouts of joy.
⁶ **They weep as they go to plant**
    their seed,
    but they sing as they return
    with the harvest.

126:1 Hebrew *Zion.*

PROVERBS 29:12-14
If a ruler pays attention to liars, all his
advisers will be wicked. □ The poor and
the oppressor have this in common—
the Lord gives sight to the eyes of both.
□ If a king judges the poor fairly, his
throne will last forever.

DECEMBER
8

HOSEA 10:1–14:9
How prosperous Israel is—
    a luxuriant vine loaded with fruit.
But the richer the people get,
    the more pagan altars they build.
The more bountiful their harvests,
    the more beautiful their sacred
        pillars.
² The hearts of the people are fickle;
    they are guilty and must be
        punished.

The Lord will break down
    their altars
    and smash their sacred pillars.
³ Then they will say, "We have no king
    because we didn't fear the Lord.
But even if we had a king,
    what could he do for us anyway?"
⁴ They spout empty words
    and make covenants they don't
        intend to keep.
So injustice springs up among them
    like poisonous weeds in a
        farmer's field.

⁵ The people of Samaria tremble
    in fear
    for what might happen to their
        calf idol at Beth-aven.*
The people mourn and the
    priests wail,
    because its glory will be stripped
        away.*
⁶ This idol will be carted away
    to Assyria,
    a gift to the great king there.
Ephraim will be ridiculed and Israel
    will be shamed,
    because its people have trusted in
        this idol.
⁷ Samaria and its king will be cut off;
    they will float away like driftwood
        on an ocean wave.
⁸ And the pagan shrines of Aven,* the
    place of Israel's sin, will
        crumble.
    Thorns and thistles will grow up
        around their altars.
They will beg the mountains,
    "Bury us!"
    and plead with the hills, "Fall
        on us!"

⁹ The Lord says, "O Israel, ever since
    Gibeah,
    there has been only sin and
        more sin!
You have made no progress
    whatsoever.
    Was it not right that the wicked
        men of Gibeah were attacked?
¹⁰ Now whenever it fits my plan,
    I will attack you, too.

I will call out the armies of the
nations
to punish you for your multiplied
sins.

11 "Israel* is like a trained heifer
treading out the grain—
an easy job she loves.
But I will put a heavy yoke on her
tender neck.
I will force Judah to pull the plow
and Israel* to break up the hard
ground.
12 I said, 'Plant the good seeds
of righteousness,
and you will harvest a crop
of love.
Plow up the hard ground of your
hearts,
for now is the time to seek
the Lord,
that he may come
and shower righteousness upon
you.'
13 "But you have cultivated wickedness
and harvested a thriving crop
of sins.
You have eaten the fruit of lies—
trusting in your military might,
believing that great armies
could make your nation safe.
14 Now the terrors of war
will rise among your people.
All your fortifications will fall,
just as when Shalman destroyed
Beth-arbel.
Even mothers and children
were dashed to death there.
15 You will share that fate, Bethel,
because of your great wickedness.
When the day of judgment dawns,
the king of Israel will be
completely destroyed.

11:1 "When Israel was a child,
I loved him,
and I called my son out of Egypt.
2 But the more I* called to him,
the farther he moved from me,
offering sacrifices to the images
of Baal
and burning incense to idols.

3 I myself taught Israel* how to walk,
leading him along by the hand.
But he doesn't know or even care
that it was I who took care of him.
4 I led Israel along
with my ropes of kindness
and love.
I lifted the yoke from his neck,
and I myself stooped to feed him.

5 "But since my people refuse to
return to me,
they will return to Egypt
and will be forced to serve
Assyria.
6 War will swirl through their cities;
their enemies will crash through
their gates.
They will destroy them,
trapping them in their own evil
plans.
7 For my people are determined
to desert me.
They call me the Most High,
but they don't truly honor me.

8 "Oh, how can I give you up, Israel?
How can I let you go?
How can I destroy you like Admah
or demolish you like Zeboiim?
My heart is torn within me,
and my compassion overflows.
9 No, I will not unleash my fierce
anger.
I will not completely
destroy Israel,
for I am God and not a mere mortal.
I am the Holy One living
among you,
and I will not come to destroy.
10 For someday the people will
follow me.
I, the Lord, will roar like a lion.
And when I roar,
my people will return trembling
from the west.
11 Like a flock of birds, they will come
from Egypt.
Trembling like doves, they will
return from Assyria.
And I will bring them home again,"
says the Lord.

12*Israel surrounds me with lies
and deceit,
but Judah still obeys God
and is faithful to the Holy One.*

12:1* THE people of Israel* feed on the
wind;
they chase after the east wind all
day long.
They pile up lies and violence;
they are making an alliance
with Assyria
while sending olive oil to buy
support from Egypt.

2 Now the LORD is bringing charges
against Judah.
He is about to punish Jacob* for
all his deceitful ways,
and pay him back for all he
has done.
3 Even in the womb,
Jacob struggled with his brother;
when he became a man,
he even fought with God.
4 Yes, he wrestled with the angel
and won.
He wept and pleaded for a
blessing from him.
There at Bethel he met God face
to face,
and God spoke to him*—
5 the LORD God of Heaven's Armies,
the LORD is his name!
6 So now, come back to your God.
Act with love and justice,
and always depend on him.

7 But no, the people are like crafty
merchants
selling from dishonest scales—
they love to cheat.
8 Israel boasts, "I am rich!
I've made a fortune all by myself!
No one has caught me cheating!
My record is spotless!"

9 "But I am the LORD your God,
who rescued you from slavery
in Egypt.
And I will make you live in
tents again,

as you do each year at the Festival
of Shelters.*
10 I sent my prophets to warn you
with many visions and parables."

11 But the people of Gilead are
worthless
because of their idol worship.
And in Gilgal, too, they sacrifice
bulls;
their altars are lined up like the
heaps of stone
along the edges of a plowed field.
12 Jacob fled to the land of Aram,
and there he* earned a wife by
tending sheep.
13 Then by a prophet
the LORD brought Jacob's
descendants* out of Egypt;
and by that prophet
they were protected.
14 But the people of Israel
have bitterly provoked the LORD,
so their Lord will now sentence
them to death
in payment for their sins.

13:1 WHEN the tribe of Ephraim spoke,
the people shook with fear,
for that tribe was important
in Israel.
But the people of Ephraim sinned by
worshiping Baal
and thus sealed their destruction.
2 Now they continue to sin by making
silver idols,
images shaped skillfully with
human hands.
"Sacrifice to these," they cry,
"and kiss the calf idols!"
3 Therefore, they will disappear like
the morning mist,
like dew in the morning sun,
like chaff blown by the wind,
like smoke from a chimney.

4 "I have been the LORD your God
ever since I brought you out
of Egypt.
You must acknowledge no God
but me,
for there is no other savior.
5 I took care of you in the wilderness,

in that dry and thirsty land.
⁶ But when you had eaten and were
   satisfied,
   you became proud and forgot me.
⁷ So now I will attack you like a lion,
   like a leopard that lurks along
      the road.
⁸ Like a bear whose cubs have been
      taken away,
   I will tear out your heart.
   I will devour you like a hungry
      lioness
   and mangle you like a wild
      animal.

⁹ "You are about to be destroyed,
      O Israel—
   yes, by me, your only helper.
¹⁰ Now where is* your king?
   Let him save you!
   Where are all the leaders of the
      land,
   the king and the officials you
      demanded of me?
¹¹ In my anger I gave you kings,
   and in my fury I took them away.

¹² "Ephraim's guilt has been collected,
   and his sin has been stored up
      for punishment.
¹³ Pain has come to the people
   like the pain of childbirth,
   but they are like a child
      who resists being born.
   The moment of birth has arrived,
   but they stay in the womb!

¹⁴ "Should I ransom them from
      the grave*?
   Should I redeem them from
      death?
   O death, bring on your terrors!
   O grave, bring on your plagues!*
   For I will not take pity on them.
¹⁵ Ephraim was the most fruitful of all
      his brothers,
   but the east wind—a blast from
      the LORD—
   will arise in the desert.
   All their flowing springs will run dry,
   and all their wells will disappear.
   Every precious thing they own

will be plundered and carried
   away.
¹⁶ The people of Samaria
   must bear the consequences of
      their guilt
   because they rebelled against
      their God.
   They will be killed by an invading
      army,
   their little ones dashed to death
      against the ground,
   their pregnant women ripped
      open by swords."

¹⁴:¹ RETURN, O Israel, to the LORD
      your God,
   for your sins have brought you
      down.
² Bring your confessions, and return
      to the LORD.
   Say to him,
   "Forgive all our sins and graciously
      receive us,
   so that we may offer you our
      praises.
³ Assyria cannot save us,
   nor can our war-horses.
   Never again will we say to the idols
      we have made,
      'You are our gods.'
   No, in you alone
      do the orphans find mercy."

⁴ The LORD says,
   "Then I will heal you of your
      faithlessness;
   my love will know no bounds,
   for my anger will be gone forever.
⁵ I will be to Israel
   like a refreshing dew from
      heaven.
   Israel will blossom like the lily;
   it will send roots deep into the soil
      like the cedars in Lebanon.
⁶ Its branches will spread out like
      beautiful olive trees,
   as fragrant as the cedars
      of Lebanon.
⁷ My people will again live under
      my shade.
   They will flourish like grain and
      blossom like grapevines.

They will be as fragrant as the
wines of Lebanon.

⁸ "O Israel,* stay away from idols!
I am the one who answers your
prayers and cares for you.
I am like a tree that is always green;
all your fruit comes from me."

⁹ Let those who are wise understand
these things.
Let those with discernment listen
carefully.
The paths of the LORD are true and
right,
and righteous people live by
walking in them.
But in those paths sinners
stumble and fall.

10:5a *Beth-aven* means "house of wickedness"; it is being used as another name for Bethel, which means "house of God." 10:5b Or *because it will be taken away into exile.* 10:8 *Aven* is a reference to Beth-aven; see 10:5a and the note there. 10:11a Hebrew *Ephraim*, referring to the northern kingdom of Israel. 10:11b Hebrew *Jacob*. The names "Jacob" and "Israel" are often interchanged throughout the Old Testament, referring sometimes to the individual patriarch and sometimes to the nation. 11:2 As in Greek version; Hebrew reads *they*. 11:3 Hebrew *Ephraim*, referring to the northern kingdom of Israel; also in 11:8, 9, 12. 11:12a Verse 11:12 is numbered 12:1 in Hebrew text. 11:12b Or *and Judah is unruly against God, the faithful Holy One*. The meaning of the Hebrew is uncertain. 12:1a Verses 12:1-14 are numbered 12:2-15 in Hebrew text. 12:1b Hebrew *Ephraim*, referring to the northern kingdom of Israel; also in 12:8, 14. 12:2 *Jacob* sounds like the Hebrew word for "deceiver." 12:4 As in Greek and Syriac versions; Hebrew reads *to us*. 12:9 Hebrew *as in the days of your appointed feast*. 12:12 Hebrew *Israel*. See note on 10:11b. 12:13 Hebrew *brought Israel*. See note on 10:11b. 13:10 As in Greek and Syriac versions and Latin Vulgate; Hebrew reads *I will be*. 13:14a Hebrew *Sheol*; also in 13:14b. 13:14b Greek version reads *O death, where is your punishment? / O grave* [Hades], *where is your sting?* Compare 1 Cor 15:55. 14:8 Hebrew *Ephraim*, referring to the northern kingdom of Israel.

JUDE 1:1-25

This letter is from Jude, a slave of Jesus Christ and a brother of James.

I am writing to all who have been called by God the Father, who loves you and keeps you safe in the care of Jesus Christ.*

²May God give you more and more mercy, peace, and love.

³Dear friends, I had been eagerly planning to write to you about the salvation we all share. But now I find that I must write about something else, urg-

ing you to defend the faith that God has entrusted once for all time to his holy people. ⁴I say this because some ungodly people have wormed their way into your churches, saying that God's marvelous grace allows us to live immoral lives. The condemnation of such people was recorded long ago, for they have denied our only Master and Lord, Jesus Christ.

⁵So I want to remind you, though you already know these things, that Jesus* first rescued the nation of Israel from Egypt, but later he destroyed those who did not remain faithful. ⁶And I remind you of the angels who did not stay within the limits of authority God gave them but left the place where they belonged. God has kept them securely chained in prisons of darkness, waiting for the great day of judgment. ⁷And don't forget Sodom and Gomorrah and their neighboring towns, which were filled with immorality and every kind of sexual perversion. Those cities were destroyed by fire and serve as a warning of the eternal fire of God's judgment.

⁸In the same way, these people—who claim authority from their dreams—live immoral lives, defy authority, and scoff at supernatural beings.* ⁹But even Michael, one of the mightiest of the angels,* did not dare accuse the devil of blasphemy, but simply said, "The Lord rebuke you!" (This took place when Michael was arguing with the devil about Moses' body.) ¹⁰But these people scoff at things they do not understand. Like unthinking animals, they do whatever their instincts tell them, and so they bring about their own destruction. ¹¹What sorrow awaits them! For they follow in the footsteps of Cain, who killed his brother. Like Balaam, they deceive people for money. And like Korah, they perish in their rebellion.

¹²When these people eat with you in your fellowship meals commemorating the Lord's love, they are like dangerous reefs that can shipwreck you.* They are like shameless shepherds who care only for themselves. They are like clouds

blowing over the land without giving any rain. They are like trees in autumn that are doubly dead, for they bear no fruit and have been pulled up by the roots. [13] They are like wild waves of the sea, churning up the foam of their shameful deeds. They are like wandering stars, doomed forever to blackest darkness.

[14] Enoch, who lived in the seventh generation after Adam, prophesied about these people. He said, "Listen! The Lord is coming with countless thousands of his holy ones [15] to execute judgment on the people of the world. He will convict every person of all the ungodly things they have done and for all the insults that ungodly sinners have spoken against him."*

[16] These people are grumblers and complainers, living only to satisfy their desires. They brag loudly about themselves, and they flatter others to get what they want.

[17] But you, my dear friends, must remember what the apostles of our Lord Jesus Christ said. [18] They told you that in the last times there would be scoffers whose purpose in life is to satisfy their ungodly desires. [19] These people are the ones who are creating divisions among you. They follow their natural instincts because they do not have God's Spirit in them.

[20] **But you, dear friends, must build each other up in your most holy faith, pray in the power of the Holy Spirit,*** [21] **and await the mercy of our Lord Jesus Christ, who will bring you eternal life. In this way, you will keep yourselves safe in God's love.**

[22] And you must show mercy to those whose faith is wavering. [23] Rescue others by snatching them from the flames of judgment. Show mercy to still others,* but do so with great caution, hating the sins that contaminate their lives.*

[24] Now all glory to God, who is able to keep you from falling away and will bring you with great joy into his glorious presence without a single fault. [25] All glory to him who alone is God, our Savior through Jesus Christ our Lord. All glory, majesty, power, and authority are his before all time, and in the present, and beyond all time! Amen.

1 Or *keeps you for Jesus Christ.*   5 As in the best manuscripts; various other manuscripts read *[the] Lord,* or *God,* or *Christ;* one reads *God Christ.*   8 Greek *at glorious ones,* which are probably evil angels.   9 Greek *Michael, the archangel.*   12 Or *they are contaminants among you;* or *they are stains.*   14-15 The quotation comes from intertestamental literature: Enoch 1:9.   20 Greek *pray in the Holy Spirit.*   22-23a Some manuscripts have only two categories of people: (1) those whose faith is wavering and therefore need to be snatched from the flames of judgment, and (2) those who need to be shown mercy.   23b Greek *with fear, hating even the clothing stained by the flesh.*

PSALM 127:1-5
A song for pilgrims ascending to Jerusalem. A psalm of Solomon.

[1] **U**nless the Lord builds a house,
    the work of the builders is
        wasted.
Unless the Lord protects a city,
    guarding it with sentries will
        do no good.
[2] It is useless for you to work so hard
    from early morning until late
        at night,
anxiously working for food to eat;
    for God gives rest to his loved
        ones.

[3] Children are a gift from the Lord;
    they are a reward from him.
[4] Children born to a young man
    are like arrows in a warrior's
        hands.
[5] How joyful is the man whose quiver
    is full of them!
He will not be put to shame when
    he confronts his accusers at the
        city gates.

PROVERBS 29:15-17
To discipline a child produces wisdom, but a mother is disgraced by an undisciplined child. □ When the wicked are in authority, sin flourishes, but the godly will live to see their downfall. □ Discipline your children, and they will give you peace of mind and will make your heart glad.

DECEMBER 9

JOEL 1:1–3:21

The LORD gave this message to Joel son of Pethuel.

2 Hear this, you leaders of the people.
  Listen, all who live in the land.
 In all your history,
  has anything like this happened before?
3 Tell your children about it in the years to come,
  and let your children tell their children.
 Pass the story down from generation to generation.
4 After the cutting locusts finished eating the crops,
  the swarming locusts took what was left!
 After them came the hopping locusts,
  and then the stripping locusts,* too!

5 Wake up, you drunkards, and weep!
  Wail, all you wine-drinkers!
 All the grapes are ruined,
  and all your sweet wine is gone.
6 A vast army of locusts* has invaded my land,
  a terrible army too numerous to count.
 Its teeth are like lions' teeth,
  its fangs like those of a lioness.
7 It has destroyed my grapevines
  and ruined my fig trees,
 stripping their bark and destroying it,
  leaving the branches white and bare.

8 Weep like a bride dressed in black,
  mourning the death of her husband.
9 For there is no grain or wine
  to offer at the Temple of the LORD.
 So the priests are in mourning.
  The ministers of the LORD are weeping.

10 The fields are ruined,
  the land is stripped bare.
 The grain is destroyed,
  the grapes have shriveled,
  and the olive oil is gone.

11 Despair, all you farmers!
  Wail, all you vine growers!
 Weep, because the wheat and barley—
  all the crops of the field—are ruined.
12 The grapevines have dried up,
  and the fig trees have withered.
 The pomegranate trees, palm trees, and apple trees—
  all the fruit trees—have dried up.
 And the people's joy has dried up with them.

13 Dress yourselves in burlap and weep, you priests!
  Wail, you who serve before the altar!
 Come, spend the night in burlap, you ministers of my God.
 For there is no grain or wine
  to offer at the Temple of your God.
14 Announce a time of fasting;
  call the people together for a solemn meeting.
 Bring the leaders
  and all the people of the land
 into the Temple of the LORD your God,
  and cry out to him there.
15 The day of the LORD is near,
  the day when destruction comes from the Almighty.
  How terrible that day will be!

16 Our food disappears before our very eyes.
  No joyful celebrations are held in the house of our God.
17 The seeds die in the parched ground,
  and the grain crops fail.
 The barns stand empty,
  and granaries are abandoned.
18 How the animals moan with hunger!
  The herds of cattle wander about confused,

because they have no pasture.
The flocks of sheep and goats
bleat in misery.

¹⁹ LORD, help us!
The fire has consumed the
wilderness pastures,
and flames have burned up all the
trees.
²⁰ Even the wild animals cry out to you
because the streams have
dried up,
and fire has consumed the
wilderness pastures.

^{2:1} SOUND the alarm in Jerusalem*!
Raise the battle cry on my holy
mountain!
Let everyone tremble in fear
because the day of the LORD is
upon us.
² It is a day of darkness and gloom,
a day of thick clouds and deep
blackness.
Suddenly, like dawn spreading
across the mountains,
a great and mighty army appears.
Nothing like it has been seen before
or will ever be seen again.

³ Fire burns in front of them,
and flames follow after them.
Ahead of them the land lies
as beautiful as the Garden
of Eden.
Behind them is nothing but
desolation;
not one thing escapes.
⁴ They look like horses;
they charge forward like war
horses.*
⁵ Look at them as they leap along the
mountaintops.
Listen to the noise they make—
like the rumbling of chariots,
like the roar of fire sweeping across
a field of stubble,
or like a mighty army moving
into battle.

⁶ Fear grips all the people;
every face grows pale with terror.
⁷ The attackers march like warriors
and scale city walls like soldiers.

Straight forward they march,
never breaking rank.
⁸ They never jostle each other;
each moves in exactly the right
position.
They break through defenses
without missing a step.
⁹ They swarm over the city
and run along its walls.
They enter all the houses,
climbing like thieves through
the windows.
¹⁰ The earth quakes as they advance,
and the heavens tremble.
The sun and moon grow dark,
and the stars no longer shine.

¹¹ The LORD is at the head of the
column.
He leads them with a shout.
This is his mighty army,
and they follow his orders.
The day of the LORD is an awesome,
terrible thing.
Who can possibly survive?

¹² That is why the LORD says,
"Turn to me now, while there
is time.
Give me your hearts.
Come with fasting, weeping,
and mourning.
¹³ Don't tear your clothing in
your grief,
but tear your hearts instead."
Return to the LORD your God,
for he is merciful and
compassionate,
slow to get angry and filled with
unfailing love.
He is eager to relent and not
punish.
¹⁴ Who knows? Perhaps he will give
you a reprieve,
sending you a blessing instead
of this curse.
Perhaps you will be able to offer
grain and wine
to the LORD your God as before.

¹⁵ Blow the ram's horn in Jerusalem!
Announce a time of fasting;
call the people together

for a solemn meeting.

16 Gather all the people—
the elders, the children, and even
the babies.
Call the bridegroom from his
quarters
and the bride from her private
room.

17 Let the priests, who minister in the
Lord's presence,
stand and weep between the
entry room to the Temple and
the altar.
Let them pray, "Spare your people,
Lord!
Don't let your special possession
become an object of mockery.
Don't let them become a joke for
unbelieving foreigners who say,
'Has the God of Israel left them?'"

18 Then the Lord will pity his people
and jealously guard the honor of
his land.

19 The Lord will reply,
"Look! I am sending you grain and
new wine and olive oil,
enough to satisfy your needs.
You will no longer be an object
of mockery
among the surrounding nations.

20 I will drive away these armies from
the north.
I will send them into the parched
wastelands.
Those in the front will be driven into
the Dead Sea,
and those at the rear into the
Mediterranean.*
The stench of their rotting bodies
will rise over the land."

Surely the Lord has done great
things!

21 Don't be afraid, my people.
Be glad now and rejoice,
for the Lord has done great
things.

22 Don't be afraid, you animals
of the field,
for the wilderness pastures will
soon be green.

The trees will again be filled
with fruit;
fig trees and grapevines will be
loaded down once more.

23 Rejoice, you people of Jerusalem!
Rejoice in the Lord your God!
For the rain he sends demonstrates
his faithfulness.
Once more the autumn rains
will come,
as well as the rains of spring.

24 The threshing floors will again be
piled high with grain,
and the presses will overflow with
new wine and olive oil.

25 The Lord says, "I will give you back
what you lost
to the swarming locusts, the
hopping locusts,
the stripping locusts, and the cutting
locusts.*
It was I who sent this great
destroying army against you.

26 Once again you will have all the
food you want,
and you will praise the Lord
your God,
who does these miracles for you.
Never again will my people be
disgraced.

27 Then you will know that I am among
my people Israel,
that I am the Lord your God, and
there is no other.
Never again will my people
be disgraced.

28*"Then, after doing all those things,
I will pour out my Spirit upon
all people.
Your sons and daughters will
prophesy.
Your old men will dream dreams,
and your young men will
see visions.

29 In those days I will pour out
my Spirit
even on servants—men and
women alike.

30 And I will cause wonders in the
heavens and on the earth—

blood and fire and columns of
smoke.
³¹ The sun will become dark,
and the moon will turn blood red
before that great and terrible*
day of the LORD arrives.
³² But everyone who calls on the name
of the LORD
will be saved,
for some on Mount Zion in
Jerusalem will escape,
just as the LORD has said.
These will be among the survivors
whom the LORD has called.

³:1*"AT the time of those events," says
the LORD,
"when I restore the prosperity of
Judah and Jerusalem,
² I will gather the armies of the world
into the valley of Jehoshaphat.*
There I will judge them
for harming my people, my
special possession,
for scattering my people among
the nations,
and for dividing up my land.
³ They cast lots to decide which
of my people
would be their slaves.
They traded boys to obtain prostitutes
and sold girls for enough wine to
get drunk.

⁴"What do you have against me, Tyre
and Sidon and you cities of Philistia? Are
you trying to take revenge on me? If you
are, then watch out! I will strike swiftly
and pay you back for everything you
have done. ⁵You have taken my silver
and gold and all my precious treasures,
and have carried them off to your pagan
temples. ⁶You have sold the people of Judah and Jerusalem to the Greeks,* so they
could take them far from their homeland.
⁷"But I will bring them back from all
the places to which you sold them, and I
will pay you back for everything you
have done. ⁸I will sell your sons and
daughters to the people of Judah, and
they will sell them to the people of Arabia,* a nation far away. I, the LORD, have
spoken!"

⁹ Say to the nations far and wide:
"Get ready for war!
Call out your best warriors.
Let all your fighting men advance
for the attack.
¹⁰ Hammer your plowshares into
swords
and your pruning hooks into
spears.
Train even your weaklings to
be warriors.
¹¹ Come quickly, all you nations
everywhere.
Gather together in the valley."

And now, O LORD, call out your
warriors!

¹² "Let the nations be called to arms.
Let them march to the valley of
Jehoshaphat.
There I, the LORD, will sit
to pronounce judgment on
them all.
¹³ Swing the sickle,
for the harvest is ripe.*
Come, tread the grapes,
for the winepress is full.
The storage vats are overflowing
with the wickedness of these
people."

¹⁴ Thousands upon thousands are
waiting in the valley of
decision.
There the day of the LORD will
soon arrive.
¹⁵ The sun and moon will grow dark,
and the stars will no longer shine.
¹⁶ The LORD's voice will roar
from Zion
and thunder from Jerusalem,
and the heavens and the earth
will shake.
But the LORD will be a refuge
for his people,
a strong fortress for the people
of Israel.

¹⁷ "Then you will know that I, the
LORD your God,
live in Zion, my holy mountain.
Jerusalem will be holy forever,

and foreign armies will never
conquer her again.
¹⁸ In that day the mountains will drip
with sweet wine,
and the hills will flow with milk.
Water will fill the streambeds
of Judah,
and a fountain will burst forth
from the LORD's Temple,
watering the arid valley
of acacias.*
¹⁹ But Egypt will become a wasteland
and Edom will become a
wilderness,
because they attacked the people
of Judah
and killed innocent people in
their land.

²⁰ "But Judah will be filled with people
forever,
and Jerusalem will endure
through all generations.
²¹ I will pardon my people's crimes,
which I have not yet pardoned;
and I, the LORD, will make my home
in Jerusalem* with my people."

1:4 The precise identification of the four kinds of locusts
mentioned here is uncertain.   1:6 Hebrew *A nation.*
2:1 Hebrew *Zion;* also in 2:15, 23.   2:4 Or *like charioteers.*
2:20 Hebrew *into the eastern sea, . . . into the western sea.*
2:25 The precise identification of the four kinds of locusts
mentioned here is uncertain.   2:28 Verses 2:28-32 are
numbered 3:1-5 in Hebrew text.   2:31 Greek version reads
glorious.   3:1 Verses 3:1-21 are numbered 4:1-21 in
Hebrew text.   3:2 *Jehoshaphat* means "the LORD judges."
3:6 Hebrew *to the peoples of Javan.*   3:8 Hebrew *to the
Sabeans.*   3:13 Greek version reads *for the harvest time
has come.* Compare Mark 4:29.   3:18 Hebrew *valley of
Shittim.*   3:21 Hebrew *Zion.*

REVELATION 1:1-20

This is a revelation from* Jesus Christ,
which God gave him to show his servants the events that must soon* take
place. He sent an angel to present this
revelation to his servant John, ²who
faithfully reported everything he saw.
This is his report of the word of God and
the testimony of Jesus Christ.

³God blesses the one who reads the
words of this prophecy to the church,
and he blesses all who listen to its message and obey what it says, for the time
is near.

⁴This letter is from John to the seven
churches in the province of Asia.*

Grace and peace to you from the one
who is, who always was, and who is still to
come; from the sevenfold Spirit* before
his throne; ⁵and from Jesus Christ. He is
the faithful witness to these things, the
first to rise from the dead, and the ruler
of all the kings of the world.

All glory to him who loves us and has
freed us from our sins by shedding his
blood for us. ⁶He has made us a Kingdom of priests for God his Father. All
glory and power to him forever and
ever! Amen.

⁷ Look! He comes with the clouds
of heaven.
And everyone will see him—
even those who pierced him.
And all the nations of the world
will mourn for him.
Yes! Amen!

⁸"I am the Alpha and the Omega—the
beginning and the end,"* says the Lord
God. "I am the one who is, who always
was, and who is still to come—the Almighty One."

⁹I, John, am your brother and your
partner in suffering and in God's Kingdom and in the patient endurance to
which Jesus calls us. I was exiled to the island of Patmos for preaching the word of
God and for my testimony about Jesus.
¹⁰It was the Lord's Day, and I was worshiping in the Spirit.* Suddenly, I heard
behind me a loud voice like a trumpet
blast. ¹¹It said, "Write in a book* everything you see, and send it to the seven
churches in the cities of Ephesus, Smyrna, Pergamum, Thyatira, Sardis, Philadelphia, and Laodicea."

¹²When I turned to see who was
speaking to me, I saw seven gold lampstands. ¹³And standing in the middle of
the lampstands was someone like the
Son of Man.* He was wearing a long robe
with a gold sash across his chest. ¹⁴His
head and his hair were white like wool,
as white as snow. And his eyes were like
flames of fire. ¹⁵His feet were like polished bronze refined in a furnace, and

his voice thundered like mighty ocean waves. ¹⁶He held seven stars in his right hand, and a sharp two-edged sword came from his mouth. And his face was like the sun in all its brilliance.

¹⁷When I saw him, I fell at his feet as if I were dead. But he laid his right hand on me and said, "Don't be afraid! I am the First and the Last. ¹⁸I am the living one. I died, but look—I am alive forever and ever! And I hold the keys of death and the grave.*

¹⁹"Write down what you have seen— both the things that are now happening and the things that will happen.* ²⁰This is the meaning of the mystery of the seven stars you saw in my right hand and the seven gold lampstands: The seven stars are the angels* of the seven churches, and the seven lampstands are the seven churches."

1:1a Or *of.*   1:1b Or *suddenly,* or *quickly.*   1:4a *Asia* was a Roman province in what is now western Turkey. 1:4b Greek *the seven spirits.*   1:8 Greek *I am Alpha and the Omega,* referring to the first and last letters of the Greek alphabet.   1:10 Or *in spirit.*   1:11 Or *on a scroll.* 1:13 Or *like a son of man.* See Dan 7:13. "Son of Man" is a title Jesus used for himself.   1:18 Greek *and Hades.* 1:19 Or *what you have seen and what they mean—the things that have already begun to happen.*   1:20 Or *the messengers.*

PSALM 128:1-6
A song for pilgrims ascending to Jerusalem.

¹ **H**ow joyful are those who fear the LORD—
    all who follow his ways!
² You will enjoy the fruit of your labor.
    How joyful and prosperous you will be!
³ Your wife will be like a fruitful grapevine,
    flourishing within your home.
    Your children will be like vigorous young olive trees
    as they sit around your table.
⁴ That is the LORD's blessing
    for those who fear him.

⁵ May the LORD continually bless you from Zion.
    May you see Jerusalem prosper as long as you live.

⁶ May you live to enjoy your grandchildren.
    May Israel have peace!

PROVERBS 29:18
When people do not accept divine guidance, they run wild. But whoever obeys the law is joyful.

DECEMBER 10

AMOS 1:1–3:15
This message was given to Amos, a shepherd from the town of Tekoa in Judah. He received this message in visions two years before the earthquake, when Uzziah was king of Judah and Jeroboam II, the son of Jehoash,* was king of Israel.

²This is what he saw and heard:

"The LORD roars from his Temple on Mount Zion;
    his voice thunders from Jerusalem!
Suddenly, the lush pastures of the shepherds dry up.
    All the grass on Mount Carmel withers and dies."

³This is what the LORD says:

"The people of Damascus have sinned again and again,*
    and I will not let them go unpunished!
They beat down my people in Gilead
    as grain is threshed with iron sledges.
⁴ So I will send down fire on King Hazael's palace,
    and the fortresses of King Ben-hadad will be destroyed.
⁵ I will break down the gates of Damascus
    and slaughter the people in the valley of Aven.

I will destroy the ruler in Beth-eden,
   and the people of Aram will go as
      captives to Kir,"
   says the LORD.

⁶This is what the LORD says:

"The people of Gaza have sinned
      again and again,
   and I will not let them go
      unpunished!
They sent whole villages into exile,
   selling them as slaves to Edom.
⁷ So I will send down fire on the walls
      of Gaza,
   and all its fortresses will be
      destroyed.
⁸ I will slaughter the people
      of Ashdod
   and destroy the king of Ashkelon.
Then I will turn to attack Ekron,
   and the few Philistines still left
      will be killed,"
   says the Sovereign LORD.

⁹This is what the LORD says:

"The people of Tyre have sinned
      again and again,
   and I will not let them go
      unpunished!
They broke their treaty of
      brotherhood with Israel,
   selling whole villages as slaves
      to Edom.
¹⁰ So I will send down fire on the walls
      of Tyre,
   and all its fortresses will be
      destroyed."

¹¹This is what the LORD says:

"The people of Edom have sinned
      again and again,
   and I will not let them go
      unpunished!
They chased down their relatives,
      the Israelites, with swords,
   showing them no mercy.
In their rage, they slashed them
      continually
   and were unrelenting in their
      anger.
¹² So I will send down fire on Teman,

and the fortresses of Bozrah will
      be destroyed."

¹³This is what the LORD says:

"The people of Ammon have sinned
      again and again,
   and I will not let them go
      unpunished!
When they attacked Gilead to
      extend their borders,
   they ripped open pregnant
      women with their swords.
¹⁴ So I will send down fire on the walls
      of Rabbah,
   and all its fortresses will be
      destroyed.
The battle will be upon them with
      shouts,
   like a whirlwind in a mighty
      storm.
¹⁵ And their king* and his princes will
      go into exile together,"
   says the LORD.

2:1THIS is what the LORD says:

"The people of Moab have sinned
      again and again,*
   and I will not let them go
      unpunished!
They desecrated the bones of
      Edom's king,
   burning them to ashes.
² So I will send down fire on the land
      of Moab,
   and all the fortresses in Kerioth
      will be destroyed.
The people will fall in the noise
      of battle,
   as the warriors shout and the
      ram's horn sounds.
³ And I will destroy their king
   and slaughter all their princes,"
   says the LORD.

⁴This is what the LORD says:

"The people of Judah have sinned
      again and again,
   and I will not let them
      go unpunished!
They have rejected the instruction
      of the LORD,

refusing to obey his decrees.
They have been led astray by the
same lies
that deceived their ancestors.
⁵ So I will send down fire on Judah,
and all the fortresses of Jerusalem
will be destroyed."

⁶This is what the LORD says:

"The people of Israel have sinned
again and again,
and I will not let them go
unpunished!
They sell honorable people for silver
and poor people for a pair
of sandals.
⁷ They trample helpless people in
the dust
and shove the oppressed out
of the way.
Both father and son sleep with the
same woman,
corrupting my holy name.
⁸ At their religious festivals,
they lounge in clothing their
debtors put up as security.
In the house of their god,
they drink wine bought with
unjust fines.

⁹ "But as my people watched,
I destroyed the Amorites,
though they were as tall as cedars
and as strong as oaks.
I destroyed the fruit on their
branches
and dug out their roots.
¹⁰ It was I who rescued you from Egypt
and led you through the desert for
forty years,
so you could possess the land of
the Amorites.
¹¹ I chose some of your sons to be
prophets
and others to be Nazirites.
Can you deny this, my people
of Israel?"
asks the LORD.
¹² "But you caused the Nazirites to sin
by making them drink wine,
and you commanded the
prophets, 'Shut up!'

¹³ "So I will make you groan
like a wagon loaded down with
sheaves of grain.
¹⁴ Your fastest runners will not
get away.
The strongest among you will
become weak.
Even mighty warriors will be unable
to save themselves.
¹⁵   The archers will not stand
their ground.
The swiftest runners won't be fast
enough to escape.
Even those riding horses won't be
able to save themselves.
¹⁶ On that day the most courageous of
your fighting men
will drop their weapons and run
for their lives,"
says the LORD.

³:¹LISTEN to this message that the LORD
has spoken against you, O people of Israel and Judah—against the entire family I rescued from Egypt:

² "From among all the families
on the earth,
I have been intimate with you
alone.
That is why I must punish you
for all your sins."

³ Can two people walk together
without agreeing on the
direction?
⁴ Does a lion ever roar in a thicket
without first finding a victim?
Does a young lion growl in
its den
without first catching its prey?
⁵ Does a bird ever get caught in a trap
that has no bait?
Does a trap spring shut
when there's nothing to catch?
⁶ When the ram's horn blows
a warning,
shouldn't the people be alarmed?
Does disaster come to a city
unless the LORD has planned it?

⁷ Indeed, the Sovereign LORD never
does anything

until he reveals his plans to his
servants the prophets.

⁸ The lion has roared—
so who isn't frightened?
The Sovereign LORD has spoken—
so who can refuse to proclaim
his message?

⁹ Announce this to the leaders of
Philistia*
and to the great ones of Egypt:
"Take your seats now on the hills
around Samaria,
and witness the chaos and
oppression in Israel."

¹⁰ "My people have forgotten how to
do right,"
says the LORD.
"Their fortresses are filled with
wealth
taken by theft and violence.
¹¹ Therefore," says the Sovereign
LORD,
"an enemy is coming!
He will surround them and shatter
their defenses.
Then he will plunder all their
fortresses."

¹² This is what the LORD says:

"A shepherd who tries to rescue a
sheep from a lion's mouth
will recover only two legs or a
piece of an ear.
So it will be for the Israelites in
Samaria lying on luxurious
beds,
and for the people of Damascus
reclining on couches.*

¹³ "Now listen to this, and announce it
throughout all Israel,*" says the Lord,
the LORD God of Heaven's Armies.

¹⁴ "On the very day I punish Israel
for its sins,
I will destroy the pagan altars
at Bethel.
The horns of the altar will be cut off
and fall to the ground.
¹⁵ And I will destroy the beautiful
homes of the wealthy—

their winter mansions and their
summer houses, too—
all their palaces filled with ivory,"
says the LORD.

1:1 Hebrew *Joash*, a variant spelling of Jehoash.
1:3 Hebrew *have committed three sins, even four;* also in
1:6, 9, 11, 13.   1:15 Hebrew *malcam*, possibly referring to
their god Molech.   2:1 Hebrew *have committed three sins,
even four;* also in 2:4, 6.   3:9 Hebrew *Ashdod*.   3:12 Or *So
it will be when the Israelites in Samaria are rescued / with
only a broken bed and a tattered pillow.*   3:13 Hebrew *the
house of Jacob.* The names "Jacob" and "Israel" are often
interchanged throughout the Old Testament, referring
sometimes to the individual patriarch and sometimes to
the nation.

REVELATION 2:1-17

"**W**rite this letter to the angel* of the
church in Ephesus. This is the message
from the one who holds the seven stars
in his right hand, the one who walks
among the seven gold lampstands:

²"I know all the things you do. I have
seen your hard work and your
patient endurance. I know you don't
tolerate evil people. You have
examined the claims of those who
say they are apostles but are not.
You have discovered they are liars.
³ You have patiently suffered for me
without quitting.

⁴"But I have this complaint
against you. You don't love me or
each other as you did at first!* ⁵Look
how far you have fallen! Turn back
to me and do the works you did at
first. If you don't repent, I will come
and remove your lampstand from its
place among the churches. ⁶ But this
is in your favor: You hate the evil
deeds of the Nicolaitans, just as I do.

⁷"Anyone with ears to hear must
listen to the Spirit and understand
what he is saying to the churches.
To everyone who is victorious I will
give fruit from the tree of life in the
paradise of God.

⁸"Write this letter to the angel of the
church in Smyrna. This is the message
from the one who is the First and the
Last, who was dead but is now alive:

⁹"I know about your suffering and
your poverty—but you are rich! I

know the blasphemy of those opposing you. They say they are Jews, but they are not, because their synagogue belongs to Satan. [10]**Don't be afraid of what you are about to suffer. The devil will throw some of you into prison to test you. You will suffer for ten days. But if you remain faithful even when facing death, I will give you the crown of life.**

[11]"Anyone with ears to hear must listen to the Spirit and understand what he is saying to the churches. Whoever is victorious will not be harmed by the second death.

[12]"Write this letter to the angel of the church in Pergamum. This is the message from the one with the sharp two-edged sword:

[13]"I know that you live in the city where Satan has his throne, yet you have remained loyal to me. You refused to deny me even when Antipas, my faithful witness, was martyred among you there in Satan's city. [14]"But I have a few complaints against you. You tolerate some among you whose teaching is like that of Balaam, who showed Balak how to trip up the people of Israel. He taught them to sin by eating food offered to idols and by committing sexual sin. [15]In a similar way, you have some Nicolaitans among you who follow the same teaching. [16]Repent of your sin, or I will come to you suddenly and fight against them with the sword of my mouth.

[17]"Anyone with ears to hear must listen to the Spirit and understand what he is saying to the churches. To everyone who is victorious I will give some of the manna that has been hidden away in heaven. And I will give to each one a white stone, and on the stone will be engraved a new name that no one understands except the one who receives it.

2:1 Or *the messenger;* also in 2:8, 12, 18.   **2:4** Greek *You have lost your first love.*

PSALM 129:1-8
A song for pilgrims ascending to Jerusalem.

[1] **F**rom my earliest youth my enemies
   have persecuted me.
   Let all Israel repeat this:
[2] From my earliest youth my enemies
   have persecuted me,
   but they have never defeated me.
[3] My back is covered with cuts,
   as if a farmer had plowed long
      furrows.
[4] But the LORD is good;
   he has cut me free from the ropes
      of the ungodly.

[5] May all who hate Jerusalem*
   be turned back in shameful defeat.
[6] May they be as useless as grass
   on a rooftop,
   turning yellow when only half
      grown,
[7] ignored by the harvester,
   despised by the binder.
[8] And may those who pass by
   refuse to give them this blessing:
   "The LORD bless you;
   we bless you in the LORD's name."

129:5 Hebrew *Zion.*

PROVERBS 29:19-20
Words alone will not discipline a servant; the words may be understood, but they are not heeded. □ There is more hope for a fool than for someone who speaks without thinking.

DECEMBER
11

AMOS 4:1–6:14
Listen to me, you fat cows*
   living in Samaria,
you women who oppress the poor
   and crush the needy,
and who are always calling to your
   husbands,

"Bring us another drink!"

2 The Sovereign Lord has sworn this
     by his holiness:
"The time will come when you will
     be led away
  with hooks in your noses.
Every last one of you will be
     dragged away
  like a fish on a hook!

3 You will be led out through the ruins
     of the wall;
  you will be thrown from your
     fortresses,*"
  says the Lord.

4 "Go ahead and offer sacrifices to the
     idols at Bethel.
  Keep on disobeying at Gilgal.
Offer sacrifices each morning,
  and bring your tithes every
     three days.

5 Present your bread made with yeast
  as an offering of thanksgiving.
Then give your extra voluntary
     offerings
  so you can brag about it everywhere!
This is the kind of thing you
     Israelites love to do,"
  says the Sovereign Lord.

6 "I brought hunger to every city
  and famine to every town.
But still you would not return to me,"
  says the Lord.

7 "I kept the rain from falling
  when your crops needed it
     the most.
I sent rain on one town
  but withheld it from another.
Rain fell on one field,
  while another field withered
     away.

8 People staggered from town to town
     looking for water,
  but there was never enough.
But still you would not return to me,"
  says the Lord.

9 "I struck your farms and vineyards
  with blight and mildew.
  Locusts devoured all your fig and
     olive trees.

But still you would not return to me,"
  says the Lord.

10 "I sent plagues on you
  like the plagues I sent on Egypt
     long ago.
I killed your young men in war
  and led all your horses away.*
The stench of death filled the air!
But still you would not return to me,"
  says the Lord.

11 "I destroyed some of your cities,
  as I destroyed* Sodom and
     Gomorrah.
Those of you who survived
  were like charred sticks pulled
     from a fire.
But still you would not return to me,"
  says the Lord.

12 "Therefore, I will bring upon you all
     the disasters I have announced.
Prepare to meet your God in
     judgment, you people of Israel!"

13 For the Lord is the one who shaped
     the mountains,
  stirs up the winds, and reveals his
     thoughts to mankind.
He turns the light of dawn into
     darkness
  and treads on the heights of the
     earth.
  The Lord God of Heaven's Armies
     is his name!

5:1 Listen, you people of Israel! Listen to
this funeral song I am singing:

2 "The virgin Israel has fallen,
  never to rise again!
She lies abandoned on the ground,
  with no one to help her up."

3 The Sovereign Lord says:

"When a city sends a thousand men
     to battle,
  only a hundred will return.
When a town sends a hundred,
  only ten will come back alive."

4 Now this is what the Lord says to the
family of Israel:

"Come back to me and live!
5 Don't worship at the pagan altars
       at Bethel;
   don't go to the shrines at Gilgal
       or Beersheba.
For the people of Gilgal will be
       dragged off into exile,
   and the people of Bethel will be
       reduced to nothing."
6 Come back to the LORD and live!
Otherwise, he will roar through
       Israel* like a fire,
   devouring you completely.
Your gods in Bethel
   won't be able to quench
       the flames.

7 You twist justice, making it a bitter
       pill for the oppressed.
   You treat the righteous like dirt.

8 It is the LORD who created the stars,
       the Pleiades and Orion.
   He turns darkness into morning
       and day into night.
   He draws up water from the oceans
       and pours it down as rain
           on the land.
   The LORD is his name!
9 With blinding speed and power he
       destroys the strong,
   crushing all their defenses.

10 How you hate honest judges!
   How you despise people who tell
       the truth!
11 You trample the poor,
       stealing their grain through taxes
           and unfair rent.
   Therefore, though you build
       beautiful stone houses,
   you will never live in them.
   Though you plant lush vineyards,
       you will never drink wine from
           them.
12 For I know the vast number
       of your sins
   and the depth of your rebellions.
   You oppress good people by taking
       bribes
   and deprive the poor of justice in
       the courts.

13 So those who are smart keep their
       mouths shut,
   for it is an evil time.

14 Do what is good and run from evil
       so that you may live!
   Then the LORD God of Heaven's
       Armies will be your helper,
   just as you have claimed.
15 Hate evil and love what is good;
       turn your courts into true halls
           of justice.
   Perhaps even yet the LORD God of
       Heaven's Armies
   will have mercy on the remnant of
       his people.*

16Therefore, this is what the Lord, the
LORD God of Heaven's Armies, says:

"There will be crying in all the
       public squares
   and mourning in every street.
Call for the farmers to weep with you,
   and summon professional
       mourners to wail.
17 There will be wailing in every vineyard,
   for I will destroy them all,"
       says the LORD.

18 What sorrow awaits you who say,
   "If only the day of the LORD were
       here!"
   You have no idea what you are
       wishing for.
   That day will bring darkness, not
       light.
19 In that day you will be like a man
       who runs from a lion—
   only to meet a bear.
   Escaping from the bear, he leans his
       hand against a wall in his
           house—
   and he's bitten by a snake.
20 Yes, the day of the LORD will be dark
       and hopeless,
   without a ray of joy or hope.

21 "I hate all your show and pretense—
       the hypocrisy of your religious
           festivals and solemn
               assemblies.
22 I will not accept your burnt
       offerings and grain offerings.

I won't even notice all your choice
        peace offerings.
23 Away with your noisy hymns of
        praise!
    I will not listen to the music of
        your harps.
24 Instead, I want to see a mighty flood
        of justice,
        an endless river of righteous living.

25"Was it to me you were bringing
sacrifices and offerings during the
forty years in the wilderness, Israel?
26No, you served your pagan gods—Sak-
kuth your king god and Kaiwan your
star god—the images you made for
yourselves. 27So I will send you into exile, to a land east of Damascus,*" says
the LORD, whose name is the God of
Heaven's Armies.

6:1 WHAT sorrow awaits you who lounge
        in luxury in Jerusalem,*
    and you who feel secure
        in Samaria!
    You are famous and popular
        in Israel,
        and people go to you for help.
2 But go over to Calneh
        and see what happened there.
    Then go to the great city of Hamath
        and down to the Philistine
        city of Gath.
    You are no better than they were,
        and look at how they were
        destroyed.
3 You push away every thought of
        coming disaster,
        but your actions only bring the
        day of judgment closer.
4 How terrible for you who sprawl
        on ivory beds
    and lounge on your couches,
    eating the meat of tender lambs
        from the flock
    and of choice calves fattened
        in the stall.
5 You sing trivial songs to the sound
        of the harp
    and fancy yourselves to be great
        musicians like David.
6 You drink wine by the bowlful

and perfume yourselves with
        fragrant lotions.
    You care nothing about the ruin
        of your nation.*
7 Therefore, you will be the first to be
        led away as captives.
    Suddenly, all your parties will end.

8The Sovereign LORD has sworn by his
own name, and this is what he, the LORD
God of Heaven's Armies, says:

    "I despise the arrogance of Israel,*
        and I hate their fortresses.
    I will give this city
        and everything in it to their
        enemies."

(9If there are ten men left in one house,
they will all die. 10And when a relative
who is responsible to dispose of the
dead* goes into the house to carry out
the bodies, he will ask the last survivor,
"Is anyone else with you?" When the
person begins to swear, "No, by . . . ," he
will interrupt and say, "Stop! Don't even
mention the name of the LORD.")

11 When the LORD gives the command,
        homes both great and small will
        be smashed to pieces.

12 Can horses gallop over boulders?
        Can oxen be used to plow them?
    But that's how foolish you are when
        you turn justice into poison
    and the sweet fruit of
        righteousness into bitterness.
13 And you brag about your conquest
        of Lo-debar.*
    You boast, "Didn't we take
        Karnaim* by our own strength?"

14 "O people of Israel, I am about to
        bring an enemy nation
        against you,"
    says the LORD God of Heaven's
        Armies.
    "They will oppress you throughout
        your land—
    from Lebo-hamath in the north
        to the Arabah Valley in the south."

4:1 Hebrew *you cows of Bashan.*   4:3 Or *thrown out
toward Harmon*, possibly a reference to Mount Hermon.
4:10 Or *and slaughtered your captured horses.*

4:11 Hebrew *as when God destroyed.*   5:6 Hebrew *the house of Joseph.*   5:15 Hebrew *the remnant of Joseph.* 5:26-27 Greek version reads *No, you carried your pagan gods—the shrine of Molech, the star of your god Rephan, and the images you made for yourselves. So I will send you into exile, to a land east of Damascus.* Compare Acts 7:43. 6:1 Hebrew *in Zion.*   6:6 Hebrew *of Joseph.*   6:8 Hebrew *Jacob.* See note on 3:13.   6:10 Or *to burn the dead.* The meaning of the Hebrew is uncertain.   6:13a *Lo-debar* means "nothing."   6:13b *Karnaim* means "horns," a term that symbolizes strength.

REVELATION 2:18–3:6

"**W**rite this letter to the angel of the church in Thyatira. This is the message from the Son of God, whose eyes are like flames of fire, whose feet are like polished bronze:

¹⁹"I know all the things you do. I have seen your love, your faith, your service, and your patient endurance. And I can see your constant improvement in all these things.

²⁰"But I have this complaint against you. You are permitting that woman—that Jezebel who calls herself a prophet—to lead my servants astray. She teaches them to commit sexual sin and to eat food offered to idols. ²¹I gave her time to repent, but she does not want to turn away from her immorality.

²²"Therefore, I will throw her on a bed of suffering,* and those who commit adultery with her will suffer greatly unless they repent and turn away from her evil deeds. ²³I will strike her children dead. Then all the churches will know that I am the one who searches out the thoughts and intentions of every person. And I will give to each of you whatever you deserve.

²⁴"But I also have a message for the rest of you in Thyatira who have not followed this false teaching ('deeper truths,' as they call them—depths of Satan, actually). I will ask nothing more of you ²⁵except that you hold tightly to what you have until I come. ²⁶To all who are victorious, who obey me to the very end,

To them I will give authority over all the nations.

²⁷ They will rule the nations with
an iron rod
and smash them like clay pots.*

²⁸They will have the same authority I received from my Father, and I will also give them the morning star! ²⁹"Anyone with ears to hear must listen to the Spirit and understand what he is saying to the churches.

³:¹"WRITE this letter to the angel* of the church in Sardis. This is the message from the one who has the sevenfold Spirit* of God and the seven stars:

"I know all the things you do, and that you have a reputation for being alive—but you are dead. ²Wake up! Strengthen what little remains, for even what is left is almost dead. I find that your actions do not meet the requirements of my God. ³Go back to what you heard and believed at first; hold to it firmly. Repent and turn to me again. If you don't wake up, I will come to you suddenly, as unexpected as a thief.

⁴"Yet there are some in the church in Sardis who have not soiled their clothes with evil. They will walk with me in white, for they are worthy. ⁵**All who are victorious will be clothed in white. I will never erase their names from the Book of Life, but I will announce before my Father and his angels that they are mine.**

⁶"Anyone with ears to hear must listen to the Spirit and understand what he is saying to the churches."

2:22 Greek *a bed.*   2:26-27 Ps 2:8-9 (Greek Version). 3:1a Or *the messenger;* also in 3:7, 14.   3:1b Greek *the seven spirits.*

PSALM 130:1-8
A song for pilgrims ascending to Jerusalem.

¹ **F**rom the depths of despair,
O LORD,
I call for your help.
² Hear my cry, O Lord.
Pay attention to my prayer.

³ LORD, if you kept a record of our sins,
who, O Lord, could ever survive?
⁴ But you offer forgiveness,
that we might learn to fear you.

⁵ I am counting on the LORD;
yes, I am counting on him.
I have put my hope in his word.
⁶ I long for the Lord
more than sentries long for
the dawn,
yes, more than sentries long
for the dawn.

⁷ O Israel, hope in the LORD;
for with the LORD there is
unfailing love.
His redemption overflows.
⁸ He himself will redeem Israel
from every kind of sin.

PROVERBS 29:21-22
A servant pampered from childhood
will become a rebel. □ An angry person
starts fights; a hot-tempered person
commits all kinds of sin.

DECEMBER 12

AMOS 7:1–9:15
The Sovereign LORD showed me [Amos]
a vision. I saw him preparing to send a
vast swarm of locusts over the land.
This was after the king's share had been
harvested from the fields and as the
main crop was coming up. ²In my vision
the locusts ate every green plant in
sight. Then I said, "O Sovereign LORD,
please forgive us or we will not survive,
for Israel* is so small."

³ So the LORD relented from this plan.
"I will not do it," he said.

⁴Then the Sovereign LORD showed me
another vision. I saw him preparing to
punish his people with a great fire. The
fire had burned up the depths of the sea
and was devouring the entire land. ⁵Then

I said, "O Sovereign LORD, please stop or
we will not survive, for Israel is so small."

⁶Then the LORD relented from this
plan, too. "I will not do that either," said
the Sovereign LORD.

⁷Then he showed me another vision.
I saw the Lord standing beside a wall
that had been built using a plumb line.
He was using a plumb line to see if it was
still straight. ⁸And the LORD said to me,
"Amos, what do you see?"

I answered, "A plumb line."

And the Lord replied, "I will test my
people with this plumb line. I will no
longer ignore all their sins. ⁹The pagan
shrines of your ancestors* will be
ruined, and the temples of Israel will be
destroyed; I will bring the dynasty of
King Jeroboam to a sudden end."

¹⁰Then Amaziah, the priest of Bethel,
sent a message to Jeroboam, king of Israel: "Amos is hatching a plot against
you right here on your very doorstep!
What he is saying is intolerable. ¹¹He is
saying, 'Jeroboam will soon be killed,
and the people of Israel will be sent
away into exile.'"

¹²Then Amaziah sent orders to
Amos: "Get out of here, you prophet! Go
on back to the land of Judah, and earn
your living by prophesying there!
¹³Don't bother us with your prophecies
here in Bethel. This is the king's sanctuary and the national place of worship!"

¹⁴But Amos replied, "I'm not a professional prophet, and I was never trained
to be one.* I'm just a shepherd, and I
take care of sycamore-fig trees. ¹⁵But
the LORD called me away from my flock
and told me, 'Go and prophesy to my
people in Israel.' ¹⁶Now then, listen to
this message from the LORD:

"You say,
'Don't prophesy against Israel.
Stop preaching against my
people.*'
¹⁷ But this is what the LORD says:
'Your wife will become a prostitute
in this city,
and your sons and daughters will
be killed.

Your land will be divided up,
  and you yourself will die in a
    foreign land.
And the people of Israel will
  certainly become captives
    in exile,
  far from their homeland.'"

8:1THEN the Sovereign LORD showed me another vision. In it I saw a basket filled with ripe fruit. 2"What do you see, Amos?" he asked.

I replied, "A basket full of ripe fruit."

Then the LORD said, "Like this fruit, Israel is ripe for punishment! I will not delay their punishment again. 3In that day the singing in the Temple will turn to wailing. Dead bodies will be scattered everywhere. They will be carried out of the city in silence. I, the Sovereign LORD, have spoken!"

4 Listen to this, you who rob the poor
  and trample down the needy!
5 You can't wait for the Sabbath day
    to be over
  and the religious festivals to end
  so you can get back to cheating
    the helpless.
You measure out grain with
    dishonest measures
  and cheat the buyer with
    dishonest scales.*
6 And you mix the grain you sell
  with chaff swept from the floor.
Then you enslave poor people
  for one piece of silver or a pair
    of sandals.

7 Now the LORD has sworn this oath
  by his own name, the Pride of
    Israel*:
"I will never forget
  the wicked things you have done!
8 The earth will tremble for
    your deeds,
  and everyone will mourn.
The ground will rise like the Nile
    River at floodtime;
  it will heave up, then sink again.

9 "In that day," says the Sovereign
    LORD,

"I will make the sun go down at noon
  and darken the earth while it is
    still day.
10 I will turn your celebrations into
    times of mourning
  and your singing into weeping.
You will wear funeral clothes
  and shave your heads to show
    your sorrow—
  as if your only son had died.
How very bitter that day will be!

11 "The time is surely coming," says the
    Sovereign LORD,
  "when I will send a famine on
    the land—
not a famine of bread or water
  but of hearing the words
    of the LORD.
12 People will stagger from sea to sea
  and wander from border to
    border*
searching for the word of the LORD,
  but they will not find it.
13 Beautiful girls and strong young men
  will grow faint in that day,
  thirsting for the LORD's word.
14 And those who swear by the
    shameful idols of
      Samaria—
  who take oaths in the name
    of the god of Dan
  and make vows in the name of the
    god of Beersheba*—
they will all fall down,
  never to rise again."

9:1THEN I saw a vision of the Lord standing beside the altar. He said,

"Strike the tops of the Temple columns,
  so that the foundation will shake.
Bring down the roof
  on the heads of the people below.
I will kill with the sword those
  who survive.
No one will escape!

2 "Even if they dig down to the place
    of the dead,*
  I will reach down and pull
    them up.
Even if they climb up into the heavens,

I will bring them down.

³ Even if they hide at the very top
of Mount Carmel,
I will search them out and
capture them.
Even if they hide at the bottom of
the ocean,
I will send the sea serpent after
them to bite them.
⁴ Even if their enemies drive them
into exile,
I will command the sword to kill
them there.
I am determined to bring disaster
upon them
and not to help them."

⁵ The Lord, the LORD of Heaven's Armies,
touches the land and it melts,
and all its people mourn.
The ground rises like the Nile River
at floodtime,
and then it sinks again.
⁶ The LORD's home reaches up to the
heavens,
while its foundation is on the earth.
He draws up water from the oceans
and pours it down as rain on
the land.
The LORD is his name!

⁷ "Are you Israelites more important
to me
than the Ethiopians?*" asks
the LORD.
"I brought Israel out of Egypt,
but I also brought the Philistines
from Crete*
and led the Arameans out of Kir.

⁸ "I, the Sovereign LORD,
am watching this sinful nation
of Israel.
I will destroy it
from the face of the earth.
But I will never completely destroy
the family of Israel,*"
says the LORD.
⁹ "For I will give the command
and will shake Israel along with
the other nations
as grain is shaken in a sieve,
yet not one true kernel will be lost.

¹⁰ But all the sinners will die by the
sword—
all those who say, 'Nothing bad
will happen to us.'

¹¹ "In that day I will restore the fallen
house* of David.
I will repair its damaged walls.
From the ruins I will rebuild it
and restore its former glory.
¹² And Israel will possess what is left
of Edom
and all the nations I have called
to be mine.*"
The LORD has spoken,
and he will do these things.

¹³ **"The time will come," says the
LORD,
"when the grain and grapes will
grow faster
than they can be harvested.
Then the terraced vineyards on
the hills of Israel
will drip with sweet wine!
¹⁴ I will bring my exiled people
of Israel
back from distant lands,
and they will rebuild their
ruined cities
and live in them again.
They will plant vineyards
and gardens;
they will eat their crops and
drink their wine.
¹⁵ I will firmly plant them there
in their own land.
They will never again be uprooted
from the land I have given them,"
says the LORD your God.**

7:2 Hebrew *Jacob;* also in 7:5. See note on 3:13.
7:9 Hebrew *of Isaac.* 7:14 Or *I'm not a prophet nor the
son of a prophet.* 7:16 Hebrew *against the house of Isaac.*
8:5 Hebrew *You make the ephah* [a unit for measuring
grain] *small and the shekel* [a unit of weight] *great, and you
deal falsely by using deceitful balances.* 8:7 Hebrew *the
pride of Jacob.* See note on 3:13. 8:12 Hebrew *from north
to east.* 8:14 Hebrew *the way of Beersheba.* 9:2 Hebrew
to Sheol. 9:7a Hebrew *the Cushites?* 9:7b Hebrew
Caphtor. 9:8 Hebrew *the house of Jacob.* See note on 3:13.
9:11a Or *kingdom;* Hebrew reads *tent.* 9:11b-12 Greek
version reads *and restore its former glory, / so that the rest
of humanity, including the Gentiles— / all those I have
called to be mine—might seek me.* Compare Acts 15:16-17.

REVELATION 3:7-22

"**W**rite this letter to the angel of the church in Philadelphia.

This is the message from the one
who is holy and true,
the one who has the key of David.
What he opens, no one can close;
and what he closes, no one
can open.*

8"I know all the things you do, and I have opened a door for you that no one can close. You have little strength, yet you obeyed my word and did not deny me. 9Look, I will force those who belong to Satan's synagogue—those liars who say they are Jews but are not—to come and bow down at your feet. They will acknowledge that you are the ones I love.

10"Because you have obeyed my command to persevere, I will protect you from the great time of testing that will come upon the whole world to test those who belong to this world. 11I am coming soon.* Hold on to what you have, so that no one will take away your crown. 12All who are victorious will become pillars in the Temple of my God, and they will never have to leave it. And I will write on them the name of my God, and they will be citizens in the city of my God—the new Jerusalem that comes down from heaven from my God. And I will also write on them my new name.

13"Anyone with ears to hear must listen to the Spirit and understand what he is saying to the churches.

14"Write this letter to the angel of the church in Laodicea. This is the message from the one who is the Amen—the faithful and true witness, the beginning* of God's new creation:

15"I know all the things you do, that you are neither hot nor cold. I wish that you were one or the other! 16But since you are like lukewarm water, neither hot nor cold, I will spit you out of my mouth! 17You say, 'I am rich. I have everything I want. I don't need a thing!' And you don't realize that you are wretched and miserable and poor and blind and naked. 18So I advise you to buy gold from me— gold that has been purified by fire. Then you will be rich. Also buy white garments from me so you will not be shamed by your nakedness, and ointment for your eyes so you will be able to see. 19I correct and discipline everyone I love. So be diligent and turn from your indifference.

20"Look! I stand at the door and knock. If you hear my voice and open the door, I will come in, and we will share a meal together as friends. 21Those who are victorious will sit with me on my throne, just as I was victorious and sat with my Father on his throne.

22"Anyone with ears to hear must listen to the Spirit and understand what he is saying to the churches."

3:7 Isa 22:22.   3:11 Or *suddenly*, or *quickly*.   3:14 Or *the ruler*, or *the source*.

PSALM 131:1-3

A song for pilgrims ascending to Jerusalem. A psalm of David.

1 **L**ORD, my heart is not proud;
    my eyes are not haughty.
I don't concern myself with matters
    too great
or too awesome for me to grasp.
2 Instead, I have calmed and quieted
    myself,
    like a weaned child who no
        longer cries for its mother's
        milk.
    Yes, like a weaned child is my
        soul within me.

3 O Israel, put your hope in the LORD—
    now and always.

PROVERBS 29:23

Pride ends in humiliation, while humility brings honor.

DECEMBER
13

OBADIAH 1:1-21

This is the vision that the Sovereign LORD revealed to Obadiah concerning the land of Edom.

We have heard a message from
the LORD
that an ambassador was sent to
the nations to say,
"Get ready, everyone!
Let's assemble our armies and
attack Edom!"

2 The LORD says to Edom,
"I will cut you down to size among
the nations;
you will be greatly despised.
3 You have been deceived by your
own pride
because you live in a rock fortress
and make your home high in the
mountains.
'Who can ever reach us way
up here?'
you ask boastfully.
4 But even if you soared as high
as eagles
and built your nest among
the stars,
I would bring you crashing down,"
says the LORD.

5 "If thieves came at night and
robbed you
(what a disaster awaits you!),
they would not take everything.
Those who harvest grapes
always leave a few for the poor.
But your enemies will wipe you
out completely!
6 Every nook and cranny of Edom*
will be searched and looted.
Every treasure will be found
and taken.

7 "All your allies will turn against you.
They will help to chase you from
your land.

They will promise you peace
while plotting to deceive and
destroy you.
Your trusted friends will set traps
for you,
and you won't even know about it.
8 At that time not a single wise person
will be left in the whole land
of Edom,"
says the LORD.
"For on the mountains of Edom
I will destroy everyone who has
understanding.
9 The mightiest warriors of Teman
will be terrified,
and everyone on the mountains
of Edom
will be cut down in the slaughter.

10 "Because of the violence you did
to your close relatives in Israel,*
you will be filled with shame
and destroyed forever.
11 When they were invaded,
you stood aloof, refusing to
help them.
Foreign invaders carried off
their wealth
and cast lots to divide up
Jerusalem,
but you acted like one of Israel's
enemies.

12 "You should not have gloated
when they exiled your relatives
to distant lands.
You should not have rejoiced
when the people of Judah
suffered such misfortune.
You should not have spoken
arrogantly
in that terrible time of trouble.
13 You should not have plundered the
land of Israel
when they were suffering such
calamity.
You should not have gloated over
their destruction
when they were suffering such
calamity.
You should not have seized their
wealth

when they were suffering such calamity.

14 You should not have stood at the crossroads,
killing those who tried to escape.
You should not have captured the survivors
and handed them over in their terrible time of trouble.

15 "The day is near when I, the LORD, will judge all godless nations!
As you have done to Israel, so it will be done to you.
All your evil deeds
will fall back on your own heads.

16 Just as you swallowed up my people on my holy mountain,
so you and the surrounding nations will swallow the punishment I pour out on you.
Yes, all you nations will drink and stagger
and disappear from history.

17 "But Jerusalem* will become a refuge for those who escape;
it will be a holy place.
And the people of Israel* will come back
to reclaim their inheritance.

18 The people of Israel will be a raging fire,
and Edom a field of dry stubble.
The descendants of Jospeh will be a flame
roaring across the field, devouring everything.
There will be no survivors in Edom.
I, the LORD, have spoken!

19 "Then my people living in the Negev will occupy the mountains of Edom.
Those living in the foothills of Judah*
will possess the Philistine plains and take over the fields of Ephraim and Samaria.
And the people of Benjamin will occupy the land of Gilead.

20 The exiles of Israel will return to their land
and occupy the Phoenician coast as far north as Zarephath.
The captives from Jerusalem exiled in the north*
will return home and resettle the towns of the Negev.

21 Those who have been rescued* will go up to* Mount Zion in Jerusalem
to rule over the mountains of Edom.
And the LORD himself will be king!"

6 Hebrew *Esau;* also in 8b, 9, 18, 19, 21.   10 Hebrew *your brother Jacob.* The names "Jacob" and "Israel" are often interchanged throughout the Old Testament, referring sometimes to the individual patriarch and sometimes to the nation.   17a Hebrew *Mount Zion.*   17b Hebrew *house of Jacob;* also in 18. See note on 10.   19 Hebrew *the Shephelah.*   20 Hebrew *in Sepharad.*   21a As in Greek and Syriac versions; Hebrew reads *Rescuers.*   21b Or *from.*

REVELATION 4:1-11

Then as I [John] looked, I saw a door standing open in heaven, and the same voice I had heard before spoke to me like a trumpet blast. The voice said, "Come up here, and I will show you what must happen after this." 2And instantly I was in the Spirit,* and I saw a throne in heaven and someone sitting on it. 3The one sitting on the throne was as brilliant as gemstones—like jasper and carnelian. And the glow of an emerald circled his throne like a rainbow. 4Twenty-four thrones surrounded him, and twenty-four elders sat on them. They were all clothed in white and had gold crowns on their heads. 5From the throne came flashes of lightning and the rumble of thunder. And in front of the throne were seven torches with burning flames. This is the sevenfold Spirit* of God. 6In front of the throne was a shiny sea of glass, sparkling like crystal.

In the center and around the throne were four living beings, each covered with eyes, front and back. 7The first of these living beings was like a lion; the second was like an ox; the third had a human face; and the fourth was like an eagle in flight. 8Each of these living beings had six wings, and their wings were covered all over with eyes, inside and out. Day after day and night after night they keep on saying,

"Holy, holy, holy is the Lord God, the Almighty—
the one who always was, who is, and who is still to come."

⁹Whenever the living beings give glory and honor and thanks to the one sitting on the throne (the one who lives forever and ever), ¹⁰the twenty-four elders fall down and worship the one sitting on the throne (the one who lives forever and ever). And they lay their crowns before the throne and say,

¹¹ **"You are worthy, O Lord our God,
to receive glory and honor
and power.
For you created all things,
and they exist because you
created what you pleased."**

4:2 Or *in spirit.*   4:5 Greek *They are the seven spirits.*

PSALM 132:1-18
A song for pilgrims ascending to Jerusalem.

¹ LORD, remember David
and all that he suffered.
² He made a solemn promise
to the LORD.
He vowed to the Mighty One
of Israel,*
³ "I will not go home;
I will not let myself rest.
⁴ I will not let my eyes sleep
nor close my eyelids in slumber
⁵ until I find a place to build a house
for the LORD,
a sanctuary for the Mighty One
of Israel."

⁶ We heard that the Ark was in
Ephrathah;
then we found it in the distant
countryside of Jaar.
⁷ Let us go to the sanctuary
of the LORD;
let us worship at the footstool
of his throne.
⁸ Arise, O LORD, and enter your resting
place,

along with the Ark, the symbol
of your power.
⁹ May your priests be clothed
in godliness;
may your loyal servants sing
for joy.
¹⁰ For the sake of your servant David,
do not reject the king you have
anointed.
¹¹ The LORD swore an oath to David
with a promise he will never
take back:
"I will place one of your descendants
on your throne.
¹² If your descendants obey the terms
of my covenant
and the laws that I teach them,
then your royal line
will continue forever and ever."

¹³ For the LORD has chosen Jerusalem*;
he has desired it for his home.
¹⁴ "This is my resting place forever,"
he said.
"I will live here, for this is the
home I desired.
¹⁵ I will bless this city and make it
prosperous;
I will satisfy its poor with food.
¹⁶ I will clothe its priests with
godliness;
its faithful servants will sing
for joy.
¹⁷ Here I will increase the power
of David;
my anointed one will be a light for
my people.
¹⁸ I will clothe his enemies
with shame,
but he will be a glorious king."

132:2 Hebrew *of Jacob;* also in 132:5. See note on 44:4.
132:13 Hebrew *Zion.*

PROVERBS 29:24-25
If you assist a thief, you only hurt your-self. You are sworn to tell the truth, but you dare not testify. □ Fearing people is a dangerous trap, but trusting the LORD means safety.

DECEMBER 14

JONAH 1:1–4:11

The Lord gave this message to Jonah son of Amittai: ²"Get up and go to the great city of Nineveh. Announce my judgment against it because I have seen how wicked its people are."

³But Jonah got up and went in the opposite direction to get away from the Lord. He went down to the port of Joppa, where he found a ship leaving for Tarshish. He bought a ticket and went on board, hoping to escape from the Lord by sailing to Tarshish.

⁴But the Lord hurled a powerful wind over the sea, causing a violent storm that threatened to break the ship apart. ⁵Fearing for their lives, the desperate sailors shouted to their gods for help and threw the cargo overboard to lighten the ship.

But all this time Jonah was sound asleep down in the hold. ⁶So the captain went down after him. "How can you sleep at a time like this?" he shouted. "Get up and pray to your god! Maybe he will pay attention to us and spare our lives."

⁷Then the crew cast lots to see which of them had offended the gods and caused the terrible storm. When they did this, the lots identified Jonah as the culprit. ⁸"Why has this awful storm come down on us?" they demanded. "Who are you? What is your line of work? What country are you from? What is your nationality?"

⁹Jonah answered, "I am a Hebrew, and I worship the Lord, the God of heaven, who made the sea and the land."

¹⁰The sailors were terrified when they heard this, for he had already told them he was running away from the Lord. "Oh, why did you do it?" they groaned. ¹¹And since the storm was getting worse all the time, they asked him, "What should we do to you to stop this storm?"

¹²"Throw me into the sea," Jonah said, "and it will become calm again. I know that this terrible storm is all my fault."

¹³Instead, the sailors rowed even harder to get the ship to the land. But the stormy sea was too violent for them, and they couldn't make it. ¹⁴Then they cried out to the Lord, Jonah's God. "O Lord," they pleaded, "don't make us die for this man's sin. And don't hold us responsible for his death. O Lord, you have sent this storm upon him for your own good reasons."

¹⁵Then the sailors picked Jonah up and threw him into the raging sea, and the storm stopped at once! ¹⁶The sailors were awestruck by the Lord's great power, and they offered him a sacrifice and vowed to serve him.

¹⁷*Now the Lord had arranged for a great fish to swallow Jonah. And Jonah was inside the fish for three days and three nights.

²:¹*Then Jonah prayed to the Lord his God from inside the fish. ²He said,

"I cried out to the Lord in my
        great trouble,
    and he answered me.
I called to you from the land
        of the dead,*
    and Lord, you heard me!
³ You threw me into the
        ocean depths,
    and I sank down to the heart
        of the sea.
The mighty waters engulfed me;
    I was buried beneath your wild
        and stormy waves.
⁴ Then I said, 'O Lord, you have driven
        me from your presence.
    Yet I will look once more toward
        your holy Temple.'

⁵ "I sank beneath the waves,
    and the waters closed over me.
    Seaweed wrapped itself around
        my head.
⁶ I sank down to the very roots
        of the mountains.
    I was imprisoned in the earth,
    whose gates lock shut forever.

But you, O LORD my God,
  snatched me from the jaws
    of death!
7 As my life was slipping away,
  I remembered the LORD.
And my earnest prayer went
    out to you
  in your holy Temple.
8 Those who worship false gods
  turn their backs on all God's
    mercies.
9 But I will offer sacrifices to you with
    songs of praise,
  and I will fulfill all my vows.
For my salvation comes from the
    LORD alone."

10 Then the LORD ordered the fish to spit Jonah out onto the beach.

3:1 THEN the LORD spoke to Jonah a second time: 2 "Get up and go to the great city of Nineveh, and deliver the message I have given you."

3 This time Jonah obeyed the LORD's command and went to Nineveh, a city so large that it took three days to see it all.* 4 On the day Jonah entered the city, he shouted to the crowds: "Forty days from now Nineveh will be destroyed!" 5 The people of Nineveh believed God's message, and from the greatest to the least, they declared a fast and put on burlap to show their sorrow.

6 When the king of Nineveh heard what Jonah was saying, he stepped down from his throne and took off his royal robes. He dressed himself in burlap and sat on a heap of ashes. 7 Then the king and his nobles sent this decree throughout the city:

"No one, not even the animals from your herds and flocks, may eat or drink anything at all. 8 People and animals alike must wear garments of mourning, and everyone must pray earnestly to God. They must turn from their evil ways and stop all their violence. 9 Who can tell? Perhaps even yet God will change his mind and hold back his fierce anger from destroying us."

10 When God saw what they had done and how they had put a stop to their evil ways, he changed his mind and did not carry out the destruction he had threatened.

4:1 THIS change of plans greatly upset Jonah, and he became very angry. 2 So he complained to the LORD about it: "Didn't I say before I left home that you would do this, LORD? That is why I ran away to Tarshish! I knew that you are a merciful and compassionate God, slow to get angry and filled with unfailing love. You are eager to turn back from destroying people. 3 Just kill me now, LORD! I'd rather be dead than alive if what I predicted will not happen."

4 The LORD replied, "Is it right for you to be angry about this?"

5 Then Jonah went out to the east side of the city and made a shelter to sit under as he waited to see what would happen to the city. 6 And the LORD God arranged for a leafy plant to grow there, and soon it spread its broad leaves over Jonah's head, shading him from the sun. This eased his discomfort, and Jonah was very grateful for the plant.

7 But God also arranged for a worm! The next morning at dawn the worm ate through the stem of the plant so that it withered away. 8 And as the sun grew hot, God arranged for a scorching east wind to blow on Jonah. The sun beat down on his head until he grew faint and wished to die. "Death is certainly better than living like this!" he exclaimed.

9 Then God said to Jonah, "Is it right for you to be angry because the plant died?"

"Yes," Jonah retorted, "even angry enough to die!"

10 Then the LORD said, "You feel sorry about the plant, though you did nothing to put it there. It came quickly and died quickly. 11 But Nineveh has more than 120,000 people living in spiritual darkness,* not to mention all the animals. Shouldn't I feel sorry for such a great city?"

1:17 Verse 1:17 is numbered 2:1 in Hebrew text.
2:1 Verses 2:1-10 are numbered 2:2-11 in Hebrew text.

2:2 Hebrew *from Sheol.*   3:3 Hebrew *a great city to God, of three days' journey.*   4:11 Hebrew *people who don't know their right hand from their left.*

REVELATION 5:1-14

Then I [John] saw a scroll* in the right hand of the one who was sitting on the throne. There was writing on the inside and the outside of the scroll, and it was sealed with seven seals. [2]And I saw a strong angel, who shouted with a loud voice: "Who is worthy to break the seals on this scroll and open it?" [3]But no one in heaven or on earth or under the earth was able to open the scroll and read it.

[4]Then I began to weep bitterly because no one was found worthy to open the scroll and read it. [5]But one of the twenty-four elders said to me, "Stop weeping! Look, the Lion of the tribe of Judah, the heir to David's throne,* has won the victory. He is worthy to open the scroll and its seven seals."

[6]Then I saw a Lamb that looked as if it had been slaughtered, but it was now standing between the throne and the four living beings and among the twenty-four elders. He had seven horns and seven eyes, which represent the sevenfold Spirit* of God that is sent out into every part of the earth. [7]He stepped forward and took the scroll from the right hand of the one sitting on the throne. [8]And when he took the scroll, the four living beings and the twenty-four elders fell down before the Lamb. Each one had a harp, and they held gold bowls filled with incense, which are the prayers of God's people. [9]And they sang a new song with these words:

"You are worthy to take the scroll
    and break its seals and open it.
For you were slaughtered, and your
      blood has ransomed people
      for God
    from every tribe and language
      and people and nation.
[10] And you have caused them to become
    a Kingdom of priests for
      our God.
And they will reign* on the earth."

[11]Then I looked again, and I heard the voices of thousands and millions of angels around the throne and of the living beings and the elders. [12]**And they sang in a mighty chorus:**

**"Worthy is the Lamb who was
    slaughtered—
to receive power and riches
and wisdom and strength
    and honor and glory and
      blessing."**

[13]And then I heard every creature in heaven and on earth and under the earth and in the sea. They sang:

"Blessing and honor and glory and
    power
    belong to the one sitting
      on the throne
    and to the Lamb forever and ever."

[14]And the four living beings said, "Amen!" And the twenty-four elders fell down and worshiped the Lamb.

5:1 Or *book;* also in 5:2, 3, 4, 5, 7, 8, 9.   5:5 Greek *the root of David.* See Isa 11:10.   5:6 Greek *which are the seven spirits.*   5:10 Some manuscripts read *they are reigning.*

PSALM 133:1-3

A song for pilgrims ascending to Jerusalem. A psalm of David.

[1] **H**ow wonderful and pleasant
    it is
    when brothers live together
    in harmony!
[2] For harmony is as precious as the
    anointing oil
    that was poured over Aaron's
    head,
    that ran down his beard
    and onto the border of
    his robe.
[3] Harmony is as refreshing as the dew
    from Mount Hermon
    that falls on the mountains
    of Zion.
And there the LORD has pronounced
    his blessing,
    even life everlasting.

PROVERBS 29:26-27
Many seek the ruler's favor, but justice comes from the Lord. □ The righteous despise the unjust; the wicked despise the godly.

DECEMBER 15

MICAH 1:1–4:13
The Lord gave this message to Micah of Moresheth during the years when Jotham, Ahaz, and Hezekiah were kings of Judah. The visions he saw concerned both Samaria and Jerusalem.

2 Attention! Let all the people of the world listen!
Let the earth and everything in it hear.
The Sovereign Lord is making accusations against you;
the Lord speaks from his holy Temple.
3 Look! The Lord is coming!
He leaves his throne in heaven
and tramples the heights of the earth.
4 The mountains melt beneath his feet
and flow into the valleys
like wax in a fire,
like water pouring down a hill.
5 And why is this happening?
Because of the rebellion of Israel*—
yes, the sins of the whole nation.
Who is to blame for Israel's rebellion?
Samaria, its capital city!
Where is the center of idolatry in Judah?
In Jerusalem, its capital!

6 "So I, the Lord, will make the city of Samaria
a heap of ruins.
Her streets will be plowed up
for planting vineyards.
I will roll the stones of her walls into the valley below,
exposing her foundations.
7 All her carved images will be smashed.
All her sacred treasures will be burned.
These things were bought with the money
earned by her prostitution,
and they will now be carried away
to pay prostitutes elsewhere."

8 Therefore, I will mourn and lament.
I will walk around barefoot and naked.
I will howl like a jackal
and moan like an owl.
9 For my people's wound
is too deep to heal.
It has reached into Judah,
even to the gates of Jerusalem.

10 Don't tell our enemies in Gath*;
don't weep at all.
You people in Beth-leaphrah,*
roll in the dust to show your despair.
11 You people in Shaphir,*
go as captives into exile—naked and ashamed.
The people of Zaanan*
dare not come outside their walls.
The people of Beth-ezel* mourn,
for their house has no support.
12 The people of Maroth* anxiously wait for relief,
but only bitterness awaits them
as the Lord's judgment reaches
even to the gates of Jerusalem.

13 Harness your chariot horses and flee,
you people of Lachish.*
You were the first city in Judah
to follow Israel in her rebellion,
and you led Jerusalem* into sin.
14 Send farewell gifts to Moresheth-gath*;
there is no hope of saving it.
The town of Aczib*

has deceived the kings of Israel.
¹⁵ O people of Mareshah,*
    I will bring a conqueror to capture
       your town.
  And the leaders* of Israel
    will go to Adullam.

¹⁶ Oh, people of Judah, shave your
      heads in sorrow,
    for the children you love will be
      snatched away.
  Make yourselves as bald as a vulture,
    for your little ones will be exiled
      to distant lands.

^{2:1} WHAT sorrow awaits you who lie
    awake at night,
    thinking up evil plans.
  You rise at dawn and hurry to carry
    them out,
    simply because you have the
      power to do so.
² When you want a piece of land,
    you find a way to seize it.
  When you want someone's house,
    you take it by fraud and violence.
  You cheat a man of his property,
    stealing his family's inheritance.

³ But this is what the LORD says:
  "I will reward your evil with evil;
    you won't be able to pull your
      neck out of the noose.
  You will no longer walk around
    proudly,
    for it will be a terrible time."

⁴ In that day your enemies will make
    fun of you
    by singing this song of despair
      about you:
  "We are finished,
    completely ruined!
  God has confiscated our land,
    taking it from us.
  He has given our fields
    to those who betrayed us.*"
⁵ Others will set your boundaries then,
    and the LORD's people will have
      no say
    in how the land is divided.

⁶ "Don't say such things,"
    the people respond.*

"Don't prophesy like that.
    Such disasters will never come
      our way!"

⁷ Should you talk that way,
    O family of Israel?*
    Will the LORD's Spirit have
      patience with such behavior?
  If you would do what is right,
    you would find my words
      comforting.
⁸ Yet to this very hour
    my people rise against me like
      an enemy!
  You steal the shirts right
    off the backs
  of those who trusted you,
  making them as ragged as men
    returning from battle.
⁹ You have evicted women from their
    pleasant homes
    and forever stripped their
      children of all that God would
      give them.
¹⁰ Up! Begone!
    This is no longer your land
      and home,
  for you have filled it with sin
    and ruined it completely.

¹¹ Suppose a prophet full of lies would
    say to you,
    "I'll preach to you the joys of wine
      and alcohol!"
  That's just the kind of prophet you
    would like!

¹² "Someday, O Israel, I will gather you;
    I will gather the remnant
      who are left.
  I will bring you together again like
    sheep in a pen,
    like a flock in its pasture.
  Yes, your land will again
    be filled with noisy crowds!
¹³ Your leader will break out
    and lead you out of exile,
  out through the gates of the
    enemy cities,
    back to your own land.
  Your king will lead you;
    the LORD himself will guide you."

3:1 I SAID, "Listen, you leaders of Israel!
You are supposed to know right
from wrong,
2 but you are the very ones
who hate good and love evil.
You skin my people alive
and tear the flesh from their
bones.
3 Yes, you eat my people's flesh,
strip off their skin,
and break their bones.
You chop them up
like meat for the cooking pot.
4 Then you beg the LORD for help in
times of trouble!
Do you really expect him
to answer?
After all the evil you have done,
he won't even look at you!"

5 This is what the LORD says:
"You false prophets are leading
my people astray!
You promise peace for those who
give you food,
but you declare war on those who
refuse to feed you.
6 Now the night will close around you,
cutting off all your visions.
Darkness will cover you,
putting an end to your
predictions.
The sun will set for you prophets,
and your day will come to an end.
7 Then you seers will be put to shame,
and you fortune-tellers will be
disgraced.
And you will cover your faces
because there is no answer
from God."

8 But as for me, I am filled with
power—
with the Spirit of the LORD.
I am filled with justice and strength
to boldly declare Israel's sin and
rebellion.
9 Listen to me, you leaders of Israel!
You hate justice and twist all that
is right.
10 You are building Jerusalem
on a foundation of murder and
corruption.

11 You rulers make decisions based
on bribes;
you priests teach God's laws only
for a price;
you prophets won't prophesy unless
you are paid.
Yet all of you claim to depend on
the LORD.
"No harm can come to us," you say,
"for the LORD is here among us."
12 Because of you, Mount Zion will be
plowed like an open field;
Jerusalem will be reduced to ruins!
A thicket will grow on the heights
where the Temple now stands.

4:1 IN the last days, the mountain of the
LORD's house
will be the highest of all—
the most important place
on earth.
It will be raised above the other hills,
and people from all over the
world will stream there
to worship.
2 People from many nations will
come and say,
"Come, let us go up to the mountain
of the LORD,
to the house of Jacob's God.
There he will teach us his ways,
and we will walk in his paths."
For the LORD's teaching will go out
from Zion;
his word will go out from
Jerusalem.
3 **The LORD will mediate between
peoples
and will settle disputes
between strong nations
far away.
They will hammer their swords
into plowshares
and their spears into pruning
hooks.
Nation will no longer fight
against nation,
nor train for war anymore.**
4 Everyone will live in peace and
prosperity,
enjoying their own grapevines
and fig trees,

for there will be nothing to fear.
The LORD of Heaven's Armies
has made this promise!
5 Though the nations around us
follow their idols,
we will follow the LORD our God
forever and ever.

6 "In that coming day," says the LORD,
"I will gather together those who
are lame,
those who have been exiles,
and those whom I have filled
with grief.
7 Those who are weak will survive
as a remnant;
those who were exiles will
become a strong nation.
Then I, the LORD, will rule from
Jerusalem*
as their king forever."

8 As for you, Jerusalem,
the citadel of God's people,*
your royal might and power
will come back to you again.
The kingship will be restored
to my precious Jerusalem.

9 But why are you now screaming
in terror?
Have you no king to lead you?
Have your wise people all died?
Pain has gripped you like a
woman in childbirth.
10 Writhe and groan like a woman
in labor,
you people of Jerusalem,*
for now you must leave this city
to live in the open country.
You will soon be sent in exile
to distant Babylon.
But the LORD will rescue you there;
he will redeem you from the grip
of your enemies.

11 Now many nations have gathered
against you.
"Let her be desecrated," they say.
"Let us see the destruction of
Jerusalem.*"
12 But they do not know the LORD's
thoughts
or understand his plan.

These nations don't know
that he is gathering them together
to be beaten and trampled
like sheaves of grain on a
threshing floor.
13 "Rise up and crush the nations,
O Jerusalem!"*
says the LORD.
"For I will give you iron horns and
bronze hooves,
so you can trample many nations
to pieces.
You will present their stolen riches
to the LORD,
their wealth to the LORD of all
the earth."

1:5 Hebrew *Jacob;* also in 1:5b. The names "Jacob"
and "Israel" are often interchanged throughout
the Old Testament, referring sometimes to the individual
patriarch and sometimes to the nation. 1:10a *Gath*
sounds like the Hebrew term for "tell." 1:10b *Beth-
leaphrah* means "house of dust." 1:11a *Shaphir* means
"pleasant." 1:11b *Zaanan* sounds like the Hebrew term
for "come out." 1:11c *Beth-ezel* means "adjoining house."
1:12 *Maroth* sounds like the Hebrew term for "bitter."
1:13a *Lachish* sounds like the Hebrew term for "team
of horses." 1:13b Hebrew *the daughter of Zion.*
1:14a *Moresheth* sounds like the Hebrew term for "gift"
or "dowry." 1:14b *Aczib* means "deception."
1:15a *Mareshah* sounds like the Hebrew term for
"conqueror." 1:15b Hebrew *the glory.* 2:4 Or *to those
who took us captive.* 2:6 Or *the prophets respond;* Hebrew
reads *they prophesy.* 2:7 Hebrew *O house of Jacob?* See
note on 1:5a. 4:7 Hebrew *Mount Zion.* 4:8 Hebrew *As
for you, Migdal-eder, / the Ophel of the daughter of Zion.*
4:10 Hebrew *O daughter of Zion.* 4:11 Hebrew *of Zion.*
4:13 Hebrew *"Rise up and thresh, O daughter of Zion."*

REVELATION 6:1-17

As I [John] watched, the Lamb broke
the first of the seven seals on the
scroll.* Then I heard one of the four living beings say with a voice like thunder,
"Come!" 2I looked up and saw a white
horse standing there. Its rider carried a
bow, and a crown was placed on his
head. He rode out to win many battles
and gain the victory.

3When the Lamb broke the second
seal, I heard the second living being say,
"Come!" 4Then another horse appeared,
a red one. Its rider was given a mighty
sword and the authority to take peace
from the earth. And there was war and
slaughter everywhere.

5When the Lamb broke the third
seal, I heard the third living being say,
"Come!" I looked up and saw a black

horse, and its rider was holding a pair of scales in his hand. 6And I heard a voice from among the four living beings say, "A loaf of wheat bread or three loaves of barley will cost a day's pay.* And don't waste* the olive oil and wine."

7When the Lamb broke the fourth seal, I heard the fourth living being say, "Come!" 8I looked up and saw a horse whose color was pale green. Its rider was named Death, and his companion was the Grave.* These two were given authority over one-fourth of the earth, to kill with the sword and famine and disease* and wild animals.

9When the Lamb broke the fifth seal, I saw under the altar the souls of all who had been martyred for the word of God and for being faithful in their testimony. 10They shouted to the Lord and said, "O Sovereign Lord, holy and true, how long before you judge the people who belong to this world and avenge our blood for what they have done to us?" 11Then a white robe was given to each of them. And they were told to rest a little longer until the full number of their brothers and sisters*— their fellow servants of Jesus who were to be martyred—had joined them.

12I watched as the Lamb broke the sixth seal, and there was a great earthquake. The sun became as dark as black cloth, and the moon became as red as blood. 13Then the stars of the sky fell to the earth like green figs falling from a tree shaken by a strong wind. 14The sky was rolled up like a scroll, and all of the mountains and islands were moved from their places.

15Then everyone—the kings of the earth, the rulers, the generals, the wealthy, the powerful, and every slave and free person—all hid themselves in the caves and among the rocks of the mountains. 16And they cried to the mountains and the rocks, "Fall on us and hide us from the face of the one who sits on the throne and from the wrath of the Lamb. 17For the great day of their wrath has come, and who is able to survive?"

6:1 Or *book.* 6:6a Greek *A choinix* [1 quart or 1 liter] *of wheat for a denarius, and 3 choinix of barley for a denarius.* A denarius was equivalent to a laborer's full day's wage. 6:6b Or *harm.* 6:8a Greek *was Hades.* 6:8b Greek *death.* 6:11 Greek *their brothers.*

PSALM 134:1-3

A song for pilgrims ascending to Jerusalem.

1 **O**h, praise the LORD, all you servants of the LORD,
    you who serve at night in the house of the LORD.
2 Lift up holy hands in prayer,
    and praise the LORD.

3 May the LORD, who made heaven and earth,
    bless you from Jerusalem.*

134:3 Hebrew *Zion.*

PROVERBS 30:1-4

The sayings of Agur son of Jakeh contain this message.* □ I am weary, O God; I am weary and worn out, O God.* I am too stupid to be human, and I lack common sense. I have not mastered human wisdom, nor do I know the Holy One. □ Who but God goes up to heaven and comes back down? Who holds the wind in his fists? Who wraps up the oceans in his cloak? Who has created the whole wide world? What is his name—and his son's name? Tell me if you know!

30:1a Or *son of Jakeh from Massa;* or *son of Jakeh, an oracle.* 30:1b The Hebrew can also be translated *The man declares this to Ithiel, / to Ithiel and to Ucal.*

DECEMBER
16

MICAH 5:1–7:20
1*M**obilize! Marshal your troops!
    The enemy is laying siege to Jerusalem.
They will strike Israel's leader
    in the face with a rod.

2*But you, O Bethlehem Ephrathah,
   are only a small village among all
      the people of Judah.
Yet a ruler of Israel will come
   from you,
   one whose origins are from the
      distant past.
3 The people of Israel will be
   abandoned to their enemies
   until the woman in labor
      gives birth.
Then at last his fellow countrymen
   will return from exile to their
      own land.
4 And he will stand to lead his flock
   with the LORD's strength,
   in the majesty of the name of the
      LORD his God.
Then his people will live there
   undisturbed,
   for he will be highly honored
      around the world.
5   And he will be the source of peace.

When the Assyrians invade our land
   and break through our defenses,
we will appoint seven rulers to
   watch over us,
   eight princes to lead us.
6 They will rule Assyria with drawn
   swords
   and enter the gates of the land
      of Nimrod.
He will rescue us from the Assyrians
   when they pour over the borders
      to invade our land.

7 Then the remnant left in Israel*
   will take their place among the
      nations.
They will be like dew sent by
   the LORD
   or like rain falling on the grass,
which no one can hold back
   and no one can restrain.
8 The remnant left in Israel
   will take their place among the
      nations.
They will be like a lion among the
   animals of the forest,
   like a strong young lion among
      flocks of sheep and goats,

pouncing and tearing as they go
   with no rescuer in sight.
9 The people of Israel will stand up to
   their foes,
   and all their enemies will be
      wiped out.

10 "In that day," says the LORD,
   "I will slaughter your horses
      and destroy your chariots.
11 I will tear down your walls
   and demolish your defenses.
12 I will put an end to all witchcraft,
   and there will be no more
      fortune-tellers.
13 I will destroy all your idols and
   sacred pillars,
   so you will never again worship
      the work of your own hands.
14 I will abolish your idol shrines with
   their Asherah poles
   and destroy your pagan cities.
15 I will pour out my vengeance
   on all the nations that refuse to
      obey me."

6:1LISTEN to what the LORD is saying:

"Stand up and state your case
   against me.
   Let the mountains and hills be
      called to witness your
      complaints.
2 And now, O mountains,
   listen to the LORD's complaint!
He has a case against his people.
   He will bring charges against
      Israel.

3 "O my people, what have I done
   to you?
   What have I done to make you
      tired of me?
   Answer me!
4 For I brought you out of Egypt
   and redeemed you from slavery.
   I sent Moses, Aaron, and Miriam
      to help you.
5 Don't you remember, my people,
   how King Balak of Moab tried to
      have you cursed
   and how Balaam son of Beor
      blessed you instead?

And remember your journey from
  Acacia Grove* to Gilgal,
when I, the LORD, did everything
  I could
to teach you about my
  faithfulness."

6 What can we bring to the LORD?
  What kind of offerings should we
    give him?
Should we bow before God
  with offerings of yearling calves?
7 Should we offer him thousands
    of rams
  and ten thousand rivers of olive oil?
Should we sacrifice our firstborn
    children
  to pay for our sins?

**8 No, O people, the LORD has told
    you what is good,
  and this is what he requires
    of you:
to do what is right, to love mercy,
  and to walk humbly with
    your God.**

9 Fear the LORD if you are wise!
  His voice calls to everyone in
    Jerusalem:
"The armies of destruction are
    coming;
  the LORD is sending them.*
10 What shall I say about the homes of
    the wicked
  filled with treasures gained by
    cheating?
What about the disgusting practice
  of measuring out grain with
    dishonest measures?*
11 How can I tolerate your merchants
  who use dishonest scales and
    weights?
12 The rich among you have become
    wealthy
  through extortion and violence.
Your citizens are so used to lying
  that their tongues can no longer
    tell the truth.

13 "Therefore, I will wound you!
  I will bring you to ruin for all your
    sins.

14 You will eat but never have enough.
  Your hunger pangs and emptiness
    will remain.
And though you try to save your
    money,
  it will come to nothing in the end.
You will save a little,
  but I will give it to those who
    conquer you.
15 You will plant crops
  but not harvest them.
You will press your olives
  but not get enough oil to anoint
    yourselves.
You will trample the grapes
  but get no juice to make your
    wine.
16 You keep only the laws of evil
    King Omri;
  you follow only the example of
    wicked King Ahab!
Therefore, I will make an example of
    you,
  bringing you to complete ruin.
You will be treated with contempt,
  mocked by all who see you."

7:1 How miserable I am!
  I feel like the fruit picker after the
    harvest
  who can find nothing to eat.
Not a cluster of grapes or a single
    early fig
  can be found to satisfy my hunger.
2 The godly people have all
    disappeared;
  not one honest person is left on
    the earth.
They are all murderers,
  setting traps even for their own
    brothers.
3 Both their hands are equally skilled
    at doing evil!
  Officials and judges alike demand
    bribes.
The people with influence get what
    they want,
  and together they scheme to
    twist justice.
4 Even the best of them is like a brier;
  the most honest is as dangerous
    as a hedge of thorns.

But your judgment day is coming
   swiftly now.
      Your time of punishment is here,
      a time of confusion.
5 Don't trust anyone—
      not your best friend or even
      your wife!
6 For the son despises his father.
   The daughter defies her mother.
   The daughter-in-law defies her
      mother-in-law.
      Your enemies are right in your
      own household!

7 As for me, I look to the LORD for help.
   I wait confidently for God to
      save me,
      and my God will certainly hear me.
8 Do not gloat over me, my enemies!
   For though I fall, I will rise again.
   Though I sit in darkness,
      the LORD will be my light.
9 I will be patient as the LORD
      punishes me,
      for I have sinned against him.
   But after that, he will take up
      my case
      and give me justice for all I have
      suffered from my enemies.
   The LORD will bring me into
      the light,
      and I will see his righteousness.
10 Then my enemies will see that the
      LORD is on my side.
      They will be ashamed that they
      taunted me, saying,
   "So where is the LORD—
      that God of yours?"
   With my own eyes I will see their
      downfall;
      they will be trampled like mud in
      the streets.

11 In that day, Israel, your cities will
      be rebuilt,
      and your borders will be extended.
12 People from many lands will come
      and honor you—
      from Assyria all the way to the
      towns of Egypt,
   from Egypt all the way to the
      Euphrates River,*

and from distant seas and
      mountains.
13 But the land* will become empty
      and desolate
      because of the wickedness of
      those who live there.

14 O LORD, protect your people with
      your shepherd's staff;
      lead your flock, your special
      possession.
   Though they live alone in a thicket
      on the heights of Mount Carmel,*
   let them graze in the fertile pastures
      of Bashan and Gilead
      as they did long ago.

15 "Yes," says the LORD,
      "I will do mighty miracles for you,
   like those I did when I rescued you
      from slavery in Egypt."

16 All the nations of the world will
      stand amazed
      at what the LORD will do for you.
   They will be embarrassed
      at their feeble power.
   They will cover their mouths in
      silent awe,
      deaf to everything around them.
17 Like snakes crawling from their holes,
      they will come out to meet the
      LORD our God.
   They will fear him greatly,
      trembling in terror at his presence.

18 Where is another God like you,
      who pardons the guilt of the
      remnant,
      overlooking the sins of his special
      people?
   You will not stay angry with your
      people forever,
      because you delight in showing
      unfailing love.
19 Once again you will have
      compassion on us.
      You will trample our sins under
      your feet
      and throw them into the depths
      of the ocean!
20 You will show us your faithfulness
      and unfailing love

as you promised to our ancestors
Abraham and Jacob long ago.

5:1 Verse 5:1 is numbered 4:14 in Hebrew text.
5:2 Verses 5:2-15 are numbered 5:1-14 in Hebrew text.
5:7 Hebrew *in Jacob;* also in 5:8. See note on 1:5a.
6:5 Hebrew *Shittim.*   6:9 Hebrew *"Listen to the rod. / Who
appointed it?"*   6:10 Hebrew *of using the short ephah?* The
ephah was a unit for measuring grain.   7:12 Hebrew *the
river.*   7:13 Or *earth.*   7:14 Or *surrounded by a fruitful
land.*

REVELATION 7:1-17

Then I [John] saw four angels standing at the four corners of the earth, holding back the four winds so they did not blow on the earth or the sea, or even on any tree. [2]And I saw another angel coming up from the east, carrying the seal of the living God. And he shouted to those four angels, who had been given power to harm land and sea, [3]"Wait! Don't harm the land or the sea or the trees until we have placed the seal of God on the foreheads of his servants."

[4]And I heard how many were marked with the seal of God—144,000 were sealed from all the tribes of Israel:

[5]	from Judah	12,000
	from Reuben.................	12,000
	from Gad	12,000
[6]	from Asher	12,000
	from Naphtali................	12,000
	from Manasseh	12,000
[7]	from Simeon.................	12,000
	from Levi	12,000
	from Issachar	12,000
[8]	from Zebulun	12,000
	from Joseph.................	12,000
	from Benjamin	12,000

[9]After this I saw a vast crowd, too great to count, from every nation and tribe and people and language, standing in front of the throne and before the Lamb. They were clothed in white robes and held palm branches in their hands. [10]And they were shouting with a mighty shout,

"Salvation comes from our God
who sits on the throne
and from the Lamb!"

[11]And all the angels were standing around the throne and around the elders and the four living beings. And they

fell with their faces to the ground before the throne and worshiped God. [12]They sang,

"Amen! Blessing and glory
and wisdom
and thanksgiving and honor
and power and strength belong to
our God
forever and ever! Amen."

[13]Then one of the twenty-four elders asked me, "Who are these who are clothed in white? Where did they come from?"

[14]And I said to him, "Sir, you are the one who knows."

Then he said to me, "These are the ones who died in* the great tribulation.* They have washed their robes in the blood of the Lamb and made them white.

[15] "That is why they stand in front
of God's throne
and serve him day and night
in his Temple.
And he who sits on the throne
will give them shelter.
[16] They will never again be hungry
or thirsty;
they will never be scorched by the
heat of the sun.
[17] For the Lamb on the throne*
will be their Shepherd.
He will lead them to springs
of life-giving water.
And God will wipe every tear from
their eyes."

7:14a Greek *who came out of.*   7:14b Or *the great
suffering.*   7:17 Greek *on the center of the throne.*

PSALM 135:1-21

Praise the LORD!

Praise the name of the LORD!
Praise him, you who serve the LORD,
[2] you who serve in the house
of the LORD,
in the courts of the house
of our God.

[3] Praise the LORD, for the LORD is good;
celebrate his lovely name with
music.

⁴ For the LORD has chosen Jacob
    for himself,
  Israel for his own special treasure.

⁵ I know the greatness of the LORD—
    that our Lord is greater than any
    other god.
⁶ The LORD does whatever pleases him
    throughout all heaven and earth,
    and on the seas and in their depths.
⁷ He causes the clouds to rise over the
    whole earth.
  He sends the lightning with
    the rain
  and releases the wind from his
    storehouses.

⁸ He destroyed the firstborn in each
    Egyptian home,
    both people and animals.
⁹ He performed miraculous signs and
    wonders in Egypt
    against Pharaoh and all his people.
¹⁰ He struck down great nations
    and slaughtered mighty kings—
¹¹ Sihon king of the Amorites,
    Og king of Bashan,
    and all the kings of Canaan.
¹² He gave their land as an inheritance,
    a special possession to his
    people Israel.

¹³ Your name, O LORD, endures forever;
    your fame, O LORD, is known to
    every generation.
¹⁴ For the LORD will give justice to his
    people
    and have compassion on his
    servants.

¹⁵ The idols of the nations are merely
    things of silver and gold,
    shaped by human hands.
¹⁶ They have mouths but cannot speak,
    and eyes but cannot see.
¹⁷ They have ears but cannot hear,
    and noses but cannot smell.
¹⁸ And those who make idols are just
    like them,
    as are all who trust in them.

¹⁹ O Israel, praise the LORD!
    O priests—descendants of
    Aaron—praise the LORD!

²⁰ O Levites, praise the LORD!
    All you who fear the LORD, praise
    the LORD!
²¹ The LORD be praised from Zion,
    for he lives here in Jerusalem.

  Praise the LORD!

PROVERBS 30:5-6
Every word of God proves true. He is a
shield to all who come to him for protection. Do not add to his words, or he
may rebuke you and expose you as a
liar.

DECEMBER 17

NAHUM 1:1-3:19
This message concerning Nineveh
came as a vision to Nahum, who lived in
Elkosh.

² The LORD is a jealous God,
    filled with vengeance and wrath.
  He takes revenge on all who
    oppose him
    and continues to rage against
    his enemies!
³ **The LORD is slow to get angry, but
    his power is great,
    and he never lets the guilty
    go unpunished.
  He displays his power in the
    whirlwind and the storm.
    The billowing clouds are the
    dust beneath his feet.**
⁴ At his command the oceans dry up,
    and the rivers disappear.
  The lush pastures of Bashan and
    Carmel fade,
    and the green forests of Lebanon
    wither.
⁵ In his presence the mountains quake,
    and the hills melt away;
  the earth trembles,
    and its people are destroyed.

⁶ Who can stand before his
        fierce anger?
    Who can survive his burning fury?
    His rage blazes forth like fire,
        and the mountains crumble to
        dust in his presence.

⁷ The Lord is good,
        a strong refuge when trouble comes.
    He is close to those who trust in
        him.
⁸ But he will sweep away his enemies
        in an overwhelming flood.
    He will pursue his foes
        into the darkness of night.

⁹ Why are you scheming against
        the Lord?
    He will destroy you with one blow;
        he won't need to strike twice!
¹⁰ His enemies, tangled like
        thornbushes
    and staggering like drunks,
        will be burned up like dry stubble
        in a field.
¹¹ Who is this wicked counselor
        of yours
    who plots evil against the Lord?

¹² This is what the Lord says:
    "Though the Assyrians have
        many allies,
        they will be destroyed and
        disappear.
    O my people, I have punished you
        before,
        but I will not punish you again.
¹³ Now I will break the yoke of
        bondage from your neck
    and tear off the chains of
        Assyrian oppression."

¹⁴ And this is what the Lord says
        concerning the Assyrians in
        Nineveh:
    "You will have no more children to
        carry on your name.
    I will destroy all the idols in the
        temples of your gods.
    I am preparing a grave for you
        because you are despicable!"

¹⁵*Look! A messenger is coming over
        the mountains with good news!

He is bringing a message of peace.
    Celebrate your festivals, O people
        of Judah,
        and fulfill all your vows,
    for your wicked enemies will never
        invade your land again.
    They will be completely destroyed!

²:¹*Your enemy is coming to crush
        you, Nineveh.
    Man the ramparts! Watch
        the roads!
    Prepare your defenses! Call out
        your forces!

² Even though the destroyer has
        destroyed Judah,
    the Lord will restore its honor.
    Israel's vine has been stripped of
        branches,
        but he will restore its splendor.

³ Shields flash red in the sunlight!
    See the scarlet uniforms of the
        valiant troops!
    Watch as their glittering chariots
        move into position,
        with a forest of spears waving
        above them.
⁴ The chariots race recklessly along
        the streets
    and rush wildly through the
        squares.
    They flash like firelight
        and move as swiftly as lightning.
⁵ The king shouts to his officers;
        they stumble in their haste,
    rushing to the walls to set up their
        defenses.
⁶ The river gates have been torn open!
    The palace is about to collapse!
⁷ Nineveh's exile has been decreed,
    and all the servant girls mourn
        its capture.
    They moan like doves
        and beat their breasts in sorrow.
⁸ Nineveh is like a leaking water
        reservoir!
    The people are slipping away.
    "Stop, stop!" someone shouts,
        but no one even looks back.
⁹ Loot the silver!
    Plunder the gold!

There's no end to Nineveh's
      treasures—
      its vast, uncounted wealth.
10 Soon the city is plundered, empty,
      and ruined.
      Hearts melt and knees shake.
      The people stand aghast,
      their faces pale and trembling.

11 Where now is that great Nineveh,
      that den filled with young lions?
      It was a place where people—like
      lions and their cubs—
      walked freely and without fear.
12 The lion tore up meat for his cubs
      and strangled prey for his mate.
      He filled his den with prey,
      his caverns with his plunder.

13 "I am your enemy!"
      says the LORD of Heaven's Armies.
      "Your chariots will soon go up
      in smoke.
      Your young men* will be killed
      in battle.
      Never again will you plunder
      conquered nations.
      The voices of your proud
      messengers will be heard
      no more."

3:1 WHAT sorrow awaits Nineveh,
      the city of murder and lies!
      She is crammed with wealth
      and is never without victims.
2 Hear the crack of whips,
      the rumble of wheels!
      Horses' hooves pound,
      and chariots clatter wildly.
3 See the flashing swords and
      glittering spears
      as the charioteers charge past!
      There are countless casualties,
      heaps of bodies—
      so many bodies that
      people stumble over them.
4 All this because Nineveh,
      the beautiful and faithless city,
      mistress of deadly charms,
      enticed the nations with her beauty.
      She taught them all her magic,
      enchanting people everywhere.

5 "I am your enemy!"
      says the LORD of Heaven's Armies.
   "And now I will lift your skirts
      and show all the earth your
      nakedness and shame.
6 I will cover you with filth
      and show the world how vile you
      really are.
7 All who see you will shrink back and
      say,
      'Nineveh lies in ruins.
   Where are the mourners?'
      Does anyone regret your
      destruction?"

8 Are you any better than the city of
      Thebes,*
      situated on the Nile River,
      surrounded by water?
   She was protected by the river
      on all sides,
      walled in by water.
9 Ethiopia* and the land of Egypt
      gave unlimited assistance.
   The nations of Put and Libya
      were among her allies.
10 Yet Thebes fell,
      and her people were led away as
      captives.
   Her babies were dashed to death
      against the stones of the streets.
   Soldiers cast lots to get Egyptian
      officers as servants.
      All their leaders were bound
      in chains.

11 And you, Nineveh, will also stagger
      like a drunkard.
      You will hide for fear of the
      attacking enemy.
12 All your fortresses will fall.
      They will be devoured like the
      ripe figs
      that fall into the mouths
      of those who shake the trees.
13 Your troops will be as weak
      and helpless as women.
   The gates of your land will be
      opened wide to the enemy
      and set on fire and burned.
14 Get ready for the siege!
      Store up water!
      Strengthen the defenses!

Go into the pits to trample clay,
and pack it into molds, making
bricks to repair the walls.

15 But the fire will devour you;
the sword will cut you down.
The enemy will consume you like
locusts,
devouring everything they see.
There will be no escape,
even if you multiply like
swarming locusts.
16 Your merchants have multiplied
until they outnumber the stars.
But like a swarm of locusts,
they strip the land and fly away.
17 Your guards* and officials are also
like swarming locusts
that crowd together in the hedges
on a cold day.
But like locusts that fly away when
the sun comes up,
all of them will fly away and
disappear.

18 Your shepherds are asleep,
O Assyrian king;
your princes lie dead in the dust.
Your people are scattered across the
mountains
with no one to gather them
together.
19 There is no healing for your wound;
your injury is fatal.
All who hear of your destruction
will clap their hands for joy.
Where can anyone be found
who has not suffered from your
continual cruelty?

1:15 Verse 1:15 is numbered 2:1 in Hebrew text.
2:1 Verses 2:1-13 are numbered 2:2-14 in Hebrew text.
2:13 Hebrew *young lions*.   3:8 Hebrew *No-amon;* also in
3:10.   3:9 Hebrew *Cush*.   3:17 Or *princes*.

REVELATION 8:1-13

When the Lamb broke the seventh
seal on the scroll,* there was silence
throughout heaven for about half an
hour. 2I [John] saw the seven angels who
stand before God, and they were given
seven trumpets.

3Then another angel with a gold incense burner came and stood at the altar. And a great amount of incense was
given to him to mix with the prayers of
God's holy people as an offering on the
gold altar before the throne. 4The
smoke of the incense, mixed with the
prayers of God's people, ascended up to
God from the altar where the angel had
poured them out. 5Then the angel filled
the incense burner with fire from the
altar and threw it down upon the earth;
and thunder crashed, lightning flashed,
and there was a terrible earthquake.

6Then the seven angels with the
seven trumpets prepared to blow their
mighty blasts.

7The first angel blew his trumpet,
and hail and fire mixed with blood were
thrown down on the earth. One-third of
the earth was set on fire, one-third of
the trees were burned, and all the green
grass was burned.

8Then the second angel blew his
trumpet, and a great mountain of fire
was thrown into the sea. One-third of
the water in the sea became blood,
9one-third of all things living in the sea
died, and one-third of all the ships on
the sea were destroyed.

10Then the third angel blew his trumpet, and a great star fell from the sky,
burning like a torch. It fell on one-third
of the rivers and on the springs of water. 11The name of the star was Bitterness.* It made one-third of the water
bitter, and many people died from
drinking the bitter water.

12Then the fourth angel blew his
trumpet, and one-third of the sun was
struck, and one-third of the moon, and
one-third of the stars, and they became
dark. And one-third of the day was
dark, and also one-third of the night.

13Then I looked, and I heard a single
eagle crying loudly as it flew through
the air, "Terror, terror, terror to all who
belong to this world because of what
will happen when the last three angels
blow their trumpets."

8:1 Or *book*.   8:11 Greek *Wormwood*.

305

PSALM 136:1-26
Give thanks to the LORD, for he is
good!
His faithful love endures forever.
² Give thanks to the God of gods.
His faithful love endures forever.
³ Give thanks to the Lord of lords.
His faithful love endures forever.

⁴ Give thanks to him who alone does
mighty miracles.
His faithful love endures forever.
⁵ Give thanks to him who made the
heavens so skillfully.
His faithful love endures forever.
⁶ Give thanks to him who placed the
earth among the waters.
His faithful love endures forever.
⁷ Give thanks to him who made the
heavenly lights—
His faithful love endures forever.
⁸ the sun to rule the day,
His faithful love endures forever.
⁹ and the moon and stars to rule the
night.
His faithful love endures forever.

¹⁰ Give thanks to him who killed the
firstborn of Egypt.
His faithful love endures forever.
¹¹ He brought Israel out of Egypt.
His faithful love endures forever.
¹² He acted with a strong hand and
powerful arm.
His faithful love endures forever.
¹³ Give thanks to him who parted the
Red Sea.*
His faithful love endures forever.
¹⁴ He led Israel safely through,
His faithful love endures forever.
¹⁵ but he hurled Pharaoh and his army
into the Red Sea.
His faithful love endures forever.
¹⁶ Give thanks to him who led his
people through the wilderness.
His faithful love endures forever.

¹⁷ Give thanks to him who struck down
mighty kings.
His faithful love endures forever.
¹⁸ He killed powerful kings—
His faithful love endures forever.
¹⁹ Sihon king of the Amorites,

His faithful love endures forever.
²⁰ and Og king of Bashan.
His faithful love endures forever.
²¹ God gave the land of these kings as
an inheritance—
His faithful love endures forever.
²² a special possession to his servant
Israel.
His faithful love endures forever.

²³ He remembered us in our weakness.
His faithful love endures forever.
²⁴ He saved us from our enemies.
His faithful love endures forever.
²⁵ He gives food to every living thing.
His faithful love endures forever.
²⁶ Give thanks to the God of heaven.
His faithful love endures forever.

136:13 Hebrew *sea of reeds;* also in 136:15.

PROVERBS 30:7-9
O God, I beg two favors from you; let
me have them before I die. First, help
me never to tell a lie. Second, give me
neither poverty nor riches! Give me just
enough to satisfy my needs. For if I
grow rich, I may deny you and say, "Who
is the LORD?" And if I am too poor, I may
steal and thus insult God's holy name.

DECEMBER 18

HABAKKUK 1:1–3:19
This is the message that the prophet
Habakkuk received in a vision.

² How long, O LORD, must I call
for help?
But you do not listen!
"Violence is everywhere!" I cry,
but you do not come to save.
³ Must I forever see these evil deeds?
Why must I watch all this misery?
Wherever I look,
I see destruction and violence.
I am surrounded by people
who love to argue and fight.

4 The law has become paralyzed,
  and there is no justice in the courts.
The wicked far outnumber
    the righteous,
  so that justice has become
    perverted.

5 The Lord replied,

"Look around at the nations;
  look and be amazed!*
For I am doing something in your
  own day,
  something you wouldn't believe
  even if someone told you about it.
6 I am raising up the Babylonians,*
  a cruel and violent people.
They will march across the world
  and conquer other lands.
7 They are notorious for their cruelty
  and do whatever they like.
8 Their horses are swifter than cheetahs*
  and fiercer than wolves at dusk.
Their charioteers charge from
    far away.
  Like eagles, they swoop down to
    devour their prey.

9 "On they come, all bent on violence.
  Their hordes advance like a
    desert wind,
    sweeping captives ahead of them
    like sand.
10 They scoff at kings and princes
  and scorn all their fortresses.
They simply pile ramps of earth
  against their walls and capture
  them!
11 They sweep past like the wind
  and are gone.
But they are deeply guilty,
  for their own strength is their
    god."

12 O Lord my God, my Holy One, you
    who are eternal—
  surely you do not plan to wipe
    us out?
O Lord, our Rock, you have sent
    these Babylonians to correct us,
  to punish us for our many sins.
13 But you are pure and cannot stand
    the sight of evil.

Will you wink at their treachery?
Should you be silent while the wicked
  swallow up people more righteous
  than they?

14 Are we only fish to be caught and
    killed?
  Are we only sea creatures that
    have no leader?
15 Must we be strung up on their hooks
  and caught in their nets while
    they rejoice and celebrate?
16 Then they will worship their nets
  and burn incense in front
    of them.
  "These nets are the gods who have
    made us rich!"
  they will claim.
17 Will you let them get away with this
    forever?
  Will they succeed forever in their
    heartless conquests?

2:1 I will climb up to my watchtower
  and stand at my guardpost.
There I will wait to see what the
    Lord says
  and how he* will answer my
    complaint.

2 Then the Lord said to me,

"Write my answer plainly on tablets,
  so that a runner can carry the
    correct message to others.
3 This vision is for a future time.
  It describes the end, and it will be
    fulfilled.
If it seems slow in coming, wait
    patiently,
  for it will surely take place.
  It will not be delayed.

4 "Look at the proud!
  They trust in themselves, and
    their lives are crooked.
  But the righteous will live by their
    faithfulness to God.*
5 Wealth* is treacherous,
  and the arrogant are never at rest.
They open their mouths as wide as
    the grave,*
  and like death, they are never
    satisfied.

In their greed they have gathered up
   many nations
   and swallowed many peoples.

6 "But soon their captives will taunt
   them.
They will mock them, saying,
'What sorrow awaits you thieves!
   Now you will get what you
   deserve!
You've become rich by extortion,
   but how much longer can this
   go on?'
7 Suddenly, your debtors will take
   action.
They will turn on you and take all
   you have,
   while you stand trembling and
   helpless.
8 Because you have plundered many
   nations;
   now all the survivors will
   plunder you.
You committed murder throughout
   the countryside
   and filled the towns with violence.

9 "What sorrow awaits you who build
   big houses
   with money gained dishonestly!
You believe your wealth will buy
   security,
   putting your family's nest beyond
   the reach of danger.
10 But by the murders you committed,
   you have shamed your name and
   forfeited your lives.
11 The very stones in the walls cry out
   against you,
   and the beams in the ceilings
   echo the complaint.

12 "What sorrow awaits you who
   build cities
   with money gained through
   murder and corruption!
13 Has not the LORD of Heaven's
   Armies promised
   that the wealth of nations will
   turn to ashes?
They work so hard,
   but all in vain!
14 For as the waters fill the sea,

the earth will be filled with
   an awareness
   of the glory of the LORD.

15 "What sorrow awaits you who make
   your neighbors drunk!
You force your cup on them
   so you can gloat over their
   shameful nakedness.
16 But soon it will be your turn to be
   disgraced.
Come, drink and be exposed!
Drink from the cup of the LORD's
   judgment,
   and all your glory will be turned to
   shame.
17 You cut down the forests of Lebanon.
   Now you will be cut down.
You destroyed the wild animals,
   so now their terror will be yours.
You committed murder throughout
   the countryside
   and filled the towns with violence.

18 "What good is an idol carved by man,
   or a cast image that deceives you?
How foolish to trust in your own
   creation—
   a god that can't even talk!
19 What sorrow awaits you who say
   to wooden idols,
   'Wake up and save us!'
To speechless stone images you say,
   'Rise up and teach us!'
Can an idol tell you what to do?
They may be overlaid with gold
   and silver,
   but they are lifeless inside.
20 But the LORD is in his holy Temple.
   Let all the earth be silent
   before him."

3:1 THIS prayer was sung by the prophet
Habakkuk:*

2 **I have heard all about you, LORD.**
   I am filled with awe by your
   amazing works.
In this time of our deep need,
   help us again as you did in years
   gone by.
And in your anger,
   remember your mercy.

3 I see God moving across the deserts
   from Edom,*
   the Holy One coming from
   Mount Paran.*
   His brilliant splendor fills the heavens,
   and the earth is filled with his praise.
4 His coming is as brilliant as the
   sunrise.
   Rays of light flash from his hands,
   where his awesome power is
   hidden.
5 Pestilence marches before him;
   plague follows close behind.
6 When he stops, the earth shakes.
   When he looks, the nations
   tremble.
   He shatters the everlasting mountains
   and levels the eternal hills.
   He is the Eternal One!
7 I see the people of Cushan in distress,
   and the nation of Midian
   trembling in terror.

8 Was it in anger, LORD, that you
   struck the rivers
   and parted the sea?
   Were you displeased with them?
   No, you were sending your
   chariots of salvation!
9 You brandished your bow
   and your quiver of arrows.
   You split open the earth with
   flowing rivers.
10 The mountains watched and trembled.
   Onward swept the raging waters.
   The mighty deep cried out,
   lifting its hands to the LORD.
11 The sun and moon stood still
   in the sky
   as your brilliant arrows flew
   and your glittering spear flashed.

12 You marched across the land in anger
   and trampled the nations
   in your fury.
13 You went out to rescue your
   chosen people,
   to save your anointed ones.
   You crushed the heads of the wicked
   and stripped their bones from
   head to toe.
14 With his own weapons,

you destroyed the chief of those
   who rushed out like a whirlwind,
   thinking Israel would be easy prey.
15 You trampled the sea with your
   horses,
   and the mighty waters piled high.

16 I trembled inside when I heard this;
   my lips quivered with fear.
   My legs gave way beneath me,*
   and I shook in terror.
   I will wait quietly for the coming day
   when disaster will strike the
   people who invade us.
17 Even though the fig trees have
   no blossoms,
   and there are no grapes on the vines;
   even though the olive crop fails,
   and the fields lie empty and
   barren;
   even though the flocks die in the
   fields,
   and the cattle barns are empty,
18 yet I will rejoice in the LORD!
   I will be joyful in the God
   of my salvation!
19 The Sovereign LORD is my strength!
   He makes me as surefooted
   as a deer,*
   able to tread upon the heights.

(For the choir director: This prayer is to
be accompanied by stringed instruments.)

1:5 Greek version reads *Look you mockers; / look and be
amazed and die.* Compare Acts 13:41. 1:6 Or *Chaldeans.*
1:8 Or *leopards.* 2:1 As in Syriac version; Hebrew
reads *I.* 2:3b-4 Greek version reads *If the vision is
delayed, wait patiently, / for it will surely come and not
delay. / 'I will take no pleasure in anyone who turns away.
/ But the righteous person will live by my faith.* Compare
Rom 1:17; Gal 3:11; Heb 10:37-38. 2:5a As in Dead Sea
Scroll 1QpHab; other Hebrew manuscripts read *Wine.*
2:5b Hebrew *as Sheol.* 3:1 Hebrew adds *according to
shigionoth,* probably indicating the musical setting for the
prayer. 3:3a Hebrew *Teman.* 3:3b Hebrew adds *selah;*
also in 3:9, 13. The meaning of this Hebrew term is
uncertain; it is probably a musical or literary term.
3:16 Hebrew *Decay entered my bones.* 3:19 Or *He gives
me the speed of a deer.*

REVELATION 9:1-21

Then the fifth angel blew his trumpet,
and I [John] saw a star that had fallen to
earth from the sky, and he was given the
key to the shaft of the bottomless pit.*
2 When he opened it, smoke poured out
as though from a huge furnace, and the

sunlight and air turned dark from the smoke.

³Then locusts came from the smoke and descended on the earth, and they were given power to sting like scorpions. ⁴They were told not to harm the grass or plants or trees, but only the people who did not have the seal of God on their foreheads. ⁵They were told not to kill them but to torture them for five months with pain like the pain of a scorpion sting. ⁶In those days people will seek death but will not find it. They will long to die, but death will flee from them!

⁷The locusts looked like horses prepared for battle. They had what looked like gold crowns on their heads, and their faces looked like human faces. ⁸They had hair like women's hair and teeth like the teeth of a lion. ⁹They wore armor made of iron, and their wings roared like an army of chariots rushing into battle. ¹⁰They had tails that stung like scorpions, and for five months they had the power to torment people. ¹¹Their king is the angel from the bottomless pit; his name in Hebrew is *Abaddon,* and in Greek, *Apollyon*—the Destroyer.

¹²The first terror is past, but look, two more terrors are coming!

¹³Then the sixth angel blew his trumpet, and I heard a voice speaking from the four horns of the gold altar that stands in the presence of God. ¹⁴And the voice said to the sixth angel who held the trumpet, "Release the four angels who are bound at the great Euphrates River." ¹⁵Then the four angels who had been prepared for this hour and day and month and year were turned loose to kill one-third of all the people on earth. ¹⁶I heard the size of their army, which was 200 million mounted troops.

¹⁷And in my vision, I saw the horses and the riders sitting on them. The riders wore armor that was fiery red and dark blue and yellow. The horses had heads like lions, and fire and smoke and burning sulfur billowed from their mouths. ¹⁸One-third of all the people on

earth were killed by these three plagues—by the fire and smoke and burning sulfur that came from the mouths of the horses. ¹⁹Their power was in their mouths and in their tails. For their tails had heads like snakes, with the power to injure people.

²⁰But the people who did not die in these plagues still refused to repent of their evil deeds and turn to God. They continued to worship demons and idols made of gold, silver, bronze, stone, and wood—idols that can neither see nor hear nor walk! ²¹And they did not repent of their murders or their witchcraft or their sexual immorality or their thefts.

9:1 Or *the abyss,* or *the underworld;* also in 9:11.

PSALM 137:1-9

Beside the rivers of Babylon, we sat and wept
    as we thought of Jerusalem.*
² We put away our harps,
    hanging them on the branches
        of poplar trees.
³ For our captors demanded a song
        from us.
    Our tormentors insisted on
        a joyful hymn:
    "Sing us one of those songs
        of Jerusalem!"
⁴ But how can we sing the songs
        of the LORD
    while in a pagan land?

⁵ If I forget you, O Jerusalem,
    let my right hand forget how
        to play the harp.
⁶ May my tongue stick to the roof
        of my mouth
    if I fail to remember you,
    if I don't make Jerusalem my
        greatest joy.

⁷ O LORD, remember what the
        Edomites did
    on the day the armies of Babylon
        captured Jerusalem.
    "Destroy it!" they yelled.
    "Level it to the ground!"
⁸ O Babylon, you will be destroyed.

Happy is the one who pays
you back
for what you have done to us.
9 Happy is the one who takes
your babies
and smashes them against
the rocks!

137:1 Hebrew *Zion;* also in 137:3.

PROVERBS 30:10
Never slander a worker to the employer, or the person will curse you, and
you will pay for it.

DECEMBER
19

ZEPHANIAH 1:1–3:20
The LORD gave this message to Zephaniah when Josiah son of Amon was king
of Judah. Zephaniah was the son of
Cushi, son of Gedaliah, son of Amariah,
son of Hezekiah.

2 "I will sweep away everything
from the face of the earth," says
the LORD.
3 "I will sweep away people and
animals alike.
I will sweep away the birds of the
sky and the fish in the sea.
I will reduce the wicked to heaps of
rubble,*
and I will wipe humanity from
the face of the earth," says
the LORD.
4 "I will crush Judah and Jerusalem
with my fist
and destroy every last trace of
their Baal worship.
I will put an end to all the idolatrous
priests,
so that even the memory of them
will disappear.
5 For they go up to their roofs
and bow down to the sun, moon,
and stars.

They claim to follow the LORD,
but then they worship Molech,*
too.
6 And I will destroy those who used to
worship me
but now no longer do.
They no longer ask for the LORD's
guidance
or seek my blessings."

7 Stand in silence in the presence of
the Sovereign LORD,
for the awesome day of the
LORD's judgment is near.
The LORD has prepared his people
for a great slaughter
and has chosen their executioners.*
8 "On that day of judgment,"
says the LORD,
"I will punish the leaders and
princes of Judah
and all those following pagan
customs.
9 Yes, I will punish those who
participate in pagan worship
ceremonies,
and those who fill their masters'
houses with violence and
deceit.
10 "On that day," says the LORD,
"a cry of alarm will come from
the Fish Gate
and echo throughout the New
Quarter of the city.*
And a great crash will sound from
the hills.
11 Wail in sorrow, all you who live in
the market area,
for all the merchants and traders
will be destroyed.

12 "I will search with lanterns in
Jerusalem's darkest corners
to punish those who sit
complacent in their sins.
They think the LORD will do nothing
to them,
either good or bad.
13 So their property will be plundered,
their homes will be ransacked.
They will build new homes
but never live in them.

They will plant vineyards
   but never drink wine from them.

¹⁴ "That terrible day of the LORD
      is near.
   Swiftly it comes—
a day of bitter tears,
   a day when even strong men will
      cry out.
¹⁵ It will be a day when the LORD's
      anger is poured out—
   a day of terrible distress and
      anguish,
a day of ruin and desolation,
   a day of darkness and gloom,
a day of clouds and blackness,
¹⁶   a day of trumpet calls and battle
      cries.
   Down go the walled cities
   and the strongest battlements!

¹⁷ "Because you have sinned against
      the LORD,
   I will make you grope around like
      the blind.
Your blood will be poured into
      the dust,
   and your bodies will lie rotting
      on the ground."

¹⁸ Your silver and gold will not
      save you
   on that day of the LORD's anger.
For the whole land will be devoured
   by the fire of his jealousy.
He will make a terrifying end
   of all the people on earth.*

²:¹ GATHER together—yes, gather
      together,
   you shameless nation.
² Gather before judgment begins,
   before your time to repent is
      blown away like chaff.
Act now, before the fierce fury of
   the LORD falls
   and the terrible day of the LORD's
      anger begins.
³ Seek the LORD, all who are humble,
   and follow his commands.
Seek to do what is right
   and to live humbly.

Perhaps even yet the LORD will
      protect you—
   protect you from his anger on
      that day of destruction.

⁴ Gaza and Ashkelon will be
      abandoned,
   Ashdod and Ekron torn down.
⁵ And what sorrow awaits you
      Philistines*
   who live along the coast and in
      the land of Canaan,
   for this judgment is against
      you, too!
The LORD will destroy you
   until not one of you is left.
⁶ The Philistine coast will become
      a wilderness pasture,
   a place of shepherd camps
   and enclosures for sheep
      and goats.
⁷ The remnant of the tribe of Judah
      will pasture there.
   They will rest at night in the
      abandoned houses in Ashkelon.
For the LORD their God will visit his
      people in kindness
   and restore their prosperity again.

⁸ "I have heard the taunts of the
      Moabites
   and the insults of the Ammonites,
mocking my people
   and invading their borders.
⁹ Now, as surely as I live,"
   says the LORD of Heaven's Armies,
      the God of Israel,
"Moab and Ammon will be
      destroyed—
   destroyed as completely as Sodom
      and Gomorrah.
Their land will become a place of
      stinging nettles,
   salt pits, and eternal desolation.
The remnant of my people will
      plunder them
   and take their land."

¹⁰ They will receive the wages
      of their pride,
   for they have scoffed at the
      people of the LORD of Heaven's
      Armies.

¹¹ The Lord will terrify them
      as he destroys all the gods
         in the land.
   Then nations around the world will
         worship the Lord,
      each in their own land.

¹² "You Ethiopians* will also be
         slaughtered
      by my sword," says the Lord.

¹³ And the Lord will strike the lands of
         the north with his fist,
      destroying the land of Assyria.
   He will make its great capital,
         Nineveh, a desolate wasteland,
      parched like a desert.
¹⁴ The proud city will become a
         pasture for flocks and herds,
      and all sorts of wild animals will
         settle there.
   The desert owl and screech owl will
         roost on its ruined columns,
      their calls echoing through the
         gaping windows.
   Rubble will block all the doorways,
      and the cedar paneling will be
         exposed to the weather.
¹⁵ This is the boisterous city,
      once so secure.
   "I am the greatest!" it boasted
      "No other city can compare
         with me!"
   But now, look how it has become an
         utter ruin,
      a haven for wild animals.
   Everyone passing by will laugh
         in derision
      and shake a defiant fist.

^{3:1} What sorrow awaits rebellious,
         polluted Jerusalem,
      the city of violence and crime!
² No one can tell it anything;
      it refuses all correction.
   It does not trust in the Lord
      or draw near to its God.
³ Its leaders are like roaring lions
      hunting for their victims.
   Its judges are like ravenous wolves
         at evening time,
      who by dawn have left no trace
         of their prey.

⁴ Its prophets are arrogant liars
      seeking their own gain.
   Its priests defile the Temple by
      disobeying God's instructions.
⁵ But the Lord is still there in the city,
      and he does no wrong.
   Day by day he hands down justice,
      and he does not fail.
   But the wicked know no shame.

⁶ "I have wiped out many nations,
      devastating their fortress walls
         and towers.
   Their streets are now deserted;
      their cities lie in silent ruin.
   There are no survivors—
      none at all.
⁷ I thought, 'Surely they will have
         reverence for me now!
      Surely they will listen to my
         warnings.
   Then I won't need to strike again,
      destroying their homes.'
   But no, they get up early
      to continue their evil deeds.
⁸ Therefore, be patient," says
         the Lord.
   "Soon I will stand and accuse
         these evil nations.
   For I have decided to gather the
         kingdoms of the earth
      and pour out my fiercest anger
         and fury on them.
   All the earth will be devoured
      by the fire of my jealousy.

⁹ "Then I will purify the speech
         of all people,
      so that everyone can worship the
         Lord together.
¹⁰ My scattered people who live
         beyond the rivers of Ethiopia*
      will come to present their offerings.
¹¹ On that day you will no longer need
         to be ashamed,
      for you will no longer be rebels
         against me.
   I will remove all proud and arrogant
         people from among you.
   There will be no more
      haughtiness on my holy
         mountain.

¹² Those who are left will be the lowly
and humble,
for it is they who trust in the
name of the LORD.
¹³ The remnant of Israel will do no
wrong;
they will never tell lies or deceive
one another.
They will eat and sleep in safety,
and no one will make them afraid."

¹⁴ Sing, O daughter of Zion;
shout aloud, O Israel!
Be glad and rejoice with all your
heart,
O daughter of Jerusalem!
¹⁵ For the LORD will remove his hand
of judgment
and will disperse the armies of
your enemy.
And the LORD himself, the King of
Israel,
will live among you!
At last your troubles will be over,
and you will never again fear
disaster.
¹⁶ On that day the announcement to
Jerusalem will be,
"Cheer up, Zion! Don't be afraid!
¹⁷ For the LORD your God is living
among you.
He is a mighty savior.
He will take delight in you with
gladness.
With his love, he will calm all
your fears.*
He will rejoice over you with
joyful songs."

¹⁸ "I will gather you who mourn for the
appointed festivals;
you will be disgraced no more.*
¹⁹ And I will deal severely with all who
have oppressed you.
I will save the weak and helpless
ones;
I will bring together
those who were chased away.
I will give glory and fame to my
former exiles,
wherever they have been mocked
and shamed.

²⁰ On that day I will gather you together
and bring you home again.
I will give you a good name, a name
of distinction,
among all the nations of the earth,
as I restore your fortunes before
their very eyes.
I, the LORD, have spoken!"

1:3 The meaning of the Hebrew is uncertain.   1:5 Hebrew
Malcam, a variant spelling of Molech; or it could possibly
mean *their king*.   1:7 Hebrew *has prepared a sacrifice and
sanctified his guests*.   1:10 Or *the Second Quarter*, a newer
section of Jerusalem. Hebrew reads *the Mishneh*.   1:18 Or
the people living in the land.   2:5 Hebrew *Kerethites*.
2:12 Hebrew *Cushites*.   3:10 Hebrew *Cush*.   3:17 Or *He
will be silent in his love*. Greek and Syriac versions read *He
will renew you with his love*.   3:18 The meaning of the
Hebrew for this verse is uncertain.

REVELATION 10:1-11

Then I [John] saw another mighty angel
coming down from heaven, surrounded
by a cloud, with a rainbow over his head.
His face shone like the sun, and his feet
were like pillars of fire. ²And in his
hand was a small scroll* that had been
opened. He stood with his right foot on
the sea and his left foot on the land.
³And he gave a great shout like the roar
of a lion. And when he shouted, the
seven thunders answered.

⁴When the seven thunders spoke, I
was about to write. But I heard a voice
from heaven saying, "Keep secret* what
the seven thunders said, and do not
write it down."

⁵ Then the angel I saw standing on the
sea and on the land raised his right hand
toward heaven. ⁶He swore an oath in the
name of the one who lives forever and
ever, who created the heavens and
everything in them, the earth and everything in it, and the sea and everything in
it. He said, "There will be no more delay.
⁷ When the seventh angel blows his
trumpet, God's mysterious plan will be
fulfilled. It will happen just as he announced it to his servants the prophets."

⁸Then the voice from heaven spoke
to me again: "Go and take the open
scroll from the hand of the angel who is
standing on the sea and on the land."

⁹So I went to the angel and told him
to give me the small scroll. "Yes, take it
and eat it," he said. "It will be sweet as

honey in your mouth, but it will turn sour in your stomach!" ¹⁰So I took the small scroll from the hand of the angel, and I ate it! It was sweet in my mouth, but when I swallowed it, it turned sour in my stomach.

¹¹Then I was told, "You must prophesy again about many peoples, nations, languages, and kings."

10:2 Or *book;* also in 10:8, 9, 10.   10:4 Greek *Seal up.*

PSALM 138:1-8
A psalm of David.

¹ I give you thanks, O Lᴏʀᴅ, with all
    my heart;
  I will sing your praises before
    the gods.
² I bow before your holy Temple
    as I worship.
  I praise your name for your
    unfailing love and
    faithfulness;
  for your promises are backed
    by all the honor of your name.
³ As soon as I pray, you answer me;
  you encourage me by giving me
    strength.

⁴ Every king in all the earth will thank
    you, Lᴏʀᴅ,
  for all of them will hear your
    words.
⁵ Yes, they will sing about the Lᴏʀᴅ's
    ways,
  for the glory of the Lᴏʀᴅ is
    very great.
⁶ **Though the Lᴏʀᴅ is great, he cares**
    for the humble,
  but he keeps his distance from
    the proud.

⁷ Though I am surrounded by troubles,
  you will protect me from the
    anger of my enemies.
  You reach out your hand,
    and the power of your right hand
    saves me.
⁸ The Lᴏʀᴅ will work out his plans
    for my life—
  for your faithful love, O Lᴏʀᴅ,
    endures forever.

Don't abandon me, for you
  made me.

PROVERBS 30:11-14
Some people curse their father and do not thank their mother. They are pure in their own eyes, but they are filthy and unwashed. They look proudly around, casting disdainful glances. They have teeth like swords and fangs like knives. They devour the poor from the earth and the needy from among humanity.

DECEMBER 20

HAGGAI 1:1-2:23
On August 29* of the second year of King Darius's reign, the Lᴏʀᴅ gave a message through the prophet Haggai to Zerubbabel son of Shealtiel, governor of Judah, and to Jeshua* son of Jehozadak, the high priest.

²"This is what the Lᴏʀᴅ of Heaven's Armies says: The people are saying, 'The time has not yet come to rebuild the house of the Lᴏʀᴅ.'"

³Then the Lᴏʀᴅ sent this message through the prophet Haggai: ⁴"Why are you living in luxurious houses while my house lies in ruins? ⁵This is what the Lᴏʀᴅ of Heaven's Armies says: Look at what's happening to you! ⁶You have planted much but harvest little. You eat but are not satisfied. You drink but are still thirsty. You put on clothes but cannot keep warm. Your wages disappear as though you were putting them in pockets filled with holes!

⁷"This is what the Lᴏʀᴅ of Heaven's Armies says: Look at what's happening to you! ⁸Now go up into the hills, bring down timber, and rebuild my house. Then I will take pleasure in it and be honored, says the Lᴏʀᴅ. ⁹You hoped for rich harvests, but they were poor. And when you brought your harvest home, I

blew it away. Why? Because my house lies in ruins, says the LORD of Heaven's Armies, while all of you are busy building your own fine houses. ¹⁰It's because of you that the heavens withhold the dew and the earth produces no crops. ¹¹I have called for a drought on your fields and hills—a drought to wither the grain and grapes and olive trees and all your other crops, a drought to starve you and your livestock and to ruin everything you have worked so hard to get."

¹²Then Zerubbabel son of Shealtiel, and Jeshua son of Jehozadak, the high priest, and the whole remnant of God's people began to obey the message from the LORD their God. When they heard the words of the prophet Haggai, whom the LORD their God had sent, the people feared the LORD. ¹³Then Haggai, the LORD's messenger, gave the people this message from the LORD: "I am with you, says the LORD!"

¹⁴So the LORD sparked the enthusiasm of Zerubbabel son of Shealtiel, governor of Judah, and the enthusiasm of Jeshua son of Jehozadak, the high priest, and the enthusiasm of the whole remnant of God's people. They began rebuilding the house of their God, the LORD of Heaven's Armies, ¹⁵on September 21* of the second year of King Darius's reign.

²:¹THEN on October 17 of that same year,* the LORD sent another message through the prophet Haggai. ²"Say this to Zerubbabel son of Shealtiel, governor of Judah, and to Jeshua* son of Jehozadak, the high priest, and to the remnant of God's people there in the land: ³'Does anyone remember this house—this Temple—in its former splendor? How, in comparison, does it look to you now? It must seem like nothing at all! ⁴But now the LORD says: Be strong, Zerubbabel. Be strong, Jeshua son of Jehozadak, the high priest. Be strong, all you people still left in the land. And now get to work, for I am with you, says the LORD of Heaven's Armies. ⁵My Spirit remains among you, just as I

promised when you came out of Egypt. So do not be afraid.'

⁶"For this is what the LORD of Heaven's Armies says: In just a little while I will again shake the heavens and the earth, the oceans and the dry land. ⁷I will shake all the nations, and the treasures of all the nations will be brought to this Temple. I will fill this place with glory, says the LORD of Heaven's Armies. ⁸The silver is mine, and the gold is mine, says the LORD of Heaven's Armies. ⁹The future glory of this Temple will be greater than its past glory, says the LORD of Heaven's Armies. And in this place I will bring peace. I, the LORD of Heaven's Armies, have spoken!"

¹⁰On December 18* of the second year of King Darius's reign, the LORD sent this message to the prophet Haggai: ¹¹"This is what the LORD of Heaven's Armies says. Ask the priests this question about the law: ¹²'If one of you is carrying some meat from a holy sacrifice in his robes and his robe happens to brush against some bread or stew, wine or olive oil, or any other kind of food, will it also become holy?'"

The priests replied, "No."

¹³Then Haggai asked, "If someone becomes ceremonially unclean by touching a dead person and then touches any of these foods, will the food be defiled?"

And the priests answered, "Yes."

¹⁴Then Haggai responded, "That is how it is with this people and this nation, says the LORD. Everything they do and everything they offer is defiled by their sin. ¹⁵Look at what was happening to you before you began to lay the foundation of the LORD's Temple. ¹⁶When you hoped for a twenty-bushel crop, you harvested only ten. When you expected to draw fifty gallons from the winepress, you found only twenty. ¹⁷I sent blight and mildew and hail to destroy everything you worked so hard to produce. Even so, you refused to return to me, says the LORD.

¹⁸"Think about this eighteenth day of December, the day* when the rebuilding of the LORD's Temple began. Think carefully. ¹⁹I am giving you a promise

now while the seed is still in the barn.* You have not yet harvested your grain, and your grapevines, fig trees, pomegranates, and olive trees have not yet produced their crops. But from this day onward I will bless you."

²⁰On that same day, December 18,* the Lord sent this second message to Haggai: ²¹"Tell Zerubbabel, the governor of Judah, that I am about to shake the heavens and the earth. ²²I will overthrow royal thrones and destroy the power of foreign kingdoms. I will overturn their chariots and riders. The horses will fall, and their riders will kill each other.

²³"But when this happens, says the Lord of Heaven's Armies, I will honor you, Zerubbabel son of Shealtiel, my servant. I will make you like a signet ring on my finger, says the Lord, for I have chosen you. I, the Lord of Heaven's Armies, have spoken!"

1:1a Hebrew *On the first day of the sixth month,* of the ancient Hebrew lunar calendar. A number of dates in Haggai can be cross-checked with dates in surviving Persian records and related accurately to our modern calendar. This event occurred on August 29, 520 B.C. 1:1b Hebrew *Joshua,* a variant spelling of Jeshua; also in 1:12, 14. 1:15 Hebrew *on the twenty-fourth day of the sixth month,* of the ancient Hebrew lunar calendar. This event occurred on September 21, 520 B.C.; also see note on 1:1a. 2:1 Hebrew *on the twenty-first day of the seventh month,* of the ancient Hebrew lunar calendar. This event (in the second year of Darius's reign) occurred on October 17, 520 B.C.; also see note on 1:1a. 2:2 Hebrew *Joshua,* a variant spelling of Jeshua; also in 2:4. 2:10 Hebrew *On the twenty-fourth day of the ninth month,* of the ancient Hebrew lunar calendar (similarly in 2:18). This event occurred on December 18, 520 B.C.; also see note on 1:1a. 2:18 Or *On this eighteenth day of December, think about the day.* 2:19 Hebrew *Is the seed yet in the barn?* 2:20 Hebrew *On the twenty-fourth day of the [ninth] month;* see note on 2:10.

REVELATION 11:1-19

Then I [John] was given a measuring stick, and I was told, "Go and measure the Temple of God and the altar, and count the number of worshipers. ²But do not measure the outer courtyard, for it has been turned over to the nations. They will trample the holy city for 42 months. ³And I will give power to my two witnesses, and they will be clothed in burlap and will prophesy during those 1,260 days."

⁴These two prophets are the two olive trees and the two lampstands that stand before the Lord of all the earth. ⁵If anyone tries to harm them, fire flashes from their mouths and consumes their enemies. This is how anyone who tries to harm them must die. ⁶They have power to shut the sky so that no rain will fall for as long as they prophesy. And they have the power to turn the rivers and oceans into blood, and to strike the earth with every kind of plague as often as they wish.

⁷When they complete their testimony, the beast that comes up out of the bottomless pit* will declare war against them, and he will conquer them and kill them. ⁸And their bodies will lie in the main street of Jerusalem,* the city that is figuratively called "Sodom" and "Egypt," the city where their Lord was crucified. ⁹And for three and a half days, all peoples, tribes, languages, and nations will stare at their bodies. No one will be allowed to bury them. ¹⁰All the people who belong to this world will gloat over them and give presents to each other to celebrate the death of the two prophets who had tormented them.

¹¹But after three and a half days, God breathed life into them, and they stood up! Terror struck all who were staring at them. ¹²Then a loud voice from heaven called to the two prophets, "Come up here!" And they rose to heaven in a cloud as their enemies watched.

¹³At the same time there was a terrible earthquake that destroyed a tenth of the city. Seven thousand people died in that earthquake, and everyone else was terrified and gave glory to the God of heaven.

¹⁴The second terror is past, but look, the third terror is coming quickly.

¹⁵**Then the seventh angel blew his trumpet, and there were loud voices shouting in heaven:**

> **"The world has now become the Kingdom of our Lord and of his Christ,***
> **and he will reign forever and ever."**

¹⁶The twenty-four elders sitting on their thrones before God fell with their faces to the ground and worshiped him. ¹⁷And they said,

"We give thanks to you, Lord God,
the Almighty,
the one who is and who
always was,
for now you have assumed your
great power
and have begun to reign.
¹⁸ The nations were filled with wrath,
but now the time of your wrath
has come.
It is time to judge the dead
and reward your servants the
prophets,
as well as your holy people,
and all who fear your name,
from the least to the greatest.
It is time to destroy
all who have caused destruction
on the earth."

¹⁹Then, in heaven, the Temple of God was opened and the Ark of his covenant could be seen inside the Temple. Lightning flashed, thunder crashed and roared, and there was an earthquake and a terrible hailstorm.

11:7 Or *the abyss,* or *the underworld.*   11:8 Greek *the great city.*   11:15 Or *his Messiah.*

PSALM 139:1-24
For the choir director: A psalm of David.

¹ **O** LORD, you have examined
my heart
and know everything
about me.
² You know when I sit down or
stand up.
You know my thoughts even when
I'm far away.
³ You see me when I travel
and when I rest at home.
You know everything I do.
⁴ You know what I am going to say
even before I say it, LORD.
⁵ You go before me and follow me.
You place your hand of blessing
on my head.

⁶ Such knowledge is too wonderful
for me,
too great for me to understand!

⁷ I can never escape from your Spirit!
I can never get away from your
presence!
⁸ If I go up to heaven, you are there;
if I go down to the grave,*
you are there.
⁹ If I ride the wings of the morning,
if I dwell by the farthest oceans,
¹⁰ even there your hand will guide me,
and your strength will
support me.
¹¹ I could ask the darkness to hide me
and the light around me to
become night—
¹²   but even in darkness I cannot
hide from you.
To you the night shines as bright
as day.
Darkness and light are the same
to you.

¹³ You made all the delicate, inner
parts of my body
and knit me together in my
mother's womb.
¹⁴ Thank you for making me so
wonderfully complex!
Your workmanship is
marvelous—how well I know it.
¹⁵ You watched me as I was being
formed in utter seclusion,
as I was woven together in the
dark of the womb.
¹⁶ You saw me before I was born.
Every day of my life was
recorded in your book.
Every moment was laid out
before a single day had passed.

¹⁷ How precious are your thoughts
about me,* O God.
They cannot be numbered!
¹⁸ I can't even count them;
they outnumber the grains
of sand!
And when I wake up,
you are still with me!

¹⁹ O God, if only you would destroy
the wicked!

Get out of my life, you murderers!
20 They blaspheme you;
   your enemies misuse your name.
21 O Lord, shouldn't I hate those who
       hate you?
   Shouldn't I despise those who
       oppose you?
22 Yes, I hate them with total hatred,
   for your enemies are my enemies.

23 Search me, O God, and know my
       heart;
   test me and know my anxious
       thoughts.
24 Point out anything in me that
       offends you,
   and lead me along the path of
       everlasting life.

139:8 Hebrew *to Sheol.*   **139:17** Or *How precious to me
are your thoughts.*

PROVERBS 30:15-16

The leech has two suckers that cry out,
"More, more!"* □ There are three things
that are never satisfied—no, four that
never say, "Enough!": the grave,* the
barren womb, the thirsty desert, the
blazing fire.

30:15 Hebrew *two daughters who cry out, "Give, give!"*
30:16 Hebrew *Sheol.*

DECEMBER
21

ZECHARIAH 1:1-21

In November* of the second year of
King Darius's reign, the Lord gave this
message to the prophet Zechariah son
of Berekiah and grandson of Iddo:

2"I, the Lord, was very angry with
your ancestors. 3Therefore, say to the
people, 'This is what the Lord of
Heaven's Armies says: Return to me,
and I will return to you, says the Lord of
Heaven's Armies.' 4Don't be like your
ancestors who would not listen or pay
attention when the earlier prophets
said to them, 'This is what the Lord of
Heaven's Armies says: Turn from your
evil ways, and stop all your evil practices.'

5"Where are your ancestors now?
They and the prophets are long dead.
6But everything I said through my servants the prophets happened to your
ancestors, just as I said. As a result, they
repented and said, 'We have received
what we deserved from the Lord of
Heaven's Armies. He has done what he
said he would do.'"

7Three months later, on February 15,*
the Lord sent another message to the
prophet Zechariah son of Berekiah and
grandson of Iddo.

8In a vision during the night, I saw a
man sitting on a red horse that was
standing among some myrtle trees in a
small valley. Behind him were riders on
red, brown, and white horses. 9I asked
the angel who was talking with me, "My
lord, what do these horses mean?"

"I will show you," the angel replied.

10The rider standing among the myrtle trees then explained, "They are the
ones the Lord has sent out to patrol the
earth."

11Then the other riders reported to
the angel of the Lord, who was standing
among the myrtle trees, "We have been
patrolling the earth, and the whole
earth is at peace."

12Upon hearing this, the angel of the
Lord prayed this prayer: "O Lord of
Heaven's Armies, for seventy years now
you have been angry with Jerusalem and
the towns of Judah. How long until you
again show mercy to them?" 13And the
Lord spoke kind and comforting words
to the angel who talked with me.

14Then the angel said to me, "Shout
this message for all to hear: 'This is what
the Lord of Heaven's Armies says: My
love for Jerusalem and Mount Zion is
passionate and strong. 15But I am very
angry with the other nations that are
now enjoying peace and security. I was
only a little angry with my people, but
the nations inflicted harm on them far
beyond my intentions.

16" 'Therefore, this is what the LORD says: I have returned to show mercy to Jerusalem. My Temple will be rebuilt, says the LORD of Heaven's Armies, and measurements will be taken for the reconstruction of Jerusalem.*'

17"Say this also: 'This is what the LORD of Heaven's Armies says: The towns of Israel will again overflow with prosperity, and the LORD will again comfort Zion and choose Jerusalem as his own.'"

18*Then I looked up and saw four animal horns. 19"What are these?" I asked the angel who was talking with me.

He replied, "These horns represent the nations that scattered Judah, Israel, and Jerusalem."

20Then the LORD showed me four blacksmiths. 21"What are these men coming to do?" I asked.

The angel replied, "These four horns—these nations—scattered and humbled Judah. Now these blacksmiths have come to terrify those nations and throw them down and destroy them."

1:1 Hebrew *In the eighth month.* A number of dates in Zechariah can be cross-checked with dates in surviving Persian records and related accurately to our modern calendar. This month of the ancient Hebrew lunar calendar occurred within the months of October and November 520 B.C. 1:7 Hebrew *On the twenty-fourth day of the eleventh month, the month of Shebat, in the second year of Darius.* This event occurred on February 15, 519 B.C.; also see note on 1:1. 1:16 Hebrew *and the measuring line will be stretched out over Jerusalem.* 1:18 Verses 1:18-21 are numbered 2:1-4 in Hebrew text.

REVELATION 12:1-17

Then I [John] witnessed in heaven an event of great significance. I saw a woman clothed with the sun, with the moon beneath her feet, and a crown of twelve stars on her head. 2She was pregnant, and she cried out because of her labor pains and the agony of giving birth.

3Then I witnessed in heaven another significant event. I saw a large red dragon with seven heads and ten horns, with seven crowns on his heads. 4His tail swept away one-third of the stars in the sky, and he threw them to the earth. He stood in front of the woman as she was about to give birth, ready to devour her baby as soon as it was born.

5She gave birth to a son who was to rule all nations with an iron rod. And her child was snatched away from the dragon and was caught up to God and to his throne. 6And the woman fled into the wilderness, where God had prepared a place to care for her for 1,260 days.

7Then there was war in heaven. Michael and his angels fought against the dragon and his angels. 8And the dragon lost the battle, and he and his angels were forced out of heaven. 9This great dragon—the ancient serpent called the devil, or Satan, the one deceiving the whole world—was thrown down to the earth with all his angels.

10Then I heard a loud voice shouting across the heavens,

"It has come at last—
    salvation and power
and the Kingdom of our God,
    and the authority of his Christ.*
For the accuser of our brothers
    and sisters*
has been thrown down to earth—
the one who accuses them
    before our God day and night.
11 And they have defeated him by the
    blood of the Lamb
    and by their testimony.
And they did not love their lives
    so much
    that they were afraid to die.
12 Therefore, rejoice, O heavens!
    And you who live in the heavens,
    rejoice!
But terror will come on the earth
    and the sea,
    for the devil has come down to
    you in great anger,
    knowing that he has little time."

13When the dragon realized that he had been thrown down to the earth, he pursued the woman who had given birth to the male child. 14But she was given two wings like those of a great eagle so she could fly to the place prepared for her in the wilderness. There she would be cared for and protected from the dragon* for a time, times, and half a time.

15 Then the dragon tried to drown the woman with a flood of water that flowed from his mouth. 16 But the earth helped her by opening its mouth and swallowing the river that gushed out from the mouth of the dragon. 17 And the dragon was angry at the woman and declared war against the rest of her children—all who keep God's commandments and maintain their testimony for Jesus.

12:10a Or *his Messiah.*   12:10b Greek *brothers.*
12:14 Greek *the serpent;* also in 12:15. See 12:9.

PSALM 140:1-13
For the choir director: A psalm of David.

1 O LORD, rescue me from evil people.
     Protect me from those who
          are violent,
2 those who plot evil in their hearts
     and stir up trouble all day long.
3 Their tongues sting like a snake;
     the venom of a viper drips from
          their lips.   *Interlude*

4 O LORD, keep me out of the hands
          of the wicked.
     Protect me from those who are
          violent,
     for they are plotting against me.
5 The proud have set a trap to
          catch me;
     they have stretched out a net;
     they have placed traps all along
          the way.   *Interlude*

6 I said to the LORD, "You are my God!"
     Listen, O LORD, to my cries for
          mercy!
7 O Sovereign LORD, the strong one
          who rescued me,
     you protected me on the day
          of battle.
8 LORD, do not let evil people have
          their way.
     Do not let their evil schemes succeed,
          or they will become proud.
                         Interlude

9 Let my enemies be destroyed
     by the very evil they have planned
          for me.

10 Let burning coals fall down on their
          heads.
     Let them be thrown into the fire
     or into watery pits from which
          they can't escape.
11 Don't let liars prosper here in
          our land.
     Cause great disasters to fall
          on the violent.

12 **But I know the LORD will help
          those they persecute;
     he will give justice to the poor.**
13 **Surely righteous people are
          praising your name;
     the godly will live in your
          presence.**

PROVERBS 30:17
The eye that mocks a father and despises a mother's instructions will be plucked out by ravens of the valley and eaten by vultures.

DECEMBER
22

ZECHARIAH 2:1–3:10
1 *When I [Zechariah] looked again, I saw a man with a measuring line in his hand. 2 "Where are you going?" I asked.

He replied, "I am going to measure Jerusalem, to see how wide and how long it is."

3 Then the angel who was with me went to meet a second angel who was coming toward him. 4 The other angel said, "Hurry, and say to that young man, 'Jerusalem will someday be so full of people and livestock that there won't be room enough for everyone! Many will live outside the city walls. 5 Then I, myself, will be a protective wall of fire around Jerusalem, says the LORD. And I will be the glory inside the city!'"

6 The LORD says, "Come away! Flee from Babylon in the land of the north,

for I have scattered you to the four winds. [7]Come away, people of Zion, you who are exiled in Babylon!"

[8]After a period of glory, the LORD of Heaven's Armies sent me* against the nations who plundered you. For he said, "Anyone who harms you harms my most precious possession.* [9]I will raise my fist to crush them, and their own slaves will plunder them." Then you will know that the LORD of Heaven's Armies has sent me.

[10]The LORD says, "Shout and rejoice, O beautiful Jerusalem,* for I am coming to live among you. [11]Many nations will join themselves to the LORD on that day, and they, too, will be my people. I will live among you, and you will know that the LORD of Heaven's Armies sent me to you. [12]The land of Judah will be the LORD's special possession in the holy land, and he will once again choose Jerusalem to be his own city. [13]Be silent before the LORD, all humanity, for he is springing into action from his holy dwelling."

[3:1]THEN the angel showed me Jeshua* the high priest standing before the angel of the LORD. The Accuser, Satan,* was there at the angel's right hand, making accusations against Jeshua. [2]And the LORD said to Satan, "I, the LORD, reject your accusations, Satan. Yes, the LORD, who has chosen Jerusalem, rebukes you. This man is like a burning stick that has been snatched from the fire."

[3]Jeshua's clothing was filthy as he stood there before the angel. [4]So the angel said to the others standing there, "Take off his filthy clothes." And turning to Jeshua he said, "See, I have taken away your sins, and now I am giving you these fine new clothes."

[5]Then I said, "They should also place a clean turban on his head." So they put a clean priestly turban on his head and dressed him in new clothes while the angel of the LORD stood by.

[6]Then the angel of the LORD spoke very solemnly to Jeshua and said, [7]"This is what the LORD of Heaven's Armies says: If you follow my ways and carefully serve me, then you will be given authority over my Temple and its courtyards. I will let you walk among these others standing here.

[8]"Listen to me, O Jeshua the high priest, and all you other priests. You are symbols of things to come. Soon I am going to bring my servant, the Branch. [9]Now look at the jewel I have set before Jeshua, a single stone with seven facets.* I will engrave an inscription on it, says the LORD of Heaven's Armies, and I will remove the sins of this land in a single day.

[10]"And on that day, says the LORD of Heaven's Armies, each of you will invite your neighbor to sit with you peacefully under your own grapevine and fig tree."

2:1 Verses 2:1-13 are numbered 2:5-17 in Hebrew text. 2:8a The meaning of the Hebrew is uncertain. 2:8b Hebrew *Anyone who touches you touches the pupil of his eye.* 2:10 Hebrew *O daughter of Zion.* 3:1a Hebrew *Joshua,* a variant spelling of Jeshua; also in 3:3, 4, 6, 8, 9. 3:1b Hebrew *The satan;* similarly in 3:2. 3:9 Hebrew *seven eyes.*

REVELATION 12:18–13:18

Then the dragon took his stand* on the shore beside the sea.

[13:1]THEN I saw a beast rising up out of the sea. It had seven heads and ten horns, with ten crowns on its horns. And written on each head were names that blasphemed God. [2]This beast looked like a leopard, but it had the feet of a bear and the mouth of a lion! And the dragon gave the beast his own power and throne and great authority.

[3]I saw that one of the heads of the beast seemed wounded beyond recovery—but the fatal wound was healed! The whole world marveled at this miracle and gave allegiance to the beast. [4]They worshiped the dragon for giving the beast such power, and they also worshiped the beast. "Who is as great as the beast?" they exclaimed. "Who is able to fight against him?"

[5]Then the beast was allowed to speak great blasphemies against God. And he was given authority to do whatever he

wanted for forty-two months. ⁶And he spoke terrible words of blasphemy against God, slandering his name and his temple—that is, those who live in heaven.* ⁷And the beast was allowed to wage war against God's holy people and to conquer them. And he was given authority to rule over every tribe and people and language and nation. ⁸And all the people who belong to this world worshiped the beast. They are the ones whose names were not written in the Book of Life before the world was made—the Book that belongs to the Lamb who was slaughtered.*

⁹ Anyone with ears to hear
    should listen and understand.
¹⁰ Anyone who is destined for prison
    will be taken to prison.
Anyone destined to die by the sword
    will die by the sword.

This means that God's holy people must endure persecution patiently and remain faithful.

¹¹Then I saw another beast come up out of the earth. He had two horns like those of a lamb, but he spoke with the voice of a dragon. ¹²He exercised all the authority of the first beast. And he required all the earth and its people to worship the first beast, whose fatal wound had been healed. ¹³He did astounding miracles, even making fire flash down to earth from the sky while everyone was watching. ¹⁴And with all the miracles he was allowed to perform on behalf of the first beast, he deceived all the people who belong to this world. He ordered the people to make a great statue of the first beast, who was fatally wounded and then came back to life. ¹⁵He was then permitted to give life to this statue so that it could speak. Then the statue of the beast commanded that anyone refusing to worship it must die.

¹⁶He required everyone—small and great, rich and poor, free and slave—to be given a mark on the right hand or on the forehead. ¹⁷And no one could buy or sell anything without that mark,

which was either the name of the beast or the number representing his name. ¹⁸Wisdom is needed here. Let the one with understanding solve the meaning of the number of the beast, for it is the number of a man.* His number is 666.*

12:18 Greek *Then he took his stand;* some manuscripts read *Then I took my stand.* Some translations put this entire sentence into 13:1. **13:6** Some manuscripts read *and his temple and all who live in heaven.* **13:8** Or *not written in the Book of Life that belongs to the Lamb who was slaughtered before the world was made.* **13:18a** Or *of humanity.* **13:18b** Some manuscripts read *616.*

PSALM 141:1-10
A psalm of David.

¹ **O** Lord, I am calling to you.
    Please hurry!
    Listen when I cry to you
        for help!
² **Accept my prayer as incense**
        offered to you,
    and my uplifted hands as an
        evening offering.

³ Take control of what I say, O Lord,
    and guard my lips.
⁴ Don't let me drift toward evil
    or take part in acts of wickedness.
Don't let me share in the delicacies
    of those who do wrong.

⁵ Let the godly strike me!
    It will be a kindness!
If they correct me, it is soothing
        medicine.
    Don't let me refuse it.

But I pray constantly
    against the wicked and their
        deeds.
⁶ When their leaders are thrown
        down from a cliff,
    the wicked will listen to my words
        and find them true.
⁷ Like rocks brought up by a plow,
    the bones of the wicked will lie
        scattered without burial.*

⁸ I look to you for help, O Sovereign
        Lord.
    You are my refuge; don't let them
        kill me.
⁹ Keep me from the traps they have
        set for me,

323

DECEMBER 23

from the snares of those who
do wrong.
¹⁰ Let the wicked fall into their
own nets,
but let me escape.

141:7 Hebrew *scattered at the mouth of Sheol.*

PROVERBS 30:18-20

There are three things that amaze me—
no, four things that I don't understand:
how an eagle glides through the sky,
how a snake slithers on a rock, how a
ship navigates the ocean, how a man
loves a woman. □ An adulterous woman
consumes a man, then wipes her mouth
and says, "What's wrong with that?"

DECEMBER
23

ZECHARIAH 4:1–5:11

Then the angel who had been talking
with me [Zechariah] returned and woke
me, as though I had been asleep. ²"What
do you see now?" he asked.

I answered, "I see a solid gold lampstand with a bowl of oil on top of it.
Around the bowl are seven lamps, each
having seven spouts with wicks. ³And I
see two olive trees, one on each side of
the bowl." ⁴Then I asked the angel,
"What are these, my lord? What do they
mean?"

⁵"Don't you know?" the angel asked.

"No, my lord," I replied.

⁶Then he said to me, "This is what the
LORD says to Zerubbabel: It is not by
force nor by strength, but by my Spirit,
says the LORD of Heaven's Armies.
⁷Nothing, not even a mighty mountain,
will stand in Zerubbabel's way; it will
become a level plain before him! And
when Zerubbabel sets the final stone of
the Temple in place, the people will
shout: 'May God bless it! May God bless
it!'*"

⁸Then another message came to me
from the LORD: ⁹"Zerubbabel is the one
who laid the foundation of this Temple,
and he will complete it. Then you will
know that the LORD of Heaven's Armies
has sent me. ¹⁰Do not despise these
small beginnings, for the LORD rejoices
to see the work begin, to see the plumb
line in Zerubbabel's hand."

(The seven lamps* represent the eyes
of the LORD that search all around the
world.)

¹¹Then I asked the angel, "What are
these two olive trees on each side of the
lampstand, ¹²and what are the two olive
branches that pour out golden oil
through two gold tubes?"

¹³"Don't you know?" he asked.

"No, my lord," I replied.

¹⁴Then he said to me, "They represent the two heavenly beings who stand
in the court of the Lord of all the earth."

⁵:¹I LOOKED up again and saw a scroll
flying through the air.

²"What do you see?" the angel asked.

"I see a flying scroll," I replied. "It appears to be about 30 feet long and
15 feet wide.*"

³Then he said to me, "This scroll contains the curse that is going out over the
entire land. One side of the scroll says
that those who steal will be banished
from the land; the other side says that
those who swear falsely will be banished from the land. ⁴And this is what
the LORD of Heaven's Armies says: I am
sending this curse into the house of
every thief and into the house of everyone who swears falsely using my name.
And my curse will remain in that house
and completely destroy it—even its timbers and stones."

⁵Then the angel who was talking with
me came forward and said, "Look up
and see what's coming."

⁶"What is it?" I asked.

He replied, "It is a basket for measuring grain,* and it's filled with the sins*
of everyone throughout the land."

⁷Then the heavy lead cover was lifted
off the basket, and there was a woman

sitting inside it. 8The angel said, "The woman's name is Wickedness," and he pushed her back into the basket and closed the heavy lid again.

9Then I looked up and saw two women flying toward us, gliding on the wind. They had wings like a stork, and they picked up the basket and flew into the sky.

10"Where are they taking the basket?" I asked the angel.

11He replied, "To the land of Babylonia,* where they will build a temple for the basket. And when the temple is ready, they will set the basket there on its pedestal."

4:7 Hebrew 'Grace, grace to it.' 4:10 Or The seven facets (see 3:9); Hebrew reads These seven. 5:2 Hebrew 20 cubits [9 meters] long and 10 cubits [4.5 meters] wide. 5:6a Hebrew an ephah [20 quarts or 22 liters]; also in 5:7, 8, 9, 10, 11. 5:6b As in Greek version; Hebrew reads the appearance. 5:11 Hebrew the land of Shinar.

REVELATION 14:1-20

Then I [John] saw the Lamb standing on Mount Zion, and with him were 144,000 who had his name and his Father's name written on their foreheads. 2And I heard a sound from heaven like the roar of mighty ocean waves or the rolling of loud thunder. It was like the sound of many harpists playing together.

3This great choir sang a wonderful new song in front of the throne of God and before the four living beings and the twenty-four elders. No one could learn this song except the 144,000 who had been redeemed from the earth. 4They have kept themselves as pure as virgins,* following the Lamb wherever he goes. They have been purchased from among the people on the earth as a special offering* to God and to the Lamb. 5They have told no lies; they are without blame.

6And I saw another angel flying through the sky, carrying the eternal Good News to proclaim to the people who belong to this world—to every nation, tribe, language, and people. 7"Fear God," he shouted. "Give glory to him. For the time has come when he will sit as judge. Worship him who made the heavens, the earth, the sea, and all the springs of water."

8Then another angel followed him through the sky, shouting, "Babylon is fallen—that great city is fallen—because she made all the nations of the world drink the wine of her passionate immorality."

9Then a third angel followed them, shouting, "Anyone who worships the beast and his statue or who accepts his mark on the forehead or on the hand 10must drink the wine of God's anger. It has been poured full strength into God's cup of wrath. And they will be tormented with fire and burning sulfur in the presence of the holy angels and the Lamb. 11The smoke of their torment will rise forever and ever, and they will have no relief day or night, for they have worshiped the beast and his statue and have accepted the mark of his name."

12This means that God's holy people must endure persecution patiently, obeying his commands and maintaining their faith in Jesus.

13And I heard a voice from heaven saying, "Write this down: Blessed are those who die in the Lord from now on. Yes, says the Spirit, they are blessed indeed, for they will rest from their hard work; for their good deeds follow them!"

14Then I saw a white cloud, and seated on the cloud was someone like the Son of Man.* He had a gold crown on his head and a sharp sickle in his hand. 15Then another angel came from the Temple and shouted to the one sitting on the cloud, "Swing the sickle, for the time of harvest has come; the crop on earth is ripe." 16So the one sitting on the cloud swung his sickle over the earth, and the whole earth was harvested.

17After that, another angel came from the Temple in heaven, and he also had a sharp sickle. 18Then another angel, who had power to destroy with fire, came from the altar. He shouted to the angel with the sharp sickle, "Swing your sickle now to gather the clusters of grapes from the vines of the earth, for they are ripe for judgment." 19So the angel swung his sickle over the earth and loaded the grapes into the great winepress of God's wrath. 20The grapes were trampled in the winepress outside the city, and blood flowed from the winepress in a stream about 180 miles* long and as high as a horse's bridle.

14:4a Greek *They are virgins who have not defiled themselves with women.* 14:4b Greek *as firstfruits.* 14:14 Or *like a son of man.* See Dan 7:13. "Son of Man" is a title Jesus used for himself. 14:20 Greek *1,600 stadia* [296 kilometers].

PSALM 142:1-7
A psalm of David, regarding his experience in the cave. A prayer.*

¹ I cry out to the LORD;
    I plead for the LORD's mercy.
² I pour out my complaints before him
    and tell him all my troubles.
³ When I am overwhelmed,
    you alone know the way I should turn.
  Wherever I go,
    my enemies have set traps for me.
⁴ I look for someone to come and help me,
    but no one gives me a passing thought!
  No one will help me;
    no one cares a bit what happens to me.
⁵ Then I pray to you, O LORD.
    I say, "You are my place of refuge.
    You are all I really want in life.
⁶ Hear my cry,
    for I am very low.
  Rescue me from my persecutors,
    for they are too strong for me.
⁷ Bring me out of prison
    so I can thank you.
  The godly will crowd around me,
    for you are good to me."

142:TITLE Hebrew *maskil.* This may be a literary or musical term.

PROVERBS 30:21-23
There are three things that make the earth tremble—no, four it cannot endure: a slave who becomes a king, an overbearing fool who prospers, a bitter woman who finally gets a husband, a servant girl who supplants her mistress.

DECEMBER
24

ZECHARIAH 6:1-7:14
Then I [Zechariah] looked up again and saw four chariots coming from between two bronze mountains. ²The first chariot was pulled by red horses, the second by black horses, ³the third by white horses, and the fourth by powerful dappled-gray horses. ⁴"And what are these, my lord?" I asked the angel who was talking with me.

⁵The angel replied, "These are the four spirits* of heaven who stand before the Lord of all the earth. They are going out to do his work. ⁶The chariot with black horses is going north, the chariot with white horses is going west,* and the chariot with dappled-gray horses is going south."

⁷The powerful horses were eager to set out to patrol the earth. And the LORD said, "Go and patrol the earth!" So they left at once on their patrol.

⁸Then the LORD summoned me and said, "Look, those who went north have vented the anger of my Spirit* there in the land of the north."

⁹Then I received another message from the LORD: ¹⁰"Heldai, Tobijah, and Jedaiah will bring gifts of silver and gold from the Jews exiled in Babylon. As soon as they arrive, meet them at the home of Josiah son of Zephaniah. ¹¹Accept their gifts, and make a crown* from the silver and gold. Then put the crown on the head of Jeshua* son of Jehozadak, the high priest. ¹²Tell him, 'This is what the LORD of Heaven's Armies says: Here is the man called the Branch. He will branch out from where he is and build the Temple of the LORD. ¹³Yes, he will build the Temple of the

LORD. Then he will receive royal honor and will rule as king from his throne. He will also serve as priest from his throne,* and there will be perfect harmony between his two roles.'

14"The crown will be a memorial in the Temple of the LORD to honor those who gave it—Heldai,* Tobijah, Jedaiah, and Josiah* son of Zephaniah."

15People will come from distant lands to rebuild the Temple of the LORD. And when this happens, you will know that my messages have been from the LORD of Heaven's Armies. All this will happen if you carefully obey what the LORD your God says.

7:1On December 7* of the fourth year of King Darius's reign, another message came to Zechariah from the LORD. 2The people of Bethel had sent Sharezer and Regemmelech,* along with their attendants, to seek the LORD's favor. 3They were to ask this question of the prophets and the priests at the Temple of the LORD of Heaven's Armies: "Should we continue to mourn and fast each summer on the anniversary of the Temple's destruction,* as we have done for so many years?"

4The LORD of Heaven's Armies sent me this message in reply: 5"Say to all your people and your priests, 'During these seventy years of exile, when you fasted and mourned in the summer and in early autumn,* was it really for me that you were fasting? 6And even now in your holy festivals, aren't you eating and drinking just to please yourselves? 7Isn't this the same message the LORD proclaimed through the prophets in years past when Jerusalem and the towns of Judah were bustling with people, and the Negev and the foothills of Judah* were well populated?'"

8Then this message came to Zechariah from the LORD: 9"This is what the LORD of Heaven's Armies says: Judge fairly, and show mercy and kindness to one another. 10Do not oppress widows, orphans, foreigners, and the poor. And do not scheme against each other.

11"Your ancestors refused to listen to this message. They stubbornly turned away and put their fingers in their ears to keep from hearing. 12They made their hearts as hard as stone, so they could not hear the instructions or the messages that the LORD of Heaven's Armies had sent them by his Spirit through the earlier prophets. That is why the LORD of Heaven's Armies was so angry with them.

13"Since they refused to listen when I called to them, I would not listen when they called to me, says the LORD of Heaven's Armies. 14As with a whirlwind, I scattered them among the distant nations, where they lived as strangers. Their land became so desolate that no one even traveled through it. They turned their pleasant land into a desert."

6:5 Or *the four winds.* 6:6 Hebrew *is going after them.* 6:8 Hebrew *have given my Spirit rest.* 6:11a As in Greek and Syriac versions; Hebrew reads *crowns.* 6:11b Hebrew *Joshua,* a variant spelling of Jeshua. 6:13 Or *There will be a priest by his throne.* 6:14a As in Syriac version (compare 6:10); Hebrew reads *Helem.* 6:14b As in Syriac version (compare 6:10); Hebrew reads *Hen.* 7:1 Hebrew *On the fourth day of the ninth month, the month of Kislev,* of the ancient Hebrew lunar calendar. This event occurred on December 7, 518 B.C.; also see note on 1:1. 7:2 Or *Bethelsharezer had sent Regemmelech.* 7:3 Hebrew *mourn and fast in the fifth month.* The Temple had been destroyed in the fifth month of the ancient Hebrew lunar calendar (August 586 B.C.); see 2 Kgs 25:8. 7:5 Hebrew *fasted and mourned in the fifth and seventh months.* The fifth month of the ancient Hebrew lunar calendar usually occurs within the months of July and August. The seventh month usually occurs within the months of September and October; both the Day of Atonement and the Festival of Shelters were celebrated in the seventh month. 7:7 Hebrew *the Shephelah.*

REVELATION 15:1-8

Then I [John] saw in heaven another marvelous event of great significance. Seven angels were holding the seven last plagues, which would bring God's wrath to completion. 2I saw before me what seemed to be a glass sea mixed with fire. And on it stood all the people who had been victorious over the beast and his statue and the number representing his name. They were all holding harps that God had given them. 3And they were singing the song of Moses, the servant of God, and the song of the Lamb:

"Great and marvelous are your works,
O Lord God, the Almighty.
Just and true are your ways,
O King of the nations.*
⁴ Who will not fear you, Lord,
and glorify your name?
For you alone are holy.
All nations will come and worship
before you,
for your righteous deeds have
been revealed."

⁵ Then I looked and saw that the Temple in heaven, God's Tabernacle, was thrown wide open. ⁶The seven angels who were holding the seven plagues came out of the Temple. They were clothed in spotless white linen* with gold sashes across their chests. ⁷Then one of the four living beings handed each of the seven angels a gold bowl filled with the wrath of God, who lives forever and ever. ⁸The Temple was filled with smoke from God's glory and power. No one could enter the Temple until the seven angels had completed pouring out the seven plagues.

15:3 Some manuscripts read *King of the ages.*   15:6 Other manuscripts read *white stone;* still others read *white [garments] made of linen.*

PSALM 143:1-12
A psalm of David.

¹ **H**ear my prayer, O LORD;
listen to my plea!
Answer me because you are
faithful and righteous.
² Don't put your servant on trial,
for no one is innocent before you.
³ My enemy has chased me.
He has knocked me to the ground
and forces me to live in darkness
like those in the grave.
⁴ I am losing all hope;
I am paralyzed with fear.
⁵ I remember the days of old.
I ponder all your great works
and think about what you
have done.
⁶ I lift my hands to you in prayer.
I thirst for you as parched land
thirsts for rain.   *Interlude*

⁷ Come quickly, LORD, and answer me,
for my depression deepens.
Don't turn away from me,
or I will die.
⁸ Let me hear of your unfailing love
each morning,
for I am trusting you.
Show me where to walk,
for I give myself to you.
⁹ Rescue me from my enemies, LORD;
I run to you to hide me.
¹⁰ Teach me to do your will,
for you are my God.
May your gracious Spirit lead
me forward
on a firm footing.
¹¹ For the glory of your name, O LORD,
preserve my life.
Because of your faithfulness,
bring me out of this distress.
¹² In your unfailing love, silence all
my enemies
and destroy all my foes,
for I am your servant.

PROVERBS 30:24-28
There are four things on earth that are small but unusually wise: Ants—they aren't strong, but they store up food all summer. Hyraxes*—they aren't powerful, but they make their homes among the rocks. Locusts—they have no king, but they march in formation. Lizards—they are easy to catch, but they are found even in kings' palaces.

30:26 Or *Coneys,* or *Rock badgers.*

DECEMBER 25

ZECHARIAH 8:1-23
Then another message came to me [Zechariah] from the LORD of Heaven's Armies: ²"This is what the LORD of Heaven's Armies says: My love for Mount Zion is passionate and strong; I am consumed with passion for Jerusalem!

³"And now the LORD says: I am returning to Mount Zion, and I will live in Jerusalem. Then Jerusalem will be called the Faithful City; the mountain of the LORD of Heaven's Armies will be called the Holy Mountain.

⁴"This is what the LORD of Heaven's Armies says: Once again old men and women will walk Jerusalem's streets with their canes and will sit together in the city squares. ⁵And the streets of the city will be filled with boys and girls at play.

⁶"This is what the LORD of Heaven's Armies says: All this may seem impossible to you now, a small remnant of God's people. But is it impossible for me? says the LORD of Heaven's Armies.

⁷"This is what the LORD of Heaven's Armies says: You can be sure that I will rescue my people from the east and from the west. ⁸I will bring them home again to live safely in Jerusalem. They will be my people, and I will be faithful and just toward them as their God.

⁹"This is what the LORD of Heaven's Armies says: Be strong and finish the task! Ever since the laying of the foundation of the Temple of the LORD of Heaven's Armies, you have heard what the prophets have been saying about completing the building. ¹⁰Before the work on the Temple began, there were no jobs and no money to hire people or animals. No traveler was safe from the enemy, for there were enemies on all sides. I had turned everyone against each other.

¹¹"But now I will not treat the remnant of my people as I treated them before, says the LORD of Heaven's Armies. ¹²For I am planting seeds of peace and prosperity among you. The grapevines will be heavy with fruit. The earth will produce its crops, and the heavens will release the dew. Once more I will cause the remnant in Judah and Israel to inherit these blessings. ¹³Among the other nations, Judah and Israel became symbols of a cursed nation. But no longer! Now I will rescue you and make you both a symbol and a source of blessing.

So don't be afraid. Be strong, and get on with rebuilding the Temple!

¹⁴"For this is what the LORD of Heaven's Armies says: I was determined to punish you when your ancestors angered me, and I did not change my mind, says the LORD of Heaven's Armies. ¹⁵But now I am determined to bless Jerusalem and the people of Judah. So don't be afraid. ¹⁶But this is what you must do: Tell the truth to each other. Render verdicts in your courts that are just and that lead to peace. ¹⁷Don't scheme against each other. Stop your love of telling lies that you swear are the truth. I hate all these things, says the LORD."

¹⁸Here is another message that came to me from the LORD of Heaven's Armies. ¹⁹"This is what the LORD of Heaven's Armies says: The traditional fasts and times of mourning you have kept in early summer, midsummer, autumn, and winter* are now ended. They will become festivals of joy and celebration for the people of Judah. So love truth and peace.

²⁰"This is what the LORD of Heaven's Armies says: People from nations and cities around the world will travel to Jerusalem. ²¹The people of one city will say to the people of another, 'Come with us to Jerusalem to ask the LORD to bless us. Let's worship the LORD of Heaven's Armies. I'm determined to go.' ²²Many peoples and powerful nations will come to Jerusalem to seek the LORD of Heaven's Armies and to ask for his blessing.

²³"This is what the LORD of Heaven's Armies says: In those days ten men from different nations and languages of the world will clutch at the sleeve of one Jew. And they will say, 'Please let us walk with you, for we have heard that God is with you.'"

8:19 Hebrew *in the fourth, fifth, seventh, and tenth months.* The fourth month of the ancient Hebrew lunar calendar usually occurs within the months of June and July. The fifth month usually occurs within the months of July and August. The seventh month usually occurs within the months of September and October. The tenth month usually occurs within the months of December and January.

REVELATION 16:1-21

Then I [John] heard a mighty voice from the Temple say to the seven angels, "Go your ways and pour out on the earth the seven bowls containing God's wrath."

²So the first angel left the Temple and poured out his bowl on the earth, and horrible, malignant sores broke out on everyone who had the mark of the beast and who worshiped his statue.

³Then the second angel poured out his bowl on the sea, and it became like the blood of a corpse. And everything in the sea died.

⁴Then the third angel poured out his bowl on the rivers and springs, and they became blood. ⁵And I heard the angel who had authority over all water saying,

"You are just, O Holy One, who is
    and who always was,
    because you have sent these
    judgments.
⁶ Since they shed the blood
    of your holy people and your
    prophets,
you have given them blood to drink.
    It is their just reward."

⁷And I heard a voice from the altar,* saying,

"Yes, O Lord God, the Almighty,
    your judgments are true and just."

⁸Then the fourth angel poured out his bowl on the sun, causing it to scorch everyone with its fire. ⁹Everyone was burned by this blast of heat, and they cursed the name of God, who had control over all these plagues. They did not repent of their sins and turn to God and give him glory.

¹⁰Then the fifth angel poured out his bowl on the throne of the beast, and his kingdom was plunged into darkness. His subjects ground their teeth in anguish, ¹¹and they cursed the God of heaven for their pains and sores. But they did not repent of their evil deeds and turn to God.

¹²Then the sixth angel poured out his bowl on the great Euphrates River, and it dried up so that the kings from the east could march their armies toward the west without hindrance. ¹³And I saw three evil spirits that looked like frogs leap from the mouths of the dragon, the beast, and the false prophet. ¹⁴They are demonic spirits who work miracles and go out to all the rulers of the world to gather them for battle against the Lord on that great judgment day of God the Almighty.

¹⁵"Look, I will come as unexpectedly as a thief! Blessed are all who are watching for me, who keep their clothing ready so they will not have to walk around naked and ashamed."

¹⁶And the demonic spirits gathered all the rulers and their armies to a place with the Hebrew name *Armageddon.**

¹⁷Then the seventh angel poured out his bowl into the air. And a mighty shout came from the throne in the Temple, saying, "It is finished!" ¹⁸Then the thunder crashed and rolled, and lightning flashed. And a great earthquake struck—the worst since people were placed on the earth. ¹⁹The great city of Babylon split into three sections, and the cities of many nations fell into heaps of rubble. So God remembered all of Babylon's sins, and he made her drink the cup that was filled with the wine of his fierce wrath. ²⁰And every island disappeared, and all the mountains were leveled. ²¹There was a terrible hailstorm, and hailstones weighing seventy-five pounds* fell from the sky onto the people below. They cursed God because of the terrible plague of the hailstorm.

16:7 Greek *I heard the altar.*   16:16 Or *Harmagedon.*
16:21 Greek *1 talent* [34 kilograms].

PSALM 144:1-15
A psalm of David.

¹ Praise the LORD, who is my rock.
    He trains my hands for war
    and gives my fingers skill
        for battle.

2 He is my loving ally and my fortress,
  my tower of safety, my rescuer.
He is my shield, and I take refuge
  in him.
    He makes the nations* submit
    to me.

3 O Lord, who are we that you should
  notice us,
  mere mortals that you should care
    for us?
4 For we are like a breath of air;
  our days are like a passing
    shadow.

5 Open the heavens, Lord, and
  come down.
  Touch the mountains so they
    billow smoke.
6 Hurl your lightning bolts and scatter
  your enemies!
  Shoot your arrows and confuse
    them!
7 Reach down from heaven and
  rescue me;
  rescue me from deep waters,
  from the power of my enemies.
8 Their mouths are full of lies;
  they swear to tell the truth, but
    they lie instead.

9 I will sing a new song to you, O God!
  I will sing your praises with a ten-
    stringed harp.
10 For you grant victory to kings!
  You rescued your servant David
    from the fatal sword.
11 Save me!
  Rescue me from the power
    of my enemies.
  Their mouths are full of lies;
  they swear to tell the truth, but
    they lie instead.

12 May our sons flourish in their youth
  like well-nurtured plants.
  May our daughters be like graceful
    pillars,
  carved to beautify a palace.
13 May our barns be filled
  with crops of every kind.
  May the flocks in our fields multiply
    by the thousands,

  even tens of thousands,
14 and may our oxen be loaded
    down with produce.
  May there be no enemy breaking
    through our walls,
  no going into captivity,
  no cries of alarm in our
    town squares.
15 Yes, joyful are those who live
    like this!
  Joyful indeed are those whose
    God is the Lord.

144:2 Some manuscripts read *my people*.

PROVERBS 30:29-31
There are three things that walk with stately stride— no, four that strut about: the lion, king of animals, who won't turn aside for anything, the strutting rooster, the male goat, a king as he leads his army.

DECEMBER
26

ZECHARIAH 9:1-17
This is the message* from the Lord against the land of Aram* and the city of Damascus, for the eyes of humanity, including all the tribes of Israel, are on the Lord.

2 Doom is certain for Hamath,
    near Damascus,
  and for the cities of Tyre and Sidon,
    though they are so clever.
3 Tyre has built a strong fortress
  and has made silver and gold
  as plentiful as dust in the streets!
4 But now the Lord will strip away
    Tyre's possessions
  and hurl its fortifications
    into the sea,
  and it will be burned to the
    ground.
5 The city of Ashkelon will see
    Tyre fall
  and will be filled with fear.

Gaza will shake with terror,
    as will Ekron, for their hopes will
    be dashed.
Gaza's king will be killed,
    and Ashkelon will be deserted.
⁶ Foreigners will occupy the city
    of Ashdod.
I will destroy the pride of
    the Philistines.
⁷ I will grab the bloody meat from
    their mouths
    and snatch the detestable
    sacrifices from their teeth.
Then the surviving Philistines will
    worship our God
    and become like a clan in Judah.*
The Philistines of Ekron will join
    my people,
    as the ancient Jebusites once did.
⁸ I will guard my Temple
    and protect it from invading
    armies.
I am watching closely to ensure
    that no more foreign oppressors
    overrun my people's land.

⁹ Rejoice, O people of Zion!*
    Shout in triumph, O people
    of Jerusalem!
Look, your king is coming to you.
    He is righteous and victorious,*
    yet he is humble, riding on a
    donkey—
    riding on a donkey's colt.
¹⁰ I will remove the battle chariots
    from Israel*
    and the warhorses from
    Jerusalem.
I will destroy all the weapons used
    in battle,
    and your king will bring peace
    to the nations.
His realm will stretch from sea
    to sea
    and from the Euphrates River*
    to the ends of the earth.*
¹¹ Because of the covenant I made
    with you,
    sealed with blood,
I will free your prisoners
    from death in a waterless dungeon.
¹² Come back to the place of safety,

all you prisoners who still
    have hope!
I promise this very day
    that I will repay two blessings for
    each of your troubles.
¹³ Judah is my bow,
    and Israel is my arrow.
Jerusalem* is my sword,
    and like a warrior, I will brandish
    it against the Greeks.*

¹⁴ The LORD will appear above his
    people;
    his arrows will fly like lightning!
The Sovereign LORD will sound the
    ram's horn
    and attack like a whirlwind from
    the southern desert.
¹⁵ The LORD of Heaven's Armies will
    protect his people,
    and they will defeat their enemies
    by hurling great stones.
They will shout in battle as though
    drunk with wine.
They will be filled with blood like
    a bowl,
    drenched with blood like the
    corners of the altar.
¹⁶ On that day the LORD their God will
    rescue his people,
    just as a shepherd rescues
    his sheep.
They will sparkle in his land
    like jewels in a crown.
¹⁷ How wonderful and beautiful they
    will be!
The young men will thrive on
    abundant grain,
    and the young women will
    flourish on new wine.

9:1a Hebrew *An Oracle: The message.* 9:1b Hebrew *land of Hadrach.* 9:7 Hebrew *and will become a leader in Judah.* 9:9a Hebrew *O daughter of Zion!* 9:9b Hebrew *and is being vindicated.* 9:10a Hebrew *Ephraim,* referring to the northern kingdom of Israel; also in 9:13. 9:10b Hebrew *the river.* 9:10c Or *the end of the land.* 9:13a Hebrew *Zion.* 9:13b Hebrew *the sons of Javan.*

REVELATION 17:1-18

One of the seven angels who had poured out the seven bowls came over and spoke to me [John]. "Come with me," he said, "and I will show you the judgment that is going to come on the great prostitute, who rules over many waters. [2] The kings of the world have committed adultery with her, and the people who belong to this world have been made drunk by the wine of her immorality."

[3] So the angel took me in the Spirit* into the wilderness. There I saw a woman sitting on a scarlet beast that had seven heads and ten horns, and blasphemies against God were written all over it. [4] The woman wore purple and scarlet clothing and beautiful jewelry made of gold and precious gems and pearls. In her hand she held a gold goblet full of obscenities and the impurities of her immorality. [5] A mysterious name was written on her forehead: "Babylon the Great, Mother of All Prostitutes and Obscenities in the World." [6] I could see that she was drunk—drunk with the blood of God's holy people who were witnesses for Jesus. I stared at her in complete amazement.

[7] "Why are you so amazed?" the angel asked. "I will tell you the mystery of this woman and of the beast with seven heads and ten horns on which she sits. [8] The beast you saw was once alive but isn't now. And yet he will soon come up out of the bottomless pit* and go to eternal destruction. And the people who belong to this world, whose names were not written in the Book of Life before the world was made, will be amazed at the reappearance of this beast who had died.

[9] "This calls for a mind with understanding: The seven heads of the beast represent the seven hills where the woman rules. They also represent seven kings. [10] Five kings have already fallen, the sixth now reigns, and the seventh is yet to come, but his reign will be brief. [11] "The scarlet beast that was, but is no longer, is the eighth king. He is like the other seven, and he, too, is headed for destruction. [12] The ten horns of the beast are ten kings who have not yet risen to power. They will be appointed to their kingdoms for one brief moment to reign with the beast. [13] They will all agree to give him their power

and authority. [14] Together they will go to war against the Lamb, but the Lamb will defeat them because he is Lord of all lords and King of all kings. And his called and chosen and faithful ones will be with him."

[15] Then the angel said to me, "The waters where the prostitute is ruling represent masses of people of every nation and language. [16] The scarlet beast and his ten horns all hate the prostitute. They will strip her naked, eat her flesh, and burn her remains with fire. [17] For God has put a plan into their minds, a plan that will carry out his purposes. They will agree to give their authority to the scarlet beast, and so the words of God will be fulfilled. [18] And this woman you saw in your vision represents the great city that rules over the kings of the world."

17:3 Or *in spirit.*   17:8 Or *the abyss,* or *the underworld.*

PSALM 145:1-21*
A psalm of praise of David.

[1] I will exalt you, my God and King,
      and praise your name forever
         and ever.
[2] I will praise you every day;
      yes, I will praise you forever.
[3] Great is the LORD! He is most worthy
         of praise!
      No one can measure his greatness.

[4] Let each generation tell its children
         of your mighty acts;
      let them proclaim your power.
[5] I will meditate* on your majestic,
         glorious splendor
      and your wonderful miracles.
[6] Your awe-inspiring deeds will be on
         every tongue;
      I will proclaim your greatness.
[7] Everyone will share the story of your
         wonderful goodness;
      they will sing with joy about
         your righteousness.

[8] The LORD is merciful and
         compassionate,
      slow to get angry and filled with
         unfailing love.
[9] The LORD is good to everyone.

He showers compassion on all
his creation.

¹⁰ All of your works will thank you, Lord,
and your faithful followers will
praise you.
¹¹ They will speak of the glory of your
kingdom;
they will give examples of
your power.
¹² They will tell about your mighty deeds
and about the majesty and glory
of your reign.
¹³ For your kingdom is an everlasting
kingdom.
You rule throughout all
generations.

**The Lord always keeps his
promises;
he is gracious in all he does.***
¹⁴ **The Lord helps the fallen
and lifts those bent beneath
their loads.**
¹⁵ The eyes of all look to you in hope;
you give them their food as they
need it.
¹⁶ When you open your hand,
you satisfy the hunger and thirst
of every living thing.
¹⁷ The Lord is righteous in everything
he does;
he is filled with kindness.
¹⁸ The Lord is close to all who call
on him,
yes, to all who call on him in truth.
¹⁹ He grants the desires of those who
fear him;
he hears their cries for help and
rescues them.
²⁰ The Lord protects all those
who love him,
but he destroys the wicked.

²¹ I will praise the Lord,
and may everyone on earth bless
his holy name
forever and ever.

145 This psalm is a Hebrew acrostic poem; each verse
(including 13b) begins with a successive letter of the
Hebrew alphabet. **145:5** Some manuscripts read *They will
speak.* **145:13** The last two lines of 145:13 are not found
in many of the ancient manuscripts.

PROVERBS 30:32
If you have been a fool by being proud
or plotting evil, cover your mouth in
shame.

DECEMBER
27

ZECHARIAH 10:1–11:17
Ask the Lord for rain in the spring,
for he makes the storm clouds.
And he will send showers of rain
so every field becomes a
lush pasture.
² Household gods give worthless
advice,
fortune-tellers predict only lies,
and interpreters of dreams
pronounce
falsehoods that give no comfort.
So my people are wandering like
lost sheep;
they are attacked because they
have no shepherd.

³ "My anger burns against your
shepherds,
and I will punish these leaders.*
For the Lord of Heaven's Armies
has arrived
to look after Judah, his flock.
He will make them strong and
glorious,
like a proud warhorse in battle.
⁴ From Judah will come the cornerstone,
the tent peg,
the bow for battle,
and all the rulers.
⁵ They will be like mighty warriors
in battle,
trampling their enemies in the
mud under their feet.
Since the Lord is with them
as they fight,
they will overthrow even the
enemy's horsemen.

⁶ "I will strengthen Judah and save
   Israel*;
   I will restore them because
   of my compassion.
It will be as though I had never
   rejected them,
   for I am the LORD their God, who
   will hear their cries.
⁷ The people of Israel* will become
   like mighty warriors,
   and their hearts will be made
   happy as if by wine.
Their children, too, will see it
   and be glad;
   their hearts will rejoice
   in the LORD.
⁸ When I whistle to them, they will
   come running,
   for I have redeemed them.
From the few who are left,
   they will grow as numerous as
   they were before.
⁹ Though I have scattered them like
   seeds among the nations,
   they will still remember me in
   distant lands.
They and their children will
   survive
   and return again to Israel.
¹⁰ I will bring them back from Egypt
   and gather them from Assyria.
I will resettle them in Gilead and
   Lebanon
   until there is no more room for
   them all.
¹¹ They will pass safely through the sea
   of distress,*
   for the waves of the sea will be
   held back,
   and the waters of the Nile
   will dry up.
The pride of Assyria will be crushed,
   and the rule of Egypt will end.
¹² By my power* I will make my people
   strong,
   and by my authority they will go
   wherever they wish.
I, the LORD, have spoken!"

¹¹:¹ OPEN your doors, Lebanon,
   so that fire may devour your
   cedar forests.

² Weep, you cypress trees, for all the
   ruined cedars;
   the most majestic ones have fallen.
Weep, you oaks of Bashan,
   for the thick forests have been
   cut down.
³ Listen to the wailing of the
   shepherds,
   for their rich pastures are
   destroyed.
Hear the young lions roaring,
   for their thickets in the Jordan
   Valley are ruined.

⁴This is what the LORD my God says:
"Go and care for the flock that is intended for slaughter. ⁵The buyers
slaughter their sheep without remorse.
The sellers say, 'Praise the LORD! Now
I'm rich!' Even the shepherds have no
compassion for them. ⁶Likewise, I will
no longer have pity on the people of the
land," says the LORD. "I will let them fall
into each other's hands and into the
hands of their king. They will turn the
land into a wilderness, and I will not rescue them."

⁷So I cared for the flock intended
for slaughter—the flock that was oppressed. Then I took two shepherd's
staffs and named one Favor and the
other Union. ⁸I got rid of their three evil
shepherds in a single month.

But I became impatient with these
sheep, and they hated me, too. ⁹So I told
them, "I won't be your shepherd any
longer. If you die, you die. If you are
killed, you are killed. And let those who
remain devour each other!"

¹⁰Then I took my staff called Favor
and cut it in two, showing that I had revoked the covenant I had made with all
the nations. ¹¹That was the end of my
covenant with them. The suffering
flock was watching me, and they knew
that the LORD was speaking through my
actions.

¹²And I said to them, "If you like, give
me my wages, whatever I am worth; but
only if you want to." So they counted out
for my wages thirty pieces of silver.

¹³And the LORD said to me, "Throw it

to the potter*"—this magnificent sum at which they valued me! So I took the thirty coins and threw them to the potter in the Temple of the LORD.

¹⁴Then I took my other staff, Union, and cut it in two, showing that the bond of unity between Judah and Israel was broken.

¹⁵Then the LORD said to me, "Go again and play the part of a worthless shepherd. ¹⁶This illustrates how I will give this nation a shepherd who will not care for those who are dying, nor look after the young,* nor heal the injured, nor feed the healthy. Instead, this shepherd will eat the meat of the fattest sheep and tear off their hooves.

¹⁷ "What sorrow awaits this worthless shepherd
    who abandons the flock!
The sword will cut his arm
    and pierce his right eye.
His arm will become useless,
    and his right eye completely
        blind."

10:3 Or these male goats.   10:6 Hebrew save the house of Joseph.   10:7 Hebrew of Ephraim.   10:11 Or the sea of Egypt, referring to the Red Sea.   10:12 Hebrew In the LORD.   11:13 Syriac version reads into the treasury; also in 11:13b. Compare Matt 27:6-10.   11:16 Or the scattered.

REVELATION 18:1-24

After all this I [John] saw another angel come down from heaven with great authority, and the earth grew bright with his splendor. ²He gave a mighty shout:

"Babylon is fallen—that great city
    is fallen!
She has become a home for demons.
She is a hideout for every foul spirit,
    a hideout for every foul vulture
    and every foul and dreadful
        animal.*
³ For all the nations have fallen*
    because of the wine of her
        passionate immorality.
The kings of the world
    have committed adultery with her.
Because of her desires for
        extravagant luxury,
    the merchants of the world have
        grown rich."

⁴Then I heard another voice calling from heaven,

"Come away from her, my people.
    Do not take part in her sins,
    or you will be punished with her.
⁵ For her sins are piled as high
        as heaven,
    and God remembers her
        evil deeds.
⁶ Do to her as she has done to others.
    Double her penalty* for all her
        evil deeds.
She brewed a cup of terror for
        others,
    so brew twice as much* for her.
⁷ She glorified herself and lived
        in luxury,
    so match it now with torment and
        sorrow.
She boasted in her heart,
    'I am queen on my throne.
I am no helpless widow,
    and I have no reason to mourn.'
⁸ Therefore, these plagues will
        overtake her in a single day—
    death and mourning and famine.
She will be completely consumed
        by fire,
    for the Lord God who judges her
        is mighty."

⁹And the kings of the world who committed adultery with her and enjoyed her great luxury will mourn for her as they see the smoke rising from her charred remains. ¹⁰They will stand at a distance, terrified by her great torment. They will cry out,

"How terrible, how terrible for
        you,
    O Babylon, you great city!
In a single moment
    God's judgment came on you."

¹¹The merchants of the world will weep and mourn for her, for there is no one left to buy their goods. ¹²She bought great quantities of gold, silver, jewels, and pearls; fine linen, purple, silk, and scarlet cloth; things made of fragrant thyine wood, ivory goods, and

objects made of expensive wood; and bronze, iron, and marble. [13]She also bought cinnamon, spice, incense, myrrh, frankincense, wine, olive oil, fine flour, wheat, cattle, sheep, horses, chariots, and bodies—that is, human slaves.

[14] "The fancy things you loved so much
are gone," they cry.
"All your luxuries and splendor
are gone forever,
never to be yours again."

[15] The merchants who became wealthy by selling her these things will stand at a distance, terrified by her great torment. They will weep and cry out,

[16] "How terrible, how terrible for that
great city!
She was clothed in finest purple
and scarlet linens,
decked out with gold and
precious stones and pearls!
[17] In a single moment
all the wealth of the city is gone!"

And all the captains of the merchant ships and their passengers and sailors and crews will stand at a distance. [18]They will cry out as they watch the smoke ascend, and they will say, "Where is there another city as great as this?" [19]And they will weep and throw dust on their heads to show their grief. And they will cry out,

"How terrible, how terrible for that
great city!
The shipowners became
wealthy
by transporting her great wealth
on the seas.
In a single moment it is all gone."

[20] Rejoice over her fate, O heaven
and people of God and apostles
and prophets!
For at last God has judged her
for your sakes.

[21]Then a mighty angel picked up a boulder the size of a huge millstone. He threw it into the ocean and shouted,

"Just like this, the great city Babylon
will be thrown down with
violence
and will never be found again.
[22] The sound of harps, singers, flutes,
and trumpets
will never be heard in you again.
No craftsmen and no trades
will ever be found in you again.
The sound of the mill
will never be heard in you again.
[23] The light of a lamp
will never shine in you again.
The happy voices of brides and
grooms
will never be heard in you again.
For your merchants were the
greatest in the world,
and you deceived the nations with
your sorceries.
[24] In your* streets flowed the blood
of the prophets and of God's
holy people
and the blood of people
slaughtered all over the world."

18:2 Some manuscripts condense the last two lines to read *a hideout for every foul and dreadful vulture.* 18:3 Some manuscripts read *have drunk.* 18:6a Or *Give her an equal penalty.* 18:6b Or *brew just as much.* 18:24 Greek *her.*

PSALM 146:1-10
Praise the LORD!

Let all that I am praise the LORD.
2 I will praise the LORD as long
as I live.
I will sing praises to my God with
my dying breath.

3 Don't put your confidence in
powerful people;
there is no help for you there.
4 When they breathe their last, they
return to the earth,
and all their plans die with them.
5 But joyful are those who have the
God of Israel* as their helper,
whose hope is in the LORD
their God.
6 He made heaven and earth,
the sea, and everything in them.
He keeps every promise forever.
7 He gives justice to the oppressed

and food to the hungry.
The LORD frees the prisoners.
8 The LORD opens the eyes
    of the blind.
The LORD lifts up those who are
    weighed down.
The LORD loves the godly.
9 **The LORD protects the foreigners among us.**

He cares for the orphans and widows,

but he frustrates the plans of the wicked.

10 The LORD will reign forever.
He will be your God,
O Jerusalem,* throughout the generations.

Praise the LORD!

146:5 Hebrew *of Jacob.* See note on 44:4.   **146:10** Hebrew *Zion.*

PROVERBS 30:33

As the beating of cream yields butter and striking the nose causes bleeding, so stirring up anger causes quarrels.

DECEMBER 28

ZECHARIAH 12:1–13:9

This* message concerning the fate of Israel came from the LORD: "This message is from the LORD, who stretched out the heavens, laid the foundations of the earth, and formed the human spirit. 2I will make Jerusalem like an intoxicating drink that makes the nearby nations stagger when they send their armies to besiege Jerusalem and Judah. 3On that day I will make Jerusalem an immovable rock. All the nations will gather against it to try to move it, but they will only hurt themselves.

4"On that day," says the LORD, "I will cause every horse to panic and every rider to lose his nerve. I will watch over the people of Judah, but I will blind all the horses of their enemies. 5And the clans of Judah will say to themselves, 'The people of Jerusalem have found strength in the LORD of Heaven's Armies, their God.'

6"On that day I will make the clans of Judah like a flame that sets a woodpile ablaze or like a burning torch among sheaves of grain. They will burn up all the neighboring nations right and left, while the people living in Jerusalem remain secure.

7"The LORD will give victory to the rest of Judah first, before Jerusalem, so that the people of Jerusalem and the royal line of David will not have greater honor than the rest of Judah. 8On that day the LORD will defend the people of Jerusalem; the weakest among them will be as mighty as King David! And the royal descendants will be like God, like the angel of the LORD who goes before them! 9For on that day I will begin to destroy all the nations that come against Jerusalem.

10"Then I will pour out a spirit* of grace and prayer on the family of David and on the people of Jerusalem. They will look on me whom they have pierced and mourn for him as for an only son. They will grieve bitterly for him as for a firstborn son who has died. 11The sorrow and mourning in Jerusalem on that day will be like the great mourning for Hadad-rimmon in the valley of Megiddo.

12"All Israel will mourn, each clan by itself, and with the husbands separate from their wives. The clan of David will mourn alone, as will the clan of Nathan. 13the clan of Levi, and the clan of Shimei. 14Each of the surviving clans from Judah will mourn separately, and with the husbands separate from their wives.

13:1"On that day a fountain will be opened for the dynasty of David and for the people of Jerusalem, a fountain to cleanse them from all their sins and impurity.

2"And on that day," says the LORD of

Heaven's Armies, "I will erase idol worship throughout the land, so that even the names of the idols will be forgotten. I will remove from the land both the false prophets and the spirit of impurity that came with them. ³If anyone continues to prophesy, his own father and mother will tell him, 'You must die, for you have prophesied lies in the name of the LORD.' And as he prophesies, his own father and mother will stab him.

⁴"On that day people will be ashamed to claim the prophetic gift. No one will pretend to be a prophet by wearing prophet's clothes. ⁵He will say, 'I'm no prophet; I'm a farmer. I began working for a farmer as a boy.' ⁶And if someone asks, 'Then what about those wounds on your chest?*' he will say, 'I was wounded at my friends' house!'

⁷ "Awake, O sword, against my
      shepherd,
   the man who is my partner,"
      says the LORD of Heaven's Armies.
   "Strike down the shepherd,
      and the sheep will be scattered,
      and I will turn against the lambs.
⁸ Two-thirds of the people in the land
      will be cut off and die," says
      the LORD.
   "But one-third will be left in
      the land.
⁹ I will bring that group through
      the fire
   and make them pure.
   I will refine them like silver
      and purify them like gold.
   They will call on my name,
      and I will answer them.
   I will say, 'These are my people,'
      and they will say, 'The LORD
      is our God.'"

12:1 Hebrew *An Oracle: This.*   12:10 Or *the Spirit.*
13:6 Hebrew *wounds between your hands?*

REVELATION 19:1-21
After this, I [John] heard what sounded like a vast crowd in heaven shouting,

   "Praise the LORD!*
      Salvation and glory and power
      belong to our God.

² His judgments are true and just.
   He has punished the great
      prostitute
   who corrupted the earth with her
      immorality.
   He has avenged the murder of his
      servants."

³And again their voices rang out:

   "Praise the LORD!
      The smoke from that city ascends
      forever and ever!"

⁴Then the twenty-four elders and the four living beings fell down and worshiped God, who was sitting on the throne. They cried out, "Amen! Praise the LORD!"

⁵And from the throne came a voice that said,

   "Praise our God,
      all his servants,
   all who fear him,
      from the least to the greatest."

⁶Then I heard again what sounded like the shout of a vast crowd or the roar of mighty ocean waves or the crash of loud thunder:

   "Praise the LORD!
      For the Lord our God,* the
      Almighty, reigns.
⁷ **Let us be glad and rejoice,
      and let us give honor to him.
   For the time has come for the
      wedding feast of the Lamb,
      and his bride has prepared
      herself.**
⁸ She has been given the finest of
      pure white linen to wear."
   For the fine linen represents the
      good deeds of God's holy
      people.

⁹And the angel said to me, "Write this: Blessed are those who are invited to the wedding feast of the Lamb." And he added, "These are true words that come from God."

¹⁰Then I fell down at his feet to worship him, but he said, "No, don't worship me. I am a servant of God, just like

you and your brothers and sisters* who testify about their faith in Jesus. Worship only God. For the essence of prophecy is to give a clear witness for Jesus.*"

[11] Then I saw heaven opened, and a white horse was standing there. Its rider was named Faithful and True, for he judges fairly and wages a righteous war. [12] His eyes were like flames of fire, and on his head were many crowns. A name was written on him that no one understood except himself. [13] He wore a robe dipped in blood, and his title was the Word of God. [14] The armies of heaven, dressed in the finest of pure white linen, followed him on white horses. [15] From his mouth came a sharp sword to strike down the nations. He will rule them with an iron rod. He will release the fierce wrath of God, the Almighty, like juice flowing from a winepress. [16] On his robe at his thigh* was written this title: King of all kings and Lord of all lords.

[17] Then I saw an angel standing in the sun, shouting to the vultures flying high in the sky: "Come! Gather together for the great banquet God has prepared. [18] Come and eat the flesh of kings, generals, and strong warriors; of horses and their riders; and of all humanity, both free and slave, small and great."

[19] Then I saw the beast and the kings of the world and their armies gathered together to fight against the one sitting on the horse and his army. [20] And the beast was captured, and with him the false prophet who did mighty miracles on behalf of the beast—miracles that deceived all who had accepted the mark of the beast and who worshiped his statue. Both the beast and his false prophet were thrown alive into the fiery lake of burning sulfur. [21] Their entire army was killed by the sharp sword that came from the mouth of the one riding the white horse. And the vultures all gorged themselves on the dead bodies.

19:1 Greek *Hallelujah;* also in 19:3, 4, 6. *Hallelujah* is the transliteration of a Hebrew term that means "Praise the Lord." **19:6** Some manuscripts read *the Lord God.* **19:10a** Greek *brothers.* **19:10b** Or *is the message confirmed by Jesus.* **19:16** Or *On his robe and thigh.*

PSALM 147:1-20

Praise the Lord!

How good to sing praises to
  our God!
How delightful and how fitting!
[2] The Lord is rebuilding Jerusalem
  and bringing the exiles back to
  Israel.
[3] He heals the brokenhearted
  and bandages their wounds.
[4] He counts the stars
  and calls them all by name.
[5] How great is our Lord! His power
  is absolute!
His understanding is beyond
  comprehension!
[6] The Lord supports the humble,
  but he brings the wicked down
  into the dust.

[7] Sing out your thanks to the Lord;
  sing praises to our God with a
  harp.
[8] He covers the heavens
  with clouds,
  provides rain for the earth,
  and makes the grass grow in
  mountain pastures.
[9] He gives food to the wild animals
  and feeds the young ravens when
  they cry.
[10] He takes no pleasure in the strength
  of a horse
  or in human might.
[11] No, the Lord's delight is in those
  who fear him,
  those who put their hope in his
  unfailing love.

[12] Glorify the Lord, O Jerusalem!
  Praise your God, O Zion!
[13] For he has strengthened the bars of
  your gates
  and blessed your children within
  your walls.
[14] He sends peace across your nation
  and satisfies your hunger with the
  finest wheat.
[15] He sends his orders to the world—
  how swiftly his word flies!
[16] He sends the snow like white wool;

he scatters frost upon the ground
like ashes.
17 He hurls the hail like stones.*
Who can stand against his
freezing cold?
18 Then, at his command, it all melts.
He sends his winds, and the ice
thaws.
19 He has revealed his words to Jacob,
his decrees and regulations
to Israel.
20 He has not done this for any
other nation;
they do not know his regulations.

Praise the LORD!

147:17 Hebrew *like bread crumbs.*

PROVERBS 31:1-7

The sayings of King Lemuel contain this message,* which his mother taught him. □O my son, O son of my womb, O son of my vows, do not waste your strength on women, on those who ruin kings. □It is not for kings, O Lemuel, to guzzle wine. Rulers should not crave alcohol. For if they drink, they may forget the law and not give justice to the oppressed. Alcohol is for the dying, and wine for those in bitter distress. Let them drink to forget their poverty and remember their troubles no more.

31:1 Or *of Lemuel, king of Massa;* or *of King Lemuel, an oracle.*

DECEMBER
29

ZECHARIAH 14:1-21

Watch, for the day of the LORD is coming when your possessions will be plundered right in front of you [the people of Jerusalem]! 2I will gather all the nations to fight against Jerusalem. The city will be taken, the houses looted, and the women raped. Half the population will be taken into captivity, and the rest will be left among the ruins of the city.

3Then the LORD will go out to fight against those nations, as he has fought in times past. 4On that day his feet will stand on the Mount of Olives, east of Jerusalem. And the Mount of Olives will split apart, making a wide valley running from east to west. Half the mountain will move toward the north and half toward the south. 5You will flee through this valley, for it will reach across to Azal.* Yes, you will flee as you did from the earthquake in the days of King Uzziah of Judah. Then the LORD my God will come, and all his holy ones with him.*

6On that day the sources of light will no longer shine,* 7yet there will be continuous day! Only the LORD knows how this could happen. There will be no normal day and night, for at evening time it will still be light.

8On that day life-giving waters will flow out from Jerusalem, half toward the Dead Sea and half toward the Mediterranean,* flowing continuously in both summer and winter.

9And the LORD will be king over all the earth. On that day there will be one LORD—his name alone will be worshiped.

10All the land from Geba, north of Judah, to Rimmon, south of Jerusalem, will become one vast plain. But Jerusalem will be raised up in its original place and will be inhabited all the way from the Benjamin Gate over to the site of the old gate, then to the Corner Gate, and from the Tower of Hananel to the king's winepresses. 11And Jerusalem will be filled, safe at last, never again to be cursed and destroyed.

12And the LORD will send a plague on all the nations that fought against Jerusalem. Their people will become like walking corpses, their flesh rotting away. Their eyes will rot in their sockets, and their tongues will rot in their mouths. 13On that day they will be terrified, stricken by the LORD with great panic. They will fight their neighbors hand to hand. 14Judah, too, will be fighting at Jerusalem. The wealth of all the neighboring nations will be captured—great quantities of gold and silver and fine clothing. [15]This same plague will strike the horses, mules, camels, donkeys, and all the other animals in the enemy camps.

[16]In the end, the enemies of Jerusalem who survive the plague will go up to Jerusalem each year to worship the King, the LORD of Heaven's Armies, and to celebrate the Festival of Shelters. [17]Any nation in the world that refuses to come to Jerusalem to worship the King, the LORD of Heaven's Armies, will have no rain. [18]If the people of Egypt refuse to attend the festival, the LORD will punish them with the same plague that he sends on the other nations who refuse to go. [19]Egypt and the other nations will all be punished if they don't go to celebrate the Festival of Shelters.

[20]On that day even the harness bells of the horses will be inscribed with these words: HOLY TO THE LORD. And the cooking pots in the Temple of the LORD will be as sacred as the basins used beside the altar. [21]In fact, every cooking pot in Jerusalem and Judah will be holy to the LORD of Heaven's Armies. All who come to worship will be free to use any of these pots to boil their sacrifices. And on that day there will no longer be traders* in the Temple of the LORD of Heaven's Armies.

14:5a The meaning of the Hebrew is uncertain. 14:5b As in Greek version; Hebrew reads *with you.* 14:6 Hebrew *there will be no light, no cold or frost.* The meaning of the Hebrew is uncertain. 14:8 Hebrew *half toward the eastern sea and half toward the western sea.* 14:21 Hebrew *Canaanites.*

REVELATION 20:1-15

Then I [John] saw an angel coming down from heaven with the key to the bottomless pit* and a heavy chain in his hand. [2]He seized the dragon—that old serpent, who is the devil, Satan—and bound him in chains for a thousand years. [3]The angel threw him into the bottomless pit, which he then shut and locked so Satan could not deceive the nations anymore until the thousand years were finished. Afterward he must be released for a little while.

[4]Then I saw thrones, and the people sitting on them had been given the authority to judge. And I saw the souls of those who had been beheaded for their testimony about Jesus and for proclaiming the word of God. They had not worshiped the beast or his statue, nor accepted his mark on their forehead or their hands. They all came to life again, and they reigned with Christ for a thousand years.

[5]This is the first resurrection. (The rest of the dead did not come back to life until the thousand years had ended.) [6]Blessed and holy are those who share in the first resurrection. For them the second death holds no power, but they will be priests of God and of Christ and will reign with him a thousand years.

[7]When the thousand years come to an end, Satan will be let out of his prison. [8]He will go out to deceive the nations—called Gog and Magog—in every corner of the earth. He will gather them together for battle—a mighty army, as numberless as sand along the seashore. [9]And I saw them as they went up on the broad plain of the earth and surrounded God's people and the beloved city. But fire from heaven came down on the attacking armies and consumed them.

[10]Then the devil, who had deceived them, was thrown into the fiery lake of burning sulfur, joining the beast and the false prophet. There they will be tormented day and night forever and ever.

[11]And I saw a great white throne and the one sitting on it. The earth and sky fled from his presence, but they found no place to hide. [12]I saw the dead, both great and small, standing before God's throne. And the books were opened, including the Book of Life. And the dead were judged according to what they had done, as recorded in the books. [13]The sea gave up its dead, and death and the grave* gave up their dead. And all were judged according to their deeds. [14]Then death and the grave were thrown into the lake of fire. This lake of fire is the second death. [15]And anyone whose

name was not found recorded in the Book of Life was thrown into the lake of fire.

20:1 Or *the abyss*, or *the underworld;* also in 20:3.
20:13 Greek *and Hades;* also in 20:14.

PSALM 148:1-14

Praise the LORD!

Praise the LORD from the heavens!
Praise him from the skies!
² Praise him, all his angels!
Praise him, all the armies
of heaven!
³ Praise him, sun and moon!
Praise him, all you twinkling stars!
⁴ Praise him, skies above!
Praise him, vapors high above
the clouds!
⁵ Let every created thing give praise
to the LORD,
for he issued his command, and
they came into being.
⁶ He set them in place forever
and ever.
His decree will never be revoked.

⁷ Praise the LORD from the earth,
you creatures of the ocean depths,
⁸ fire and hail, snow and clouds,*
wind and weather that obey him,
⁹ mountains and all hills,
fruit trees and all cedars,
¹⁰ wild animals and all livestock,
small scurrying animals and birds,
¹¹ kings of the earth and all people,
rulers and judges of the earth,
¹² young men and young women,
old men and children.

¹³ Let them all praise the name
of the LORD.
For his name is very great;
his glory towers over the earth
and heaven!
¹⁴ He has made his people strong,
honoring his faithful ones—
the people of Israel who are close
to him.

Praise the LORD!

148:8 Or *mist*, or *smoke.*

PROVERBS 31:8-9

Speak up for those who cannot speak for themselves; ensure justice for those being crushed. Yes, speak up for the poor and helpless, and see that they get justice.

DECEMBER
30

MALACHI 1:1–2:17

This is the message* that the LORD gave to Israel through the prophet Malachi.*

²"I have always loved you," says the LORD.

But you retort, "Really? How have you loved us?"

And the LORD replies, "This is how I showed my love for you: I loved your ancestor Jacob, ³ but I rejected his brother, Esau, and devastated his hill country. I turned Esau's inheritance into a desert for jackals."

⁴Esau's descendants in Edom may say, "We have been shattered, but we will rebuild the ruins."

But the LORD of Heaven's Armies replies, "They may try to rebuild, but I will demolish them again. Their country will be known as 'The Land of Wickedness,' and their people will be called 'The People with Whom the LORD Is Forever Angry.' ⁵When you see the destruction for yourselves, you will say, 'Truly, the LORD's greatness reaches far beyond Israel's borders!'"

⁶The LORD of Heaven's Armies says to the priests: "A son honors his father, and a servant respects his master. If I am your father and master, where are the honor and respect I deserve? You have shown contempt for my name!

"But you ask, 'How have we ever shown contempt for your name?'

⁷"You have shown contempt by offering defiled sacrifices on my altar.

"Then you ask, 'How have we defiled the sacrifices?*'

"You defile them by saying the altar of the Lord deserves no respect. 8When you give blind animals as sacrifices, isn't that wrong? And isn't it wrong to offer animals that are crippled and diseased? Try giving gifts like that to your governor, and see how pleased he is!" says the Lord of Heaven's Armies.

9"Go ahead, beg God to be merciful to you! But when you bring that kind of offering, why should he show you any favor at all?" asks the Lord of Heaven's Armies.

10"How I wish one of you would shut the Temple doors so that these worthless sacrifices could not be offered! I am not pleased with you," says the Lord of Heaven's Armies, "and I will not accept your offerings. 11But my name is honored* by people of other nations from morning till night. All around the world they offer* sweet incense and pure offerings in honor of my name. For my name is great among the nations," says the Lord of Heaven's Armies.

12"But you dishonor my name with your actions. By bringing contemptible food, you are saying it's all right to defile the Lord's table. 13You say, 'It's too hard to serve the Lord,' and you turn up your noses at my commands," says the Lord of Heaven's Armies. "Think of it! Animals that are stolen and crippled and sick are being presented as offerings! Should I accept from you such offerings as these?" asks the Lord.

14"Cursed is the cheat who promises to give a fine ram from his flock but then sacrifices a defective one to the Lord. For I am a great king," says the Lord of Heaven's Armies, "and my name is feared among the nations!

2:1"Listen, you priests—this command is for you! 2Listen to me and make up your minds to honor my name," says the Lord of Heaven's Armies, "or I will bring a terrible curse against you. I will curse even the blessings you receive. Indeed, I have already cursed them, because you have not taken my warning to heart. 3I will punish your descendants and splatter your faces with the manure from your festival sacrifices, and I will throw you on the manure pile. 4Then at last you will know it was I who sent you this warning so that my covenant with the Levites can continue," says the Lord of Heaven's Armies.

5"The purpose of my covenant with the Levites was to bring life and peace, and that is what I gave them. This required reverence from them, and they greatly revered me and stood in awe of my name. 6They passed on to the people the truth of the instructions they received from me. They did not lie or cheat; they walked with me, living good and righteous lives, and they turned many from lives of sin.

7"The words of a priest's lips should preserve knowledge of God, and people should go to him for instruction, for the priest is the messenger of the Lord of Heaven's Armies. 8But you priests have left God's paths. Your instructions have caused many to stumble into sin. You have corrupted the covenant I made with the Levites," says the Lord of Heaven's Armies. 9"So I have made you despised and humiliated in the eyes of all the people. For you have not obeyed me but have shown favoritism in the way you carry out my instructions."

10Are we not all children of the same Father? Are we not all created by the same God? Then why do we betray each other, violating the covenant of our ancestors?

11Judah has been unfaithful, and a detestable thing has been done in Israel and in Jerusalem. The men of Judah have defiled the Lord's beloved sanctuary by marrying women who worship idols. 12May the Lord cut off from the nation of Israel* every last man who has done this and yet brings an offering to the Lord of Heaven's Armies.

13Here is another thing you do. You cover the Lord's altar with tears, weeping and groaning because he pays no attention to your offerings and doesn't accept them with pleasure. [14]You cry out, "Why doesn't the LORD accept my worship?" I'll tell you why! Because the LORD witnessed the vows you and your wife made when you were young. But you have been unfaithful to her, though she remained your faithful partner, the wife of your marriage vows.

[15]Didn't the LORD make you one with your wife? In body and spirit you are his.* And what does he want? Godly children from your union. So guard your heart; remain loyal to the wife of your youth. [16]"For I hate divorce!" says the LORD, the God of Israel. "To divorce your wife is to overwhelm her with cruelty,*" says the LORD of Heaven's Armies. "So guard your heart; do not be unfaithful to your wife."

[17]You have wearied the LORD with your words.

"How have we wearied him?" you ask.

You have wearied him by saying that all who do evil are good in the LORD's sight, and he is pleased with them. You have wearied him by asking, "Where is the God of justice?"

1:1a Hebrew *An Oracle: The message.*   1:1b *Malachi* means "my messenger."   1:7 As in Greek version; Hebrew reads *defiled you?*   1:11a Or *will be honored.*   1:11b Or *will offer.*   2:12 Hebrew *from the tents of Jacob.* The names "Jacob" and "Israel" are often interchanged throughout the Old Testament, referring sometimes to the individual patriarch and sometimes to the nation.   2:15 Or *Didn't the one LORD make us and preserve our life and breath?* or *Didn't the one LORD make her, both flesh and spirit?* The meaning of the Hebrew is uncertain.   2:16 Hebrew *to cover one's garment with violence.*

REVELATION 21:1-27

Then I [John] saw a new heaven and a new earth, for the old heaven and the old earth had disappeared. And the sea was also gone. [2]And I saw the holy city, the new Jerusalem, coming down from God out of heaven like a bride beautifully dressed for her husband.

[3]I heard a loud shout from the throne, saying, "Look, God's home is now among his people! He will live with them, and they will be his people. God himself will be with them.* [4]He will wipe every tear from their eyes, and there will be no more death or sorrow or crying or pain. All these things are gone forever."

[5]And the one sitting on the throne said, "Look, I am making everything new!" And then he said to me, "Write this down, for what I tell you is trustworthy and true." [6]**And he also said, "It is finished! I am the Alpha and the Omega—the Beginning and the End. To all who are thirsty I will give freely from the springs of the water of life. [7]All who are victorious will inherit all these blessings, and I will be their God, and they will be my children.**

[8]"But cowards, unbelievers, the corrupt, murderers, the immoral, those who practice witchcraft, idol worshipers, and all liars—their fate is in the fiery lake of burning sulfur. This is the second death."

[9]Then one of the seven angels who held the seven bowls containing the seven last plagues came and said to me, "Come with me! I will show you the bride, the wife of the Lamb."

[10]So he took me in the Spirit* to a great, high mountain, and he showed me the holy city, Jerusalem, descending out of heaven from God. [11]It shone with the glory of God and sparkled like a precious stone—like jasper as clear as crystal. [12]The city wall was broad and high, with twelve gates guarded by twelve angels. And the names of the twelve tribes of Israel were written on the gates. [13]There were three gates on each side—east, north, south, and west. [14]The wall of the city had twelve foundation stones, and on them were written the names of the twelve apostles of the Lamb.

[15]The angel who talked to me held in his hand a gold measuring stick to measure the city, its gates, and its wall. [16]When he measured it, he found it was a square, as wide as it was long. In fact, its length and width and height were each 1,400 miles.* [17]Then he measured the walls and found them to be 216 feet thick* (according to the human standard used by the angel).

[18]The wall was made of jasper, and the city was pure gold, as clear as glass.

¹⁹The wall of the city was built on foundation stones inlaid with twelve precious stones:* the first was jasper, the second sapphire, the third agate, the fourth emerald, ²⁰the fifth onyx, the sixth carnelian, the seventh chrysolite, the eighth beryl, the ninth topaz, the tenth chrysoprase, the eleventh jacinth, the twelfth amethyst.

²¹The twelve gates were made of pearls—each gate from a single pearl! And the main street was pure gold, as clear as glass.

²²I saw no temple in the city, for the Lord God Almighty and the Lamb are its temple. ²³And the city has no need of sun or moon, for the glory of God illuminates the city, and the Lamb is its light. ²⁴The nations will walk in its light, and the kings of the world will enter the city in all their glory. ²⁵Its gates will never be closed at the end of day because there is no night there. ²⁶And all the nations will bring their glory and honor into the city. ²⁷Nothing evil* will be allowed to enter, nor anyone who practices shameful idolatry and dishonesty—but only those whose names are written in the Lamb's Book of Life.

21:3 Some manuscripts read *God himself will be with them, their God.* 21:10 Or *in spirit.* 21:16 Greek *12,000 stadia* [2,220 kilometers]. 21:17 Greek *144 cubits* [65 meters]. 21:19 The identification of some of these gemstones is uncertain. 21:27 Or *ceremonially unclean.*

PSALM 149:1-9

Praise the Lord!

Sing to the Lord a new song.
  Sing his praises in the assembly
    of the faithful.

² O Israel, rejoice in your Maker.
  O people of Jerusalem,* exult in
    your King.

³ Praise his name with dancing,
  accompanied by tambourine
    and harp.

⁴ For the Lord delights in his people;
  he crowns the humble
    with victory.

⁵ Let the faithful rejoice that he
    honors them.

Let them sing for joy as they lie on
    their beds.

⁶ Let the praises of God be in their
    mouths,
  and a sharp sword in their
    hands—

⁷ to execute vengeance on the nations
  and punishment on the peoples,

⁸ to bind their kings with shackles
  and their leaders with iron chains,

⁹ to execute the judgment written
    against them.
  This is the glorious privilege of
    his faithful ones.

Praise the Lord!

149:2 Hebrew *Zion.*

PROVERBS 31:10-24

* **W**ho can find a virtuous and capable wife? She is more precious than rubies. Her husband can trust her, and she will greatly enrich his life. She brings him good, not harm, all the days of her life. ☐She finds wool and flax and busily spins it. She is like a merchant's ship, bringing her food from afar. She gets up before dawn to prepare breakfast for her household and plan the day's work for her servant girls. ☐ She goes to inspect a field and buys it; with her earnings she plants a vineyard. She is energetic and strong, a hard worker. She makes sure her dealings are profitable; her lamp burns late into the night. ☐Her hands are busy spinning thread, her fingers twisting fiber. She extends a helping hand to the poor and opens her arms to the needy. She has no fear of winter for her household, for everyone has warm* clothes. ☐ She makes her own bedspreads. She dresses in fine linen and purple gowns. Her husband is well known at the city gates, where he sits with the other civic leaders. She makes belted linen garments and sashes to sell to the merchants.

31:10 Verses 10-31 comprise a Hebrew acrostic poem; each verse begins with a successive letter of the Hebrew alphabet. 31:21 As in Greek and Latin versions; Hebrew reads *scarlet.*

DECEMBER 31

MALACHI 3:1–4:6

"Look! I [the LORD] am sending my messenger, and he will prepare the way before me. Then the Lord you are seeking will suddenly come to his Temple. The messenger of the covenant, whom you look for so eagerly, is surely coming," says the LORD of Heaven's Armies.

2"But who will be able to endure it when he comes? Who will be able to stand and face him when he appears? For he will be like a blazing fire that refines metal, or like a strong soap that bleaches clothes. 3He will sit like a refiner of silver, burning away the dross. He will purify the Levites, refining them like gold and silver, so that they may once again offer acceptable sacrifices to the LORD. 4Then once more the LORD will accept the offerings brought to him by the people of Judah and Jerusalem, as he did in the past.

5"At that time I will put you on trial. I am eager to witness against all sorcerers and adulterers and liars. I will speak against those who cheat employees of their wages, who oppress widows and orphans, or who deprive the foreigners living among you of justice, for these people do not fear me," says the LORD of Heaven's Armies.

6"I am the LORD, and I do not change. That is why you descendants of Jacob are not already destroyed. 7Ever since the days of your ancestors, you have scorned my decrees and failed to obey them. Now return to me, and I will return to you," says the LORD of Heaven's Armies.

"But you ask, 'How can we return when we have never gone away?'

8"Should people cheat God? Yet you have cheated me!

"But you ask, 'What do you mean? When did we ever cheat you?'

"You have cheated me of the tithes and offerings due to me. 9You are under a curse, for your whole nation has been cheating me. 10Bring all the tithes into the storehouse so there will be enough food in my Temple. If you do," says the LORD of Heaven's Armies, "I will open the windows of heaven for you. I will pour out a blessing so great you won't have enough room to take it in! Try it! Put me to the test! 11Your crops will be abundant, for I will guard them from insects and disease.* Your grapes will not fall from the vine before they are ripe," says the LORD of Heaven's Armies. 12"Then all nations will call you blessed, for your land will be such a delight," says the LORD of Heaven's Armies.

13"You have said terrible things about me," says the LORD.

"But you say, 'What do you mean? What have we said against you?'

14"You have said, 'What's the use of serving God? What have we gained by obeying his commands or by trying to show the LORD of Heaven's Armies that we are sorry for our sins? 15From now on we will call the arrogant blessed. For those who do evil get rich, and those who dare God to punish them suffer no harm.'"

16Then those who feared the LORD spoke with each other, and the LORD listened to what they said. In his presence, a scroll of remembrance was written to record the names of those who feared him and always thought about the honor of his name.

17"They will be my people," says the LORD of Heaven's Armies. "On the day when I act in judgment, they will be my own special treasure. I will spare them as a father spares an obedient child. 18Then you will again see the difference between the righteous and the wicked, between those who serve God and those who do not."

4:1*THE LORD of Heaven's Armies says, "The day of judgment is coming, burning like a furnace. On that day the arrogant and the wicked will be burned up like straw. They will be consumed—roots, branches, and all.

[2]"But for you who fear my name, the Sun of Righteousness will rise with healing in his wings.* And you will go free, leaping with joy like calves let out to pasture. [3]On the day when I act, you will tread upon the wicked as if they were dust under your feet," says the LORD of Heaven's Armies.

[4]"Remember to obey the Law of Moses, my servant—all the decrees and regulations that I gave him on Mount Sinai* for all Israel.

[5]"Look, I am sending you the prophet Elijah before the great and dreadful day of the LORD arrives. [6]His preaching will turn the hearts of fathers to their children, and the hearts of children to their fathers. Otherwise I will come and strike the land with a curse."

3:11 Hebrew *from the devourer.*   4:1 Verses 4:1-6 are numbered 3:19-24 in Hebrew text.   4:2 Or *the sun of righteousness will rise with healing in its wings.*
4:4 Hebrew *Horeb,* another name for Sinai.

REVELATION 22:1-21

Then the angel showed me a river with the water of life, clear as crystal, flowing from the throne of God and of the Lamb. [2]It flowed down the center of the main street. On each side of the river grew a tree of life, bearing twelve crops of fruit,* with a fresh crop each month. The leaves were used for medicine to heal the nations.

[3]No longer will there be a curse upon anything. For the throne of God and of the Lamb will be there, and his servants will worship him. [4]And they will see his face, and his name will be written on their foreheads. [5]And there will be no night there—no need for lamps or sun—for the Lord God will shine on them. And they will reign forever and ever.

[6]Then the angel said to me, "Everything you have heard and seen is trustworthy and true. The Lord God, who inspires his prophets,* has sent his angel to tell his servants what will happen soon.*"

[7]"Look, I am coming soon! Blessed are those who obey the words of prophecy written in this book.*"

[8]I, John, am the one who heard and saw all these things. And when I heard and saw them, I fell down to worship at the feet of the angel who showed them to me. [9]But he said, "No, don't worship me. I am a servant of God, just like you and your brothers the prophets, as well as all who obey what is written in this book. Worship only God!"

[10]Then he instructed me, "Do not seal up the prophetic words in this book, for the time is near. [11]Let the one who is doing harm continue to do harm; let the one who is vile continue to be vile; let the one who is righteous continue to live righteously; let the one who is holy continue to be holy."

[12]"Look, I am coming soon, bringing my reward with me to repay all people according to their deeds. [13]I am the Alpha and the Omega, the First and the Last, the Beginning and the End."

[14]Blessed are those who wash their robes. They will be permitted to enter through the gates of the city and eat the fruit from the tree of life. [15]Outside the city are the dogs—the sorcerers, the sexually immoral, the murderers, the idol worshipers, and all who love to live a lie.

[16]"I, Jesus, have sent my angel to give you this message for the churches. I am both the source of David and the heir to his throne.* I am the bright morning star."

[17]**The Spirit and the bride say, "Come." Let anyone who hears this say, "Come." Let anyone who is thirsty come. Let anyone who desires drink freely from the water of life.** [18]And I solemnly declare to everyone who hears the words of prophecy written in this book: If anyone adds anything to what is written here, God will add to that person the plagues described in this book. [19]And if anyone removes any of the words from this book

of prophecy, God will remove that person's share in the tree of life and in the holy city that are described in this book.

²⁰He who is the faithful witness to all these things says, "Yes, I am coming soon!"

Amen! Come, Lord Jesus!

²¹May the grace of the Lord Jesus be with God's holy people.*

22:2 Or *twelve kinds of fruit.*   22:6a Or *The Lord, the God of the spirits of the prophets.*   22:6b Or *suddenly,* or *quickly;* also in 22:7, 12, 20.   22:7 Or *scroll;* also in 22:9, 10, 18, 19.   22:16 Greek *I am the root and offspring of David.*   22:21 Other manuscripts read *be with all;* still others read *be with all of God's holy people.* Some manuscripts add *Amen.*

PSALM 150:1-6

Praise the LORD!

Praise God in his sanctuary;
     praise him in his mighty heaven!
² Praise him for his mighty works;
     praise his unequaled greatness!
³ Praise him with a blast of the ram's horn;
     praise him with the lyre and harp!
⁴ Praise him with the tambourine and dancing;
     praise him with strings and flutes!
⁵ Praise him with a clash of cymbals;
     praise him with loud clanging cymbals.
⁶ Let everything that breathes sing praises to the LORD!

Praise the LORD!

PROVERBS 31:25-31

She is clothed with strength and dignity, and she laughs without fear of the future. When she speaks, her words are wise, and she gives instructions with kindness. She carefully watches everything in her household and suffers nothing from laziness. □ Her children stand and bless her. Her husband praises her: "There are many virtuous and capable women in the world, but you surpass them all!" □ Charm is deceptive, and beauty does not last; but a woman who fears the LORD will be greatly praised. Reward her for all she has done. Let her deeds publicly declare her praise.